AGAINST THE TIDE

TONY BENN
Against the Tide
DIARIES 1973-76

ARROW BOOKS

This volume is dedicated with love and gratitude to Caroline, who has sustained my faith during more than forty years, to our family, and to our grandchildren who, as members of the next generation, may find these experiences helpful in understanding our society; and to comrades in the socialist movement.

Arrow Books Limited
20 Vauxhall Bridge Road, London SW1V 2SA

An imprint of Random Century Group

London Melbourne Sydney Auckland Johannesburg
and agencies throughout the world

First published in Great Britain by Hutchinson 1989
Arrow edition 1990

© Tony Benn 1989

The right of Tony Benn to be identified as the author of this work has been asserted by him in accordance with the Copyright, Designs and Patents Act, 1988

Random Century would like to thank the following for their kind permission to use various cartoons in this volume; © Colin Wheeler, *New Statesman* (p.63); Gibbard, © *Guardian* (p.67) © Garland, *New Statesman* (p.156; p.381); Cummings, © *Express Newspapers* plc (p.183; p.312; p.393; p.545); Garland, © *Daily Telegraph* (p.374; p.689); Jak, © *Evening Standard* (p.385; p.681); and for kind permission to reproduce all the inside photographs, which are listed with credits on pages vi, vii and viii.

Printed and bound in Great Britain by
The Guernsey Press Co Ltd
Guernsey, C.I.

ISBN 0 09 968390 3

Contents

ILLUSTRATIONS   vi

ACKNOWLEDGMENTS   viii

EDITOR'S NOTE   ix

FOREWORD   xi

1 THE LAST DAYS OF EDWARD HEATH   1
  January 1973 – February 1974

2 SOUNDING THE RETREAT   113
  March – October 1974

3 REFERENDUM   236
  October 1974 – June 1975

4 THE LAST DAYS OF HAROLD WILSON   392
  June 1975 – March 1976

5 THE DEATH OF CONSENSUS   551
  April – December 1976

PRINCIPAL PERSONS   695

APPENDIX I – Shadow Cabinet 1973   715

APPENDIX II – Cabinet and Ministers   716

APPENDIX III – NEC Committees 1973/1976   722

APPENDIX IV – Alternative Economic Strategy   725

APPENDIX V – Abbreviations   728

INDEX   731

List of Illustrations

First Section

The Diarist at work in his basement office (Camera Press)
The Benns, 1973 (Tony Benn's Private Collection)
Canvassing voters in Bristol, 1974 (Tony Benn's Private Collection)
With future voters in Bristol, 1974 (Tony Benn's Private Collection)
Dennis Johnson, chairman of Meriden (Press Association)
Meriden workers assemble a 'Bonneville' bike (Press Association)
Day trip in Concorde, 1974 (Tony Benn's Private Collection)
Michael Clapham and Campbell Adamson (Popperfoto)
Tea by candlelight during three-day week (Camera Press)
Checking the lists for power cuts (Camera Press)
Arthur Scargill with flying pickets, 1972 (Press Association)
Demonstrators support industrial strikes, 1974 (Camera Press)
Lawrence Daly and Joe Gormley (Camera Press)
Pit Deputies impose overtime ban (Camera Press)
Mick McGahey addresses Scottish miners, 1974 (Camera Press)
Stockpile of coal, Battersea Power Station (Popperfoto)

Second Section

Heath at pro-Market rally, 1975 (Popperfoto)
Referendums on continued membership of Common Market (Rex Features)
Prime Minister and his Dissenting Minister (Camera Press)
Neil Kinnock (Camera Press)
Denis Healey (Popperfoto)
Shirley Williams (Popperfoto)
Roy Hattersley (Syndication International)
Judith Hart (Syndication International)
Eric Heffer (Syndication International)

Joan Maynard (Syndication International)

Trade and Industry against the Market (Camera Press)

Talking to workers, Robertson's factory (Rex Features)

First North Sea oil, June 1975 (Syndication International)

Anthony Eden, Ted Heath and Harold Macmillan (Syndication International)

Margaret Thatcher and Willie Whitelaw (Popperfoto)

Conservative Party Conference, 1976 (Syndication International)

Jack Jones, General Secretary TGWU (Camera Press)

Members of NEC sing Auld Lang Syne (Popperfoto)

Michael Foot at Conference, 1976 (Popperfoto)

Wilson faces press after resignation (Syndication International)

Wilson leaves Downing Street by car (Popperfoto)

Knight of the Garter, June 1976 (Popperfoto)

Sir Anthony Part (Universal Pictorial Press)

Bernard Ingham (Universal Pictorial Press)

Francis Cripps and John Smith (Tony Benn's Private Collection)

Frances Morrell, political adviser 1974-9 (Universal Pictorial Press)

Secretary of State for Industry's office, 1974 (Tony Benn's Private Collection)

Acknowledgments

These diaries are the product of a huge collective effort.

Ruth Winstone, the Editor of this volume and of the whole Benn Diary series, has supervised and worked with the team which has transcribed nearly two million words from tape, and proposed the cuts to bring it down to a manageable length, whilst retaining the essentials and preserving the balance and integrity of the original. She has also been responsible for the preparation and checking of facts, notes, biographical material and appendices to render the material as intelligible and accurate as possible for readers and scholars alike.

Ruth Hobson and Sheila Hubacher have worked hard and conscientiously on the transcription and provided invaluable editorial advice on the text; I am deeply indebted to them for their commitment and understanding.

I must also repeat my personal thanks to Century Hutchinson who have undertaken this long-term publishing project, and particularly to Kate Mosse and Richard Cohen who have managed its publication with their usual sympathy and care.

Tony Benn
1989

Century Hutchinson would like to thank the following for their kind permission to use various photographs in this volume:

PHOTOGRAPHS
Popperfoto; Syndication International; Rex Features Ltd; Carmen Press Ltd; Bristol Evening Post; Eddy de Jongh; Universal Pictorial Press & Agency Ltd; Rolph Gobits; the Press Association Ltd.

CARTOONS
© Colin Wheeler, *New Statesman* (p. 63); Gibbard, © *Guardian* (p. 67); © Garland, *New Statesman* (p. 156; p. 381); Cummings, © *Express Newspapers* plc (p. 183; p. 312; p. 393; p. 545): Garland, © *Daily Telegraph* (p. 374; p. 689): Jak, © *Evening Standard* (p. 385; p. 681).

Whilst every attempt has been made to clear copyright for all illustrations used, in some cases this has not been possible. The publishers would like to apologise in advance for any inconvenience caused.

Editor's Note

The event which dominates this volume of the Benn Diaries is the crisis of autumn 1976. Its impact on the future of the Labour movement and British political life has been described by Tony Benn in the Foreword: it also had its effect on the shape and balance of this book for a number of reasons.

When James Callaghan sacked Barbara Castle as Secretary of State for Social Services in March 1976 the Cabinet lost its only other serious diarist (Dick Crossman having died in 1974). The debates between colleagues, and the decision-making in the months following Wilson's resignation leading up to the Cabinet decision to take an IMF loan in December 1976, were recorded daily by Tony Benn: he therefore provides a unique commentary on among other things, Cabinet, Cabinet committee and NEC proceedings. This has meant that a greater degree of detail has been preserved in Chapter Five, and certain other important issues, for example energy policy, have been covered only in bare outline: oil policy will in any case be given greater prominence in Volume IV, of the Benn Diaries. The emphasis in the last chapter has also fashioned the editorial considerations for the preceding three years' diary: the effect has been to trace the threads connecting Labour's dilemma in December 1976 to Labour in opposition in 1973, when the Party was preparing its Manifesto and programme for a future Government.

This volume has been reduced to about one sixth of the length of the original transcript from cassettes: the years 1973–1976 comprise 1,750,000 words in total, of which 325,000 are published here. The greatest challenge in cutting such a huge proportion of the text has been in preserving continuity and balance. It has been my aim to ensure the continuity of themes, but inevitably the published diary represents the tip of an iceberg, and conceals the huge workload which accompanied every issue faced by a Secretary of State. Within the constraints imposed by Chapter Five, I have endeavoured to maintain the balance of the original, which reflected the conflicting demands on a politician who was Cabinet Minister, NEC member and constituency MP. Preserving the integrity of the original has been facilitated by Tony Benn's commitment to candour in publishing this record of a political life.

The inclusion of chapter notes and occasional footnotes has, as in

Volumes I and II, been largely a matter of personal judgment. While hoping to clarify certain points, particularly where reference is made to some specific event which has occurred before the start of this volume, (eg the 'Pentonville Five' case), I have had to assume a basic knowledge of the period on the part of readers of all ages. Appendices give biographical notes on the major figures appearing in this volume, as well as lists of all the members of the Labour Shadow Cabinet, Government and National Executive Committee from 1973–6.

The Benn Diaries are buttressed by a comprehensive system of archives that include documents, manuscript notes, speeches, press cuttings, photographs and films which have been consulted in the preparation of the Diaries: this has been invaluable in the checking of names and facts, but nevertheless apologies must be made in advance for any errors or mispellings which may have crept in.

In the past fifteen years, starting with the Crossman Diaries, various attempts have been made using the thirty-year rule, the Official Secrets Act, the Radcliffe Report on ministerial memoirs, and – in the case of Crossman and Peter Wright – the courts, to persuade or compel individuals not to publish accounts of their experiences. To an outsider looking in on the political world through this detailed record of events it is absurd that any such account could, or should, be prevented from being made available to a wider audience, on the grounds of national security or interest. Knowledge of the political process, in its widest sense, is already limited by the way news and information is purveyed: *Against the Tide* with the original text which is available for research, exposes those limitations and by doing so enriches the quality of debate.

Ruth Winstone
July 1989

Foreword

Momentous events that were to shape the politics of the Eighties and will have a profound influence in the future occurred in the four years, 1973 to 1976. These years facilitated the entrenchment of monetarist policies when the Conservatives returned to power in 1979, and some of the militarism can be traced back to the decisions of a Labour administration.

The publication of a political diary after an interval of ten or fifteen years is a conscious political act designed to open up the recent past to more detailed scrutiny than is possible through the media or memoirs. It is an intervention coming between press reports of the time and history books which have not yet been written, providing documentation of events in detail that journalists could not have known about and about which historians would never know without this sort of raw material.

The original diary for this four-year period amounts to approximately one and three quarter million words. The task of reducing it has been a hard but necessary one, to meet both the limits of patience that could reasonably be expected from readers and those imposed by publication itself. Many of the immensely detailed accounts of Cabinet and Party proceedings have been sharply cut, but some key meetings have been published almost in their original form along with one or two of the crucial Cabinets under Callaghan's premiership that accepted the IMF diktat – during which period I was the only Cabinet diarist.

However, a Diary is a record of a learning process and I have not attempted to remove many of the opinions I expressed and actions I took, which now embarrass me. The editing process has been to clarify but in no case alter the meaning of the words – a rule learned from Hansard Parliamentary Reporting which has earned its reputation for integrity.

With the advantages of hindsight, it is clear that the significance of these eventful years was not apparent to the public at the time, partly because of the short term nature of most contemporary political debate. For example, the long and passionate discussions about Common Market membership were conducted with little reference to federalism. This vision, always in the minds of the most committed advocates of British membership, was brushed aside in order to avoid real public debate on that question.

Similarly, the victory of world bankers in the IMF over a Labour Cabinet clearly marked the beginning of what subsequently came to be known as 'Thatcherism', for the adoption of money supply targets was an integral part of the bankers' demands, and indeed had first been raised as early as 1969, when Roy Jenkins as Labour Chancellor of the Exchequer notified his colleagues that money supply had to be controlled in order to win world financial approval.

So, it is possible to perceive in some of the basic ideas which have characterised Conservative Government in the 1980s their victory ten years earlier, in the preceding Labour Government. In short, though there was a change of administration in 1979, which was clear and sharp in electoral terms, there was a continuity in thinking about central questions which stretched from Labour to Conservative rule, one paving the way for the other.

That role of Labour in preparing the way for the Conservatives was identified in my diary in July 1975, when I put my ideas into a paper and confided my fears to Cabinet colleagues.

> 'We were elected on the basis of the Social Contract, full employment and an interventionist industrial policy to which the movement is seriously committed. Now we are being told not only to adopt real pay cuts but to accept rising unemployment, to accept public expenditure cuts of two to three billion, to push for rising prices to get profits up and then to hope that this will lead to investment through the market mechanism.'

Socialist historians will ask *why* it was that a Labour Government could have gone down to such a disastrous defeat at the end of the 1970s, opening up a decade of right wing politics. If these diaries serve any purpose I hope it may be to provide some understanding of precisely how that happened. I hope also that they will dispose of the absurd mythology, which has been allowed to develop unchallenged, that Labour lost the 1979 General Election because it was too radical in its thinking: in truth it was rejected by its own supporters because it had abandoned almost all pretence to radicalism, and those who had given it its earlier majorities felt disappointed at Labour's inability in office to pursue the policies on which it had been elected.

The question that interested me then – and interests me even more now – is how this philosophical surrender came to take place. Why was there a collective failure to understand what was really happening to us all and to produce remedies that were relevant?

I believe that the rapid rate of global technological change which has been accelerating for more than a century had by the Seventies outdated many of our institutions and changed the structure of society in a way that necessitated changes in political thinking. These changes did not take place.

The post-War Labour Government of Clement Attlee was able to carry through its social revolution because the planning mechanisms it had inherited from the war-time coalition were at hand to deal with the task of reconstruction, and a war-weary public retained a sense of community which made it into a willing partner in the establishment of the welfare state and the rebuilding of our industrial base.

But the institutions chosen for that purpose, which included a substantial expansion of the public sector, lacked an essential democratic element and came to be seen as centralised and bureaucratic and hence increasingly unacceptable to post-War generations.

It is one of the strange paradoxes of political life that the Left in the Labour Party has always been accused of advocating centralised state planning. Actually the greatest commitment to Morrisonian nationalisation has come from the right wing of the Labour Party, while the pressure for industrial democracy and participation has come from the left-wing which as a result has been denounced by the so-called 'realists' in the Party leadership.

Similarly it has been the Left which has favoured open government, the accountability of the security services, the referendum on Europe, and all those ideas which have now reappeared as symbolic interests of the centre or liberal element of the political spectrum.

Partly because of the need to respond to day-to-day political pressures and partly because of a lack of interest in what were sometimes dismissed as 'arid constitutional wrangles', Labour Ministers never turned their minds to the problems created by having to work with obsolete institutions nor considered how they might be reformed.

Indeed the most important policy decisions, such as those concerning the EEC and the IMF, both of which involved a major shift of power to international organisations, were reached without any serious examination of their impact on the democratic process and in complete disregard of the growing countervailing pressure to decentralise political power.

In parallel with this institutional weakness was the abandonment of a serious socialist analysis of the changes that were taking place in capitalism as it became more global and powerful and Labour was left increasingly at its mercy with no parallel international organisations representing working people, which might have acted as a check and balance on the unrestrained excesses of international financial and industrial power.

Another great failure of thought stemmed from the way in which Labour Cabinets, as much as – if not more than – Conservative Cabinets, chose to follow American policy in respect of international issues, notably the Cold War. In this volume the reader stumbles across the decisions to upgrade the Polaris nuclear missile, a matter reported almost casually to the Cabinet under the heading 'Refurbishment'. This apparently modest decision marked the start of the Chevaline missile project without the knowledge of Parliament or the electorate.

It was, of course, Attlee who agreed to the positioning of the US bases here after the War and I can think of only one occasion, that of Harold Wilson's temporary dissociation from American policy in Vietnam, when a Labour Government was prepared to take a line independent from that dictated by the White House and the Pentagon. Thus did Labour allow itself to be sucked into the high military spending and Cold War posture insisted on by the Americans, and failed even to move as far as General de Gaulle or Chancellor Willy Brandt who both saw the importance of seeking better relations with the Soviet Government. It may be for this reason that the Gorbachev reforms – glasnost and perestroika – have taken us so completely by surprise. For any understanding observer could have seen these changes slowly emerging inside the USSR from the Krushchev initiatives onwards.

The Labour Government's myopia and attachment to US policy, requiring military expenditure at home and abroad well beyond our means, gobbled up unacceptable chunks of our national income and denied us the advantages that would have flowed from a redirection of resources into civil production and industrial investment.

It is too soon to reach any final judgement about the Labour Party, in and out of office, during those years. Although these diaries record a deal of sharp criticism of my colleagues and their decisions, there were formidable achievements which improved the standard of life of those we represented and tilted the balance of power towards them in health and safety, in education and other social provision.

The factors which bound us together and the many personal friendships that existed during this period also should not be overlooked in what is primarily a political and not a personal diary. My purpose is not to identify individual heroes or denounce traitors but to show the enormously powerful nature of the forces ranged against the Labour Government and Labour movement: the City of London, the media proprietors, the upper ranks of the administration and, as we now know, elements within the Security Services.

Despite all my criticisms, I am proud to have participated in the Government and the Party during this period in British history.

                                                            Tony Benn

1
The Last Days of Edward Heath
January 1973–February 1974

By January 1973, Edward Heath's Government, unexpectedly elected in June 1970, had been through its famous 'U-turn' on policy and the Conservatives were in retreat from the monetarist approach adopted early in their term of office. Preoccupied with Europe, Heath had seemed unable to appreciate the seriousness of the growing economic problems facing his administration and pursued a rigid and unpopular statutory prices and income policy. These problems were exacerbated by the massive OPEC increases in oil prices in 1973 which made the miners, in particular, a formidable opponent.

The Conservative Government's ruthless approach towards 'lame ducks' – industries such as Rolls Royce and Upper Clyde Shipbuilders, which were allowed to go bankrupt – had given way under pressure to a new Industry Act which provided subsidies to industry and wide ranging powers of government intervention, an Act which owed its parentage to the work of Labour's 1966–70 Ministry of Technology. Meanwhile, the Government's curbs on trade union activity in the Industrial Relations Act of 1971 had been challenged by a successful miners' strike in 1972 and the release of the 'Pentonville Five', dockers imprisoned by the Industrial Relations Court and subsequently summarily released after enormous trade union demonstrations and opposition.

The Labour Party, having restored its relations with the TUC, was also radicalised by the experience of the Heath Government, which was then considered extreme, and was in the process of developing a major new socialist Programme for Britain for presentation to the 1973 Conference. But, as the early pages of this volume record, Harold Wilson, concerned at the commitment to taking some profitable firms into public ownership (a plan which became known as the 'Twenty-five Companies') threatened to use his personal veto to prevent it from appearing in Labour's Election Manifesto.

Heath's main achievement had been to secure a positive vote in the House of Commons – with the support of Labour MPs who defied a three-line whip – authorising Britain's entry into the Common Market in 1972. At the point at which this chapter opens, Britain had become a member of the Market and for many people it looked as if that long argument was over. In reality it was simply moving to a new stage as the Labour Party began an anguished debate on whether the next Labour Government would commit itself to a Referendum vote to remain or withdraw from the European Community. Roy Jenkins, an ardent pro-European, had already resigned the deputy leadership in 1972 mainly on this issue.

Originally in a minority of one in the Shadow Cabinet and the National Executive, I continued throughout 1973 to argue for a Referendum on this vital constitutional question; the proposal was a popular one in the Party nationally and the campaign in support developed strength, appealing to some Labour leaders as a way of getting the Party off the hook politically, and preserving its unity by sub-contracting the decision to the electorate as a whole.

I had just completed my year as Chairman of the Party and was intimately involved in the development of Labour's 1973 Programme and Election Manifesto.

Wednesday 17 January 1973

Nothing on television but Edward Heath's press conference at Lancaster House, with the world's news media gathered, to announce Phase 2 of the pay and prices freeze. Parliament has been totally pushed to one side and now MPs simply sit at home watching television to find out what Government policy is, as opposed to people sitting at home watching the House of Commons' interrogation of the Prime Minister. Really this is the end of parliamentary supremacy.

I feel I am living in a dream world at the moment. The attitude of the Shadow Cabinet to the freeze, broadly speaking, is not to stick its neck out, and hope to be popular.

I just don't believe in the Labour party under the present leadership, pursuing its present policy. Now, there is a sort of Democrat/Republican division within Britain so the real effort will have to come through pressure from the outside.

Tuesday 23 January

The Parliamentary Labour Party meeting this morning began with Douglas Houghton's tribute to Len Williams* who died in Mauritius during the Christmas recess.

Harold Wilson then introduced a discussion on the Tories' prices and incomes policy, saying that we should vote against the White Paper and the Counter-Inflation Bill: Tory Government policy wasn't fair, it was one-sided, it was rigid on wages and weak on prices. We should broaden out the attack to cover the whole economic position, but we shouldn't attack the concept of *any* policy against inflation.

Stan Orme welcomed the Shadow Cabinet's line. 'We must not be defensive about the trade unions. The memorandum by Maudling

---

* Former Labour Party General Secretary; knighted in 1968 and appointed Governor General of Mauritius.

[former Chancellor of the Exchequer] published in *The Times* last autumn pointed to the political dimension of power and the development of capitalism. *We* can't mobilise without Hugh [Scanlon] and Jack [Jones]. We must offer an alternative to a mixed economy, challenge the heart of the system – the banks and insurance companies – because these institutions operate with our money and the money we create: this Government is moving towards a corporate state, whereas the trade unions are bound to be socialist in their approach.'

'Although prices are the immediate issue, we must be more fundamental,' Eric Heffer said. 'The postwar consensus has broken down and therefore there is a crisis of capitalism. Parliament will be irrelevant under this Bill. The trade unions are bound to resist and it is no good saying the law must be obeyed; if workers break the law we must support them because the law is not above life and class. Law is created by man for his own purposes.'

This is the general line that is now beginning to develop on the Left.

Winding up the discussion, Denis Healey said that it was refreshing to be going into the battle united. The Government had reversed its policy and somersaulted. This is a crisis of capitalism, the central problem being low growth. Living standards rose 7 per cent in 1972; whereas this year they would have to be cut back on average by 1 per cent. If growth survives we will have a massive balance of payments deficit; if the Government devalues or floats down, prices will rise. We must therefore broaden the attack to cover the whole economic situation. The Government is giving the Labour Party an arsenal for socialism.

Former American President Lyndon Johnson died last night.

Thursday 25 January
There was a joint meeting of the Shadow Cabinet and the National Executive today, opened by Bill Simpson.

Early in the discussion, Reg Prentice declared, 'People are cynical about politics and politicians. We must capture imagination and idealism – political leadership should be an educative role, and social spending requires that we be known as a party of high taxation.'

Tony Crosland said he was more optimistic about winning the next Election but less optimistic about what we would be able to achieve. A grave economic crisis would face us and would colour the pledges we could make; we would have to have direct action on exports and investment.

Then I presented the paper I had prepared on the links between the trade unions and the Party. I said that cynicism would be worse if Heath's promises failed; the Government knew there was an economic crisis ahead. We had everything to gain by the polarisation of the debate and the main argument in my paper dealt with relations with the trade union movement, to which we should give top priority. The idea of a powerful and really strong policy alliance with the union movement would have wide appeal and could lift a cloud of anxiety from the whole community. I said the role of the mass media in presenting the trade union movement unfairly to the public was important. If we want the electorate to support us, we must identify with their struggle and I saw no prospect of them looking to us unless we had confidence in them. I thought cynicism about politics was a direct reflection of how British political leaders have thought of people in the past. There was a serious vacuum between government and people which was dangerous for democracy.

'Nationalisation poses problems of compensation,' Jim Callaghan said, 'and the banks and insurance companies have intangible assets, and therefore we must outflank them by setting up our own organisations, instead of trying to take them over.'

Ted Short talked in philosophical terms, saying he had no objection to pragmatic policies but that we needed to 'fill out our philosophy' because the Tories had a stronger framework of ideas than we did. We must show we care for the individual, develop a strong sense of social responsibility.

'We haven't done badly since 1970,' said Michael Foot, 'but we need to rebuild the relations with the unions. It is a tragedy that we didn't destroy the Government over the Common Market. The socialist argument is now relevant again. Investment failure is a failure of the system and socialisation of investment is the only answer. This drives us to a more fundamental criticism of society and we are moving towards socialism but we must be internationalist, not anti-American or anti-Asian.' Michael added that we had to face the problem of the super-blocs and he didn't want to see one in Western Europe.

Joan Maynard said you could only justify a prices and incomes policy in a socialist society. We must defend the trade unions by attacking the other side and argue the case for socialism. Unless we take control of the economy, it will take control of us and we had to legislate for our class.

Peter Shore saw a year of crisis ahead, both economic and political. He thought there might be an early Election since the Government might have no alternative but to seek a fresh mandate, but he was afraid that the crisis might not actively help us. We must generate confidence, confidence was the most important thing.

Summing up, Harold said it had been a very worthwhile discussion. We were united, the Common Market argument was over and undoubtedly the NEC Conference policy was right.* Heath's economic policy

* The 1972 conference opposed membership on the terms accepted by the Conservative Government and called for a radical renegotiation of many of these terms by a future Labour Government and their endorsement in an Election or a Referendum.

is not really a U-turn. We are facing permanent legislation. He agreed with Michael on the commanding heights of the economy, that the finance houses of the City and not just industry must be dealt with. He liked the idea of a socialisation of investment with more interest in channelling funds into socially desirable purposes. We must use the pension funds for social purposes and stop Stock Exchange speculation.

It was a good day's discussion, something we don't often have.

Sunday 28 January

Ray Buckton drove me to Doncaster for a meeting on the railways. I like Ray: he is an interesting man, and a great friend of Clive Jenkins. Since he became General Secretary of ASLEF, he has been playing a very active part in trade unionism and is regarded as a great rather than a dangerous radical. He was cautious with me in the car – I suspect most trade unionists are cautious with all parliamentary people – but at the same time very friendly. He told me how the railwaymen had succeeded last year in helping the miners to prevent oil getting through to the power stations and, indeed, without the ASLEF ban on oil supplies he didn't think the strike could have succeeded. He also told me that someone from the Post Office Engineering Union had warned him that he, Ray, was having his telephone line bugged during the strike. These examples of working class solidarity being used, tentatively, to defend people against the Government impressed me. I felt that they were preparing themselves, not in any sense for a revolution but for a transfer of power of an important kind.

Monday 29 January

Big news today arising from the Poulson hearing.[1] A claim was made that Tony Crosland had been given a £500 coffee pot by Poulson. Tony, very sensibly, called a press conference immediately, produced the coffee pot which he had had valued at £50, returned it at once and said he wished he had never seen the damned thing. By acting really quickly, he disposed of the issue straight away.

Wednesday 31 January

Lunch with Arnold Weinstock, Managing Director of GEC, and as always it was a pleasant bantering lunch. He said he loathed Crosland, particularly after he had heard Tony's speech on bashing the rich. He was worried by Rolls Royce and the aero-engine guarantee the Government had given to Rolls, which he thought was extravagant. He predicted that a large number of unnecessary people working for Rolls would have to be got rid of if Rolls was to become profitable.

Monday 5 February
At tea in the Commons Tea room the Labour MP for Bolsover, Dennis Skinner, turned on me on the Clay Cross question,* attacking me for having voted 'the wrong way' on the National Executive. He has campaigned hard against the Housing Finance Act and is very upset about the unsympathetic attitudes on the NEC and in the Shadow Cabinet. But he was completely wrong about my vote.

This evening the Association of Cinematograph, Television and Allied Technicians blacked out TV screens in retaliation against the IBA, who had banned a film on Poulson. This raised a very important question, rather in line with what I had said last year at Conference about the responsibilities of those working in the broadcasting industry.

Wednesday 7 February
John Biffen, the Conservative Member for Oswestry, came to see me on a private visit to tell me on which points certain Tory MPs would be voting against the Government on the Counter-Inflation Bill.

Wednesday 14 February
The Times reported a story saying that I had claimed that if Heath went on attacking the trade unions, there would be a civil war. What I had actually said was that Heath was waging civil war against the trade unions, so I rang the editor's office to complain and I was put through to John Groser, the lobby correspondent, who said it was absolutely contrary to the report he had put in. I received an abject apology and they promised to print a correction tomorrow. I am glad I acted quickly because it was completely misleading.

Friday 16 February
To a conference about Concorde at the ASTMS headquarters attended by the British and French unions with Clive Jenkins in the chair. It was the first time there had been a joint meeting of all the unions involved and it was really due to Clive Jenkins's enthusiasm. He said that he felt it was important to have a united position by the workers.

Then I went to Peterborough to do *Any Questions* with an awful

---

* Clay Cross Council, Derbyshire, on which Dennis Skinner's brother, David was a councillor, had refused to raise rents under the Conservatives' controversial Housing Finance Act, 1972, and as a result, councillors were fined and disqualified. The NEC was criticised by the Conference for not supporting them strongly enough. The row rumbled on throughout 1973 and 1974.

man, Lord Hewlett, Jeremy Thorpe and Antonia Fraser.* It was
unspeakable; just a terrible knockabout. I drove Antonia Fraser home
and she told me she was thinking of standing for Parliament herself.
Now that she is forty she feels she has to think about the direction of
her life again.

Sunday 18 Febraury

The *Observer* attacked me in its leading article today for being hysterical
over the civil war issue. Heath obviously is trying to present himself as
a middle-of-the road politician with extreme left-wing militant unions
on the one hand and extreme right-wing Powellites on the other, and
this is a particularly sensitive issue since the *Observer* is taking the line
that my defence of the unions puts me in an extreme position.

Wednesday 21 February

To Lincoln to speak at a by-election meeting with Phillip Whitehead,
Labour MP for Derby North, whom I like very much. I had a quick
meal, then on to the meeting which was attended by about a hundred
people but the mass media absolutely dominated. There was a film unit
on a great big platform occupying most of the left of the hall. We had
to make our entrance a second time for the benefit of the cameras with
the bright lights and the crowd in darkness. It was an illustration of
just what happens when the media takes over. A by-election belongs
to the people not to the mass media, and I didn't like it a bit: it
confirmed everything I had said at the Party Conference last October.
I didn't talk about Taverne† but I did talk about the need to strengthen
democracy. Phillip Whitehead thought Taverne had been wrong,
although he is a close friend of his.

Saturday 24 February

I arrived home at about 2 am from Bristol to find the children still up
and that Caroline had gone to Brighton because Hilary had been kicked
in the back playing football and had been admitted to hospital with
serious kidney damage. Caroline stayed with him overnight. I had a
few hours' sleep then drove down to Brighton, found Hilary in a bad
way and we authorised an emergency operation. Rosalind his fiancée
was very worried.

---

* Lady Antonia Fraser, writer and historian, daughter of the Earl of Longford; was
married to Conservative MP Hugh Fraser until 1977. She subsequently married
playwright Harold Pinter.
† Dick Taverne, QC, MP for Lincoln, 1962–72, was forced by his local Party to resign
over his pro-Common Market stance, and won the resulting by-election in March as
a 'Democratic Labour' candidate.

Monday 26 February

To the Campaign Committee where my paper on splinter parties and community politics was briefly discussed. Harold Wilson reviewed the whole political situation and launched into a great attack on my speech on race relations during the 1970 Election: how I had lost thousands of votes in the Midlands with the attack on Enoch Powell. I let it pass but it was an indication of how unfriendly he is at the moment. I just note it down because I think he is still smarting under the difficulty he thinks I put him in at last year's Conference on the Common market question.

Wednesday 28 February

National Executive this morning. The TUC-Labour Party Liaison Committee statement was approved, having been to the TUC and to the Shadow Cabinet.

My motion came forward that 'the National Executive Committee pledges its full support to the Trades Union Congress in its opposition to the unfair and unworkable policies now being pursued by the Government and resolves to campaign with the trade unions in support of the proposals contained in the joint statement approved by the TUC and the Labour Party'. I had tabled this deliberately because it looked as if the TUC was going to come out in open opposition to the Government and I wanted it to be absolutely clear that this was the line we would support, and we would not allow Reg Prentice, Jim Callaghan or anyone else to come out attacking the trade unions as happened with the Pentonville Five last summer. Unfortunately, my motion came up so late in the Executive that I can't really pretend it was discussed in any way, but at least it did go on the record.

There was an all-day ASLEF strike today. The industrial disputes at the moment – the gas workers, the hospital workers, the railway engine drivers and the teachers – do represent a major Government confrontation with the trade unions, something which is creating a great deal of public agitation and nervousness on the part of the political leadership.

Thursday 1 March

Geoff Bish, Stuart Holland and Margaret Jackson came in this morning to discuss our Green Paper on the development of our industrial policy. I presented the outline I had made of existing Government powers and the new powers that we would need in order to succeed. Stuart Holland is a very bright guy who worked at Number 10 with Harold during the last period of Government. He is dissatisfied with Harold now and is rather attaching himself to me, though I don't see much prospect at the moment of my own chances improving since I am still living in the shadow of my year as Chairman of the Party and the events of the Conference.

I went to Bristol for the AGM and afterwards watched the result of the Lincoln by-elections; Taverne won overwhelmingly. It was very depressing because Taverne was cock-a-hoop and the TV coverage has been so pro-Taverne, there was not even a pretence of being fair.

Sunday 4 March

This evening we held a party for George Doughty [General Secretary of TASS], Eric and Doris Heffer, journalist Hugh Macpherson, Michael Meacher and his wife Molly, who are a bright pair, Stuart Holland and Frances Morrell. Eric's book called *The Class War in Parliament* is coming out shortly and he promised he would send me a copy, although he warned me that there were references critical of the 1964–70 Labour Government and my part in it.

Wednesday 7 March

I went to the Commons today and found I had not been put down to speak in the Budget debate, the first time for about four years; I felt it was something to do with the Lincoln result and Harold trying to disengage from me. So I bearded him in the corridor. 'I see I haven't been put down to speak in the debate.' He said, 'Oh, I didn't know. The names are not picked by me.' But this got around and I heard that Peter Shore and Michael Foot had decided to make a fuss and when we came to the Shadow Cabinet, it was put right immediately by Harold himself.

Dick Taverne was introduced into the House this afternoon by Dick Crawshaw and Andrew Faulds, two Labour MPs, which created enormous bitterness. It was awful.

Wednesday 8 March

There were two bombs in London, one outside Scotland Yard and one in Whitehall. The violence of the IRA appears to have come to the surface and this has created a new political atmosphere in a way. It is frightening people, and fear always turns them to the Right.

Monday 12 March

We had the TUC-Labour Party Liaison Committee to discuss the TUC's proposed national day of stoppage in protest at the control of wages. Sid Greene, General Secretary of the NUR, said they were not yet committed to a stoppage; Reg Prentice said he hoped it would not take place because it appeared to be contrary to an earlier decision of the TUC General Council's special congress.

Jack Jones interrupted him. 'You weren't there and you can't say what the General Council decision was.' Reg said he thought the action was a political strike and therefore he was in favour of a low-key response, otherwise it would give Heath a chance to exploit it.

Jim Callaghan said we must remember that 'women didn't like strikes' and the Labour Party got the backlash.

Jack said the unions were part of the labour movement and he turned to Reg. 'Now Reg, I wish you wouldn't accept admiration from people who are not friends of this movement,' – a clear reference to the fact that Reg has been highly praised in 'Crossbencher' in the *Sunday Express* recently.

I said Hugh Scanlon's speech at the Special TUC Congress appeared to say that the TUC had made a tremendous offer to the Government at Chequers last September and was ready to try to enforce a maximum increase of £3.40 if only this Government would accept it. Sid Greene explained that this was not quite what had been said, but £3.40 was what had been offered. I am beginning to probe the line Scanlon has been putting about and I don't think Jack Jones likes what Scanlon has been saying. I added, 'If you're going to be in a position to offer this to a Tory Government, it would certainly be helpful to us to know what sort of offer *we* might get.'

Denis was concerned that it was not really clear where we went from here. He said the Labour Government had calculated that all the sweat of a statutory incomes policy only produced a gain of about 1 per cent and if we didn't believe in it, perhaps we should tell people so.

Douglas Houghton said, 'We're moving towards a controlled economy, and in whose interests is it to be controlled? We would like to know what the TUC wages policy would be. We have got to consider the role of the public sector,' and Jim Callaghan added, 'Winning an Election requires a much clearer statement by the trade union movement. Wages policy is an attitude rather than a policy.'

After this rather crabby exchange, Jack suggested it would be a good idea if we had a royal commission on the pay question. This was seized by Harold as a most constructive suggestion.

Vic Feather handed round a paper indicating the TUC's view on what should be substituted for the existing Industrial Relations Act. Then we broke up.

At the Home Policy Committee of the NEC there was a discussion about the next Labour Government. They all felt that the programme was so complicated and full that it would take three Parliaments to implement. So I chipped in and said I was uneasy about this; we really couldn't wait for twenty-five years. What we wanted was a substantial and irreversible shift in the balance of power and wealth in the *next* Labour Government and that it wouldn't necessarily cost money if we were prepared to act swiftly.

Jim Callaghan said we should go more slowly and 'leave our humane imprint on the social legislation of our time'. I declared that wasn't enough for me and I would need an Industrial Powers Act if I was going to carry through the sort of industrial policy a Labour Government would need. This little clash was well worth having and I was much tougher than I have been for a long time at that committee.

Wednesday 14 March

Had dinner this evening at the Speaker's house with a Russian parliamentary delegation. I talked to Smirnovsky, the Russian Ambassador whom I haven't seen for about eighteen months. I sat next to a man from the British desk of the Foreign Ministry in Moscow and I told him how deeply conservative our Foreign Office was, how hostile it was to the Soviet Union and what a difficult job it was in the 1960s at Mintech to get technological agreements going.

The Russians really do hate the British at the moment. They think us negative, much more negative than the French, and I got a strong sense that they had a chip on their shoulder. The fact is that the Russians, to whom I don't want to be hostile at all, are most unattractive: they are bureaucratic, and the invasion of Czechoslovakia in 1968 certainly separated them from most of the young, left-wing people in the West.

Saturday 17 March

Geoff Bish, Stuart Holland and Margaret Jackson came in to tidy up the industrial policy paper. I had prepared a great chart showing what our objectives were and adding equality and redistribution of power under the general heading of 'A fundamental and irreversible transfer of power and wealth', as the main objective of the next Labour Government. We have also included an advisory structure whereby Ministers would have personal cabinets attached to them, as well as using the Central Policy Review Staff ('Think Tank'), which the Prime Minister would obviously want.

Tuesday 20 March

Had dinner with Judith Hart. We agreed that the time had come when the works of Karl Marx would have to be rehabilitated in the Labour Party because the Party without Karl Marx really lacks a basic analytical core. I also tried to discuss with her the idea of the State Holding Company and get her to see that we didn't need to have a second industrial department which she wants. I personally think that it would be a great mistake, but she is obviously building herself up for the job of Minister of Public Industry when Labour is returned to power.

Friday 23 March

Beautiful weather. Went to Bristol and spoke at a Sixth Form Conference on the Common Market. Then canvassing in the municipal elections; it is well worthwhile for keeping good relations with Labour councillors there because my constituency is terribly marginal.

Sunday 25 March

Had an all day conference at the Channing Hotel in Clifton on election organisation. It was a good meeting, although none of the things we talked about have been carried out in the constituency.

I drove home in the afternoon feeling exhausted, so I stopped by the roadside and slept for half an hour: I was woken by a policeman who wanted to know if I was all right.

Wednesday 28 March

The NEC met this morning and I had given some consideration as to whether I should proceed with my resolution supporting the day of protest. I decided to raise it as an item from last month's Executive minutes which contained a resolution pledging the full support of the Party to the trade union movement. So I said, 'I take it that we do support the day of protest and stoppage which the TUC have now agreed upon, this being, of course, 1 May.'

Joe Gormley said the TUC didn't want political interference by Labour politicians; they want it to be purely a day of industrial action by the unions. Jim Callaghan was against a political strike and said he himself did not intend to speak on 1 May. Bill Simpson suggested that although the TUC saw this primarily as an industrial day we should ask the TUC to indicate to us what attitude they wanted adopted towards May Day, and then send letters to the affiliated unions telling them that we would be supporting the day of protest and stoppage.

Harold Wilson said, 'The TUC don't regard it as a political strike. It is an industrial action,' and Bill Simpson said, 'Well, I propose to put my suggestion as a resolution.' I seconded it. Jim Callaghan wished to vote against it, so there was a vote of the NEC and Bill Simpson's motion was carried by 17 votes to 6 with Denis Healey, Fred Mulley, Tom Bradley, Jim Diamond and Joe Gormley supporting, and Jim Callaghan and Harold Wilson abstaining.

Also on the agenda was a proposal for an amendment of the Party constitution which provided that the Leader of the Party should be elected annually by Conference. This was a significant amendment and since I strongly support it, I really wondered what I should do. But Ron Hayward took the view that since constitutional amendments were being considered next year, the best thing to do was to leave it until then.

On the Home Policy Committee report, Harold Wilson complained bitterly about the leaks of policy documents. The last TUC-Labour Party Liaison Committee had resulted in a major leak about Reg Prentice and his clash with Jack Jones. There was also a leak of Terry Pitt's Campaign Committee document indicating the lines on which the Labour Party might have to develop a rapid Election manifesto. Harold was absolutely furious.

I went to a lunch for Hugh Scanlon held by all the political lobby correspondents. Hugh appeared to be talking off the top of his head without any notes. He began by saying that the TUC was not trying to usurp the power of Parliament but you couldn't expect the trade unions to accept a law just because it is the law when it purported to change the basic nature of one of our oldest institutions. He said that in a free market, you couldn't restrict the working class from selling the only commodity it has at its disposal which is its labour; the trade union movement had offered the Tory Government, last September at Chequers, the best deal they had ever offered any Government and it had been turned down. This was the point Hugh had made at the special TUC Congress and the point on which I had probed Jack Jones at the TUC-Labour Party Liaison Committee.

There were questions, and Hugh was asked whether he supported the Labour Party's refusal to send members to the European Parliament. He said – which I know to be true – that he wasn't pro or anti-European in principle and whether we were operating in a British or European context, we were dealing with capitalism. But things were changing in the trade union movement and he said that trade unions had to deal with the question of representing their members in the context of European membership. He thought that this change in trade union attitude would be reflected during the year. This was a very important answer because Hugh Scanlon himself had moved the AUEW resolution at last year's Conference which had called for Britain to withdraw from the Common Market when Labour was elected.

He was asked about the Industrial Relations Act and he said that the Government should make two amendments in the Act. One, to make it necessary for specific Government approval for actions before the National Industrial Relations Court; the second, to end the registration of unions which was costing the AUEW (I think he said) £50,000 or £150,000 a year.

I had no idea whether Hugh was aware of the significance of what he was saying but it got enormous press coverage; the pro-Europeans saw it as the beginning of the undermining of the position of the Party on Europe at this year's Conference; and the Government saw it as a weakening of the trade unions in the face of their insistence on Phase 2, and indeed the Industrial Relations Act.

Admittedly, Hugh Scanlon was being used to embarrass the Labour Party but such wide coverage was also an indication of how power has now passed from parliamentarians to people outside, and that what is said by major industrialists or major trade unionists is now much more significant than what is said by parliamentarians facing each other in the Chamber of the House of Commons. To this extent, there has been a genuine social revolution that has taken place regardless of which party is in power. In the old days, the ex-President of the Oxford Union, Mr Heath, facing the ex-President of the Oxford Union, Mr Jenkins or Mr Crosland, with the ex-President of the Oxford Union, Mr Jeremy Thorpe chipping in, would have been the centre and source of power. But now the debate is, if you like, between Enoch Powell representing right-wing working class people and Hugh Scanlon representing left-wing working class people. This is what has happened in Northern Ireland as well – the breakaway from Terence O'Neill on the one hand and the Catholic hierarchy on the other so that one is now dealing with Gerry Fitt and Ian Paisley*. This is a significant and important transfer of real power and unless we get hold of this and understand it properly we shall miss a great deal by thinking of power purely in electoral terms.

Thursday 29 March

The row over the NEC supporting the day of protest and stoppage was in the papers and of course Jim Callaghan has emerged as a hero. Indeed, it appeared in the evening papers last night in detail and Jim said he wasn't sorry it had appeared. His line, which is an interesting one, is that he wants to appear as the right-wing parliamentary Labour leader. He assesses that this is the way the PLP and the country is going

* Lord O'Neill of the Maine, Unionist Prime Minister of Northern Ireland, 1963–9; Gerry (later Lord) Fitt, Leader of the Social and Democratic Labour Party; the Revd. Ian Paisley, Protestant Unionist MP for Antrim North, founder of the Free Presbyterian Church.

and I wouldn't be at all surprised if he hadn't briefed the press himself.

At 5.30 I went to the Public Sector Study Group to consider their State Holding Company* proposal – Judith Hart, Stuart Holland, Tommy Balogh, Tony Banks, Mik and others. They have worked very hard on this and it is an important addition to Labour industrial policy. We went through their report and discussed how much public enterprise we would need to have during a period of Labour Government and whether or not we would want to name the top twenty-five companies, i.e., the leading companies in each industrial sector which we would want to bring into public ownership.

Friday 30 March
Went up to Manchester with Ron Hayward to meet USDAW and an interesting thing emerged from my talk with Ron. He told me that Sir Denis Greenhill [Permanent Under-Secretary of State at the Foreign and Commonwealth Office] had one of his best men working at Transport House.

We chatted all the way up to Manchester. I had said to Ron that I thought we ought to try to broaden out the Party – in terms of aiming at a wider base towards a popular front, rather as in France. But he had warned me not to do this because it would get me into trouble. I do think the Labour Party needs some Marxist analysis and this is what the Young Socialists bring in. Also it has to take a new view of Communist movements in other countries, if not in this country: certainly when we begin seriously in Europe, we won't just be working with the Social Democrats, but with the Communists as well, there is no question about that. But with the drift to the Right at the moment, this is a difficult argument to get across. It may come after the next Election, which I am beginning to think we shall lose.

Sunday 1 April
To the Institute for Workers' Control Conference, where I shared the platform with Walter Greendale, a docker from the TGWU in Hull. Joan Maynard was in the chair. It was a mixed bunch, a sort of market place of the extreme Left – International Socialists, the International Marxist Group, the Militant group of Young Socialists, the Communists, Labour stalwarts and so on. I didn't know what sort of reception I would get. I described the TUC-Labour Party Liaison Committee, absolutely coldly – no attempt to excite them. I said that amendment of the Companies Act would be necessary, that the TUC was working out its response to the idea of industrial democracy, and that the next

* The holding company, to be called the National Enterprise Board, would hold shares in joint public-private and wholly government-owned companies, and extend public control and ownership.

Labour Government would seek to 'carry through a fundamental and irreversible shift in the balance of power and wealth in favour of working people' which was the key point to get across.

Walt Greendale, who is a member of the National Dock Labour Board, said industrial democracy would be easiest to achieve in the docks. He said the 1964–70 Labour Government had let the dockers down. Nationalisation without workers' control was worse than private industry, and worker directors on the European model were no answer.

Then we had a boilermaker from Shotton who made a brilliant speech castigating the last Labour Government for its condemnation of the National Union of Seamen, for 'In Place of Strife' and its productivity drives, for its closure of the mines and railways, and then attacking the idea of law being absolute. He said, 'Bugger the law! Anyway what we want is the right to work by law.' It was extremely interesting.

Audrey Wise, Labour's candidate for Coventry South-West, said, 'The Tories haven't hesitated to take the powers they need. Let us learn from their boldness and carry through an Enabling* bill.'

Tuesday 3 April
My forty-eighth birthday and when I got home in the evening there was a lovely birthday cake and a party for me.

Wednesday 4 April
Dashed to the House of Commons for the Shadow Cabinet at which we discussed the Diplock recommendations.[2] Diplock does include detention without trial and there is some division in the Shadow Cabinet as to whether we should support the Government, whether we should oppose the report outright, or let the Bill go through on second reading and put in amendments.

The next question concerned the collapse of interest in the House of Commons. Michael Foot said this was serious. No one took part in debates, it was necessary to have more three-line whips. Somebody else said it was because a lot of committees were sitting all the time. Michael said he had always been opposed to committees for this reason. It was a depressing discussion reflecting how the House of Commons has lost a lot of its vitality: power has gone to Brussels, to the TUC and the CBI, and we are just a rubber stamp. Unless we make a real fight to get some powers back, people will wonder whether it is worth being in the Chamber. We are not even televised, the House of Commons turned

---

* An Enabling bill is a piece of primary legislation that give powers to Ministers to make regulations covering a wide range of matters, sometimes subject to parliamentary approval but without the passage of further legislation.

that down. I said I thought it was more fundamental than a matter of lazy MPs but Harold, quite characteristicaly, thought it was mainly that members just sat about in the Tea Room.

I got a lecture from Frank McElhone saying I was alienating the PLP badly by my continued links with the Left and my line on May Day. He was worried I wouldn't get back on to the Shadow Cabinet.

Thursday 5 April

Hilary came out of hospital and we are profoundly relieved that he will be able to get married on Saturday as planned.

Caroline was co-opted again as a member of the Inner London Education Authority.

At the House of Commons there was a meeting of the Industrial Policy Committee to discuss Judith Hart's State Holding Company document, the National Enterprise Board.

Tony Crosland immediately raised three questions: were we clear about whether we wanted these companies to be profitable or not? Could we get efficient management? How would we justify the choice of companies for public ownership? He was in favour of a smaller experimental start.

Judith Hart said the Committee had deliberately not revealed the companies they had identified. We said in the paper that twenty to twenty-five companies would be needed to yield significant control of the economy and she didn't think the management opposition would be an insuperable problem.

Stuart Holland emphasised that anything less than twenty companies would be a mere salvage operation. To be effective you needed a much larger number and Continental experience had shown this would work.

Edmund Dell said that by not naming the companies concerned, you are giving greater hostages to fortune. You could exaggerate the benefits against the cost involved; when you come to power there could be a crisis and this would all create short-term disruption. Management was a real problem that couldn't be brushed aside and it would be better to have a slow advance.

Eric Heffer didn't really like the State Holding Company and he would only accept it as a halfway house because we needed a better perspective. He was in favour of spelling out the names of the companies. Management problems couldn't be a reason for not going ahead and we may have to pay over the odds to get good managers. As to industrial democracy, he was in favour of self-managing socialism.

I said that the conditions after the next Election might be very serious with accelerated job losses as a result of EEC competition. If we were returned to power, since we have price and profit control in mind, we might as well develop a powerful capacity to increase investment. As to management, after my experience dealing with private management, I couldn't say I was very struck by it. Top management was not particularly efficient and the good management was just underneath it. On the choice of firms, we couldn't really make that selection now and this was inherent in the problem. On industrial democracy, we were waiting for the TUC to come forward. But certainly on the central question of whether the next Labour Government would introduce some control of the economy I am sure all Ministers would agree that bribing, cajoling and merging industry could not continue.

Judith Hart said that you couldn't extrapolate from existing experience of public ownership because conditions would be different. The Conference resolutions were our remit, and this remit required us to advance substantially; profitable manufacturing companies were the areas in which we should move. She thought the twenty-five companies should be named but we would be taking over going concerns and there were serious problems to be faced.

Anyway, the paper was more or less agreed after a good discussion. Crosland has got his eye on Trade and Industry in the next Labour Government and this is why he attends all these meetings religiously.

Saturday 7 April
Hilary and Rosalind married at the Kensington Register Office this morning with all the family there. We held the reception and they spent the night at our house after watching *Match of the Day* on television!

Wednesday 18 April
National Executive, and an important letter from Tom Jackson, General Secretary of the Union of Post Office Workers, was read out, criticising the Party for supporting the TUC day of protest and stoppage, and saying that the Party sometimes seemed to have a death wish advocating political strikes. He regretted the decision and thought it was short-sighted and wrong. He believed there was a gap between the National Executive and the rank-and-file membership. He then enclosed £5000 from the Union for Party funds and another £5000 for the hospital workers.

The next item from the International Committee was quite significant. Mikardo presented a defence statement in which there was a paragraph which rehearsed the policy resolutions passed at Conference. It stated, 'With this as a background, a Labour Government participating in multilateral negotiations will formulate its attitude and as a first step would seek the removal of American Polaris bases from Great Britain.'

Jim Callaghan moved an amendment so that the paragraph read: 'With this as a background, the policy of a Labour Government, participating in multilateral negotiation, will be that the remaining US bases on the territories of European states including Britain should be discussed within the context of the present negotiations on nuclear and conventional disarmament; on the limitations of strategic arms and on mutual and balanced force reductions.'

In effect, Jim was saying was this whole issue would be discussed, and there would be no commitment even to seek the withdrawal of American nuclear bases. After a long discussion Jim summed up by saying that he was trying to safeguard the future position of a Labour Government, and he insisted on a vote. His amendment was defeated by 17 to 3.

I should note that before we came on to the defence statement, Mikardo referred to the Russian invasion of Czechoslovakia and drew attention to Harold Wilson's visit to Czechoslovakia which has just taken place, during which he was alleged to have said that the events of 1968 were forgotten. Mik very much regretted this comment. So Jim said that he regretted Mik's reference to Harold Wilson, particularly as Harold wasn't present. He suggested we leave out a reference to Czechoslovakia in the statement so that it didn't look as if we were criticising Harold.

I sat next to Harold on the Front Bench yesterday and he is hopping mad at the way in which this Czechoslovak visit has been built up in order to damage him. But he shouldn't have said what he did in quite that way. He just got it wrong, but he did bring out with him David Hathaway, a Nonconformist minister who had been arrested eighteen months ago for allegedly smuggling Bibles into Czechoslovakia. Harold is very proud of his Scarlet Pimpernel role and he told me this was the seventy-second person he had got out of jail since he had been Leader of the Opposition. But he is very resentful of the fact that a number of Labour MPs tried to put down a motion criticising his visit. He said, 'What's the point? They elect a Leader in November and then attack him all year.' He is touchy and sensitive but his combative spirit is really strong.

Friday 20 April
Good Friday. Stansgate. I was absolutely exhausted. I've never been more tired, so I had a lie in. Walked a bit and then went with Caroline, Hilary and Rosalind to St Lawrence Church and St Peter's on the Wall. Did a bit of carpentry just to get my mind off politics.

Sunday 22 April
Easter Sunday. There is no doubt, looking back, that my chairmanship and my final speech at Conference strongly criticising the media did me a great deal of damage. In return, they attacked me bitterly for

several weeks and then let me rot in silence for a time.

I go up and down, get depressed as things go wrong and then cheer up again afterwards. But I have got from now until the end of July, three months' hard work, to build up support in the House of Commons, make my Trade and Industry group work better, and continue to develop good relations with the trade unions. The crunch question now is how to get the Party to adopt a radical policy and the parliamentary leadership to accept it.

I have written to Alastair Hetherington, Editor of the *Guardian*, Harold Evans, Editor of the *Sunday Times*, and Hugh Cudlipp, Chairman of IPC, saying I would like to see them again. I want to put across to them that the goodies and baddies theory of the Labour Party ought to be reviewed. Values are changing and discontent has to be resolved by more radical policies. The historical function of the Left is to carry these policies through and of the Right to capitulate. If one could get this across, the present situation would be seen as much less frightening and threatening.

Tuesday 24 April
Up at 4.15 in the morning and left for the Labour Party Young Socialists' Rally in Skegness. I was scheduled to debate with Ted Grant who is the leader of the Militant Tendency. The LPYS Conference attended by 850 young people had been held over the weekend and the rally was today with about 400 young people.

Andy Bevan was the chairman. John Forrester of the AUEW introduced the session, and paid a tribute to the Young Socialists. He said the Labour Party must be a moral crusade, talked about the creation of wealth by the workers, and said that workers felt that, morally, factory equipment and its products belong to them. He said that one trouble with the Party was that it was too aggressive towards comrades who didn't agree and the quality of humanity was, in his book, more important even than the quality of Marxist or socialist thought. He said that the movement would have to accept that there would be differences and we couldn't go on clobbering each other.

Before I spoke I had a brief word with Ted Grant whom I had never met before. He is a South African, in his fifties, a Trotskyite, and when I asked him where else in the world they were interpreting Trotsky correctly other than his own faction, he corrected me: 'Not faction, our own tendency.' Then he said, 'Well, there is no one else in the world who follows Trotsky correctly.' This confirmed my feeling that he is really a theological leader, a teacher by instinct. He has got a tremendous influence over the young people. Listening to him speak, he is absolutely rational, logical and analytical up to a certain point and then he just goes over the top and keeps talking about 'the bloody settlement that the capitalists are preparing for the workers' and quotes Brigadier Kitson, the guerrilla warfare expert, who advocates CS gas and more riot shields for civil disturbances. This gives Ted Grant a justification for his message and then no doubt Brigadier Kitson reads Ted Grant and orders more CS gas. But really they are both on the fringes of British politics.

In his speech, he paid a tribute to me for the work I had done in trying to introduce more democracy into the Labour Party. He said the spirit of democracy and discussion was a great tradition and the Militant Tendency could only gain from it. He then attacked the Right of the parliamentary Party and Michael Foot and the 'so-called Left'. He quoted from Trotsky's book, *Where is Britain Going?*, which he had recommended to me before the meeting began. He said that the preparations of the Tories in the twenties and thirties were for civil war and that the Labour Party had good intentions; but the next Labour Government would either split, or betray the workers, or fight and be resisted by force.

I wound up my speech by dealing with the Housing Finance Act and what we had done. I said how much I welcomed a dialogue and was opposed to bans and proscriptions in the Party. The problem was one of persuading people, that was the real difficulty Militant faced, not the view of the leadership.

I said that if I had to criticise Ted Grant's analysis, I would disagree with the view about a bloody settlement. If I believed it, we wouldn't be here passing resolutions, we would be planning guerrilla warfare. If the young people, with all their passion and energy and idealism, were diverted to thinking in civil war terms, it would weaken rather than strengthen their influence. I got more than a polite clap at the end, which was unexpected.

Friday 27 April

The Watergate scandal[3] in America has reached astonishing proportions and today Patrick Gray, the head of the FBI, resigned. It is thought he destroyed relevant records in the case. This could well have a desperately damaging effect on Richard Nixon's last term and reveal him for what he really is, which we know from his early days as a muckraking, anti-Communist McCarthyite.

Over the holidays I composed a resolution for the National Executive, calling for how people vote on motions and amendments to be recorded in the minutes of the Executive; for these to be checked at the next meeting and made available in the library; sent to Labour Parties and affiliated organisations who were prepared to pay the cost; and printed and circulated with the NEC's annual report to Conference. It will cause great ill feeling among those who want to keep their activities quiet but it does involve a major transfer of power from elected Executive members to rank-and-file delegates. There is no question that I shall get some support, though how much, I don't know.

Sunday 29 April

At noon Antonia Fraser came to see me about biographies. She has written a well-received life of Mary Queen of Scots and of Cromwell, and has been invited by the BBC to do a programme in the *One Pair of Eyes* series for August. In this programme she is interviewing the Conservative MP Nigel Fisher, who wrote Macleod's life, Macleod having left no papers when he died in 1970. She is interviewing Professor Hugh Thomas who wrote John Strachey's life; James Pope-Hennessy the biographer of Queen Mary and Michael Holroyd who wrote the life of Lytton Strachey; and she wants to do some contemporary filming of me at a May Day rally in Birmingham in order to examine the possible role of film in biography.

As I sat and talked about it all with her it became quite clear to me that if one is going to record every minute as fully and completely as this, one does have to ask oneself the central question: 'Am I a participant in life and politics or am I an observer?' and if there is any conflict between the two, one must be a participant. It is rather like filling up the North Sea with oil instead of taking it out. One creates a great archive which may or may not be of interest to anyone else. What one is bequeathing is one's working papers and documents; watching life simply to be able to make it interesting is not enough.

Antonia Fraser said that she had met Anthony Eden a couple of years ago in Barbados, and how pleased he was to talk to her. She described how her mother Elizabeth Longford, who lived in Hampstead and was a friend of Hugh Gaitskell's, bitterly hated Harold Wilson; how contemptuous she was of his style of life in Hampstead Garden Suburb. This explains a great deal of Wilson's dislike for that snobbish Hampstead establishment of upper middle-class socialists and Fabians.

Monday 30 April

Today the US Attorney General, Richard Kleindienst and two of his closest aides, Ehrlichman and Haldeman, were sacked; tonight Nixon is due to make a great television broadcast about the Watergate scandal.

Tuesday 1 May

May Day, the day of national protest and stoppage called by the TUC. I was asked to go to their May Day by the Birmingham Trades Council and I am the only member of the Shadow Cabinet actually speaking.

Yesterday in the House of Commons Jim Callaghan told me that he would deliberately not be in his Cardiff constituency for the day. Eric

Heffer was going to be in Liverpool with Jack Jones. Frank Allaun told me he would be participating in London: it is a disgrace, I believe, that no members of the Shadow Cabinet itself should be taking part.

Caroline and I got up just before six and drove to Birmingham. The march was to begin at the Digbeth Civic Centre. Only one Labour MP, Ray Carter, turned up. There was a curious announcement that Julius Silverman, the Labour MP for Aston, was prevented by the rail strike from getting there. Roy Hattersley was speaking in Sheffield but otherwise there was no support from the Birmingham MPs.

One of the great things about a May Day march organised by the unions is that the speakers don't lead but march behind their banners. This situation has led to massive ordering of new banners by the trade unions.

It was a beautiful day and we marched for two to three miles with twenty-five thousand people, with tens of thousands more who watched. We were led by a Scottish pipe band with the police marching beside us. When I asked one of them whether he was there to protect the crowd from us or us from the crowd, he said he didn't really know why he was there at all. It was immensely good natured. The BBC film unit, filming for *One Pair of Eyes*, was there and in the hall.

It was certainly the biggest and best May Day meeting that I have ever attended and it was reminiscent of those prewar years; indeed, no doubt, of the Twenties and of the times during the nineteenth century when the Labour Movement was stirring itself for change.

Outside the Town Hall all the sects were selling their papers: the International Marxists with *Red Weekly*; the Socialist Labour League with *Workers' Press*; the International Socialists with the *Socialist Worker*; the Communist Party with the *Morning Star*; the Labour Party with *Labour Weekly*. This gathering around the Labour movement of all these sects was a very important part of the exercise and we bought all the papers.

The meeting began with the chairman telling the meeting that Roy Hattersley couldn't be there, at which there was such a lot of booing that he couldn't get it across that Roy was actually speaking in Sheffield at a similar meeting, which was quite to Roy's credit. But it was an indication of the Militants' anger. The SLL were in the balcony opposite the platform and on the left were others with red banners which the groups tried to hang in the view of the BBC television cameras.

The leading shop steward in the Austin Morris works, Dick Etheridge, who is a Communist, spoke and he made the collection speech brilliantly. It was all tremendously informal and friendly.

After that, Harry Urwin, Assistant General Secretary of the TGWU spoke, a most formidable and powerful speech, strong, clear, explaining what was happening; comparing Dick Taverne with Oswald Mosley in advocating the corporate state. 'The Establishment in this country before the war was in favour of the corporate state and it's in favour of the corporate state today,' he said. Strong stuff. Afterwards Caroline said she had been struck by the number of Marxist phrases that had crept into the argument: the workers who create the wealth, a confrontation between different class interests, etc. A marvellous meeting.

Afterwards we chatted to one or two of the youngsters with their various sectarian papers. One lady of about seventy came up to us and turned to a young Trotskyite, a worker I should think in one of the factories, and said, 'Nice to see you and don't you think Harold Wilson is wonderful?', and off she went with her shopping bag.

Incredible as it may seem, the ITN six-o'clock news put the one-day strike not only below the Nixon Watergate speech of last night, but also below the food negotiations in Luxembourg and below one or two other items. Then they began the 'stoppage' news by showing the chaos for commuters and a film of an interview of a motorist who couldn't get into the Horse Guards Parade car park and a soldier who was acting as traffic warden, '... And to add to the congestion were the May Day strikers marching into Central London where fourteen people were involved in scuffles.' Not a single reference to a single speech that had been made, when something like a million and a half people had come out on strike. That is the mass media against which one has to fight and battle. One's first instinct was to blow up but that wouldn't do any good.

Nixon's address to the American people was awful, a speech in which he accepted responsibility for what had happened because he was at the top, his office had to be preserved, it would be cowardly to do otherwise and there could be no whitewashing in the White House – a really gimmicky PR phrase. But he didn't answer the fundamental questions and even defended the people he had sacked on the grounds that perhaps their zeal had been in a cause in which they deeply believed (namely his own re-election as President).

When the dust has settled on Watergate, the time will come to make a speech warning people that there is a police state in every Western country, more discreet, more civilised, and without the violence of the Stalin period, but surveilling political activity. Of course, telephone tapping does go on in this country and nobody ever questions why the Communist Party headquarters in King Street are continually tapped. The authorities just draw a distinction between acceptable parties and non-acceptable parties to tap.

Wednesday 2 May
At the end of the Shadow Cabinet I raised the question of whether I should issue a statement drawing attention to our 'nationalisation

without compensation' discussions in order to frighten off speculators from buying up bits of Rolls Royce which the Government have put on the market. Shirley Williams thought this might be the occasion for redundancies which the Government could blame on us. There was a generally discouraging atmosphere. Somebody said, 'Why do we always make Tony into a bogeyman? At any rate, he does draw these things to our attention.' So I let it slide. There is no point in going to the stake for one controversial statement.

Thursday 3 May
Coming back on the train from a meeting in Brighton, Ron Hayward told me about how Marcia Williams was 'running Harold', how she and her brother, Tony Field, and her sister worked with him, how Joe Haines was in Harold's confidence, Alf Richmond, a press aide from the *Daily Mirror*, was the baggage master, and Gerald Kaufman was round and about. This is the kitchen cabinet – Harold's court. It has always been like that but it still annoys Ron Hayward who has not got a lot of time for Harold. But Harold is a very shrewd political operator and one must not forget that.

Friday 4 May
Drove to Bristol and canvassed in Knowle Ward. I knocked at the door of one white-haired mustachioed, retired sergeant-major type, who had been with Standard Telephones and Cables, which is the British subsidiary of ITT. He invited me in and attacked the international companies, condemned them for running the world, though there wasn't much we could do about them. He loathed them. He was a Labour supporter. Then he said, 'I want to put a point to you on which my children strongly disagree with me. I think everything is run by Jews. Look at Lord Melchett, Lord Goodman, Derek Ezra, Arnold Weinstock – the Jews are everywhere.' For the first time I began to see an anti-semitic element returning. Previously it has been the Blacks or the Pakistanis or the Indians who were to blame, but here was the basic ingredient of old prewar fascism returning.

I said, 'Look, concentrate on the issue – should anyone have so much power? What about the Scots taking over, or the Welsh taking over, or men taking over?' I felt it was a straw in the wind, very alarming.

Had a rest this afternoon and then went and recorded *Any Questions*. On the team were the Tory MP Nicholas Scott, Beryl Grey of the London Festival Ballet and journalist Bernard Levin. I haven't actually spoken to Bernard Levin for some twelve years and during that time he has launched into the most violent attacks, by calling me Mr Zig-

Zag Loon and other things in *The Times* – really perpetual, obsessional hatred.

Afterwards I heard he was going back to the Royal Hotel in Bristol and I offered him a lift. I brought the car round, put his bag in for him, drove him twenty miles into Bristol, talked to him about the old city, about the new Catholic Cathedral, about St Mary Redcliffe Church, and I was as charming as could be. It was absolutely heaping on coals of fire. Most satisfying!

Monday 7 May

Rang Harold Wilson in Liverpool and got his general approval to put out my statement saying that those who are thinking of acquiring shares in Rolls Royce Motors should take serious notice of the official policy of the Labour Party in calling on the next Labour Government to 'renationalise, without compensation, public assets which are sold off by the present Government'.

At the Home Policy Committee industrial policy was brought up early and I got my paper accepted: the objective of a 'fundamental and irreversible shift in the balance of power and wealth in favour of working people'; an industrial powers act; planning agreements between companies, unions and the Government on national economic priorities; a State Holding Company; regional policy; monopolies and mergers. I got it all agreed except that Shirley Williams attacked the industrial powers and said they sounded authoritarian. I said, 'Well, some of these powers the Tory Government have *already* taken.' Shirley argued, 'But that isn't to say we want them.' I replied, 'We have got to make up our minds whether we are going to be serious about this.' I was very sharp with her, because she comes out on the right-wing on everything.

Jim asked, 'Couldn't we have this as a Green Paper – sort of interesting discussion stuff?' in order, of course, to avoid any commitment.

'Be quite clear,' said Denis. 'This is the programme of the commitment in the Manifesto.'

Tuesday 8 May

Frank McElhone told me an interesting story. He had been talking to Gus MacDonald who used to be a fitter in Upper Clyde, was taken on by *Tribune* as their industrial correspondent and is now head of the *World in Action* team. Apparently after my speech at Conference last year attacking the media, Arnold Goodman [Chairman of the Newspaper Publishers Association] had gathered together the newspaper proprietors and probably TV people as well. They had all agreed that the speech constituted a direct threat to them and they called on Harold to repudiate me. But they pressed him too hard and he declined to do so, though he dissociated himself last year from the statement. Also Gus told Frank that there was a great deal of support in the press and television for what I had said but these people were fearful for their jobs, so kept quiet.

Into the House, and sat next to Harold. My statement on Rolls Royce was in the papers this morning and messages began coming in. Peter Walker and Tom Boardman, the Minister for Industry, had made statements criticising me for irresponsibility. Sir Ian Fraser, the Chairman of Rolls Royce, had attacked me, and they all implied that I had spoken without consultation with colleagues.

The telephone at home rang continually. Apparently Douglas Houghton had issued a statement saying that he was concerned about what I had said. When I saw Harold he made no reference to it and I gather it was just Douglas trying to get me into difficulty. Walter Johnson, the Labour Member for Derby South, had expressed his concern and tonight Keith Standring of APEX announced that my words had been ill-timed and might prejudice the employment of the workers involved. Of course, once investors are caught up in the debate, then there is real trouble and that is the explanation of the Government's attitude.

The BBC came and interviewed me for the ten o'clock news and their parliamentary correspondent implied that I had made another boob as I had at the Conference and that Harold Wilson would issue a statement. It is getting exciting.

Ken Coates rang to say he approved. I phoned Peter Shore, Ron Hayward and Michael Foot to ask them to give me full support at tomorrow's Shadow Cabinet and to emphasise that I had cleared it with Harold. I even left a message for Crosland. I am not having this – I am not going to be dropped in this one. I did indicate to the press that in fact Harold had been consulted but I want to keep that back until we thrash this out tomorrow.

I rang Nicky Kaldor* who is entirely on my side, and he is going to ring Harold, Tommy Balogh and Denis Healey. So I am building up for quite a tussle. I will also try to get the Shadow Cabinet to agree to a motion of censure on the Government for their handling of Rolls Royce, leaving the taxpayer to pick up the cheque for the expensive RB-211.

Wednesday 9 May
The Times said that Wilson was gravely concerned and that four senior colleagues had been to see him to complain about my Rolls Royce statement. The other papers had the same general line. The *Daily Mail*

* Professor of Economics, University of Cambridge; Adviser to the Labour Government, 1964–70 and 1974–9.

had an attack, saying I was a mobile disaster area. The *Guardian* had a more friendly leader saying that I should clarify. There was a cartoon in the *Telegraph* showing me as a clown. *The Times* also had a leading article on the principle of consent, attacking me for getting my facts wrong. Only the *Morning Star* wrote a piece in support.

I rang Harold and the first thing he said was 'I didn't do any briefing.'

'Well, it was in all the papers this morning.'

'Well I didn't. I tried to stop it.'

So I let it rest for a second and then he said, 'Anyway, you made a brilliant speech on Monday. I read it in Hansard – a marvellous speech,' so I knew he was feeling extremely guilty.

I said, 'Well, look Harold, I think we should put down a motion of censure on the Government on Rolls.' I concentrated on building up the Shadow Cabinet; but he is obviously nervous and under pressure from both sides.

Had a word with Frank McElhone. I thought he would have been driven absolutely up the wall with it all, but he had been attacked by thirty Members last night in the Tea Room and he just hit back and sloshed them. 'You are always going for Tony Benn. Of course his statement had been cleared with the Leader.' He told me that Labour Members Don Concannon, Dennis Skinner, Eric Heffer, Stan Orme and Norman Atkinson are all going to make statements in support of me. It's got to the point where even Frank has to stand and fight because he knows what I'm up against. That was encouraging.

Shadow Cabinet, and after regular business we came to Rolls Royce. Harold began and, in fairness to him, he did say that I had let him see a piece of paper some time ago that unfortunately had got lost, that he had missed the Shadow Cabinet last Wednesday, hadn't realised that there was a great row brewing and that most people had been critical. He added that I had rung him on Monday and although he had made a couple of changes to my statement, he had assumed that this was the position and had passed it.

Then Jim Callaghan said, 'Tony was very sternly criticised last Wednesday and the overwhelming majority were against him saying anything.'

Ted Short disagreed. 'No, I think what happened was that Tony said he would take account of how the discussion had gone and then he would raise it with you.'

I asked them to pass round the five-page aide-mémoire that I had written which was enormously valuable and if I hadn't had that I would have been massacred. I took them through it page by page: the policy statement to the Executive; Harold's speech at Conference; the Conference resolutions; my winding up; the words of Labour's

Programme for Britain; then my recent statement; the legal position; and finishing up by saying we should now have a motion.

Harold then produced a statement beginning, 'It is *not* the policy of the next Labour Government to nationalise Rolls Royce motors without compensation', and so on. Insofar as it was incompatible with my statement, it was intended to be a rebuke.

I let the argument rage on. At one stage I came in and said, 'Denis last night on the radio mentioned something about Concorde and the next Labour Government. I had a phone call within twenty minutes from a Labour candidate saying that it had undone a year's work trying to build back the confidence of the aircraft workers.'

Denis interrupted and said, 'I didn't say the next Labour Government would do it. I said this Government should do it.' I said, 'Well, there is nothing in that but you might have consulted me because that does affect 2,500 jobs directly.' Denis said, 'I made that statement on the Front Bench in the Budget Debate. You heard me.' I said, 'You may have done but you didn't consult me. I am not going to be picked out, I'm telling you, I'm not going to be budged.'

Peter Shore came in, his face white. 'I think this is outrageous. The real offence is not Tony Benn's statement. We all know there are complications and problems about how you implement Party policy and we must retain the right to say what we want, and how it should be done. But the real offence is that four colleagues and somebody associated with, or claiming to speak for Harold, put out a statement that got Tony in trouble; that is absolutely intolerable.'

Michael Foot was very skilful and said, 'You know, really Tony's got it right, he's put it right. Surely the best thing to do would be to have a debate on Rolls Royce and Tony would say all this.'

Jim said, 'I want to speak. I am critical, and I am critical of Tony to his face. He has caused a lot of trouble. Look at his line on May Day.' The problem for Jim is that he is in a minority. But I let him go on. An execution was being planned and I saw it happening.

Fred Peart was a bit worried about confiscation, and Jim said he had never been nor would be in a Party that believed in confiscation. Ron Hayward came in. 'Look, Tony has referred quite accurately to the NEC statement and the Conference resolution.' There was a Division in the middle and gradually it began to settle. It was agreed that there would be a 'Supply Day' debate, I would open it, I would be allowed to wind up the debate, if necessary to deal with outstanding points and Harold would put out a statement which would include a repudiation of the press stories about a row.

Thursday 10 May

Press comment today was all over the place. *The Times* had a heading, 'Wilson approves Benn's statement', and a malicious account of what happened at the Shadow Cabinet. The *Mirror* and the *Sun* said I was rapped.

Had a phone call from Clive Jenkins who said that trade unionists couldn't understand what the row was about and asked if it would help if the ASTMS conference this weekend had an emergency resolution in support of me; I said it certainly would.

I went to see Ron Hayward and together we went to the TGWU Finance and General Purposes Committee to talk about relations between unions and the Party. 'The real problem is this,' I said. 'Of course we should consult on legislation, but we should consult on immediate situations. As an ex-Minister I know very well that the whole set-up is for Government to interact with the Establishment – with management, the City, and civil servants. If we want to be different we have got to deal not only with the Official Secrets Act which is immensely imporant, but also with the whole problem of liaison and secrecy and changing the Companies Act. This is what it is all about.'

Jack Jones was very interested. 'If we could present openness as an aspect of industrial democracy that would be fine,' he said. He went on to suggest that Labour leaders weren't vigorous enough and a Protection of Employment Act was needed. Referring to Labour leaders, he said, 'I am not criticising Tony but there are others who are not as good as he is.' As we got up to go I said, 'By the way, Jack, I wouldn't object to a little bit of support on my Rolls Royce fight. They are trying to crucify me.' So Jack held up his hand and stopped the meeting, although they were just about to go on to the next item. 'Look, couldn't we support Tony Benn in what he is doing?' and they all said, 'Yes' – about twenty-five of them. So I was able to tell the press afterwards that the Finance and General Purposes Committee of the TGWU had backed me, which was very welcome.

Went to the Tea Room to see if I could stir up support in case the matter was raised at the PLP meeting and found Joan Lestor and Frank Judd [Labour MP for Portsmouth West] actually drafting a favourable resolution, so I showed them my memorandum. Charlie Pannell said he would support me. 'Talk about the Loneliness of the Long Distance Runner. What about the loneliness of the first batsman?' he said. 'When I look along that Front Bench and I think the number of times each of them have made me gasp with what they have said.'

I went to the Mass Media Group of MPs where they were discussing broadcasting. We are trying to get a Green Paper out and at the end of the meeting I summed up what I thought we should say: 'The

Labour Party believes the media are not serving the people adequately and are dominated by privileged power groups. We shall seek to deal with the situation by a broad policy of democratic ownership and control. We therefore absolutely reject any system based on Government censorship or central control as well as control by direct or indirect commercial interests. We believe that our objectives should be:

1. To establish a firm public service framework of supervision for broadcasting and the press;

2. To assert the principle of public ownership in the technical transmission facilities;

3. To accept the principle of centrally gathered revenue by public funding however divided, and by channelling of other revenues through the same fund;

4. To seek to decentralise the operating units as far as practicable;

5. To encourage the widest possible access to the media of all kinds;

6. To entrench the principle of democratic control at every level covering workers and with proper opportunities for others to make their comments;

7. To safeguard the right to publish and broadcast a diversity of views;

8. To guarantee that all media and management issues are openly discussed and regularly reviewed; and therefore

9. The Labour Party will set up an executive commission whose job it will be to consider the above objectives after there has been a Green Paper published. When that paper has been agreed by Parliament the commission will be invited to report on certain applications, problem and priorities. When these recommendations are made they will be discussed and the commission itself will have responsibility for implementing them.

This may involve a change of structure but the executive commission will have no control whatsoever over the content of any programme, and it will be simply structural and advisory and executive as and when it is necessary to make changes.'

This was broadly accepted and indeed widely welcomed.

Friday 11 May

The papers are full this morning of the total failure to float Rolls Royce. Only £7 million was purchased by public subscription, only 360 of the 900 workers applied for shares and it was generally admitted that my speech had played some part in stopping it, which is a great achievement. Even so, the institutions have promised to pick up the remainder, so the flotation will take place. The *Financial Times* reported the support given me by the TGWU, and the *Daily Telegraph* had a fierce denunciation entitled 'Limousine Socialism', saying that unless the Government adopted Labour's policy of threatening to reverse existing policies, Labour would be in power whether in or out of office – a marvellous comment in view of the fact that the House of Lords and the City of London have kept the Tory Party in power in and out of office for years.

Clive Jenkins rang to say that the ASTMS Annual Delegate Conference was going to have an emergency resolution along the lines that 'This Conference welcomes the statement made by Tony Benn in support of the defence of public assets and in defence of the security of the people whose jobs depend upon them.' This will be debated on Monday. Also next week is the debate on Rolls Royce. So the Government are going to be in a real difficulty.

Sunday 13 May

The *Sunday Telegraph* today had a leader, 'Bolshevik Benn'. Nora Beloff of the *Observer* had a long piece saying that Denis Healey and Tony Crosland privately had a contempt for me but couldn't say it publicly because they might not be re-elected, but in any case, the Labour Party never took any notice of its Conference resolutions. I stayed up till 3 am digging into the background of Rolls Royce for Questions tomorrow and the debate.

Monday 14 May

Tony Banks came in this morning and told me what facilities the AUEW research department, under his guidance, could put at my disposal.

Department of Trade and Industry Questions in the afternoon, during which I got an answer about the amount of money that had been put into Rolls. Clive Jenkins rang to tell me the emergency resolution had been passed.

From 2 till 7 the Shadow Cabinet met to consider the Party's policy programme. Harold Lever wanted to remove the phrase 'irreversible transfer of wealth and power' and attacked me on Rolls Royce. So I said to him, 'Say it publicly; don't say it privately to the press or to this meeting. Say what you think publicly.' Jim was in favour of leaving 'irreversible' in the document. Then Tony Crosland attacked the planning agreements and I again said, 'Argue your case publicly. Don't just leak it to people and then leave the Party to believe this is right.' Shirley Williams attacked the Industrial Powers Bill as being undemocratic. Harold Lever said he was reminded of a corporate state. He didn't believe in public ownership; planning agreements; and the regional machinery needed clarifying.

I said, 'Look, we must have some perspective. Twenty years ago 100 companies produced about 25 per cent of our output, now they produce 50 per cent and will shortly be producing 55 per cent. We must be ready to answer the question – do we actually wish to control this power or not?'

Harold Wilson thought we could take over as and when we needed to. Then we came to the nationalisation of the financial institutions. Harold Lever said, 'You don't need a mandate as a Government. You can do as you like. We will recommend nationalisation of building societies and yet some of them are cooperatively owned. Why nationalise? The small depositors will remove their funds. But nevertheless the banks, insurance companies and building societies have defects and the Party will have to remedy them.'

Harold Wilson said, 'A Committee of Inquiry into the Stock Exchange would be the right thing to do. It is an amateurish casino and should be an investment market. We should try to see whether we could use the pension funds for public purposes.'

'We are aiming at the wrong targets. The City may be immoral but you can't control the banks,' declared Jim.

Harold replied that last year's Party Conference only called for the nationalisation of banking and insurance because it hadn't defeated the platform all week, and if we took the wrong decisions we would be in opposition for another thirteen years.

I commented that the Right should argue its case with the Conference to which Jim replied, 'If you have a debate, it splits the movement.'

Shirley thought there was declining support for public ownership and the problem was how to reconcile the desire of Conference activists with a public which doesn't accept their view. 'Well, the public doesn't necessarily accept your attitude on race, but you go on saying it, and quite rightly,' I said.

Then we came on to Scotland and Wales, and the issue of Ministers having 'personal cabinets'. I said, 'Well, we have got a reference to them in the programme and we must have them.'

'Don't worry,' said Harold. 'I shall have a Central Policy Review Staff man in each Department.'

'Oh no you won't,' I replied. 'I am not having one of your people in my Department. I am going to have my own advisors, working with yours.'

What the meeting made absolutely clear was that the parliamentary leadership is well to the Right of the movement.

Tuesday 15 May

I went to the Commons and opened the Rolls Royce debate. I began by saying that we had never advocated confiscation, and developed ten charges against the Government. When I had finished, Peter Walker got up and tried to mock the whole thing. He didn't address himself seriously to anything I had said. There was quite a big crowd there, I think mainly to see me slaughtered. Heseltine attacked me. Judith Hart and Charlie Pannell spoke for me; then I wound up. Frank McElhone had whipped up a lot of support.

In the evening, I was asked to appear on *Midweek* with Heseltine and I discussed Rolls Royce with him there, calmly and quietly. Of course he was in a more difficult position on the public platform because of the amount of money that has gone into Rolls Royce. He had tried to catch me in the House on the question of whether the workers would be consulted by a Labour Government if we wanted to nationalise, and I hadn't given a very good answer. But I had thought about it meanwhile, so on the programme I said, 'I think it's a very interesting idea. If the workers want nationalisation, they should be able to have it – a sort of Heseltine doctrine. I would like to think about it some more.' It was really most successful.

Wednesday 16 May

This morning at the Churchill Hotel we started a joint meeting of the National Executive and the Shadow Cabinet on Labour's major policy statement. Jim was in the chair. Harold started by saying that this was a very good policy statement but perhaps we should consider publishing it as a book. Bob Mellish said it represented twenty years' work for the next Labour Government.

Reg Prentice said, 'This document is intended for an interested public. But the public is tired of exaggeration.' He warned against giving a pledge, for example, that there wouldn't be high taxation. He said, 'This is a statement of aspirations and we should take out the extreme passages, including references to public ownership.'

Crosland also questioned whether this was the right stance for the Party. 'We must be responsible and not make promises we can't keep. We must recognise that when we come to power, economic growth will be booming and we may have to reduce it and reduce public expenditure. A democratic society is what we want and therefore we have to be in tune with the mood of the country which is towards the Centre. There is no evidence that the country wants us to move to the Left. The document lacks a theme. Our priorities are: 1. Stable prices; 2. An attack on poverty; 3. The redistribution of wealth; 4. Social equality; 5. Redistribution of power towards workers' control and consumers' control; 6. Environment and transport and 7. Foreign policy.' Those were Crosland's great thoughts which were leaked to the press as the most brilliant intellectual contribution of the day.

Douglas Houghton pointed out that we had left the Common Market out of our thinking and it would dominate the next Parliament if we didn't confront it. Did we *really* want a Referendum on whether to endorse membership of the EEC?

Denis said the annual cost of our programme was twice to three times what we would get from existing revenues and we would have to face this.

I said, 'I think we should stick to our programme. It is a rolling programme designed to be developed each year. It is thought-out and constructive. It is available for consultation in detail, it was for Conference to pronounce upon and the Manifesto will be drawn from it. When do we implement it? It used to be said it would take one Parliament, then two Parliaments, then three, now twenty years and finally it is suggested we publish it as a book. This is where the doctrine of the mandate comes in, that Conference wants us to do more than we are evidently ready to do. Of course, we will have to have priorities where costs are concerned but there are other things, for example dealing with voluntary schools, which costs nothing at all.'

I said we really had to have a political perspective. There was growth though we didn't know how secure it was. We also had to face the fact that we were confronting a growth of corporate power and the political link with that corporate power in the Tory Party was very important. Now that capital had new freedom of movement within the Common Market and links with the mass media, with the Third World, with African wages, with ITT and Chile, we were facing a new feudalism. We had a supreme opportunity now to expose and reveal the nature of that corporate power and its link with the Tory Party and to win people over to a change in the power structure without which none of the interesting things that Tony Crosland had said could be done. We were looking to make a fundamental and irreversible transfer in the balance of wealth and power.

Peter Doyle, the Young Socialists' NEC member, said he had first read about this document in the press and it had been described as Wilson's nightmare so that he himself had thought it must be a pretty good programme; but when he read it he couldn't understand what the fuss was about. He said, 'The Party is trumping for change. Ninety per cent of the Party supported Tony Benn on Rolls Royce. They are worried about unemployment and a minimum wage.'

Ian Mikardo questioned the Party's objective. We should not be defensive. Those who stand by the present order in society should be asked to justify the system. For example, one seventh of the population is below the family income supplement level.

Michael Foot said, 'Look, we start with the repeal of the Tory Acts. We look at the Common Market; we repeal the Pay Board; we get rid of the Industrial Relations Act and the Housing Finance Act. Then we go on from there. The Common Market is the key issue both in the next Election and in the next Parliament. Public ownership is the only way to make our society democratic.'

'We must start with philosophy' said Shirley Williams. 'Our object is to transform society: but we must get elected. How could you cope with an electorate which was very sceptical? Only by showing you mean what you say. Priorities can be radical but they must be realisable. The public is not yet persuaded in favour of old-fashioned public ownership.'

Joan Lestor agreed that we did lack a philosophy and this had lost us a whole generation of young people. Education must be among our top priorities, particularly pre-school education. We must come out for high taxation. Public ownership was essential but it must be real and within democratic control. Party credibility depended on our being ready to do what we said we would do.

Renée Short of the Women's Section said there was insufficient reference in the document to women.

Jim Callaghan quoted Maxton: 'If you can't ride two horses, you ought not to be in the circus.' The object of the document was to state our position, to enthuse our supporters *and* to win the Election. We could come to power when the economy was slowing down and it could be more difficult than 1964.

On incomes policy, John Forrester said that the workers simply wouldn't accept wage restraint if everything else was decided by market forces. Denis Healey said, 'We have got to try with a statutory prices and voluntary incomes policy.'

Harold made some reference to the balance of payments and the multi-nationals, and Harold Lever launched into a great attack upon planning agreements. He said there was no relationship at all between the remedies we proposed and the problems faced by the last Labour Government. Parrot cries about public ownership or the media or planning would get us nowhere. We were, in effect, trying to assert that we couldn't run a mixed economy.

We broke for lunch and, as I left the room at the Churchill, some journalists came up and asked me to comment on George Brown, who had attacked me on the BBC last night, describing me as 'an ageing young man, like Stafford Cripps before he saw the light'. As I hadn't heard the broadcast, I refused to comment on George Brown, but I said I was very honoured to be compared with Stafford Cripps who was my predecessor – I recalled that George Brown had moved the expulsion of Stafford Cripps from the Party! Then I was asked about this morning's meeting and I said it had been very good natured. Harold was fussing round like an old chicken saying, 'Look at him, look, he's briefing the press, he's briefing.' The man seems paranoid.

I sat at lunch with Jim and Harold. I think Harold's a bit frightened of me at the moment. Jim took me aside and said, 'My dear boy, I know what you've been going through over the past few days. This is what happens to every political leader as he breaks through to become a major figure and I want you to know that I understand how you feel.' I can't help liking Jim; he is so avuncular and agreeable. At the same time, it was an indication that he recognised I was in earnest.

After lunch, I opened on industrial policy, saying that Mik would deal with the details of public ownership but the real question was whether public ownership was old hat or was our defence against the new feudalism. None of us was credible unless we were talking from our own experience. I looked back on my experience at the Ministry of Technology (I made friendly references to Harold Lever) and public ownership did seem to me to be a central issue. We were short of powers. We didn't realise the importance of the workers' role. We hadn't learned the lesson of Heath. The Common Market Bill was itself an Enabling bill transferring powers to others to make rules. We must have all these powers. We would use them for different purposes, and we would use different methods to devolve these powers and make them all democratically accountable. But these powers were essential and explicable; they cost nothing; and they could be acquired in a single bill in our first session.

Ian Mikardo said the Lever doctrine of watering down our programme had been tried and had failed. North Sea oil and gas must be nationalised. The workers *did* want public ownership. We did well when we had a confrontation with the Tories over it as in the 1964 Election. As to the twenty-five companies, that was put in to tie the leadership and he would therefore be prepared to delete the reference if we had the Industrial Powers Act.

Judith Hart said, 'The National Enterprise Board is the major theme and as Harold said . . .' at which point Harold Wilson interrupted, 'Do you mean me or Harold Lever?' I said, 'While you're at it, when people talk about Tony, they might make clear who they mean too.' Judith continued that the British public sector was smaller than most and the last Government had relied on demand management, indicative planning and the little Neddies which weren't sufficient.

Fred Mulley came back to ends versus means and said, 'Don't maximise the opposition by being too explicit.' Roy Hattersley was against powers in an Enabling bill. 'We know what we want to take over – about six to eight companies.' Frank Allaun said that our greatest weakness was that there was no apparent difference between the Parties.

Crosland argued that there was no link between public ownership and equality, no link between powers and control. He said he couldn't answer questions in his own constituency about what would happen to the companies there. The public would accept nationalisation in individual cases but not as the general case.

Denis Healey said, 'Capitalism in Britain needs structural change.' The National Enterprise Board had been tried in Italy, planning agreements in France; an Enabling bill would give the Tories their great chance. He was against public ownership by statutory instrument, or an Industrial Commissioner or the NEB's power to invest.

Harold Wilson was in favour of the National Enterprise Board as a shareholding body but he wanted an Industrial Reorganisation Corporation, which revealed that his thinking hadn't altered much since 1964. He said he quite liked the planning agreements but he was opposed to nationalisation by statutory instrument and said, 'We simply pass a bill to take over when we want to.' He was also against the twenty-five companies and said, 'Who's going to tell me that we should nationalise Marks & Spencer in the hope that it will be as efficient as the Co-op.' As to the City, banking and insurance, he said, 'We only take notice of Conference resolutions when it suits us, everyone knows that.' He then launched into an attack on the Stock Exchange, saying that there was a case for merging and amalgamating building societies under state supervision. On insurance companies, he thought we should start with motor insurance, but we couldn't nationalise the merchant banks; we would take over one bank and then someone else would set up another one next door. A state unit trust run by the Post Office Giro for investment in industry might be desirable.

Willie Ross said, 'We mustn't be afraid of being radical. After all, in 1964 my Highlands and Islands Board had been attacked. We must be relevant but shouldn't give hostages to fortune.' He favoured an Enabling bill and he said, 'We must modernise parliamentary procedure.'

I quoted what Heseltine had said to me on television last night about workers and public ownership and Bob Mellish said, 'You were marvellous on television but don't wreck us by putting it forward now.'

At this point the meeting was closed, so I said, 'We really need to continue this discussion.' I didn't want it ended, it was so important.

Friday 18 May

Had a long phone conversation with Arnold Weinstock who rang me. He is on the board of Rolls Royce, and he wanted to pass on a vaguely friendly political message in the light of the Booz-Allen report on shipbuilding. He said, 'Why did the Tories commission American consultants to attack the British ship building industry? And why did they then arrange for that attack to be published since it would be used by people all over the world? Did you know that Booz-Allen was the firm of consultants that they used to plan and prepare their changes in the structure of government, including the Rayner reorganisation of the Defence Procurement Executive?* Should this not be probed? But don't mention my name.'

Having formerly been the villain of the piece, I am now worthwhile getting in touch with. He is undoubtedly worried about public ownership.

Saturday 19 May

I should report that every day this week the Watergate hearings have been on and are being shown simultaneously on television by satellite. It is absolutely riveting. Ludovic Kennedy of the BBC has gone over there. When I saw him doing *Midweek* this week, I told him the scoop of the century would be to get an interview with Alger Hiss when Nixon finally falls because Nixon was his chief congressional prosecutor in the Un-American Activities Committee; Kennedy was taken with the idea. Hiss, who was named as a Soviet agent during the McCarthyite period, was jailed for perjury, and has continually protested his innocence to this day.

Watergate is clearly going to bring Nixon down.

Monday 21 May

To the TUC-Labour Party Liaison Committee meeting at Congress House, and in the lift I said to Jack Jones, 'We must nationalise the aircraft industry, and I want a bit of help from you on this.'

While we were sitting waiting for the meeting to begin, there was some joking about what positions we would like to hold. Jim Callaghan said he'd like to be head of the IMF. Douglas Houghton wanted to be General Secretary of the TUC. Harold said, 'No doubt Tony would like to be the Archbishop of Canterbury.' It was a very snide remark. So I said, 'Do you know, Jim, I had a dream about you that you *would* join the IMF' (these rumours have appeared in the last few days) 'and that you would come back on a mission when the next Labour Government was in power and wreck that Government too.' It was going very near the mark but he did have the courtesy to laugh.

We spent an hour or so discussing the Labour Party's comments on

---

* In 1970 Derek (later Lord) Rayner, a director of Marks & Spencer, was attached to the Civil Service Department to head a team of businessmen examining defence procurement. In 1972 he was appointed Chief Executive of the new Procurement Executive. Subsequently he became Chairman of Marks & Spencer. He served as chief adviser on efficiency to the Prime Minister, 1979–83.

the TUC's proposals for replacing the 1971 Industrial Relations Act.[4]
Vic Feather said, 'We want a clear-cut repeal of the Industrial Relations
Act, a restoration of the pre-1971 position, then an employees' protection act, a new industrial relations act, and then industrial democracy.'

After much discussion, Jack said, 'Look we *must* have repeal,' and
Harold Wilson agreed.

Hugh Scanlon said, 'We're going round in circles. We can't have
registration of trade unions as at present replaced by certification under
a new act. I am fundamentally opposed to this.'

'Look, we are only proposing to go back to the pre-1971 situation –
registration on an optional basis – which would have no implications
for you at all,' Douglas Houghton explained.

Harold Wilson said we proposed to have two acts, one repealing the
Tory Act and another within three months.

Wednesday 23 May
At the NEC, when we came on to my motion on open decision-making
at the Executive, Bill Simpson asked me to defer it because there was
a lot of business. I insisted and moved it in about ninety seconds. It
provided that we should record the NEC motions and votes, make
them available as minutes once they were agreed and publish them in
the Party's annual report. The argument against was that it was a big
change and it might put pressure on members of the Executive. The
argument in its favour was that delegates were entitled to know; and
the General Secretary's press briefing after each NEC was a move in
this direction. There was no reason for secrecy.

I was interested but should not have been surprised to find that
Michael Foot attacked this, saying that we must have secret minutes;
it would alter the nature of the Executive, it would make meetings
more formal and injure the NEC's effectiveness, and would push real
discussion elsewhere.

Harold Wilson said he agreed with Michael's conclusions but he did
deplore the leaks and to this extent agreed with me – Harold himself
always abstained on voting and that was understood.

It was agreed that Ron Hayward would make a paper available at
the next NEC.

Afterwards, Michael Foot was absolutely violent. He contended my
procedure was like that in Communist countries and would drive the
NEC back to secret discussion. He is an élitist parliamentarian and he
doesn't like the relationship with the rank-and-file if it means they put
pressure on him; he's a parlour pink to this extent. Altogether it was
rather sharp.

Thursday 24 May
The papers are absolutely crammed with the Lambton resignation; Lord Jellicoe, Leader of the House of Lords, has also resigned[5] admitting that he had had affairs with call-girls. It is astonishing when this happens. You get two Ministers resigning and the press behaves as if the whole world is coming to an end.

Sunday 27 May
Stansgate. Twelve hours in bed. The Lambton and Jellicoe affairs dominated the papers today – articles by A.J.P. Taylor and by Montgomery Hyde, leaders on private and public standards, historical parallels. 'Is it a Communist plot?' The Bishop of Leicester is sympathetic. Comments by the Chairman of the Church Committee for Social Responsibility, and so on.

Monday 28 May
I woke up at 1.15 in the morning because I had so long in bed, so worked until 4.30 finishing my memorandum on the Official Secrets Act and the appointment of outside advisers to Ministers.

A lovely afternoon and the river was full of boats.

Wednesday 30 May
To the Churchill Hotel for the final National Executive meeting to discuss the programme, where we began with a long argument about pensions with Barbara Castle defending Dick Crossman's earnings-related pension scheme with the support of Harold Wilson, Shirley Williams and Denis Healey. On the other side Judith Hart, Bill Simpson, Peter Doyle, who made a marvellous speech about his father, a retired busman, and Joan Maynard arguing for a new scheme which was not funded and was based on raising the basic pension from general taxation.

On health we had an argument about fluoridation. I asked, 'Why do we have to put fluoridation into the programme at all? It splits both the Left and the Right straight down the middle and it is putting teeth into our programme quite unnecessarily,' at which there was much laughter.

Then we had a considerable debate about Ministers having personal cabinets. I argued strongly for them and Harold said we could have them. Jim said they just inflated the egos and ambitions of Ministers. Fred Mulley was against them. Much to my surprise, on a vote the motion was defeated by 11 votes to 8 with Lena Jeger, a former civil servant, coming out against. Barbara was strongly in favour.

A discussion followed about how we should handle immigration. Jim

Callaghan wanted us to put in specifically the control of numbers. I managed to get added to the phrase that our immigration policy would not be dictated by racial consideration, 'nor dictated to us by EEC rules'.

After lunch we came on to housing and land, where there was a great discussion about whether we would acquire land automatically if it came up for development and that was carried by 11 to 1, Shirley voting against. In the end the issue of the Enabling bill came up which I got through by making adjustments on phrases. Harold supported it, even nationalisation of companies by the Enabling bill, although nationalisation of whole industries might still require individual acts of Parliament. The Industrial Commissioner is going to be called Public Trustee and will go in when a company has betrayed its workers or has violated the national interest. So I was immensely pleased.

On re-nationalisation, we had an argument about how we would handle re-acquisition of parts of an industry that had been hived off, without compensation. I tried the form of words that 'while accepting the Conference resolution, we re-affirm the view that we have expressed that those who have bought hived-off assets cannot expect to make any profits through compensation from another Labour Government'. But Frank Allaun, Joan Maynard and Peter Doyle were absolutely determined to stick to their guns. When Michael Foot suggested we simply delete the whole passage and look at it separately, it was carried by 10 votes to 3. I did emphasise we have not repudiated the Conference resolution and I hope that is accepted.

Then we moved on to the National Enterprise Board and the question of the twenty-five companies. Harold tried to tone it down and say they simply would keep the equity shares in a public safe deposit! I said this wasn't good enough and I argued for a substantial increase. To my amazement, although most of the Left had disappeared early so that by the time we actually came to it, the Left seemed to just about balance the Right, a vote to preserve the commitment to the twenty-five companies was carried by 7 votes to 6. The seven were myself, Joan Maynard, Frank Allaun, Judith Hart, Peter Doyle, and I think John Chalmers and Joan Lestor; against, Michael Foot, Shirley Williams, Jim Callaghan, Walter Padley, Sid Weighell [Assistant General Secretary of the NUR] and Denis Healey, who recommended we delete it altogether. It was astonishing. Harold said he would have to reserve the position of the Shadow Cabinet. But although 7 to 6 was not a famous victory, it did reflect the balance of opinion on the Executive and that was important.

That was more or less all. I left at 9.40 pm and caught a bus home. Today has been successful. The Party is now firmly launched on a left-wing policy, which I am strongly in favour of, and although no doubt there will be some concessions made in the Manifesto, it is a remarkable development of views that we have achieved in three years of hard work. I quoted today the little booklet in the 1935 Election, 'Fifty Reasons for Voting Labour', which included the nationalisation of banking, credit, insurance and so on. Jim quite properly said, 'Remember what happened in the 1935 Election; we only got 150 seats,' but circumstances were different. So I feel it has been a good job and nobody can argue now that there is no difference between the Parties. Now we have got to carry the argument and fight the battle.

Wednesday 6 June
To the *Financial Times* lunch with about 250 bankers representing between them assets of £95,000 million.

Charles Villiers [Chairman of Guinness Mahon] introduced me very courteously and I got up and delivered my speech. It was like trying to shoot an elephant with a humane killer. I said nothing that wouldn't have been regarded as normal at a Labour Party Conference, but the fact that I had the effrontery to say it here was frightening for them, because they realised I was serious. Charles Villiers then stood up and said, 'A very important speech and I can assure you that Tony Benn loves his country as much as you or I do' implying that after such a speech they would assume that I was a traitor. It was a most significant comment to make.

After lunch, Caroline and I went to Oxford. She went off to see Marilyn Butler and had dinner at St Hugh's, while I gave my seminar at Nuffield College and talked about ministerial advisers. That awful man (whose name I've forgotten), a Tory who fought Joan Lestor at Slough,* was there on a year's special fellowship. Of course, nobody agreed with me about ministerial advisers.

Later that evening, I met a student who told me she had been working on a study of urban poverty for the Home Office. I asked why the Home Office. 'Well,' she said, 'they have a lot of economists they don't know what to do with, so they put them on this job.' I said, 'Surely the useful thing to do would be to carry out a study on what to do with redundant economists.' Here is a woman who has been to public or direct grant school, had a scholarship, or paid to go to Oxford, got a good degree and, having had all these advantages ladled upon her, was about to earn a very good living studying poverty, when the poor could have done so much more with her salary. I found the whole thing revolting.

* Nigel Lawson, elected Conservative MP for Blaby, 1974; Chancellor of the Exchequer from 1983 until his resignation in October 1989.

Friday 8 June
Enoch Powell has made a great speech implying that he might recommend his followers to vote Labour in the next Election on the grounds that only the Labour Party would offer an opportunity to the people of this country to vote against the Common Market. This has created an enormous sensation: Will he be thrown out and what are his motives?

Saturday 9 June
To Bristol, and visited the University Settlement at Barton Hill for the opening ceremony of their new hall. I then raced up to Manchester to attend the first National Community Action Conference at the Institute of Science and Technology. Des Wilson was there, very much a media figure, a journalist who has gone in to championing the underprivileged; and David Sheppard, the Bishop of Woolwich, a cricketing vicar who was wearing a purple shirt to signify his episcopacy and a purple ring – a trendy left-wing bishop of a kind disliked by the Establishment.

The Conference turned out to be extremely unruly. Before I went on there was a good little play produced by Prunella Scales, a TV actress associated with the Socialist Labour League. I was due to speak at 8 o'clock and my slides didn't work for some time, so there was a lot of ribald laughter and they shouted, 'It's an insult to our intelligence. We've been betrayed,' and so on. But I stuck it out and hit back.

'You think you've discovered pressure groups and community action. The trade union movement began community action 130 years ago and you have separated yourself from it. That's why you are ineffective and are not achieving what you hoped to.'

When I sat down, a very dishevelled woman of about thirty-five with a Tyneside accent spoke. 'I have got five children, my father's a disabled pensioner and I look after him as well. This is the first time that I have ever come in a university building in all my life. I came to this conference and you,' she said pointing contemptuously at all the people who had shouted, 'you wouldn't let me listen to that man,' pointing at me. It was the working class revolt against the intellectuals. The questions and answers went on but this sense of betrayal was very evident. These people had absolutely no confidence in me or in the Labour Party.

Sunday June 10
Brian Walden, the Labour MP for Birmingham All Saints, came to the house at 11 o'clock and stayed until 3. I had asked him to look in. He drank quite a lot, and talked continuously but I learned a great deal. He told me that he had been Hugh Gaitskell's script writer and that it was he who wrote 'Fight, fight and fight again', which was the speech that triggered off Harold Wilson's candidature against Hugh Gaitskell

for the leadership in 1960. Also, in respect of the Common Market, Brian had invented Hugh Gaitskell's phrase about 'throwing away a thousand years of British history'. So these two phrases, for which Gaitskell is most clearly remembered, didn't actually even come from him. As one of Hugh Gaitskell's older script writers myself, going way back to 1956, I was fascinated to hear this.

Anyway, Brian took it that I had wanted his advice and proceeded to give it me. He said he thought that I could possibly be the Leader of the Party and that I had to turn my mind quickly and carefully to the problem of why I wasn't getting across to Labour MPs. He thought the reason was that I was frightening them. They had their constituencies, a good job in the House of Commons and I disturbed them, disrupted life and made them feel they might lose. What they wanted was reassurance: Harold Wilson was always reassuring them and I was worrying them. This is not so different from what Frank McElhone says.

We went on to talk about economic policy and the mixed economy. He talked compulsively. 'Of course we want a mixed economy but a real one, in which the big companies and major corporations are either run or owned by the state; if people pay their taxes and are treated decently, and provided for properly, particularly with their pensions so that they are not humiliated in retirement, then we can have competition and capitalism at that level, where it really applies.'

Of himself he said he would never hold office and he intended to retire from Parliament when he was fifty. Although he wanted to go on with politics, it didn't pay enough. I urged him to think again but I think he was probably deeply hurt that he hadn't been given a job by Harold Wilson, just as Dick Crossman was that he hadn't been given a job by Clem Attlee in the 1945 Government. So Brian has compensated by using his natural brilliance in order to make money and to secure his own future.

Monday 11 June
Parliamentary Questions and Geoffrey Howe, the Solicitor-General, in answer to one of my questions said that the government thought a mixed economy was preferable to the 'neo-Socialist and neo-Communist doctrines of the Right Honourable gentleman': so now, actually in the House, I have been called a Communist.

I dashed to the Organisation Committee where the big item was that we abolish the list of proscribed organisations. Really a notable change, signifying the end of the Cold War in a Labour Party context, just as the visits between Nixon and Mao and Brezhnev marked its end in an international context. It was a great gain.

Stephen came with June [Battye] to dinner at the House of Commons this evening. We walked on the terrace and Jim Callaghan was extremely friendly, awfully courteous to them, and we talked a bit. It appears that that French vetoed his appointment to the IMF and he was disappointed.

Tuesday 12 June

Jack Jones and Geoffrey Goodman, Industrial Editor of the *Mirror*, came to dinner. It was a most interesting evening and it confirmed what I had long suspected, that Jack Jones, far from being a left-wing radical, has settled down into a central position which could best be described at the moment as the Healey stance, Jack obviously having a very high regard for Denis. I seem to remember from reading the security report on Jack which was once sent to me, that he had been a Communist. But at any rate, here they are, both in their middle fifties, both anxious to get rid of Heath. In effect, what Jack said was that we must concentrate on priorities. We must deal with prices and pensions. We must relate everything we say to the problems. We didn't want airy-fairy stuff. Nationalisation was unpopular; it failed. We were not a socialist party and it was too late to convert us into one. He said he understood Harold Wilson's position on all this and rather shared it. Then he asked me again, 'Why don't you make a speech on pensions instead of all this airy-fairy stuff?' He went on to say that Heath was in many ways more advanced in his thinking and his relations with the trade unions than the previous Labour Government had been.

We went on to talk about Harold's veto on policy. I said that if Enoch Powell came out in the Election and supported the Labour Party policy on Europe, we would be in danger of having our commitment to the Referendum vetoed by Harold at Roy Jenkins's insistence. Jack said, 'Well you would have to let Roy go and you would have to accept Powell's support on Europe.' I agree with that.

Geoffrey Goodman has just come back from a trip to China with Hugh Cudlipp. He said Hugh had been deeply moved and impressed by China, was now trying to introduce workers' participation in the *Mirror*, and was going to commission a series of articles on workers' participation.

Wednesday 13 June

Had a talk to Jim Sillars, the Labour MP for South Ayrshire, and he told me that the Tribune Group was unanimously against the Leader's veto and also 70 per cent against the twenty-five companies proposal. He told me a bit about the Scottish position and how he himself had become a convinced Scottish nationalist: he thought that when the Kilbrandon Report on the Constitution came out, this would cause deep divisions in the Parliamentary Party. I foresee very real difficulties on this score.

In the evening Walter Greendale of the TGWU, the Hull docker I met at the Institute for Workers' Control Conference in Nottingham in March, came to see me at Ken Coates's suggestion to see how we could follow up public ownership of the twenty-five companies. He had had the idea of calling a national shop stewards' conference to discuss it. But I said I thought the best thing to do was to stimulate debates actually in the factories or workshops, or among shop stewards of one particular company at a time, so one could begin to test the extent to which support would build up within a company for the public ownership of that company. If such debates could really be started, it would be tremendously effective in strengthening our hand politically, making it easier for us when the time comes, indeed making it inevitable.

Wednesday 20 June

Shadow Cabinet all day, where we had a full and important debate. Tony Crosland started by saying, 'What is the electoral strategy of the Left? The polls don't seem to imply any rise in militancy, and nor do the by-elections. There is no swing to the Left, and, if anything, there is a swing to the Liberals. There is anxiety about undemocratic local parties and trade unions. Labour MPs are more in touch with local Party members than members of the Executive. The trade union bloc votes are unpopular.' As a result, he couldn't either see or understand a lurch to the Left.

Michael Foot said the twenty-five company proposal was crazy and he believed I had committed an error in submitting it. The Manifesto Committee was a joint body and not two bodies. He didn't want to have a vote on the twenty-five at the Conference and therefore we had to find a formula beforehand to avoid difficulties. Ron Hayward should start discussions on public ownership and we should put a statement to Conference that would wipe out the issue of the twenty-five companies, so that there would be general agreement. If we couldn't sort it out we were not fit to be here.

Jim Callaghan thought the twenty-five companies issue was a symptom of changes in the attitude of the NEC which sought to alter the relationship between itself and the PLP. He gave four examples. One was the overt encouragement to the rebels in the case of the Housing Finance Act; second, the NEC proposal that there should be no compensation for the re-acquisition of the hived-off assets; thirdly, its ill-judged support for the day of protest and stoppage; and finally the case of the twenty-five companies. He said this represented a changing approach by the NEC and he did not regard the National Executive as representative of the Labour Party. Harold Wilson was a most popular leader and, except for a small group of envious and jealous people, everyone agreed with his veto statement.

Harold said the next Election would be fought on 'prices at a stroke'. He was sorry that the twenty-five companies row had let Lambton and Jellicoe off the hook. The Leader had to assert himself, and the PLP had urged him to take a line. A resolution for Conference on public ownership which excluded the twenty-five companies was the answer. He then made another contemptuous reference to candidates for the NEC looking for votes – which was obviously a reference to Judith Hart and me. Generally speaking he appeared unattractive and uninspired.

Then I said this was the most important discussion we had had for a long time. I didn't take a tragic view of our disagreements. One thing that was encouraging was that in all the polls, twice as many people believed the Labour Party cared about what the electorate thought as believed the Tories did, and this was what a mature democracy was about. I said this was a debate, it wasn't personal, we all had confidence in Harold Wilson, it wasn't a reference to him, and the Manifesto could exclude the twenty-five so long as it included the word 'substantial'. The real discussion was whether we were being led by an economic boom back to consensus politics, as seemed to be implied. I didn't take that view. I thought that there was a certain breakdown of society requiring radical solutions. I understood Jim and Shirley's point about democracy being threatened by the NEC, but I took a much graver view that democracy was being strangled by entry into the Common Market, by the corporate state, by the power of business, and by the mass media. The way to win was to attract support from our own people. I pointed to the fall of 13 per cent in the turnout at the thirty-six polling stations in my constituency over twenty years.

I said I wasn't prepared to go back and try to bribe businessmen to do what was not in the interests of their shareholders. As to Party democracy, I couldn't object to what Harold had said about the veto because he had only said publicly what had been said privately for years. But the case for taking some notice of the Conference was that when you looked back over the conflicts between the Conference and the Labour Cabinet in the years we were in office, the Conference had very often been right. But, I said, I thought there was a danger of double standards in saying some things privately and other things publicly.

Denis Healey blurted out, 'Well, Tony Benn has just advocated absolute madness – that we should debate this publicly – absolutely mad.' He was livid. Denis is a management man. He sees everything in terms of looking tidy and neat and efficient.

Then Michael Foot asked me, 'Are you *really* going for the twenty-five companies? Do you think we could win the Election? Do you *want* to win the Election? What are you up to? What are you saying?'

By the time I finished lunch, the rumour was already going round that Michael Foot had accused me of wanting to lose the Election, suggesting that I wanted to do it simply in order to become Leader of the Party. This story had been leaked immediately after the Shadow Cabinet and appeared in all the papers tonight: 'Foot Bashes Benn', 'Foot Stamps on Benn'. I declined to comment because I could immediately see the advantage of not trying to combat this story but to let it ride as having come from others. So I said nothing.

Collected the papers at midnight and cut out all the headlines. This is exactly what I wanted; leaks from the Shadow Cabinet that couldn't possibly have come from me and that will help me to put across my argument that the Shadow Cabinet proceedings should be made public.

Thursday 21 June

Jim rang up to tell me that I had been badly used and he said, 'You know, we could work well together.' He also told me he was writing a preface of a book on Giro and asked if I could help him with it. So I went back to my files and dug out my original article of June 1964 in the *Guardian* about the Post Office, Jim's letter to me when he was Chancellor, expressing great caution about it, and the text of my speech announcing it, and sent them all off to him.

Michael Foot came into my room at the House, very shamefaced because he has been described in the papers as the man who destroyed me at the Shadow Cabinet. He thought I would be angry but I wasn't. He didn't agree with it; he told me that Jack Jones was against the twenty-five which I knew anyway. He said he had written to the papers saying the report that had appeared was inaccurate. He said, 'We can't have a confrontation over the veto and the NEC should submit a statement on public ownership which would ease the difficulty of compensation and the twenty-five companies.' I said I thought it was, in the end, a matter of honest politics, whether one was ready to say publicly what one said privately. I don't think Michael liked that very much.

Saturday 23 June

We prepared for a party today. About sixty people came including, Michael Foot and Jill Craigie – both a little embarrassed – Dick Clements [Editor of *Tribune*], Norman Atkinson and his wife, Eric and Doris Heffer, Ron and Phyllis Hayward, Frances Morrell, the Zanders, Robin Day, Margaret Jackson, Tony Banks, Alan Evans of the NUT, Peter Shore, Stuart Holland, the Harts, the Arnold-Forsters and the Meachers. It went on until about 2 in the morning, and it was jolly and friendly. We agreed to form the 'Twenty-five Club' committed to the nationalisation of the twenty-five companies.

Sunday 24 July

Had dinner with Frank Judd, Frank Field, Jack Straw, Joan Lestor and someone else from one of the pressure groups. The middle-class pressure groups think differently from the trade unions. Frank Judd's background is Fabian in the sense that his father was the Secretary of the League of Nations Union and the United Nations Association. Frank Field is a weak character, Director of the Child Poverty Action Group. Jack Straw is a young lawyer on the make who has come up through the National Union of Students. They were sort of tempted by what I was saying but they think of socialism very much in terms of race relations – somewhere else rather than at home.

Later I read H. N. Brailsford's book, *The Levellers*, which Antonia Fraser's book on Cromwell triggered me to read. The criticisms made by the Levellers of the people in seventeenth-century England who cared more about a few Christians captured by the Moors or held as slaves by the Turks in Constantinople than the condition of the people at home reminded me of Nye Bevan who was so scornful of those for whom socialism began south of the Sahara. There was a touch of that about this evening, but still I enjoyed it.

Tuesday 26 June

I have been really absorbed by my reading on the English Revolution and I asked Jack Mendelson the Labour MP for Penistone, a former University lecturer, if he would give me a private tutorial on the English Revolution. We had about an hour in the Tea Room on the Levellers and the Diggers or True Levellers, who comprised a radical group in Cromwell's army. It was fascinating. He gave me a reading list including Christopher Hill on Cromwell, so I have set aside Antonia Fraser's book now and am concentrating on the serious ideological and historical stuff.

All the parallels with the situation today are there. The argument with the King and his court: Heath and the City of London, with the big corporations. Then one can see the right wing of the Parliamentary Labour Party as the Presbyterians, rigid, doctrinaire, right-wing, but officially on the side of puritanism or socialism. The Socialist Labour League and the International Socialists on the Left are the Agitators. The Levellers are broadly the Labour movement as a whole. There is the argument about the pulpit and who has access to it, which could be seen as the whole debate about democracy today. I had no idea that the Levellers had called for universal manhood suffrage, equality between the sexes, biennial Parliaments, the sovereignty of the people, recall of representatives and even an attack on property: concepts which later emerged in the constitution of the United States and indeed in the French Revolution.

Wednesday 27 June

At the NEC, we came to my motion calling for the publication of the minutes. I introduced it briefly and circulated the press reports that had appeared after the last meeting, both from *The Times*: one describing the voting figures and who had voted for the twenty-five companies; the other, Harold's comment that the Shadow Cabinet would not hesitate to use its veto.

Denis Healey said if you did publish the minutes, you must also publish the reasons; the Party didn't like hearing about disagreement, it damaged morale. He didn't see why, if there were individual examples of bed-wetting, we should go in for collective incontinence. A very amusing analogy.

Michael strongly supported Denis. He argued that from a practical point of view, the press would play up our disagreements. There was no democratic principle involved. The NEC must act as an Executive; we must have some secret meetings and if we weren't allowed to have them here, the effect would be to transfer the discussions into even more private meetings.

I dealt with this briefly in winding up. I said, 'You don't publish the reasons in Hansard for voting. My name is often published in the Division list when I haven't made a speech.' I said that we were all accountable; that it wouldn't be expensive. I said the decisions we make were important, why shouldn't the Party know what we were doing? The cure for leaks was to ensure that people got the information they were entitled to. I thought it would tend to bring us all together.

To the Shadow Cabinet where I had moved the same resolution on the publication of Shadow Cabinet minutes. Tony Crosland said he would like to have minutes of the Shadow Cabinet, he didn't see why we couldn't.

Harold Wilson said, 'We are here to wage a war and we shouldn't reveal our thinking to the enemy.'

I was defeated in effect 12 to 1 so that was the end of that exercise in democracy.

Friday 29 June

Up at 5.45 to go to Bristol for the Clifton Cathedral consecration. I had been invited by the Catholic Bishop Rudderham. Cardinal Heenan, the Archbishop of Westminster, was there and also the apostolic delegate from the Vatican, thirty-one bishops, several abbots, four Anglican bishops, and my friend Father Norbury from the Jesuits.

I don't think I had ever been to a Catholic service in my life, I thoroughly enjoyed it. I was impressed by the simplicity of what one expected to be a very elaborate service and the humbleness of the cathedral itself – the fact that Catholic Bishops don't now wear elaborate robes but very simple yellow mitres and saffron capes; the fact that the service itself is in English and very simple. The whole thing is quite unlike the Latin mass from which the Anglican service is taken, so that they have begun to remove the barriers between the priests and the public. They did have the relics of the saints which were concreted into the altar to satisfy the faithful. They burned the incense and blessed the twelve points in the cathedral; but by Anglican standards there was nothing too fancy about it.

Cardinal Heenan gave a homily in which he said that, unlike the Age of Faith, the Christian Church was now a minority religion and he contrasted the present position rather unfavourably. I asked him afterwards whether the Age of Faith was a reference to the pre-Reformation. He said, 'Oh no, that would have been very unecumenical!' I said how much I had enjoyed and been moved by the consecration, one didn't just go in and watch, one had to help to turn the building into the cathedral. The congregation had something to do. When we were outside Bishop Rudderham's chauffeur was standing there and he asked what we thought about the musicals *Godspell* and *Jesus Christ Superstar*; Heenan thought this was all rather trendy and hadn't got much to do with real religion.

Tuesday 3 July

Caroline and I drove to Keele to see Stephen receiving his BA degree. We were asked to join in the most revolting prayers: praying to Almighty God to see that a suitable supply of qualified manpower was there to run society. I must say Keele is, as somebody put it to me, a country offshoot of Oxbridge. Princess Margaret was the Chancellor, a stubby, dull, ageing princess.

Thursday July 5

Lunch with the German Ambassador, Karl von Hase, at the Embassy. He and his officials conducted a sort of interrogation but I actually quite enjoyed it. The Ambassador said to me, for example, 'Marxism is becoming pretty widely understood in the Labour Party now, isn't it, as it is in Germany?' He presumably wanted to tempt me into saying I was a Marxist. I said, 'I don't know really; it is a foreign ideology. The British Labour movement is fundamentally based on Christianity, expressing itself through the trade unions, through the distrust of power, through socialist ideas of cooperation; and the only difference between me and Harold Wilson is that he boasts of the fact that he has got through three pages of *Das Kapital* whereas I am ashamed of the fact that I *only* got through three pages.'

We went on to talk about Watergate and they hoped Nixon would survive, whereas I said I thought it was necessary that some example should be made of the abuse of power and that it would be a good thing if he was toppled.

Then I drove to Bristol for a long surgery. Went to the General Management Committee where there were two resolutions being considered for Conference. One was promoted by the Young Socialists calling for total democracy with the power of local parties to force the resignation of MPs; for MPs to receive the annual average wage to keep them in touch with workers; for election of the Leader by Conference and so on. This was not accepted but the one on nationalisation without compensation was accepted.

Monday 9 July

John Poulson, the architect, and Andy Cunningham, who is on the NEC, have been arrested. At the House today, I spoke to John Cunningham, the Labour MP for Whitehaven, who is Andy's son, and I just said, 'If there's anything I can do, let me know because your father has always been very kind to me.'

Wednesday 11 July

The Times published my article on secrecy and political advisers. I went to the PLP meeting on industrial policy and I opened very briefly.

When Harold Wilson spoke, he said it was a tragedy that 'twenty-six words out of 70,000' had done so much damage. This was a first-class policy, but Tory Central Office would read the twenty-five companies section very carefully and try to distract us. This was not a Left–Right issue, giving the impression that it was between the nationalisers and consolidators and, apart from the twenty-six words, it was a good document. He said the selection of twenty-five companies would be like picking names with a bodkin from the Yellow Pages. He would like to see the Co-op Development Agency come forward, and the workers' industrial future lay in creeping nationalisation with wider distribution of profits – *not* in controlling firms.

Harold's speech went down badly – it was immensely pedestrian and defensive, it concentrated entirely on the industrial scene, and afterwards there was a great row. Eric Heffer got up and said it seemed that there was a further withdrawal from the position on public ownership and he would be writing to Harold seeking clarification. In the Tea Room I chatted to Hugh Fraser. He told me that when he was Secretary of State for Air, he was in Washington at the time Profumo resigned, so he went to see John McCone, the Director of the CIA, to tell him that the CIA needn't worry because Profumo knew no real secrets. McCone had said to him, 'Thanks for telling me, we knew Jack was an early morning worker,' i.e., the CIA had known about his affair with Christine Keeler even before the British Government knew.

Monday 16 July

The *Sunday Post* had a poll in Scotland: who would you like to lead the Labour Party if Harold Wilson went? Thirty-five per cent said me, 33 per cent Michael Foot, Shirley Williams, 1 per cent and Roy Jenkins, 2 per cent.

At ten past ten, after a Division, I watched Lady Antonia Fraser's programme in the *One Pair of Eyes* series, about her work as a biographer. The first fifty minutes consisted of interviews with precious biographers and clever historians, with her wandering round the places she had visited when she was writing the biographies of Cromwell and Mary Queen of Scots. Then she talked of the difficulties of being a biographer of a modern subject. She said she had been to Birmingham to photograph a contemporary event, and there she was, watching the crowd with the pipers marching by, and shots of me with my pipe and grey hair, and bits of my speech into which she cut her commentary.

Tuesday 17 July

Lunch at Quaglino's with the 1972 Industry Group of Labour businessmen masterminded by Rudy Sternberg, Sir Joseph Kagan, Wilfred Brown, Arnold Gregory, Derek Page* and one or two others who have offered to advise the Labour Party on industrial matters. They are very close to Harold and hope to be put in positions of authority under a Labour Government. I am rather cynical about them.

Still reading books about the Levellers, Gerrard Winstanley and the 'True Levellers' – the Diggers. Of course, the Levellers lost and Cromwell won, and Harold Wilson or Denis Healey is the Cromwell of our day, not me. In a sense I feel these ideas are there to be called upon but if I pursue them to their logical end, the election of everybody and popular sovereignty and referenda and so on, I shall not carry support. That is the problem I face unless I can really carry through a major revolution.

Thursday 19 July

Bill Rodgers came to dinner. Hilary and Rosalind had bought some

---

* Sir Rudy Sternberg, Chairman of Sterling; Sir Joseph Kagan, Chairman of Gannex; Lord Brown, Chairman of Glacier Metal Company, Minister of State at the Board of Trade, 1965–70; Arnold Gregory, industrial consultant, Labour MP for Stockport North, 1964–70; Derek Page, businessman, Labour MP for King's Lynn, 1964–70.

strawberries and I gave him a good bottle of wine in the back kitchen of my basement office, where we talked for about three hours. First I tried to get him to assess the political situation – the prospects of winning. He thought there was a chance of winning but he didn't believe a radical change would be in tune with public opinion. On public ownership he felt that the case hadn't been made out and that we shouldn't really be doing it.

Then we got on to Harold and he said that Harold was a liability. He was meaner than he used to be, he hadn't matured as a statesman after he had been in power, that the middle of the Party was getting disillusioned with Harold. The new MPs had come into Parliament in 1970 thinking he was wonderful, and the more they had seen of him, the less they liked him.

Monday 23 July
Debate on the Price Commission and Pay Board reports. Enoch Powell gave a brilliant academic analysis of the cause of inflation and called for a restriction of the money supply. In winding up, I decided I would attack Enoch: people listen to him fascinated by his intellect and clarity and he mesmerises Labour MPs like rabbits caught in a headlamp. First, I dealt with the politics of inflation in my speech, and I came on to the Tory Party which had abandoned its Conservative philosophy and was destroying itself, and then I mentioned Powell. I said he had made a brilliant speech and people had admired him for breaking with his Party, but what he was calling for meant unemployment; and that there would be other effects on our society, including the possibility that people who were unemployed might turn upon immigrants. I said the country would be ill-advised to take his advice. Geoffrey Howe wound up with an awfully pedestrian speech.

Friday 27 July
The pound has fallen to 20 per cent of its value a year ago and the interest rates were raised to 11.5 per cent – critical rates. The situation is very serious now.

Spoke to Jeremy Thorpe about the possibility of a coalition government and whether Home would replace Heath, then invite Roy Jenkins, Harold Wilson, or Jeremy himself to join the coalition. Jeremy thought Home wouldn't be any good because he didn't know anything about economics. But I wouldn't rule out the possibility that it would be Home's qualities which would attract people rather than his particular knowledge on economic problems. Jeremy was cock-a-hoop, of course, and his bandwagon is rolling.

I rang Peter Shore to discuss the by-election results.* He sees a massive national crisis coming and says we must politicise it. He said, 'Of course there could be more than one coalition,' and he sort of indicated that there might be some Tory anti-Market people who would bring Heath down and we would then find ourselves with two coalitions – the Centre–Right European coalition with some Conservative leader other than Heath, and an uneasy correspondence of interests between the Left and the anti-Market right of the Tory Party, Neil Marten [Conservative MP for Banbury] and others, with Powell in the background. This would be extremely difficult. Peter thought Labour would have to advocate a 'doctors' mandate' which appealed to the nation as a whole and beyond the trade union movement, whose consensus support we would need. I said I was afraid of a doctors' mandate with Wilson in charge because I didn't trust him, but Peter said it would be different from the old image of Dr Wilson, doing everything for you, it would mean emergency measures to deal with the Market and a siege economy. He said that no thinking had been done, and nobody had really given any consideration to what these measures might be.

Well, I have *certainly* given a great deal of thought to the measures we might need. I think we would need the Emergency Powers Act and an emergency Industrial Act which would give the Minister absolute power to deal with the situation. Peter is quite right, we do have to make a national appeal. We must not use a great crisis of capitalism as an excuse for postponing reform, we will have to carry reform through on the wave of the capitalist crisis and this is what we must think about.

These are very stirring times.

Sunday 29 July
On *World at One* today, Roy Jenkins attacked Barber for his handling of the economy and called for tougher measures. Cecil King was interviewed, warning that there were no politicians in Britain who could lead the country out of its present difficulties and that he thought the parliamentary system was on its way out, although he didn't know what would replace it. When he was pressed he said he thought some businessmen should be brought in – so we are back to Great Britain Ltd.

---

* By-elections at Ripon and Isle of Ely, caused by the deaths of the sitting Conservative MPs, were won by the Liberals David Austick and Clement Freud. In both cases the Labour candidates dropped to third place.

Thursday 2 August
Twenty-five years ago today, I met Caroline.

A very bulky package arrived in the post, which was the Department of Trade and Industry's inquiry into the affairs of Rolls Royce, conducted by Mr MacCrindle QC and Peter Godfrey, a Fellow of the Institute of Chartered Accountants. What astonished me was that although I had been interviewed at length and quoted, they had not interviewed any of the Ministers responsible for Rolls Royce during the last two-year period. So there was in fact no criticism or comment about the Government's handling, a complete whitewash. It most unjustly blamed two men, Sir Denning Pearson, the Chairman of Rolls Royce in 1969–70, and David Huddie, the Chairman of the Aero-Engines division.

I discovered that twenty-five million shares had been bought at knockdown price when the company was bankrupt by an American nominee company and now of course these shares are worth 30p – so about £7m is going to American speculators that will be paid for out of the sale of Rolls Royce Motors. I had raised this issue in May and got into real trouble.

Sunday 2 September
Had drinks with the Croslands. I haven't seen them for a long time and I thought I might as well mend my fences as Susan and Tony are old friends of ours. Tony said that in all the years of Opposition, the only useful thing he had done was to develop the idea of a building society stabilisation fund. For him it was the working out of effective detailed policies that was the function of Opposition, whereas for me it was quite different. It was connecting the Party to the unions, working on future policy, encouraging people, explaining things and so on.

He said he was afraid that Roy Jenkins would stand for the Shadow Cabinet and would want the job of Shadow Secretary of State for the Environment and he, Tony, had no intention of moving as he particularly wanted to nationalise land. I told him that his interests in industrial policy had led me to believe he wanted to be Secretary of State for Industry, as a former President of the Board of Trade, but he replied he wasn't interested.

Thursday 6 September
To Bristol for the General Management Committee. Cyril Langham said that he was not able to accept any veto on our policy and that he hoped there would be resolutions at Conference on it. Bert Roach asked how Labour could fight its enemies. I said we would have to decide whether the crisis we had inherited would be the excuse for doing nothing or the occasion for doing something. Herbert Rogers said

the nationalised industries were being run by enemies who were not interested in the people. I was stimulated by the meeting; the arrival of the Beckinghams has greatly helped to encourage activity.

Friday 7 September

I rang Ron Hayward and he said, 'By the way, you are not introducing the industry debate at Conference. Harold is.' I saw red at that – I shouldn't have done, it showed a great lack of self-control, but I did because here was the man who had been trying to stop the industrial policy all summer, who threatened to veto it and now wants to present it. This was *my* subject, the thing I had worked on so hard. So I found out where he was and rang him. Stephen was with me, which I really felt necessary. I just lost my temper. 'I have just spoken to Ron about the industrial policy debate and he has told me that you don't want me to open it. I cannot believe that this is true. We spoke today and you made no reference to it. It would be a direct repudiation of me and the policy for which I am doubly responsible as Chairman of the NEC Policy Committee and the Front Bench industry spokesman. I actually drafted the eight points of the Industry Act and after your veto speech if I don't introduce it, it will be seen as a repudiation.'

Well, Harold played it down and said I misunderstood him and he had never intended that I was not to do it. In fact, I know that he had told Michael Foot that he wanted *him* to wind up the debate because Michael had been doing his dirty work for him all summer to try to get him off the hook. Subsequently, he told Michael that I had objected not to him, Harold, opening, but to Michael winding up. So he really played it dirty, as he usually does. I shouldn't have got so angry but maybe it wasn't a bad thing.

Saturday 8 September

In the evening we went to dinner at Claridges and then on to see Alec Guinness in *Habeus Corpus*.

It is the hottest September for many years. Very pleasant.

Monday 10 September

At 3 I went to see Harold and was with him for about fifty minutes in his room at the House of Commons. I had decided not to mention the angry telephone call but Harold brought it up and told me he had looked up precedents and found that the Leader of the Party had often opened debates at the Conference when he chose to do so, but he was quite content for me to wind up. He didn't tell me that he had already arranged for Michael Foot to wind up and was using my protest as a way of getting rid of Michael. He said that he thought that perhaps the answer to the problem of the veto was that we should have a very early meeting to fix the Manifesto. As I later discovered, his intention was that we would actually get the Manifesto drawn up before the Conference, with the Executive and the Shadow Cabinet meeting together and agreeing a statement on public ownership which would then go to Conference.

Tuesday 11 September
Today there was a coup by the Junta in Chile and President Allende was murdered.

Friday 14 September
In the evening, Stephen and I went to see Alvaro and Raquel Bunster. Alvaro was the Ambassador in London for what was Allende's legitimate Chilean Government. The Naval Attaché, an Admiral, has thrown him out of the Embassy today. We went to see if I could be of any help. I took my tape recorder and recorded his account of what happened during the coup as far as it affected him, and an interesting record it is. Raquel has been ill and she asked me to get a message to her mother in Santiago so I spent most of the night trying to get through to Chile on the phone. The Post Office in London said they couldn't connect me; I tried a friend in Cincinnati who said he would try; finally I got through to ITT in New York and all their lines to Santiago were open, which infact confirmed what Bunster had said, namely that ITT were in on the coup. I daresay we shall find out when the coup is over.

Monday 17 September
I attended the BAC–Rolls Royce aircraft workers' meeting at the extramural department of the university where Ron Thomas* was in the chair and Lew Gray, Bill Gilchrist and others from BAC-Rolls Royce were there having prepared their Workers' Control Plan. It was really complete municipal socialism with 100 per cent election by the workers and I strongly urged that it be published in time for the Labour Party Conference.

Tuesday 18 September
There was a waterburst at the convent next door and I went in to help the nuns and got absolutely soaked.

---

* Lecturer at Bristol University whose initiative with shop stewards at BAC–Rolls Royce led to the publication of the influential report, *A New Approach to Public Ownership* in August, 1974. Ron Thomas was subsequently elected Labour MP for Bristol North-West.

Wednesday 19 September
Jim Callaghan invited me to have lunch with him. It is all part of Jim's campaign for the leadership but still, I like him. We had a most pleasant time and talked about farming. He said, 'Of course, I am finished, past it,' and I said, 'Rubbish, we are moving into an era where much older people take over the leadership. Look at Churchill, de Gaulle, Mao and Tito.'

Friday 21 September
Peter Shore's pamphlet was published today recommending that an incoming Labour Government should boycott all the institutions of the Common Market and discontinue all payments. I agree with this strong line.

I offered Frances Morrell a job as a political adviser in my department if we won the next Election.

Tuesday 25 September
Industrial Policy Committee at Transport House, where Reg Prentice said we wanted a definitive statement on industrial democracy in the New Year. David Lea [Joint Secretary of the TUC-Labour Party Liaison Committee] said the TUC had been working on this for years and the Congress had called for equal treatment for the nationalised industries. The TUC had an Industrial Democracy working party and was calling for comments by the end of the year; it also insisted on 50 per cent representation on boards from the trade unions.

I said that surely all you have got to do is to ask the workers two questions – one is, 'Are you in favour of public ownership?' And the second is, 'How would you like the management run?' Reg was very much against seeking the workers' view.

Tommy Balogh gave the example that in Yugoslavia and Hungary it was all chaos, that it was irrelevant and dangerous to consult the workers because you had to have incentive systems.

Then Stuart Holland said that the problem with Yugoslavia was that there was a lack of state control of prices and regional policy, and our proposed planning agreements represented a strategic control of major firms which would permit democratic management within them.

Tony Banks pointed out that the workers were not unanimous at all about this; of course the AUEW is opposed to having workers on the boards at all.

Reg Prentice said that what was important was the repeal of the Industrial Relations Act, then legislation for an Employment Protection Act, and an Industrial Democracy Act. He was in favour of single channel bargaining and thought more elements should go on the collective bargaining agenda.

Albert Booth thought the TUC opposition came from those in favour of industrial democracy. We must satisfy the workers that it wouldn't damage their powers of collective bargaining and we can't really separate ownership from control. Peter Parker* said this was hard to grasp and we must be practical in the Election. We needed a glossary and the Party had never thought of the problems of management.

Anyway we agreed to go ahead on the basis of maintaining contact with the TUC, pushing for more disclosure, joint control at shop-floor level, with everything negotiable, TUC membership was the key, experimentation should be phased, and we should invite consideration by the shop floor and the shop stewards combine committees – that was the first time the Labour Party had ever agreed to consult the combines, a considerable gain. It was an important meeting.

Wednesday 26 September
Press conference at Transport House, Bristol, to launch the BAC–Rolls Royce shop stewards' statement on workers' control, which provides the workers with an elected council to hire and fire the management – brilliantly simple. On the eve of Conference, I believe the Labour Party has achieved good relations with the trade union movement. I don't think the trade union leadership altogether trusts the PLP – rightly, in my view – but still, formally, there is an agreement.

The Labour Party leadership, by an overwhelming majority, is still suspicious of the trade unions. Tony Crosland said at one of our Shadow Cabinet meetings that it wasn't Marxism that was the problem, because nobody really believed in Marx, but whether the Labour Party ought to be so tightly linked to the unions. He wants a consumer-oriented Swedish type of socialism, and yet it is this link with the workers, in my judgment, which offers the only serious chance of major social, political and industrial change. The most significant development in my own thinking in the last three years has been a recognition that the trade union movement not only has to defend its own rights and should be supported by us but ought to have a joint programme with the Party. That has been brought about and the programme will be a joint one. All the Labour leaders like Douglas Houghton and Jim Callaghan, who in the old days used to urge the need for strong links with the unions, take a very different view now that trade unions are under left-wing and not right-wing leadership.

Another element in the current situation is the introduction into the centre of the leadership of three people. There is Michael Foot, who decided after the 1970 Election that he would go on to the Front Bench

---

* A Labour industrialist, Chairman of Rockware Group, who was later appointed Chairman of British Railways Board.

and play a more active part; he is what the ultra-Left accurately call fake Left, is parliamentary-orientated, although he cultivates good relations with some individual trade union leaders and is reasonably well trusted by the rank and file. But he has lost the sharp cutting edge of his socialism.

Michael has brought with him Jack Jones – every Labour leader requires a major trade union backer: Clem Attlee needed Ernie Bevin; Hugh Gaitskell would have liked the T&G backing but Frank Cousins was General Secretary at the time and that was what all the trouble was about, so Gaitskell had to rely on right-wing leaders such as Tom Williamson and Jack Cooper of the GMWU, and Sam Watson of the NUM; Harold has now got a working relationship with Jack Jones.

There is no doubt that Jack Jones has completely abandoned his serious left-wing position. He is quite crudely against the adoption of the socialist programme because he is for sticking to the bread-and-butter issues – pensions, food subsidies, repealing the Industrial Relations Act and so on. I think the incident in the summer of 1972 when the dockers broke into his office, threw an ashtray at him and abused him was a deep shock. Hugh Scanlon and Jack have now in effect divided; I think Hugh detects in Jack something of an abandonment of the old course.

Looking around, Denis Healey is struggling as Shadow Chancellor. He is a tough character, a thug really. My relations with Denis are at their poorest, and yet I can get on at a superficial level of cordiality. But he hates my guts and I must say I reciprocate. He wobbles about according to which way the wind is blowing. He is utterly unscrupulous in the use of argument to get what he wants. I shall never forget in February 1968, Cecil King, Chairman of IPC, making him the candidate for leadership of a coalition government.

Jim Callaghan is very charming, much better after his prostate operation, an agreeable and skilful politician, marvellous at getting his own way. He is basically very conservative with a feel for what people will put up with, and comes round in the end when the argument has been won. He is a shrewd political figure with a lot of useful life ahead.

I have been running a very dangerous course over the last two or three years, pushing leftward, having been persuaded by looking back at our period of Government that this is the only way of bringing about any change. But I am not very adept at organising a personal group, I tend to be a bit of a loner. Frank McElhone despairs of me a lot of the time. On the other hand, I think he recognises that the stream of opinion which I represent cannot be ignored.

Labour Party Conference: Blackpool

At the NEC meeting traditionally held on the eve of the Party Conference, a huge row broke out over the proposal by Harold Wilson to have a joint Shadow Cabinet/NEC meeting, before Conference opened, to present a united front, particularly over the contents of the Party's Election manifesto. In essence, the argument centred on public ownership and the inclusion of the Twenty-five Companies plan, Wilson turning it into a confidence issue. The NEC rejected a joint meeting.

New Statesman, 28 September 1973.

Friday 28 September
The Shadow Cabinet was held in Harold's hotel suite on the first floor. It began with Harold giving a colourless account of what had happened at the NEC. Michael Foot said, 'Well, we don't want to take a tragic view; it's not too bad. We tried and it didn't work.'

Reg Prentice thought it was disgraceful that the Executive had refused to meet the Shadow Cabinet and it was essential that we made it clear that the parliamentarians would have the final decision. The Twenty-five Companies was a futile proposal because everybody knew it wouldn't be carried out and it would be better to tell Conference that.

Shirley wanted a confrontation. 'Harold, I'm very depressed. We have got to face this one. You will have to say at the Conference on

Tuesday what you have said about the Twenty-five in the past. You must sort this out. You've got to do it right.'

I said, 'The press are absolutely determined to destroy us, and if they don't pick this, they'll pick something else. They are trying to present us as a Marxist Party and we have just got to face it. We can't run away at the first sign of press criticism.' I turned to Reg. 'Look, Reg, if you want to know why the Executive didn't want to meet us, it was in part because of your speech, reported in *Labour Weekly* last week and what you have just said now: they suspect that you are actually trying to exert the power of the Shadow Cabinet over the NEC at the Conference.' Then I commented to Shirley, 'With the best will in the world, Shirley, this idea of the psychology of confrontation is half the trouble. If we have this psychology of confrontation, we really miss the mood of the Party. As far as your anxieties about society and law and order disintegrating are concerned, this is always said on the eve of great reforms because, in a sense, it is true before great reforms. Don't worry and don't be so concerned about it.'

Harold said, 'We all know what the National Executive is like on the eve of the re-elections; it goes through a menstrual period.'

I replied, 'Harold, there are other elections. There are elections to the Shadow Cabinet, and there is a very different electorate at General Elections.'

'It might be a very good idea if you paid more attention to that electorate,' replied Harold.

'I have no interest in losing the General Election. I have a marginal seat with a lot of workers. What worries me is not Nora Beloff's crowd but the Labour people who don't vote; turnout dropped from 83 per cent to 66 per cent in my strongest Labour areas. I think this programme will bring them back out.'

Reg Prentice jumped in with, 'The Twenty-five Companies won't.'

'Well, maybe not, but the general feeling that we are fighting for the workers may. That's what it's about.'

Harold then went on about leaking, saying he knew it was the same person who had leaked in 1967 as it was now on public ownership, on the Common Market stories, and on what happened at the Shadow Cabinet. I am sure he was referring to me, that was the only interpretation one could put on it. He sort of spat it out. Then he turned to me. 'You talk about your workers in Bristol. Well, I was in Derby the other day and all they asked me was, why did Tony Benn make those silly statements.'

'I do my meetings around the country and I think I can assess the mood of the Party as well as anyone else can,' I replied.

He really was terribly hostile and I am the main object of his anger at the moment. I have got to face that fact.

After that Douglas Houghton said, 'I agree with what Michael, Bob Mellish and Tony Benn have said.' I interrupted, saying that I wished he would give me that in writing. He went on, 'I think this really is a matter of vision. I see the programme as our vision and the Manifesto as our priorities and if you put it like that you understand what it is about.' A very sensitive speech and much appreciated. Although the two extreme right-wingers, Reg Prentice and Shirley Williams, were absolutely determined to precipitate a confrontation, the rest were just crying in their beer really and it annoyed them enormously when Michael and I said that there was no need to take a tragic view and that it would all work out in the end.

Later, I asked Jim to come and have a chat and, pacing up and down my room, he said, 'You know Harold was accusing you of leaking. We must get you closer to Harold.'

'I remember in 1966,' I said, 'you told me how bitterly resentful you were that Harold thought you were engaged in a plot, and now it's me.' I told him about Harold's behaviour over the winding up of the industry debate at Conference.

'I thought Harold had got over that bitchy behaviour now.'

'Maybe it doesn't happen to you any more but it certainly happens to me,' I said.

Saturday 29 September

I got buttonholed in the bar by Tommy Balogh, who is such a bore. We were talking about North Sea oil and he was continuing his fight against civil servants whom he remembered and who had no doubt humiliated him. 'Moreover, Tony, we must see to it that we never have any more lower middle-class Ministers like Dick Marsh* and Roy Mason who are just bullied by these fascist civil servants. We need public school boys like you to stand up to them.' That just about sums up his view of politics. You put in your aristocratic friends, who then are able to down the civil servants. I said, 'If this country changes, it won't be because of public school Labour Ministers beating public school civil servants. It will be because the people at a Conference simply won't accept the explanations given from the top and will just go on demanding change until they actually get it.'

Sunday 30 September

Caroline and I went to the Conference church service at which Colin

---

* Richard (later Lord) Marsh, Minister of Power, 1966–8 and Transport, 1968–9; Labour MP for Greenwich, 1959–71, resigning his seat to become Chairman of British Railways Board.

Morris, General Secretary of the Methodist Church Overseas Division, gave an excellent sermon.

In the evening, we went to the TGWU party and Caroline talked to Bert Ramelson, the Industrial Organiser of the Communist Party, an ageing, friendly, cautious man. Really, how these people are presented as the bogeymen passes my understanding.

I also attended the Bertrand Russell Peace Foundation fringe meeting with Alvaro Bunster who made an excellent speech. There was one eighteen-year-old Young Socialist from Birmingham, absolutely booming with confidence, who said, 'I warned the Ambassador when I came to see him eighteen months ago that unless the workers in Chile were prepared to use force and defeat the armed forces, the civil service and the business leaders, this would happen. I warned him.' She was so confident, it gave one quite a boost. Then another Young Socialist, an apprentice from Newcastle, said, 'We have got Chilean Navy ships in the yards and we are dropping spanners in the machinery and issuing leaflets.' He said they had asked the Post Office Engineering Union to help. Very encouraging.

Tuesday 2 October

I dropped to third place in the National Executive vote, down by thirty-three thousand votes; but everybody fell a bit. Harold opened the public ownership debate with a speech which was somehow uncomfortable. It lacked any particular inspiration but he was immensely tough about the things on which everybody knew he was weakest, giving a long list of what we would nationalise, how we would deal with it and so on.

My winding up went down well and the Conference responded marvellously. People latched on to the phrase, 'We shall use the crisis we inherit as an occasion for making the fundamental changes and not as an excuse for postponing them.' This pledge will be the test of sincerity of the next Labour Government.

Went to a late lunch and Frances Morrell was so pleased about the speech that she bought some champagne.

Did *Midweek* with Alf Robens, Fred Catherwood,* Ludovic Kennedy and Robin Day. Robens was pretty offensive and unattractive. Ludovic Kennedy simply hadn't read the policy statement, and Robin, sitting beside me, was furious that a man who was so poorly briefed should be handling the programme. I was sharp with Robin who tried to bully me. The interviewer's most effective role is to help bring out what the

---

* Lord Robens, industrialist, former Labour MP (Wansbeck, 1945–50, Blyth, 1950–60) and former Chairman of the National Coal Board. Sir Fred Catherwood, Director-General of the National Economic Development Council, 1966–71.

Guardian, 3 October 1974.

interviewee wants to say and convey the doubts and let him deal with them, not to treat the person as if he were a criminal on trial for his life. Robin, as a former barrister, has never understood this. All he does is build up public sympathy for the person he bullies.

Wednesday 3 October
The NEC met in the evening to elect its Chairman. It is Jim Callaghan's turn and an important chairmanship it is going to be because 1974 is likely to be an Election year. He has come two years after me because I knocked him off the Executive when I was first elected in 1959, and he lost seniority.

Went to the Tribune meeting and Jack Jones made a speech praising Michael Foot to the skies and saying he was worth ten times any other member of the Shadow Cabinet: I must say I took that amiss and let it be known I did, because on the Shadow Cabinet Michael has been compromising like anything. Still, he has a thirty-year record as the leader of the Left and the Tribune meeting is very much the annual occasion of his fan club.

Eric Heffer made a speech in which he said we should introduce trade unions into the army to prevent a development of the Chilean situation here. It was a very courageous speech and I think it's right, but I haven't got the courage to say it: I know if I proposed it, there would be a tremendous row.

At the meeting Michael Foot said it would be a scandal if I wasn't re-elected to the Shadow Cabinet. He put his protective cloak around me because it was known that there would be attempts to get me off the Shadow Cabinet.

Thursday 4 October
There was a boycott of the bars today because of the poor pay the bar staff receive. I heard Harold Lever went through the picket lines saying, 'You're just a lot of thugs.'

In the afternoon Alvaro Bunster addressed the Conference, an historic moment since it was a facility that hadn't been offered to a foreign socialist since Leon Blum spoke in the Thirties at the time he was Leader of the French Popular Front. He made a most moving speech which earned him a standing ovation.

In the debate on the Common Market there was a vote of 5 to 1 for the policy which included the Referendum.

Friday 5 October
The usual end of Conference, and I am absolutely exhausted, but it has been fun.

Home to find Melissa and Joshua both asleep in front of the television.

Monday 8 October
I had a talk to Stephen who is going to do his thesis on American political advisers [the White House Staff] from Roosevelt to Nixon.

Tuesday 9 October
This evening I went to Chesterfield to speak on behalf of Eric Varley. Eric was a raging left-wing trade unionist when he came into Parliament in 1964 and Harold took him up. Then he became a friend of Gerald Kaufman, and they are key figures in Harold's kitchen cabinet. Harold is pushing him forward, wants him to be the next trade unionist in the Cabinet now that Dick Marsh has gone and Roy Mason is the only one left. He is an able guy but as he gets older and absorbed into the parliamentary system, his early left-wing ideas are beginning to be eroded, as is the fate of so many.

Wednesday 10 October
The Middle East war* is still raging, and the news from America is that Vice-President Spiro Agnew has resigned following scandals from the time he was Governor of Maryland and extending right through to his period as Vice-President. This has knocked a prop away from Nixon who is still battling through the Watergate affair and now is really in retreat. With Agnew gone and a new Vice-President to be appointed, this means there is an alternative to Nixon, which in turn makes his position much more difficult.

Sunday 14 October
Bill Rodgers came to see me this morning for nearly two hours. I had asked him to come for a chat because it is a way of keeping indirectly in touch with Roy Jenkins. Bill was opposed to a Referendum on the EEC and would say so in any forthcoming Election campaign. He would vote with the Tories against a Referendum bill if one was brought forward by a Labour Government, and he said that Roy would resign if one was proposed. He thought the Labour Cabinet would favour membership after re-negotiation of the terms and that there would be four or five anti-Europeans who could resign to fight the Cabinet during the Referendum campaign itself. But Roy would not accept the Referendum.

He said that Roy himself had not at that moment decided whether to stand for the Shadow Cabinet and whom he would replace. I said I was sorry that Roy had ever resigned from the Shadow Cabinet, which indeed I was. He thought the middle of the Party wanted Roy back on the Shadow Cabinet and that if I were to urge the Referendum now, it would be divisive. He thought the European Parliament issue should not be raised this session. He himself was going to support me for the Shadow Cabinet and wanted to assure me that there would be no campaign to get me off it. He said the Party needed me; I was often infuriating but he recognised my contribution. But he advised me to de-escalate the pressure I was building up. He said he thought 'Benn the Statesman' would be the right line now. 'After all,' he said, 'you might be Leader one day and we would have to be reconciled to you then. Be very careful that what you say now doesn't lead to you being blamed for the defeat of the Party if we lose the Election.' He was friendly and professional and in a sense was offering a deal.

Monday 15 October
Went to the CBI dinner which was held at 8 Smith Square. I hadn't

* The Yom Kippur war between Israel and Egypt backed by Syria was at its height in October 1973 and the US organised a huge airlift of arms for Israel.

been there since the late 1920s when I was three, so I said to Sir Michael Clapham, 'I haven't been in this house for forty-five years or so.'

'What do you mean?'

'Last time I was here, I was visiting the MP for Smethwick in 1928.' They didn't believe it and I pointed out that it had been Oswald Mosley's house and it was there that I made my first public speech. 'Boys and girls and sailors, thank you for the tea party!'

From the CBI, Michael Clapham, Sir John Partridge, Campbell Adamson, Sir John Whitehorn, Lucien Wigdor and Alex Jarratt were there. On our side, Harold Wilson, Denis Healey, Ted Short, John Gilbert [Labour MP for Dudley], Harold Lever, and myself. Harold Wilson was late and he said little of interest during the dinner. He began by asking, 'Who leaked the fact that we were meeting?'

Campbell Adamson replied, 'Well, I think I have said we were having regular talks with the Opposition.'

'Well, who leaked it?' said Harold.

That was absurd, because there's absolutely no reason why the meeting should be kept secret at all. During the dinner Harold went on to say, 'We're on the side of industry. We are against finance. You're the fall guys.'

Denis Healey was at the end of the table and was very offensive about public ownership. 'Of course we want a little public ownership but Tony goes much further than most of us.'

Harold Lever said that what we needed was a new scheme for distribution. 'Got to see that the loot is better distributed.' Everybody always laughs at Harold Lever; he's funny, but also they know in their hearts that he is not in any way threatening. He went on, 'The trade unions should be disbanded, ideally, and what we need is tax concessions for managers.'

The CBI were utterly gloomy. Campbell Adamson said, 'Another Labour Government must control the unions but price controls would be acceptable only if they were used to control pay – though we don't really believe in controls.'

Wigdor added, 'The balance must go back in favour of capital. It has tipped too far towards labour.'

Partridge thought management was disillusioned, and Whitehorn said, 'You should tax capital and not income.'

I laid into them. 'You're all so gloomy and depressed. You're licked, pessimistic. There is more vitality on the union side than there is on the management side. We have all agreed that we have got to have a managed economy. The question is in whose interest do we manage it? We have got to have a re-distribution of power and establish a new social contract. This is what we are all about.'

Harold looked awfully cross and as soon as I began speaking, he said,

'Well, now I think we had all better go home.' He obviously didn't want me to have a chance to develop the argument.

Ted Short, I think, finally got Harold round the corner to Lord North Street where he lives. I suppose Harold was trying to neutralise the CBI, make them feel they had nothing to be afraid of. My feeling is that we had better be honest and tell them what we are going to do. I felt the evening was a complete waste of time, having a discussion in which we never really got to the root of the issues at all.

Tuesday 16 October
Fortune magazine published an article about dangerous socialists all over the Western world: they cited Mitterand in France, Gough Whitlam in Australia, Wolfgang somebody in West Germany, the left-wing leader of the Japanese socialists, and me from Britain. They said that the democratic socialists who had been regarded as the front-line of defence of American capitalism against Communism in the Fifties had now recovered their radicalism. It was a shrewd article, describing exactly the differences between the Shirley Williamses and the Jim Callaghans, the Tony Croslands and the Reg Prentices, all of whom are perceived as being on the Left of the capitalist front against Communism, but the article then almost naively said that this wasn't enough.

Wednesday 17 October
At the Shadow Cabinet there was a row over whether Britain should continue to supply arms to Israel during the war. Fred Peart said he didn't want a three-line whip. Tony Crosland also wanted a free vote.

Merlyn Rees said, 'Well, in 1967 we sent arms to Israel clandestinely even though we had announced an embargo.'

'The US is supplying the extra arms to Israel and spares are not urgent,' said Jim.

Denis said, 'Israel wants to commit the British to the war, it's politically important and that's why they want the arms.'

Jim said that the difficulty was that the Leader and Deputy Leader, Harold and Ted, were really opposed to the Party policy on Israel.

Ron Hayward said, 'Let's support the sending of arms. It will help with the by-election.'

Peter said we had to condemn aggression, but Harold Lever was not prepared to accept the arms embargo that the Government had introduced. 'Conscience works all ways,' he said.

Douglas Houghton said, 'The Shadow Cabinet should follow the Leader on this.'

Willie Ross warned that a free vote would mean that everyone would abstain, which is true.

Harold said, 'I'll appeal to Heath tonight to lift the embargo.' He believed we should supply both sides.

Later, I sat on the bench beyond the Members' Lobby talking to Maurice Miller, the Labour MP for Kelvingrove, who is leading the campaign on behalf of the pro-Israeli group. I said I thought the only thing was an imposed solution with Soviet-American agreement putting a ring of steel round Israel. That was the only security I could see, but I'm afraid that as a result of saying that and not coming out wholly for arms for Israel, Maurice Miller wrote me off as anti-Israeli. I do feel tremendous pressure from the pro-Israeli lobby bearing down on me; there is no question that it is there.

Thursday 18 October
Up at 6.30, feeling lousy, for a three-day visit to the North-East and Scotland to look at North Sea Oil installations. It was all Frank McElhone's idea and until I got there I hadn't realised the magnitude of the North Sea Oil development. It really is huge and has completely transformed the political situation in Scotland. British industry is not equipped to deal with it and we are a developing country now with the multi-national oil companies working here. It's like the gold rush and is producing the same results.

Friday 19 October
Arrived at Aberdeen and drove to Inverness in terribly cold weather. Peter Allison from the Scottish Party and Gavin Laird, Scottish organiser of the AUEW, met me. To Dingwall and then to Nigg Bay to see the rig, and met MPs and the head of Wimpey which is associated with Brown & Root who are building the rig.

To Banff overnight, still feeling awful.

Saturday 20 October
Peter Allison, Gavin Laird and I went from Banff to Peterhead where we met the Provost. The Labour candidate took us round and again I felt this gold-rush atmosphere.

Flew back to London. A most interesting three days which absolutely convinced me of the need for public enterprise to come in to North Sea oil development, otherwise one is handing over the future entirely to international companies.

Sunday 21 October
Nixon sacked Professor Archibald Cox, the Watergate special prosecutor, and Elliott Richardson, the Attorney-General, has resigned in protest: this gives the whole Watergate crisis a completely new impetus because Nixon has alienated the immensely powerful legal lobby, a sort of breach of constitutional rights.

Had a long telephone call from Stephen who said he had been invited to St Antony's College, Oxford, for the weekend and since that is the great spy school, it wouldn't surprise me at all if they try to recruit him.

Monday 22 October

Had lunch in the Tea Room with Jim Sillars who brought me up to date on how wildly Scottish Nationalist the Scottish TUC had become, and how, if Britain stayed in Europe, he would become a Scottish Nationalist member.

At 5 we had the Shadow Cabinet and the Channel Tunnel came up, since it has now become inextricably linked with the Common Market. Peter Shore and Michael Foot are strongly opposed to it, as I am, with Tony Crosland in favour.

Wednesday 24 October

In the evening Caroline and I went to Robin Day's fiftieth birthday party and met all the old Gaitskellites – Davenport who writes in the *Spectator*, Woodrow Wyatt of the Mirror Group, a Labour lawyer Ben Hooberman, Rees-Mogg and Roy Jenkins. A real gathering of Fleet Street ex-liberals.

Sunday 28 October

Caught the train to Glasgow for a meeting in Govan for the Labour candidate, Harry Selby. It was well attended but the Govan campaign has really gone bad on us in a big way. These by-elections do provide some sort of a test of how we are going to do and there is a great deal of anxiety about them, particularly as the Scot Nats have made such a tremendous impact. I think it is the effect of the oil giving them more confidence.

Sunday 11 November

Big family lunch with Frances Morrell, Tony Banks, Bryan Stanley (the General Secretary of the POEU), Alan Sapper who is the General Secretary of ACTT, Dick Clements and Joan Lestor, where we planned a great national campaign based around the Labour–TUC Liaison Committee. When you talk to the parliamentarians they get completely demoralised by a bad election result.* In their eyes, everything rotates around the House of Commons. The trade union people, on the other

---

* By-elections were held on 8 November 1973 at Berwick-upon-Tweed, Hove, Edinburgh North and Govan. At Berwick (previously held by Lord Lambton), the Liberal Alan Beith won; Hove and Edinburgh North were held by Conservative candidates, Tim Sainsbury and Alex Fletcher; in Govan, Margo MacDonald (Scottish National Party) defeated the Labour candidate.

hand, are very stabilising because they are engaged in a longer-term battle, and I found Bryan Stanley and Alan Sapper reassuring in this discussion. I am going to hold a series of these meetings at home.

Monday 12 November
I went to see the Prime Minister of Israel, Golda Meir, speaking at the Churchill Hotel. She's a remarkable old woman. She spoke with great feeling, passion and warmth about the war and how she had seen so much suffering all her life. The trouble is that she just cannot see the other side at all. She simply cannot see the Arab case or the Palestinian case, so this makes it difficult for her to listen to the arguments.

Monday 19 November
Trade and Industry Group of MPs. We planned our work and I suggested we got Eric Varley, Peter Shore, Reg Prentice and John Silkin to consider the oil/power situation on a daily basis as it affected various sections of the community. I put this to the Shadow Cabinet and it was agreed. I also suggested we have a series of meetings with the trade unions.

From 12 November 1973, the NUM started an overtime ban in support of their pay claim which conflicted with Phase 3 of the Government's counter-inflation policy. This, combined with action in the electricity industry and a cutback in oil supplies from the Middle East as a result of the Yom Kippur war, led to fears of nationwide power shortages, and the Shadow Cabinet agreed that the Trade and Industry Group of MPs should start monitoring the oil/power situation daily.

Saturday 24 November
The Sunday papers reported a speech by Reg Prentice at the Labour Parliamentary Association dinner at County Hall in which he said, 'Moderate members of our Party must stand up and be counted. By moderate, I do not mean people who are half-hearted or namby-pamby, I mean the majority of the rank and file who are not Marxists, who are not hell-bent on nationalising everything, who are fed up with the sillier forms of trade union militancy, but who are sincerely dedicated to the social democratic traditions of the Labour Party.'

Drove up to Ilkeston, Ray Fletcher's constituency, for a meeting. ITN were there to see whether I was going to reply to Prentice. The local Party had laid on a bazaar and there was an old fortune teller, 'Madame Eva', in one of the side rooms with a crystal ball covered with a black velvet cloth (she was, of course, also an ordinary Labour Party stalwart). I was sitting in the hall working, having arrived early, and she came and sat down and began uncovering her crystal ball. I would *never* have gone to her for a prediction but I did talk to her, and after we had finished talking, she told me how she saw things in the ball, and how she had predicted various events. As I left she said to me, 'You are going to have a great shock in February, a terrible shock. You are going to get the blame for something you haven't done. Then in September, it will all be all right again.'*

Monday 26 November
At the TUC-Labour Party Liaison Committee, there was a brief discussion on my proposal that the Committee should be used for discussing political strategy. Harold said no. Denis said it would be better if we had an evening booze-up. Douglas Houghton supported me. George Smith of UCATT said political strategy was for the Shadow Cabinet. Ron Hayward said the Committee's role was to discuss the nuts and bolts.

Wednesday 28 November
At the Shadow Cabinet we discussed the mining dispute and Harold said that talks had broken down by 18 to 5 with 4 abstentions. He favoured a ballot of miners. I suggested why not support the miners and trust them. Harold Lever said that the miners were engaged in a political strike; Crosland thought the miners couldn't be trusted.

Thursday 29 November
Had lunch with Roy Wright, the Deputy-Chairman of Rio Tinto-Zinc, who was very gloomy. He said, 'Of course, we are heading for a major slump. We shall have to have direction of labour and wartime rationing.'

In the evening, had a drink with John Silkin who thought it was just possible that there could be a coalition; the Tories would get rid of Heath, and Whitelaw would suggest that Jim become Prime Minister of a coalition. Most interesting.

Friday 30 November
Went early to see Harold Evans and Hugo Young of the *Sunday Times* and they listen attentively to my political analysis. I said, 'Look, both parties have failed. There is an energy crisis, and there may be a slump. The crisis is a crisis of confidence shared by the Establishment. It is not just a case of crooks governing morons. There is something else wrong.

---

* This woman's wretched words preyed on me all winter and then as the Election got nearer and nearer, I became convinced we were going to lose, and I was going to get the blame. I assumed something would happen in September vindicating me. It just shows how people must be terrorised by witch doctors.

It is a crisis of consent as in the late colonial period. We have got to convert negative to positive power and that means more equality and more democracy. You can have a right-wing dictatorship or a left-wing dictatorship, but we want more democracy and equality and not a national Government. A coalition Government would be crazy.' Harold Evans, of course, has got his own candidates for a national Government and so have I. He asked, 'Why are you so unpopular with the press?' so I said, 'Because you write such unpleasant things about me. That's why.'

I don't know if I really made any impression but it was an attempt.

Monday 3 December

Dinner with Wilfred Brown who also believes we were heading for a slump and food riots and there must be a national Government. If this is what the businessmen are saying, it is significant.

At the Commons I saw John Biffen who told me, 'Enoch Powell is waiting for the call.' Also at the House, Peter Shore told me that Michael Foot – who he thinks is marvellous – must be the next Leader of the Party.

Friday 7 December

Travelled to Bristol and my election agent, Ennis Harris, warned me I'd lose the Election because my left-wing views were not acceptable. In the evening I went to Knowle Ward for a meeting where there were only four people, despite having distributed 700 leaflets. It really was awful. There is a great sense of crisis everywhere.

Saturday 8 December

Out visiting all the Party stalwarts. Went to a pensioners' rally and came back to London with Len Murray. He really is a nice, formerly radical, bureaucrat. Everyone in that position gets bureaucratic and there is no enthusiasm at the top at all. The whole atmosphere is always so flat. I think this is what political leadership does for you: you become a manager, you have management responsibilities and all your imagination and vision is crushed out of you. It is essential to offload some of this management on to people who are not at the top.

Sunday 9 December

The Sunday papers all described Britain under siege. The workers at Aldermaston who actually produce the atomic warheads are in dispute again. They claim that the Poseidon developments with multiple warheads are on their way and that the Atomic Weapons Research Establishment police are armed.

Monday 10 December
Ken Coates phoned to say that an ASLEF driver in Hull had reported that lots of oil was going to power stations and that Lawrence Daly [General-Secretary of the NUM] knew this. Jack Jones is to be told. The way they are building up on the work-to-rule by the miners to imply that they are responsible for the crisis is quite wrong.

Wednesday 12 December
We had a joint National Executive/Shadow Cabinet meeting to finalise our Election Manifesto in the event of a snap decision by Heath. We started by discussing the crisis, which gets worse every day. Jim Callaghan said that our policy was intended for the natural end of a Parliament but the present crisis meant that we should expect emergency Tory measures and we might ourselves have to move quickly in response to the situation.

'You can't separate our policy from the crisis and therefore we should appeal to the British people with our analysis of the crisis. Pensioners mustn't suffer,' I said.

Then on the Manifesto defence proposals, Frank Allaun wanted £1,000 million cuts and the closure of the Polaris bases. Jim felt that this would break up NATO and create pressure for a German nuclear force. Judith Hart then said defence spending by a Labour Government couldn't be sacrosanct. I argued that there was such a tough military-industrial complex in existence that we ought to be hard at this stage, or we never would be. Ted Short commented that the Tories would accuse us of leaving the country defenceless.

Finally, Jim suggested that Michael, Barbara, Tony Crosland, Terry Pitt and I draft the Manifesto within a month.

Thursday 13 December
The trade figures came out with £270 million deficit. Went to the House of Commons and Heath made his statement on the crisis. It was tremendous – he announced a three-day working week to reduce energy consumption. There was a realisation of the great depth of the crisis.

Sunday 16 December
Phoned Ken Coates, Michael Barratt Brown, who is a sympathetic economics lecturer at Sheffield University, Michael Foot, Dick Clements and others, so as to begin building up ideas to combat the 'coal crisis', the Government's three-day week and to find out whether coal stocks really justified the panic. Michael Barrett Brown thought the Government's motive was to try to get the balance of payments right, and asked why there was no consultation with the unions about the

energy crisis. I jotted down a lot of figures about the stocks. A useful day.

Monday 17 December
At the TUC-Labour Party Liaison Committee, there was a TUC document on energy and the balance of payments. 'The three-day week is a scandal,' Len Murray declared. 'We think the emergency Budget should not cut deep, it should deal with the oil and energy situation and we should look for deep and drastic cuts in personal consumption. But a wage freeze would create an impossible crisis. The unions *must* be free to negotiate wages. Trade unions can tackle the problems.'

Jack asked, 'Where are the oil supplies going to? The Labour Party must not attack the trade unions but the multi-nationals.'

Jim said, 'We must now consider an immediate statement. The scenario will be that the Government will introduce a series of measures nationally and this will open an option for an Election.'

I insisted that we should look at this from a political perspective. There was no real coal crisis – it was more a row between the Government and the miners, with the three-day week taken as a political decision. The CBI and the TUC should monitor the energy situation and there should be a joint Labour Party-TUC meeting, perhaps with the National Council of Labour, to issue a statement.

Sid Greene said that coal stocks were strong, the rail dispute should not be allowed to cloud the real situation. Without the coal dispute the country should still be in trouble and the Government were exploiting it. Wages must not take the knock. David Basnett, the General Secretary of the GMWU, spoke. He has always impressed me, tall, lanky, quiet, a former RAF pilot, very shrewd and quite radical. Clive Jenkins gets on well with him as, I think, does Jack Jones. He said, 'We must issue a statement. There are really three crises. One is an economic crisis – the balance of payments and inflation. The second is the energy crisis, short and mid-term; the Government is pretty apathetic about that. The third is the industrial relations crisis with short-term disputes and a longer-term problem.' Even the CBI, said Basnett, was moving to the idea of price control and free bargaining, and the repeal of the Industrial Relations Act had a part to play. 'Therefore,' he concluded, 'we should press for the reversal of the counter-inflation and industrial relations policy.'

Harold argued that there was a basic economic crisis which pre-dated the energy crisis and the Government was trying to muddle them up together. We should issue a statement today, because Heath's statement had been made without any consultation with industry and was highly political and likely to encourage panic. The three-day week was not right. The tripartite monitoring of energy (which was my suggestion) might be considered and the multinationals would have to be looked at. The Government would not go for social justice and we must remove the industrial relations poison. The basic crisis would have happened anyway, and we were all really saying the same thing.

Jim thought a statement on the three-day week wasn't necessary. Tripartite monitoring might be worth having but the Government should control oil and he thought the OECD should monitor the situation. He himself thought the miners should get more money but the train drivers should accept conciliation.

Len Murray came in, saying we should check the coal stocks and hold tripartite monitoring over because the TUC itself had not agreed to that yet. We should really attack the three-day week, go back to collective bargaining and issue a statement. He did not like the Government intervening in industrial disputes; and he didn't want political interventions either pro or anti. He thought it would be better if the politicians shut up, and he didn't want us to refer to the mines or the railways. The relative cost of the lock-out versus the cost of a settlement had to be balanced.

Ted Short said, 'We are being too managerial. We want leadership and inspiration. The Government is responsible for 80 per cent of the crisis. The real answer is in a different economic and social policy.' He added that if the Government were going to try to fight on a 'unions versus Britain' basis then Labour and the TUC must stand shoulder to shoulder.

We then tried our hand at drafting a statement, but in the event we put out a very short one saying, 'The Government has created a grave industrial position by its unnecessary panic in imposing on British industry a compulsory three-day week from today, with related cuts in wages. It is threatening the livelihood of millions and causing untold hardship and chaos over wide areas of British industry.'

At 3.30 the Chancellor, Anthony Barber introduced his emergency measures, which were generally thought to be a complete fiasco. There was some reduction of land and buildings, home demand, taxation of income, 10 per cent surcharge on surtax, and so on.

Healey welcomed the realism; Powell congratulated Barber, and seemed to be coming round to support the Tories, despite his earlier declarations.

At 5 o'clock, the Shadow Cabinet. I said that we must look at the situation politically and the attack on the miners and the unions was something we had to resist. We had to look to an Election and the possibility that Powell was now back in the Tory camp. The public reaction to the three-day week was one of anger, and the TUC/Labour Party statement was important. Phase 3 had been killed and the nation really had to make a choice. How far did we want to go? Did we want to take over? We had to speak for the national interest.

Ted Short thought we must take seriously the possibility of an early Election. Harold Wilson said that the Labour Government should be the 'national Government' and we must go for national unity. He rather wished I wouldn't keep referring to the risk of a national or a coalition government!

Tuesday 18 December
IRA bombs in London.

First day of the economic and energy debate. Harold spoke and I wound up. Heath is beginning to crack. I felt somehow that there would be an Election and that this would be the last speech I would make for a very long time in Parliament. It was probably that silly old fortune teller in Derbyshire but somehow, the whole day I felt obsessed with the worry, which did nothing for my speech.

Wednesday 19 December
The first item at the NEC was the TUC-Labour Party Liaison Committee report. I proposed a joint plenary meeting between the three bodies: the whole NEC, the whole Shadow Cabinet and the whole TUC.

Jim said, 'No. Perhaps an NEC-Shadow Cabinet on 9 January, and a NEC-TUC on 7 January. Remember, the TUC isn't political.'

I was really trying to consolidate the very useful alliance between the trade unions and the PLP because this is the source of our strength, and despite everything Shirley, Jim, Reg Prentice, Douglas Houghton, Tony Crosland, Harold Lever and Roy Jenkins say, this is the thing that will win us the Election. If we turn on the trade unions in the hope that we will be popular with the Nora Beloffs and *Guardian* readers, we are sunk.

Thursday 20 December
To Bristol, delayed by the big West Ealing train crash, for the Trades Council meeting on the three-day week. Dai Francis from the South Wales Miners spoke on the miners' claim; I must say those miners are the natural leaders of the working class; they put spirit into the Trades Council, and all the teachers' and nurses' representatives who were there, wobbling on the fringe of the TUC, were really strengthened. An exciting evening.

Sunday 23 December
I overslept and had a lazy day at home. Three more IRA bombs in London.

I tidied the office and wrapped Christmas gifts. We have decided not to go to Stansgate, because I felt I had to be ready for the possibility of an Election. The oil price was doubled again today, the second doubling since September.

Tuesday 25 December
Christmas Day. Absolutely marvellous family day. No politics at all.

Saturday 29 December
I wrote to Heath asking questions about the level of fuel stocks and this, I must be absolutely candid and admit it, was because Ken Coates bullied me into doing so. Having checked the letter with Eric Varley and Harold Wilson, I delivered it to Heath, to the newspaper offices, then I phoned Ray Buckton and Lawrence Daly. Generally speaking I prepared myself for a political battle in a big way.

Sunday 30 December
There was very good coverage in the *Sunday Times* of my questions to Heath. The *Telegraph* came along to take a picture, and I was continuously on the phone.

Teddy Sieff was shot in his home in Queen's Grove.*

In the evening we had a big gathering – Michael Meacher, Hugh Macpherson of *Tribune*, Joan Lestor, Frances Morrell, Tony Banks and Ken Coates – to work on a Labour response to the crisis. We talked for about six hours, planning our future action, then we worked out a lot of questions. Will the Government take action to protect people who can't afford mortgage and hire purchase payments because of the cuts in wages due to the three-day week? What is the Government going to do to inform the people of the benefit rights to which they are entitled? What additional discretionary powers have been given to DHSS managers? Will they suspend the three waiting days?

The whole thing is beginning to take off. I was enormously grateful for the help given to me by colleagues.

Monday 31 December
I set up our Monitoring Service to gather and publish information on the true nature of the fuel crisis. I also produced a bulletin of my own, and I drafted a second letter to Heath.

Ken Coates and I agreed that the main object of the exercise was to pin the responsibility on the Government and get the attention of the media. A big accusation. Why was there no three-day working week

* Joseph Edward Sieff, President of Marks & Spencer, who was also Vice-President of the Zionist Federation, was shot and severely injured apparently by a Palestinian attacker.

in 1972? It hadn't been necessary during a six-week, all-out strike and yet the miners were currently only on a work-to-rule. What was the cost to the country in excess of a settlement? What was the cost to the worker? Heath's lock-out would bankrupt Britain. We should challenge Heath to call off the three-day week, end the lock-out. The chaos was being caused by the three-day week and not by the miners. We must support and identify with the needs of the people and report what the Labour Party is doing, call for a General Election and demand either work or full pay.

I had a tremendous number of telephone calls, including Nicky Kaldor who mentioned the work of a bright chap, Francis Cripps, in Cambridge. Michael Meacher promised to get on to Shelter. Frank Field said he would do a survey of the effect on child poverty. David Piachaud, a Labour academic, was working out figures on coal stocks. I kept ringing Number 10.

The Secretary of the South East Derby Labour Party rang up to say there was a lot of coal being delivered at the power stations. Tony Banks said he would help by trawling trade unions in the Midlands for information on stocks. When you really ask the workers to provide you with information, the stuff pours in. You probably need a crisis to bring it about but it can be done and this is what we have achieved.

Tuesday 1 January 1974
I rang Harold and asked him if we should demand an early recall of Parliament. He said, 'That's for the Shadow Cabinet to discuss.' So I asked for an early meeting of the Shadow Cabinet and he didn't want that.

The BBC came and interviewed me and I prepared a series of questions for the Labour Monitoring Service, and Donald Ross, the editor of *Labour Weekly*, and Percy Clark [Labour Party Director of Information] will put out a Labour press bulletin every day from Transport House. Ken kept ringing with information on coal stocks. I got on to British Rail about movements of coal, and the NCB about stocks of coal at power stations and asked the sewage people whether there was a risk of sewage in the streets.

Caroline typed out a further letter to the Prime Minister and Stephen and June drove me to Number 10 after lunch to deliver it. Robin Butler, the Prime Minister's Private Secretary, said the Prime Minister hoped to get a reply to me today and also that the Government would be issuing some figures. Then I went to the St Ermine's Hotel, where Percy Clark had arranged a press conference.

Later, Heath's letter arrived, indeed two letters – the advance copy sent from Number 10, then the actual signed letter from Chequers. I immediately put out a statement saying I welcomed the fact that the

Prime Minister had been forced to give more information, and that his Ministers were being told to make some response to the crisis which the Government was creating.

Before I went to bed, I was interviewed by *Newsdesk*. I am now extremely tired. The *Guardian* have asked me to do a 1,200 word article for lunchtime tomorrow and I have got Donald Ross coming in the morning. For Heath to challenge me to support Phase 3 shows the man must be absolutely desperate because he has known from the beginning that the Labour Party is opposed to Phase 3 as unfair and unworkable. And so it is.

But it is very stimulating and exciting. When we meet the TUC on Friday, I think there will be some recognition that the Party has been active in this battle.

Wednesday 2 January
The 7 o'clock news had last night's interview, replying to Heath's challenge to pledge myself in support of Phase 3. Went out to buy all the papers and by the time I got back Capital Radio had already telephoned and woken Caroline up. At 7.30 they turned up with a radio transmitter car and fed me straight into the network, live from my living room. The *Morning Star* and the *Sun* had front-page coverage.

At 4 o'clock I went to the House of Commons and saw Harold and Eric Varley. Harold said, 'You have helped to fill in a couple of rather thin news days and you have caught Heath off guard.'

We discussed the possibility that Heath might ask for a dissolution if he was forced into a corner. I suggested Whitelaw might offer a coalition and we might then have an Election under difficult circumstances. Harold's main concern is that the Labour Party should come out of this situation without doing itself damage with the middle ground.

This morning I repeated in a press release my answer to Heath's challenge, pointing out that the three-day week would cost £2,000 million a year and for a fraction of that he could introduce food subsidies and higher pensions and freeze rents, which would transform the industrial situation. Indeed, I challenged him to do that.

Thames Television interviewed Ray Buckton, General Secretary of ASLEF, just after the talks with the British Railway Board. They were not successful because the Board will not negotiate with the loco men until the industrial action ends, and Buckton's men won't do that until negotiations start. During the interview, Ray came out strongly in my support – the first endorsement I've had in this crisis from a trade union leader.

I had several phone calls expressing support. I need it because Lord Carrington said tonight that this is just a personal campaign by me.

Harold is showing no signs of saying anything publicly yet – I'll just have to hope he will defend me.

Thursday 3 January
The phone rang continuously. Eric Heffer called to say that the oil fired stations were able to operate even with coal shortages. Also, in Liverpool, 80 per cent of the sewage went into the sea untreated anyway, so there were no grounds for a sewage scare based on lack of power for treating it!

Alan Williams, the Labour MP for Swansea West, rang to say there was plenty of coal at all the power stations in Wales, and I had a phone call from NATSOPA to say that the General Secretary, Dick Briginshaw, was publishing a letter of full support. Harold rang to say he was issuing a thousand-word statement which would be on all broadcasts.

I discovered that public meetings are not to be exempted from electricity restrictions, which will affect old age pensioners' clubs and community groups, whereas cinemas, strip clubs, bingo halls and commercial entertainment are allowed to continue. So I wrote to Peter Walker demanding that these restrictions be lifted, so that democracy could function.

Went in to Transport House after lunch. Ron Hayward has agreed to run the Monitoring Service and the statements will come from Transport House, with Donald Ross publishing his information bulletins.

At the Drafting Committee, I asked whether Michael Foot was right to compare our attitude to the situation with that in 1940 and 1945 because in 1940 Britain had a coalition Government, to which Jim said, 'Well, *I'm* in favour of a national Government.'

I repeated, 'A national Government?'

'Yes,' he confirmed, 'if it adopted our policy.'

'What – a coalition Government?'

'Yes, but I know they wouldn't,' he said.

'What you are saying is that you would be in favour of excluding from the public the choice between two policies.'

'I think a coalition Government, a national Government, would be a good thing if it would follow our policy,' was his reply.

John Silkin had said to me before Christmas, that he thought Jim might be won over to a coalition Government; and John's theory was that Whitelaw – who had a great admiration for Jim – might offer him the premiership. I'd thought it a far-fetched idea, but this was a minor confirmation of it.

Took part in a television discussion with James Prior [Leader of the House of Commons], Arthur Scargill, who is President of the Yorkshire

Mineworkers, and three other miners. I was heavy and slow and didn't say much, but the children were satisfied with it and thought Prior looked confused and muddled.

Friday 4 January
To the TUC-Labour Party Liaison Committee at 10.30 at Congress House with Sidney Greene of the NUR in the chair, and Jones and Scanlon both absent. However, Harold Wilson, Denis Healey, Bob Mellish, Jim Callaghan, Douglas Houghton, Norman Willis (the new TUC Assistant General Secretary), David Lea, Ken Graham, head of the TUC's industrial relations department, and George Smith were all there.

I was asked to introduce Labour's industrial policy proposals so I went through the thirteen points, saying they conformed to the policy agreement we had reached with the TUC. Jim described how we were dealing with the incomes policy and asked if the TUC could help us.

Norman Willis thought people were worried about prices and he urged the Party to be a party of reconstruction. He reminded us what Harold had said in 1963: 'If socialism hadn't existed, it would have had to be invented to deal with the scientific revolution.' How you deal with oil, with waste, is about socialism and the whole national situation, and incomes fall into place. He said our policies were practical: we did well in 1964 and we should do well again now.

We moved on to the industrial situation and Harold opened, saying that since 17 December, Labour and the TUC had been speaking with one voice.

I made some practical points. First, we should renew our call for an end to the three-day week; second, we should draw attention to problems like the steel industry which would be badly hit; third, we should say something about the protection of families – and I mentioned the idea of a short-run increase in family allowances during the crisis – and finally, we should consider joint demonstrations.

Reg Prentice believed this was a profoundly serious crisis. 'We must look for national unity when we attack the three-day week. We must recognise there is a deteriorating situation, a curtailment of production is inevitable and, demonstrably, the miners should be paid more. But the miners' action is not justified, they are aggravating and inflicting hardship on millions of workers and weakening the national economy and it should be called off.'

Harold Wilson asked, 'What would happen if you made a speech like that, Reg? The right-wing moderates can't hold their own on the NUM Executive, they can't hold their own people. And if the Labour Party told the miners to go back, it would lead to an all-out strike and the miners would feel deserted.'

Jim Callaghan said, 'Reg is wrong. The moderates can't dominate the NUM any more. There will either be an Election, or Heath will concede to the miners, or he will be replaced. Heath himself doesn't want an Election on "Who runs Britain?".'

Then Jim reported that Lord Lloyd of Kilgerran, President of the Liberal Party, had written to him, as Chairman of the Labour Party, suggesting talks between them and Lord Carrington, Chairman of the Tory Party, on the industrial situation. Jim said he was deferring his reply until after today's Shadow Cabinet.

'The TUC is in a box, which is locked from the outside,' Len Murray said. 'Reg's idea is simply not on. There is an alternative to the three-day week which is a sensible negotiated agreement. This is destroying the possibility of constructive Government–industry cooperation.'

Denis Healey warned, 'The Election will come if there is a full-scale strike. Tory opinion may shift.' He saw the TUC and the CBI converging and welcomed Michael Clapham's speech on having a statutory price policy and a voluntary incomes policy. He wanted to avoid any clash that might imply class confrontation. 'We want to make it a confrontation between industry and the Government.'

'Well, it is the class war and we have got to face it,' I said.

Mikardo believed that many industrialists actually think Heath has gone mad. 'Couldn't we get some individual industrialists to say something publicly; could we get the unions to get some employers to speak out?' to which Len Murray said, 'We'll try.'

At 2 o'clock at Shadow Cabinet, Harold Wilson reported on the situation and finished by saying, 'As for Tony's little exercise over Christmas, I think we can agree it was useful – and harmless to us.' He then attacked the policy of confrontation, adding, 'We are not against all action under Phase 3. We must recognise that the miners are a special case. It would be a pity if they got into a full-scale strike.'

Jim Callaghan supported the recall of Parliament. He again mentioned the letter from the Chairman of the Liberal Party.

There would be great pressure on the Government, an Election would solve nothing and he was dubious about Harold Wilson's tributes to Whitelaw – a thing I have often said to Harold – for fear that Whitelaw might succeed Heath.

Willie Ross believed we should attack Heath. Peter Shore said, 'Supposing there *is* a miners' strike, is it against the law?' Reg said it was and I pointed out that it was only against the law if the Pay Board brought an order against the miners and the Attorney-General decided to prosecute. Peter Shore said the Government was being punitive. He hoped we wouldn't hurry the Manifesto. We shouldn't link it to the crisis. Michael Foot pointed out that there was no commitment to publish on Wednesday after the joint meeting.

The last contribution came from Reg. 'I won't speak out publicly but I will return to my theme because this could develop into a conflict with the law and the miners must accept the national interest. Millions have accepted Phase 3 and the miners are contributing to the hardship.' He said the NUM moderates felt unable to take charge, therefore the militant tail in the NUM wagged the moderate dog and the moderate dog wagged the TUC and the TUC wagged the Labour Party.

Sunday 6 January
The *Sunday Times* had a centre-page spread called 'Why Tony Benn Got His Sums Wrong', about the coal stock position but, read very carefully, it implied that I was right, that the problem isn't due to coal but reduced oil supplies to the power stations. It also made clear that a 20 per cent cut in domestic consumption would be sufficient to meet the problem.

On the news we heard that planes at Heathrow are being defended by rings of police and tanks and the press say this is due to the rumour that there might be an SAM missile attack on London Airport, as some missiles have disappeared from the Middle East. Doing it as an exercise was one thing, but when we heard that it might be kept up for six weeks, I began thinking about its significance. My suspicious mind led me to the possibility that Carrington wanted to get people used to tanks and armed patrols in the streets of London. I thought I would draft a statement demanding the reasons. Caroline was against this. 'After all,' she said, 'you're not the Defence spokesman.' But I am the Aviation spokesman, and airports and airlines are my responsibility. I called Harold and told him. I also rang Fred Peart who said, 'I support the Government if it is security and anyway it will get the troops off their bottoms' – a most cynical view. I said, 'I am only telling you what I have done. But perhaps Carrington might have told you in advance as a courtesy.'

Then Michael Heseltine rang, saying they had had tip-offs since Christmas that there would be missile attacks on aircraft as they come in to land at London Airport, and that the tanks were therefore to protect the airport. It was interesting to get the story confirmed. I said to Heseltine, 'You could have at least let Harold know privately – and I hope there will be some sort of a statement made when Parliament meets. Will you keep me posted?'

Monday 7 January
There was a cartoon in the *Daily Mail* depicting me as a stormtrooper with a swastika on my shoulder, ordering Joe Gormley and Ray Buckton to torture the British public, saying, 'We have ways of making you suffer.'

Went in to the Organisation Sub-Committee at 3.30 which was held by candlelight and camping gas because Transport House does not have light on Mondays. On the question of the 20 January meeting on the Common Market, the Poplar Civic Theatre was not available because of the electricity cuts and the Government's refusal to make an exception for political meetings, so the committee wanted to cancel the meeting.

'You must be mad', I said. 'We must go ahead with the meeting, we must bring pressure to bear on the Poplar Labour Party.' John Cartwright [Director of the Royal Arsenal Cooperative Society], who was in the chair and who is the leader of the Labour Group on Greenwich Council, then said, 'We can't because the safety of the audience is at stake,' and Tom Bradley added, 'We might be breaking the law by having the meeting.' 'For God's sake,' I said, 'if necessary we'll have the meeting in the street and explain this is a ban on freedom of assembly. I have written to Peter Walker about it.'

Finally, it was agreed to issue a statement that we would go ahead with the meeting, but these chaps would capitulate to anything. If the Labour Party had been made illegal, they would have gone off to Wormwood Scrubs, mumbling under their breath 'obey the law' as they were bundled into the black marias. None of the top Labour leadership has any guts.

At the end, I raised another item on the agenda. 'I want to suggest that we give a red alert to the Party and say "prepare at once for an Election". First, it is possible there will be an Election. Second, it would show our confidence and might make the Cabinet think twice. Third, with the three-day week, the time and energy are available to mount an Election at a time when the unions are committed to us. Also, it would be a great morale booster.'

'Oh,' they said, 'how would an Election help?'

I replied that the only way in which an Election would *not* help would be if the Tories won. If we won, we would get the problems settled. This defeatism, inactivity and pessimism is embedded in the Right.

Later, I saw Tom McNally [International Secretary of the Labour Party] in the café opposite Transport House, who said, 'Thanks for all you've done in the last week,' which was surprising because he is not an admirer or supporter.

Tuesday 8 January
Woken up at 7.45 by Nicky Kaldor on the phone saying how shocked he was by the press attacks on me. He said the Government had adopted

the technique of the big lie as with the 'Zinoviev letter' in 1924.*

The Information Committee meeting at 11.30 considered slogans for simplicity, such as 'Back to Work with Labour'.

We discussed the present crisis and Barbara said, 'We are landed with the defence of the miners, and we must maximise our advantages and give reassurance; the Tories themselves are frightened at having a fanatic in charge and they are afraid Heath will destroy social democracy. Polarisation had frightened a lot of people.' She had heard that Heseltine was raging against Heath.

Dashed to another meeting where Francis Cripps, Michael Meacher, and Donald Ross and Don Brind of *Labour Weekly* and I went over the coal stock figures. Granada TV were there filming the discussion. We analysed the need for further questions: Why was the oil cut back? When was the decision taken to shift back to oil after the miners' dispute began? And so on.

Campaign Committee in the afternoon, and I was asked to report on the Information Committee recommendations. Harold was there, Jim was in the chair. Shirley said, 'Women don't like strikes, women don't get wage increases, women are frightened of militancy, they like "normalcy".' Fred Mulley thought it was no use going to the unions, since they would do nothing to help with the women's vote. I said we should give a lead to women and not just wait for the pollsters. We should ask them to defend trade unionists and defend themselves.

At 6 we had the Shadow Cabinet and, as we gathered, we heard that Carrington had been appointed Secretary of State for Energy.

Harold announced that there would be a Private Notice Question by Fred Peart about London Airport, obviously as a result of my telephone call. Roy said, 'I'm against this line. It just gives the Government an excuse to make their case, gives them a platform; we mustn't be seen to be against *everything*.'

I told them that Heseltine had rung about the reports that SAM missiles might be used against aircraft. Jim Callaghan, who had seen Robert Carr last night, interrupted to say that wasn't true.

Went to Deptford for the Workers' Control conference in the Town Hall, with about 200 people present. Granada Television filmed it, and there were some tremendous questions such as, 'How are you going to get rid of Harold Wilson?' and so on. I summed up at the end and said, 'We mustn't be pessimistic about the outcome. The Labour movement

* The forged letter allegedly from the Communist International to the British Communist Party urging them to start a revolution, which when released during the 1924 Election campaign contributed to the downfall of the first Labour minority Government.

is very strong. Democracy is what we have built up and we must use it.'

Wednesday 9 January
Rang the DTI and was told that Peter Walker's letter was on its way. It finally reached me with rude scribbles in Peter Walker's own handwriting on the top and bottom of the letter:

'Dear Tony,
(or would you prefer Benn)'
'Yours sincerely (I notice that yours was not sincere!)
Peter (Walker to you)'

In the House, Heath gave a pedestrian speech justifying the three-day week and how necessary Phase 3 was. He was quite intransigent. Harold was boring to begin with but when he read out the TUC Economic Committee statement, which held out a small olive branch to the Government, Heath jumped in twice to say it wasn't a satisfactory assurance; the first time, Robert Carr put one hand to his head, and the second time he put his head in both hands and looked terribly gloomy. Heath has lost the confidence of his people and many Tories openly admit they think he is destroying the Party and the country.

Thursday 10 January
The press was full of Barber's rejection of the TUC offer after the Neddy meeting and the ASLEF crisis has worsened because Dick Marsh has now said that drivers who don't work will not be paid.

John Biffen came up to me while I was having tea and said, 'I have been asked whether there should be an Election and I have said no because I think Wilson would win it unless you made an extreme speech and frightened people back into the Tory camp. I say this as a man who is not without considerable admiration for you.'

Saturday 12 January
Election rumours continue to grow at a fantastic rate.

Sunday 13 January
A survey commissioned by the *Observer* and *Weekend World* showed that within a few weeks the three-day week would bring the country to a halt. Jack Jones and Hugh Scanlon were interviewed on *Weekend World*, both very good, urging the TUC peace proposals; Scanlon saying that his basic claim of £3 a week would still be within Phase 3. There were also three industrialists on the programme – Lord Stokes, Chairman of British Leyland, Peter Parker, and Monty Finniston, Chairman of British Steel – all hoping that the TUC proposal would be taken up by

the Government. But Patrick Jenkin, the new Minister for Energy under Carrington, a rather pompous and self-satisfied man, said he didn't think the TUC proposals were any good.

Monday 14 January
Michael Foot rang and asked me if I had noticed that the trade figures had been postponed by a week. The reason given in the *Sunday Times* yesterday was that the DTI officials couldn't read the computer print-outs by candlelight. Very suspicious! So I wrote another letter to Peter Walker, telephoned it to his office, told the press, and then got a very angry reply back from him denying my accusation that he was suppressing the figures.

Ken Coates rang. Mitterand has declined to sign the joint letter with me to Brezhnev about the treatment of oppositionists in the Soviet Union. Apparently Mitterand is going to the Soviet Union soon and doesn't think it would be productive.

Tuesday 15 January
Up at 6 and left for Bristol. It is the first time I've been by car since the energy crisis began in earnest and with a fifty mph speed limit it took me about three and a half hours.

I heard later tonight that Taverne is definitely intending to put up a candidate here in readiness for an Election and he is coming to Bristol for a big meeting at which he will no doubt announce the candidature. In a way I am confident, because there is a massive trade union and socialist backing for me; even if I get defeated there will be no dishonour in it.

Went to Temple Meads and the cafeteria was shut because of a strike so I went into the taxi drivers' café which was friendly.

At 5 I did a surgery, masses of people with heartbreaking problems, particularly housing.

Wednesday 16 January
The main news today was a report of Enoch Powell's attack on Heath, Powell maintaining that an Election would be a fraud. The Governor of the Bank of England said we would have ten years of austerity. The pound dropped to its lowest level ever, I think, to $2.16.

To the Shadow Cabinet and Harold opened by saying, 'We won't discuss whether there is going to be an Election or not; but let's assume that the Cabinet is divided. Some Ministers are talking openly against Heath. If he fixes 7 February, it would be outrageously short, particularly with the printing difficulties and the three-day week. If it's 14 February, it's still an outrage because the electoral register used will be the old one within forty-eight hours of the new one becoming effective so we must make a maximum attack on that. The Government fear the worst now. The Governor of the Bank of England's statement was very important. I'll do a speaking tour: we must all speak with *one* voice on the basis of the Manifesto when we agree it. No private enterprise and no gimmicks. I will be in London every day of my press conference and I invite colleagues to join me from time to time. We must make no Party capital out of the OPEC oil crisis.'

Michael Foot said we mustn't give the impression we could do nothing. 'As Tony Benn said at the Conference, we would not make the crisis we inherit the excuse for not implementing our programme but the occasion for carrying it through. We must convince people we will do what we say.'

Jim Callaghan wasn't convinced there would be an Election. He thought people would be nervous of voting if the street lights were out. What do we say to the miners? We must be simple and rather repetitive; don't broaden it out too far. 'Confrontation versus conciliation' would be one theme and 'Equality can't await growth' would be another. He hoped our party political broadcasts would be flexible.

Later, Harold said, 'Ignore Enoch Powell because last time the attack on him lost five seats.'*

I interrupted and said, 'Look Harold, I've heard you say this two or three times before and never contradicted you, but it just isn't true.'

'Well, I've said five times that you lost us five seats.'

'Let me deny it once,' I said, 'and then you can proceed.'

That was more or less it. But I did say to Joe Haines outside, 'I'm going to be the bogeyman.'

'Oh yes, they're expecting you to proclaim the revolution,' Joe replied.

'Well I'm tape-recording everything I say and every question and answer and every radio and television interview, so there will always be a complete transcript available: but I'm sure even that won't prevent me being misrepresented.'

Thursday 17 January

The papers this morning had a full account of Dick Taverne's statement that he was going to put up James Robertson as his candidate in Bristol South-East, a blue-blooded Tory City man who, up to a few months ago, was working for the Tory Government, Heath and Lord Rothschild.

Rang Jennifer Jenkins today and asked whether Roy would send me

* Wilson had been critical of my attack during the 1970 Election on Enoch Powell for his stance on immigration and race relations (see *Office Without Power*, Chapter 3).

a message of support although if Roy wasn't able to send me a message, I would understand. He needn't mention my name. He could say 'I hope that electors in Bristol South-East vote Labour.' She said she would put it to Roy.

At 3 Heath was in the House for Questions and everybody wanted to know what the Cabinet had decided about the TUC initiative. The Government has obviously reached no decision. It is deeply divided, of that there is no doubt. Heath was stonewalling but looking miserable, as were all his Ministers, and I think they have now got second thoughts about it all.

Jim Callaghan, sitting on the Opposition Front Bench, offered to come to Bristol during the campaign and Michael Foot offered to come and speak for me. I said that would be marvellous. Neil Kinnock, Labour MP for Bedwelty, suggested a couple of miners from South Wales and I said I'd thought of it but hadn't liked to ask. So he's going to lay that on. Dennis Skinner came up and said, 'Keep steady, keep quiet now. Let the others climb on your bandwagon.'

I wound up the debate on the Companies Act, taking a very strong line first of all on the three-day week and the Government deceit, then on the evils of capitalism, and on the right-wing organisation Aims of Industry, comparing their methods with Watergate and saying how corrupting they were. Finished up with workers' control and public ownership. I can't be got for libel because I'm covered by parliamentary privilege – that's what it's for. I took my Sony in a box into the House and recorded the whole speech with interruptions. I think I shall do it again, keep my own Commons archives. I daresay I'd get into terrible trouble but I don't know that it is an offence to take a tape-recorder into the House of Commons.

It doesn't look as if there's going to be an Election now. I think Heath has lost 7 February as an option and he might very well find that after he has brooded over it at Chequers this weekend that he misses the 14th; he may try either to ride the miners out and hope to provoke them into further action or say they've solved the problem because we can go back to a four-day week.

This is the most thrilling experience of campaigning so far in my life and I get the feeling that the attack on me by Taverne in Bristol is going to stimulate and encourage support. I should be surprised if Robertson picked up more than a few hundred votes,* and if a humiliating defeat is imposed on Taverne, pushing him into a lower position than the Labour candidate achieved in Lincoln, it will avenge the Left. Of course, if the Labour Party wins the Election on the slogan 'Back

* In the event, James Robertson received 668 votes, fewer than the National Front candidate.

to Work with Labour' (which Don Concannon thought up and which the Shadow Cabinet have accepted) then the balance of power in the Labour Party is absolutely firmly on the Left; because one of the great arguments of the Right is that you can't win an Election with a left-wing programme. If you have a left-wing programme and you win an Election, then the Right will have lost that argument, and that will be a historic moment in the history of the British Labour movement.

Monday 21 January
To lunch with the Iranian Ambassador in honour of Harold Wilson. The Ambassador is a bit of a playboy, has racehorses and so on. At the lunch were Harold, Jim, Ted Short, Eric Varley, Gerald Kaufman, Lord Greenhill, the Permanent Secretary at the Foreign Office, Sir Martin Charteris, the Queen's Private Secretary, and others.

Sir Martin Charteris called me Tony which I thought was friendly. I said, 'Oh, you're just the man I want to see to ask about dissolution and the rules governing it.'

He replied, 'Well, the Queen has absolute rights.'

So I said, 'Yes, of course, but I remember a discussion I had with the Queen's former private secretary Michael Adeane at Hampton Court in 1966 where I got the impression that the Queen was not anxious to get too involved in controversial matters and was therefore quite pleased that the Conservative Party, for example, had chosen a system of election for their Leader to avoid the invidious task of her having to make a choice.'

'Yes, that's right. But as to a dissolution, she has absolute rights.'

So I said, 'Let's discuss it hypothetically because I realise that we can't discuss the present position. But I take it the Queen would consult.'

'Yes, she has an absolute right to consult.'

'Well, I assume that she would consult former Prime Ministers. Does she consult the Speaker?'

'No, I don't think she does.'

'Well, the Speaker is a Privy Councillor. He's the man who knows about the House of Commons better than anyone else and from a completely detached position so, on questions of a dissolution, as to whether or not a man or a series of men might command a majority, the Speaker would be a very good person to advise.'

He said he had never thought of that and that it had never been done.

I said, 'I know it hasn't been done, but it would allow the Queen to distance herself slightly from the controversy by calling in the Speaker while preserving her absolute right.'

'Oh yes,' he replied. 'We must preserve her right because I think there has to be some risk attached in order to provide excitement for the monarchy. And, of course, in the end, the Queen's judgment would have to be tested by the events.'

He presumably meant that if the Queen refused dissolution to Heath, and then Heath was in some way defeated, this would be embarrassing to the Palace. So he said, 'In 1926, Bing, who as Governor-General of Canada was the Crown's representative, refused a dissolution to the then Prime Minister, Mackenzie King; King then resigned and got his government re-elected. The Governor-General's relations with him were much strained afterwards.'

Obviously the palace has been busy thinking about dissolutions and how to handle them, and maybe my suggestion about the Speaker will be noted. I was particularly interested when he said there must be some risk for the monarchy to make it exciting.

At lunch I was sitting with Frank Giles of the *Sunday Times* and Sir Eric Drake, Chairman of BP, who said he couldn't understand why all politicans wanted to be Prime Minister.

I said, 'Well, yes it's true, they do. But think of the number of *businessmen* also waiting at their Colombey les Deux Eglises for the call; Beeching, Robens and all those people.'

'Would Carrington be able to renounce his title to become Leader?' he asked.

'No, not under existing law but of course the Government can do what it likes.'

'Well, Carrington's a very good chap.'

That was an interesting view from Drake, who is a right-wing Tory. All of a sudden, I could see a new Lord Home appearing out of the shadows – and Carrington might be the businessman's choice.

'Of course,' I said, 'that's how Home got it because everyone thought he was out of the running with his peerage.'

On my right was the Managing Director of the *Financial Times*, Alan Hare, and during the discussion he said, 'Of course, the *Financial Times* is completely non-political.'

I laughed. 'Oh, come on, you can't expect me to let a comment like that go unchallenged. What you mean by non-political is Conservative, but you consciously abstain from the wilder excesses of political polemics.' Then I said, 'It is a very odd thing, you see, that no newspaper in Fleet Street will allow any politician to be taken seriously who doesn't accept three key elements. One is the statutory incomes policy, the second is the Common Market, and the third is anti-trade union legislation. If you don't accept one of those three things, then you are out. You're either mad, ambitious, or Communist.'

I argued about the need to enfranchise five hundred thousand shop stewards by introducing industrial democracy if you were going to solve the problems of society. I am addressing the *Financial Times* lunch shortly and I might use this as a theme.

Hare then said, 'Well, another Labour Government would have to have a statutory incomes policy; all your Shadow Cabinet people admit this privately.'

'Maybe they do but they haven't got the courage to say it publicly because they know it is a non-starter and they wouldn't get away with it. It just wouldn't be on. Something else will have to give.'

'What do you mean by that?' he asked.

'There will have to be reforms of another kind.'

He said, 'You'll take on the City of London?'

'No,' I said. 'There'll just have to be reforms of another kind. The reason I am most bitterly attacked by the ultra-left is because they know that I am really the only guy who might save the parliamentary system by making the necessary reforms.'

Afterwards Jim Callaghan drove me back to the House and expressed his anxiety about the power of the trade unions.

'Maybe, Jim, but look at the Government, run by the City of London, and nobody says the City is too powerful. It's a question of whose side you are on. It's a gut issue.'

'They're much too powerful,' he replied.

'Well, I don't believe in powerful leaders. I believe in spreading the power among the rank-and-file. Anyway, you were always pro-union when they supported your view.'

'Yes,' he said, 'but they are still much too powerful. This is our problem.'

Jim, in fairness to him, has always thought there wouldn't be a snap Election.

Tuesday 22 January

There may be a full-scale miners' strike now because the Government is standing firm and so the prospect of an Election is increasing quite sharply again. Enoch Powell in *The Times* denied having recommended people to vote either Tory or Labour in the next Election, so he is keeping everybody guessing.

Wednesday 23 January

At the TUC-Labour Party Liaison Committee, I moved an emergency resolution – which I drafted in the middle of the night – 'that the National Executive Committee of the Labour Party pledges its full support to the Trades Union Congress in its proposals to bring about a settlement of the present dispute in the mining industry, and calls upon the British people to back the National Union of Mineworkers in their efforts to achieve a fair and honourable settlement of their claim'.

Before the Shadow Cabinet, Roy approached me. 'I want to see you afterwards. I should have spoken to you.' This was in reference to my phone call asking if Roy would send me a message of support. Later he said, 'I have considered your request and I think in the event of an Election, I might find it possible.'

'If you can't do it, I quite understand. You needn't mention my name if you find that difficult, simply say to former Labour voters you hope they will vote Labour.'

He replied, 'In principle, yes.' But he was so red either with anger or embarrassment or I don't know what, that I felt I'd put him in a difficulty by asking him. I shall write him a note thanking him for agreeing in principle to send me a message and leave it at that.

Watched Harold on television. All this 'national interest', 'working together', 'keep calm and keep cool', and 'a Labour Government will knit the nation into one', seems absolute rubbish to me now.

Thursday 24 January

I notice that the attitude of the Parliamentary Labour Party, including the Right and Centre, is now completely changed. Today Bob Maclennan, Labour MP for Caithness and Sutherland, who has been very anti-me for a long time, said that at the Scottish Committee this morning he had been described as a 'Bennite' socialist. I laughed with him about that. There's been a sort of breakthrough.

Tony Crosland came up to me today and said, 'We ought to have a talk and see how far apart we are.' That was a sign of something; Denis Healey is also being very respectful lately – and he's a great old weathercock.

At the PLP meeting, Sydney Bidwell, the MP for Southall, got up and attacked Reg Prentice for his speech last weekend in which Reg declared that Mick McGahey, the NUM Vice-President, was as much an enemy as the Tories.

Saturday 26 January

The miners are making it clear that if a strike is called, they are intending to stop the movement of coal completely and other resources to power stations. This, of course, will lead to confrontations between pickets and police, and it is in this atmosphere of anarchy and chaos that the Government hopes to get re-elected, and I have no doubt of that. Unless we are able to challenge on the real argument, then there is no hope for us. There is to be a strike ballot on Wednesday.

Monday 28 January

I heard from the *Bristol Evening Post* that the National Front intended to put up a candidate in Bristol South-East, so now that's the Tories, the Liberals, the Tavernites and the National Front as my opposition.

This morning a journalist called Jacob Ecclestone from *The Times* rang and said he wanted to see me urgently. My secretary, Mary Lou Clark, protecting me from a possible spoof, asked him to leave a note at the Commons and he left a letter for me saying that last night an article had been printed in the first edition of *The Times* by a Tim Congdon headed, 'An Economic Case for Giving Miners More'. It referred to a study published at Cambridge and the piece ended with the words, 'The 35 per cent figure is, of course, significantly above the miners' demands. But the logic behind it is overwhelming.'

According to Ecclestone, when William Rees-Mogg, the Editor, saw this first edition, he rang the Night Editor and wanted the whole article removed from subsequent editions. However, the final instructions were to delete the last paragraph and to substitute a new heading for the whole article called, 'An independent view. A Cambridge case for giving miners more.' This had really annoyed Ecclestone and his colleagues and he thought I ought to know about it.

I referred to it in the House during Questions with Peter Walker without mentioning Ecclestone. I decided that if *The Times* does not print this exchange tomorrow, I shall write a letter charging them with suppressing press freedom by a direct order from the Editor, and saying if a satisfactory answer is not given, I shall report the matter to the Press Council and invite the NUJ chapel of *The Times* and Lord Thomson [Chairman of the Thomson Organisation, publishers of *The Times*] to consider it. I think I have caught William Rees-Mogg out on a most obvious case of editorial political censorship.

I later rang Ecclestone and he said he hadn't spoken to the Editor himself but he was sure it had come from him. I suggested he raise it at *The Times* chapel meeting on Wednesday and he courageously said that he would be prepared to confirm it publicly.

After Campaign Committee, I went to the Mass Media Seminar Committee where I hoped the final draft of our policy would be before us. We went through the communications Green Paper and the main argument was whether an element of internal democracy should be included. Chris Mayhew argued strongly that the mass media were too important to let democracy be applied; he was pretty much in a minority. There was a division at 7 and I walked out with Chris Mayhew, who said, 'This is disgusting, woolly, Marxist stuff. You will have Communists running newspapers.'

'What about William Rees-Mogg?' I said, and I recited what had happened at *The Times*.

'I'd rather have William Rees-Mogg running newspapers, given he believes in parliamentary democracy, than Alan Sapper and the Marxists.'

I said, 'That's just an indication that you feel socially more at ease with William Rees-Mogg than you do with a prominent trade union leader.' He was angry. It is not really worth having him on the Committee, but I have to take account of his views.

I think Jim is edging himself into position for a coalition Government. Prentice has apparently attacked McGahey again and McGahey is in a difficulty because, on the radio tonight, he said, 'Many of the troops which may be mobilised are the sons of miners, and if they come to dig coal, we shall appeal to them and explain our case to them.' A perfectly reasonable argument, nothing revolutionary in that. But people are now talking about sedition. I think we're heading for trouble and I am tempted to make a speech in advance which warns that the full moral and criminal responsibility for what might happen will fall on the Prime Minister's head.

Tuesday 29 January
The Times reported the exchanges in the House yesterday. The *Guardian* also said a statement from the Labour Party attacking Communists was imminent, and that some back benchers were saying they hoped Mr Wedgwood Benn would keep out of it. Spent the morning drafting a letter to the Editor of *The Times*. Peter Jay, the Economics Editor, rang to say that the staff were very upset but he did confirm informally that Rees-Mogg himself had censored the article.

On the 1 o'clock news was a report of a statement drafted by Hayward and Callaghan which began, 'We speak for every member of the Labour Party as well as for millions outside it in sending the mineworkers our good wishes and support.' Then it went on '... But communists and other extremist leaders of the NUM say they have wider political objectives ... We utterly repudiate any attempts by Communists or others to use the miners as a political battering ram ...' and so on.

Then came Wilson's Early Day Motion that had been put on the Order Paper signed by himself, Ted Short, Douglas Houghton, Bob Mellish, Eric Varley and others attacking McGahey by name. Jim was interviewed on the news and he attacked McGahey's reference to the troops. He said, 'Who would take notice of the miners appealing to the troops? It's rubbish', and that there would be a long and bitter strike. This was obviously designed to dissuade the miners from voting for a strike. Petre Crowder, Tory MP for Ruslip-Northwood, was asked about his proposal for the establishment of vigilantes and he said he hoped he would have the chance of driving a lorry through a picket line. Then Jill Knight, Conservative MP for Edgbaston, said strikers were the enemy of the state.

Went to the House for Questions and Norman Tebbit, the Tory MP for Epping, asked the Prime Minister whether he would arrange for the title of Lord Stansgate to be resuscitated. Another Member got up and asked whether Harold Wilson agreed with the statement I had made at the weekend, that it was not for Labour to instruct the miners on how they should vote. Harold got up and floundered a bit. I saw the Early Day Motion circulated by Harold Wilson attacking McGahey; indeed Harold said in the House that McGahey and Heath were the two extremists. I decided to do a bit of research and so looked up *The Times* for 1912; what was interesting was that in March 1912, the miners were balloting on a strike, the Government were rushing the Minimum Wages Bill through – which is like the Relativities Report – and Tom Mann said the troops should assist the miners and was being prosecuted for sedition. Josiah Wedgwood, Bertie Russell and others set up the Defence of Free Speech Committee to defend Tom Mann. *The Times*'s leading articles were fulminating every day about syndicalist revolutions. And Ramsay MacDonald issued a statement warning against syndicalism but saying that the Labour Party wished the miners well. So there's been no real change in the Labour Party since 1912!

After dinner Michael Foot and I had a chat and he told me that Dick Crossman is dying, which is very sad.

Wednesday 30 January

This morning there were massive attacks on Mick McGahey and the *Guardian* actually ran a leading article saying, 'Poor Mr McGahey, there's not much difference between him and Mr Benn.'

Rang William Rees-Mogg's secretary at *The Times* and she read his letter to me which hasn't yet arrived. 'Dear Anthony, I took your letter to be a request for an explanation as to what had happened.' He thought the original article wasn't justified on the basis of the study and that logic was seldom overwhelming, particularly as pay wasn't the only factor in getting miners into the pits – by which he meant that unemployment was another way. That is no doubt in the Government's mind as well.

Went to the House at 3.30. The debate (on the Ten Minute Rule Bill) for the televising of Parliament was defeated by about thirty votes. I voted for it.

In the Shadow Cabinet, Michael Foot said he wished to refer to the Early Day Motion condemning Mick McGahey, and to Jim and Ron's statement. There had been no consultation on these. He said he disliked the attack on McGahey; McGahey might have been misreported, and anyway, he didn't like Jim's statement because it referred to extremists. Who were these extremists? Lawrence Daly?

Bob Mellish said that MPs had wanted a statement. There was a fear of a 'Reds under the bed' Election campaign by the Tories, so Jim had therefore drafted a statement on the Monday night, and issued it yesterday.

Harold Wilson said a great deal of damage had been done by McGahey. The Party had been very feverish after the Heath broadcast on television. The miners' MPs had not objected to what he, Wilson, had said, indeed, most of them had supported it: as Leader, he had to say something. Douglas Houghton strongly supported Harold. He thought the Party had benefited generally and we should back the Leader.

Ted Short said he supported what had been said. The Leader had had no option and with an Election almost certain, it was essential to make clear that we were not linked to the Communists.

Then Roy Mason pointed out that Arthur Scargill, the Yorkshire President and Mick McGahey, the Scottish President, were competing for the vacancy that would be created when Joe Gormley retired.

Reg Prentice supported Jim's statement. Denis Healey said that the majority of the nation agreed with it and he was amazed at the naïvety of Michael Foot in not facing what he should have realised was a major threat to the social fabric of society. He wasn't so surprised at *my* naïvety.

I interrupted, 'Well, I, at least, am not an ex-Communist,' which shook the Shadow Cabinet.

'Well,' said Denis, 'perhaps it would have been better if you had been through these experiences when you were young.'

Douglas Houghton finished the meeting by saying that he was deeply troubled and the whole fabric of our society would be shattered.

It was a long, bitter and tough meeting.

I went back to my room in the House and found a message from Joe Haines to ring James Margach of the *Sunday Times*. I rang him and he said, 'You know, Rees-Mogg has the same relationship with Heath that Geoffrey Dawson [former Editor of *The Times*] had with Chamberlain before the war.' He quoted two entries from Dawson's diary for the same date, 23 May 1937; 'I do my utmost night after night to keep out of the paper anything that might hurt their susceptibilities' – 'their' referring to the Nazis; and secondly, in a letter to Lord Lothian, 'I spend my nights dropping in little things which are intended to soothe them' – again referring to the Nazis.

James Margach was very tough about it, so all of a sudden, I feel rather inspired. I deeply appreciated it, and told him I was grateful for a friendly reference in an entirely hostile press. Came home feeling much better.

Thursday 31 January

I was working quietly at home when I had a message to get to the Shadow Cabinet at midday. It wasn't fully attended, but Harold had called it because of Heath's statement in which he has now in effect proposed that the TUC would have to accept Phase 3 and the Pay Board and the Relativities Board. Even in that event, he wouldn't, on that basis, offer cash to the miners, but he would offer something soon afterwards.

Harold thought the wisest thing to do was to leave it to the TUC to respond and not interfere at the moment. I was sure that Harold was right, that we shouldn't be drawn into the negotiations. I thought we ought to follow our present line which, in effect, was supporting Joe Gormley as President of the NUM: therefore we ought to support his approach – i.e., there must be cash on the table.

I sat on the Front Bench for a bit; actually went to sleep during Question Time which is a difficult thing to do.

Then to the Polling Committee where Bob Worcester [Managing Director of MORI], Denis Healey, Shirley Williams, Tony King of Essex University and others were gathered. I did manage to get removed the idea that we would ask Taverne how much support his party had. I said it was outrageous to ask a renegade Labour MP who picks his own candidates. They all really wanted to test the strength of Taverne and I felt I was up against a little Gaitskellite clique, but I stuck to my guns.

Sunday 3 February

Herbert Rogers rang this morning, livid about the statement attacking McGahey. But when I rang Frank McElhone last night he thought that I would probably need to support the Early Day Motion condemning McGahey to restore my credibility with the PLP. Well, I just won't do it.

This evening we had a small party at home. Francis Cripps came down from Cambridge and it was the first chance I had for a proper talk to him. He said that he and a group of people who had been economic advisers to the last Labour Government, and had worked with Nicky Kaldor and the Treasury, felt that they would never take the Official Secrets Act again because decisions in the Treasury were not taken on a scientific basis. The technical people produced the figures and then the Treasury mandarins discussed them and came to their hunch conclusions and then told the Chancellor what they thought he should do; in the case of Labour Chancellors, they usually did it and the Cabinet never altered it. He prophesied that when the next Labour Government came to power, the Treasury would get hold of Denis within five minutes and tell him the situation was critical: the international monetary community would insist on this and that, and we would have absolutely massive measures announced within twenty-four hours.

Brian Walden thought that this would happen. Harold Wilson had been going around the City saying that they had no cause for worry. He too did not think the next Labour Government would be particularly radical, in fact, all we would do would be to nationalise land and after that have swingeing taxation with an end of all our Election pledges. It will be a right-wing Cabinet, just as Harold wants it.

I said that in those circumstances I could see myself being in and out of the Cabinet within a week: I certainly would not resign, but I would make political speeches describing the nature of the decisions that would have to be taken.

It was a very useful evening and I must say, of all the economic advisors whom I have met so far, I think I would regard Francis as the most able guy to have. He did say that he had advised Jenkins, Healey and Taverne after the 1970 Election, but he did not feel that advising men of power to reach their own decisions was really the right way of going about things.

Monday 4 February
This morning I had a third call from the *Bristol Evening Post* on the instructions of its Editor, Gordon Farnsworth, to ask me why I had not signed the motion on McGahey. I said I had no comment but, off-the-record, I was not going to be driven into signing a denunciation of anybody; I thought it ill-conceived, it was better left to the miners to sort out and I had made up my mind that, since 'Reds under the bed' was the theme of the Election, I was going to have nothing to do with it.

The result of the miners' ballot was 81 per cent voting for the Executive recommendation to strike – 188,000 to about 41,000 – so I put out a little statement saying now that the silent majority have stood up and been counted beside their leadership, the whole nation should support the miners' just claim for an honourable and fair settlement to get the nation back to work.

Went over to the CBI where there was a dinner laid on. I sat next to Lucien Wigdor, who thought that the strength of the unions was the great obsession of the CBI and that pressure groups should not be allowed to finance political parties – a traditional CBI argument.

I think the CBI have lost confidence in their own capacity to solve these problems, and so they are pleading now with the Labour Party to stand up against the unions because they see that the Tories cannot do it. This plea for a coalition approach to the problem of trade union power is wrongly aimed unless the Labour Party deserts its true function which is to support working people.

We are on the eve of a great strike and the only choices open to Heath are to settle; to have a strike and an Election; or be replaced. If he tries for a dissolution he might be removed by the Tories before he could get one. Meanwhile the Labour Party leadership is hovering about, hoping to be popular.

Tuesday 5 February

Went to the House for Prime Minister's Questions. It was clear from Heath's answers that, with the announcement that the miners' strike would begin on Saturday night, the Cabinet had in effect decided to go to the country. Heath was busy burning his bridges and his boats and everything else. The whole atmosphere was of the hustings, no question about that.

Speculation is starting among MPs that Heath will now go for an early Election, possibly as soon as 28 February.

Wednesday 6 February

In view of the imminence of the Election, I duplicated a short letter and sent out a postal vote form and a copy of the campaign document to 1,000 of my known supporters.

I went to the House at 3.30 and Barber made a strongly polemical Election speech in which he attacked me twice. He was completely floored by Enoch Powell who asked him why, if oil prices were reckoned to be deflationary, world food prices were not deflationary. He got Barber in such a muddle that he didn't know the difference between inflationary and deflationary. Barber finished up by saying that anyone who opposed the Government's prices and incomes policy, its statutory wage policy, was leading the country towards totalitarian Communism. He got a poor hearing.

I went and had a cup of tea in the Tea Room, and next in the queue was the Tory MP for South Buckinghamshire, Ronald Bell. I asked him, 'Are you a hawk or a dove?'

'As you know, I am a supporter of Enoch Powell.'

'What will Enoch do?'

He said, 'His view is pretty clear and Heath has to have an Election to save his skin because if he doesn't have one, we'll get rid of him.' He spoke so disloyally that one could see the most tremendous ructions developing in the Tory Party.

At 5 o'clock, the Shadow Cabinet met and Harold said that Carrington had let it be known to the press that there would be three resignations – his own, Prior's and Barber's – if there was any cash on the table for the miners; Whitelaw would like to resign if there wasn't. But you don't resign just before an Election.

Thursday 7 February

At 12.40, the Secretary of the PLP rang me to say that the General Election was to be on 28 February and this was announced on the 1 o'clock news.

I had to cancel my lunch engagement with Clive Jenkins and David Basnett, and Clive said over the phone, 'We will send two full-time organisers into your constituency, buy a loudspeaker for your use and give £250 to your Election funds.' David Basnett said, 'Contact Larry Whitty' (who was formerly my Private Secretary at the Ministry of Technology and who is now head of the Research Department at the GMWU), 'and tell him what you want, and we'll see what we can do.'

In the House it was like the end of term, with cheering and counter cheering and shouting and so on. I must say, as I walked out at 3.30 I wondered if it was the last time I would be in that place.

Tonight Enoch Powell decided not to stand as a candidate because he feels the Election is a fraud and he can't put forward a policy which he knows the Tory Government would break if they got elected. This is a very important factor. Many Tories will be extremely worried by Enoch's defection and it will do Heath an immense amount of damage; it is bound to have an effect in pushing us up in the polls. If only Harold would look and sound a bit more convincing, we might have a good chance.

Friday 8 February

At 10.30 I went to Transport House for the meeting on the Manifesto, attended by Shadow Cabinet members and members of the Executive.

Despite Joe Gormley's efforts, the miners have decided to go ahead with their strike and it remains to be seen whether the Government will try to impose a cooling-off period under the terms of the Industrial Relations Act.

Saturday 9 February

Went to Pudsey where I talked to Party members. The Labour candidate is the former Reverend Ken Targett who has corresponded with me over the years. The press were there and I stressed the point that I am now taking up urgently, namely that we should listen to the older people in this Election. 'Talk to your grandfather, he's been through it all before.' One man there, Ambrose Robinson, said he remembered Robert Blatchford, had read the *Clarion* as a child and that he had been a friend of Victor Grayson's.* Someone else said he had known the

---

* Robert Blatchford, author of *Merrie England* and editor of the *Clarion*, a socialist paper; Victor Grayson, Socialist MP for Colne Valley from 1907, who disappeared mysteriously at the beginning of the First World War.

dockers hero, Tom Mann and had even been a pall-bearer at his funeral. Came back on the train with two journalists who are covering my campaign for the whole of the Election period – Brian Woosey who is now with the *Sun* and has been told to massacre me, and Tim Devlin, a Tavernite from *The Times*, a bright, ambitious young man.

Sunday 10 February
Went off to *Weekend World* to do a fifteen-minute discussion with Margaret Thatcher and John Pardoe, Liberal MP for North Cornwall, on the miners' dispute, with Peter Jay in the chair.

Caroline and I got to the Unicorn Hotel in Bristol at 10 pm where we have two rooms on the top floor. We unpacked, had a meal, and I rang Frances Morrell. She thought the General Election campaign had not got off to a good start from the Labour point of view. The mining dispute was bound to complicate it. The Labour challenge was not coming across clearly enough and the whole thing was being presented as Heath's great gamble; Heath's battle for fairness; Heath and the moderates. She thought this impression had to be destroyed if we were to make progress and we must be stronger. We had to invite the public to confront the reality of the trade union movement and its role, that it did not want to 'run Britain' but it did represent a growing group of important people with whom we should learn to govern jointly, just as the Tories, when they were in power, governed Britain jointly with businessmen.

David Butler also rang this morning to say he foresaw a Tory landslide; he was afraid that the Labour Party couldn't survive.

Monday 11 February
After lunch I went to Stockwood, the most difficult area in my constituency. It was windy and cold and pouring with rain. What was worrying was that out of fifteen houses there were three women – housewives between twenty-five and thirty-five – who had voted Labour in 1970 but were impressed by the arguments about the unions, about the miners, about Communists, about Militants, about strikes and about being fair but firm. So Heath's propaganda seems to be getting across and he is doing it on a big scale.

Came back absolutely persuaded that I would lose Bristol and that there would be a Tory landslide. Now, at midnight, having watched a lot of television and seen Heath doing a brilliant party political broadcast and Harold floundering away about the price of petrol, I am going to bed tired, exhausted and rather depressed.

Tuesday 12 February

A letter of support from Trevor Huddleston came in and I received a message of goodwill from Donald Soper.*

In the afternoon, I went out on my own. Labour people are deeply worried, undecided and not knowing what to make of it all. The Government line about fairness and more discipline and so on, has had an effect. This, coming from a strong Labour area, indicates to me that we have got to make a great deal of progress in two weeks.

I came back to the hotel this evening and watched Jim Callaghan on television sandwiched between Part One and Part Two of a violently anti-Communist programme about the KGB – which made it look as if the Labour Party was almost a part of the KGB. A most unfair programme slot.

I will try to assess the position at this stage. There has been a powerful Conservative opening, clear, strong, simple, warnings of higher taxation if Labour is elected and so on. Wilson is really fooling about on the fringes, seen at press conferences and ticket-only meetings; whereas Heath is on the streets in walkabouts, giving a sort of De Gaulle impression. I have a choice as to whether to play it quietly or get my idea of the campaign launched and find that it could be repudiated by Harold.

Wednesday 13 February

Caroline rang to say that Roy Jenkins had sent the following:

> Message to Tony Benn from Roy Jenkins. You asked if, through you, I would send a message about the electoral situation in Bristol which I willingly do. My call to the electors of Bristol is to give their support to you as to the other official Labour candidates.
>
> Roy Jenkins

Caroline had thought it wasn't worth using but the more I thought about it, the more it seemed it was. So I set it on one side for use at tomorrow's press conference.

Thursday 14 February

In the evening, I went to Redfield School to my first public meeting. When I arrived at 7.15, *Midweek*, Swedish and German television, *The Times*, the *Observer*, the *Mail*, everybody was there – but no audience. So I quickly left the school, jumped in my car and drove up and down

---

* Trevor Huddleston, Suffragan Bishop of Stepney; Donald (Lord) Soper, sometime President of the Methodist Conference. Both socialist Christians.

the streets announcing on my loudspeaker, 'Labour meeting begins in five minutes at 7.30 at Redfield School. BBC television cameras are there. Come and put your questions to the nation.' When I got back at 7.40 there were a few people sitting there with the media.

Monday 18 February
Two big issues are emerging tonight – North Sea Oil, about which both Heath and Wilson have spoken, and Concorde, where the French appear to want to cut production of the existing models and go for a huge new modification programme costing £150 million. This is a direct threat to Bristol.

But the Election is gradually settling. People are consolidating and returning, I think, to traditional loyalties. Everyone seems to think it will be close: it could be Labour just ahead with the Liberals perhaps holding the balance or Labour ahead in Parliament but with only 40 to 45 per cent of the national vote. One simply can't tell.

About fifty miners turned up this morning and we got them out canvassing. There was some trouble about whether they would canvass or just distribute their own strike literature but whatever way it is, it is getting across the message.

Tuesday 19 February
The Times had a leader calling for my defeat and removal from Parliament. The Concorde cut-back was headlines.

At 12 Melissa came with me to the Lord Mayor's service. Typical Church of England, Tory Party-at-prayer service, with the Bishop preaching a Tory sermon. Afterwards we looked in at the Lord Mayor's parlour in the Council House.

Stephen told me my picture was one of four used on the Tory party political tonight. Wilson, Jenkins, Callaghan and Benn – the Labour moderates, the middle of the roaders and extremists, as if there were several Labour Parties.

Friday 22 February
Bristol Transport House at 9.30. Sylvia Sims came to the press conference. She is a lovely woman, acting this week at the Theatre Royal, Bath, in *Odd Girl Out*. She is the daughter of a trade union leader, born in Deptford and has got her roots deep in the Labour movement. Then went with her to Barton Hill where she made a rousing speech and we met lots of people who were all friendly.

At 6.55 Harold Wilson, who had flown in to Lulsgate, came in to Bristol Transport House and I took him over to the Central Hall: Harold has got the whole thing organised to an extraordinary extent with huge placards behind him and a special microphone with a cut-off switch to introduce him as the next Prime Minister. I found the whole personality cult a bit offensive. He looked a bit nervous and I think he does realise that he is perhaps within a week of the end of his political career. Anyway, he made a speech that was applauded enthusiastically. It was the Entertainer, the old Harold Wilson, but it didn't have any depth or substance. He did, however, pay a tribute to me on the Referendum: 'When Tony first suggested it, we hadn't quite realised its importance. Now we will have it.'

Saturday 23 February

Today Enoch Powell made his big Birmingham speech – of which I have only heard the briefest reports – where he began to indicate that he would be recommending people who believed in re-negotiation and the sovereignty of Parliament to vote Labour. That is going to be a major issue in this Election. The Common Market has come into its own in the last week. It is the big question because it touches at food prices, at Heath's misunderstanding of the character of the British people and also at the basic questions of the freedom of Parliament and the people. Focusing attention on it is the main contribution that I have been able to make to Party policy over the last three years.

Monday 25 February

The second poll came out today and instead of a 4.5 per cent lead, I now have a 14 per cent lead, that is about 37 per cent of the vote with 23 per cent for the Tory, 11 per cent for the Liberal, less than 1 per cent for Robertson and none at all for the National Front. At the same time the 'don't knows' and undecideds are still about 35 per cent when you gross them together, so there really could be any result at all.

Wednesday 27 February

Later in the day, Hilary arrived from London with a copy of the *Evening Standard* containing an article by Kingsley Amis describing why he was going to vote Tory, and saying that I was 'the most dangerous man in Britain'.

Up to Gypsy Patch Lane for the factory gate meeting of about 300 people outside Rolls Royce. Clive Jenkins arrived in a leather jacket with a fur collar. I said, 'Ah, Blücher arriving at Waterloo.' He was very amusing and made a good speech.

The stewards at Rolls Royce had arranged for a mixed grill for us in the canteen but later we were told that the security guards would not admit us to the canteen and would bring the grill out to the car. Then a steward came back and said, 'It's all right. You can go back in. I have said that if they don't allow you to eat there, we will have a strike of the canteen staff.'

The national polls today show that the gap is closing between Labour and the Tories. We are only 2 per cent behind and it does look as if we might possibly get more seats if the Liberal intervention is mainly anti-Tory.

Thursday 28 February
Polling Day.

We went to one polling station in Windmill Hill where there was a Young Socialist sitting with his YS badge and his Tony Benn sticker, and a boy taking numbers for the Tories. Later in the evening, we met the same boy in our Labour Committee rooms in Windmill Hill helping us to knock up late voters because he had been persuaded by the Young Socialist that he had gone wrong.

After that we went and had a meal at the Golden Egg in Clifton. Back to the hotel and I had a quick nap before going back out from 5 to 9.30, doing a final round of major committee rooms. Canvassers were pretty contented. There were thirty cars available in Brislington. The place was absolutely crammed with people, with very little sign of Tory activity.

At 10 pm we were back at the hotel and we had a couple of hours there. By then the first results were out and it was quite clear that the swing was not uniform, that the Liberals were doing well in Tory seats and knocking the Tories out but not having anything like the same impact in Labour seats. So it all looked quite encouraging.

At 12.15 we all went to the Brislington School where the count was being held, and found there two complete television crews. The media appeared to have taken charge, with gossip writers, etc, no doubt all waiting for my defeat. Harlech Television had taken the domestic science room on the ground floor and had a canteen there with a big notice 'HTV staff only'. Caroline made such a row that we were allowed in for some baked beans and coffee.

I took my portable TV and we put it in one of the classrooms outside the count so people could watch the results as they poured in through the night. The Campaign for Social Democracy agent was there, who had been a Tory. He told Caroline that the Tories were furious with him for having joined Taverne's party. He was feeling uneasy about it all. He told Caroline that they had expected a lot of rough house from Labour people. But by us absolutely ignoring them their campaign had fallen flat.

I had a word with Reg Bale, the National Front candidate and we sat down together. I said, 'Now look. We are a working class party. The Tories only stay in power because they divide the working class. They divide the women from the men, the pensioners from the young, the lower paid from the better paid and now you are dividing the white workers from the black workers. It's all part of the strategy to keep the working class under Tory control and there are some very unpleasant people in the National Front.' He was rather touched: 'Well, I've been in a turmoil in my mind for the last two years. I nearly emigrated but my wife loves Windmill Hill so much.' So I said, 'Let's have a word afterwards and see if we can't find a way of making the Labour Party more responsive to the needs of your people because I accept that there has been a problem.' He told me that the Young Socialists had abused him today. I asked him to introduce me to his wife and told her how sorry I was about this, and that it certainly wasn't at my encouragement.

I did also hear a rumour that Robertson, the Taverne candidate, had been financed by the Editor of the *Observer* David Astor, who had sent one of his relations down to be treasurer of the campaign.

Talked to a couple of old Liberals wearing the red rosette which is the old Liberal colour in Bristol East.

The counting didn't begin until 1.35 am and it was 4.35 before the result came out. But well before then one could see that I was well in the lead, and in the end the result was dazzling – a majority of 7,914.

Notes
Chapter One

1.   (p. 5) In 1972 a public bankruptcy hearing against an architect, John Poulson, had led to the resignation of Reginald Maudling, the Home Secretary, who, among other public figures, was referred to in the evidence. Following the hearings, a series of trials was held in 1973 and early 1974 at which a number of men, mainly public officials, were convicted and imprisoned for corruption, including John Poulson himself, T. Dan Smith, Chairman of the Northern Economic Planning Unit, and Andy Cunningham who was a trade union representative on the NEC from 1964 to 1974.

2.   (p. 16) Lord Diplock was appointed Chairman of the 'Commission of Legal Procedure to deal with Terrorist Activities in Northern Ireland' in September 1972 after a huge increase of violent activity and death in the province that year. The Commission recommended among other measures the trial of suspected terrorists by courts without a jury, because of the threat of or actual intimidation of jury members. Diplock courts continue to operate in Northern Ireland.

3.   (p. 21) The Watergate scandal started shortly after Richard Nixon's re-election as President in November 1972, and was so called after the Democratic Party headquarters in the Watergate building Washington were burgled during the American election campaign. Throughout 1973 and 1974 Nixon's involvement became more and more obvious. After refusing to hand over tapes

of all the conversations between himself and White House staff, Nixon finally resigned in August 1974.

4.   (p. 40) The Industrial Relations Act introduced by the Heath Government in 1971 was the centrepiece of Edward Heath's programme. The Act introduced measures such as the registration of trade unions with a Government Registrar and the establishment of a National Industrial Relations Court which would control the activity of unions and penalise them for non-compliance with the provisions of the Act. It became the source of great conflict between the Government and the trade union movement, provoking enormous demonstrations and stoppages, and a demand by the TUC for an assurance that a future Labour Government would repeal the Act.

After the election of Labour in 1974, and the repeal of the Act, Edward Heath announced that if re-elected the Conservatives would not re-enact the legislation.

5.   (p. 41) Lord Lambton was a Conservative MP who renounced his peerage on succeeding his father in 1970, in order to remain in the Commons (but retained his courtesy title). He was very supportive during my own peerage fight in 1963. As Under-Secretary of State for Defence for the Air Force he was forced to resign his seat and his office in May 1973 as a result of his involvement with a 'call-girl' whose husband, Colin Levy, attempted to sell compromising information to the press. Following Lord Lambton's resignation, Earl Jellicoe, Lord Privy Seal and Leader of the House of Lords, also resigned due to rumours of casual 'call-girl' affairs. Although Lord Jellicoe resigned in the wake of the Lambton investigation, a Security Commission report concluded that there was no connection between the two cases and also concluded that in the event, there had been no security threat in either case.

2
Sounding the Retreat
March – October 1974

The Labour Government that was formed on 5 March 1974, after Heath's negotiations with the Liberals had failed, lacked an overall majority in Parliament. But with leading industries in serious trouble and desperate for Government support, the economy reeling from the troubles that had brought Heath down, and the Conservative Party demoralised and divided, it was a golden opportunity for the Labour Government to initiate its programme of radical socialist policies.

The industrial plan, as set out in our Manifesto in February 1974, was quite straightforward. We intended to set up a National Enterprise Board as a channel for public funds into industry, which would also allow for the acquisition of some prominent companies that occupied a key role in the economy. Although no figure was mentioned in the Manifesto, rumours quickly spread that twenty or twenty-five top British companies were to be 'seized' for public ownership. In addition, we proposed the concept of planning agreements with major companies – to be discussed with both management and the workforce through their local unions – which would provide a better framework for securing investment and an extension of industrial democracy at the workplace. The Government was dependent from the first on a workable voluntary agreement – the Social Contract – with the trade union movement, securing trade union cooperation while Labour was pushing through a programme of reforms advantageous to the mass of workers.

But from the start, the CBI and the press began to criticise the new industrial arrangements, first on the grounds that they would lead to some kind of Eastern European or Stalinist form of state direction, and later as a Trotskyite plot for full-blooded workers' control: both criticisms were equally wide of the mark. But the 'enemy within', as interpreted by the certain parts of the Establishment, came to be the focus for surveillance: the targets were trade union leaders who had Communist connections, Ministers who had been explicit or outspoken in favour of socialist policies, and others on the Left in active politics.

Peter Wright's Spycatcher, amongst others, now confirms that destabilisation attempts were made to deflect the Government from its path. Harold Wilson, of course, had no revolutionary plans of any kind, but he saw it as his function to return Britain to 'normalcy', so that by the second General Election in autumn

1974 (which he knew would be necessary) the fears of the Establishment of a socialist transformation would be laid to rest. So, just as Ted Heath completed the 'U-turn' that cost him his job, Wilson executed an even quicker U-turn on the programme agreed at the 1973 Conference and published in the February 1974 Election Manifesto. These were indeed months of retreat, concealed from the public gaze but nevertheless real.

Tuesday 5 March

Sir Antony Part, the Permanent Secretary of the old Department of Trade and Industry, rang me at 8 this morning, anxious to have a word. I told him I intended to move in to Peter Walker's old office to establish my centre there and that Peter Shore could go into Sir Geoffrey Howe's old office next door. I said we would be fighting hard to prevent the Industry Department from being carved up.*

Harold rang me at 11 and told me he was also giving me Posts and Telecommunications.

At 12 there was a meeting at Number 10 with the TUC. Len Murray said they hoped for an agreement with the new Government, they were glad that we were seeing both them and the CBI. 'We hope to translate the Labour-Trade Union compact on industrial relations into reality.' The TUC would like to be given the chance to work with the CBI and as a priority they wanted the repeal of the Industrial Relations Act. As to the economy, said Len, we must get the miners back to work, and resume five day working by negotiation; we didn't want Draconian solutions. The balance of payments couldn't be solved this year.

Jim Callaghan hoped the legislation for the repeal of the Industrial Relations Act was well advanced.

In the afternoon, it was the turn of the CBI to come to Number 10. Campbell Adamson was assuming an early return to work, but he hoped that there would be commercial and domestic restraint until industry was back to normal.

I had to hurry off to the Palace to be made Secretary of State, and there I found the Queen's Private Secretary, the ADC and so on. We were ushered in and Michael Foot, Eric Varley, and an Australian judge took the oath as Privy Councillors and then I got my seals of office.

Went to the Cabinet and there was really very little discussed. Harold said we would adopt Christian name terms in Cabinet, 'following what Tony Benn suggested years ago'. On the miners' dispute, we agreed to let the NCB start negotiating at around the figure that the Relativities

---

* One of Harold Wilson's first administrative changes was to split the old Department of Trade and Industry into two.

Board had recommended, which was well above what Heath had been prepared to accept.

A week ago, I thought I might be out of Parliament and now I am in the Cabinet as a Secretary of State. I feel I have to keep the hopes of the Left alive and alight. The job is enormous and the press is entirely hostile and will remain so. I have to recognise that in putting forward my proposals to the Cabinet, all will be opposed: but there are four powerful Secretaries of State on the Left – myself, Michael Foot, Peter Shore, and Eric Varley – and we are a formidable team.

Wednesday 6 March

The National Executive met at 9.30. Jim talked about the need for better coordination between the Government and the NEC and policy committees, and the TUC-Labour Party Liaison Committee. The NEC supported the formation of a minority Government and pledged its full support.

Frances Morrell, Francis Cripps, my personal secretary Mary Lou Clarke, Frank McElhone and I had a long talk about how we would use public ownership in the first instance as an ambulance for failed firms – because British Leyland and one or two other firms are in serious difficulties. Frances and Francis have been both been appointed officially as advisers; they are going to get about £4000 a year and share a big office on the same floor as me.

The miners' strike is over with a settlement of £100 m, twice what the Tory Government offered but still about £25 m below their full claim.

Thursday 7 March

At 9.30 I met Secretary* and he told me that Harold had specially arranged to transfer the Printing Division of the old DTI, which has responsibility for sponsoring the newspaper industry, to the Board of Trade; this is clearly so that Harold can keep me entirely away from the mass media. For the same reason broadcasting policy has been sent over to the Home Office. I also heard that all political advisers have to be negatively (i.e. secretly) and then positively (i.e. openly) vetted.

At 11.55 I was summoned over to see the PM who said, 'About Ministers, I will let you have Michael Meacher as your Parliamentary Under-Secretary and I am giving you Gregor MacKenzie and Eric Heffer as Ministers of State.' Brian Walden apparently would not accept because he can't afford to take office and give up his other activities.

---

* The Permanent Secretary at the Department of Industry, Sir Antony Part, was known by convention as 'Secretary'.

At 2 we had the Concorde meeting with David Jones, Deputy Secretary of the Department and Ken Binning, an Under-Secretary, both of whom I knew from my Mintech days. They told me in effect that there was unanimous official advice now throughout Whitehall for the cancellation of Concorde, and they had agreed that it was unsaleable in its present form. My own view is that we should continue with the present Concorde programme. This is one of the most difficult problems I have to tackle and I will have to fight it with tremendous care because it could be a disaster politically for me both in Bristol and personally.

To Cabinet, where we discussed the wording on the Common Market for the Queen's Speech. The relevant phrase was that we would 'seek changes in the policies in the European Community' and, when the choice had been put to the people through the Referendum, 'looked forward to playing a full and useful part in Europe' which was a complete watering down of our Manifesto position which committed us to retain parliamentary control over our regional, industrial and fiscal policies.

We went on to the Social Services section. Barbara is unchanged from the old days: she wanted her entire legislative programme spelled out in the Queen's Speech. She is just politically greedy, that is the only way of describing her.

An Industry Bill will be introduced, consolidating and developing existing legislation to promote industrial expansion; it is exactly right, giving no hostages to fortune. We shall put it forward modestly but it *will* be the Industry Bill.

I caught the train to Bristol for the GMC. There were a lot of youngsters there and I thanked them for the campaign, told them we had got the landslide in Bristol that could have been achieved elsewhere by fighting on the programme with the trade union movement, the Young Socialists, the miners and the constituency. There were three hundred helpers in Brislington alone on polling day and forty cars in a single ward: so when the Labour movement is mobilised there really is nothing you can't do.

Friday 8 March
I had a message from Harold suggesting Bill Nield* as a further Minister of State. Well, Part was unhappy about Nield. I asked what the difficulty was. Had they had a row? After some hesitation, Part explained: 'Well, quite frankly, the position is that Sir William Nield

---

* Sir William Nield, Deputy Chairman of Rolls Royce Ltd, had been permanent Secretary in the Cabinet Office; in the late Thirties he worked for the Labour Party Research and Policy Department.

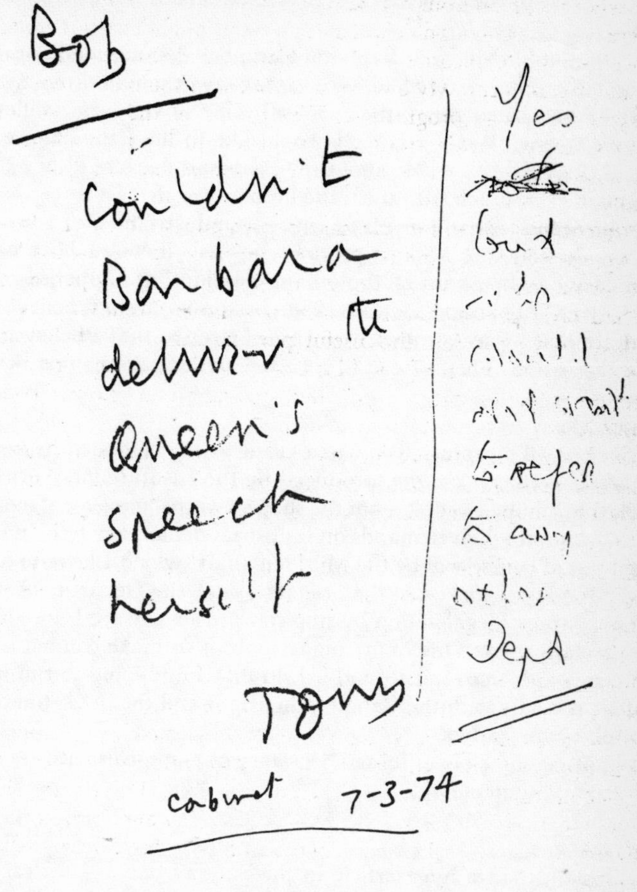

Bob

couldn't
Barbara
deliver the
Queen's
speech
herself

Yes

but

... to refer
to any
other
Dept

Tony

Cabinet   7-3-74

Cabinet note from Tony Benn to Bob Mellish, 7 March 1974.

ran the negotiations for our entry into the Common Market and was given a GCMG [Knight Grand Cross of the Order of St Michael and St George] which all of us on the 'Home' side thought was a bit much. They give GCMGs to everybody in the FO but in the Home Civil Service they only give KCMGs [Knight Commander of the Order of St Michael and St George] and this is a real problem.' I told him to think it over and have a word with Sir William Armstrong.

Later, Part came back and said he had thought about it and was prepared to accept Nield, but by this time I had heard from Armstrong that Nield wasn't available.

At 3.30 I met Sir Michael Clapham, Campbell Adamson and others from the CBI. They wanted to know what my responsibilities were, and after I had listed them, they showed some anxiety, particularly about investment. 'Well,' I said, 'I would like to have the chance of talking to the CBI as a whole about my proposals because although I have been in close touch with the trade unions over the last three years, I have not been so closely involved with top industrialists, so I would like to go through the Labour programme with them.' I hoped we wouldn't have to break off of 'diplomatic relations' as happened over the Industrial Expansion Act in 1968, because I didn't believe in confrontation as a way of moving forward. I stressed that I believed in genuine discussion. They agreed to get a few industrialists along.

Saturday 9 March
Stayed in bed all morning. Ken Coates rang and I suggested he insert in the *Workers' Control Bulletin*, produced by the Institute for Workers' Control, that I hoped people from the shop stewards' movement would begin to formulate their demands on industrial democracy to help me. The real test of course will be the Meriden affair[1] which I have to deal with on Monday. I looked at the brief and since the Department says I can't encourage illegal action by stop stewards, I can see I am going to have a clash there. One of my biggest jobs is to make contact with the shop stewards' movement, and if I do that I am going to run into difficulties not only with the Cabinet, the Right and the press, but also with trade union leaders.

Joshua made some beautiful red Secretary of State seals with sealing wax – a splendid memento.

Sunday 10 March
Tony Crosland had a huge article in the Sunday papers – extracted from a book he is writing – which constituted a major attack on Labour policy, headlined as Crosland's view in contrast to Benn's view. This is clearly the way Fleet Street is going to build up its its campaign: Crosland is the hero, I am the villain. I feel totally isolated at present – by my civil servants, by the press, by the Tories and the Liberals who attacked me on *The World this Weekend* today, by my colleagues and by Harold. I am sure that the Department interpreted my caution of the first few days in office as an indication that I did not intend to proceed with the Industry Bill and the NEB, so I have got to stiffen my stance tomorrow when I meet them all.

Rather a gloomy evening, to be truthful.

Monday 11 March
At 10 o'clock we had a meeting about Norton Villiers Triumph at Meriden. Jack Jones came with Harry Urwin, Bill Lapworth (the Divisional Organiser of the TGWU at Coventry) and Dennis Johnson, the shop stewards' convenor.

I agreed that we would make expert advice available to the people in the factory – probably taking on consultants who would work for the shop stewards in preparing a case for viability. Second, if they needed any further information from the company, I would ask Dennis Poore, Managing Director of NVT, to make it available and I may even use my powers to put a director on the Board. Third, I would ask Poore to desist from any attempt to harass the cooperative. Fourth, we would try to find some way of getting the bikes to America to meet the summer demand. This was the best I could do and we agreed to a press statement afterwards, stating that 'I had considered the position sympathetically and was helping the cooperative to get their case put forward in the best possible way.'

I agreed with my Ministers that I would leave home at 8.30 every morning, meet the press office advisers just after nine, and have a 9.30 'prayer' meeting with advisers and Ministers only.

About 2.30 I went over to the Neddy (NEDC) meeting which was a waste of time, a ritual dance. The plain truth is there is no sense of real economic, social or political crisis at all. When these people get together, they just live in a mush of consensus. It is difficult for me, observing it fresh from the hustings, to get a proper assessment. My own belief is that this consensus is in fact coming to an end and that although we shall have a short honeymoon, we are going either to see it crack under inflationary pressure in which wage demands will play a part, be driven back to statutory wage control which is quite unacceptable, or to some other form of control of the trade unions. To this extent, I do believe that society is actually in the process of break-up. But to get anybody else to share my view is extremely difficult.

When I looked around at that Neddy meeting, I realised we have turned all our institutions into the 'dignified' parts of the constitution. There were three groups present: the industrialists who, eight days ago, were financing a Conservative campaign designed to show that the trade unions were threatening parliamentary democracy and that the Labour Party was led by extremists; the trade unions who were financing up to the hilt a Labour Party campaign directed against big business; and Labour Ministers, who were saying one thing on the hustings but behaving here as if they were part of an old-boy network inextricably linked with business and the City, while the trade unions played along.

Immediately afterwards, Frances came in and described her lunch with Bernard Donoughue, Joe Haines and Geoff Bish at Number 10. She had got the impression that Bernard Donoughue really saw his main role as spying on Ministers. It is a tremendous help to have Frances, who is in touch with the political network through Number 10 and Transport House; as well as Francis Cripps with his access to outside economists, Nicky Kaldor in the Treasury, and Frank McElhone, who keeps me in touch with the PLP.

To Number 10 for the eve of session drink, where Harold read the Queen's Speech to us. Eric Heffer said he felt miserable that he was locked up in the Department and thought that he might betray his links with the working class movement outside. Frances later told me that Eric had gone to the Palace today to be sworn in as Minister of State which she thought had somewhat affected him: he had been pleased to go but felt that, by being pleased, he was somehow betraying the working class movement. These are the complicated class elements in our society whereby the Queen sucks you away from your supporters and makes you feel you are only there because she appointed you. Harold gave a lecture about the need to shut up on everything, to forget we are politicians and simply be Ministers.

Wednesday 13 March

To Number 10 for the first meeting of the Economic Strategy Committee of Cabinet. The first paper from Michael Foot suggested that the Tories' Pay Board should be continued for a period but its operation should be made more flexible. Denis went further and said it should continue until we made real the voluntary compact with the TUC.

In effect, this means that for the moment we have abandoned our policy of returning to normal industrial negotiations to which we were clearly and deeply committed in our Manifesto. I let the argument rage but I did say that I took it that we would be back to the position in September 1972. Then, Heath was saying, 'I'll have a statutory policy if you don't agree a voluntary one' whereas we would be saying, 'If you don't agree to a voluntary one, we won't relax the statutory one.' But these arguments did not prevail.

Back to the office and worked on my speech and went to the House at 2.30 to deliver it. Actually, it was thought a dull, ministerial speech, with a few minor interruptions. Afterwards Frank McElhone said the right-wing of the Labour Party was delighted: I am under heavy pressure from him to move to the Right.

Got home at about 11 o'clock feeling depressed, and then had to spend four hours on my boxes. The workload at the moment is too heavy and I am not getting enough sleep.

Thursday 14 March

At 10.15 I managed to see Harold and I said, 'There is only one thing I want to raise with you, and that is getting the facts out on Concorde while there is political mileage, because if you simply announce the cancellation then the facts will be overlooked and we will never get the credit for having opened the books.' He agreed and suggested, 'What about a Select Committee to look at it?' I was perfectly content at that.

When the Cabinet met, we had parliamentary affairs, and a long discussion about whether we would be defeated on Monday by the Liberals and the Tories voting together. I think we'll be left to try to salvage as much as we can of the immediate situation and when it gets out of hand, there will be a huge clamour for a national government and moderates in the Liberal, Tory and Labour Parties – no doubt including Jim Callaghan, Roy Jenkins, Reg Prentice and Shirley Williams – will agree to join it: we will then absolutely be clobbered.

I had a meeting of my Department and there was a long discussion on the Industry Act in which they all tried to nibble away at the National Enterprise Board. How would it differ? What was the point of public ownership? Was the role of Government going to be eroded by the NEB and the Industry Bill?

I said, 'Look, I obviously gave you a bad steer. The long-term job is to prepare an Industry Bill which will meet all the requirements – allow us to set up the National Enterprise Board, allow us to nationalise by statutory instrument and allow us to introduce planning agreements. Once we get that we can examine possibilities under existing powers in what will be a difficult situation.'

Later, I was told that Dennis Poore of NVT had started legal action against the Meriden cooperative. Then Poore himself came to see me for an hour and a half. In effect when NVT had taken over the company, it had been on the basis of closing the Meriden plant in 1973 and transferring the work to the Birmingham or Wolverhampton sites. The closure went ahead, and the men had subsequently occupied the plant; but as the Conservatives had put in money the men were sitting on valuable assets. When I pressed Poore he admitted that the motorcycle trade was improving, that the long-term prospects were good, that the cooperative workers had taken a wage cut, were full of enthusiasm and could certainly produce bikes for the next three years.

'Well, why don't you come to an arrangement with them?' I said. 'I'll put in a little bit of money and you become the president of the cooperative; you hire your management to help in areas the workers don't know anything about.' A meeting was arranged for next week.

Saturday 16 March
Peter Shore thinks we may be defeated in the House on Monday night. If that happens then Harold would try for a Dissolution, and the question is would the Palace give him one? I don't know what else the Queen could do. Then we would have another Election campaign immediately.

Sunday 17 March
I read all the Post Office briefs and put a note in my box saying that I would like a series of commemoration stamps issued as soon as possible in honour of the British trade union movement, showing some of the great leaders of the Labour movement and some trade union banners.

Frances came in the evening and helped me to draft a press statement on Concorde. Then I had a few people in: Eric and Doris Heffer, Albert Booth, Michael Meacher, Francis Cripps. We agreed on our main objectives: the development of long-term policy, notably the Industry Act on which we could not conceivably hope to make any progress during the present session with the precarious majority; the full utilisation of existing industrial powers to make as big an impact as possible now; the development of a new relationship designed to persuade the trade union leadership to allow us to reach the shop-floor level of industry.

Tuesday 19 March
The big news is a brilliant speech by Michael Foot yesterday which led the Tories to withdraw their motion of no-confidence against the Government. This obscured the fact that what Michael was doing was accepting the continuation of the Pay Board and the statutory pay policy which is exactly what the whole Establishment wants. As we have no parliamentary majority we are not in a position to remove it. But unless this great source of energy – the industrial leadership of Britain – is harnessed to constructive purposes no government is going to be more than just a cork tossed on the sea of unsettled industrial power relationships.

Rang Sir Kenneth Keith, the Chairman of Rolls Royce, who was angry that I was seeing all the Rolls Royce shop stewards before seeing him, but that of course is the relationship which I intend to establish.

Then I went to the Cabinet Office and had the Oath of Office administered to me as Minister of Posts and Telecommunications by Sir Godfrey Agnew, Clerk to the Privy Council. Afterwards I asked him about the administration of an oath because you do nothing except stand there with your hand raised while it is read to you. You don't even have to assent. But, the Lord President being present, it apparently constituted a binding oath. I told him I had affirmed out of respect for Charles Bradlaugh, who had struggled to get the right to affirm established and that I didn't want to swear because I didn't believe in taking the name of the Lord in vain. I added that the atheists who didn't really believe in swearing or affirming, saw the oath by God in favour of the sovereign as a ritual exercise. I don't think the arguments had ever occured to him.

Then I drove to Bristol with Roy Williams, my new Private Secretary, and Frank McElhone to meet the Concorde trade union representatives. When we arrived there was a huge press corps waiting.

At Transport House, Bristol, I saw Ron Nethercott of the TGWU and others and I said to Ron, 'Not to put too fine a point on it, there is enormous pressure to cancel Concorde. I have got a few days' grace but I don't know how long. You must use these few days to bring pressure to bear. You must get on to Jack Jones, tell him to go and see Harold Wilson.' In the absolute confidentiality of the room that was sufficient for him.

Then I went downstairs and met the shop stewards, Lew Gray and John Blackley, and the trade union-British Aerospace liaison committee. That was followed by a second joint meeting of the Bristol Trades Council and the TUC South-West Regional Advisory Committee. I went over the ground again and some powerful points were put. They included a demand for a Concorde inquiry, the need for a select committee, a request for an interview with the Prime Minister and so on. Civil servants are upset because I said I would put the resources of the Department at the disposal of the trade union officials to prepare their case as best they could. Antony Part is very worried about this because he is not sure that I have the power. The whole idea that one should use officials to help workers, as distinct from helping management to make money, has just not penetrated into Whitehall yet.

It has been a extraordinary day because I have been performing both the functions of a Minister of the Crown, and the role I assumed in Opposition, namely of getting Bristol to fight for its survival. Of course what I was saying then was, 'Fight for your survival' and what I am saying now as the Minister is, 'I am here to consult': but if you put the two together they are the same thing. My officials, who are partly nervous that I will do myself damage with my colleagues, and partly unfamiliar with political and trade union activity, are a bit flummoxed. But, candidly, I could not remain as a Minister if the Cabinet betrayed me by cancelling Concorde three days after publishing the figures. So I think I am going to win. Indeed, I heard a rumour that Treasury officials were recommending to the Chancellor that he should now proceed by consultation.

That's the end of the day. I am immensely tired but greatly stimulated. Gordon Farnsworth, Editor of the *Bristol Evening Post*, wrote a leading article that nobody has done more than Tony Benn to fight for Concorde. If the Cabinet do decide to cancel, then I might have to declare my intention to consult my people in Bristol and let them decide whether I should continue in the Government or not. I would not wish to resign but I would not feel able to continue unless they renew their confidence in me.

Wednesday 20 March

To Bristol Rolls Royce where I met the new Managing Director, and the Board who explained their programme. Then I went to see the senior management, followed by the shop stewards. They had put a note on my table saying, 'Our jobs depend on Concorde. Your job depends on us!' But they were very friendly.

The last engagement was a mass meeting held at the airport with 12,000 people. I played that cool and quiet, with no rhetoric, and then withdrew from the meeting.

Undoubtedly my civil servants were highly alarmed by the whole exercise which they knew would annoy the Treasury. Frances expressed her feeling that the publicity had gone to my head and I had damaged my chances of being taken seriously as a political figure.

On the other hand, when I got back to London and discovered a telegram from the French saying that under no circumstances would they agree to cancel, and when I heard that Denis Healey wanted a decision to cancel taken at the Cabinet tomorrow, I really felt that I had done the only thing I could in mobilising support outside.

One very sad bit of news – I heard tonight that Auntie Rene – Father's sister – died last night after a road accident. She was ninety-two, was walking home from visiting a friend south of the Thames on a wet day and was hit by a car. She was taken mortally wounded but conscious to St Thomas's Hospital, where she died two hours later. She was a remarkable woman, the last link with my ancestors, and a woman who throughout all her life took such an enormous interest in other people, lived through them and for them, supporting them and backing them up. She first visited the House of Commons in 1892 as a girl of ten, when my grandfather was elected. Everyone who knew her will really be sad.

At home I found Stephen preparing for his visit to Cincinnati tomorrow with Caroline. She is going to see her mother, who is dying, so there was a sense of the passing of generations. The next time round it will be us.

Thursday 21 March

The Government is in an interesting position. Harold depends on Michael, Michael brings with him Jack Jones's loyalty and that triumvirate is *the* most important group in the whole Goverment. I think Roy Jenkins is being bought off. As to the rest, they are less important figures. Harold, of course, thoroughly enjoys this risky political position because it means he can do what he likes; so do the right-wing members of the Cabinet because they can always use the Liberals' parliamentary strength as an excuse for delaying any programme that they don't believe in. But this can't go on for long; there will have to be another Election – September at the latest.

Went over to the Cabinet at 10.45 and parliamentary affairs was followed by free family planning on the Health Service which Barbara got the Cabinet to agree to. Denis said it would have to come out of her budget.

Then Concorde. I said, 'I will try to be helpful and brief but it is a very important issue. My recommendation is that even though Concorde won't gain money for us, we need time and possibly a select committee.' I went through all the points: that the figures were not agreed; there was no alternative plan; we couldn't cancel on Budget day which Denis wanted. We couldn't reach a secret decision; there were the relations with the trade union movement; the necessity to keep good faith; and the good name of the Government.

Michael Foot supported me. Even Jim Callaghan said he had been swayed by what I said. It was clear then that I was winning. Denis argued as hard as he could, saying it was uneconomic and the sooner we cancelled it the better. But in fact he was driven back.

I feel much more cheerful today because I have really scored a notable Cabinet success, not by bullying but by the weight of argument. I think that Denis won't now be able to announce the cancellation in the Budget and the thing will drag on because the French will ensure that it does!

Friday 22 March
At 10.45, Sir Kenneth Keith, Chairman of Rolls Royce, accompanied by Sir William Nield, came in with the Secretary, Frank Beswick and David Jones present, to do a *tour d'horizon* of the whole Rolls Royce picture. I have known Keith for some time, a tall, arrogant man who thinks that because of the critical press comments of me, he can simply lay down the law.

He began from notes. 'I want to tell you, Minister, the circumstances in which I was appointed. I was approached by Sir William Armstrong in 1972 who asked me if I would take on a job in the national interest. I said, "Yes, but why do you ask without telling me what it is?" He said, "Because the Prime Minister [Heath] cannot have his request refused and won't put it if it is likely to be refused." Then Sir William told me it was Rolls Royce. I went to see the Prime Minister and he said, "This is a most important job. Will you take it on?" So I answered, "Yes. I will take it on so long as I am not buggered about by junior Ministers and civil servants and officials." And that is the basis on which I accepted it.'

He went on to describe his attitude to the future of the company, to the need for the RB-211–524, to the fact that Bristol was a great headache with so many strikes. He said he was looking for new hardware, travelling the world to try to help Rolls Royce and doing it without a penny's recompense. He made some reference to 'that ass Scanlon' and so on. He spoke for about half an hour and I listened carefully. It was a most offensive presentation of the case.

When he finished I said, 'Well, since you have put your cards on the table and told me how you became Chairman of Rolls Royce, let me tell you how I became Secretary of State for Industry. In February. I had a marginal constituency. I got the support of the trade unions in Bristol and thousands, many of them aircraft workers, turned out on polling day and returned me to Parliament, and the Prime Minister asked me to become Secretary of State for Industry.

'I don't know how long this minority Government will last but while I am in charge I will not accept chairmen of nationalised industries indicating to me that they won't be mucked about by junior Ministers and civil servants: Rolls Royce is a nationalised company and must be accountable for what it does. As for your proposals for the stretched engine, I have some knowledge of Rolls Royce from my years as Minister of Technology, when I dealt with Sir Denning Pearson, and I remember very well the application for Government funding of the RB-211 and the case made for it. On the trade union side, I know the Bristol Rolls Royce workers very well and I can only tell you that that plant there has been very badly managed indeed. Anyone with any sense would know that the real problem in Bristol is the anxiety the workers have experienced arising from the uncertainty of the Concorde project. They have not been involved in decisions until the decisions have already been made.'

I think all this came as something of a shock to Keith who spoke at best as if he were an army officer talking to the troops and at worst as the most arrogant right-wing Tory boss. At one stage when Keith said, 'I can't bother with politics, I am in business ...' Frank Beswick intervened and I said, 'Well, politics is politics and while we retain the power to change our Government by democratic means, we expect industry to take account of decisions that are reached.'

It was a bitter exchange and at the end he said, 'I hope we can get on well together with you as my Minister.' I added, 'And the owner of your company.' So he said, 'But not my employer.' I said, 'I am inclined to say to you what my sergeant said to me in the war: "You play ball with me and I will play ball with you." '

I was extremely angry, I must confess. My Private Secretary said he never realised how easy it was to become a socialist until he heard Keith.

Saturday 23 March

One titbit; Jack Jones rang Harold yesterday and Harold told him there would be no cancellation of Concorde in the Budget so Jack passed the word down the line. If there is a charge that I leaked the news, at least I know exactly where it came from.

Sunday 24 March

Eric Heffer rang me tonight, horrified because we were going to supply warships to Chile. He said he was going to write to the Prime Minister. This is the beginning of the old game which I remember so well, where our moral position on foreign policy is completely eroded as soon as we get into office. It is a long uphill struggle against colleagues for whom the Manifesto is simply a piece of paper to be torn up as and when convenient.

Monday 25 March

I mentioned to Eric Heffer yesterday that Sir Antony Part had told me that he had been warned by the security people that the MP whom Eric wants to appoint as his PPS is not considered suitable. So I had asked Part to find out what the reason was and I just notified Eric of this so he would be in the picture.

Budget Cabinet at 11.30. I dislike Budget Cabinet intensely anyway, because one learns secrets twenty-four hours in advance and I don't like sitting on secrets as valuable as that. But I must confess listening to Denis my gloom mounted. He can't do anything about introducing a wealth tax this year. He was strongly urged by Jim Callaghan and Harold Lever not to upset international confidence by any action on the gift tax. On income tax he is making a move, but it is a Budget that will undoubtedly disappoint the Party and the movement, one which as I listened to it, I was convinced was written by the Treasury and not by Ministers. Harold Lever used to talk about frolicking on the margins of policy and this was the most vivid example. Harold himself, being at Number 10 Downing Street, is free to look at the Budget with the Chancellor, but the Treasury will not let anyone else in – and that includes Cabinet Ministers. There is absolutely no reason why these discussions about whether it should be a reflationary, deflationary or neutral Budget shouldn't be discussed in outline with the Cabinet, absolutely no reason why we shouldn't be able to discuss different sorts of taxes and make our contribution felt.

There was a worrying report in the *Sunday Telegraph* that the Government had decided to continue to supply the warships ordered by Chile and that Jim Callaghan had approved the decision.

Leaving the Cabinet, I asked Jim if this report was true. He said, 'Yes. The warships are finished. What are we going to do with them? We hope that Chile will become a democratic country and this is a way of influencing her.' When I recall all the endless trouble there was over even the peaceful trade with South Africa, this seems to me to be a foolish policy to adopt and there will be a hell of a row in the movement. Indeed, I heard a rumour that Eric was going to resign – which I hope he won't. But this does us great damage, breeding the deepest cynicism about whether a Labour Government is serious on matters of this kind.

I worked on my box and I came on to a third item of gloom for the day: the way in which the Common Market re-negotiations are being handled. Night after night I get a note that there is to be a meeting of the European Coal and Steel Community at which the British Steel Corporation is to be represented, or that there is to be a meeting of European Postal and Telecommunications Ministers or a meeting on Regional Policy or a meeting of the Committee on Research in Science and Technology. Always, the Department says we should go to safeguard British interests, to adopt policies that are in our interest, and to show willing. Each time I say that I am against that and each time I am over-ruled. I was over-ruled today by the Foreign Secretary in a minute which said I couldn't control steel prices because it might bring the Commission or the European Court into action against us. One can see how democracy is completely undermined, once officials start getting together, and there is no proper ministerial or democratic accountability at the top. The more I see the Common Market from the inside, the more I want Britain to get out of it and live on its own, cooperating with others but not in any way bound by treaty obligations: a loose, joint harmonisation arrangement, perhaps linked to a customs union, that is all we need.

Tuesday 26 March

Clive Jenkins, who is preparing figures on Concorde, came in for a talk. He expressed grave doubts about my having a trade union advisory committee, and thought it would be impossible to establish contacts with the shop floor because it would undermine the hierarchies and bureaucracy of the trade union General Secretaries. He did offer to lay on a dinner at which these things can be discussed informally and I agreed to that.

I went over and listened to the Budget; slept through great chunks of it.

Wednesday 27 March
At the National Executive at 10 o'clock, Joan Maynard asked about warships for Chile and Jim said it couldn't be raised there. So I wrote a little note to Jim:

> Dear Jim,
>
> You will of course be aware of the generalised anxiety that is being expressed within the PLP, including by some Ministers, about the press report forecasting your parliamentary statement on Chile. I have not seen that statement but if it does authorise the delivery of the warships, there will be severe criticism. Could the statement be deferred to allow Cabinet discussion?
>
> Tony

Michael Foot added:

> I very much agree with Tony. Could we have a discussion tomorrow?
>
> Michael

I passed it up to Jim. Just as I was leaving, he came up. 'Look, about this Chile thing. I don't understand it. It is in line with what we did with South Africa. I mentioned it to Harold and he said to go ahead.'

So I said, 'Well, I know a lot of MPs are worried, including Eric Heffer.'

'Well, Eric had better be careful. He is seen in the Lobby flailing his arms about and people are beginning to ask whether he is a member of the Government or not.'

I said, 'I haven't seen the statement but I just put it to you that there might be trouble which the Cabinet might want to think about before it goes ahead with the statement.'

'Well, read the statement,' said Jim, so I did and commented, 'It's pretty mild but I would be guided simply by what the Chief Whip said on a situation like this. I remember being crucified over South Africa on the uranium deal from South-West Africa and it just is terribly costly in political support at this juncture.'

Jim then began to be struck by the argument and said, 'Well, will you tell Harold that you have spoken to me?'

'No, Jim, I can't butt in on your business. You had better have a word with him yourself.'

I dropped him back at the Foreign Office and in the car on the way he told me how miserable he was that the ministerial committee on the

Common Market kept trying to write his speeches line by line and word by word.

Thursday 28 March
Cabinet, beginning with the question of warships to Chile. Jim gave the case for supplying them, i.e., that there was a major export interest involved and that one of them had already been handed over to a Chilean Navy crew. Roy Mason confirmed that we had orders worth £200 million in Latin America as a whole and we would be regarded as very unreliable if we reneged.

Bob Mellish warned, 'It will cause a lot of internal political trouble. There are ninety MPs who have signed a critical motion. Wouldn't it be more sensible to consult?'

With the exception of Bob Mellish, Michael Foot, Peter Shore, myself, Barbara, Harold and Ted Short who were broadly in favour of consultation, and Merlyn and John Morris who were wobbling, the majority of the Cabinet took the view that you had to take a tough decision and this consultation business was nonsense. But in the end it was agreed that Jim should consult the leaders of the Back Bench committees.

At 5.30 pm I went to the CBI meeting with the Prime Minister. It was just one long moan. Michael Clapham said there was deep disquiet about the Budget; there was no incentive to invest, nor to export; nothing to curb inflation; the remedies were based on the wrong diagnosis; company profits would fall and the investment squeeze would tighten. Large companies were only just maintaining their investment programme. There would be a downturn next year and liquidity would be made worse. The pay crunch would come because the Budget was inflationary.

Denis just sloshed out and, being a great fighter, said he was very distressed and he had tried to take their advice. He mentioned all the things they had asked for which he had included in the Budget. The CBI sounded absolutely licked. Like all these businessmen, they are trying to run a system that simply doesn't work any more. They want confidence which is essential for investment – then they refuse to invest.

Friday 29 March
With a tremendous team, I flew in the HS-125 jet to Paris for a Concorde discussion. With the Ambassador, Sir Edward Tomkins, we were taken to see M. Achille-Fould, the French Minister for Transport, in a succession of cars with two motorcyclists with their horns bleeting through the streets of Paris. When we arrived, there was a huge crowd of about fifty struggling cameramen.

I had a half an hour's heart-to-heart with the Ambassador and

Achille-Fould who is a charming man, a Tory wine-grower whose family have owned their own vineyard since the seventeenth century. In the course of the private talk we didn't deal much with the substance but it was quite clear that the French are determined to go on with Concorde. I said, 'You know my interest in it, but there are serious problems. The best thing is to be absolutely candid and fair with you.'

During the lunch Achille-Fould repeated a cynical but amusing saying: 'The art of politics is to take money from the rich and votes from the poor by persuading each of them that you are going to protect them against the other.' A very perceptive description of the Tory politician.

Monday 1 April

At 12 Sir Ray Brookes, the Chairman of Guest Keen and Nettlefolds, Henry Grunfeld, the President of Warburg's and Jasper Hollom, the Deputy-Governor of the Bank of England, came to see me about the imminent collapse of Alfred Herbert Ltd, the machine tool company. Ray Brookes plonked on my desk a note that he had written that morning saying he would take over Alfred Herbert if I would put up money and support his concept of a Machine Tool Corporation with a small Government holding, which would buy and lease machine tools and equalise the market and underwrite the whole thing. It was a fantastic scheme, requiring me to accept, at the drop of a hat, a complete policy for the machine tool industry and leave him free to run it as he thought best.

Had a short talk to Hugh Brown, the Labour MP for Provan, and Frank McElhone about the possible support for a feasibility study on setting up a cooperative newspaper to replace the collapsed Beaverbrook Press in Glasgow.

Tuesday 2 April

Had lunch with George Woodcock [former General Secretary of the TUC] whom I hadn't seen for a long time; he is sixty-nine and very slow now. We talked about how 'In Place of Strife' was mishandled in 1969 by the Labour Government, and about the growth of shop-floor power. We moved on to how we should consult the unions and he said, 'Well, go and see Len Murray, then talk to the Executive and ask them to agree that you should contact the shop floor. Go at it patiently and slowly. You'll make some progress.' I walked with him towards Victoria Station as far as the Department of Trade.

Came back at about 10 o'clock to hear that President Pompidou had died. This is very important for Concorde, because French Ministers will now be unable to move until there is a replacement, so Achille-

Fould will probably not come to London next week and the whole Concorde decision will be held up.

It is now 1.45 in the morning of my forty-ninth birthday. Just going to bed very, very tired with a tremendous weight of work on my shoulders. My goodness me, you don't have much time for thinking. But as Frances Morrell said to me, all Ministers have problems. Defence has got to make cuts, Crosland has to deal with mortgages, Jim Callaghan has to cope with Europe and Shirley Williams has got to deal with prices. Being a Minister is not an easy job.

Wednesday 3 April
Birthday presents from the family. The papers are full of Pompidou's death and its possible implications.

I went in to the office and Eric Heffer had started instructions to make Merseyside into a special development area, together with Chesterfield, Eric Varley's constituency, and also Leith to make it look good. I had to say to him, 'Look Eric, you mentioned it yesterday, but I think we will have to consider it collectively before you initiate it with all its implications.'

He was furious. 'Well, if that's the case I shall resign.'

'But you see the point, Eric, it is a big expenditure.'

'Fifteen million pounds,' he said.

'I know, but we have to consider it against the context of possible substantial cuts in public expenditure that the Chancellor of the Exchequer is proposing. Anyway, with expenditure of that kind, you would still have to put it before the Cabinet.'

He cooled down a bit. 'I'm sorry I got excited – I am worried. But I shall resign.'

I said, 'Well, let's give each other seven days' notice of resignation.'

A bill is being proposed to save Dr Michael Winstanley, the Liberal MP for Hazel Grove, from being unseated due to a 'technical office of profit' he has held while an MP; his medical practice advised the Ministry of Health and he continued to receive money from it after entering Parliament. That has made Dennis Skinner hopping mad because of the Government's refusal to indemnify the Clay Cross councillors. I cannot understand why we can't just have an amnesty which wipes out their surcharges/fines and the disqualification. After all, Governments can do whatever they like. If we don't, Dennis is threatening to denounce us all and I really don't blame him.

Frank McElhone came to see me. The truth is that I have left him out in the cold and he was angry, like Mary Lou who feels isolated. He denounced me for ignoring the PLP, so I told him to fix things up, and he said, 'I have fixed them up and they have all been cancelled. You are devoting yourself to the wrong priorities.' So I have to placate Mary Lou and Frank; I have got to re-allocate my work better so I spend more time with MPs; and I have got to keep the Ministers sweet, particularly Frank Beswick and Eric Heffer. I have got to be a better manager of people and I'm not very good at that, that's my trouble. I had a knocking from him for forty minutes.

I came home and there was a birthday cake for me, and then I settled down to my boxes.

Thursday 4 April
Cabinet began with a brief reference to the statement to be made on Clay Cross, in effect saying we would aim to legislate for the removal of the disqualifications but there could be no public funds to help the surcharged councillors. I said we ought to look at the possibility for an amnesty, and we agreed to come back to it at the end of Cabinet, when it was suggested that we strengthen the statement which should include some reference to law and order. Harold Wilson said it was only a holding statement. Tony Crosland reckoned that if we did anything to help financially, it could cost £1.5 million of public expenditure. That is an absurd way of looking at it when we are talking about wiping out penalties imposed by the Tories. Jim was strong on the law and order line, as were Roy and Reg. Eric Varley said most of the people at Clay Cross were Trotskyites.

Michael Foot said we hadn't considered it sufficiently and I supported Michael. We had a commitment to consider. We should look at precedents of retrospective legislation, including the Michael Winstanley case. This argument went back and forth, so I said 'Let's take the parallel with Northern Ireland. What are we doing about the rent and rates strike?'

Merlyn Rees said, 'They are all paying the money back.'

'Yes,' I said 'but there is no penalty involved. Here is Gerry Fitt in West Belfast who has been advocating the rent and rate strike and now they are being let off if they pay the arrears. Why can't we do that with Clay Cross?'

Harold said, 'In Northern Ireland, with internment, democracy has broken down.'

'That is still a breach of the law. If the law is the law, it is as much an offence in Northern Ireland. You make martyrs of these people and even the Tories were clever enough not to let the Pentonville Five* become martyrs; they used the Official Solicitor to solve the dilemma.'

---

* Five dockers imprisoned in 1972 by the Conservatives' National Industrial Relations Court over picketing and swiftly released after huge protests by the Labour movement.

Jim said, 'There was wide public support for the Pentonville Five.'

'Not to begin with,' I said. 'It built up later and it will do so later for the Clay Cross people.'

I lost the argument, but at least I retained my self-respect; as I had chaired the Conference in 1972 when the Conference expressed its view on this along such lines, I felt I was obliged to fight.

Friday 5 April

At the Cabinet Public Enterprise Committee, we had a brief talk about the feasibility study, masterminded, I think, by the Scottish Nationalists, which the journalists in Glasgow want for their own newspaper in the wake of Beaverbrook's collapse there. Eric Heffer is up there today. But there was a general feeling that this was very hot to handle because it was an unlikely innovation to support a press cooperative.

Later I went over to see Len Murray at the TUC. Spent about an hour with him, and told him that our consultation should be real and the Department of Industry's relations with the unions should be as close as they are with management. I was particularly interested in getting clearance from him to see the General Secretaries *and* the people on the shop floor about industrial democracy. 'You'd better be careful about that,' he said. 'Be very careful. Don't interfere, because we are handling it.'

Saturday 6 April

I wrote a note to Anne Crossman following Dick's death yesterday. Dick was a remarkable man, immensely intelligent and kind when he wanted to be but, of course, the teacher throughout his life – always preferring conflict, which cleared his mind. He was absolutely unreliable in the sense that he often changed his views, but he always believed what he said, which is something you can't say of others. He was also capable of being unpleasant and my friendship with him had deteriorated sharply in recent years. At any rate, he will be remembered through his diaries which will be the best diaries of this period ever published; though I hope my own, if they are ever transcribed, will also turn out to be a reasonable record.

Monday 8 April

George Thomson, who is now an EEC Commissioner, came at 12.30, and I asked him about the Regional Development Fund. He said he would like us to go snap on it now because it would confirm our desire to remain in the Community, whereas if we left it until later, it might be part of a package in the renegotiations which would take a year.

I asked him whether he thought there could be some parliamentary approval for decisions made by the Community. He said that where regulations were in draft, they could be ad referendum to the House of Commons, but where the Commission had derived power to make rules and regulations enforcable throughout the Community, there was no scope for parliamentary approval.

Finally, I explained to him, quite plainly, my feelings. I said I had never been on an explicitly anti-Market platform in my life but since we had been in the Community, I felt the House of Commons had become a spectator of great events, and that too much power had drained away to Europe through all the official committees that had been set up. When I had been campaigning in the Election, hostility to the Market was strongly expressed by council house tenants and others, and I felt this was a problem. He just said, 'There is nothing you can do about that.' As far as he is concerned, we are in and that's the end of it. But I was very friendly and I said I would like to go and visit him in Brussels.

Sandwich lunch with Ministers, where we discussed two problems. One was open Government where the trade unions are just as reluctant as civil servants or Ministers to see the books opened or things published. The second was the Common Market where there is a pretty fair agreement between Eric Heffer, Frank Beswick, Gregor MacKenzie, Michael Meacher and myself that the Common Market is just not on in the long term. When the British people discover what it really means, they will oppose it and we have got to set out our alternative which is harmonisation with Europe, a free-trade area and cooperation on an ad-hoc basis.

Tuesday 9 April
At Cabinet, the Chile warships came up again. Jim Callaghan reported that he had met a group of Labour MPs on the previous evening, half of whom had been in favour of releasing the existing warships. He said it would require legislation to stop the release, and how would you get the Chilean sailors off the ship already doing trials off the English coast, and so on and so on.

Michael Foot came out very strongly against and I said, 'It is absolutely untrue that it would require legislation. What about the arms embargo against Israel during the recent war? What would we say if we discovered that the Russians had put in an order for some fighters from British Aircraft Corporation? Of course we can do it, it is a decision we are absolutely free to take.'

I raised the question of the repair and overhaul of Rolls Royce engines at East Kilbride for the Hawker Hunters which we had sold to the Chilean Government. I said, 'This is even worse because these Hawker Hunters may actually be used to strafe guerrillas with bombs.'

We lost. Only two of us spoke against it, Michael Foot and myself. Barbara Castle was silent, so was Peter Shore perhaps because, as Trade Minister, he was worried about the threat to copper supplies, which might be stopped in retaliation if we don't go ahead with the deal.

At 4, I had the TUC Steel Industry Consultative Committee with Dai Davies, Johnny Boyd, Moss Evans*, amongst others, with Frank Beswick and Michael Meacher flanking me. Dai Davies went through the situation in the steel industry and criticised the corporate plan, although actually he has largely gone along with the Chairman of BSC, Monty Finniston, and his embarrassment arises from the fact that now there is a lot of protest from the people affected by steel closures.

Johnny Boyd was most offensive, what Clive Jenkins called a 'high degree of institutionalised indignation'. He called me 'boy' saying, 'I can only tell you, boy, that we are sick of all this parliamentary double talk. What are you going to do about these closures?'

I read out what was in the Manifesto. 'We are going to do that; we are going to stick to it.'

He said, 'Well, none of your usual kidology.'

I said, 'Look, we've just been through it and if you're not satisfied, let's go through it all over again. I am not going to leave this room until I am satisfied that you are in agreement with what has been proposed.' In the end he shut up and Dai Davies apologised, saying that Johnny was often like that. But it was something of a trial of strength, and I think it was a surprise to them that I fought so hard.

Wednesday 10 April

To Cabinet, where there was an important agenda. We started with the Industrial Relations Act on which Michael had put in a memorandum covering three points. On picketing, he said that we were bound by the High Court decision that pickets couldn't stop cars to get their message across. Elwyn Jones fully supported Michael and, I think, was partly responsible for insisting that the High Court decision be upheld. The second point was that we were going to set up a tribunal to deal with workers who were sacked by the unions in firms with closed shop agreements. The third referred to existing cases now going through the courts under the Industrial Relations Act.

On picketing, of course, what we are doing is accepting a completely Tory view. On unfair dismissal, I asked why we were picking out the trade unions for unfair dismissal when we hadn't even worked out our general provisions for unfair dismissal by employers. On the existing

* Dai (Sir David) Davies, General Secretary of the Iron and Steel Trades Confederation; John Boyd, executive member of the AUEW, General Secretary 1975–82; Moss Evans, National Organiser of the TGWU, General Secretary, 1978–85.

cases, it is quite clear that there will be another £70,000 fine on the AUEW which they won't pay, and they will therefore have all their assets seized. On compensation for unfair dismissal, the T&G has got £1 million still to pay.

I said, 'This is absolute nonsense. We can't stand by and let the unions be fined because of previous Tory legislation. We took a strong line in Opposition that you should obey the law but that the law should be changed and now we have the power to change it.'

Elwyn said it would be unconstitutional to extinguish existing rights of employers against the unions.

'To hell with that,' I said. 'The Tories extinguish the rights of trade unions and of elected councils under their legislation. Why can't we extinguish the rights of their people? After all, if we take the view that the law is the law and it must be obeyed, then when we change the law, that will have to be obeyed. What we need is an amnesty, wiping the slate clean.'

So Roy said, 'Let's explore this. An amnesty means that when a criminal offence has been committed, you forgive them.'

'Well, yes, but I am talking about wiping the slate clean.'

Harold suggested we accept a Back Bench amendment on this. I said, 'Why not do it ourselves.' Anyway it was agreed to look at it all again. I somewhat shook them. But, my God, when you hear those people, they are instinctively Tory.

At 5 o'clock I went to the second Cabinet meeting, held for the first time in Harold's room in the House. Harold made a reference to Marcia and her brother Tony Field and the press allegations of improper land deals. He says he felt he had driven the press into a corner but he continued, 'I must tell you, there are two other members of the Cabinet, whose names wild horses wouldn't draw from me, who are being pursued by the press. One has been tailed for five years and on the other they have got a dossier two feet thick. They both would be regarded as being in the leadership stakes if I went. So I just want to warn you.'

This was Harold telling us that if any of us made a move against him, he might take action against them. It was an extraordinary thing and showed him in his cheapest light because if he really had any information about two people in the Cabinet who were being tailed the decent thing would have been to tell them.

Northern Ireland came up next and Merlyn Rees reported that the situation was getting extremely serious; the IRA were involving women and using hostages to drive bombs into areas. Under a pledge of the utmost secrecy, we were told it was decided to surround Belfast and prevent any cars entering. This is to be announced soon.

It was agreed, again under the highest secrecy, that we would begin considering the implications of a total withdrawal. Of course, if that got out, it would precipitate bloodshed but we felt we simply had to do it. Roy took that view. Jim looked very doubtful but thought it needed to be done. Fred Peart, Peter Shore and Willie Ross are 100 per cent pro-Protestant. So the Cabinet would divide on Catholic-Protestant lines in the event of this happening.

Later we went into Eric Heffer's room and he read the text of a speech he was going to make saying he understood and shared the disquiet about the decision to supply the existing warships to Chile. We went through the speech carefully and I got him to remove the words 'and share', and then there was masses of stuff about what we had said in Opposition. I warned him that he might well be fired but he was prepared to take that risk. Indeed if he didn't take it, he would resign on it. He feels so strongly because in March 1972 he went to Chile with a message from Harold to Allende and it just turns his stomach to see the Cabinet doing this. It is an important test case because if he is fired, there will be a big row and if he isn't fired, then the way will be open for anyone to oppose the Government. I advised him to send the text to Harold as a courtesy.

Thursday 11 April
At 12.15 Sir Antony Part came to see me. He hummed and hawed a bit and then said, 'Minister, do you really intend to go ahead with your National Enterprise Board, public ownership and planning agreements?'

'Of course.'

'Are you serious?' he asked.

'Of course. Not just because it is the policy but because I was deeply associated with the development of that policy.'

He said, 'Well, I must warn you, in that case, that if you do it, you will be heading for as big a confrontation with industrial management as the last Government had with the trade unions over the Industrial Relations Act.'

'I am not going to jail any industrialists. I am not going to fine them. We have just got to move forward.'

'I know,' he said, 'and I will try to lubricate things, if that's really what you mean.'

'Well, of course it is. I know I can't do it now but we have got to move in that direction.'

Then, blow me down, he put in a paper and tried to get me to agree verbally to a proposal that because of the extra burden on industry, which has reduced their liquidity position, we should allow them to put all wage increases through the Price Commission as an allowable cost which would give an extra £600 million to industry at the expense of the consumer. I said, 'That is an even more relaxed view of price control than the previous Government agreed.'

'It's the only way' he replied. I refused. 'You can put your analysis of liquidity to the Treasury if you like, but I won't accept that.'

This is the way in which the Department of Industry acts, simply as a mouthpiece for the CBI, and that is what I won't have.

Saturday 13 April

Eric Heffer rang to say he had had a letter from the Prime Minister telephoned through to him, telling him that his speech was incompatible with his position as a Minister. His agent is besieged with press inquiries. By 8.30 tonight, that is in about half an hour's time, I would think Eric will have been thrown out of the Government. But Harold has taken on a great new incubus because though it may make him feel he has been tough and strong in dealing with a rebellious Left, the Party won't have it. Eric's only fear is that perhaps the Party won't understand what he is doing. To that extent, I think he may be right because the publicity given so far to the supply of these warships has been minimal. But I hope that by tomorrow the issue will be fairly clear. If I am asked about it, I shall simply say 'I greatly regret his dismissal', because I feel that he is a most sincere man and the Government really must contain within it people who are able to recognise the anxiety of Party members. But Eric is taking a great risk. He speaks his mind and is respected for that, but he finds the compromises of office very difficult to take. I understand it, and there have to be people like that in politics. Office isn't the only thing. Indeed, I so often feel like that myself that I almost share his desire to be in a position where he is free to argue his view openly and without the restraints imposed by Harold.

Harold bases himself on his 'Procedure for Ministers',[2] which he dictated to us and was not itself collectively agreed, and I feel it raises very important questions which need to be discussed in the movement; the Procedure for Ministers is not published therefore nobody knows the restraints under which Ministers operate. This is partly the problem.

Sunday 14 April

This morning the BBC came to do an interview with me about investment. They threw in a question on Eric Heffer's speech on warships for Chile. When it came to the 1 o'clock news, they had cut my answer in respect of the Chile issue. So I rang up *The World This Weekend* to complain, and asked them to send me the full text of what I had said in the interview.

When I rang Frances, she advised me not to make a row. 'Harold is in real trouble and rows of this kind don't do the Party any good and you ought not to be tied up with it.'

I had various calls from Eric and advised him to say nothing more
at all. Then Judith Hart rang me up to say she had been very worried
by Eric's speech because it had put her in a difficulty and she wondered
whether *she* should make a statement, or resign. I told her to keep quiet,
say nothing and leave it. Since I find myself saying to other people
what Frances says to me, perhaps it would be better if I took my own
advice and kept quiet.

Monday 15 April
On the 1 o'clock news, Jim Callaghan gave an interview about Eric
Heffer. He said it was contrary to collective Cabinet responsibility but
Eric was inexperienced and he recognised his sincerity and he hoped
Harold wouldn't sack him.

In fact the advice that I gave the Cabinet, which was that there
would be a hell of a row, has turned out to be absolutely right and if
they had handled it differently, it might never have happened. But
there you are.

Tuesday 16 April
The papers this morning were still full of Eric Heffer. *The Times* had a
leading article. Generally speaking, he has done extremely well. Jim
Callaghan's broadcast made it clear that he should not be dismissed
and I suspect now he won't be. Of course, there is widespread support
for him in the Party and I think this could well put him on the NEC,
and I personally would be pleased if it did.

Wednesday 17 April
Worked on letters and my box, where there was a report of Harold's
meeting with Willy Brandt, the Chairman of the SPD, at Pompidou's
funeral. The account made it clear that Harold had said he could get
what he wanted for Britain without an amendment of the Treaty of
Rome or the Treaty of Accession. This was the first clear line I had of
Harold's attitude to the Market, acting the pro-Marketeer again as he
had when he was last Prime Minister.

A scrambler telephone was fitted at Stansgate.

Tuesday 23 April
After lunch Bill Ryland came for a private talk about his position as
Chairman of the Post Office. He wanted to go on for three years. I had
offered him eighteen months, but said I could let him stretch it out to
two years. I asked him about a series of stamps featuring the trade
unions which I very much want – and he said it was difficult because
they were political, and they therefore could not be done. This of course

is rubbish, since they are printing Churchill stamps next year for the centenary of his birth.

Caroline and I went to Locket's for the husbands-and-wives' left-wing dinner: Barbara Castle talked about nothing but the need to bribe consultants to accept whole-time service in the Health Service. But mainly we talked about Chile and agreed that we would have to put up a fight at the National Executive tomorrow morning.

Wednesday 24 April

NEC this morning, and the key item was the discussion on Chile. Jim Callaghan began by justifying what had been done. He mentioned other arms contracts abroad, the repercussive effects of threats of retaliation on copper supplies, and he repeated the question of how we would remove the Chilean sailors from the ship, and so on.

Michael Foot said – and this is interesting because it was the first time a Cabinet Minister had done so for a long time – that this had aroused a lot of feeling and that he doubted a lot of the arguments; we would never have sold arms to a fascist country before the war and the Government should review the decision.

I came after Michael and said that we all had to accept collective ministerial responsibility as Cabinet Ministers for what had already been decided but there are much wider issues involved here. We were in for a long period of Government and there were bound to be occasions when central policy issues arose on which the Party Conference had taken a stand – where there are differences between the Government and the Party – and when anxiety is expressed by the movement. The question was how should we deal with it. We had to accept that Ministers do hold collective responsibility but should not use it as an excuse for fending off criticism.

I had a brief talk with Secretary who really came in to find out why I was seeing Lord Rothschild. When Rothschild arrived I reminded him we had met before and that I had supported him on the customer-contractor relationship. I said there was a grave economic crisis and I had wondered if the Think Tank* might like to try to identify the main problems facing Britain in terms of regional imbalance and investment and balance of payments, as a background against which a debate could get going.

We moved on from that to the machinery of government and open government. Rothschild was rather creepy-crawly. Considering he had

* The Central Policy Review Staff, or Think Tank, was established in 1970 by Edward Heath, comprising a multi-disciplinary array of talents to serve the Cabinet. Lord Rothschild was its first Director-General, until October 1974 when Sir Kenneth Berrill took over.

worked under Heath for three and a half years, he might have been a bit more loyal about Heath but still he said he had tried to get the Tory Cabinet to discuss some basic issues but without success. I said I was always in favour of discussing things and not just reading papers.

Thursday 25 April

I was very tired today. At Cabinet at 10.30 the first item was a speech by Roy Mason yesterday in which he had hinted that British troops might be withdrawn from Northern Ireland. Harold said that Ministers must consult with the FO, and in particular with the Northern Ireland Secretary before saying anything. Merlyn told me he was desperately worried and that Gerry Fitt was furious at Roy's speech and it encouraged the idea that the British Labour Government was a soft sell. Harold said the speech was a breach of the Procedure for Ministers and he used these words: 'Ministers have no other existence than as Ministers.'

At about 12 we began an enormously long discussion on Europe, that went on till 5.45. There were three papers before us: one on the Budget, one on the Common Agricultural Policy and one on the developing world and trade. The key paper in the whole document was Annexe 2 to the Budget paper showing that in 1980 it was expected that the GNP per head in the Community countries would be: Germany, 7,600; Denmark, 6,345; France, 6,195; Belgium and Luxembourg, 5,925; the Netherlands, 5,575; Italy, 3,285; UK, 3,235; Ireland, 2,370. That is the extent of the difference – with Germany more than twice as rich per head as we are.

I said, 'Well, if you look at the long-term figures, we are heading for development area status in the EEC. Why don't we start at a bargaining position with a request for more of the Budget than the others?' There was general laughter at the idea.

Jim said we had a choice between a quick solution to the re-negotiation, which would mean we would fail, and a slow one which would mean we might succeed. Denis made a very powerful speech saying that when the autumn came and the defence review began, and the Germans realised how much we were subsidising them, that would be something for us to bargain with; and similarly when the oil came along, whenever it was, we would be in a stronger position. But he said, as to Europe, it was absurd the way the bureaucracy was growing there. Nobody believed in it – they just took their hat along because they felt they had to join in. Nobody knew what it was about at all.

Roy Jenkins said that if we went for a quick solution, the future of the Government would be in grave danger, which was a sort of vague threat of resignation.

I said that we would find that industrial and regional policies were central – not peripheral – to the re-negotiation. The fact was that we were facing the problems of long-term decline. This would blow back on us through the domestic and political system, and the electoral consequences would be obvious. It wouldn't be enough to say, 'Don't worry, we are trying to get a bigger share of the Budget.' It just wasn't on to unarm ourselves at this moment when we were about to adopt a new policy. Whatever form our new policy took, it would inevitably involve a systematic distortion of free competition and control of the market. I had certainly noticed, as a Minister, how much power had gone to Brussels and that already options were not open to us, and domestic decisions had to be cleared with the Foreign Secretary. There was a great pessimism about the future of Britain. The myth of Empire had been replaced by the myth of Europe.

Friday 26 April
The Confederation of Shipbuilding and Engineering Unions, led by George Doughty, came to see me about British Leyland. They were concerned about press stories that British Leyland was cutting back on the investment programme and selling off its operations in Basingstoke and Spain.

They pointed out that British Leyland was the only British motor firm in existence, 170,000 people were involved, and they thought that Government intervention was inevitable. British Leyland was in fact more important than Rolls Royce. Any public money that went in must be open to public scrutiny and controlled in the public interest. The policy of the Confederation was that this must be done through public equity and industrial democracy. The interests of the Confederation were to try to maintain job security: they pointed out that Renault was nationalised twenty-four years ago, that Volkswagen in its heyday had been publicly owned, that the share value of Leyland had now dropped substantially. They also referred to their 1970 resolution which had called for public ownership in engineering.

I thanked them for coming, said I welcomed their visit, understood their anxiety, that the press stories had not originated with me, there had been no specific approach and I was grateful to them for putting their view on record. 'Do you want to let it be known that this talk took place?' They said no, fearing it might endanger the company.

Saturday 27 April
At 11.15 the Prime Minister of Malta, Dom Mintoff, and the Maltese High Commissioner came to see me. Dom said that he hoped that the new relationship with the Labour Government would be cordial. He described projects they were promoting in Malta: shipbuilding with the support of the Arab countries, possibly the development of large

tankers; a £70 m project with Libyan, Kuwaiti and Saudi money, which the UK would be welcome to join in; a cement project the Germans were interested in; perhaps diesel engines or hydraulic pumps or aluminium production. He thought the UK technical assistance proposal offering up to £1 m would be a useful point of entry. He indicated his great anxiety about defence cuts which might affect the Malta base. We agreed, because the Foreign Office, the Department of Trade and the Overseas Development Ministry were present, that a broadly based mission should go and look at it.

But, of course, my official briefing was wildly antagonistic towards Malta. I was told the problem was that, after their talks had failed years ago, the Tories had written off Mintoff. He was thought completely unreliable.

As we left I told Mintoff I admired his skill in keeping an island of 300,000 going by getting support from all over the place; and how the Common Market looked so big and bureaucratic. He said life looks much more difficult when you are at the bottom end of the scale. Mintoff is a very good negotiator and an attractive guy. Extremely difficult – but then you can't survive if you are the Prime Minister of Malta without being difficult.

Sunday 28 April

I received the figures I wanted on the support given to private industry by Government. It runs to about £750 million a year, and has done for the last four years. That is in effect about £2 million a day for four years, and a very useful figure to have because it throws private industry completely on the defensive. Either it represents a remission of taxation to that amount, or alternatively you could argue that that part of their dividends which is distributed has in fact come from Government.

As I look at it, I can see my way through now in breaking industry's resistance to my policies. I shall win over the managers and the small businessmen, and I shall get the nationalised industries to welcome the planning agreements; I shall isolate the big Tory companies, then show how much money they have been getting from the Government, and if they don't want it, they don't have to have it.

Geoffrey Goodman rang up and said he detected among senior businessmen a general belief that there will have to be an authoritarian government until the oil comes ashore, in order to control the trade unions; otherwise they are absolutely sunk. It may be that if there is a great crisis, Heath will come back and say, 'This is why I was fighting the miners: to prevent inflation and to control the unions,' This is a serious possibility.

Monday 29 April

To dinner with Caroline at Glyn's Bank with Richard Lloyd, the Chief Executive, Sir Jasper Hollom of the Bank of England, the Earl of Airlie who is a businessman and Dundas Hamilton, Deputy Chairman of the Stock Exchange – all accompanied by wives. After an agreeable dinner, the men stayed behind at the table and Lloyd asked, 'How do we fit in to the planning agreements?'

I said, 'Well, the problem is, we are not getting investment, we haven't solved industrial relations and we haven't solved the problems of regional imbalance. We have to cooperate a bit more directly. I don't know much about the City and you will have to tell me what you can do.'

'We must restore confidence.'

'What is the political price of restoring confidence?'

'Well, you have got to have better dividend distribution, otherwise equities will collapse.'

I said, 'Maybe we have come to the point where we can't operate like that; public sector investment isn't a problem because we'll always need telephones and railways and steel. I don't think you appreciate the fact that there has been a very substantial shift in the balance of power, that the statutory wage policy led to the three day week and the collapse. We have all got to start again.'

'Perhaps the system's breaking down.'

I said, 'I know it is breaking down but we have got to find a way of increasing investment, that is all. The Government has been putting £2 m pounds a day into industry and it is not a very effective system. I'd like to look at it again.'

On the whole it was a friendly discussion, but I found them as licked as the CBI because they, too, in their hearts, believe the unions have to be brought under control, and that is politically not on. I told Dick Lloyd that the unions had defeated the Labour Party in 1970 by withdrawing their support, and had defeated Heath by mobilising their support, and we all had to come to terms with this reality.

But they were interested in meeting us all. Harold was bashing the Earl of Airlie, an old reactionary, over the head. I left it that Jasper Hollom or somebody would come to talk to us about the general problems and how they thought we could overcome them. I told them there was endless time for consultation, we were not in a hurry, we hadn't got a parliamentary majority and we had got to look at things afresh. They were talking about workers' participation and involvement and getting workers to buy shares, and all that Tory crap. The guys were mainly hereditary bankers who sent their kids away to public school and they had no fight, never been through the fire; whereas the up-and-coming trade union leaders and stewards are very formidable, and in the end they will win. When somebody asked Caroline, 'Are you against capitalism?' she answered, 'I'm quite objective about it.'

Tuesday 30 April

We heard this morning that Caroline's mother died in Cincinnati. She had a most distressing last few months.

I went into the office and we discussed the commemorative trade union postage stamps. The Post Office have now said they can't find room for them next year although in their memorandum they listed the European architectural historical year, the Royal Yachting Association, Jane Austen, Turner – the most extraordinary upper-class liberal arts preferences, without any regard to the interests of working people. So I sent a stiff minute back and spoke to Bill Ryland about it when he came later in the day.

We had a meeting on Meriden at which the Department produced their recommendation – on the proposals put up by Geoffrey Robinson and the cooperative – that we couldn't go forward with Meriden. I instructed that these comments be made available to the cooperative and to Geoffrey Robinson and asked the Department to prepare a paper arguing *in favour* of Meriden which we will put before colleagues.

Wednesday 1 May

I went at 10 to the Overseas Policy and Defence Committee where the only item on the agenda was the engines, spares and overhauls for the Hunter aircraft for Chile. I presented my paper, arguing that we should discontinue and terminate the contracts. Peter Shore supported my view and was against the overhauls.

Jim Callaghan favoured the supply of the engines and the continuation of the overhaul arrangements. 'It would be a victory for the British Communist Party if these overhauls were stopped.'

Then Harold came in and it was quite obvious that he saw it pragmatically. He said there was a lot of anxiety about it, and I felt he was moving in my direction.

Edmund Dell said that *all* the regimes in Latin America depended on the goodwill of the army and therefore we should supply the arms. Roy Jenkins didn't think this issue mattered very much. Church people didn't care much about Chile (as Harold had implied), it was a remote country of which he knew very little and there was no philosophical basis for differentiating between these overhauls and the supply of warships in general.

Friday 3 May

To Number 10 for the Energy Committee. There was a very good paper from Rothschild's Central Policy Review Staff on the whole question of energy conservation. Predictably, none of the Ministers wanted it published. Fred Mulley said it would upset various bodies with which the Department of the Environment was involved. Others felt the same and the Treasury in particular thought it would create pressure for public expenditure that they were not prepared to meet, for example fiscal incentives to encourage the development of electric cars.

I said, 'Look, we all know what has happened. Officials have been ringing each other up around Whitehall to say it will upset the French, and telling Fred Mulley that it will upset the building industry, and telling me that it will upset somebody else.' Harold accepted publication; mind you, Sir John Hunt, the Cabinet Secretary, told me afterwards that he had briefed the Prime Minister to support it, so Rothschild was pleased.

I said perhaps the Rothschild report should be published as a Blue Paper – you hold it in a gloved hand, light it and retire immediately and it should have a statement on it, 'Treasury Warning. Reading this report may damage your wealth.'

Went over to Transport House and Jack Jones and the TGWU gave me, on loan, a beautiful old banner 'The Workers Union', about nine feet by nine feet. I'll have to give it back if there is a change of Government.

Jack asked about Meriden and I said, 'I saw them and have told them to prepare a case against what officials are advising.'

He said, 'I know that and I appreciate it. What can I do to help?'

'You can press Denis Healey, Harold and Michael Foot at the critical moment when it comes before Ministers.'

Back to the office to see the Russian Ambassador, Mr Lunkov. I was just in the process of hanging up my banner and he took a lot of interest in it. My office is getting to look more and more messy, like my basement office at home.

After that Secretary came in, very worried about the radical nature of our policy and the resistance there would be in industry. I recognise this and I have got to get the argument right and deal with the real difficulties and make the policy intellectually defensible. It can't be done easily. It is much too big and the implications are enormous. The Secretary is pessimistic about it but then he is broadly a market economy man. It is like talking to a Tory all the time, except he will do what I ask in the end.

Eric Heffer looked in, furious that he had received a letter from Harold saying that his speech on Chile had gravely embarrassed the Government.

I said, 'Whatever you do, Eric, don't make another speech about it on May Day. I am trying to win a battle now on the supply of aero-engines for Chilean aircraft and if you go and make a speech about it, we are absolutely finished.'

Monday 6 May
At 11 o'clock we had the TUC–Labour Party Working Party on the nationalisation of the aircraft industry with George Doughty of TASS, David Lea of the TUC, Jack Service of the CSEU and others. They agreed to bring out an urgent paper for the CSEU conference in the summer. George Doughty was in the chair and I was there as an ordinary member of the Committee.

The more I think about this, the more I see that if you are going to have socialism, you have to have a secondary power structure in which Ministers sit in but are not the dominant figures. All of a sudden it came home to me that if I sat there with a TUC member in the chair, while retaining the rights of a Minister to do things as and when I thought necessary and as agreed, it would be much better than having trade unionists coming in to see me with petitions to Ministers, with the Whitehall machine in the saddle. This concept of a working-class power structure, democratic and organised in parallel with the Government structure – in effect joint government of the country by the Labour Party and the trade unions – makes an awful lot of sense. I think it is wholly compatible with all that is best in parliamentary democracy: we would govern in conjunction with the trade unions just as the Tories have always governed in conjunction with the City and big business.

Had a working lunch with the Secretary, Professor Alan Peacock (the Department's Chief Economic Adviser) and Anne Mueller, a Permanent Under-Secretary who is also the wife of James Robertson who stood against me as a Social Democrat candidate in the Election. Francis Cripps had written a paper with three recommendations intended as interim proposals for the Cabinet, including transitional employment subsidies for firms where there were closures or major redundancies in developed areas and cheap loans for small businesses.

It was the first time we had sat in the office with the banner on the wall and psychologically it was a tremendous advantage to us. I could see the Secretary's head framed with 'Unity is Strength' as I listened to him.

Professor Peacock, Anne Mueller and Secretary opposed the paper, and Eric Heffer immediately lost his temper. 'Well, I don't know why I am in the Government. *This* paper is just propping up capitalism. I want to take it over. I want to bring it under the people's control.' It wasn't exactly an outburst but a strong statement of his view and it did them a hell of a lot of good to listen because it drove them on to the defensive.

Francis Cripps had the brilliant idea that we would consider options he knew that the Chancellor was considering, put in a paper on those options, and in this way he would force the Cabinet to discuss Treasury options even though the Treasury itself had not brought them to our attention.

I went to a dinner in honour of Sir Frank Wood, the retiring Permanent Secretary of the Ministry of Posts and Telecommunications. William Armstrong, head of the Civil Service, was there, drunk and more decayed than my recollections of him. His parents were in the Salvation Army, and I had thought rather highly of him but I think he was destroyed by Heath.

Tuesday 7 May

Dinner with Kuzmin, the Soviet Deputy-Minister of Foreign Trade, and Lunkov, the Ambassador. Lunkov knew Khrushchev well and said he was a very temperamental and excitable man. I asked Kuzmin whether Henry Ford or Karl Marx had done more for socialism. At the end, the Ambassador made a little speech saying I had been the 'inspirator', a mixture of inspirer and conspirator, of the Anglo-Soviet technological agreements, and that he regarded me as a friend.

So I replied that I attached a lot of importance to this; Academician Kirillin [Chairman of the State Committee on Science and Technology] and I were old friends and we had tried to make technological agreements work. They indicated the seriousness with which we approached not just trade and technology but political relations. We had to see in what we were doing not an attempt to change each other's systems because we had to learn from each other, but a way of building world peace in the wider Europe of which we were all members.

Wednesday 8 May

Gilbert Hunt, who is President of the Society of Motor Manufacturers and Traders and Chairman of Chrysler UK (formerly Rootes), came to see me. He was tremendously amenable and said that Rootes Motors had had a bit of experience of planning agreements through his being on the Simca board in France. 'Detroit is nervous that you are going to bully the multinationals,' he said.

I told him I would like to have lunch with him and the head of the Chrysler organisation in Europe. I asked why there had been so few strikes in France – there hadn't been one at his Simca factory for twenty-two years. He replied that the Ministry of the Interior passes on political information about subversives, and I told him that we did not want surveillance of trade unionists here.

Thursday 9 May
Peter Shore and I had a drink in the office and we talked a little bit about the EEC. He said that Helmut Schmidt, who is likely to succeed Willy Brandt as Chancellor, is much more Atlantic orientated. He is a great friend of Giscard d'Estaing and the whole Community would take a very different direction than it had when Germany had been led by Brandt and France by Pompidou.

It is astonishing, the number of heads of state that have fallen recently. Trudeau, the Canadian Prime Minister, fell today and there is going to be an Election there. Brandt's resignation is an extraordinary one because it now contains a hint of scandal: an East German spy, Gunter Guillaume, has been to Norway on holiday with Brandt and has taken compromising photographs of him.

Friday 10 May
I overslept this morning, and dashed into the office where Mr Flanigan, a presidential adviser at the White House and also one of the Council of Economic Advisers, came to see me to urge the American view that at the OECD conference on 29/30 May we should agree to review the rules of international investment generally, which would include multinational companies.

Flanigan is a young man, socially and intellectually well-connected; he had a big tie with the crest of the President of the United States on it and he was surrounded by three people, all of whom looked vaguely English, representatives of the East Coast Establishment.

My brief from Anne Mueller simply said, if he says this the Secretary of State had better not comment, if he says that the Secretary of State might find it better not to respond, if he says the other then the Secretary of State might indicate that no decision has been reached: a completely neutralising brief.

In fact I argued with him and told him that these were big political problems, particularly in relation to the multinational companies, which affect every country in the world. Multinationals are about power; they affect the trade unions, they affect Britain not only as a home country of many big multinationals, but also as a developing country with the oil companies operating in the North Sea. We have to look at them politically. National governments are bound to protect the interests of their own people.

He pressed me and said, 'Your response implies that you might take the same view about the pledge on no import restrictions on trade.'

'Not necessarily. But in the end we have to justify our policy to our own people and we have huge areas of unemployment into which we must get resources. It is no good going to Scotland and telling them that I would like to have pushed a firm in their direction but under the international rules, it had to go somewhere else. I am bound to push to see that they get it.'

I pressed the argument home. 'After all, you interfere with the market on medical care just as we do with our NHS; you interfere with the market on environmental questions just as we do.' I have no doubt that he had been fully briefed by the American Embassy and was not much surprised by what I said.

After he went the Secretary came in and we had a chat about my workers' control draft speech which has scared the pants off him. He said that it would create terrible fears and that it was one thing to say this in Opposition but another to say it in Government. It was a classic statement.

My attitude is a de-centralising one in favour of the extension of democracy and openness. I said, 'I am not a milk-and-water Stalinist' – a phrase he found very offensive – 'who wants to bring everything under bureaucratic control. I want the whole thing to be opened up. I am much more likely to cause trouble in Whitehall for trying to de-centralise than for centralising.'

Later, George Ball, former Under-Secretary to Kennedy and Johnson, came representing United Airways aircraft with a proposal for some arrangement by Pratt and Whitney for a link with Rolls. He is an old New Dealer who has ended up working in the big corporations.

When he had finished Frances Morrell asked him what John Kennedy had been like. He said that he was a man with no great intellectual power and no experience – he had only been a junior Senator – but he learned quickly and appointed good people. He had had very little conceptual vision, and was always interested in the here and now. Ball added, 'I was with him every one of the 1000 days he was in the White House. Johnson, who was destroyed by the Vietnam War, was a much abler politician than Kennedy.' It was interesting to get that view of Kennedy, as a nice, able, Boston Irish political glamour boy.

As we walked out I asked him about Nixon. 'He will certainly be impeached this year, no question now that the *Chicago Tribune* has dropped him. He will probably prefer to resign in return for a Bill of Immunity than be impeached and be pushed out with prosecutions against him.'

Sunday 12 May

One little thing today pleased me. Tomorrow I have a meeting with François Ortoli, the President of the European Commission, and I remembered that he had come to me in the spring of 1970, when he was Minister for Industrial and Scientific Development. So I checked it in my Five Year Diary – found the exact date and pulled out the cassette, recorded on 7 April 1970, of my daily diary, and in a few minutes I found the account – what I thought of him, what sort of a man he was, what we discussed and so on.* A very useful reminder. These taped diaries stretching over another fifteen years of political life will mean something like twenty-five years of recollection recorded nightly. It is very satisfying.

Frances said this afternoon that she was convinced that the Department of Industry was sabotaging my industrial proposals. I feel the same. Sir Antony Part is making no progress, they just turf back things I want with their objections and I then have to force them to carry out my wishes – as I had to do with Meriden, with all the European questions, and so on. Frances says that on the planning agreements, the National Enterprise Board and the Industry Act, the officials are simply skating over the really difficult questions so they are never explored properly. It is as if I'm trying to swim up the Niagara Falls.

Professor Peacock is utterly wedded to laissez-faire, and it is extremely difficult to operate with that sort of advice coming to you. I just have to think of ways of out-flanking them. One way is by public speeches that commit them to a public policy that they then have to defend; another is to resuscitate the idea of a meeting in the Central Hall, Westminster, where I would talk to the entire Department and tell everybody roughly what our policy is and invite them to help achieve it.

Monday 13 May

Sir Antony Part came to see me at 9.45 and I told him that I was really very unhappy about the way things were working out. I had to rely on the Department to put forward proposals that I strongly believed in and I hoped that he would bend. I think this shook him a bit and word went round the office, obviously as a result of his meeting later with the Under-Secretaries, that I was unhappy. Later, Peter Carey had asked Frances Morrell whether I thought the Department was entirely conservative.

At 12.15 Ortoli arrived with a huge collection of staff – a German, a Dutchman, an Italian, Sir Michael Palliser, who was formerly a Private Secretary at Number 10, and so on.

After welcoming him I said he would already know my view, that I was against entry into the EEC under the negotiated terms which I did not think were in the interests of the British people, and I had been largely responsible for the Referendum campaign. My view had not in any way altered but, at the same time, I was anxious to discuss it with him because, as I saw it, the vital area was industrial policy. The

* This meeting is to be found in *Office Without Power 1968–72*, Chapter 3.

Community was developing its industrial policy and we were developing ours, and it was the divergence or convergence between the two which we needed to consider.

Ortoli replied, 'Perhaps I should tell you that I speak as an old colleague and not as the President of the Commission. I am very keen on regional policy, I was responsible for regional policy under de Gaulle. Indeed I proposed the original regional fund. But, at the same time, macro-economic policies are essential; we must have harmonisation and there is a great dynamic mechanism here which will help us.'

I said I fully shared the view of the importance of regional policy, but Britain had been putting £2 m a day into industry over the last four years and we had not produced results. 'Look at Scotland,' I said, pointing to the bottom of the map (which hangs upside down on my wall). 'There is our Southern Italy. You can see what a tremendous problem we have, and this is something to which we have to respond.'

Ortoli was intrigued by the upside down map and he said, 'Perhaps your policy has not been very effective, perhaps putting all this money in is not the best way of doing it. Perhaps you should get other things right.'

'Yes,' I said 'That's exactly what we're working on.'

He continued, 'Do not assume that there is a divergence. The Commission is seeking to coordinate, not to impose.'

I said I accepted all that but the pressures on me came from the people I represented and the Commission was above all that. The democratic link was what really mattered, the accountability of power, the pressure through the ballot box, the need to respond as I might have to when the representatives of the City of Edinburgh come to ask for special development status. For me, democracy meant the power to remove the man who makes the policy and to change the policy. As to voluntary harmonisation, that was quite different. We were most law abiding, but this supra-nationality made things difficult.

Ortoli admitted that the Treaty of Rome gave the Commission powers but there was always the potential for dialogue – and the Court of Justice in case of disagreement; and the European Parliament had the power to dismiss the Commission.

I said I understood all that. 'I have never spoken on a specifically anti-European platform but what I fear is that the Commission will decapitate or apply the guillotine to British democracy.' This is not just the British being difficult, it is a problem the Community will have to face – how to root a faith in these institutions in the hearts and minds of the people.

'Well,' said Ortoli, 'you say it may take a long time to do this, but we haven't got a long time, we have got to do the work of a hundred years in ten years.'

I do find him a charming, delightful man. I said I wished we had more time to talk; this was a new perspective, frankly, on the problems of government and of Europe which the Commission may not entirely recognise and accept.

After he had gone, I had a sandwich lunch and asked Antony Part his view of whether there would be a slump. He said there might be. Then he added, 'We're reaching the point of the crossing of the Rubicon and your speech about workers' control will lead to tremendous opening of fire on us because industrialists fear you are going to establish it.'

'I am not trying to cross any Rubicon, I am sitting on the banks of the Rubicon, waiting for consultation before I proceed but if *they* cross the Rubicon and attack me that is a very different thing.'

Tuesday 14 May
There was an article by Walter Terry in the *Daily Express* suggesting that Michael Foot and myself, Judith, Joan Lestor, Ian Mikardo and Hugh Scanlon were really trying to work towards an Allende-type Marxist Government in Britain. Michael Foot was the amiable one and I was the serious one who said less, which Frances thought was the nicest tribute to me that she had read.

At 10.15 Secretary came in and we had a further discussion on my speech on workers' control next Friday. He told me again that this was the crossing of the Rubicon because the words 'workers' control' were mentioned. He said, for the third time, that I must consult the Prime Minister. While we were talking, in came a letter from Robert Armstrong at Number 10 to Roy Williams saying, 'I understand that your Minister is making an important speech in his constituency on Friday and the Prime Minister wants to see the text.'

So I asked, 'How did Number 10 know? Nobody knows except Roy Williams, and you, Permanent Secretary.' He maintained he didn't know what I was talking about and I said, 'This information has been handed over to Number 10.' I must say I did blow up.

Another minute came in from Harold about collective Cabinet responsibility, reminding us of the Cabinet statement he read on 3 April 1969 following Jim Callaghan's opposition on the NEC to 'In Place of Strife.'

Wednesday 15 May
At 10 to Transport House for the Campaign Committee. I was asked to introduce my paper on Party strategy and I went through it bit by bit. It contained the key phrases about Ministers remaining political and being free to argue the case beyond the confines of their own in-

trays and also a note about the need to retain the enthusiasm of our supporters. Harold commented first. The British people need sympathy and understanding. People don't want to be told they must make a choice. There is a City crisis and we could have a serious world crisis because of the oil situation and the monetary crisis.

I said, 'We have to both present the crisis and be reassuring.'

Shirley said, 'The public may turn to a coalition. There is a fear that the plurality of our society will disappear and it would become like Eastern Europe.'

'I am not a Stalinist.' I said. 'I am in favour of a Referendum, of spreading power. I am in favour of democracy. You know that, Shirley.'

'Well, you are unique,' Shirley replied.

'This has got to stop,' said Jim. 'It's getting like a seminar.'

Thursday 16 May

Cabinet, where we began with Chile. I presented my paper that we should ask Rolls Royce to terminate the aero-engine contract. Jim maintained that the contract should be honoured, it was a political matter. The Communists were in favour of stopping supplies and the International Committee of the NEC was unrepresentative. Jim believed we should not isolate the Chileans. He proposed we should say to Rolls Royce, 'We don't wish to assist the regime, and there will be no further arms. But we will fulfil existing contracts and progressively bring them to an end.'

I complained of the fact that this was being made a Communist issue and Sir Thomas Brimelow, head of the Diplomatic Service, had been circulating Departments – or maybe just my Department – to find out how many Communists there were. Anyway, I won.

Then we moved on to the sale of Wasp helicopters to South Africa, and the Attorney-General warned that failure to supply the Wasps would be a breach of contract. Jim said, 'Don't send them because of Nigeria.' Denis and Harold said, 'Don't send them.' So we won on that.

I had a briefing on the Anglo-Soviet Joint Commission. Interestingly, the Foreign Office were warned that the Soviet aim was to dislodge us from the Common Market. I pressed Sir John Killick [Deputy Under-Secretary at the Foreign Office] on this and asked for evidence.

'By inference,' he said.

'What inference. After all the Russians deal with the Italians, the French, the Germans; why in our case should this be their objective?'

Of course they hadn't got a case, they were just scaremongering. We are apparently supposed to stop them pressing for a bigger trade delegation in London because it is thought it would be full of KGB people, apparently 80 per cent of them are, so the FO claim. But how can they know?

New Statesman, 17 March 1974.

Saturday 18 May

Went to Bristol to address the Workers' Educational Association on workers' control, which Harold had heard about and queried. They listened intently. I said it was a modest account of what a Minister could do, and there were some excellent questions about the working class's intelligence and how education needed to be re-shaped. We are at the beginning of a great movement that hasn't yet caught on – but it is coming.

Sunday 19 May

My relations with Harold are absolutely rock bottom. Tomorrow night there is a dinner at Number 10 for Academician Kirillin, and Harold hasn't invited me, though I am one of the principal Ministers (not that I want to go particularly). But I will have to consider how to improve my relations with him. He really does think that my public statements about 'open government' and so on, are destroying the Labour Party, whereas I think it is the only hope.

Monday 20 May

To Harold's room where the TUC-Labour Party Liaison Committee was having its monthly meeting. I wanted to be there because I had a paper in on the work of the Department to mobilise the support of the unions. It was a great innovation because Ministers don't normally present papers to Party colleagues describing what they are later going to put to Cabinet colleagues. But of course with Hugh Scanlon, Jack Jones, Alex Kitson of the TGWU, David Basnett and Alf Allen from USDAW there, not to mention Geoff Bish and others, it did open up the whole area of Cabinet discussion and developed very fully the idea of a parallel power structure.

Dashed away at 11.30 for the Anglo-Soviet Commission. There was no simultaneous translation which was a scandal, and the British interpreter was really lousy. At lunch, I had an interesting talk, sitting between Ambassador Lunkov and Kirillin. I asked what they thought of Giscard d'Estaing, the new French President. Kirillin said Giscard was chairman of the Franco-Soviet Commission and they liked him very much.

On the Common Market, Lunkov said Kosygin had asked him about the British re-negotiation and he had told him he thought the French would try to help with British problems. 'Of course,' he said, 'we don't like the Common Market but have to accept it as reality.' He believed we had to move towards a broader Europe.

Lunkov said the Soviet press didn't report much about the Watergate scandal, they simply based their news on the American press reports. But Walter Annenberg, the American Ambassador in London, had told Lunkov that Nixon would never resign even if he was impeached.

Dinner at Number 10 for Kirillin. I had queried the fact that I hadn't been invited so Harold put me back on his guest list. Harold spoke, beginning with a long, detailed description of all the negotiations with the Russians, describing dates, places, times, projects, what had happened. It was a display of his virtuosity of memory – amusing, though a bit egocentric.

As they were leaving, Peter Shore, Harold and myself stood on the steps of Number 10. It was a beautiful warm May evening and there were a few people watching from the other side of the road. Harold described how the Foreign Office had tried to get round the Cabinet proposals on the Chilean aircraft contract. He reminded us of a Ministry of Works memorandum to Attlee saying, 'We have read the Cabinet's proposals.' Attlee replied, 'The Cabinet does not propose, it decides.' So he has had a great fight with the Foreign Office and he is making a statement tomorrow on the Chile situation, which will be total victory. It couldn't be better. The Rolls Royce engines will not be overhauled and that is it.

I came home from the dinner feeling extremely happy. Stephen was here and that always cheers me up.

Tuesday 21 May

At 5 o'clock the conference room was crowded with fifty or sixty Rolls Royce/BAC shop stewards from Bristol, Herne, Fairford and Weybridge, and John Gilbert from the Treasury, Albert Booth, Frank Beswick and, bless him, Michael Foot which was really nice since he is so busy. They presented the case for Concorde. Then I said, 'My job is to represent the opinions submitted. Would it be right to say that the following was the case?' and I read out fourteen arguments which, in fact, were the contents of my Cabinet paper. I read it to them without saying it was a Cabinet paper and without saying it was my view, but simply stating that this was the view I was trying to represent. They were delighted with it.

Wednesday 22 May

The Public Enterprise Committee at Number 10 met this morning with Harold Wilson in the chair for the first time. I got the Meriden cooperative taken first, describing the background, the amount of effort the workers had put in, the support of Jack Jones, Geoffrey Robinson's contribution and the need to give them financial backing in the order of £4.5 – 6 million. I said it wasn't easy to find a project where you could have a degree of commitment as great as this, with workers prepared to take a drop in wages.

Joel Barnett was sympathetic but argued strongly that what I was suggesting would be disastrous: there was no real prospect of the project succeeding and it would wreck Dennis Poore's operations at Norton Villiers Triumph.

But it was agreed by the Committee that in principle we would support the proposal, provided the arrangements were worked out in detail.

In the evening I went over to the Russian Embassy, where I talked to Mikhail Suslov, a member of the Soviet Politburo, who, it is said, is a great KGB figure. He told me, 'All Foreign Office officials are useless. You can't talk to officials.' I said, 'That's our problem! We have to fight for what we want.' He said, 'Get an initiative taken at the top because we shan't take the initiative unless the British Government does.'

Kirillin had said a couple of things at dinner on Monday night which I forgot to record. I asked him about Trotsky, and he replied, 'No one in Russia has ever heard about Trotsky.' 'Don't you have Trotskyite groups? What do you discuss? What do young people talk about politically?' I asked.

'About Stalin.'

'Was Khrushchev's speech at the Twentieth Congress published? Is it still available?'

'It was never published.' He said something like, 'You should have a one-party state and then you needn't worry about Elections'. It was one of his jokes, pretty crude.

I mentioned to Terence Garvey, the British Ambassador in Moscow, who was at this evening's reception, what Suslov had said about the Foreign Office. He thought Suslov was just trying to make trouble for the British Government, between Ministers and officials and with the Americans and all that, and he pointed out that that was what one would expect from a senior member of the KGB.

Thursday 23 May

Today was quite a day. Almost the full text of my paper to the TUC-Labour Party Liaison Committee was in the business pages of *The Times* and was a major revelation of the work going on in the Department. The *Financial Times* had a summary of the Labour Party Working Party on Company Law. Other papers also had the full text or extracts of the new draft Manifesto (which Geoff Bish had written in case there was a n early Election) which contained a number of new commitments that hadn't been discussed in the Party's policy committees.

It was against this background that I went to the office for the ministerial meeting at 9.15. Eric Heffer, Michael Meacher and Frank Beswick were there. We discussed our growing dissatisfaction with the Department. First, there had not been the degree of help and commitment in the proposed Green Paper on industrial policy that was expected. Second, we knew that the Department played some part in stirring the Treasury to get Denis Healey to send on Monday a critical minute, denouncing my industrial policy. Third, the Department continued to put before us proposals on European issues that involved acceptance of the principle of entry. Fourth, in the case of my speech on workers' control, it was the Permanent Secretary who notified Number 10 in advance. Fifth, in respect of IPD, the old Fisher-Bendix works at Kirkby in Wilson's constituency, which is in trouble, Eric Heffer had not had enough help. Sixth, the Department had resolutely argued for cancellation of Concorde and had done all it could at official level to bring this about. These were some of the complaints and there were others, including the long delay in bringing forward Francis Cripps's proposals for handling the interim situation, and opposition to our plans for the Meriden cooperative.

At Cabinet we discussed Concorde and Elwyn Jones reported on the legal implications of cancellation. After I had given all the arguments in favour of carrying on, Denis Healey then launched into a long speech in which he said this was the moment to grasp the nettle; the money would come out of other Ministers' departmental budgets if it wasn't cancelled and that we should terminate regardless of whether the French agreed or not, though we could keep production going until October.

Jim, however, came out in favour of the aircraft, as did Peter Shore.

Roy Mason made a powerful speech in favour of continuation, citing the VC-10 and other cases.

Roy Jenkins said it should be cancelled, as did Reg Prentice, and it was quite clear that the only three Ministers who were in favour of cancellation at *any* cost, whatever the French said, were Healey, Jenkins and Prentice.

Harold began summing up that there was a general opinion in the Cabinet in favour of cancellation and that I should go and talk to the French Government to get this agreed.

I won one point – which would buy me more time – in saying that we would come back to the Cabinet to clear the negotiating brief after it had been considered by the Ministerial Committee for Concorde to which it will now be referred. I felt this discussion represented a major defeat but Harold said afterwards, 'You won, really.'

There was a massive crowd of Concorde workers outside Number 10. I went and had a chat with them, then slipped out through a side door to avoid the main body of demonstrators.

At 3.30 I had a meeting on appointments to public boards, beginning with the problem of finding suitable people for the Post Office and Rolls Royce. I announced that I wanted to publish all the vacancies with salaries and job specifications so that anyone who would like to be considered can write in, instead of people's names coming forward unofficially.

The Secretary objected strongly and said it would mean a thousand letters and twenty thousand staff-hours. I said, 'I will take responsibility if you will provide facilities for sending out acknowledgments with forms for people to fill in.' This threw him a bit. Michael Meacher said, 'If you got even one good one out of a thousand, that would be enormously worthwhile.' But the truth is I am eroding the Department's power to recommend people for appointments. It was a fascinating tussle.

Ray Tuite, Roy Williams, Frank McElhone and I went to Stanstead Airport and caught the HS-125 to Glasgow. I am dictating this at midnight in the Central Hotel.

The amusing news tonight is that Harold has made Marcia Williams a peer.

Friday 24 May

At 8 o'clock I went down for a working breakfast with John Warne, the Department of Industry's director for Scotland, the Regional Officer of the DTI, Ray Tuite, Roy Williams, Frank McElhone, Hugh Brown, MP for Provan, and the three people from the workers' cooperative who are trying to set up the *Scottish Daily News* – Allister Mackie, Chairman of the Action Committee, Hooper and MacGee. We talked for three quarters of an hour but although I gave my general sympathy and support I couldn't promise any money.

Afterwards, with Bruce Millan, Minister of State at the Scottish Office, to the STUC for two and a half hours. I described the outline of my general approach and then we discussed in some detail oil, steel and shipbuilding and other issues. A lot of old friends were there. I was told there was a deputation of yard conveners from Barclay Curle, which was owned until yesterday by Swan Hunter, who had sold it to Yarrows: the men had come because their workers had not been consulted.

Four men came in in their working clothes, intelligent pawns in the game, expressing their bitterness that they had been encouraged by the management to do 'consultative exercises' with them to improve relations in the yard, and just as they reached a peak, they were told the yard had been sold and they would now have to queue up for a job at Yarrows. They would lose money out of it, might well be dismissed, and you could see them just wringing their hands with rage at the way the workforce had been treated. Nobody cares what happens to workers. The Establishment just take them for granted. If the middle class were treated in the same way, the country would have a full-blooded revolution within twenty-four hours. It is astonishing how class-oriented we are.

I went to the Central Hotel and gave a press conference at which I spoke most sharply about the way both the newspaper workers and the Barclay Curle workers had been treated.

Afterwards, I had a word about oil with the Lord Provost, Bill Gray, a rather dreamy, philosophical, distinguished-looking man, a lawyer by profession. I went to meet the Reverend Geoff Shaw, Labour leader of Strathclyde Council representing 2.5 million people.

We talked about the development of my industrial policy and I said I hoped local government would develop an industrial role. Just as we were leaving the Glasgow City Chambers, I had a message that I was to fly back to London at once for a Cabinet; but since I hadn't the least desire to miss any of the rest of the programme and as the jet couldn't be got up in time, I ignored it.

To the Post Office where I was introduced to the Regional Director, the Head Postmaster and the management, the union representative,

UPW and others. I told them we were going to deal with their pay problems separately. A complete syndicalism has developed between management and labour, they just come together in a way one would never have thought possible before. It is a most interesting development in the nationalised industries.

From there to the Scottish Business School where I talked with all the youngsters from Strathclyde, Glasgow and Edinburgh Universities. I was asked a wide range of questions which were quite immature because although they had learned all the techniques of business management, they had no experience. It confirmed my suspicion of qualifications as a pre-requisite for positions of authority. What we need is more experience, with education available as a back-up to supplement and deepen that experience.

A Rolls Royce delegation from Hillingdon came to see me about Concorde and I was as candid as I could be. At the end I took the convener aside and said, 'Just one word – very important and don't ever say it came from me, but everything depends on the French Government standing firm. I am going to fight Denis Healey like a tiger to see he doesn't get rid of Concorde.'

That was the end of my official programme and I was still being followed in a car by two Special Branch men who had been tailing me all day. Finally, at about 9.45, I arrived at Abbotsinch Airport, said goodbye and caught the plane to Stanstead. Ron Vaughan picked me up and I slept in the car, and got home at 1.15, washed out and exhausted. But it was useful and enjoyable and I am at my happiest out of the office.

Tuesday 28 May

The Irish situation is getting even more serious and Brian Faulkner, Leader of the Unionist Party, and the power-sharing executive have resigned today. Harold, being basically pro-Catholic as I am, will not want to have much truck with the Protestants. On the other hand, he is a realist and he won't want the Cabinet to reach any decision at all until he is absolutely sure that he has the support of all the Cabinet members including the Catholics – Bob Mellish and Shirley Williams – and the pro-Protestants Fred Peart, Willie Ross, Peter Shore, Jim Callaghan, Merlyn Rees. It will be interesting to see how the rest divide.

Wednesday 29 May

Francis Cripps thinks there is a big Treasury counter-attack coming and the proposed Green Paper on industrial policy needs to be re-drafted a bit to take account of the points they are likely to make. He thinks there are four lines of attack. First, suggesting the planning agreements be limited to the top twenty-five companies instead of the top 180. Second, that the paper covers a more limited range of activities. Third, that we leave the big companies with their existing incentives. Fourth, that the National Enterprise Board be simply a State Holding Company and that the public ownership be done by acquisition through individual Acts of Parliament. Of course, if this were the policy, it would completely destroy everything that was contained in the Labour Party Manifesto.

Friday 31 May
Roy Williams came in to check the amendments I had proposed, concerning specific industrial and regional points, to Jim Callaghan's speech on the renegotiation of the terms of British membership of the EEC. However, I noticed in a telegram that had been copied to me, that Jim had already sent the advanced draft of his speech yesterday to the Ambassador in Brussels to show to other EEC Governments, and therefore the original draft, even without my own amendments, is bound to be the basis for his speech. Put simply, he has sold out on the central question of British sovereignty, and appears to think that the industrial and regional policy aspects are not worth emphasising as major points for re-negotiation. This is not accidental. It means, first of all, that he doesn't attach importance to industrial policy and secondly that if the Common Market rules prevented us developing our own industrial policy in accordance with the Manifesto, he would not be sorry to see these restraints imposed on me in the present political situation.

This is the only conclusion I can reach. I will consider writing Harold a personal letter through my private network saying that a political point I want to make and get on the record is that I am not at all happy with the way the re-negotiation policy is going. I don't want him to be under any misapprehension about the line I am likely to take at the end of the re-negotiation. I don't trust the Civil Service network.

Sunday 2 June
Lord Rothschild rang to say he was interested in my ideas to get public appointments made more open and asked if he could send me a private letter at my home address. I feel I get on well with him. Also I have supported some of the papers prepared by his Central Policy Review Staff and suggested they should be published; Rothschild is a great believer in open government and has upset Whitehall which, of course, doesn't like it. He supported me a bit on Meriden, which I appreciate, so I think he is quite a useful ally to have. Certainly he would be a dangerous enemy.

Roy Jenkins has refused to let the Price sisters serve their sentence in the Armagh jail in Northern Ireland, which I think is a great mistake. Whether they will actually starve themselves to death is another matter.* But you cannot treat people who regard themselves as prisoners of war exactly as if they were common criminals. You just can't do it.

At 6.30 people began arriving for our party: Albert Booth, Eric Heffer, Michael Meacher and Ken Coates. We had a really good evening talking about Ireland and the need ultimately to have a strategy of withdrawal from Northern Ireland.

Monday 3 June

I went to speak at Eastbourne to the National Union of Sheet Metalworkers, a very old union. My speech, which had been very carefully prepared, went down like a pancake on a wet pavement. No real response. Afterwards we sat round and talked about it to some of the men. They said, 'Workers are suspicious. They don't believe what's happening. They think all this involvement is a substitute for real power, and they know that they have real power, if they want to use it. They want socialism', and so on.

I think many unions are in a sense saying, 'We want the whole thing or we shall just use our veto because we can deal with management at any time we like so long as Government keeps out of the way.'

An Irish prisoner Michael Gaughan died of pneumonia tonight during his hunger strike and there was a big demonstration outside Roy Jenkins's house. We locked all the windows and doors in case they decided to come round and have a crack at us, since we don't have police protection. Political life is just full of hazards, and there is nothing you can do about it.

The first day's debate on Northern Ireland today showed the two Front Benches absolutely at one in their view and I think I may well be in a minority when I say in Cabinet that I believe we should withdraw from Northern Ireland as soon as we can on a phased, orderly basis, beginning by setting a date.

Tuesday 4 June

There was an amusing incident today. The visiting Bulgarian Minister of Trade had given me as a parting gift a tablecloth and a little Bulgarian calculating machine, a tiny hand-held one in beautiful yellow, which had a memory. It was a lovely thing. The department that advises on gifts said I could keep the tablecloth but that the

---

* Dolours and Marion Price, serving life imprisonment sentences in Brixton for car-bombings in London in 1973, were on hunger strike to try to get themselves transferred to Northern Ireland prisons. In March 1975 they succeeded.

calculator was too valuable and it should be for office use only. I asked today what had happened to it and was told it had been sent away to be debugged in case it had a recording device in it, and when the technicians had looked at it closely, they had were been enormously impressed by the quality of its circuitry, which they said was the best they had seen among American, German and Japanese examples. They were very puzzled by how the Bulgarians could have got hold of such marvellous technology. So it could be that Britain is reduced to copying the Bulgarians, though if that happens we really are finished!

Had tea with Norman Buchan, who is a Minister of State at Agriculture, Fisheries and Food. He poured his heart out to me. 'Do you realise that Fred Peart has abandoned his opposition to the Market?'

'Of course. I think everybody in the Cabinet knows he has completely swung over. He is just a shell of his former self.'

'It's worse than that,' said Norman, 'he doesn't read his papers. He signs everything he is given and is drunk half the time, and anyway he was only against the Market when he was last Minister of Agriculture because Sir John Winnifrith, his Permanent Secretary, was passionately anti-Market, and now the man who guides him on these matters, Freddie Kearns, is passionately pro-Market.' I am not surprised about Sir John Winnifrith's influence. He is a very tough character.

A group of Scottish Labour MPs – Hugh Brown, Tam Dalyell, George Lawson, John White, Harry Ewing and John Robertson – came to see me at the House about the workers' newspaper cooperative in Glasgow. They were absolutely persuaded that the workers were serious people who ought to be supported. The most amazing thing of all was that George Lawson, who is a dour, tough, right-wing, pro-Market MP and a stern critic of mine, said he believed the workers' cooperative was something that reflected the best in my ideas and he felt it was something we should support. It was like getting a kiss and a hug in public from Roy Jenkins. It did indicate that there has been a shift of opinion. I told them to go and canvass other Ministers and I would do my best.

Wednesday 5 June
The gunfire in the press about our industrial policy continues, with the *Daily Telegraph* reporting an attack by Marcus Sieff, 'Marks, Marcus and Marxist – St Michael Versus St Anthony'.

At 9.30 Miscellaneous Committee 28 met at the Cabinet Office. Coming out, I talked to Michael Foot and said I would put in a note to him of my view on the next stage of our incomes policy, along the lines that:

1. All salaries should be published.

2. Top salaries should be negotiated like all wages using a standard pattern of negotiation without all these review bodies.

3. The Treasury might have a ten-to-one ratio, saying that salaries more than ten times as much as the lowest paid person in the firm or organisation would be subject to tax penalties.

4. There should be a universal threshold and a flat rate rise for everybody which would deal with the problem of inflation.

5. Most wage negotiations should be conducted at the plant level and we should be quite candid and say that incomes policy *is* unfair but in asking people to accept unfairness, we are offering them greater power and some perspective of social change.

Michael was quite struck.

Lunch at Locket's with Hugh Scanlon, the first time we had had a proper talk together. We began on Northern Ireland and he thought Len Murray had been wrong to go on that march to stop the Ulster Workers' strike* because you shouldn't strike break. A very interesting point, considering the intimidation by the Ulster Workers' Council.

We moved to my Green Paper on industrial policy and I asked him, 'Why don't the unions push harder to get the Labour Government to implement radical policies?'

'Because they don't think it is real. What they say to themselves is "Why go out on a limb now for a policy to be published which we know can't be implemented?"' He went on, 'Tony, as far as you are concerned, you must not get isolated from the trade union movement. The trade unions support you very strongly but don't go out on a limb now and get the blame for losing the next Election.' It was an incredibly cautious thing to say. He then asked if I'd talked to Jack Jones about it all.

'Yes,' I said, 'but does Jack Jones really care about the transformation of society?'

'Exactly. He is up to his neck in it with Harold Wilson. Right up to the top.'

So I commented, 'I think Harold Wilson, Michael Foot and Jack Jones run the country. But what happens if there isn't an early Election? We may find then that our policy has gone by the board.'

'I had assumed that there was going to be one in September and therefore you would only have to wait a few weeks.'

---

* A general strike was called by the Protestant-led Ulster Workers' Council in May 1974, and speedily ended the experiment in power-sharing in the province, inaugurated at the Sunningdale meeting in December 1973.

'Well, how can I get the case across if I can't publish the Green Paper now?' Then I added, 'Hugh, I know you are neutral on the Common Market, feeling that it is not a matter of principle.'

'Yes,' he replied. 'If capitalism is going to survive, it doesn't matter whether it survives here or in the Common Market and while we have got it, we may as well have prosperous capitalism. That's been my general attitude. After re-negotiation, I think the AUEW will still be firmly against, except I must tell you that Reg Birch, on our Executive, who is a member of the Communist Party (Marxist/Leninist), has come out strongly in favour of the Common Market in line with what is being said in Peking because the Chinese are now very anti-Russian and pro-Common Market. He has joined forces with Johnnie Boyd. I think you will find the TUC are wobbly about this in the end as they were on the National Industrial Relations Court. I can't be absolutely sure but I think they would vote against staying in on unacceptable terms.'

Went back to the office and Jack Spriggs the AUEW convener and Dick Jenkins the TGWU convener from the old Fisher-Bendix works in Kirkby, came to see me. Harold Wilson as the local MP had got Fisher-Bendix sold-off to Thorn Electrical in 1971 and the firm was then bought by this odd set-up called IPD which is now not viable and is asking us to save more than 1,200 jobs. I must say, Spriggs and Jenkins made a powerful impression. I told them what the position was, and they said, 'The plain truth is the last Government was ready to help us and you apparently are not.' It was the human case against the chartered accountants' case and every time I hear it, I am struck by it.

Thursday 6 June
Lunch at ICI with Chairman Jack Callard, and his directors – Robert Haslam, Maurice Hodgson and Ray Pennock. They asked me bluntly, 'Do you believe in profits?'

'Yes, if you mean a return on capital. No, if you mean an unequal distribution of income.'

Then they asked, 'What about ICI? Will you give a promise that ICI won't be nationalised?'

One chap, whom I liked very much, said, 'You know, as a citizen, I agree with you entirely but of course ICI is a successful company. What about profitable companies?'

I said, 'Let me put it to you like this. I couldn't nationalise ICI unless there was a case for it. You are successful, you have a good investment record, good exports, good industrial relations. What concerns me at the moment is poor industrial performance. You know, the arrangements are all wrong, the framework is all wrong, we haven't solved basic problems.'

'Can I quote you on that at a shop stewards' meeting?' asked Callard.

'Well, you speak for yourself and I'll speak for myself. I'll come and address the shop stewards, if you like!'

We went on to discuss democracy, and I pointed out that I was accountable to a lot of people, and they said, 'Yes but you ought to show leadership.'

'Maybe,' I said, 'But these people are suffering great injustice and they want to correct it. I think they are right.'

'Well, tell them to work harder – an honest day's work for an honest day's pay.'

It was very primitive stuff, and there was a deep feeling that people were ignorant and you couldn't trust them. That is the key – the main political question is whether you trust people or whether you don't, and if you don't, then you are left with excuses for retaining power yourself.

Friday 7 June
Roy Williams rang me in Bristol to say that Number 10 were livid that I had agreed to do *The World This Weekend* on Sunday without consulting them, and the Prime Minister wanted a written statement from me about it. Harold had also heard about my Nottinghamshire Miners' Gala speech tomorrow and wanted that sent across. How Number 10 got to hear about that I don't know. The real issue between Harold and me is the right of a Minister to be political, and Roy Williams and Ray Tuite said they had never known a Minister treated in this way. I shall write to Harold saying I understand that it not being sent across was an oversight, and just leave it at that. It doesn't help to look provoked at the moment: and if I don't react, it gives me a position of moral ascendancy over Harold, which I think is important.

Saturday 8 June
Got to Mansfield, having been driven from Derby, and marched with Len Murray and Don Concannon on the Nottinghamshire Miners' Gala. Ken Coates was there; the Bishop of Southwell made a speech of dedication, then Len Murray talked about the need for unity and the need for the trade union movement to restrain its own demands.

Sunday 9 June
The papers all covered the speech in Nottinghamshire yesterday, more or less in full, which showed the benefit of a short clear press release.

Ronald Butt of the *Sunday Times* had an article called 'The Vacuum at the heart of the Tory Party,' saying there was a complete collapse of intellectual activity in the Tory Party and that the Labour Party was driving ahead confidently and developing its policy over a wide area, notably in the Department of Industry. It indicates that we must look more frightening to them then we do to ourselves.

Monday 10 June
There was a meeting with George Edwards, Chairman of BAC, about Concorde. He handed me a letter attacking the British Airways figures and I suggested he might give me further information on the French. Roger Hird, my second Private Secretary, was in the room writing away, and I said, 'Put down your pencil, we are having a private talk.'

In the corridor and the lift, I had a further chance to talk to George and I told him the whole story. 'The Cabinet have told me to go forward and suggest that we discontinue, but if the French insist on producing sixteen planes we shall go ahead. Therefore, without breathing a word that you have heard this from me, your job is to persuade the French to make such a demand and then we shall have to build them. It is not very reputable but I have reached the point where I shall fight any way I can to keep it going because I know it is right, and there is a complete collapse of morale in the top leadership of this country. I know you don't agree with my ideology, George, and a lot of things I say but unless we pull ourselves up by the bootstraps, we are finished.'

So we left it that I could contact him any time I like – I have his home telephone number now.

I had a word at 12.30 with Part, who was in a very detached mood. He had been on holiday although he knew these were the two weeks when the Green Paper should have come forward, and now he has arrived back hoping it would be on its way to Whitehall where he could say he had nothing to do with it. But he is back just in time for some very important discussions. I told him he would get a draft of the Green Paper in his box tonight and we would discuss it again tomorrow. Frances Morrell had wisely said, 'You have got to commit Part, as your principal adviser, to it. That is what he is paid to do and he must sit through it.' So I am not doing this without the Secretary being present and I more or less pointed this out. 'Well,' he said, 'the planning agreements are all right but the NEB will cause trouble. The question is, do you want to alienate people for that little extra advantage?' That is the way in which he treats the Manifesto commitment; but I am much tougher now and I dug my toes in.

At 3.30 I saw Maurice Edelman [Labour MP for Coventry North-West], George Park [Labour MP for Coventry North-East], and unions from the machine tool manufacturers Alfred Herbert in Coventry. The Alfred Herbert contingent said they had no confidence in the management. Two years ago there were no orders because of the recession, now the finances were shaky and they were borrowing money they would have to repay, and they would go bankrupt.

I said, 'I'm glad you came to see me before there's real trouble. You read the papers, you know the score as well as I do. I personally think the firm ought to be brought into public ownership but I haven't got the powers to do that. So I suggest that I write to Neale Raine, Chief Executive of Alfred Herbert, and say that you have been to see me to express your anxiety, your lack of confidence in the management, and I will suggest that a management study be set up to look at the company, to receive evidence from and report to the unions, the management and the Government. In the light of that, you can make recommendations to me and I'll consider what to do.'

They were delighted. My officials looked sick. I have never seen two people look so shocked at the way in which I handled it. But somehow, I have seen a shaft of light; I know clearly why I am there. I am there to look after our people, and what good people they are. The brief given to me – 'that the Secretary of State thanked them for coming' and 'he is well aware of the importance of the firm' – is just a complete con.

At the Tribune Group there were about forty MPs present and I was asked to say a word. I briefly spoke about the note I had put out to the TUC-Labour Party Liaison Committee. I said, 'I would have liked help from the movement. It is not that I mind being on my own but the movement has got to be clear whether it wants this policy carried through or not.'

I felt it was warm and friendly. Towards the end of the meeting, Audrey Wise said. 'If you look round, big business is only attacking the Department of Industry and we can't leave Tony to take the fire himself.'

Then Dennis Skinner who was in the chair took it up and he said, 'We [i.e. the Tribune Group] should have collared all the specialist groups but we didn't organise for it. We can still join the Trade and Industry Group. We can go to the PLP meeting on Wednesday when Tony is describing the work of his Department and we can support him there against members of the Party who are critical of the policy.'

At 5.30 I went to the Home Policy Committee of the NEC and the item I was interested in was taken out of turn because I had to go to see the Meriden men. I said, 'I have nothing very much to say except that my TUC-Labour Party Liaison Committee paper has been leaked to the press and I would just like permission to declassify it and issue it as an information note.'

Fred Mulley said, 'That's most unusual, to declassify because a thing is leaked. If Tony Benn wants to issue it, he can issue it himself but we as a committee ought not to release it.'

I replied, 'But *I* never classified it. It wasn't private, I didn't leak it.

But now it is out, it would be very helpful to be able to give people an indication of what we are doing.'

In the end, it was agreed it would be declassified and I will get it circulated in the Whip's Office and available for the PLP meeting on Wednesday.

So I left early and at 6.30 Bill Lapworth and Dennis Johnson from Meriden came to see me. I told them that Harold Lever and Joel Barnett had seen Poore, and Poore had been negative – which they no doubt encouraged – and therefore they were recommending to Cabinet that regretfully we didn't support the cooperative. The men were very shocked; how they hated Harold Lever who had said he didn't believe in cooperatives.

So then I said, 'Let's be simple. Let's sit down together and plan how we beat it. First of all, tell me what will happen if this recommendation goes through the Cabinet.'

Dennis Johnson said, 'Poore will take legal action. He will move in trucks. His writ names thirty-one people, including Bill Lapworth. I am not going to respond to the writ and I may be arrested. There will be mass demonstrations in Coventry.'

I said, 'Thank you very much for telling me that because I have a duty to alert the Cabinet. I suggest you issue a statement to the press tonight so it's in the papers tomorrow morning, saying you have been to see me and that if Poore sabotages the cooperative you will produce a new scheme in which Meriden operates on its own, and you ask for time to prepare that and submit it.' So they did that from my room. While they were sitting there, I scribbled on a piece of paper 'and the Minister said he would give full consideration to the proposals made'.

Tuesday 11 June
Had an hour and threequarters' meeting on the draft Green Paper. Part said he thought that the new draft needed re-writing and ended up by saying that the NEB would be highly controversial in Whitehall; other Departments were already saying at an official level that it was a Marxist document.

'Well, the policy is in the Manifesto,' Eric Heffer reminded him.

After some discussion I spoke. I was very grateful to the Secretary, glad to have him back and I thought there was an awful lot in what he said. The Green Paper was really an argument. I thought we should underplay it much more. It does need re-writing. We were looking for a new consensus around which people could rally.

Part responded, 'If you talk about social objectives, there would be a lot of assent. Officials, however, at the moment will think it is a political tract – all dogma and no content – and therefore they will tend to wash their hands of it.' For example, he thought Michael

Meacher had gone too far on the multinationals.

Peter Carey then said he thought it was too polemical for Whitehall, and Ron Dearing [Under-Secretary, Department of Industry] said, 'Don't attack the multinationals.'

'All right, we won't attack them, but we mustn't defend them,' retorted Eric.

Part said, 'The multinationals are growing and we mustn't be like King Canute.'

It was a good discussion and at the end I said. 'OK, Alan Lord [Principal Finance Officer] will re-write the preface; Michael Meacher, Ron Dearing, Francis and Frances will look at the NEB again; the officials should write the planning agreement and we will meet again next Monday.'

There were three items on the agenda at the Public Enterprise Committee of Cabinet, first being the Meriden crisis. Joel Barnett and Harold Lever recommended that in view of what Geoffrey Robinson and Dennis Poore had said to them, the whole thing should be dropped. I fought like a tiger – I have never fought harder than I did there. To my amazement I got away with it. I have lost all respect for Harold Lever and Barnett too, the way they have handled this. If I had accepted their recommendation, there would have been endless trouble.

On IPD, I said I was very reluctant, but I felt you could not sack 1200 people even though it was a bum firm. So it was agreed that the firm should go bust, that we should tell the Receiver we intend to buy the factory and set up a company for it, have a feasibility study and save the jobs as best we could. A sort of legalised work-in. That was not a bad conclusion.

I dashed over to the husbands-and-wives' dinner, with Barbara and Ted, John Silkin and Rosamund, Peter and Liz and Tony and Judith. I told them I have now declassified my Home Policy Committee document, and it will be available at the PLP for them to see tomorrow. I added that I was under heavy pressure and I wanted a bit of support.

Barbara turned on me. 'You with your open government, with your facile speeches, getting all the publicity, pre-empting resources – "I'm the big spender, I can't do it without money" – trying to be holier than thou and more left wing than me.' She was extremely angry with me. 'I know we can *only* get this expenditure if we go for a statutory wages policy,' she said, revealing once again her hatred for the trade unions.

I said, 'Look Barbara, I haven't spent a penny, you've had pensions, the nurses' increase, I haven't been allowed to spend a penny. I'm thinking about future policy, and the only job I've been given is to sack 21,000 people in my own constituency on Concorde. I have never said anything about pre-empting resources because I know that has got to be done collectively, but I am simply developing a case.'

But she retorted, 'How are we going to solve the problems?'

'We're going to solve them by trading off wealth for power,' I replied. 'We have got to admit it is an unfair society, and give people a perspective, and I am not prepared to accept that Britain is declining.' My God, Barbara's hatred really came out. I think she is feeling guilty.

Wednesday 12 June

A remarkable day. The papers this morning were full of headlines like, 'All Out Attack on Benn', 'Wilson Rebuffs Benn', 'Wilson to Take Over Industrial Policy' after my interim report on industrial policy to the TUC-Labour Party Liaison Committee had been published.

We had our weekly political meeting this morning. We began with my minute on the political work of my Ministers. Eric didn't like that. He didn't like being told that he was collectively responsible for Government decisions. He didn't like being told that the Prime Minister's Minute on Procedure was there to guide us all. He told me that he was so fed up with getting minutes from Harold about speeches, that he asked his office to tell Number 10 that he didn't wish to have any more minutes from Harold on this subject. I must say his effrontery is superb.

Then we went on to discuss the reports about Harold taking over the Department of Industry. Frances said, 'Don't get worried. It's an old news story. It may not be true.' Eric blew his top again. 'Of course, Harold can't take over the Department of Industry; it just can't be done.' In fact, Number 10 rang up to say they hadn't given that briefing. But Joe Haines gave a further briefing at lunch time, all of which appeared in the *Evening Standard*. The fact is that there is a war between us and Number 10 at the moment and there is no point pretending there isn't. But we want to keep very calm.

This morning on the way in to the office, Ron Vaughan told me he had heard on the news that the BSC plant at Cruise Hole in St George in Bristol had a fire last night and families were evacuated. So I rang the *Evening Post* from the car to get the details and then gave orders that the plant was to be closed for two days. I rang back the *Evening Post* again and said, 'Clear your front page and say "Benn shuts plant".' Actually it was all *ultra vires*; I don't think I had any power to do it and this was brought to my attention by officials later in the day.

Thursday 13 June

The press this morning reported Ted Heath's attack on me yesterday where he called me a Commissar and compared my plans with those of Eastern Europe. 'Commissar Benn by Ted' was one paper's headline. But there was a sensitive article by Maurice Corina in *The Times*, saying

I had been working hard on this policy and I hadn't been glad-handing it around.

Flew to Blackpool for the POEU conference and straight to the Savoy Hotel, and I tried to sleep for an hour because I hadn't got to bed until 3.30 and was up at 7. I was extremely tired, almost too tired to sleep.

My speech was cleared and ready. An old Welshman, who had picked me up from the airport, came and spoke to me just before I got up to address the conference. He said, 'You know, Tony, not many people in the movement express themselves very well but you really have got into a position where the grass roots understand what you are saying. And I will tell you that nine years ago when you first came to a POEU conference, I tape-recorded your speech and I played it as I went round the country as a political education officer for the union and people used to applaud the tape. I just wanted you to know that.' I was deeply touched.

I got a marvellous welcome from the delegates. Of course, the Heath attack on me as a Commissar was a gift and, as I took off my coat and stood up in a blue shirt with a POEU tie, I said, 'I am wearing my Commissar's uniform, and my tape-recorder is my bodyguard so that when I read about it in the *Daily Express* tomorrow, I will know what I really said.' I gave the speech which was really a plea for workers' control in the Post Office.

Back in London I had a meeting about British Steel Corporation appointments because Ralph Bateman, the President of the CBI, (who incidentally today delivered a tremendous attack on me in Bath about Communism and my being a disaster) has resigned from the BSC. I had them all in and I said, 'Well, I'll advertise the vacancy.' This was a slight shock.

Secretary said, 'That would have to go to Number 10.'

I replied, 'That is entirely for me to deal with on the ministerial net. I don't want this to go to Number 10 on the official network,' not then knowing – and I still can't prove – that there had already been some leakage to Number 10. 'I might make a short-list of names.'

'Well,' said Secretary, 'Perhaps you shouldn't announce that at the same time. If you do it later, you will get twice the publicity.'

'That is a very cynical remark, Secretary.' I'm afraid that my relations with Part are absolutely at rock bottom.

At 6.30 we had an enormous meeting on Meriden in my room at the House of Commons which lasted about four hours. I told them that I had been given authority to try to see if we could set up a cooperative. I was absolutely determined not to let the Meriden people down. We really had to choose between two basic solutions: the first, the Robinson plan to make Meriden work within NVT; and the second, whereby I shall go flat out to try to get the independent Meriden cooperative working.

Friday 14 June

There was a message from Number 10 that the Prime Minister has said I am not to make any more speeches on industrial policy until he has had the chance of a word with me, with no date fixed for that. So I said to Roy Williams, 'I shall take no notice of that whatsoever.' You can't tell a Secretary of State not to make speeches.

Robert Armstrong had also sent a message from Number 10 referring to a piece in the *Daily Telegraph* on Monday that I was thinking of changing the system of appointments by letting it be known publicly that there were vacancies: the Prime Minister has said that is not to be done without consultation with him because it affects the whole Government. I shall take no notice of that either.

Because I am using my authority, I am being stopped at every point. Harold Lever and Joel Barnett had protested about the Meriden meeting last night, particularly that a statement had gone out to the press. Well, there was nothing wrong with that, so I had a sharp word with Harold Lever and said he couldn't have read the statement or he would have understood. He was simply hopping mad behind the charm and friendliness. He is, of course, bitterly hostile to any type of industrial change and when you press beyond the smile, you come up against the hard man. I said he wasn't Secretary of State for Industry; he wasn't asked to report on what I had done.

Roger Hird came in and asked if I would agree my brief for my Brussels visit on Tuesday. I said, 'What do you mean? I never agree my brief, I am just given my brief.'

'Yes', he said, 'but the FO want you to agree it.'

'I am not going to.'

If I am asked to agree my brief for Brussels, that, in effect, means I read the Foreign Office brief in favour of staying within the Community and once I have agreed it, it then becomes a document that can be quoted back to me: 'Secretary of State agreed in his brief on 18 June . . .'

'In that case,' he said, 'how have you consulted with the Foreign Office?'

'The Foreign Secretary can have a word with me if he likes and the Foreign Office can send notes over. But if I change the brief because I don't agree with it, it will go back to the Foreign Office who will change it back, with a minute from the Foreign Secretary saying I have got to do what he tells me. After that I will be stuck. If I simply receive the notes without comment that's fine.'

So Roger Hird said, 'You may be in breach of collective Cabinet responsibility.'

'I know that but that is my problem, not yours,' and he went out.

Then I had a candid talk to Roy Williams. 'Look. This is what is really happening. All my industrial and regional policy in respect of Europe is being taken away and put under the Foreign Secretary's control. My Green Paper is being blocked by the Treasury, by the Chancellor's minute. My day-to-day business is now being watched by Harold Lever and Joel Barnett. All my speeches are controlled, and indeed I have been told by the Prime Minister not to speak or broadcast. And as regards appointments, the Prime Minister has said I am not to proceed even by letting it be known there are vacancies. This is the position I am in and do you wonder that, frustrated within Whitehall, I turn outside, where my support is?'

Roy Williams, who is a shrewd chap, said, 'Well, you know, Secretary of State, having seen you at Blackpool at that POEU conference, I do realise what fantastic support there is and what a strength it must be.'

'Honestly, Roy, it is not that I want a boost, but that is where the support is and whether I am a Minister or not is of marginal interest to me because all of that will continue after I leave office. I will just have to run this as best I can. You mustn't worry and if the worst comes to the worst, I'll discontinue press releases and do street interviews instead.'

Saturday 15 June
This morning, the papers said 'Wilson Backs Benn', which is very fraudulent in view of what he is doing privately, but still he felt he had to come out and support me, which is good. My speech in Bristol in favour of free enterprise for the small firm was well reported in terms of the small firms being enterprising and the big firms being remote and impersonal. But the difference between the big firm and the small firm is what the mixed economy argument is all about, and this is the way I shall present it in the forthcoming motion of censure put down by the Tories against the Government's industrial policy.

James Margach said to me today, 'Your colleagues now see you as a new Bevan or Stafford Cripps and they are very frightened.'

Tomorrow is our silver wedding anniversary party and Caroline has done all the work for it. I have done nothing at all, but I did record a whole selection of family sound archives including the first record I gave to her, in 1948 and hers to me, our recording at Coney Island in 1949 just before we were married, our wedding, and other family occasions.

Monday 17 June
At 2.30 I went to see Harold. Frances had said to me, 'Just make three points. The campaign is going very well and the Tories are on the run;

you come along and brief against me and it undermines my position; and that gives the Tory campaign a fresh lease of life.' So I went along to say that and, God, he made about thirteen points during the course of that hour and a half. He was red and angry and sounded bitter.

'What is your strategy?' he asked gruffly.

So I described it to him. I said I didn't disagree with his view on industrial policy.

'Why are you having this "debate"? You are only helping the Tories. Why haven't you produced a bill? Anyway, who said there should be a Green Paper? We don't want a prolonged *debate* about it. We want legislation. You have been lazy, you haven't got on with it, you have just been making all these speeches. We are in Government now. Why don't you get on with the policy? As to Ministers on the National Executive just causing confusion voting against each other, we might have to consider Ministers not being on the Executive.'

'I would greatly regret that, Harold, but you sent round a note about Ministers on the Executive, reminding us of your rebuke to Jim Callaghan over "In Place of Strife" years ago.'

He said, 'I notice you have been disobeying all my rules of Procedure for Ministers.'

'I didn't reply to any of them but I do not accept them. They have never been published. They have never been collectively discussed with me and I do not accept them.' So I got that on the record.

'What about this NEC resolution about the Common Market?'

I said, 'That's fair enough. That's the Party preparing itself for the end of the renegotiation period.'

'It's a direct attack on the Cabinet.'

I said, 'Not at all. It's nothing to do with the Cabinet.'

'You can't separate yourself.'

'I don't agree with that,' I said. 'I am also a member of the Party. I am concerned with the Party business.'

'I can only tell you Jim has threatened to resign.'

'That's up to him. A lot of people threaten to resign.'.

'Why are you doing it? Why are you doing it *now*? *Why*?'

I said, 'Look Harold, I read in the *Sunday Times* a complete account of what happens in the Cabinet Committee on Europe –'

'Of which you are not a member,' he interrupted.

'No,' I said. 'But it was quite accurate, saying the Foreign Office had beaten the Party; the Party needs to be reassured. I must tell you honestly, Harold, that I have been fairly neutral on the Market up until the Election.'

'Oh no you weren't. Do you remember what you said at Tiverton in 1972?'

'About boycotting the European Parliament?'

'Yes,' he said, 'and that if the Conference decided to vote for Britain to withdraw, the leadership would have to accept it.'

'Yes, but I changed that when it was taken to be personal to you. Anyway, I was saying that I *was* neutral. But now that I have been a Minister and have seen the effect of the Common Market destroying the authority of Ministers and parliamenary democracy, I am bitterly hostile, I may as well tell you. And if the Party wants a special Conference on the Common Market you will have to give your view.'

He said, 'What happens if I don't go to the Conference?'

'That's up to you.'

'And what happens if the Cabinet disagrees with the Conference?'

I said, 'That might happen anyway. We have got to face the facts and I am certainly not pursuing pro-Marketeers. They would be free to disagree.'

'Oh, so you think that as a member of the Cabinet you would be free?'

I said, 'We have never discussed that. I don't know what view would be taken.'

'Why are you doing it now?' he repeated. Then he continued, 'I hear also from Jim that you are going to call for Treaty amendments when you go to Brussels tomorrow.'

'I am doing no such thing. I will do exactly what the Party requires. I am going to probe.'

He went on, 'Why don't you work harder instead of making all these speeches? Why don't you behave more as you did when you were in the Ministry of Technology?'

'I work very hard indeed.'

'But why do you make all these speeches instead of putting your policy forward?'

I said I didn't agree with that assessment.

'Well, you are not working as a member of a team.'

'I absolutely reject that, Harold. Not only do I make speeches in support of all Ministers, but when my civil servants turn up with a letter to undermine another Minister, I tear it up. I won't send it. That's more than can be said for other Ministers.'

'Well, they don't think you're a member of the team. Now, on broadcasting, why do you get all this exposure?'

I said, 'I get messages twice a day saying I'm *not* to broadcast – one even came in stopping me from doing *The World at One* before I had actually been invited.'

'Well, that's because we knew you were preparing for it. You realise why I didn't want you to do *The World at One*.'

'I was told you thought it would blank out your speech at Swansea.'

'Yes, and Shirley doesn't get the publicity you get, nor does Barbara.

I can't, because the press concentrates on you simply because you are doing damage to the Party. You are like Hugh Scanlon.'

'Really, Harold, I don't accept that.'

Then on the forthcoming motion of censure against our industrial strategy, he said, 'I think you had better speak alone.'

I told him there would be two Tory speakers and if I am alone it will leave out Eric Heffer who had done all the work on the working party; secondly if I speak alone it looks as if I am on my own.

'Well, if Eric speaks, every word he says will have to be looked at. You know what is happening. I had to restrain a senior Minister this weekend who was determined to make a speech attacking your policy.'

'I'm sorry but that's up to you,' I said.

'Well it's my problem. Maybe you don't care.'

I said, 'I do care, but this is Party policy. If Ministers want to make a speech attacking Party policy...'

'How would you like it if Ministers attacked your policy on the Executive?' asked Harold.

'Well, I believe in debate and discussion – there's nothing very wrong about a disagreement. It goes on all the time and when we come to future policy then of course we must be free to discuss it and there will inevitably be disagreements.'

Then we got on to Concorde. 'What do you think your job is anyway?'

'Well, you gave me a job with two elements in it. One was to help you cancel Concorde in my own constituency!'

'You've won on that,' he said.

'I don't know that I have yet. Anyway, the other was to work on this policy and I have been working on a few little problems, like Meriden, which is difficult. I have been working extremely hard.'

The truth is that he is furious that I have turned Industry, which was intended to be a non-Department, into one of the most exciting departments in Whitehall. The one general thing that really emerged was the extent of his anger.

Tuesday 18 June

Went to London Airport and caught the plane to Brussels with members of my Private Office. We were met and taken straight to the Commission for a series of meetings. I had given a great deal of thought about how I should handle this. Jim had told Harold that I intended to say that it would be necessary to re-negotiate the treaties, which was never my intention. I saw it purely as a fact-finding meeting and intended to draw as much out of the Commission as I could, while saying as little as I could. I welcomed the visit, said it was fact-finding, described the responsibilities of my Department, talked a little about our policy, how and why it would work with the National Enterprise Board and planning agreements. Re-negotiation was for Jim Callaghan, but the decision was for the British people.

My first meeting was with Altiero Spinelli, the EEC Commissioner for Industry who said he had been dealing with some of these problems in the old Steel and Coal Community. There was no problem about nationalisation – the Community couldn't intervene in that – but the nationalised industries must not be managed so as to destroy the Common Market. Steel prices and investment were matters for the Community. A German Director-General said, 'I must tell you, there is very little left to the national Government in respect of steel. Over-all planning is a matter for the Community: the Community is planning all steel investment, but we are ready to talk to Governments as long as they recognise that. Moreover,' he continued, 'the BSC had a dominant position and therefore came under Community control. No British control is allowed over the private steel sector. Manufacturers cannot fix the prices, the Commission has all the power.'

On nationalisation, he said that we couldn't interfere with competition or create a monopoly and it would be best to have an industrial policy framed within the Community. If you put money in on a non-economic basis then it would create difficulties.

I said that the market economy in Britain had failed and we were deliberately distorting the competetive market economy in order to get what we wanted.

Then I went to see Commissioner Simonet on energy policy and he talked about the difficulties, the strain, the need to have a perspective. I didn't make much progress with him. It showed me how a political Commissioner would handle delicate things and of course they had no doubt been briefed to win me round. An exhausting day of visits and discussions and television coverage.

This huge Commission building in Brussels, in the shape of a cross, is absolutely un-British. I felt as if I was going as a slave to Rome; the whole relationship was wrong. Here was I, an elected man who could be removed, doing a job, and here were these people with more power than I had and no accountability to anybody.

Later, I walked over to meet the British Counsellors – people from the Foreign Office, education departments, trade, industry, customs, chancery, treasury and legal departments and I said I would like to hear how they saw it all. They said there had been a pause after the Election but things were moving again since 4 June.

I said, 'Look, let me put a point to you. I find an enormous difference as a Minister between now and 1970 when I left office, because this huge area of Community business has opened up and I am not in charge of it.'

They replied, 'We are all officials from different Departments but we are all seconded to the Foreign Office and responsible to it.'

'That completely explains how I feel: when I come here I am a Foreign Office official too, a Parliamentary Under-Secretary of State in the Foreign Office. I find that the things I would like to do, the options that would interfere with Community obligations are just closed: they are not mentioned because they can't be achieved.'

This made it crystal clear to me: the Community does centralise power in Whitehall inasmuch as the Foreign Office is in charge. Jim can always refer to a resolution agreed at a committee of which I am not a member, and after that the only option I have is to take it back to Cabinet. But Cabinet can't revise it because it is a once-for-all decision, taken in connection with re-negotiation. In fact, what has happened is that Community practice has fed back into British Government, and it has completely destroyed the informality of British Government, our freedom of action and the very nature of Cabinet Government.

Lunch at this huge, overpowering gathering, with George Thomson and Peter Carey and Spinelli, who told me his life story. He was a Communist as a young man, jailed in 1927 by Mussolini for sixteen years. When he was in prison, with Georgio Amendola, a leading Italian Communist, Spinelli opposed the Russian purge trials and Amendola conveyed the decision to him that he had been expelled from the Communist Party. So he was expelled while in prison. He came out in 1943, worked for a time and then decided to give himself to the European movement and has been a passionate European Federalist ever since. He is a man one couldn't help liking, full of enthusiasm and sweetness, with a dream and a vision. I told him when I saw him in London, and I felt it again today, that I loved his passion but hated his directives!

Afterwards, I saw Commissioner Borschette and told him our object was to replace the market economy in certain areas in Britain: he would recognise that this would affect competition policy in Britain, but would it affect it in the Community?

'No,' he said, 'our general approach is that there is no difficulty. Intervention of course must be within the common discipline. As to the National Enterprise Board, we would have to report the degree of intervention. Other states would have the right to complain. The Commission would approve the upper limits of aid to industry. If Britain were to increase capacity then the Commission would step in. On shipbuilding there is overcapacity and the Community should agree on capacity levels and some yards would probably disappear.'

Then I went to see Ortoli. 'How do you see industrial democracy?'

he asked. 'Have you been influenced by the fifth directive?'*

'It is a factor,' I replied, 'but I see withdrawal of consent from our system and the development of industrial franchise as the key. Even the most Trotskyite solutions are really just the municipal model, where the workers or the people hire and fire their management.'

'Ah,' said Ortoli, 'but you can't consult people because they want incompatible things.'

That is the key to every élitist argument – you get it from the right-wing of the Labour movement, from the Tories, from the Civil Service, from academics, from Fleet Street and of course from the élite of élites, the Commissioners themselves.

My visit confirmed in a practical way all my suspicions that this would be the decapitation of British democracy without any countervailing advantage, and the British people, quite rightly, wouldn't accept it. There is no real benefit for Britain. Though depressing and gloomy, I found it a most fascinating day.

Friday 21 June
We were defeated yesterday by 21 votes in a motion of censure against our industrial strategy, moved by Heath. But at least it forced Harold to defend the Manifesto in Parliament. The papers of course were full of it.

Saturday 22 June
I began getting telephone calls asking for my comments upon a statement by Eldon Griffiths, Conservative MP for Bury St Edmonds, that I had named the top twenty companies.

Sunday 23 June
'Benn Names Top 20 Companies' was splashed all over the press with a degree of vitriol expressed which surpassed anything one could have expected. It is lucky that I had a baptism of fire two or three years ago over Upper Clyde and the Common Market, the Pentonville Five and the mass media, because now it is like water off a duck's back; but briefings by colleagues against me is depressing and that is where the stuff really comes from. If the Party stuck to its policy this sort of thing wouldn't happen.

Monday 24 June
To lunch with Jack Jones at Locket's. It was an interesting lunch because he was trying, as usual, to bully me. He began by saying,

---

* An EEC proposal for workers' participation based on the German codetermination system, under which workers would sit on supervisory boards.

'You're looking shaky at the knees, dear! You'll feel better if you lie down and rest!'
Sunday Express, 23 June 1974.

'Harold Lever says Meriden isn't viable. They just want £7 million of public money. I am going to see him again in a couple of days.'

'Well, Harold Lever doesn't want this to work.'

'Oh, I'll have to see him about it,' Jack replied, making it quite clear that he is now bypassing me and going straight to Harold Lever.

We moved on to the general issue of companies that are going bust. 'Nationalisation is no good,' he said. 'People don't want it. Management in nationalised industries is very bad.'

'I haven't much faith in British management, but it's certainly no worse in the nationalised industries than in private industry.'

'But people don't want nationalisation.'

'Well, we may have no alternative if firms go bust.'

'What do you mean if firms go bust?'

I gave him some examples – Fisher-Bendix, Beaverbrook's *Scottish Daily Express*.'

'You don't want to support the Scottish newspaper workers,' he snapped.

I said, 'It's a very big political issue in Scotland whether they are entitled to have a newspaper of their own.'

'You don't want to do that. You don't want to save every lame duck.'

'What about British Leyland?' I asked.

'Why couldn't you sell it?'

I said, 'To whom?'

'Why don't you sell it to General Motors?'

When Jack Jones recommends that the British Government sell British Leyland to General Motors of America, there is an indication that the criticisms of him from the Left are correct. He was reinforcing everything Denis Healey says.

We moved on to the Common Market and I told him my view of the true position. He said, 'I have spoken to Harold and he says that the Common Market will never accept our proposals and that we will be out in six months.'

'You must be joking,' I said, 'Jim made one speech for domestic consumption and now he is in the process of selling out to the Market.'

Came back to the office where Richard Bullock and John Lippitt, two of my senior officials, were waiting to discuss Court Line.[3] They said they had been working throughout the weekend and had produced a scheme in accordance with what I had suggested, namely that we should buy the shipyards for £60 million, which gives me all the shipyards and ship repairing yards and I think that is a great gain. So I said, 'All right, go ahead and put in that paper.'

In the House, Michael Meacher was sitting next to Jim Callaghan and asked, 'What do you think of our draft Green Paper, Jim?'

'You'll have to drop the first part.'

'What do you mean, the first part?'

'The National Enterprise Board,' said Jim. 'We can't have it. We will just go for the planning agreements.'

So that was a word of warning, put quite crudely. If I look at the position we are in at the moment, there is enormous hostility to our programme and indeed to the Department of Industry Ministers, from the Prime Minister, the Foreign Secretary, the Chancellor of the Exchequer and the Home Secretary – and that is a fairly formidable line up to lick.

Wednesday 26 June

The press had another field day this morning. The *Daily Express* said 'Benn Spreads Grab to Tiny Companies' or something, then listed 4,000 companies that were owned by the Top Twenty. Fleet Street is having a sort of nervous breakdown at the moment because nobody has ever dared to argue the case openly and without embarrassment. If they really thought it was so unpopular, they wouldn't be devoting so much space to trying to stop it but they know in their hearts that there is a favourable response of some kind. So I feel perfectly happy.

I arrived a bit late at the NEC. Ian Mikardo proposed a motion that 'the National Executive Committee welcomes and supports the speeches in which Harold Wilson and Tony Benn have expounded and reinforced the sections of the Manifesto dealing with industry and would like to see this example followed by all other Ministers in relation to the sections of the Manifesto for which they are responsible.' By then we were nearly inquorate but it just got through. It gave me a hell of a kick.

Had lunch with Frank Chapple. I asked him about the Communist Party, of which he is a former member. He said it had no appeal for young people any more. I asked him a number of questions. 'You made a very profound remark last time I saw you at an Anglo-Israel lunch when you said, "Look, I agree with a lot of what you say but we will just have to do it when the time comes, we don't have to talk about it; events will take us there." Do you think events have got us there now?'

'Very nearly,' he answered. 'Still, why *do* you have to talk about it? Why not do it?'

'You have got to win the argument first', I replied.

I got on well with him, which was slightly surprising.

Made a statement in the House on Court Line. It was absolutely hilarious. It was a cautious statement, which was attacked by Heseltine; so I replied that I couldn't understand why he should worry because I had nationalised 16 companies under his old legislation each with the support of the firm. Then to another question I said I had consulted the CBI and they were quite happy. The Labour benches were packed and they were just hooting with laughter.

Then John Davies got up and tried to say something about Upper Clyde so I congratulated him on being the author of the legislation [the 1972 Industry Act] that I had used for this widespread expansion of public enterprise.

Thorpe got up and asked if his little Appledore shipyard in North Devon was safe. I replied, 'Yes. Nationalisation by a Labour Minister saved it. It's a pity the Rt Hon gentleman didn't prepare his people for the merits of our policy.'

It was just a pushover.

Thursday 27 June

Cabinet at 11 o'clock. On Concorde, Harold reported his talks with Jacques Chirac, the Minister of the Interior. He said Chirac had raised Concorde straight away. Harold had mentioned the costs, and then asked, 'What would you say if we suggested that we discontinued it? What would your answer be?' Chirac had simply replied, '*Negatif, negatif.*'

I congratulated Harold on having done the difficult job and asked how he would like it settled. Would he like it settled between himself and President Giscard d'Estaing or between me and Cavaille, the Transport Minister. As he had done the hard part of the job, perhaps he would also like to do the popular part!

At 2.30 I went over to the House for the EEC Monitoring Group, a joint committee set up to watch the re-negotiations. Mik, Lena Jeger, Roy Hattersley and one or two other members were there. I was elected chairman. We discussed the Referendum and agreed to consider a paper which the Government might publish as a White Paper before the Election.

The Secretary came to see me at 4.10. The first thing he did was ask me about the aircraft nationalisation report that had recently been published by the Confederation of Shipbuilding and Engineering Unions, and he said, 'I hope you are nothing to do with it.'

I replied, 'Of course I'm to do with it – I am a member of the committee which produced it.'

'Well, your name can't appear on it.'

'Why not?'

'I have to remind you of the Procedure for Ministers which is that Ministers cannot separate themselves from their ministerial tasks. I have to tell you that my duty as Permanent Secretary is to help Ministers to fulfil the requirements of the Procedure laid down.'

So I said, 'Well, I've told the Prime Minister that I don't accept the Procedure and it's very embarrassing for you to discuss political matters with me – Party matters – I am quite happy to do so in a personal capacity but I am not prepared to discuss my Party work with a civil servant.'

Then he came on to my speech due to be made tomorrow at Buxton on regional policy. 'How did you get to see that?' I asked.

'The office here asked me to check the figures and they sent me a copy.'

I said, 'It's a political speech that's being made and the press release is going out through Transport House.'

'Well, Minister, don't you think that what you're doing is inflaming the North against the South?' That was a reference to the phrase 'industrial policies being discussed in the comfortable atmosphere of Westminster, Whitehall and Fleet Street' and to the fact that I describe other parts of the country, perhaps patronisingly, as the regions.

Well, I pointed to the map on the wall showing the assisted areas and I said, 'That's the most important map in Britain – that's where our support lies.'

'Well, you're inflaming people,' he said. 'You're raising temperatures.'

I said, 'Not at all – I'm using very clear language.' I went over and opened the Manifesto. 'The first objective of the Manifesto is about a fundamental and irreversible shift in the balance of wealth and power in favour of working people and their families,' I read.

'Well,' he said, 'I have never known a Minister in the whole course of my life in any Party who has been like you.'

'Well, I'm sorry but as far as I am concerned my work as a manager or a Minister is nothing like as important as my work as an educator and spokesman – speaking for people.' Of course, Antony Part simply didn't understand that. He has a completely different way of thinking and just does not seem to be really trying to assist me in getting things done. He just comes along and warns me: that I've crossed the Rubicon, that I've done this and that. At a suitable moment, after the Election, I may ask for him to be replaced because of a breakdown of confidence between us.

Friday 28 June
To the Industrial Development Committee of the Cabinet at Number 10, with Harold in the chair. I opened, saying that my Green Paper was a major policy initiative and should be seen against a background of industrial decline and a forecast of further decline. Our policy was well known, I wouldn't deal with it in detail – it was to introduce a National Enterprise Board and planning agreements: the object was to argue and explain the policy, and to discuss the transition.

I said the old policy hadn't worked and what we had to go for was better value for money. As to the problem of whether firms would go abroad, they were doing that anyway: for example, Ford, under the Tory Government, decided to use the profits at Dagenham to invest in Spain.

Denis Healey favoured a mixed economy which must be profitable. We had had lower productivity and he thought there might be a case for planning agreements in the NEB. His worry was that this policy would not provide an adequate return on capital and would be a way of propping up lame ducks like Concorde. The main purpose, which was to make profit, had to be made clear. Workers' control was no good and he wanted that to be understood. As to private industry, confidence was important, and vague threats had led to a blight on investment. We must make clear what we wanted.

Jim agreed entirely with Denis. He said that the uncertainty argument that I had used was ingenious but in fact this was causing an investment blight; Para 58 had to be rewritten completely. ' I am not agreeing to this policy – it will tear the Party in two, and we won't accept it.'

Harold spoke. 'I accept fully the Manifesto and the planning agreements and the NEB. I cannot however support an NEB outside the control of Ministers regardless of Government policy, and I resent other Ministers saying they are custodians of parts of the Manifesto.' (That was a reference to Eric Heffer who had said that.)

Crosland said he had just written a book on all this – *Socialism Now and Other Essays* – and hoped it would be circulated among members of the Cabinet. He knew of no great debate in Britain between those who would rather work for the North Thames Gas Board than ICI. Denis Healey was right about the need to increase profits, and the NEB had not been properly thought out.

Shirley Williams thought that unclear proposals were very dangerous and might precipitate a collapse or recession. 'Tony has alarmed industry. We must carry industrialists with us, they are on the edge of total non-cooperation.'

Harold Lever agreed with all the criticisms, but Peter Shore defended me. 'Labour can't build up confidence while it is re-distributing wealth and power,' and there was a new abrasiveness as compared with 1964 when there had been consensus. 'We have to establish a new consensus; we can't retreat.' The weaknesses of the paper, however, were that people couldn't manufacture without a new structure, without planning agreements which didn't seem to frighten ICI at all.

Willie Ross wanted to tell the Committee that on the previous day a thousand people in the carpet factory in Ayr had lost their jobs and people had withdrawn their confidence from the system. Planning agreements were absolutely essential. 'As for the attacks on Tony Benn, if it had been my job to produce this policy, the attacks would have been on me.' That was warm support.

In winding up, I said that I wanted to make it absolutely clear that I liked my colleagues and thought they were able, keen, brilliant, good, true, hard working and well meaning. But we faced a great crisis and I quite frankly didn't think that the odd speech by Harold Lever would restore confidence. Profits would fall and the problem was one of collapse. I accepted what had been said. I would listen carefully and I agreed with Peter that we were seeking a new consensus and I knew I must persuade people, not least my colleagues. Many of the points made by critics were an outright attack on the Manifesto but that was their problem and not ours. I accepted the mixed economy but the very big firms would be either publicly owned or publicly controlled and the small firms, which comprised 999 out of every 1,000, would be encouraged to go ahead on a free enterprise basis. Uncertainty was inevitable and all the other policies of the Government had created uncertainty, but probably the biggest two areas of doubt were nothing to do with me. One was the Common Market – which Jim was presiding over – because of the Referendum principle, and the other was North

Sea Oil. I did not accept for one moment that this uncertainty was due to my speeches alone.

On workers' control or the workers' role, I said we learned during the three-day week that if there was a slight shaking of the rigidities of the management hierarchy, higher productivity was possible. I referred to the redundancies at the Ayr carpet factory which Willie Ross had mentioned, Meriden, Leyland, Alfred Herbert; we had to operate quickly to deal with these problems. We had also to face the fact that, against a background of the control over the steel industry being transferred to Brussels, we couldn't give development area status to Leith without the permission of the Commission and we mustn't suppose it was going to be so easy for us to control the situation.

Harold declared, 'I have decided what I will do. I will circulate a paper and it will come back to Ministers in a week's time for discussion. Then it will go to an official committee who will report back to a small group of Ministers. Then it will come to this committee again and back to Cabinet.'

That was how it was left. It was the most fascinating discussion and I went away feeling, in a way, that it had been a success not least because they have all blown their tops and expressed their anger, which I knew was going to happen anyway: now they have got it off their chests.

Saturday 29 June
I went to the Churchill Hotel to meet Itzhak Rabin, the new Israeli Prime Minister. Eric Heffer was the only other Minister there, with some Labour and Tory MPs.

Rabin started off, 'There is no objectivity in foreign policy. I am looking at these problems through the eyes of the Israelis. Peace is a vague term and it must fulfil five requirements. One, if there is to be real peace, the Arabs and Israel have got to be reconciled to the existence of each other. Second, the parties to the conflict must agree to a peaceful solution. Third, there must be a free flow of information and trade. Fourth, there must be some solution to the Palestinian problem. And fifth, the peace must be between peoples and not just between diplomats.' He said there would have to be a transitional phase and various steps and the key role lay with Egypt. 'We won't give up territory until Egypt removes some of its obstacles to real peace.'

Nixon had airlifted arms to Israel in the Yom Kippur war and had got a warmer welcome, even in Cairo, than anyone else, which proved that the tough line pays off. A strong Israel *reduces* the risk of Arabs choosing the military option. Terrorists were working to prevent peace and to create tension and Lebanon was the only country that really allowed them. Rabin told a current joke about Israel: 'It's just like

Moses to have wandered for forty years in the desert and then taken
the Jewish people to the one place in the Middle East where there was
no oil.'

Brian Magee, the Labour MP for Leyton, asked, 'What about a
national home for the Palestinians?'

'I don't know what that means,' replied Rabin. He said there was
no democracy in the Arab world and he quoted Abba Eban, the Israeli
Foreign Minister, 'National suicide is not an international obligation.'
In any case, he didn't think the terrorists spoke for the Palestinians.

Sunday 30 June

The front page of the *Sunday Telegraph* read 'Benn's Effrontery', attacking me for taking Frances Morrell to a normally all-male industrial
dinner. There will just be buckets of dirt of one kind and another tipped
over me and I intend to take no notice of it.

Peregrine Worsthorne had an excellent article in the *Sunday Telegraph*.
'Are we all socialists now?' he asked. Will the slump make it necessary
for everybody to adopt Benn's view?

My phone has been out of order with mysterious clicks and one or
two weird incidents. When I spoke to Jeremy Thorpe early on Friday
morning, giving him the conditions under which we are going to help
Court Line so that he would be able to go off to Devon without anxiety
over the Appledore Shipyard, the telephone call was heard by someone
who was phoning me from Paris at that moment. Then Caroline made
a call on the home phone and got a crossed line so she picked up the
office phone and got the same crossed line, which seems to suggest that
our calls are being taken together and tapped, or something. Then
today, both phones were working outwards but if I dialled one of our
numbers on the other number, I couldn't get through. So there is
something funny going on and I am toying with the idea of writing to
the Post Office for an explanation, and then writing to Roy Jenkins,
'Will you give me an assurance that there is no warrant out for my
phone to be intercepted,' with a copy to Harold. That would throw
them into disarray.

Monday 1 July

The *Sun* and the *Mirror* had huge coverage of the Frances Morrell
story: 'Wedgie's Stag Night Guest Who Stops Blue Stories' and 'Benn's
Bombshell'. The back page of the *Guardian* reported that Harold was
going to turn down our industrial policy, a product of his briefing, and
The Times said, 'Harold Calls for Clear Frontiers Between the Private
and the Public Sector.'

Lunch at 1 o'clock with Antony Part and Ministers present. Part is
working away with other Permanent Secretaries on what, in a sense, is

the policy for a government of national unity and it is absolutely clear that civil servants are already preparing for such a government.

At 4 I went to the Economic Strategy Committee which went on until 6.45 – an enormously long and boring discussion. As we left Jim Callaghan and I walked to the front door and he said, 'I heard you were very nice on Friday in winding up the discussion on the Green Paper.' (He had had to leave after his slashing attack on it.)

I replied, 'Not at all. I simply said I loved my colleagues; I thought they were marvellous, able, nice, decent, reasonable people but that their rhetoric wouldn't solve our problems.'

In the Division Lobby I saw John Golding [Labour MP for New-castle-under-Lyme] who is parliamentary officer of the Post Office Engineering Union and I told him about my telephone. 'Would you ask Bryan Stanley to check and see if my line is being tapped?' He said, 'Yes, I certainly will.' Bryan Stanley himself is very angry because he is sure his own phone is tapped.

Peron of Argentina died today.

Tuesday 2 July
At 9.30 the Ministers and Ray Tuite came in. Ray said the press officers were in revolt over the way that Joe Haines was working from Number 10. Nobody had ever known so many restrictions placed before.

At 2.30, I had a discussion with Professor Peacock. He is what Tony Crosland calls a 'progressive right-winger'. He came to talk about a study by Cardiff University on dislocations in the Labour market, for which I have withdrawn financial support. I told him, 'I think this money ought to be given to the trade unions in Wales to spend on research that *they* think is relevant' and I read from our 'Programme for Britain' that money would be given to the trade unions to sponsor research. I said, 'It is much more likely that the research would be relevant and that the recommendations would be implemented if it has been commissioned by the trade unions.'

This really set Peacock and his colleagues aflutter. He said, 'What about academic standards?'

'I am not suggesting that the Welsh TUC wouldn't want to hire academics, but the academics would be working for them and not for the Government.'

At 4 o'clock Lord Stokes, Chairman of British Leyland, came to see me. Obviously he had heard all the rumours that I was going to intervene and nationalise British Leyland. So I said, 'Look, I have never made a statement to anybody. But do let me know if you get into trouble because I really wouldn't like to know at the last minute.'

'Oh no, we are all right,' he said. 'We might need a bit of money in the spring of next year but we are managing. But, of course, we can't sustain our investment programme.'

'Why not?'

He said, 'I can't get the money.'

'Well, work out a shadow investment programme which is higher than the one you can afford but which is still rational and sensible and let me look at it.'

Wednesday 3 July

At 10.30 we had the Neddy meeting in the Millbank Tower. This was hailed as a very big meeting because of the breakdown of confidence which had allegedly taken place between the Government and industry. Harold took the chair. The discussion was of a paper by the CBI and Bateman said he was pleased at the Social Contract, but the present situation was dangerous; everyone is asking how do we get out of our problems; there is an anxiety about company profitability, cash flow, investment and jobs.

Thursday 4 July

I had a word with Frances and Francis about the Prime Minister's minute which I had received this morning saying I couldn't be on the committee to monitor the Common Market legislation and re-negotiations. It also informed me that I couldn't move my motion on the Common Market at the NEC and that I wasn't behaving as a member of the team. Frances Morrell thought that there might be something in this argument. It was a real shot over my bows.

Cabinet at 11, where we talked about the EEC. I said that when the Referendum was held, I should certainly be opposed to membership. George Thomson had indicated that there would be little more than a pledge to look at our budgetary contribution again and winning a second Election required us to make the Referendum and a free vote of the people into a much more central issue. I would like to see us publish a White Paper on the Referendum before the Election to make this clear. We therefore also had to begin thinking about an alternative to the EEC. I could see the United Kingdom with Ireland, Denmark and Norway and a new EFTA working very closely with the Six in the reduced Common Market, all within a framework of the European Security Conference which was being steadily built up.

Jim said, 'Repeat those again.' So I went through the alternatives once more, and he wrote it down.

Harold thought the odds were against staying in the market and his mind was moving towards either an Election or a Referendum. I said, 'Harold, if we have an Election, we've got to face the fact that the only way in which you could give people a real choice would be if the Labour Party were firmly opposed to remaining in and the Tories were in favour of staying in. Therefore in the present circumstances a Referendum is the only way you could offer that choice.

Sunday 7 July

I cycled over to see Tony Crosland this morning. He is an old friend and I thought I should mend my fences. Frances said that I really should try and not be so difficult. So I'm going to see a Minister a day.

Susan was in bed with a virus and Crosland was working on his red box. I asked him about his Department and he said he had nine Ministers and he had to spend most of his time on psychiatric work – comforting those who thought they ought to be in the Cabinet.

Monday 8 July

I went over to the Foreign Office and spoke to Jim Callaghan for twenty minutes. I hadn't been in that office since, I think, George Brown or Michael Stewart was Foreign Secretary. It is a huge room overlooking the park, enough to make any Secretary of State feel totally isolated. It is like living in the royal suite of a big hotel. There was nothing in the room to identify with Jim at all.

I mentioned that I didn't like just meeting in the Cabinet when we had the grinding business to get through. He felt I criticised him on the European policy and I thought he was very critical on industrial policy. 'Well, let's have lunch sometime,' Jim said.

Tuesday 9 July

At 5.30, the Industrial Development Committee met at Number 10 to consider a new paper on industrial policy that has been put in by Harold Wilson under the names of the Secretaries. It really was a disastrous paper. I'd only got it at 10 last night and I'd stayed up late reading it. It was completely different in character from the policy on which the Party had fought the Election. I did get my Private Secretary to ring Number 10 to see if they would agree to postpone it, but they wouldn't.

Under this paper, the National Enterprise Board would control all the nationalised industries and the planning agreements would be the responsibility of the little Neddies. Absolutely crazy.

The whole two-hour meeting was a disgrace. Harold suggested we should have a general discussion first, so I started and said, 'Look, you've put me in a really difficult position, Prime Minister. I was a Minister for four years in this area from 1966 to 1970. I then spent four years working on the industrial policy for the Election and, since the Election, four months in implementing that policy and putting it before you. Now, it is thrown away. Four hours are given to us to consider a policy that is fundamentally different and I wish we could defer it and consider it again.'

'Oh no,' said Harold, 'we'll have a discussion on it.'

Tony Crosland announced, 'We can't put the nationalised industries under the National Enterprise Board.' Denis agreed and Harold Wilson said that it was never clear in the policy whether this was intended or not. So I replied, 'I'm very sorry but it was never mentioned, it was never even suggested that the nationalised industries should be under the NEB.'

That was the opening exchange and it couldn't have been worse.

Then on the NEB itself, I described the five circumstances under which you might need to take industries in to public ownership.

'Well,' Harold replied, 'you can't have a marauding NEB going round the country grabbing firms.'

Jim said, 'You can't write a Manifesto for the Party in opposition and expect it to have any relationship to what the Party does in Government. We're now entirely free to do what we like.'

Then we came to the question of a list of companies. Harold Wilson was adamant that we had to avoid a list. I thought we ought to be flexible.

In the end, after much poor argument it was agreed that the National Enterprise Board would not cover the nationalised industries, and that aircraft, shipbuilding and ports should be handled separately and would have statutory boards.

Today, Chris Mayhew joined the Liberals – not that that marks any change because he's been a Tory Liberal all his life – but of course it is hot news and it is dominating the headlines.

Thursday 11 July

I had a briefing meeting with Hugh Brown, Gregor MacKenzie, Peter Shore and Eric Deakins, Peter's Parliamentary Under-Secretary, and the Glasgow newspaper workers, with all our officials.

The Action Committee had put up a request for £1.75 million, my officials had suggested it wouldn't be viable, and I had sent the men their report. They attacked it and said it was unfavourable and unfair. I listened to these London officials telling Glasgow newspaper workers that it wasn't on, and they were so arrogant. It would have converted me to Scottish Nationalism if I had been one of those guys. They knew I was friendly, however, and in the end I told them that if they could find half the money from somewhere else, if they would accept that there was a risk, if they recognised that the workers, being equity holders, would come at the bottom of the pile for redundancy pay if the venture went bust, and if they accepted that it was only £1.75 million and no more, then we would consider it.

Friday 12 July

At 12.30. Clive Jenkins came to see me, I thought in anticipation of tomorrow's meeting with ASTMS. But, in fact, he went on to talk about the Security Services. He suspected that his telephone was being tapped and I said that I thought mine was too.

Clive has a lot of members who are the top electronic experts in the country and he got them to come and 'sweep' his office. They discovered that his office and his switchboard were bugged. He offered to lend me his piece of electronic apparatus to sweep my house, which I might just use.

Clive is very optimistic because he really feels that the trade union movement has come to power, whoever is in office, and I think that is right. He himself, when he gets on the General Council is hoping to get members to see their enormous potential – not a revolutionary potential but simply a structure of power to rival the Establishment.

I said that once I realised that the working class would come to power complete with its own institutions, then the bourgeois system just wouldn't be relevant or would have to be adapted.

Monday 15 July

To Locket's for lunch with Roy Grantham, General Secretary of APEX. I'd never really spoken to him before. He's a sandy-haired man, a year younger than me, with gold-rimmed spectacles and looks like a Baptist preacher. A teetotaller and a non-smoker, he was born in 1926, the son of a silversmith who was regularly out of work in Birmingham. By the time he was twelve, Roy was a socialist. During the war he was a Bevin Boy, that's to say he worked in the mines. He became a civil servant and then joined the Clerical and Writers' Union. He is himself a practising Anglican, though very much on the Low Church side, married to a Catholic.

He thought that the period we were going through was rather like the Reformation. Intellectuals had no role and Britain would either go Powellite, a sort of right-wing, working-class, Peronist-type of organisation, or it would go Left, though he couldn't quite see how.

He believed consumers had a bigger role to play. He absolutely concurred with my mass media argument and compared the media today exactly to the old Church pulpit, which is Brailsford's point in his book, *The Levellers*. He's a right-wing pro-Common market General Secretary, but I found him very pleasant to talk to.

At 4.30, Jack Spriggs, the convener from IPD came to see me with Kenneth Cork, the Liquidator/Receiver, and the consultant Ingrams. Cork and Ingrams thought the factory would sustain 450 people. Jack Spriggs said that all the workers should be employed. So I worked out on the back of an envelope that the difference between employing them all and employing part of them would be roughly – by the time you took the gross costs into account – less than the cost of keeping them unemployed for twenty-six weeks, roughly £390 per job, and much below what was expected. I said I'd give them six months to work it out.

Dinner with Jim Callaghan. He talked about how he didn't let the Foreign Office bully him, had only one red box every night and read the telegrams.

We discussed the Election which he thought would be in October, and that we would win. He didn't think there would be an economic crisis between now and then.

We went on to the Party and the Left. He knows nothing about the Left at all. Never heard of the ultras, never realised that the Trotskyites were critical of Jack Jones and Hugh Scanlon, of Michael Foot, myself and Eric Heffer as 'fake' Left. He simply knew nothing about it.

He was worried about Communists in the Party because 'I know documents pass across'. I was sure he, as a former Home Secretary knew these things, but he said that it wasn't from being in the Home Office but from other sources. I said that I remembered him discussing with me the possibility of preventing Hugh Scanlon's election to the AUEW. I told him I wasn't worried about the Communists. They had no appeal whatever to the young, they were very bureaucratic and stick-in-the-mud.

Then he asked me about the industrial policy and how I felt about being a bogeyman. I said I didn't take it personally. He thought that if we lost the Election, people would blame me. I doubted that. Finally, he told me that he might give up next year, and I said, 'Now look, Jim, you're sixty-two, Churchill became Prime Minister at sixty-four. You've got ten more years of political life in you if you want it. That's the decision you've got to make. You've got to keep yourself available.'

Well, then he declared that he didn't want to be Leader. He repeated it so many times that it was obvious that he did. He said he had told Harold that if Harold was going to retire, he must give Jim three months' notice so that Jim could retire before him.

I pointed out that we didn't know what was going to happen. I stressed that I knew that Jim disapproved of me very much and didn't agree with me, but nevertheless I liked him very much. I told him that I couldn't talk like this with Roy or Denis.

Returning to the theme of the General Election, he thought it would be a very bitter period if we were to lose. I said that we mustn't lose, but that it would still be a bitter period if we won. Jim wasn't sure he'd want to be leader during such a period. Then he'd be sixty-six before the Election in 1979. He'd obviously worked it all out. I said that he must be available, that's all, like Cincinnatus.

Today, Archbishop Makarios has been deposed in a coup in Cyprus and rumour has it he may well have been killed.*

Tuesday 16 July
Had dinner with Sir Ray Brookes of GKN at GKN House in Kingsway, with Otto Clarke [former Permanent Secretary, Ministry of Technology] and various other Directors. They received me very courteously but when we sat down Brookes declared that if I didn't remove GKN from the list of top companies for nationalisation within a month, they would cancel all their investment plans for next year. During the dinner, I asked him to confirm what he had said, which he did. So I responded that he knew very well that there was no such nationalisation list and never had been. However, GKN was among the names of the top twenty companies in this country, given to me by the Department, and I had asked my Department to check how much public money they'd had.

He said that everybody in Europe thought that GKN was going to be nationalised. I told him he knew that wasn't true but I pointed out that his company subscribed to a right-wing organisation that went round the country declaring that this was the case – so he was harming himself. It was clear that we may be facing a strike of capital.

Wednesday 17 July
I talked to Frances for a bit about the problem of self-control in a situation where Harold is driving me to desperation and I am just hanging on, and being courteous and am not even complaining.

I went over to the Northern Ireland Committee at Number 10 very briefly, on the collapse of Harland and Wolff which will cost £35 million. Harold wanted it to be taken out of the budget for Northern Ireland.

Secretary came in to see me about the Post Office chairmanship. I had in fact been aiming to tell Harold my decision, that we should appoint Lord Peddie, former Chairman of the Prices and Incomes Board, as a non-executive chairman. But, in fact, Part hinted that he himself would like to be Chairman of the Post Office.

Then I told Part about GKN and said that I had been concerned to hear Ray Brookes say that he would be cancelling his investment programme unless I gave an assurance that we wouldn't nationalise GKN. Part said that was the view of the more militant industrialists; the others would sit on their hands. The Chairman of Hawker Siddeley,

* President Makarios of Cyprus was overthrown by Greek officers in the Cyprus National Guard, an event which was followed on 20 July 1974, by the invasion of Cyprus by Turkey which led to the partition of the island.

Arnold Hall, will probably cancel the HS-146 aircraft project: he won't say it is due to us but it will be obvious. He thought other firms would simply postpone their investment.

Finally I said to Part, 'Now, can I say a word about the Department,' and I went over the Department of Industry being cut down in size and all the erosions and the splits in responsibility.

'Well, it's all due to the fact that you are out of step with your colleagues and there is a severe strain in the Government.'

'Maybe,' I said, 'but in addition to that, I have to contend with the fact that my civil servants are working to rule. No doubt they read in the papers that there is great resistance to my views and feel that they can do so.'

'That's a very serious charge.'

I said, 'It's not really a serious charge. I am observing it quietly and calmly and I think that is what is actually happening.'

Having said it wasn't the case, he added, 'Of course, they are all very worried about lack of viability and all that.'

'Well, I know that. But civil servants have no experience of the Labour movement. I shall make it absolutely clear that they have just got to make things work. It's up to them. Some of the ideas may fail, but the policy is very important.'

Then he went off. Roy Williams said afterwards to me that he had been impressed by the reception I got over Court Line from the Parliamentary Labour Party. He said, 'If you didn't exist, the Party would have to invent you.' He thought everybody else in the Cabinet was out of touch with the rank-and-file of the Party and that the Cabinet didn't like the Manifesto.

I told him that I was really an old-fashioned radical Liberal who looked ahead a bit and saw what was coming. I was a realist, I wasn't a wild left-winger and so on. That was why *Workers' Press* attacked me and why I read it so carefully. I think all this sunk in, but it probably won't last for long.

Went to dinner with the Chinese and Algerian Ambassadors. We talked about Heath's visit to China. I had, in fact, already heard that when Heath went to China as Leader of the Opposition, there was a tremendous reception for him at Peking Airport without, however, a guard of honour. The Ambassador told us that Mao had asked Chou, 'Why wasn't there a guard of honour and a band playing the national anthem?' and Chou said, 'It might have upset Mr Wilson.' Mao is reported to have said, 'What does that matter.'

Heath of course met Mao, and when he left there was a huge guard of honour with six foot two inch Chinese standing immaculate and a band playing 'God Save the Queen'.

I said I assumed he had been well received because of his attitude to the Common Market. They said, 'Yes, because he stood against the hegemony of the Great Powers.' We had quite a talk about Europe. They said of course war was inevitable between America and Russia, which worried the Algerian Ambassador.

I said to the Chinese Ambassador, 'I can understand why the Chinese people are in favour of Britain joining the Common Market, but you should take more account of *our* people's attitude.'

'We think you would be better off,' he said.

'The last time there was a united Europe with military power, in 1942, it was fighting both the Americans and the Russians and the British haven't forgotten that,' I said.

The Chinese party said, 'You have got to stand against the Russians. The Russians are very well armed.'

'That may be but they are very weak because they can't hold their own people in Eastern Europe. You sound like Mr Dulles who, at the time he was Secretary of State in America, said war was inevitable, and Chou-en-Lai went to Bandung and said peace was possible. Now *you* say war is inevitable and *Nixon* says peace is possible.' They laughed at that.

It was an interesting discussion, particularly talking about the Russians and how strong the Chinese thought they were. They said, 'In our view Stalin was seven-tenths correct and three-tenths incorrect; his attitude towards the occupation of Eastern Europe and changing the boundaries of Poland and his seizure of part of Finland was incorrect.'

'That's what Dulles said. He talked about liberating these territories.'

They said, 'We don't know why Stalin did it. If he did it to safeguard the Soviet Union's interest, then he was correct. If he did it for imperialist reasons, then he was incorrect.'

It was a sort of game really. But I teased them and got on very well with them and I must say the Ambassador was very much brighter and more charming than any of his predecessors. He even told a funny joke about Walter Ulbricht of East Germany. 'What is the difference between a disaster and an unfortunate incident? Well, if Herr Ulbricht fell off the top of a television tower to the ground and was killed, that would be an unfortunate incident. But if he got up and walked away, it would be a disaster.'

Thursday 18 July

A really filthy leader appeared today written by Anthony Shrimsley, editor of the *Daily Mail*, saying that my objective was to destroy democracy as we know it in this country. A piece of yellow journalism that passes belief.

At 9.30 I had three-quarters of an hour with Ministers and Ray Tuite to discuss the state of play. Ray made it absolutely clear that relations with Number 10 were as tense as they had ever been. He was incensed that when Jonathan Dimbleby had offered me half an hour on *This Week* to answer the attacks made on me by the press, Harold Wilson, after a twenty-four-hour delay, had personally banned the broadcast.

At 10.30 Edmund Dell and two Treasury people from the public expenditure side came to see me about Giro. The Treasury is absolutely opposed to the Giro and always has been.

I said, 'Well, you know, Edmund, the Giro is the only public service bank we have.'

'Oh, no,' he said. 'The Trustee Savings Bank is a cooperative. Why do you make a philosophical difference between them.'

'That's the whole point. I don't but you do.'

In the end he capitulated, but the Treasury official, Unwin, was angry. I just went for him and said, 'Look, the Treasury has always been against the Giro. It opposed the Giro under the Tories during the 1950s when the Post Office wanted it; in the early 1960s it beefed up Jim Callaghan to oppose it when I introduced it; it helped to get it reviewed under the Tories. Now it's a small element but it is important.'

Edmund said, 'Well, it's very small.'

'Of course it is small; that's why you don't have to worry about it.'

At 11.30 there was a Cabinet with Harold in the chair. We began with a word about parliamentary business, then Cyprus and the UN role. Jim described the dangers, and that there might be a Turkish invasion. The Americans didn't want to upset the Greek Colonels. Harold announced a Cyprus committee made up of himself, the Foreign Secretary, Chancellor, Defence Secretary and I think the Home Secretary and one or two others.

Peter said, 'Surely when democracy is undermined we ought to support it.' This put Jim on the defensive.

Friday 19 July

Ron picked me up at 7.15 and drove me to Northolt from where I went up to Newcastle with Ray Tuite and Martin Vile, my Assistant Private Secretary, in an Andover of the Queen's Flight.

At Newcastle, I had an hour with the trade union representatives and the management of Court Line shipbuilders. The management were very nervous, like a defeated army who had come to surrender. They said how glad they were to be in the public sector; how they would work for their new employer as well as they would have done for their old one. It was rather a weird feeling. Fortunately, being in Geordieland, the relations between the management and the workers were pretty good. The workers made a lot of demands but had high regard for their management. We ended up by asking, 'Will you prepare together a corporate strategy for these yards and then we will have a look at it.' The great thing was to keep ship repairing and shipuilding separate.

While I was there I heard that sixteen Concordes had been authorised by Harold after his visit to Giscard d'Estaing, which was good news.

Had dinner at the Durham Miners' Gala, sitting next to Ted Short. Ted showed me the false bank statement which listed entries into a Swiss bank account.* I feel sorry for Ted. I don't know what's going on, or whether he knows what's going on; but it is very unpleasant and I think it probably is doing us all a bit of damage.

Saturday 20 July

Up at 6.15 and at 7 I was driven to the Bearpark. I had breakfast in the Methodist hall and then went round the village with the band. It was the usual intensely moving experience with the old people coming out and waving and the women in their curlers and babies in arms and the band playing, people treating it in a homely way. It was a lovely warm morning. The BBC *Midweek* team were there covering it. Some bitchy media woman asked questions like 'Don't the miners now control the Labour Party?' and 'Why do you bother to continue coming?' I just treated it gently and let it roll over me.

At 8.30 the band adjourned to the Dog and Gun, and I had a mug of tea at the Royal County Hotel in Durham. Then I heard that Harold had to go off because of the Cyprus crisis – the Turks have invaded this morning.

Watched from the balcony and there was the usual moving feeling of deep political commitment. I find it very thrilling.

Monday 22 July

To Cabinet and Jim reported on Cyprus where we are concentrating on getting our own people out. We have come out of it very ingloriously, but then even in Cyprus we are no longer a serious military power.

Lunch in the office with the Secretary and most of the Ministers. We talked about the power of the Treasury and why it is that Cabinet didn't have collective control over the Treasury like any other Department. Antony Part said, 'Ah well, the Treasury is in a special position and you can't confide to Ministers because it would all leak,' – whereas, of course, officials are reliable! I commented, 'I suppose we ought to be grateful to the Treasury officials for confiding in the Chancellor.'

But, of course, democracy doesn't exist at the centre of British government. It has to be recognised that if one really were to reform British

---

* In July 1974, a bank statement from a Swiss account in Ted Short's name was anonymously circulated, detailing payments into it of several thousand pounds. The statement was a forgery and no such account existed. The perpetrators of the smear have never been discovered.

government it would have to start with the collective control of the
Treasury which at the moment is under the personal control of the
Chancellor. This means, in fact, that the Chancellor is under the
collective control of the Treasury, because no Chancellor has really
broken with its concepts.

Afterwards, Mary Lou came in and we tried to sort out the telephone
problem. I have got to change the number because of the eternal
harrassment on the phone over the last few days.

Dinner at Locket's with Leonard Woodcock, the President of the
United Automobile Workers in America, and Jack Jones, Glyn Hawley
and Moss Evans, the three top people from the TGWU. We had quite
a talk about the state of the Labour Party and planning agreements
and industrial democracy. Later Michael Foot, Jill Craigie and Eric
Heffer joined us.

During the discussion, Jill said, 'We have got to win the Election.
We stuck by our principles for twenty years and where did it get us?'
And Michael added, 'We have got to dress up our vote-winning policies
as principles and and dress up our principles as vote-winning policies.'

Eric said he was deeply shocked by this. I think his view of Michael
is completely shattered.

Tuesday 23 July

At 11 to a meeting to discuss the HS–146. It is a big civil aircraft that
the Tories had agreed to support when they were in power on the
grounds that it was the one civil project of any substance that Britain
had, and they planned to put £40 million into it, with provision for
review. When I last saw Arnold Hall, the Chairman of Hawker Siddeley, he said they were re-examining it, but John Lidbury, the Deputy-
Chairman, wrote to the Deputy-Secretary David Jones, saying Hawker
Siddeley wanted to cancel it and giving two or three pages of very
inadequate reasons. David Jones told him to put this in writing formally
and that letter, which arrived yesterday, said that the main group
board of Hawker Siddeley would be bound to recommend cancellation,
and seek agreed cancellation with the Government. I was very angry
because David Jones had sent me a minute recommending that we
agree to this – which would mean up to 8700 job losses in the aircraft
industry by 1978 – saying that the Treasury would agree to recommend
to the Chancellor that he acquicsce in the cancellation, and suggesting
I might write to the Prime Minister in this vein. This meant David
Jones had already spoken to the Treasury about it without consulting
me. I was hopping mad.

At the Industrial Development Committee we considered the workers' Action Committee in Glasgow; I recommended that we accept
their scheme on certain conditions. Joel Barnett felt it was very danger-

ous; the arrangement was open-ended and would create a precedent for workers who became redundant; it would make it impossible to get transition to more economic employment.

In fact I got the go-ahead to write to them and make an offer. But I think it is so harsh that they won't survive.

The next thing was IPD (Fisher-Bendix) on which I had proposed that we acquire the factory for £3 million and give them a subsidy of about £300,000 for the unutilised labour – about 600 jobs – till the end of the year, so that the feasibility study would have a chance of getting off the ground.

Joel Barnett said this would work out at £40,000 a job. It was quite scandalous to quote that figure because he was mixing the capital acquisition and the uneconomic jobs which we were holding for a few months. Harold Lever thought this was the economics of Peter Pan. Although there was some support for buying the factory and employing the 600 people, there was no support for the other subsidy so I said I'd take it to Cabinet.

If these discussions were broadcast, people would leave the Labour Party in droves. There is such cynicism and hostility from Labour leaders about the needs of working people. The gap between me and the right wing, or even the unimaginative, run-of the-mill Labour politicians, is vast and I just don't know how it can be narrowed. I have to keep my temper and be restrained, as I was.

Back at my car, Roy Williams was waiting for me, looking very bedraggled. He said that Robert Armstrong, the Prime Minister's Private Secretary, had rung him tonight to find out if I was persisting in the resolution to the NEC on the special conference on the Common Market at the Executive tomorrow.

I said, 'You'd better tell him that I didn't feel able to discuss Executive business with him.'

I will have to make up my mind what to do. Roy hinted that Harold would sack me if I went ahead with it, and he may. If I were fired on this it would be an awful waste. On the other hand, it has come to the point where you have to stand up for what you believe in. If I am fired I shall just spend the next two months campaigning for the return of a Labour Government which I desperately want, and I shall say nothing critical of Harold whatever. He is the Leader of the Party and as such he has my full support.

Wednesday 24 July
The Greek Government has fallen* and Karamanlis is back in power.

* As a result of events in Cyprus the military government collapsed and a civilian government was formed with Konstantinos Karamanlis, Prime Minister between 1955 and 1963, at its head.

Talked to Frances about the National Executive this morning because I felt threatened by Harold's message last night, half expecting at this stage to be sacked. She told me I should keep my mouth shut on everything, particularly over the EEC Monitoring Committee, and reserve my views for the special conference.

Jim was in the chair to begin with. The question of Clay Cross came up. Frank Allaun pointed out that in early August the Clay Cross councillors would be faced with an £8,000 fine, bankruptcies, or restraints on their properties. He moved that £8,000 from Party funds be paid to them and that we should ask the Government to look again at the Clay Cross issue and other disqualified councillors.

On paying the £8,000 only three of us voted: myself, Joan Maynard and Frank Allaun. On the request for the Cabinet to reconsider the whole question, Jim said, 'I take it that means that the Executive wishes to express its dissatisfaction with the Cabinet.'

I interrupted. 'Wait a minute, Jim. Don't say that because if you press that, the Cabinet Ministers here can't vote for it. If it is just the Executive asking the Cabinet to reconsider, they can vote.' That was a very important distinction. Anyway, by 20 votes to 2 – Jim and Shirley voting against – we agreed to send a deputation to see Harold.

Finally at 12.30 we came on to my motion calling for a special conference on the Common Market and I moved it formally. Mik supported me and it was carried by 12 votes to 4, with Shirley, Tom Bradley, John Cartwright and Hickling voting against.

I went to Carmelite House for lunch with Vere Harmsworth, proprietor of the *Daily Mail* and *Evening News*, who is the grandson of Sir Harold Harmsworth, Lord Northcliffe's brother. He had all his top brass there, the Managing Director of the Associated Newspaper Group, the two managing editors and the editors of both papers. Anthony Shrimsley (of the *Mail*) had written that vicious piece about me.

I was very charming to Vere Harmsworth and said how my grandfather and grandmother had known his great uncle. I admired the room in which we had lunch, which was Northcliffe's old office. At lunch I said we needed older people in politics, and moved on to the subject of wisdom and to Enoch Powell, and from there on to the Tory Party and the fact that it had laid down the Union Jack as a symbol because of Common Market membership. Then we had a great discussion about industrial democracy; about the Action Committee in Glasgow; about Meriden; about how you had to institutionalise power to make it constructive.

Shrimsley chipped in, 'Yes but you want to destroy democracy.'

I said, 'Look it is very difficult to discuss these ideas if you suggest that there is simply Che Guevara on one side and a fascist junta on the other; we have to make adjustments in our society from time to time. The change I am proposing is no more dramatic than the New Deal, or 1945, and we must discuss it seriously.'

At the end, Harmsworth said, 'I must tell you, we have had many politicians to this table but I have been very impressed by what you have said.'

At a meeting in my office of Eric Heffer, Frank Beswick, Michael Meacher and Gregor MacKenzie, I got Part, who has been made a Knight Grand Cross of the Order of the Bath, GCB, to bring out his ribbon and chain and cross which he had received this morning from the Queen. I took lots of photographs of him and somehow he looked so ridiculous taking such simple and innocent pleasure from it all, that it gave me a feeling of being one-up for the rest of the morning.

Hilary and Rosalind came over to the House of Commons and we had dinner together. Hilary came up to see my room and to use the lavatory, and there was Roy Jenkins smoking a big cigar, having forgotten to lock the door!

Thursday 25 July

The press this morning presented the Executive's decision yesterday to have a special conference on the Common Market as a great victory for the anti-Marketeers.

At 9.30 I went over to Number 10 for the joint meeting of the Cabinet and the NEC to consider the draft Manifesto for the next Election, which is expected within three months. Fred Mulley was in the chair as Jim was tied up with the Cyprus crisis. Harold began by saying the Tories were in a shambles; we had a good Manifesto; the spending priorities have got to be watched carefully; and there should be a drafting committee, and later a further joint meeting.

Bill Simpson was the first to get up. He thought we should add a note on Tory tactics which were to pretend to put nation before Party and we must attack the idea of the coalition. We must also bring forward the whole question of public ownership to a much earlier part of the programme. The Aims of Industry campaign, particularly 'the ugly face of Wedgwood Benn' written by Yorick (who may be Norman Macrae, the Deputy Editor of the *Economist*), needed to be confronted and taken head on. Public ownership should be the centrepiece of our introduction.

Mikardo raised the question of forthcoming White Papers and said they might pre-empt the joint meeting between the Cabinet and the Executive to discuss the Manifesto.

Harold Wilson said, 'We can't have a situation where Government stops and the Party takes over.' But he agreed that a Manifesto drafting committee can see the draft White Papers and consider them bearing this in mind.

Denis Healey thought we could only take on limited commitments; the Social Contract was the key to everything and the guidelines contained in it were laid down by the TUC.

I said that the Social Contract really had to be seen as dealing with broader issues than simply wages. (Harold added, 'Yes, it covers pensions and wealth.') It was our fundamental commitment to implement the programme.

Then we came to the Common Market. Jim Callaghan had left behind a letter saying he thought the total timescale for conclusion of the Referendum question, as to whether we recommend Britain to stay in or come out, should be about twelve months.

Then Roy Jenkins said he wanted to put on record his deep-seated objection to a Referendum. He feared it would threaten the cohesion of the Government and it would be impossible to have a Referendum on this matter and on nothing else. The adhesion to the EEC was certainly no more fundamental than questions that might subsequently arise about the unity of the United Kingdom; and the problem would then be whether we should then have referenda on these matters as well. We might be pushed into one on capital punishment; on immigration; on race; on public ownership. He felt the sovereignty of Parliament was at stake.

Mik said that the PLP had had a good meeting last night. Everyone who spoke had been in favour of a Referendum; it was the key to electoral victory and to the handling of the Common Market issue and it was much too late to raise the whole principle again now. 'Let the people decide' had been an absolutely binding pledge.

Tony Crosland was against it. He thought the crux of the matter was that we didn't want to re-start the argument. We could stick to the words we used in the February Manifesto. Michael Foot had reservations about a Referendum but thought we should stick to it. Barbara was in favour.

Then I spoke. I thought it had been well worth discussing the problem. This was a high constitutional matter of letting the people decide and, of course, it was the sovereignty of the people, not the sovereignty of Parliament that we were concerned with. A Referendum offered to each person complete respect for his or her views and he or she would be allowed to vote any way they chose, even those in the Cabinet.

Friday 26 July

At 10 o'clock there was a Cabinet devoted mainly to public expenditure.

After Denis, Michael Foot and Tony Crosland. I was called and said I was grateful for the chance of a talk, that within the assumptions of Denis's paper containing the Treasury proposal for public expenditure, we had very little room for manoeuvre. It would certainly involve a tight restraint on public expenditure including social services, and a great deal would hinge on the wage restraint that we were told in the paper we needed. I went through ten assumptions stemming from Denis's analysis, saying that if all these assumptions were re-examined, we might develop alternative strategies. During the ensuing discussion Harold got very cross. He said no one was to make notes. 'It is absolutely against practice for Ministers to write down what other Ministers are saying.' So I put my pen down.

This evening, news came out that Roy Jenkins had made a major speech in support of continued membership of the Common Market.

Saturday 27 July

Roy Jenkins's speech on Europe is front page headlines in the *Daily Mail* ('Jenkins Slams Benn Men'), *The Times* and the *Financial Times* and the *Mirror*. The *Sun* said 'The Most Courageous Speech of His Courageous Career'. Mayhew, Taverne and George Brown rushed to Jenkins's support later today. I just decided to bite my tongue – there is nothing for me to say.

Sunday 28 July

The press this morning was still full of Jenkins's speech and the attack on it by Eric Heffer, Syd Bidwell, Ian Mikardo and the Newport MP, Roy Hughes. This is exactly what the Tory press have been waiting for – signs of a serious split. There was also a leading article in the *Sunday Times* attacking the idea of a Referendum, which has obviously very much frightened the right-wing Establishment. Later today Shirley Williams and Reg Prentice came out in support of Roy Jenkins, so the line-up is becoming fairly clear. I'm just keeping out of it.

Monday 29 July

My first appointment was with Michael Foot at the Department of Employment, as part of my strategy of canvassing members of the Cabinet. We turned to Roy Jenkins's speech and I said that I was in favour of free speech, of people saying what they think.

'This morning,' said Michael, 'I predicted to Jill that you'd say you were in favour of free speech. But Tony, don't say it publicly; you'll be bitterly attacked in the Party.'

'Well, of course,' I said, 'Roy wants us to lose the Election because of Europe.'

At 11 I went over to Number 10 and saw Roy in the anteroom, so I smiled at him. 'Well, you know I always support free speech.' He smirked.

Crosland said, 'Nobody ever reports *my* speeches.'

'Well, they are not interesting enough!' I retorted. 'Roy is interesting.'

When we went into the Ministerial Committee on Economic Strategy (MES), I heard Tony Crosland ask Ted Short what he thought of Roy's speech. 'Bloody awful,' barked Ted. 'I agree,' Tony replied. 'And if I'd had any doubt about it, Tony Benn's glee would have convinced me.'

At 12 I went to Cabinet. Harold reported on the White Papers, referring to the progress on my industry White Paper.

We discussed pensions, or rather Barbara spoke for twenty-five minutes. Then Denis made two points which Barbara answered. This went on for about forty minutes and in the end she lost. She should have simply said, 'Well, this is pretty non-controversial. I have no doubt everyone has read it; and it has been agreed by the Social Services Committee', and she should have left it at that. She really talked herself out, not for the first time.

I passed a lot of little notes to Bob Mellish during this carry-on. 'As Chief Whip, can't you move the closure?' and 'Perhaps she will have to stop for lack of food' and 'It looks as if only the Dissolution of Parliament will stop her.'

At 4.30 Sir Arnold Hall and John Lidbury of Hawker Siddeley came to see me to repeat the reasons why they wanted to cancel the HS-146 by agreement. It was the usual stuff: inflation, the cost of energy, the hazardous world situation, rocky airline finances, slower demand, higher incidence of costs. They said the aviation board and the group board were unanimous and it was a judgment based on the assessment of the commercial viability of the plane.

Well, I wasn't having that. I went through every point separately and I don't think they did very well in answering me. I asked them if they would consult the unions.

'Oh,' said Arnold Hall, 'they have nothing to contribute.'

'Maybe not, but I will have to consult them before I can give you a measured reply. You see, the Government is involved in the long-term future of the aircraft industry: Concorde is running down, the defence review is coming and this is the last major civil project, involving probably hundreds of millions of pounds on the balance of payments – a huge Government investment. Also people will argue that this has happened because of fears of nationalisation.'

Wednesday 31 July

Caroline and Joshua arrived at 12 and came over with me to the House. Jim Callaghan was making his statement on Cyprus and I followed with my statement on Concorde. I got some hostile questions, some friendly ones, and the Bristol MPs spoke. It was really exciting: I have saved Concorde and that is now off my chest.

The next statement on shipbuilding was also mine and I had the enormous pleasure of announcing the nationalisation of the shipbuilding industry. I worked so hard on the problems as Minister of Technology when I knew things weren't right, so I had given a solemn pledge that I would nationalise, a pledge which I was able to discharge. It gave me a tremendous thrill.

Of course, the Tories were very critical but they simply couldn't win because shipbuilding production has been absolutely stationary for twenty years. World orders have gone up five times and our percentage of world orders has dropped from 28 per cent to 3 per cent.

To the meeting of the Cabinet committee on my White Paper *The Regeneration of British Industry*, set up and chaired by Harold. The NEB's main strength in manufacturing would come from the acquisition of a number of key firms – that is to say, profitable firms, not just lame ducks. There was a great struggle but I think I got my way.

We came to future acquisitions and there was a real battle over whether or not we would say that if we provided regional grants, that would lead to public ownership. I said that when we were considering suitable firms for acquisition, we should add, 'The NEB will act also as a means to a further substantial expansion of public ownership through its power to take a controlling interest in relevant companies in profitable manufacturing industry.'

Harold wouldn't have that so I pointed out to him, 'Well, those are your very words from the Conference,' a very provocative remark to make. 'That was part of a longer sentence,' he said.

So I read him the words again, from the Manifesto, from the Labour Programme, and from his speech. I dug my toes in and something of that will survive, including the power to protect British firms from foreign takeovers.

We had a big argument on whether we should say that no other companies would be taken compulsorily into public ownership beyond ports, oil, land and so on. I tried to get that proviso removed.

Then, would compulsory acquisitions be by specific Act of Parliament? We got that in, but if there were circumstances of compelling urgency, we would by pass the need for an Act by the use of Statutory Instrument.*

* Statutory Instrument enables a Department to deal with circumstances that could not have been foreseen in the original drafting of legislation.

Dashed back to the office. It had been two and a quarter hours of absolute agony and bloodshed.

At 5.30 I had to go back to the Cabinet Committee because I had put in a paper on handling regional policy in discussions with the Commission. I simply said we should coordinate, consult and harmonise but that the ultimate power would remain with the UK Parliament and I quoted the Manifesto.

Jim said, 'Well, if we are going to blunder on like this and be obstructive, I don't know where we are.'

I turned to Jim. 'I very much resent the suggestion that as the responsible departmental Minister, my paper is taken to be blundering and obstructive, while the Foreign Office paper is taken to be constructive. There are two views and I will defend my view vigorously. It must go to Cabinet.'

Jim was livid. The Committee broke up and as we went out he said to me, white with anger, 'I'm absolutely fed up with you, absolutely fed up. You have split the Party in two.'

'That's the opposite of the truth Jim, and you know it very well.' Of course, he was angry not only about this Committee, but also the special conference on the Common Market which I pushed through last week.

Frances and Francis were at the office and they told me they had had a marvellous meeting on economic strategy with other advisers, and their paper on their five alternatives had gone down extremely well. The five economic strategies are: the Selsdon strategy; 'Stop and Go'; borrowing to get us through; reconstruction (which is really the Manifesto strategy); and isolationism. They said Maurice Peston from the Department of Education and all the others had been mesmerised and had agreed with the analysis. The paper had been written by Frances Morrell who had extracted the intellectual content from Francis Cripps and explained it all clearly. They are a marvellous combination. She said she was amazed that all these distinguished economists, Ham from the Treasury, Matthew Oakeshott from the Home Office, Maurice Peston and Andrew Graham from Number 10, had been tremendously excited and thoroughly enjoyed it.

Thursday 1 August
Banner headlines attacking the nationalisation of shipbuilding in the *Daily Mail*, the *Daily Express*, *The Times*, the *Financial Times*, and so on. The employers are hitting back but the case is so powerful, I don't think we have to worry.

At 9.30 Part came to see me with two really tough items. First, the idea of a popular version of the Industry White Paper: I had said I wanted a million leaflets to go out to industry and he replied that, because it was near an Election and it would be controversial, we probably wouldn't be able to do it. I asked, 'Why not? There's either an Election or there isn't and it would certainly be no more controversial than the White Paper.'

He said, 'I can only tell you that it would not be possible.'

Frances, who was sitting there, chipped in, 'Secretary, if you say that, that would be taken by people to be a political judgment by the Civil Service.'

Part picked up his folder, began to pack it and half stood up. 'Unless Frances withdraws that, I'm not continuing the discussion.'

'Half a minute,' I said. 'I'm not speaking for her, she'll speak for herself. But quite frankly what you said about the leaflet being controversial could only mean politically controversial. It isn't controversial for the Government, therefore it must be the Opposition who think it is. What is the Opposition objection? It's political.'

This went on for a long time and Frances said, 'I can't withdraw my comments. All I said is that your remark will be seen by others to be politically motivated, that's my best judgment.' In the end, she did say, 'It wasn't meant to be a criticism of you.' So then Part subsided.

The next thing he strongly objected to was my letter to the TUC in which I had offered them £20,000 to carry out research on job problems instead of giving the money to Cardiff University.

'You can't do that.'

'Why not?'

'The Department has decided to conduct a different sort of programme,' he explained.

'Who is the Department? It's me,' I said.

'But you can't give money to a trade union.'

'Why not? We give it to management, and to academics, why not to a trade union?'

He left and I must say it was exhausting. Part has been working to rule since we arrived and has done nothing to help me. He has just detached himself, and insofar as he has said anything, it has been completely obstructive. I think it all began when he asked me, 'Are you seriously going to try to implement your programme?'

Francis Cripps came to tell me about his lunch with Sir Douglas Henley of the Treasury who had told him and Frances, 'Of course, all the trouble over the White Paper has been caused by your Secretary of State because he is unreasonable. If he had just taken up the planning agreements and not pushed for the NEB, officials would have got it through in eight weeks but he has put up a huge fight and refused to do what the officials recommended; the Civil Service can't cope with a Minister who won't accept recommendations. It puts great strain on them. Officials who try to be loyal to their Departments can't be loyal when they have a Minister like that.' Frances and Francis were shocked.

Harold Wilson was on television tonight being interviewed about public ownership by Robin Day, who asked, 'Who speaks for the Labour Party, Tony Benn or Harold Lever?' Harold answered, 'I'm in charge. I'm in control.'

Friday 2 August

Cabinet met today – the key meeting to consider the Industry White Paper. Harold reported on its progress, then we went through it, beginning with the planning agreements, then the NEB and returning to the introduction at the end.

It was impossible to take any notes because the battle was too hot. Denis Healey said we had to remember that the collapse of business confidence was now a major factor and this meant we simply could not approach this policy rationally.

Harold Lever said this policy, as it was, would be a ruinous blow to industry.

Shirley's general contribution was that confidence was very low, things had changed since we had published our policy a year ago and were elected to govern. Politics meant we had to take charge of the situation so we couldn't be tied by what we had said before. She was as unhelpful as she could be on absolutely everything. Shirley is, without doubt, the most reactionary person I know. She gives the impression of being so nice yet she feels society is crumbling and she herself has no confidence in any of our policy. But she is now being built up as the great heroine: 'Shirley keeps our food prices down, Shirley protects our shopping baskets' and so on when she is, in fact, doing nothing beyond broadly doling out money to industry.

Clever Tony Crosland knows it all, very much disliking the policy, of course. He pretends it is meaningless; it doesn't matter; it has got nothing to do with anything.

Next to Tony is Jim Callaghan, deeply conservative, much less destructive than I thought he would be but absolutely insistent on the issue of not nationalising by Statutory Instrument on constitutional grounds.

On the other side of the table was Willie Ross, giving me strong support. Fred Peart said practically nothing. Ted Short was on the whole quite helpful. Denis Healey was not as bad as he might have been, quite frankly, still scornful and skeptical but he's more or less learned to accept it.

On the planning agreements, I said, 'Now look, here is a fundamental question. Are you going to give me any leeway because if I can't use the planning agreements to negotiate investment and jobs with the big companies, I will have absolutely no leverage at all?'

This led to a tremendous argument. Harold said he had never realised that the planning agreements were intended to be used for that purpose.

'Of course they were,' I shouted, and I read out a chunk under Investment on page 10 from Labour's Programme for Britain that 'planning agreements would be the means by which all regional aid was going to be channelled.' I said, 'It isn't just a theoretical question, it's a highly practical question.'

This was fought over very hard. 'I'm only asking for an experimental beginning but I think we must do something here.' I not only lost, but Harold even wrote in a special pledge that regional development grants would continue to go to the big companies, and not be a matter for negotiation in planning agreements.

I read out Harold's speech to the 1973 Conference and tried to make the words mean something. I said this was a central part of our policy; it was of fundamental importance. If we let this go by, it would be a change of policy. Moreover, we couldn't get jobs into the regions, with 8 per cent unemployment in Merseyside, if we didn't use the planning agreements as leverage against the big companies.

Harold said, 'If you do use them that way, you would have 18 per cent unemployment in Merseyside.'

It was a very bitter struggle and an important defeat for me. I said I wanted my dissent recorded in the minutes of the Cabinet.

We came to the National Enterprise Board and I said that on this nobody could have any doubt what our policy had been. It was substantial expansion of public ownership into profitable manu-facturing industry and that, as such, ought to be taken out of the main paragraph and made one of the open objectives. So that was done. Also new ventures and joint ventures were made a second objective. So that was a victory.

'The NEB will be the instrument by which the Government ensures the nation's resources' was accepted.

Then we came on to the paragraph dealing with acquisitions. There was an argument about whether we should use a phrase that Harold had added about 'vast industrial empires built on the basis of asset stripping'. Harold Lever tried to remove it and I mildly concurred because I knew it was just rhetoric, but I didn't press it because I didn't want to annoy Harold any more.

There was a long discussion about whether to state that the intention was that all holdings would be acquired by agreement. I got removed a provision which suggested that if a company was given special regional assistance, the NEB shouldn't take a shareholding. It was finally agreed that acquisition would be voluntary except in compelling urgency, where the Government would bring the issue before Parliament and any action would require specific parliamentary approval. So I didn't do too badly on that.

After that, I managed to get through the Cabinet the agreement that we should upgrade Edinburgh, Leith and Cardiff to development area status, Chesterfield and Derby to intermediate area status and Merseyside to special development area status. This will cost £25 million and it was a bit of a struggle.

That was three and a half hours of Cabinet mainly fighting this policy, and frankly what I have got is far better than I expected. I gather Harold did a briefing saying that the moderates won. Well, he can do that if he likes but when people say, 'If this is what the moderates think ...' then it is going to be great. I couldn't be more pleased. If people think I have been defeated, the Left will realise how hard I have fought, and I shall welcome it and say it is 95 per cent of our policy.

Came home late and had a meal with the kids. There was a cartoon in the *Evening Standard* tonight with two civil servants in the Department of Industry outer office, in front of a door marked A. Wedgwood Benn; one was saying to the other, 'Tony's not well. He hasn't nationalised anything all day.'

Saturday 3 August

The *Daily Mail* said, 'Wilson Goes Cold on Benn' and every other paper took up the same theme on its front page or inside. It was a very, very dishonest briefing by Number 10 and Harold knows it.

Roy Williams, Ray Tuite, Caroline and I were flown in a Beagle to Fairford for the Concorde test flight, where we met Brian Trubshaw, the chief test pilot, who is an old friend of mine. We saw the shop stewards, all Labour, had a few photographs taken and then we had lunch with the executive management of BAC, all of whom, of course, are Bristol Tories, albeit friendly ones.

At 1.40, about sixty of us climbed into the Concorde, and the great plane rumbled to the take-off point. There were a couple of American Airforce colonels from Edwardes Airforce Base on board, and the plane was crammed with technicians, because it was being treated as a proper test flight.

Some of the shop stewards had never flown before, even one of them who had been in the aircraft industry for thirty-seven years. Another had gone to confession last night, and another had made his will. Some of them had been up during the war but not since. It was astonishing that in the aircraft industry, nobody had thought of asking them to fly. Indeed, they had themselves asked many times and the management had always turned them down, and I insisted on taking them all up this time.

The whole plane shook. You could see the front portion, because it is a very long plane, just wobbling. Then this roaring take-off. We climbed through cloud, not steeply but quite quickly. We went out to a point off the coast of Cornwall and down to the Bay of Biscay; we reached Mach 1 as we went supersonic at about 700–800 miles an hour. It rose to 2.02 which was something like 1800 nautical mph. Absolutely no sensation in the plane at all. Somebody made a threepenny bit stand up on his table in front of him. We just behaved like people on a coach trip to Weston-Super-Mare or Southend, taking photographs and talking. I did a radio interview for Bristol, introducing the morning show from the plane.

We came back over Bristol and turned and swung over the city, went to RAF Lyneham, flew over the airfield and landed at Fairford. I had another very brief interview with a couple of journalists about the flight. Then we went into the hangar and I thanked all the shop stewards and they thanked Brian Trubshaw.

It was an unforgettable day. I feel very pleased to have nursed that plane through its final crisis before its entry into service.

Monday 5 August

Eric Heffer turned up and just at that moment the latest draft of the White Paper arrived with a little note from Sir John Hunt saying the Prime Minister had read it and didn't feel a drafting committee was necessary. So we looked at it with great trepidation and read it through. It is amazing, everything is in except the question of channelling all regional assistance to the top one hundred companies through the planning agreements. We were never specific about that in public, although those who followed the documentation knew that this was what we meant. The National Enterprise Board is an absolute dream, hardly a word I would change except 'each compulsory acquisition would be by Act of Parliament', and we have said that in urgent cases – failure of a firm or loss of control to a foreign power – it would be subject to special parliamentary approval. That is the Enabling legislation and if I am asked about it, I will have to say they have got to await the Industry Bill itself because there are aspects of this we haven't settled. Eric was just beaming. So that was a marvellous conclusion. With the assisted areas and Meriden and Glasgow, we have, in five months, done exceptionally well.

Tuesday 6 August

Big news in this morning's papers that Nixon had known about the cover-up. It has always been alleged that he lied about the cover-up and yesterday he made a statement which really amounted to a confession. It may well be that by the end of the week he will be out; Congress will have forced his resignation, or will accelerate his impeachment, or there will be some Indemnity Bill passed in return for his resignation. It looks as if the Nixon era is moving to its end. Why he made the statement, I don't know. It shocked all his friends, and even his lawyer expressed his horror; I should think the White House is now an absolute nightmare, it must be like the bunker in Berlin in 1945.

Wednesday 7 August
Came home with Frances Morrell for dinner and afterwards we came down to the basement office and hammered out how to present the industrial policy to the public. In the end the general theme was that Britain faces a grave economic crisis. Everybody knows we are going to have some years of real austerity, shortage and difficulty. It is a deep-seated crisis, exacerbated by the oil price rise and the collapse of confidence. It is absolutely essential that during this crisis Britain re-equips itself with new plant and equipment to make it competitive. It is also essential that we end completely the confrontation between the unions and the community; therefore, they must have much more democratic control and we must have more equality than we have had. If we get these three things right, we can emerge from this period of difficulty with our factories and our nation re-industrialised and re-equipped and Britain will be a major industrial power once more, with its own oil reserves.

Thursday 8 August
A Court Line meeting in the afternoon. It appears that the company is in a much more serious position than when we decided to acquire the shipyards. The whole company will go into liquidation next week and we must be sure that the shipbuilding interests are safeguarded. The holding company which owns Court Line Shipbuilders is just a shell and the whole thing is utterly rotten.

Two things amused me today. For the Honours List it was recommended that I should appoint for a knighthood a banker from Scotland, followed by Monty Finniston; Rupert Nicholson, the Rolls Royce receiver, on the grounds that he had done such a good job of selling off Rolls Royce last year; Gilbert Hunt, the Chairman of Chrysler; and an English industrialist.

So I thought to myself, if there has to be an Honours List I will strike some of the names out and add new ones, in a different order: Monty Finniston; Group Captain Fennessy of the Post Office; George Doughty of the Confederation of Shipbuilding and Engineering Unions; David Gentleman, the designer; Ken Alexander from Strathclyde; Geoffrey Robinson of Jaguar.

Secretary said, 'Well, I won't argue with you over this because I know I wouldn't win.'

The other amusing thing is that I am hosting the Lancaster House reception for those who attend the Farnborough Air Show. My office had alerted me to the fact that the South Africans would be there. So I thought about it and made up my mind and announced that invitations were not to be sent either to the South Africans or the Spanish and Chilean Ministers, diplomats, defence attachés or military officers.

By today, messages had come over from the Foreign Office saying it would create great offence if the Spanish Minister was not invited. So my officials said to me, 'I suppose you could get Lord Beswick to host it.' I said, 'Yes, perhaps.' Then they said, 'But unfortunately your name has already been printed on the invitation' as if to say, 'therefore, you will have to have these people.' So I said, 'If my name is printed, then I insist that these people are not invited; if the Foreign Office want to go ahead with the invitations, they will have to get somebody else to host it.' I just dug my heels in. I will not be photographed with these people. I won't have them to the party and if there is a row, so much the better. So that's that. There will be a squeal from the Foreign Office but they will just have to put their own Minister in.

Came home and Melissa arrived back from two weeks in France looking great.

My holiday is about to begin and it has been a remarkable five months in office. I have achieved most things I wanted, no doubt about it, except for one or two minor points. I have made an impact on thinking about industrial policy and with the publication of the White Paper on Thursday of next week, a new era begins in which I have to try to get it across and win support. I am lucky with my Ministers: Eric and Michael are very competent, Frank Beswick does an extremely good job, Gregor MacKenzie is a dab hand and keeps at it. My three advisers, Frances Morrell, Francis Cripps and Ken Griffin are all excellent. I am not sure the holiday will be a long one as I guess that a month from now we shall be into the Election and I shall be surprised if it isn't an extremely hard one.

Friday 9 August

I stayed up to watch the special *Midweek* programme and at 2 am London time, Nixon gave his final broadcast as President. He made no real reference to Watergate and spoke as if he was a Prime Minister who had lost his parliamentary majority, full of the usual corny Nixon morality. An extraordinary broadcast. There was the fascination of seeing a great figure crushed; it was like a public execution.

In the evening I listened to Nixon's emotional farewell to the staff of the White House, and President Ford's inaugural speech, full of Mid-West homespun philosophy.

Caroline and I went down to Stansgate. Very tired but awfully nice to be away.

Monday 12 August

Ron came to collect my red box. Worked all day. Melissa and her friend Gina arrived from London which was fun.

Thursday 15 August

Today, at Stansgate, Caroline and Joshua rescued two men from the river after their dinghy had capsized.

Went up to London to the office and worked on my final press statement for the White Paper. Frances had helped to reduce it to two minutes, just the right length. I must confess, I was unusually nervous. The press conference was jam packed and they were turning people away from the cinema at the Department of Industry. I went in and there were about a dozen photographers standing right in front of me, as if it were a Party Conference, and two television cameras recording it all. I was questioned for about an hour and a half.

I finished at about 1. I had a loose tooth and an abscess forming so I got the office to fix for me to go to the dental hospital at 2.

Friday 16 August

Papers full of the White Paper and Court Line, which did finally collapse yesterday, the significance of which is gradually beginning to seep in. The *Daily Express* attacked Caroline for rescuing the two people and not telling the coastguard so they could call off the helicopter search – as if she could possibly have known. As far as she was concerned she had helped two people ashore, given them a cup of tea, they had phoned their friends, and she had driven them home.

Saturday 17 August

At 2 Caroline and I flew to Coventry where we were met by the Lord Mayor. We were driven to the Triumph workers' co-op at Meriden. It was a fantastic spectacle. There was the freshly painted factory with an old picket tent and brazier on the gate and a couple of bikes out front, with Bill Lapworth of the T & G, Dennis Johnson, the chief shop steward, John Gratton from the AUEW and their wives to meet us. We went round the factory and talked to the men; the conveners and the stewards themselves took us round, and it was just like going round a Chinese factory – they were speaking with such confidence about their own skill and their work and how they wouldn't need as many supervisors and so on. Then we went into the canteen where tea was being served and Dennis Johnson introduced me briefly and I said a word; then Geoffrey Robinson spoke. There were one or two questions, and I described our industrial policy, and then they sang 'For he's a jolly good fellow' which was very touching.

Sunday 18 August

This morning the headlines were terrible. The *Sunday Express* had a banner headline 'Court Line – was it a Labour Plot?' to prove the failure of private enterprise. The papers also violently criticised the White Paper.

Monday 19 August

Spoke to Part who had heard I had rung Number 10 to suggest there should be an inquiry into Court Line. He was against this and said it would not help me. I asked him what he meant by 'would not help me'.

'You said something in the House on 25 June which did give the impression that the Government was underwriting Court Line.'

'I did not.'

'Well, Minister, you did say that the Government would safeguard the holidaymakers who were hit by Court Line's collapse and I notice that you altered that answer yourself, so you have altered the draft put before you.'

I said, 'I have no recollection of changing any words put before me, but in any case the phrase is no different from what was said on 1 July which was that "the board of Court Line accept that this should enable the holiday operations to continue." ' But Part was obviously trying to abstract the responsibility of the civil servants from me and was implying that I was really in trouble.

I must admit I am beginning to wonder whether the public anger against me, based on the belief that I'm responsible for losing them their holidays through Court Line, won't actually lead to some incident. It is very rough on the family and they are incensed by the lies that are told.

Tuesday 20 August

Rang the office and spoke to Part. 'That change you said I made in the parliamentary answer was not in my handwriting.'

He said, 'No, but you had written the original draft of the answer.'

'You will recall very well that I went to a Cabinet Committee that morning and reported, and when I came back from that meeting I was the only one in a position to draft, but it was in fact cleared by the whole Public Enterprise Committee.'

At 11.45 Martin Vile rang and read me Harold Wilson's statement on Court Line, and it was quite unacceptable because it talked about 'grave allegations against Ministers which should be substantiated or withdrawn'. I can just see the headlines 'Prime Minister Wilson speaks of grave allegations against Benn' and we would never recover. In the event, Harold dropped the statement and it is now in the Department of Trade's, i.e. Peter's, hands.

Wednesday 21 August
Stephen's twenty-third birthday.

At 1 Peter phoned and we argued over my suggested amendments to his statement. He was very unwilling to say that the Government had not given any guarantee or underwritten Court Line or even suggested underwriting it. 'People just won't believe that,' he said.

I said, 'They will only not believe it because nobody has said it firmly. We have got to put our own case on the record and the Department of Trade inspectors will reach their own conclusion. If we don't put our own case on the record, we are leaving the field to the Tories.'

He said, 'We mustn't be contentious.'

I got angry with him and said, 'You must stand up and fight on this.' He's incapable somehow of seeing or acting.

Later this afternoon, by which time I had got four boxes ready to go back to London, Peter rang and told me that the statement was agreed and going out tonight.

This morning, the *Daily Express* had a picture of Stansgate describing it as being protected by barbed wire and brick walls and so on. Melissa was upset and Joshua thumped the table with anger.

Thursday 22 August
Papers carried the disclosure by *Peace News* of documents from the extreme right-wing organisation GB '75, organised by Colonel David Stirling, who set up the Special Air Service, a right-wing intellectual soldier of the kind often seen operating in other countries. One of the documents said I was the greatest danger facing this country and this has led to further discussion about the possibility of a right-wing military coup. This is really the extreme Right marshalling itself. For example, we've had Sir Walter Walker (a retired General from NATO) and Oswald Mosley waiting in the wings. Although I don't for a moment take any of them seriously, there is no doubt that it is intended to create a feeling that anarchy is about to break out, and therefore we need a strong authoritarian Government. This is no doubt why there were alerts at Heathrow, which are intended to lead people to the coalition concept. While there is a serious possibility that a radical policy might be enacted, this sort of campaign will be waged against it.

There was a letter in the *Guardian* today from Michael Ivens, head of Aims of Industry, comparing the NEB with Mussolini's pre-war scheme to reconstruct Italian industry with state support.

Sunday 25 August
When the crisis comes, and it will probably be over a slump or Europe, a few people will go: Reg Prentice, Shirley Williams, Roy Jenkins and one or two others are bound to slip away into the centre ground, and the Labour Party will have to build itself up again.

Tuesday 27 August
Cold and windy. Worked all day fitting a seat on to the top of the car for the Election. We tested it up and down the road, with the loudspeaker.

Monday 2 September
At 10.30 Jack Spriggs, Dick Jenkins, Eric Heffer, Kenneth Cork (the Liquidator), Frances Morrell and a host of other people, including the consultants, came and we had a first look at the proposals that Spriggs and Jenkins had put forward for IPD. It was a marvellous meeting and the transformation in these people from the time they first came here is extraordinary. They arrived as militant trade unionists, bitter, hostile and suspicious, and gradually they have been won over to seeing that we have no interest in the old IPD. We want these guys to do more than save their jobs, we want them to take responsibility for their own future. I find it really moving and impressive to see Jack producing his management chart, his marketing estimates and capital needs. We went through it together and we cut it down to about £4.5 million. Jack seemed quite happy and he is going to seek the support of the TUC leaders in Brighton this week; I promised to put forward his proposals when they come in.

To Farnborough by helicopter where I was met by the Deputy Director of the Society of British Aerospace Companies. I looked at some of the planes, walked through the stands, had drinks and lunch with the SBAC. Met the Duke of Kent and King Hussein of Jordan who had decided to turn up with twenty-seven members of his retinue. Hussein called me 'Sir' which made me feel that I ought to call him 'Your Majesty' at least once. I had a talk to him about security risks, what planes he flew and so on.

I watched the flying display and talked to the Duke of Kent who said he had been in Cyprus and his sympathies were on the Greek side because, 'As you know, I'm half Greek myself' referring to his mother Princess Marina.

Tuesday 3 September
Arthur Scargill was interviewed by that awful woman Anne Scott-James in the *Evening Standard* last night, where he said he would like to see me as Prime Minister and Roy Jenkins and Shirley Williams thrown out of the Labour Party. He said he was a democratic Marxist which is a new category the British can't really understand. He's a bright guy and I like him. The point is how, if we get a working majority in the Election, we can use that analysis to try to carry through some changes within the Party, particularly in its internal democracy, and the re-selection of MPs, if local parties want it, between Elections.

Friday 6 September
Travelled up early to Liverpool, where I was met by Eric Heffer and we went to IPD where we walked round the factory with Jack Spriggs, met the stewards for a short meeting, then met the management – those who had remained – and addressed a mass meeting.

I went on to the North-West Council of the TUC where we had an excellent discussion. The trade unionists are so much more impressive than the management. They are not pessimistic, but practical, serious and appreciate what is at stake.

Sunday 8 September
To Bristol for my local Executive's meeting and we planned the Election campaign. Back in the evening and Francis Cripps looked in. He said he thought the Treasury would move fast after the Election to get a Budget in which it would borrow to preserve jobs but in return for borrowing it would be immensely macro-economic in its approach, resisting industrial policies it didn't like, trying to postpone national-isation and generally pursuing right-wing policies. It would try to get the support of the trade unions by saying this would save jobs. In fact, said Francis, it would be propping up capitalism by moving money into the corporate sector, by easing the price code and cutting taxation and we would have a big struggle on our hands. I agreed with him that he must prepare a paper on an alternative economic strategy.

Tuesday 10 September
At 2.15 I had a briefing for the IDV meeting at 3. I asked the Committee to note that the workers' cooperative at IPD was coming along well, and to authorise money for the Receiver to keep it going until the end of November. I was deeply committed to this and I believed we must succeed.

Harold Lever sat there bursting with laughter and Denis Healey thought it was crackers. Harold Wilson said, 'It was in my last Election address; we'll have to do something until the Election is over.' Utterly cynical. Frankly if that little discussion had been recorded, it would have destroyed the credibility of the Party completely.

Anyway, I said, 'Well, *you* tell me how you are going to get people to take a £20 a week wage cut as is happening in Coventry now to work for the cooperative. And you tell me where you will get people to exercise the responsibility that they are able to show. Merseyside is an absolute desert, a battlefield, and we must deal with it.'

At 4.30 Sir Douglas Allen, the new Permanent Secretary at the Civil Service Department, came to see me. He used to be at the Department of Economic Affairs with George Brown and told some funny stories about him.

We talked about the Treasury, the Department of Economic Affairs and the DTI, and how you needed a counter-balance without splitting the Treasury. He said, 'Of course, the real thing is for the Treasury decisions to be put in commission like everybody else's.'

I said, 'Of course, but the Treasury would never have it.'

'Oh no,' he said, 'it's the *Chancellor* who wouldn't have it. The Treasury wouldn't mind a bit.' Very interesting.

Thursday 12 September

Cab'net was dominated by Cyprus. Jim reported and said it was pretty clear that the Turks wanted the whole north-east of the island; they might even declare an independent state and there didn't seem much that could be done about it.

'What about the United Nations?' asked Michael Foot. 'Surely this attempt to settle international affairs by force is unacceptable to us. Why don't we use the UN?'

Jim Callaghan said, 'Well, the Turks got away with it by force and we have just got to accept that fact. Anyway, there's no point taking it to the United Nations; they've got no powers.'

Michael said, 'Surely the whole point is that the United Nations is there for the people who don't have power.'

Jim emerged disgracefully from the exchange. I didn't join in but Michael and Ted Short did very well.

Friday 13 September

I had a visit this morning from two Polish Ministers, the Vice Premier, Mr Olszewski, and the Minister of Machine Building. After talking about the big tractor deal they've signed with Massey-Ferguson, we moved on to Polish economic reforms and the need to decentralise, and how the big Super Powers didn't seem to me to be the future. Olszewski said, 'Yes, decentralise up to a point with economic reforms but of course workers just want more money and less work.'

He fitted in exactly to the tycoon image which I suppose every kind of society throws up, whether it be the landowners, or the king, or the capitalists, or the Communists twenty-five years after their revolution. A working-class tycoon, if you like; he was actually a qualified engineer, but representing a working-class movement. He had as low an estimate of the intelligence and capacity of his own people as do, say, Denis Healey or Sir Jack Callard of ICI or the old right-wing trade union bosses.

I talked to Olszewski about the role of the Central Intelligence Agency and the admission by the CIA to the Congressional committee that they had, I think, spent $4 million undermining the Allende Government by creating chaos. I said how undesirable the work of the Intelligence services was in pursuing their own policies. He agreed.

Then I went on to say that Willy Brandt, who had conducted an active Ostpolitik, had been undermined, so it appeared, by East German Intelligence agents.

He said, 'Yes, that was a great pity.'

'Well, how do *you* control them?' I asked.

'We have much greater political control', he said. 'There's much greater freedom than there was. We don't want to repeat Stalinism again, we are anxious to develop liberty, and we must get political control of Intelligence.'

I said, 'Yes, but what about international espionage? You see, you are building on the desire for greater freedom and we want socialism, but we don't want to go through Stalinism.'

'Oh well, that arose out of revolution and war,' he said.

At about 6 o'clock or thereabouts, I gave a 'farewell' party for the Private Office and some of the senior officials. I clearly am not going to give a party if we're defeated, and if I'm moved, it would be hard. So we agreed to have it while I was still there, which was much nicer.

Saturday 14 September

I am not sure about the Election – my thoughts go up and down. I must record here too that Caroline is finding the strain appalling. She feels that, being under the shadow of a Cabinet Minister, everything she does is dismissed. I agree that this is a real sacrifice that the wives of politicians have to make.

Sunday 15 September

To the Campaign Committee and Executive in Bristol. We had 6000 window bills, 8000 leaflets and 1000 addressed envelopes, and so the ward organisers' work is pretty clearly set up. I was asked to read my Election address and various criticisms were made – that it made no reference to women, that it didn't stress the crisis enough, that one passage sounded like Speech Day at a public school, and so on. I was rather resentful until I came to the conclusion that I was sounding like Harold, when he said 'In the end I will decide what I say', so I accepted all the amendments and thanked them. Indeed, I think there is something to be said for regarding the Election address as being the collective voice of the local Party.

Ferranti is in financial difficulties and I issued a statement that after discussions with the Department of Industry and the Ferranti Company, the Government have agreed to provide the company with support under the 1972 Industry Act.

I suppose this will enable me to hammer home most purposefully the main political lessons: Ferranti subscribes to the Tory Party to get Government out of industry's hair, and then comes round with its begging bowl, when it gets into trouble, for help from a Labour Government. This is the lesson of modern capitalism and the Government's policy is highly relevant, while the Opposition are being odiously hypocritical.

Monday 16 September
The Central Intelligence Agency, through William Colby, the Director-General, has been giving evidence in Washington and has openly admitted that the CIA spent $4 million undermining the Allende Government in Chile. This of course is far worse than Watergate though it receives very little public comment, and it is a candid admission of how they do it. One has to keep an eye out for the role of British Intelligence here at home. Apparently a man called Cord Meyer was sent to London by the CIA to work with the British Labour movement, and one would be foolish to underestimate the extent to which American business is secretly mobilising in order to defeat the Labour Government, and particularly policies on which we are going to fight the Election.

To Number 10 at 9.30 to the big State Dining Room to work on the new Manifesto. We were given half an hour to read it, then Jim introduced it and Harold said he had not seen it till this morning, because he did not want to be in a more advantageous position than others.

Looking back on the meeting briefly, there are three achievements in the new Manifesto, not without importance: that the industrial policy has remained in its entirety; that the Referendum or ballot box vote on the EEC within twelve months of the Election and binding on the Government is crucial; and that the phrase 'fundamental and irreversible shift in the balance of wealth and power in favour of working people and their families' has remained as the only broad perspective.

But I am sure that when the Election is over there will be a determined push to the Right and there will have to be an immediate effort to halt it. If we get a working majority, so much the better.

Tuesday 17 September

At 10 a huge delegation arrived representing Ferranti workers from all over the UK, led by the CSEU, the STUC and the individual unions and stewards. They all said much the same thing – even the senior management – namely, that they wanted the company kept in its present form, that they didn't want to see jobs lost, that they rejected a take-over by others (in their minds was a Weinstock take-over), and that they wanted Government support which should carry accountability with it. The senior management identified themselves as employees which is what they are, and I promised to give consideration to their requests. Afterwards Bob Wright of the AUEW and Jack Service came and we drafted a reassuring statement.

Wednesday 18 September

I had a word with Len Murray – or Lionel, as he likes to be known – about the Scottish Action Committee of workers producing the new *Scottish Daily News*. He was very negative about it. 'The unions will say, "God bless you but you mustn't think we will give you much money."' He said the print unions were in trouble and he can't recommend to his members to help the paper. In effect, the trade union bureaucracy has come to a similar conclusion to that of the official bureaucracy, that it is not viable, it is too risky and although it may be a good cause, 'count us out'. I shall have to report that frankly to the committee of Ministers tomorrow.

A Cabinet had been called this morning and Harold said, very solemnly, as if he were announcing a great event, 'Colleagues, I must tell you that Her Majesty the Queen ...' There was some chatting going on and he said, 'Silence, order. I am telling you that Her Majesty the Queen has assented that there should be a Dissolution of Parliament and an Election on Thursday 10th October, and that the announcement will be made at 12.45.' Well, since everybody knew quite well that that was what it was about, there wasn't much excitement.

There was some discussion about smears, and Barbara Castle said that she had heard that the *Sunday Times* was going to reveal that Ted Short owned six houses; and Harold said there was a rumour that his income tax returns had been photocopied, and so on.

Jim warned us of the danger of attacking a coalition too much because there was such a will to survive among the British people, and Bob Mellish said that the British people with their sense of fair play liked to feel that we would talk to anybody. Michael Foot argued that we couldn't let the argument about coalition go by default. I said I hoped we would ignore the public opinion polls as far as we could.

Friday 20 September

Frances and Francis came in for a final pre-Election talk and we agreed the general line for the media: namely no press conferences during the Election, no interviews for the press except for sympathetic papers like the *Mirror*; I would offer to write articles or answer written questions, do television and radio interviews as and when I want, and no TV units when I am canvassing.

I came home for about half an hour and saw Mary Lou. Caroline and I went down to Bristol to the Campaign Committee at Unity House. It was amusing because the tension between Herbert Rogers, who had planned to run the campaign, and Ennis Harris who had agreed to be the agent, was just under the surface, with Cyril Langham, the chairman of the local Party, being on Herbert's side and me supporting Ennis's right to be the agent.

I was officially readopted, for the eleventh time, and I made a little speech thanking them and saying how deeply I valued my links with them. I said how important the Election was in the current situation, and what a cheat the whole question of the coalition was.

Ken Coates rang to say he was launching some sort of an appeal to Labour leaders about the CIA intervention against Allende in Chile. Of course, everyone is just a little bit anxious about whether this might be going to happen in Britain as well, particularly with the big international companies' interests in operations here. Martha Mitchell, the wife of John Mitchell, US Attorney-General, said on a television interview tonight with David Frost that she thought Nixon had instructed or – at least – approved the attempt to kill Governor George Wallace of Alabama. Caroline made the point that Nixon might be polished off because he knew too much. This is the general atmosphere of politics at the moment.

The other consideration is the extent to which the CIA might engineer a run on the pound or provoke some crisis during the Election. If that were to happen, then the whole situation could go bad in a very big way. If it became a really major crisis, Harold and Denis, no doubt Jim and perhaps Roy and Michael (and hopefully myself), together with the big union leaders, would have to get together to consider emergency action. I just don't think this is going to be an ordinary Election. I think something very big is going to blow up on us – I just feel it. Whether it will defeat us we won't know until two weeks on Thursday.

Saturday 21 September

Caroline had a letter from Graydon, her brother in Cincinnati, describing how a reporter, purporting to be from the *Sunday Times*, told him she was doing a profile of their father, James Milton de Camp. Graydon expressed surprise at this because their father was a provincial lawyer who had died thirteen years ago, and the girl had said, 'We want to know the origins of his great wealth.' So this is the *Sunday Times* snooping in order to provide a background for the profile that I understand is to appear in tomorrow's edition.

Sunday 22 September
The profile appeared in the *Sunday Times* today: 'The Man the Tories Love to Hate' by William Shawcross and Bruce Page, a generally offensive piece, full of in-group jibes which would mean absolutely nothing to anyone who wasn't in the Fleet-Street-senior-civil-servant-academic-world coterie.

Tonight it was announced that Lord Chalfont has decided to leave the Labour Party and join Dick Taverne, a *Times* plot of some kind so far as timing is concerned, but entirely without significance because being a peer, Chalfont has no vote. Who's ever heard of him anyway? But it will excite Fleet Street again. They do live in a closed little world, playing out their dramas to each other, while the great big world outside makes practically no impact on them and vice versa.

Tuesday 24 September
Went to the office very briefly then to the Broadwalk for a short go on the loudspeaker. I must say I got a very warm welcome. People came up and reminded me of things I had done for them and so on.

Wednesday 25 September
Heard that Joan Lestor had been told by an International Socialist journalist friend that a big financial scandal or smear was being prepared against me for the last week of the campaign. It is slightly disturbing and worrying, but my inclination is to say that I have been warned that such a story might appear and as it is not true, I do not intend to make any further statements about it, and leave it at that. Rang Frances and she didn't think it would make any difference whatever to the Election and I think, curiously, that is true. People just forget these things.

I travelled to Derby and went to the Midland Hotel and found they had given me the suite where Queen Victoria stayed on 25 September 1849. Slightly mysterious feeling dictating this in a room where Queen Victoria slept.

I was driven to one of the clubs where I met the stewards from Rolls Royce and other works. I talked to the Transport and General Workers first, then to the ASTMS shop stewards from Rolls Royce – there is no doubt, this is the audience, this is the group which really understands what it is about and to which I am responding.

Then we went to a school where the BBC had got a video feed into the news. It is the second time they have done this to me and I find it very distressing because one is talking under lights and knowing that every word could be picked up. All they probably used on the news was a bit about Lord Chalfont – I said the peers didn't have a vote, that the House of Lords was the Madame Tussauds of British politics, and I knew that because I had escaped from it. Everybody laughed and it was quite a harmless and amusing contribution. But it might have encouraged our people a bit so perhaps it was worth it.

The really big news today is that Shirley Williams at the Transport House press conference said that if the Referendum went against Britain's continued membership in the Common Market, she would resign from public life. Well, that's a bit blown up but if we lose the right-wing members of the Party one by one, Mayhew, Chalfont, Williams, it won't be a disaster. Not that I would drive her out, but if she can't persuade people, then that is her problem not mine. I had a message from Transport House saying Shirley had made a remark directed at me at the press conference today, 'Please act as a member of the team and preserve the image of the team.'

Thursday 26 September
Roy Jenkins reiterated what Shirley said: the Right is clearly just seeking to wreck the Party's front on Europe because, above everything, they are determined not to consult the people. They don't want a Labour Conference; they don't want a Referendum; they want to impose their will. It has done the Right an awful lot of damage.

Friday 27 September
Worked on my box this morning. There are a lot of cases of collapsed firms and I have had to give rapid instructions: ask the National Research Development Corporation to help; ask the managements not to go ahead with the closure; consult the workforce; promise we will consider help so long as we don't assume legal responsibility; deal with the Receiver; prevent lay off of people at Fisher-Bendix. A most extraordinary succession of problems.

At 10.30 I went to collect Caroline from the station and it is lovely to have her here. The Election begins in earnest only when she arrives.

We settled into the Unicorn Hotel, and who should arrive but Frances Morrell, Francis Cripps and Clive Jenkins. We sat and had a drink together. Clive is very amusing, though he is perhaps a man who needs to be kept under the most severe democratic control.

Saturday 28 September

To London by train with Frances and Francis and we discussed the text of what I should say at the Labour Party press conference at Transport House. Ron Hayward told me that Harold had been very angry with Shirley Williams over her Common Market statement, and had more or less warned her that there were plenty more in the Second Eleven who could replace her. That's a story that I do not believe.

Caught the train to Bath and was met by Caroline who had come over from Bristol, and Donna Haber of ASTMS, who's attached to Clive Jenkins's campaign. We were taken to the headquarters where there was a huge crowd of people, with a few Tories. I walked over to the precinct by the Pump Room and made a political speech in the pouring rain through a most inadequate loudspeaker with a lot of heckling from Mayhewites, Tories and a National Front chap.

Sunday 29 September

The *Observer* says that it is likely I will be dropped as Secretary for Industry, the policy will be completely modified after the Election, and the Cabinet simply couldn't believe their ears when they heard me say that the system was breaking down – which they all thought must mean parliamentary democracy was breaking down. Ronald Butt in the *Sunday Times* said there were rumours that I'd be removed. This story comes no doubt from both the right-wing members of the Cabinet who are always quoted as hating my guts but are never named and perhaps Harold thinks it is prudent to reassure industry at the moment.

Went over to Transport House in Bristol at 10 and someone there showed me a very expensively printed colour booklet entitled 'I challenge Heath', which attacks Ted Heath in the most scurrilous and disreputable way, and alleges he is a homosexual. It was written by the woman, Karen Cooper, who threw ink at him when he was in Brussels to sign the Treaty of Accession to the Common Market, and she had tried to get Ken Coates to publish it as a trailer to her book which is due out soon. It was filthy, and in it the author alleged she was a member of the Labour Party, so one wonders whether it wasn't really designed to damage us. British politics is getting more like American politics every day, where this sort of thing has been going on for some time.

Monday 30 September

Vera Cox from the Bristol Party drove me to South Molton in North Devon where I spoke for a moment in the village square. Then on to Appledore to the Court Line shipyard where there was a tremendous welcome, with masses of press and television. They had got a big mug of tea, sandwiches and Mars Bars ready for me.

After lunch I was introduced to an old stalwart called Ernie Tuttie, in his late sixties, I would think. He had been in the Party for fifty years and somebody told me, 'He's like a piece of seaside rock. If you split him down the middle, you'd find Labour written all the way through.' Earlier this year when the local Party couldn't get any envelopes for this Election, he had taken on the job of buying 70,000 labels and writing all the addresses by hand.

I put my hands on his shoulders and said, 'Well my friend, you certainly have worked hard', at which point he burst into tears and said, 'I am overcome with emotion at this moment.' He took off his spectacles and mopped his eyes and put his arm around me like a son and we walked along together until he had recovered his composure. He came from Smethwick years ago and has worked in North Devon. There is a tiny band of supporters there; they only get 6000 votes and it was a big political occasion.

We went to the canteen and talked to the women who did a twenty-five-hour week for £10: they had no union. Then I went up on the hillside and addressed about 800 shipyard workers, a marvellous meeting. Of all the meetings I have recorded, this would have been one of the best, but I forgot to press my tape-recorder. I told them the story of Court Line and how we had saved their yards, and how the Tories and the Liberals would sell them back to private enterprise. We wanted them to work with their management and produce a corporate plan. You could have heard a pin drop. Then we walked around a covered yard, the most modern in the world, I should think, producing tugs for the North Sea. Of course, it had all been equipped by the Shipbuilding Industry Board when I was Minister and was now in the public sector. There was a tremendous sense of excitement, a very impressive occasion.

After that we went into Bideford and from there I was driven on to Barnstaple with a loudspeaker blaring. Mike, one of the Party workers, had equipped the car not only with these enormously powerful loud-speakers, but also with a two-way radio that kept in contact with a Land Rover which was never very far from us, so there was a lot of 'Over to you, over' and 'Mike 1 to Mike 2, are you reading me? Out.' They were having a whale of a time.

Drove to Exeter with Vera Cox, very tired by then. I was due to be back in Bristol by 11 but I got a phone call to say that John Pardoe, the Liberal economic affairs spokesman, had said we were deliberately bankrupting British industry, Heseltine had alleged that I was going into board rooms like an undertaker, and Heath had attacked back-door nationalisation. The Party wanted me to do the ITN news bulletin at 10, so one of the members got in his Daimler and drove me from Exeter to Plymouth where we arrived just in time. I slept in the car. Robert Kee interviewed me in a most hostile way but still I got across a few points.

Wednesday 2 October

Caught the train to London with Caroline. Ron Vaughan met us at the station and took us home where Mary Lou was waiting. Stephen had a fabulous time in America of which I shall be reporting more. He and June met Alice Roosevelt Longworth in Washington DC, the 'girl in the Alice Blue Gown', the daughter of President Theodore Roosevelt. He went to the White House press briefing and said something to President Ford who nodded and smiled at him. He also met the senior policy analyst from the State Department.

This morning, Hilary went for an interview for a job in the research department of the EETPU.

Harold Lever or someone is busy selling the idea that I am going to be moved from being Secretary of State for Industry, and that we will put £1,000 million into the banks as a way of dealing with the cash flow situation. So I said to Francis Cripps, 'Will you prepare a paper for the Cabinet suggesting that we take over the National Westminster Bank, which I think is the largest. How much would it cost?'

'Between £100 and £200 million.'

I said, 'If Harold Lever is going to suggest we put in £1,000 million, let's counter it with the suggestion we take over a bank and see what happens.' Francis Cripps was doubtful but later Frances Morrell told me he became quite motivated by the idea, went out to buy some cigarettes, saw a branch of National Westminster and said how exciting it was to think this might be ours.

In the Department, Secretary was making one last rear-guard action against my writing to the Secretary of the Welsh TUC, George Wright, to approve the broad outlines of his plan for the use of the research grant. Secretary sent me a minute opposing my doing anything more at this stage than acknowledging his letter. But I am determined to reply to Wright before the Election, confirming my acceptance. Secretary had tried to suggest first that I would need the approval of the Welsh Office (whose opposition he had stirred up); then he said I'd need the support of the Common Market, which is quite untrue. Today, when I dictated my letter, Part told Roy Williams that in his capacity as Accounting Officer, he would need a directive before he was ready to spend the money. 'Well,' I told Roy, 'I am quite happy to give him a directive but all I am doing now is approving the draft proposals.' Roy asked me to see him and I said, 'No. I can't be persuaded. I am quite clear in my mind what I want to do. Will you please send the letter off.'

Thursday 3 October

Got to the Central Hotel in Glasgow at around 8, and had a good breakfast. Gavin Laird of the AUEW met me and we went to the old *Daily Express* office and I was asked to address the staff briefly. I paid a tribute to the staff as individuals but said the *Express* had been unhelpful to Labour. I described my interest in the *Scottish Daily News* project, and how we had published a pamphlet encouraging people in the media to reject Government control but at the same time to try to limit commercial control of the mass media.

Went to the Hillingdon Estate at 12.30 for a tremendous meeting with about 3000 people from Rolls Royce. Bruce Millan was there and we had lunch with the management.

Then at 2.45 we went to Linwood for a meeting with the shop stewards from Chrysler, with Norman Buchan.

I went to speak for Harry Ewing, Labour Candidate for Stirling, Falkirk and Grangemouth, in the Town Hall, and back to the BBC where I was interviewed by Robin Day for *Midweek*. He was most offensive, touching on subjects as wide-ranging as industry and proportional representation. I kept my cool, but he lost his at the end.

Friday 4 October
Caroline and I got to Euston at 5.15 and we were met and driven to Bristol.

It certainly has been a fantastic week, just slogging away at the campaign all over the country, but on the whole the feeling is good.

Sunday 6 October
To the Walter Baker Hall for a very crowded meeting, attended by my Marxist-Leninist opponents from the Revolutionary Communist Group and IS. Cyril Langham was in the chair. A record of Stafford Cripps speaking in 1935 was played and it was remarkable, much of what he had said being far more radical than anything that we are saying today.

I decided to talk to the people about their own achievements, looking at the history of the Party right back to 1918; paid a tribute to Herbert Rogers, talking about his early years in the movement. I read Clause 4 and talked about Stafford Cripps and the near defeat in 1931; how the employers in Bristol had lit a fire in the chimneys in the corset factory, which had been closed, to give people the impression that there would be jobs if the National Government was re-elected, and how the Party had stood against MacDonald's betrayal; how Stafford Cripps had called for a popular front and had been expelled from the Party by a resolution at the annual conference moved by George Brown; how the Party, or Herbert at any rate, had supported the ILP against the electoral truce.

Monday 7 October
The papers this morning printed my speech at the University Labour Club yesterday, where I said the telephone lines were hot between

Jeremy Thorpe and the Tory headquarters about preparations for a coalition. I got a very angry telegram from Jeremy Thorpe saying, 'Your suggestion is ridiculous. I have no contact with other Party Leaders apart from my open letter to Mr Wilson and Mr Healey and I call upon you to substantiate or withdraw.' Of course, the coalition idea is now running into serious difficulties because it is becoming a major issue in the Election.

To Bristol Commercial Vehicles and the Liberal candidate, Mr Wardle, was there. He followed our car shouting through his loud-speaker. His posters say 'Vote Wardle to Beat Benn' and apparently some Liberals have found this so offensive, they have blanked them out to leave 'Vote Wardle'. The Middle-Class candidate, Wing-Commander Gooding, is putting out material saying, 'Ban the Benn – Vote for Gooding the Middle-Class Candidate'. His message to the electors is incredible; 'pure Monty Python' as one pensioner said to me. I am collecting all this Election ephemera.

Thursday 10 October
Polling Day. To Transport House where the *Daily Mirror* was waiting – they photographed me at a couple of polling stations and on top of the car with my loudspeaker.

At 1 o'clock we had lunch and I made a further thermos so I could drink tea from my tin mug while sitting on top of the car. The seat was so hard, I got really sore. Fortunately, there was very little rain but it was cold up there and I had my anorak and blanket round me.

Josh arrived in the afternoon. He and Stephen went around together all afternoon and were terrific. We worked right through, had a cup of tea with George Easton, then finished at about 8.45 and went back to the hotel for a meal.

The results began coming in. The polls this morning were showing on average a 5.5 per cent Labour lead but it became quite clear that this distribution of our lead varied very much according to which part of the country it was, and in the Tory marginals where they were fighting like hell, they did actually manage to hold their own. The computer began by predicting a 66 over-all majority, but it narrowed and narrowed as the night went on.

To the count at about 12.10. BBC and ITN television said that mine was the only result they intended to show from the South-West, and when I asked all the Labour agents who were gathered in the classroom, which we had booked and provided with a kettle, milk, teabags and sugar, there was an overwhelming vote against letting the cameras in to the declaration. ITN and the BBC were extremely angry. The result came out at about 1.15 am, a great deal earlier than in the last Election. My majority was 9,373 compared with 7,912 in February. I had a 17.7

per cent majority and my percentage of the vote rose from 47 per cent to 49.1 per cent. It was an absolutely superb result.

I went back to the hotel and watched the results until about 4 am. The computer prediction was of a Labour majority of five by the time I went to bed.

NOTES
Chapter Two

1.   (p. 118) In 1973, under the Conservative Government, Norton Villiers Triumph (NVT) were given a grant to attempt to reorganise the British motorcycle industry. To this end, one of the works, at Meriden, near Coventry, was to be closed with the redundancy of 1750 workers. The workforce resisted the closure and introduced a 'work-in' during which bike production was continued, followed by a 'sit-in' to protect the assets of the factory, including 2000 finished motorbikes. An attempt at setting up a workers' cooperative had already been tried by the time I arrived at the Department of Industry in February 1974, and it was one of the early industrial crises I inherited.

2.   (p. 139) Harold Wilson, like all incoming Prime Ministers, produced his own 'Questions of Procedure for Ministers', laying down 'guidance' on ministerial conduct for the attention of all members of the Government over a wide range of activity. I did not accept that this Procedure was binding on me or my departmental Ministers and issued a minute of my own in June 1974 which concluded: 'We are still ourselves, Labour Party and trade union members, as well as Ministers; and our accountability is to our consciences, to the people, to the Party and to the Movement, as well as to the Government.'

3.   (p. 184) Court Line, the giant leisure group, which also owned the North Devon Appledore Shipbuilders as well as ship repairing yards in the North-East, had approached the Government for financial assistance. In June 1974, I announced in the House of Commons that the Government was ready to acquire the entire shipbuilding and ship repairing interests of Court Line. Because of Court Line's holiday business (it owned Clarkson's and Horizon), a collapse – which in fact happened in August 1974 – would have had serious implications for holidaymakers travelling abroad with Court Line. The affair became the subject of a Trade Department inquiry.

3
Referendum
October 1974–June 1975

Over the eight months following the October Election, in which Labour gained a precarious three-seat majority, I was preoccupied with the forthcoming Referendum on Common Market membership, and with attempts to advance an increasingly frustrated industrial policy.

The Labour Government's position on the Common Market was that the terms under which the Conservatives had formally entered the Market in 1973 would be re-negotiated and the new terms would be put to the British people for rejection or acceptance. That principle at least had been won, but nothing else had been resolved.

The central point argued by me and others opposed to the Common Market was that the British electors would lose their right to enact through Parliament the laws they wished, and to uphold this legislation against Community law. However, there was never any doubt in my mind that the Prime Minister and James Callaghan – who personally conducted the re-negotiations – were convinced long before the June Referendum that Britain should remain in the EEC, that the Cabinet would so recommend and that the public would be persuaded to confirm that decision. The Conservative Opposition under Margaret Thatcher, who successfully challenged Heath under new rules to elect the Conservative Party Leader, was happy to sit back and leave the Labour Party to fight out this particular issue.

The initial work of the Department of Industry began to bear fruit by 1975 in the worker cooperatives, the protection of major firms such as Leyland, Ferranti and Alfred Herbert from bankruptcy, and the publication of Bills negotiated with the appropriate unions dealing with the shipbuilding and aircraft industries. The Industry Bill itself was also published. But resistance to the Manifesto's industrial proposals both from within the Labour Government ranks, and by the Civil Service and industrialists, also hardened during this period. This was demonstrated most effectively when my Permanent Secretary sent me an 'Accounting Officer's Minute', for which some explanation is needed.

The procedure derives from the direct responsibility that the Permanent Secretary, or some other senior civil servant, has for the accounts in each Department, which have to be reported to the Comptroller and Auditor-General who, in turn, is responsible to the Public Accounts Committee. In normal circumstances these accounts are certified by the Accounting Officer as a matter of course, but if he or she believes that the expenditure which the Minister wishes to authorise is in an area in which the policy is new or unclear, he may issue an Accounting Officer's Minute to that Minister, asking for specific instructions to spend the money. If, subsequently, the Accounting Officer is questioned by the Public Accounts Committee – a not uncommon practice – he will report accordingly and the Minister may then be asked to explain his policy personally. There is, however, a particular type of Accounting Officer Minute which carries the implication that the Minister is seeking to authorise expenditure which is deemed improper. In these circumstances, the charge can be a serious one.

Just before the Election I had been warned that Sir Antony Part, as my Accounting Officer, was preparing to send me such a minute over various items of disputed expenditure; this event erupted after the Election into a major issue with much wider implications, and led to a showdown within the Department and with the Prime Minister.

Saturday 12 October

The *Economist* has demanded my dismissal as Secretary for Industry. Frank McElhone rang to say he thought it was quite possible that Harold might move me – that is very much the rumour. But Jack Jones, I think, probably wouldn't favour that. Nobody can now claim that I did the Party any damage in the Election. Harold's own Election campaign was trifling and unimportant, with no real content; that man is capable of being Prime Minister four times without doing anything to change the structure of power in society.

Sunday 13 October

Caroline's birthday, with family presents this morning. Mother came to lunch and Stephen showed us films he had taken in America.

In the evening we had a political gathering of Frances Morrell, Francis Cripps, Michael Meacher, Ken Coates, Bryan Stanley, Clive Jenkins and Stephen. The whole discussion was about political strategy. It seemed to me that we had two objectives: one was to get Britain out of Europe in the next twelve months and the other was to get our industrial policy across.

Clive said that there had been various feelers put out to test out how trade union leaders would react if I was moved to the Department of Health and Social Security – a very big Department, requiring a big shake-up. He said the word had gone back to Number 10 that this was not acceptable. So it looks as if Harold has been putting his toe in the water and has had his initiative rejected and rebuffed.

This morning the *Sunday Telegraph* said that the Industry Bill was going ahead full steam. The *Observer* and the *Sunday Times* have called for my removal by Harold Wilson mainly because they think I would wreck the re-negotiation of the Common Market. This is all part of a scenario that Harold no doubt is working on at Chequers over the weekend.

Monday 14 October

Rang up Len Murray who said he couldn't see me until tomorrow as he was going to see Harold Wilson this afternoon.

Hugh Scanlon eked out an hour of his time and I went to see him this afternoon. All he wanted to talk about was my own position. 'Have you been reappointed? Have soundings been made about you possibly being moved?' I said I didn't want to discuss that. But he said, 'If you are moved my Executive Council will issue an immediate statement denouncing it.'

He was most friendly. 'Now, this is the moment to speak frankly,' he said. 'We won't always agree but you have stood up for the trade union movement. You have been bashed; you have been the bogeyman. You and I would both have been scapegoats if we had lost the Election.'

Tuesday 15 October

At 9 to see Len Murray, who criticised me for giving the £20,000 to the Welsh TUC. I must say, I laughed because it proved how bureaucracies all think alike. I told him, 'Sir Antony Part, my Permanent Secretary, threatened to report me to the Public Accounts Committee for that and if you are against it too, I haven't got a friend in the world.' So he responded, 'Well, we'll think about it.'

'If you have a drumhead court martial, give me a chance to say something before you sentence me to death,' I said.

At 10.30, I went to Number 10 for the Cabinet. On the way in, I saw Crosland and I said, 'Congratulations on your appointment.'

'What do you mean?' he asked.

'Haven't you seen Harold?'

'No.'

'Didn't you see him last night?'

'No.'

'Oh good heavens, perhaps I shouldn't tell you . . .'

'What is it?'

'It's Defence,' I said.

Harold Lever was standing beside me and he said, 'Yes. Surely you must have heard.'

'What?' Crosland exclaimed.

'Defence,' I repeated. 'After all, a paratrooper, wartime record, an obvious appointment. I think it's simply marvellous. You must really deal with the defence cuts and put your mind to the administrative problems.'

'You're kidding.'

'No. Why should I be kidding?'

'I just don't believe it.'

I said, 'For heaven's sake, don't tell Harold I've told you when you go in and see him.'

I absolutely had him. Then he said, 'Do you mean it.'

I said, 'Of course I don't.' And all of a sudden he was very relaxed.

As we went into Cabinet, all Harold Wilson said was, 'We won.' He's only going to make one or two minor changes among junior Ministers. 'The most important thing,' said Harold, 'is that we revert to the tightest rules on broadcasting and articles in the press. These problems must stop. We will go ahead with the Manifesto but on presentation we must be careful and we don't want any of that "we are the masters now" sort of stuff.'

Jim Callaghan spoke. 'I would like to congratulate you, Harold. The points I would make are these. There is great unease within the middle classes; there is the balance of payments debt fear; we are being classed internationally on a par with Italy; the oil economy measures must be taken in a more draconian form; public expenditure must be cut; we should be tough at the beginning and ease up later; and the Social Contract must be made to work because we can't have a statutory wages policy. The Tories are in disarray and although we are really the national party, we still can't win the middle ground and there is a great fear of the power of the unions; they have got much too much influence on all Governments and we must rectify and remedy the situation.'

When I was called I said there were one or two points I wanted to make that hadn't been raised. 'First of all, I think the Election campaign has ended cynicism, in that very violent attacks have been made upon us and we've been through a sort of trial by ordeal. But at any rate it has left us with our integrity: people think we mean what we say. Secondly, even if the public don't like us as much as we'd wish, our policy is relevant and there is no alternative available.

'The defeatism of the middle class is a factor because the Tories don't have anything to offer. But we do, and we could win their support, particularly on planning agreements. Industrial salaried management are very keen on this idea and we could sell it. We mustn't have a confrontation with management, we must act by persuasion.

'Of course we would like national unity and all that but what we are moving towards are changes that will make a new national consensus possible, a consensus that will last for ten years or so. Nothing we can say or do will prop up the present system, which has absolutely lost the confidence of a lot of important people. And if there are sacrifices to be made, we will have to have some perspective, some vision.'

Crosland made a long contribution. 'I won't dwell on sacrifices because they are inevitable. Rents will go up on 1 April next year by more than under the Tories' Housing Finance Act. Rates will go up 65 per cent. Nationalisation is irrelevant and in constituencies that have nationalised industries, Labour did very badly because the industries are so unpopular; we only did well where they were lame ducks.'

He thought planning agreements and the NEB would have a minimal impact and was very skeptical about their value. He hoped that Harold would recognise that the Conference and the National Executive, in their thinking and statements, were completely out of line with the attitude of Labour voters as a whole and he hoped there would be an early showdown between the Government, the National Executive and Conference, such as Attlee had engaged in in 1945. He thought this was necessary, particularly given the Conference resolutions that would be coming forward. As to the trade unions, he said most people feared them, they were too powerful and wherever you had a strong trade union, equality was set back.

I went back to the office and I asked Roy to check with Number 10 whether I had been reappointed. He did this and said no, I hadn't as yet. I felt really aggrieved; after all, we all shared the victory and Harold was the only one who was getting the prizes.

At 4 o'clock, I went to Number 10 for a meeting with the TUC and the CBI, and in the lobby I met Ron Hayward who said, 'Congratulations.'

'On what?'

'On being reappointed.'

I said, 'Well, I don't know whether I have.'

He said, 'Harold has told me that he has reappointed everybody.'

So that was actually how I heard – from the General Secretary, outside the Cabinet Room. I must say, I am still affronted.

Members of the CBI began to arrive, among them Sir Donald MacDougall, Lucien Wigdor, Dick Marsh, John Partridge from Imperial Tobacco, Ralph Bateman (who just looks like a Madame Tussaud's industrialist of 1910 vintage), Campbell Adamson, Adrian Cadbury and Lord Plowden.

Lord Plowden said he's never known confidence so low in all his years, half as a civil servant and half as an industrialist, and the uncertainty about the industry White Paper and about the Common Market was affecting investment, profitability and cash. Orders were simply not coming in. He was glad that the Prime Minister had at least talked about a healthy private sector.

Harold said, 'Well, I quoted from the White Paper. Of course, we want voluntary arrangements, we are happy to give you reassurance, and colleagues are well aware of industrial anxiety. We want to fix the boundary between the public and the private sector clearly.'

I went back to the office and now I knew I was confirmed, I felt in a stronger position.

My general impressions of the day are that a Labour Cabinet will have to be cleaned out one day and maybe the Europe dilemma will do it in order to get things right. You can't go on with a bunch of right-wing people like that. They are now to some extent a minority, or at any rate they haven't got a clear majority in the Cabinet. But there will be a bust-up some time, whether it is over Europe or whether it is the breakdown of the Social Contract.

Wednesday 16 October

I slept for three-quarters of an hour after lunch, then at 3 I had a long discussion about our strategy on the Budget with my senior officials – Antony Part, Peter Carey, and Raymond Prosser – and Alan Lord, the Department's Principal Finance Officer.

I must say it was a most fascinating meeting. Part was furious when I said that we must safeguard jobs; he said, 'Well that's why you have a reputation for being a con man, because you are not safeguarding jobs.'

'Oh, I've been called a lot of things,' I said. 'I am not particularly worried about that.'

This afternoon a note arrived from Robert Armstrong. 'Last Friday, you put your office at the disposal of the Prime Minister to permit a reconstruction, and now the Prime Minister has asked me to let you know he will be glad if you would continue. Robert Armstrong.' So I get back formally into the Cabinet via a Private Secretary's letter – most insulting.

Came home and read the Think Tank paper for Cabinet tomorrow which is a Tory rewrite of our Manifesto. It would never have got through the Conference, through the Executive, or through the Cabinet and it is quite unacceptable; a coalition document which I shall strongly attack.

Thursday 17 October

Cabinet and the Think Tank document. Rothschild has left the CPRS and Sir Kenneth Berrill is now in charge.

Jim Callaghan concentrated on international aspects – which were graver than at any point in our lifetime. 'The international monetary mechanism might break down.' He was still afraid we would be classed with Italy and the idea was taking hold that we couldn't govern ourselves. He was in favour of oil rationing. What we needed was the

Dunkirk spirit, although he himself found it embarrassing to refer to it because it has become such a cliché.

I came in. 'In the nicest possible way, I want to say some difficult things.' I felt the paper revealed the Establishment on a psychiatric couch because the whole discussion was shot through with a complete lack of confidence in our own people. I disliked the document because it was really an alternative manifesto. 'Let's be quite clear about qualified managers and getting our policies across. The plain truth is that some of the silliest things that have been done have been done by the cleverest people. Look at the closure of the railways and the mines. And we, after all, as a profession, as politicians, are wholly unqualified.'

Jim interjected, 'But we care.'

'The point isn't that we care,' I said, 'it is that we are accountable, we have to be re-elected. We have to listen whether we like to or not. This idea that somehow you could solve the problem by having more qualified civil servants is rubbish. If I had ten thousand PhDs in Business Studies in my Department of Industry, it would contribute absolutely zero to our productivity.'

Denis said, 'You will need them for the planning agreements.'

'No, I won't, and you will understand why when it comes forward. The real contribution will be made when the workers have some say in running their own affairs, not in having people in the Department who know what to do. The real art is to listen to the crackpots and see which of them has the grain of truth in what they say. We have got to support those people and when they have got further support, capitulate gracefully to them.

'As for extremists, we are told they are people we have got to fight. But, looking back, who was right on the Industrial Relations Act? Was it you, Reg? Or was it the AUEW, who fought it? Would we ever have got the Scottish National Assembly if there hadn't been a lot of extremists in Scotland who made life hell for Willie Ross? It isn't that people have lacked confidence in democratic institutions – as the report says – but that democracy is being progressively squeezed out in a society where power is becoming more and more centralised.' Everybody laughed at my contribution but, as a mattter of fact, it was quite a good one.

Jack Spriggs and Dick Jenkins came at 2. IPD (Fisher-Bendix) had put in a proposal for £3.9 million and predictably my officials were totally obstructive: it isn't viable; it won't work; the manning is too high. Jack was marvellous. He said, 'Look, we know better than you. We are the people who are really experienced. Don't try to persuade us we don't know our business. We will build this up from scratch.'

Caroline and I went to Tommy Balogh's house for the left-wing dinner. Judith Hart was upset and told me that Harold had called her

The Diarist at work at home in the basement office.

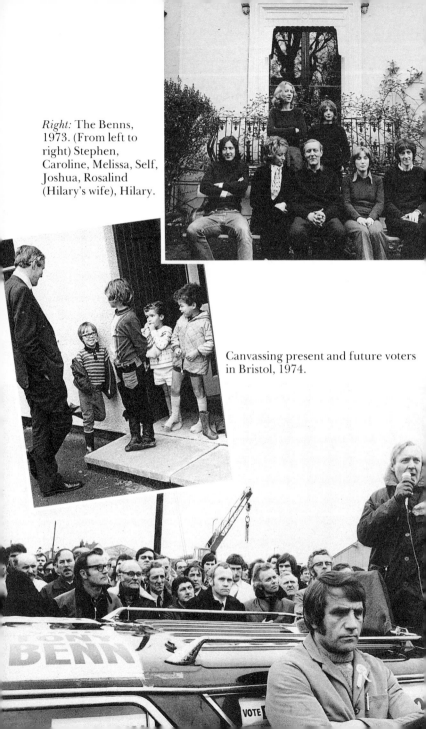

Right: The Benns, 1973. (From left to right) Stephen, Caroline, Melissa, Self, Joshua, Rosalind (Hilary's wife), Hilary.

Canvassing present and future voters in Bristol, 1974.

Left: Chairman of the Meriden motorbike cooperative, Dennis Johnson, tackling the paperwork, 1975.

Below: Meriden workers assembling a 'Bonneville' bike.

Above: A day trip in Concorde, 1974, with the people who built i – for some their first ever air flight.

Left: The honeymoon is ending: President of the CBI, Michael Clapham (left) and General Secretary Campbell Adamson, at Number 10, May 1974.

Heath's own 'winter of discontent', 1973-4

Tea by candlelight during the three-day week, when electricity was rationed.

Checking the lists for power-cuts.

'King Arthur', President of the Yorkshire miners, with flying pickets at Saltley Coke Depot, 1972.

Demonstrators show support for proposed industrial strikes, Trafalgar Square 1974.

The Miner's Leaders: Lawrence Daly (left) and Joe Gormley, putting the NUM case to the Relativities Board, February 1974.

Pit Deputies impose an overtime ban.

Above: Mick McGahey, Vice-President of the NUM, addressing Scottish miners, 1974. His class loyalties led to his denunciation by Wilson as well as Heath.

Left: Battersea's most famous landmark looms behind a coal stockpile in anticipation of the miners' all-out strike, February 1974.

in at 2.30 and had said, 'I can't appoint you back to your Department because I understand you have got Communist connections.'

She said to Harold, 'I have never been a Communist.'

'No,' said Harold. 'But I understand you have been contacted.'

She said, 'Well, my son is a Communist.'

'It's nothing to do with that,' said Harold.

'Well, I did ring John Gollan, the Secretary of the Communist Party, in September to say I couldn't speak at the Chile meeting in Scotland because Jimmy Reid [a leading Communist Party member] would be there.'

'Oh,' said Harold, 'that's getting nearer the mark.'

She told me she got angry and decided that if she was sacked, she was sacked, and went back to her office to wait, but was called by Harold at 6 o'clock and told it was all right.

It is significant that the Security Services decided to pick off Judith Hart, very significant.* And it is significant that Harold decided to take it up, having known her since 1959; he would have to pitch his judgment against the Security Services judgment. It shows the sort of thing we are up against. It means the Security Services will pick me off if they have half a chance.

Judith said she was just angry with Harold but in fact she was weeping, she was so distressed.

Friday 18 October

Alfred Herbert has gone to the brink and the whole question is do we let it go or keep going like Ferranti. Of course the Industrial Development Advisory Board wants to let it go, as does the Treasury, no doubt. I wanted to keep it going. Bullock, one of my Deputy Secretaries, sat in my office and said, 'They wouldn't face reality.'

I said, 'I don't want to punish the trade creditors; the shareholders, I am told, we can deal with later. What I want to do is to get the company on its feet again.'

Then at 2.30, a big meeting to consider the threat to the HS-146. I thought the meeting was to be with the Confederation of Shipbuilding and Engineering Union people – Ken Gill, Jack Service, Roy Grantham, Bob McCusker and Bill John. But when I went to the conference room, I found the Confed Executive with all the stewards and they said, 'We haven't quite finished our consultation.' I said I'd

---

* Judith Hart was the target of MI5 undermining which reached a peak in October 1974. Part of their case rested on a confusion of her with Mrs J. Tudor Hart, who had visited Warsaw in 1950, and was a member of the British Communist Party.

go away and they said, 'No, come and sit in.' So I was present as a sort of Back Bench member of the meeting, while the stewards briefed the national officials about how to approach me – it was open trade unionism of a most extraordinary kind.

At the end of the briefing, Ken Gill, the new General Secretary of TASS, who has just been elected to the TUC General Council and who is a Communist, said to the stewards, 'Now I think you had better go away while we see the Minister.'

They said, 'Hey, we came to see the Minister too.'

'Oh no, *we* see the Ministers.' Then he turned to me, 'Do you mind slipping out for a minute while we sort this out.'

I said, 'No. Come up to my office when you're ready.'

They came up to the office and brought a representative collection of shop stewards with them. I handed round the letters I had written to Arnold Hall, though I hadn't in fact got permission from him to allow them to see his letters to me. My letters to Hall, however, made it clear I had been fighting this case since July. They were delighted. I issued a press release enclosing the documents and I told my office to persuade Hall to agree to release his half.

After asking my officials to slip out, I said to them, 'Now look. You know what the argument is about at the moment: do we put huge sums of money into industry or do we put it in selectively; do we put it in accountably; do we put it in for projects like this; do we put it in to make our industrial policy live? That's the issue. Do we come through the recession surviving in areas where we need to be strong?' They saw the whole thing immediately. I said, 'It is going to be a hell of a struggle – like the Concorde. You know that.' And they understood.

I took Ken Gill aside and I said, 'The Treasury wants to cancel this.' He said. 'I know.' So they have got the whole score now and, of course, the thing that was really touching is their complete confidence in me.

I discussed Judith's story with Frances and speculated again as to why the Security Services had chosen this moment to go for Judith and why Harold had done it that way. I told Frances I had been very surprised that Harold had rung me up during the Election in Bristol and asked me if I knew anything about Bickenhall Mansions; had I been lured there to a flat to smoke cannabis? He had told me a story about Marcia's handbag having been taken and someone telling her to collect it from a certain flat, and she was afraid if she did she would be compromised in some way. I told Frances I had thought nothing of it.

She said, 'Oh yes I heard that story during the Election.'

Saturday 19 October

Frank McElhone rang, shocked by Keith Joseph's speech in Birmingham, and saying that it would thoroughly upset the Catholic

Church. Joseph's speech on 'The remoralisation of Britain' was an attack on permissiveness on the Mary Whitehouse model, but had advocated birth control for poor families so as to reduce the number of children they would produce, since the mothers were unfit to look after them. It was a complete master-race philosophy; the theory that the problem is the immorality of the poor rather than poverty is a most reactionary idea bordering on fascism.

Frank is very bitter about Harold's appointment of junior Ministers, notably John Smith [MP for Lanarkshire North] and Harry Ewing [MP for Sterling, Falkirk and Grangemouth], to the Scottish Office instead of himself. He believes the whole devolution policy will be designed to strip the Department of Industry of its powers by spreading them among the Scottish and Welsh Offices, leaving me with the Department of Industry in England.

Sunday 20 October

The papers today covered Joseph's speech. The churches have already attacked it and I must say it will do a great deal to repel people from the Tories; I think he may have thrown away the Tory leadership by being so explicit. His plan to deal with inflation by throwing people out of work, then when they are poor implying they are not fit to have children and that they are immoral, is so easy to destroy.

Herbert Rogers rang. At the GMC on 7 November we will get a resolution passed on the Common Market and start work on campaigning for the Referendum, writing to all other local parties and distributing literature. Herbert said that a crunch is coming; capitalism has served its historic purpose and will have to be replaced by socialism.

Monday 21 October

Went in to the office after lunch and I had a meeting with Secretary about advisers. Part treats me like a consultant psychiatrist would a particulary dangerous patient, and at any moment I expect him to ring a bell and a fat, male nurse in a white jacket will come and give me an injection.

Frances came in to look at my paper on industrial democracy and I looked at the paper she and Francis had written on the economic situation. It was very precise and we are beginning to identify the new criteria that go beyond the crude definitions of viability. We also knocked a *Labour Weekly* article into shape. Frances is very good at that, although I admit I find it slightly irritating when she changes my drafts.

Tuesday 22 October

I went over to the House for the PLP meeting, with Mik in the chair.

Harold Wilson and Ted Short were re-elected Leader and Deputy-Leader *nem-con*.

Then Harold made a very tough speech. He'd written it all out and he stood there reading it – how he would implement the Manifesto, there'd be no backsliding, everyone had come in under these terms. He just cannot speak without a text. It was really a warning to the Right. It is Harold at his most dishonest, when you know what a backslider he is in Cabinet and how at Conference he is so radical. But still . . .

Wednesday 23 October
At 4 I went over to the Ministerial Committee on Economic Strategy. Denis began, in effect, by taking the whole cash crisis problem on board and accepting it.

Sir Kenneth Berrill said, 'Look, profitability is the Number One issue. No one at the moment will invest, borrow or lend. If you get profitability right, you don't need anything else.'

This gave the whole game away. That is the Tory philosophy presented as official advice.

I hurried back to the office and had about an hour on the HS-146 which my officials want to cancel. I had the serried ranks of Part, David Jones, the solicitor Michael Kerry and Anthony Warrington [an Under-Secretary].

I simply dug my toes in. 'Arnold Hall may be breaking the contract. Why don't we publish it?'

'Oh, it's not clear that he is breaking it,' Michael Kerry said.

'Well, the workers think that he is and I think he is.'

'Oh, you can't say that without my advice,' he said.

'Well, I can give my judgment and say I agree with them.'

It was really just a defence of property rights. The Ministry of Defence won't publish the HS-146 contract because it is 'confidential'.

'The workers have an interest in the contract – their jobs,' I said. 'And I represent them. That's why I am here.'

Thursday 24 October
Harold began Cabinet by stating that he thought that no Minister should make any broadcasts until after the Queen's Speech. He complained about one Minister who had refused to acccept this decision from him, which was a reference to Eric Heffer.

Jim made a statement on the recent visit of Royal Navy ships to South Africa, because last night's *Evening Standard* had a banner headline that he was furious with Roy Mason and the Admirals. And it was in all the papers this morning.

It turned out that the manoeuvres in South Africa had been agreed between Bill Rodgers and Roy Hattersley at the Foreign Office, claiming that they were operating under a decision of the Overseas Policy Committee on 17 July.

Friday 25 October

I heard the amazing news that Hawker Siddeley had capitulated and given the HS-146 a reprieve for a month. That absolutely transforms the situation and I've got to mobilise the unions now.

I dictated a minute to Harold Wilson objecting strongly to his Cabinet Procedure for Ministers. Then Secretary came to see me and we had a long talk. What it really came down to was that he was unhappy about the relations between me and civil servants. Some, for example, had been upset when I appeared to imply that they were hostile to shop stewards when shop stewards came to see me on closure cases.

'Well,' I said, 'Secretary, I don't want to embarrass them in any way, but I must tell you frankly, officials do just put up barrier after barrier when they know quite well that I'm trying to find new criteria for support. If they don't believe that worker enthusiasm is worth anything in a proposed workers' cooperative, for example, then why don't we say, "Let's assume that enthusiasm is worth 5 per cent of costs, and re-work the figures on that basis." Why don't they try and help me, instead of simply obstructing me and being difficult? I feel as if I'm swimming against the tide all the time – it's exhausting for me too.'

He then told me that officials had also been shocked that I had described the planning agreements as an extension of collective bargaining into bargaining for power. The officials who had been discussing this at the CBI now felt that they'd been engaged in a complete confidence trick.

I said, 'I'm very sorry but what did you think the fundamental and irreversible shift in the balance of wealth and power was all about if it wasn't this? I've made endless speeches about this over the years and you must take them seriously. If people don't take them seriously and choose to present the argument in another way, well that's a problem for them. What I'm trying to do is to take the enormous power of the trade union movement and harness it to productive effort.'

'Well, Secretary of State, the problem is that you are trying to proceed with seven league boots, and we think you've got to go more slowly,' he replied.

'Maybe seven league boots,' I said, 'but I've been in the Department for seven months and I'm not aware of having done anything, made any progress at all. I've spent no money, got no legislation through, and I'm trying to get some indication that things are moving at all.'

Then he said that other officials felt that I was difficult to work with, and although they were absolutely loyal in interdepartmental discussions, officials in other Departments had said on occasions that the Secretary of State for Industry had gone completely off his rocker.

'My view is perfectly straightforward. I try to say the same thing at the Conference, in Parliament and in the Department – and I don't agree that these ideas are so very absurd. Of course, I'm in a minority in the Cabinet.'

'Ah well, you're thought of as a devious Minister who mobilises people outside in support of your view in the Cabinet.'

I said, 'Well, mobilising is what it's all about. Of course I do. Of course I go to where the support is, which is largely in the trade union movement, but my colleagues in the Cabinet who don't like me leak everything to the mass media. I read all these reports by the lobby correspondents that senior Ministers have great doubts about my judgment or whatever. I'm not even complaining. If they think it's better to go and talk to Nora Beloff and say what they think about me, I'm certainly not going to stop talking to *our* people so that they can bring their influence to bear. I've protected the Cabinet from making some terrible errors because they didn't know what the consequences of certain courses of action were.'

Whether he was threatening to resign or not, I don't know, but there was a sort of vague hint of warning in the exchange. Part really is an impossible man, and I would get rid of him if I could. Roy Williams said it was quite untrue that officials found me difficult to work with. There were a lot of them who were extremely attracted by the ideas, and loyal to them. He thought that Secretary was speaking more for himself.

Monday 28 October

Mary Lou typed out my three-and-a-half page resolution for the Bristol South-East Constituency Party on the Common Market, which I'm hoping to take with me to the GMC next week. The problem is that if you say 'don't split the Party', which is Harold's line, and now Ron Hayward's, the effect is that the pro-Market people outside and within the Cabinet have total control over the situation and the Party can't be mobilised. If, on the other hand, I were to start mobilising the Party, then it would be seen as a split and I would be held responsible. I'm not at all sure how to handle it and I think I've got to take advice on this, collectively.

Michael Clapham was in the chair for the meeting at my Department with the CBI. I welcomed them, saying that we would of course be meeting again at Neddy meetings and I hoped for a good relationship. We were united by our problems and our proposals were sincerely meant. I said that I thought the CBI were realistic and that I'd be guided by them as to how they wanted to proceed.

Michael Clapham was the first to speak and he thought that consultation had not got very far and he particularly hoped that the CBI would participate in the drafting of the Industry Bill.

Then Campbell Adamson chipped in to say that he had to make it absolutely clear that the CBI was bitterly opposed to the proposals for the NEB, and he wanted to know how the various paragraphs on the role of the NEB were construed. He wondered, referring to what I'd said in the White Paper, on what basis short-term market force influences might have to be overridden.

I said, 'Well, this is not uncommon: we do it with advanced technology, aircraft, computers and to deal with declining technologies like shipbuilding, and to deal with the regions; it seems to be quite a sensible proposal.'

Lord Watkinson, the Deputy President, said, 'Yes, but it's not what you say, it's the way that you say it.'

'Well,' I replied, 'you really must separate what I've said from what it is said that I've said.' I drew attention to the meeting with the CBI in Wales when the CBI had referred to the bitter attacks I had made on management in the White Paper. When I'd asked them to point these attacks out, they had been completely flummoxed because there weren't any.

Everyone laughed and someone chirped up that I should have published the White Paper in Welsh.

Then Watkinson continued, 'If we're going to discuss this and you stick to your view, there's not much point in consultation.'

I said, 'Well, I am listening. It's a very valuable discussion for me, but acquisitions of industries by Government have always been done by parliamentary decision, and I think you'll acquit me of ever trying to conceal my intentions. My views are very well known and, having put our policy before the electorate in two Elections, I think we're entitled to proceed.'

Michael Clapham said that they saw great dangers in this, and Campbell Adamson objected to equities being taken in profitable companies.

'I take it, you don't want the public sector to be unprofitable?'

'No,' said Adamson, 'we don't.'

I said, 'Well, in that case, if the public sector is to be profitable, the Government will own profitable companies, and if you agree that where we put in money it is reasonable that we should have the same return as anyone else and have control over who puts in money, then you've got some sort of an explanation.'

At that, we left discussion of the National Enterprise Board. At least they'd got it off their chest. We agreed to have further talks after the Queen's Speech, and I asked if they wanted to make them tripartite with the TUC. They said they'd prefer to begin by making them bilateral. It was very useful and as a result of it, I had the feeling that we had broken the deadlock, and we are not going to have an absolute revolt on our hands, as I'd half expected.

I took them right down to the front door and Eric Heffer stayed behind and he said, 'Look, I've been thinking about my own position. I'll stay for the session and then I'll go back on to the Back Benches.' I have to conclude that Eric is an unhappy man and I sense he misses the Back Benches.

I went over to Number 10 and had a talk to a few people at the Eve of Parliament reception. Harold banged the table and told Bob Mellish to guard the door. Mr Speaker was there. It's all a silly, silly ritual. Harold delivered a homily on how we were Ministers first and everything else came second; collective responsibility was all-important, and if we didn't like what the Government did we should nevertheless defend it or keep quiet. If we criticised it we were out. Wherever we were, we were always Ministers. The usual absolute rubbish. He went on about speeches, broadcasting, articles – it was quite unacceptable.

Then he read the Queen's Speech, and I slipped away quickly. Came home and did my box.

The big news today is the bomb in Denis Howell's wife's car. Another bomb went off in Birmingham today. There may have to be major security for all Ministers. It is a slight anxiety for the family. Joshua and Melissa are bit worried, but I don't think there's anything we can do.

Tuesday 29 October

I heard that there is a plan to put armed guards to protect all Cabinet Ministers, which I hope isn't the case.

Frances Morrell was in the office at 8.50. She suggested that I shouldn't write to Harold Wilson about the Cabinet Procedure for Ministers because Prime Ministers can't be defeated on principle, they can only have their authority eroded; since I'd written a piece in *Tribune*, I ought to leave it at that.

Then she said that I should not put my resolution on the Common Market to Bristol South-East because it would immediately put me at the head of the attack on the Common Market, and that would be damaging. So on these two main issues she has come out against me.

I had lunch with Frank McElhone, and his general advice, as usual, is to swing to the Right. It always makes me angry and he knows that. His advice is fine if one wants to challenge Shirley Williams for the leadership, but I'm not sure whether the leadership thing is as important as I thought it was. Freedom to speak is the most important thing of all in politics.

Wednesday 30 October

At the Executive, Mik said we'd better remove from the EEC Monitoring Committee those Ministers who by Harold's diktat were not permitted to come. I said that I thought the problem was its name and suggested we rename it the 'EEC Liaison Committee'. That was agreed.

Then it was agreed to send Mik to the Roumanian Communist Party Conference in Bucharest, a very important innovation. Finally Mik's motion deploring the Government's action in holding combined naval exercises in South Africa was carried with an amendment that we welcome the Foreign Secretary's initiative in reviewing the Simonstown Agreement.* I voted for it.

Thursday 31 October

This really is a day to remember. So much has happened that I am having to rely heavily on my memory and impressions despite dictating my diary on the evening of the very day.

The papers this morning had a lot about yesterday's National Executive, notably about the fact that the EEC Liaison Committee had been set up by the NEC on my motion. Second, the motion criticising the Government for the Simonstown exercises received massive publicity; *The Times* had a banner headline, 'Labour Government – Clash Between Government and Party. Benn says, I defy Wilson.'

At 10.30 Harold began the Cabinet by saying, 'Before we come on to the agenda, something very grave has happened. There has been a serious breach of collective Cabinet responsibility by some members of the Executive yesterday. Only on Monday night, on the Eve of Parliament reception at Number 10, I had to remind Ministers – and it was intended for new Ministers – that they are always primarily Ministers, above all other things. They are totally and collectively responsible for everything done by Government. Any of them who do not like these restrictions are absolutely free to follow the logic of their actions and go back to the freedom of the Back Benches and there are plenty of people on the Back Benches who would give their eye teeth to be in the Cabinet and have the honour of putting our socialist programme on to the statute book.'

This was clearly directed at me. He went on to say that he didn't know exactly what had happened about the Monitoring Committee, but he had made it absolutely clear that he was not prepared to have Ministers on the Monitoring Committee representing the Executive. He was not against 'liaison' but Ministers could not be put on representing the Executive. It appeared that he had been defied. As to

---

* The agreement between South Africa and Britain allowed the Royal Navy to continue to use Simonstown as a naval base, after being handed over to South Africa in 1957.

Simonstown, it was most unfortunate that at a moment when the Government was itself reconsidering the agreement – and Ministers concerned would have been quite aware of that – they should have lent themselves to a rebuke which could only make it look as if the Government had capitulated to pressure.

Jim came in at this point, 'Harold, I must make it clear that I couldn't be at the Executive yesterday because I had the Japanese Foreign Minister to see me. I was deeply shocked by what had happened. If this is the way the Executive is going to behave, I think I had better resign from it, as should all Ministers who feel the same way, so that it can be seen what a pitiable body of people are left.'

'Well,' said Harold, 'I think that is something we would have to consider.'

Michael Foot spoke up. 'I was at the Executive yesterday – not for the whole day, but certainly for the EEC Liaison Committee discussion – and I don't think that the way it has been presented is altogether right. Tony behaved quite reasonably. He simply said, "We don't want this idea of monitoring; we just want to have the idea of liaison." ' (By the way, this incident had occurred after Harold had left the Executive yesterday, although it would have made no difference whatever if he had been there.)

He continued, 'I had left before the South African resolution came up but had I been there, I might have done the same thing. I think we had better discuss all these problems because they are really very difficult and we have got to get them right.'

'First of all, Harold, can I explain what happened yesterday,' I said. 'As you know, the Monitoring Committee was set up at the suggestion of Jim, and I was put on it by the Home Policy Committee, though I might have been on as a Minister because of my regional and industrial responsibilities. But let's start with one thing, and be absolutely clear: if we are going to have rules, they are going to be the same for everybody. It is no use saying that Ministers are not to represent the National Executive side on these liaison committees because Jim himself is on the major liaison committee – in his capacity as Chairman of the Party, not as a Minister.'

'In that case,' said Jim, 'I will resign.'

I went further, 'Let's be clear that there are committees on which Ministers sit as members of the Executive and they liaise with the Government of which they are also Ministers. In a sense, the whole Executive monitors all our work all the time because, after all, that's what the Executive does: it considers the work of the Government. Moreover, I remember very well that when Jim was a member of the Executive in 1969, he voted against "In Place of Strife".'

Jim interrupted, 'I did not vote against it.'

'Well,' I said, 'you spoke against it publicly.'

'Yes,' said Jim, 'and I was sacked from the Inner Cabinet as a result.'

Then Harold came in, 'It was never acceptable to me.'

'Well, I know that, Harold. As a matter of fact, looking back on it, Jim's was a prophetic warning; we were all wrong and he was right.

'Anyway, I might add, there are a number of outside bodies beside the Executive. There are many of us here who aren't members of the Executive, perhaps even some who are, who brief the press. I have never complained about this. But, for example, there was a very high level Economic Strategy Committee on Europe of which I was a member, and in the *Sunday Times* the following weekend every word I had said was quoted, handed over by somebody who was present at that meeting – another Minister. I don't complain about that. Nor do I complain about the fact that when journalists come to see me they always start by asking, "What do you say to your critics in the Cabinet?" And when I ask who these critics are, they say they are not in a position to disclose their names. Some people go to Nora Beloff and say exactly what they think of their colleagues, but I don't leak and I don't brief. We must have the same rules for everybody. Take the rebuke about South Africa given to Roy Mason which appeared in the *Evening Standard* last week. Now Jim denies it.'

Harold snapped, 'We are investigating that.'

'Perhaps. But you can't tell me that the press isn't used by some Ministers against others. Then there is another aspect, if I may speak absolutely frankly: double standards. During the Election, in an answer to a question at a press conference, Shirley Williams said that if the Cabinet recommended against Europe – '

'No,' said Shirley correcting me. 'If the Referendum went against Europe – '

'Well, whatever it was you said, you stated you would not be able to stay in public life if, as a result of it all, we left Europe. During the Election, I defended Shirley consistently from bitter critics in the Party who felt she had completely let the side down, because, after all, she was only stating her view. I have never said what I would do at the end of the re-negotiation though, as a matter of fact, I think everyone knows what my attitude is, and that the issue is all about sovereignty. But you can't have one standard for one group and a different standard for another.'

I finished, 'I must absolutely repudiate the idea that I defied you, Harold, and I hope we are old enough in this game not to believe everything we read in the papers.'

Denis simply said, 'Prime Minister, the remedy is entirely in your own hands', indicating quite clearly that as far as he was concerned, the sooner Harold sacked me the better.

That was more or less the end of that, except I did say I hoped we could discuss the matter at Chequers. Michael said to me at the end, 'If you get a letter from Harold' – who had said he was going to write to us all individually – 'let's consult about it.'

During the discussion, Bob Mellish passed me a note, 'You have a lot of good common sense. We have difficult times ahead. Let's have a private word some time; you have a tendency to go into minefields without a detector. I was in the Royal Engineers for six years and can help you.' I wrote back, 'The real issue here is the link between the Government and the labour movement. That key link was broken and we lost the '70 Election; the reason we won in 1974 was that we re-established that link. We mustn't accidentally destroy it again.'

I came back to the office, then to Cabinet again at 4.45. I asked for the evening paper to be brought to me and there in the *Evening Standard* was 'Benn & Co are told to toe the line or else. Cabinet Storm, Wilson gives sack warning.' I showed it to Michael and he said in Cabinet, 'Look Harold, in view of what has been said this morning about leaks, can you explain how this got into the evening papers?'

So the paper was passed across to Harold who pretended to be very surprised. He said, 'I don't understand that at all. Of course, I did have to tell Haines that if this morning's story came up, he should say I would be getting in touch with Ministers. But I don't understand this; I just don't understand how it could have happened.' The paper was handed round the Cabinet. It did Harold an awful lot of damage because of course everyone knew who was responsible.

Harold went on, 'Anyway, what do you expect me to do? Just after I warned Ministers about collective responsibility, this happens. Do you want the press to think I am spineless.' Well, that gave the whole game away.

The whole thing got very bitter and unpleasant.

Friday 1 November
Secretary came in and told me that my make-up last night on television had made me look like Frankenstein.

At 12 I went to meet the entire board of Alfred Herbert, 100 shop stewards from the Confederation, Bob Wright of the AUEW and officials. I began by saying, 'This is a great company with great skills, a great history, great future, and of great importance to our economy. It has got into trouble, and I don't see any point in looking back over the past to lay blame. We have the choice of putting Alfred Herbert into the hands of the Receiver or dealing with it so as to avoid punishing the workers and trade creditors, so I would like to know what you think. Would you be ready to tackle it on this basis?'

The Managing Director, Neale Raine, responded. 'This is a great social experiment and we certainly welcome what you suggest. We would be prepared to go for complete disclosure and discussion.'

Bob Wright said, 'Well, the policy of the Conferation of Shipbuilding and Engineering Union is that there should be nationalisation; but you have got limited powers at the moment and we think the proposal you make is a very sensible one.'

A series of other people got up, and somebody else from management asked, 'Can we export our goods to Eastern European countries?' Gradually out of it all came an agreement that they would set up their own consultative arrangements covering the whole plant; that I would make consultants available to the workers and the management; that there would have to be a network of accountability – that is to say that the management must be accountable to the workers – that the workers must take responsibility for seeing that it is a success, and that I was accountable to Parliament for the money we put in. I came out delighted. It was a great innovation without any legislative change, just a new way of tackling problems.

Went to the Algerian Embassy party. I had had a note saying the Foreign Office was not very keen on Ministers going, but I was glad I made up my own mind because the African National Congress people came up and thanked me for what I had done on Simonstown. Other African Ambassadors and diplomats were there and it was marvellous.

Came home and found several minutes which Harold had re-issued, reminding Ministers about collective responsibility and re-stating the rule that where any conflict of loyalties arose, the principle of collective responsibility was absolute and overriding. He recalled that my vote in support of the motion on Simonstown on the Eve of Parliament had been a clear breach and said in the last paragraph:

> I must ask you to send me, in reply to this minute, an unqualified assurance that you accept the principle of collective responsibility and you will, from now on, comply with this requirement and the rules that flow from it in the National Executive Committee as well as in all other circumstances. I must warn you that I should have to regard your failure to give me such an assurance or any subsequent breach of it as a decision on your part that you did not wish to continue as a member of this administration. I should, of course, regret such a decision but I should accept it.   HW

I tried dozens of draft replies. A slightly unpleasant end to the day.

Saturday 2 November

In the afternoon I rang Frank McElhone who, surprisingly, thought I was in a strong position because of the hostility of the centre of the Party to the South Africa Simonstown agreement. He said this is worth between 15 and 50 votes, which is the way he calculates all these issues.

When talking later to Frank Cousins on the phone, he gave me good advice. 'I wouldn't make this a challenge. That little man actually asked me to stay in the Government in order to help him to keep Britain out of the Common Market.'

'That's a good story,' I replied. 'But we must be gentle. Maybe all Prime Ministers have to be like that.'

'Well,' said Frank, 'I cherish the hope that that isn't true and we could have a Prime Minister who isn't. But don't get thrown out on this one. In the next few months, you're going to get pressure for the statutory incomes policy brought back and pressure on Europe; you must be in position for that fight.' He was very wise.

Sunday 3 November
Judith rang. She and Joan Lestor have received similar minutes from Harold on the Simonstown motion. Judith told me her local Party was furious and wanted her to stand up for her rights. That was her instinct and Joan felt rather the same. So Judith arranged to come round at 9.30 tonight – Joan may come too – and we will sort out roughly how we are going to respond.

It is possible that in seven days from now – indeed even twenty-four hours from now – I might be out of office and a Back Bencher. If it happens, I have got the consolation of knowing that there is a lot of support, and maybe this country does have to go through the experience of seeing people ready to give up their offices for their beliefs, in order to believe in them again. But I would rather it didn't happen now, since I have got certain responsibilities in this. Frances and Francis would lose their jobs and I have a duty to try to advance the industrial policy. But nobody is indispensable on the ministerial side. What really is indispensable, however, is some evidence of principle in Government. Although I haven't been very active on South Africa and I have compromised all over the place over the years, the political role of the Minister is the most important aspect.

I rang Bob Mellish and said, 'Look, I have had this minute from Harold and I have got to write a reply of some kind. I am anxious to defuse it. I don't want an argument. It's a pretty nasty minute of the "dog licence" kind warning me I only have one bite.' I read him my current draft reply.

Dear Harold, Thanks for your minute. I can most certainly assure you, without any qualification, of my loyalty to the Labour Party, Labour policy, and our Labour Government which all Ministers have a collective responsibility to sustain and which all members of the Party, especially those who serve on the NEC, want so much to succeed in its historic task of who serve on the NEC, want so much to succeed in its historic task of carrying through our Manifesto. Our success must depend on maintaining the closest relations of trust and confidence in the Party and as a Minister, I shall certainly work in every way I can to strengthen that trust and build up our confidence in each other.   Tony

Bob said, 'That's fine. Why don't you include a phrase about "further discussions".' So I added, 'I would welcome further discussions about how this could be achieved.' Bob told me, 'You know, I had a word with Harold about you not so long ago. He has got an absolute thing about you. He thinks you are brilliantly able, but that you have no judgment.'

'I am very well aware of that. I feel he hates my guts, to be perfectly honest.'

'I don't think he hates your guts, but he is terribly conscious of his own status, so when he over-reacts it obviously explodes all over the place. I think at one time he thought you were trying to get his job.' 'Well, I certainly am not,' I said. 'He'll be there for another twenty years.'

'Oh God, I hope not.'

'Well, Churchill was eighty when he went and Harold is only fifty-eight. So he probably will be.'

'I'm no Wilson stooge by any means,' said Bob, 'but I do think it would be a good idea if we talked about it because it is a difficult problem. Come and see me and we'll lock the door and have a talk. You see, Harold can't bear to appear to be responding to pressure.'

I said, 'My idea of politics is that it's all about responding to pressure.'

In the evening, Michael Foot rang me up and asked what I was going to say to Harold, so I read him my reply too.

'Well look,' he said, 'if that doesn't satisfy Harold and he sends you another minute, I'd be very happy to come and see him with you. But we must keep the Government together at least until we have repealed the Industrial Relations Act.'

John Lestor also rang and asked what she should say. I told her to make it short, sweet and generally loyal.

Then I talked to Eric Heffer who read to me over the telephone what Harold had said to him in his letter of 27 October headed 'Personal, Confidential'. It was very interesting.

Dear Eric, Thank you for your letter of 19 October. I can understand your feelings about the naval exercises. Although there has been some discussion about the general problem of relations with South Africa, no decisions had been taken. I was quite unaware that the exercises were due to be held at this time and so, I believe, was Jim Callaghan. I have called for a full report and shall be taking this up with the colleagues involved during the next few days.   Yours, Harold.

That proves conclusively that Harold didn't know, and puts me in a strong position though I will have to be careful how I make use of the advantage. So, the position now is that Harold will either not accept the letter and sack me, which I doubt; or he will ask for further assurances which will mean I will have to think about it; or he will accept the letter and put it out through Joe Haines that I have grovelled to him in order to keep my job. I think that's the most likely course of action.

Monday 4 November

I talked in the House to Judith Hart, Joan Lestor and Margaret Jackson, the new MP for Lincoln who made her maiden speech today. We agreed that if we all got a second letter from Harold we should wait until the following night and try to play it cool. There is a general impression that Harold has gone over the top.

I showed Frank McElhone my reply to Harold, which I have now sent. He said I should have been tougher but instead I had been very clever which would make Harold angry. But he didn't think for one moment Harold intended to sack me, though he might pick off Joan or Judith to make a point.

Tuesday 5 November

The first item at Cabinet was Clay Cross. Tony Crosland presented the report agreed yesterday by a group of Ministers under Harold Wilson's chairmanship, in which local authorities would be asked to raise rents or rates to get back the money that had been lost through non-implementation of the Housing Finance Act. The disqualification of the councillors would be repealed but Clay Cross would still have to pay the £7,000 which they had incurred. Tony said he found it distasteful, but he hoped to present it to the House in such a way that Dennis Skinner would not walk out of the Chamber.

Jim said he had been opposed to doing this all along but thought he had to go along with it now.

I said I warmly recommended the proposal to remove the disqualification which was in line with what the NEC and Conference had asked for, but I thought we should wipe out all the penalties for these reasons. First, the non-implementers were defending the people they were elected to represent. Secondly, they were sticking to their pledge to those electors. Thirdly, they were defending the principle of local democracy. Fourthly, they had played a notable part in educating the public in the evils of the Housing Finance Act and hence helped in our Election – I added that I thought history would put them in the same category as George Lansbury and the Tolpuddle Martyrs and some of us would live to see the day when they were honoured.

There was an outcry from the Cabinet. 'What are the objections to it?' I asked. 'First of all retrospective legislation. There is no legal objection to the removal retrospectively of a penalty or conferment retrospectively of a benefit. It was argued that they were breaking the law, but illegal Pakistani immigrants have had an amnesty and they were breaking the law; all work-ins are illegal – Fisher-Bendix which Harold has helped with, and Meriden, have involved people occupying property they didn't own. It is said we are yielding to pressure but we often yield to pressure – the most recent case being on Thalidomide.'*

I got my reply from Harold in the evening: an absolutely uncompromising letter. I discussed it with people in the Lobby. Neil Kinnock and Mik said, 'Don't resign.' Bob Hughes, the MP for North Aberdeen, came and said, 'I'll resign if you would like me to.'

Went upstairs and saw Joan and Judith. We all agreed the next stage was to ask Harold if we could see him.

Michael had said he would come so I suggested it, but he was going anyway. Jim Callaghan told Judith, 'Give the man what he wants.' Bob Mellish said, 'Go and give him a kiss.' I don't think it's as simple as that. I think he does intend to have a showdown.

Frances's advice was, 'You will simply have to grovel but find a loophole if you can.'

That's the end of a pretty hideous, grim day with Meriden crumbling and the row with Harold reaching crisis point.

Wednesday 6 November
In the end I decided to send Harold a letter along these lines:

Dear Prime Minister,

In my last letter I made it clear that I accepted the principle of collective ministerial responsibility and hence all the requirements that flow from it.

Yours
Tony Benn

Then, during the course of the most boring NEDC meeting I have ever attended, I got a note from Harold Wilson in his own hand:

* Distillers Company manufactured and marketed an anti-sickness in pregnancy drug in the 1960s which caused severe limb deformities in the children born to women who took it. After a prolonged legal battle, a fund was established to compensate victims.

Dear Tony,

Thank you for your letter giving me the reassurances that I sought. I regard the matter as closed.

At 6 Arnold Hall and John Lidbury came to see me about the HS-146: Eric Heffer and Michael Meacher were present and the meeting began with a fight. Hall was burning with rage about what he alleged I had done to him publicly. I didn't refer to his letter to his workers before the Election but I simply said, 'You declined to have any tripartite meetings; you wouldn't discuss plans with the unions.'

He said, 'I have no obligation to discuss the contract with anyone but a contractual partner.'

'Yes, but if a contractual partner requires to have the case argued out.'

'Well, I'm not doing that.'

I said, 'What are you going to do. Are you going to destroy the aircraft drawings?'

'That's an outrageous suggestion,' he replied.

I said, 'Quite frankly, if I worked for you and was treated by you in the way you have spoken of these people, I would be suspicious of everything you intended to do.'

It was a great stand-up row. I said, 'You have wrecked this aircraft, and I am advised you're in breach of contract.'

'Well, that will go to the courts,' he said.

It was very rough, extremely rough.

Before this, in the afternoon, I had a word with Joan Lestor who was extremely upset and said, 'You promised last night you would consult and we would all write to Harold and say we would like to see him. Now you and Judith have written separate letters. That's a complete betrayal.'

'I did ring Judith in the middle of the night. But I decided in the end that I would simply reaffirm what I had said in my first letter, which didn't seem to me to change the position very much, and Harold accepted it.'

Joan said, 'I can't speak. I am too upset.'

But it worried me very much, especially after Eric Heffer said, 'Look, you have grovelled to Harold. I am sorry to say it, but you have grovelled.'

To dinner with a Roumanian delegation. Ron Hayward and Mik were there so I had a brief word with them. Ron told me, 'I saw Harold for ninety minutes today. Don't reply to any letters. It's all over, it's finished.' Mik agreed with him, 'Michael saw him today and it's all over.'

So, looking back on it, if I had held my hand for another five hours, the thing might have ended without any further correspondence. But, as it is, I may have lost credibility. These matters are difficult to judge.

Thursday 7 November
The papers contained a briefing put out by Joe Haines about the assurances I – along wth Joan Lestor and Judith Hart – were supposed to have given to Harold Wilson, on the basis of which the Prime Minister is said to have regarded the matter as closed. I didn't read them very carefully because I was humiliated by the whole experience, and the 'dog licence' approach to ministerial appointment is one that I find absolutely odious. But I recognise that the Left is going to be worried by it. They will think I have sold out and I am afraid that somehow, without quite knowing how it happens, I will slip back into the position that I occupied between 1964 and 1970, when I went along with a lot of policies that I really thought were wrong.

Friday 8 November
I was taken to Birmingham by helicopter. It was misty and raining, and the cloud base was about 300 ft, so the helicopter just scooted in to Birmingham at treetop level. It was quite exciting as we were going about 120 mph. Landed at Elmdon where I had done my first flying training in 1943 on Tiger Moths, and there was the same old terminal building, where Bill Lapworth of Meriden was waiting. A threat had been made that the 'Red Flag 74' would blow me up, so I had two police cars and motor cycles, and two Special Branch people followed me all day.

To the NVT motorcycle works at Small Heath for what turned out to be a very hostile meeting with about fifty shop stewards. I made a short speech and then they turned on me. 'You're just a tin pot king thinking you can impose your will. You don't care about the jobs here. Why should Meriden have help? Is it really a cooperative? Why didn't you listen to us?'

From there I went in to the mass meeting in the canteen, where there were two or three thousand workers. Not a single shop steward wanted to come on the platform with me so I climbed on by myself, sat on the table and picked up the mike. It was a pretty rough, hostile meeting. I described what had happened and that I would try to give them an assurance of their future if we could get an expansion programme going.

Poore had clearly recognised that the feelings of the shop stewards and of the workers at Small Heath were against the Meriden cooperative. He had said this to me many times and I hadn't believed him, but it seems that he was to some extent right.

After that, Bill Lapworth, Dennis Johnson, John Grattan, Geoffrey Robinson and I talked until 9. Broadly the strategy we worked on was this: we would get the shop stewards from all three plants together, and work for the objective of public ownership for all three plants in a British motorcycle corporation.

Caught the train back to London and got home exhausted.

I did get a clear feeling from today's events of an alarming situation; there was the militancy of people sticking to their jobs, which I fully support, but at the same time, the fear of slump means that workers will turn against workers and working-class solidarity will be strained to its utmost.

Monday 11 November

At Cabinet we discussed the Industrial Relations Act. The situation is that we were committed before the February Election to its complete repeal. But it has not yet been repealed in full because, due to Harold Lever's absence from a vote in the summer, the Tories managed to retain the special clause providing for a judicial tribunal to examine cases of dismissal from work due to the operation of a closed shop.

Michael Foot stressed that the TUC did not want the tribunal. Elwyn Jones said this was absolute surrender to the trade union movement. Why should we blow the trumpet of surrender so soon?

I agreed strongly with Michael. 'I cannot understand this theory that the test of the virility of Labour Ministers is that they really must have a row with the trade union movement. Why didn't we take the high moral line that a man's employment was put at risk by companies who just threw him out of work for their own profit and loss reasons?'

It became clear that only about six members of the Cabinet were against Michael, but Roy Jenkins said he wanted a minute of dissent to be recorded in the Cabinet minutes. 'Well,' Harold stated, 'that procedure was dropped ten years ago.' Roy was furious. Then tactically at the end, Michael somehow got the Bill put back a week or so.

In the afternoon, I went to one of the most inspiring meetings I have ever attended; it was organised by the Lucas Aerospace Shop Stewards' Combine Committee, the best organised combine in the country with all the unions represented. There were sixty or seventy people there and they presented their case for public ownership. I said the Government had not yet made a statement; there were two options for the airframe industry which the Labour Party and the TUC had not thought sensible; and there was the possibility of it coming under the NEB. They have quarterly meetings in Sheffield and they are in fact a complete shadow administration of a very important kind. I found myself wholly in sympathy with them.

Wednesday 13 November

After the Industrial Development Committee today I had a word with Stan Orme. 'Stan, as a member of the Tribune Group, you can see what is being done. The whole policy is being eroded in such a way as to make it very difficult for us at Industry to proceed. Denis says he has to go for Tory measures because he has no socialist instruments. When he's criticised he says, "Ah but the socialist instruments are coming." Then when he does have them he says, "We can't have socialist instruments" and tones them down. The thing is a fraud and I am going to have to fight to the death to restore vitality to the policy.'

I am going to have to build up massive support now through major speeches. I had assumed that after the White Paper was published the battle was won, but of course it wasn't. There is a systematic social-democratic betrayal of socialist policy and the Cabinet has got nothing in common with the aspirations of the movement. But the social democrats are much cleverer than Gaitskell who killed by confrontation: they kill the policies by deceit and double talking, saying one thing publicly and doing another thing privately. I don't intend to be defeated like that.

Thursday 14 November

Just before Cabinet, I gave Michael a copy of my draft minute to Harold, asking for Ministers to be free in the Referendum campaign to pursue their own arguments – for him, Peter and me all to sign.

At lunch in the House, I sat at the Scottish table and talked to Frank McElhone, who is very dissatisfied that he hasn't seen enough of me. Harold had told him that Don Ryder would be Chairman of the NEB, which is probably quite a sensible appointment.

Later, I met Jim Sillars and David Lambie [Labour MP for Central Ayrshire] to talk about Scottish aviation and whether it should be nationalised. They told me there had been a tremendous explosion of Scottish nationalism, exploiting every grievance, against steel closures, against the Government for the industrial disputes, against the English unions.

Jim Sillars said that if the English majority in the forthcoming Referendum was sufficient to overturn the Scottish and Welsh opposition, then the United Kingdom would split. Therefore, for the sake of preserving the unity of the UK, he would prefer an entirely separate Scotland within the Common Market. That was quite an interesting development, and I think he's probably right.

Friday 15 November

I went over to the Economic Strategy Committee on Europe. I tried to raise the important general question about sovereignty and the impact of the EEC on the unity of the United Kingdom, and so on, and Harold said, 'We've got other very important business and we can't go into that.'

I had prepared a list of all the issues in which I have been involved and on which I've had to go to the Community for assent or on which my work was monitored. Although our pragmatic experience might indicate that no real difficulties were being created, the fact is that power has shifted and that our industrial policy will be incompatible with this degree of monitoring and approval.

I wanted to discuss the pressure for a closer union – the federal escalator – and direct elections. Once you have elected Members of a European Parliament with a larger geographical area to look after and at least half our legislation to watch, then the House of Commons becomes an inferior assembly. I wasn't concerned with parliamentary sovereignty as such but with the electors who controlled the House of Commons. They would be put in an inferior position.

However, this was all pushed aside and instead we went on to the harmonisation of tariffs on 1 January.

As we were leaving the meeting, Michael signed the letter to Harold requesting that Ministers should be free to take their own line in the Referendum campaign. Peter also signed it but he wanted to delay sending it for a week, since he felt we shouldn't push our luck and it looked a bit like a demarche.

Back to the office and found I had kept Donald Stokes waiting for half an hour. 'We talked in the summer,' he said, 'and you asked me to tell you what increase would be necessary in our investment programme. Well, I need £250 million, part of which I will be able to get from the banks but they won't give it to me until they know what your attitude is. I want it in equity: I can't get it from the market, and I can't get it from Finance for Industry.'*

We decided that there would be deeper discussions between British Leyland and the Department, and we would agree their strategy for approaching the banks. I would minute the Prime Minister, telling him that something was on the way. Meanwhile, we would work out a package and before we issued a statement, we would call in the unions for discussions and then we would work out the details. It would probably involve £50 million equity stake, which would be about 20 per cent equity holding in BL, plus possibly another 20 per cent in convertible loan stock which would be a substantial move towards British Leyland becoming part of the NEB.

Sunday 17 November
All-day Cabinet at Chequers. I read the papers on my way there. The front page of the *Sunday Times* carried the introduction to Dick

---

*Finance for Industry (FFI) was a fund designed to work with the NEB to mobilise private capital for the purpose of stimulating investment.

Crossman's diary. He was determined that the myth that we call parliamentary democracy should be exposed. Therefore, he had left his diary and hoped his colleagues would forgive him for the unfriendly references made to them. But, he said, his own follies were equally revealed.

His reasons for writing the diaries were similar to mine, indeed, I think I got the idea of putting them on tape from him. He kept a diary from 1952 to 1970. Mine are nothing like as complete as that but they will overlap with Dick's from 1964 to 1970 and insofar as we were at the same Cabinets and on the same committees, there will be some cross check. My diary does document, with enormous precision, the 1970 to 1974 period, including the first seven months of this Government.

The publication of Dick's diaries is important because if collective responsibility extends even after a man is dead, then the public is cheated for ever of knowing what really happened.

Chequers has been completely redecorated since I was last there, in 1970. I should think they must have spent half a million on it. All the panelling has been scraped of its dark stain and varnish so it was much lighter – a great improvement. The wallpaper was a bit garish. Heath really did spend an enormous amount of money on making his days at Number 10 and Chequers comfortable. Of course the press say nothing about it when it is a Tory.

The Cabinet gathered at about 10.30 in the Gallery on the first floor, with Harold saying he hoped the meeting would be informal. Sir Kenneth Berrill opened with a Think Tank paper. As far as the balance of payments was concerned, we had to decide on ways of closing the gap. We had the problem of inflation. There was anxiety about oil. We had to be competitive.

Productivity was crucial, said Denis Healey. There would be a slump or devaluation and if we went on like this, we would drop to a Spanish standard of living. Even so, despite our reduced military and economic strength, we still had a far greater influence on international thinking than people imagined.

Roy Jenkins's view was that we shouldn't be too economic. There had been a very substantial ten-year change in the balance of world alliances. The US power to run the world, which we had experienced after the war, had gone. China had come on to the scene and if they saw any evidence – as a result of the oil-price crisis – that capitalism was breaking down, this might lead the Russians and the Chinese to come together again and decide to end detente with the West because they no longer needed to live with capitalism. He, for his own part, feared a pre-emptive strike by the US against the oil countries and thought it might be another Suez.

Eric Varley argued that self-sufficiency in oil was what we should aim for. He talked about the Scargill mafia. 'We mustn't frighten the oil companies away from the North Sea; we must be absolutely sure they are profitable.' I must say, seeing a former militant miner attacking Scargill, saying we must be nice to the oil companies, was a fine reflection of what being in Government can do to people.

Ted Short said, 'We must mobilise people, operate by persuasion and consent. For example, Tony Benn is encouraging worker cooperatives and I absolutely agree with him.'

I came in at this point. 'We must make up our minds as to how we can get a new domestic consensus as well as a new international consensus, and just as we rule out a pre-emptive strike against the Arabs – which Roy suggests the Americans might go for – we must also rule out one against the forces at home who are asserting their rights. If we have a slump, the only way people will get through the crisis is by being given a new perspective.'

We would have to consider whether we wanted bigger or smaller units. Was it true the world was going 'big'? Were there just going to be Super Powers who would run everything – Russia, America, the Common Market, China, and Japan? When I looked round the world, what I saw was the Russian empire breaking up, and the possibility that China might disintegrate when Mao died. The Americans, though not breaking up geographically, might very well find themselves under considerable stress because of their domestic problems, for example of race and the urban crisis which would paralyse them and prevent them acting internationally. We had to recognise that the world was tending to go smaller, not bigger.

Jim Callaghan pessimistically said that every morning when he shaved he thought that he should emigrate but by the time he had eaten breakfast, he realised there was nowhere else to go. He thought the collapse of confidence was absolutely critical. He didn't think there would be an American Suez against the Gulf, but he did think the Americans would be drawn in if Israel got involved. The Palestinians had a case and although he recognised the Labour Party was a pro-Israeli party, we did have to understand the needs of the Palestinians. He thought Britain was going down hill so fast that we might well lose our seat on the Security Council, then go on sliding down. There was no solution, that he could see, to our problems.

Denis Healey thought it was no good giving up being the world policeman simply to become the world parson.

In summing up the morning, Harold Wilson suggested that American leadership had gone. The UK had great influence with America through Jim's friendship with US Secretary of State Kissinger, and we also had friendly relations wth Russia. He thought there should be some attempt at joint Anglo-French exploration of the oil in the Channel, and a five-year agricultural plan should be looked at.

After lunch I got the opportunity to ask Bob Mellish whether he thought Cabinet Ministers would have the freedom to speak during the Referendum campaign. He said, 'There's no alternative. Michael Foot won't be shut up, nor will you, nor Roy, nor Shirley.' He believed Harold was thinking along the same lines. If that is the case, it is very encouraging. Peter, however, still declines to send the letter off to Harold yet, although he has now agreed it can go on Thursday afternoon without further consultation with him.

Tuesday 19 November

Frances Morrell was upset in the office because there has been a row to try to prevent her going to the Labour Party Conference. She was fed up with the way the civil servants were trying to clamp down on the advisers. I encouraged her and told her it was exactly what happens in respect of Ministers and the Prime Minister.

At 5.15, I went over to Number 10 and saw Harold. We talked about the Post Office, and I said that I had saved Bill Ryland for another term as Chairman and that I got on well with him. The unions wanted him. Then, on the chairmanship of the NEB, I understood that he had Don Ryder in mind and I said I'd be happy to appoint him. I knew him, had a lot of time for him, he was very energetic and seemed sympathetic. So that was agreed.

Wednesday 20 November

The only important item on the Cabinet agenda was defence. Harold reported on consultation with the Americans and the Germans on our proposed defence cuts. The Germans were a bit anxious about reductions of troops in Europe and the Americans were worried about our withdrawal from the Gulf and from the sovereign bases in Cyprus. It's the old story. They never want you to cut defence because, as the argument goes, we're going against our NATO allies. When we do cut, it is always too little and too late.

So we came on to whether we should continue with the nuclear deterrent. Harold said that in fact we were not intending to develop the Poseidon submarines. He reminded people of the discussions that had taken place up to 1970 and the reservations that were made at the time. He told us that all that was being proposed was a very minor addition to the present nuclear weapons system, without the multiple re-entry vehicles (MIRVs).

He felt there were a number of reasons for retaining the deterrent. First of all, the European position: we didn't want the French to be the only ones who had nuclear weapons, with the risk that the Germans might go in with them. Second, our influence in the US through Jim and Henry Kissinger was thought very important. Third, it brought us into the Hot Line and we were consulted. Fourth, the Soviet Union had never objected and had valued our independent judgment.

Then Jim said that he shared the Prime Minister's view, particularly on the risk that if we pulled out the Germans might come in; he recognised that this was a matter on which the Prime Minister had greater knowledge than anyone else.

Michael prevaricated and declared that it was very difficult. He didn't like nuclear weapons but he was ready to go along with the proposal that we retain them, particularly if the Manifesto commitment – to move towards the removal of American nuclear bases – was preserved.

£24 million a year for ten years – £240 million – was a lot of money in Barbara's view, money she could use in the Department of Health and Social Security. It wasn't a serious contribution.

Roy Mason talked about the great value of this strength with the rundown of conventional forces. At this stage, Harold Wilson left to go to a service to unveil a plaque for Churchill, and Ted Short took over the chair.

Reg Prentice crossed and uncrossed his hands, sweated and looked pious and sanctimonious, said how anxious he was. But in the end he predictably came out in favour of nuclear weapons. He thought we might bargain them away later in return for a settlement.

Peter Shore argued that British power was weakening everywhere; that the French had nuclear weapons, the Israelis might have them, so we mustn't contemplate a reduction in British power of this kind.

I said I had never been a unilateralist, I'd never marched to Aldermaston, and my *instinct* was to keep them – the Americans had them, the Russians, the French, the Chinese, the Indians, the Israelis. But I could see a certain contradiction in arguing that whereas the Indians had destroyed their moral position and lost influence in the world by exploding nuclear weapons, we wished to gain or at least retain influence by keeping them. So my *mind* told me that it was not right to retain them.

Secondly, I thought that they were clearly unusable – though I wasn't one of those who would want to use them. They were ineffective as a means of defence because – as I'd pointed out at a Cabinet a couple of weeks ago – the only wars that had been won since 1945 were by guerillas defending their own country.

Third, I doubted whether there was real political control over this aspect of our military establishment. These weapons were very expensive and Aldermaston was always arguing that we needed a permanent, skilled crew to maintain them, and therefore that the best thing to do was to employ the workforce to produce a new generation of weapons. I also said that it was a very expensive rental to the Hot Line and I wondered whether we wouldn't be entitled to a word for sanity in a crisis without having nuclear weapons.

Perhaps worst of all, however, the retention of nuclear weapons misled us about our influence in the world. The bomb somehow made us feel very powerful. Indeed there were many people in Britain who thought that the Queen and the bomb were the only two weapons we had left. I said I didn't think either of them were much use.

If the forecasts of the decline of our economy, to which Jim Callaghan had referred, were true, then a further defence review would be necessary. So, all in all, I was in favour of not continuing with them.

This created a bit of a stir, but the rest of the debate went on predictably. The Vietnam war had convinced John Silkin that we should have nuclear weapons; John Morris was afraid that if we didn't have them, conventional weapons would have to be increased.

Harold Lever said that the Vietnam war has also convinced him that we should have them, and he agreed with what Harold had said earlier.

Jim Callaghan believed that nuclear weapons stabilised the position, and their removal would be destabilising.

Willie Ross complimented me by saying, 'At least Tony Benn is consistent, because twenty years ago he resigned from the Front Bench where he was the Number Two Air spokesman, as he didn't honestly feel that he could join in a defence strategy which contemplated the use of nuclear weapons.' Amazing that he should recall that.

Bob Mellish said that you simply couldn't give up the bomb, the British people would never understand it. Shirley came back with a sort of unctuous, 'Let's keep them, but can we be assured that we can bargain them away?'

One point I made in my speech was that I recognised that in decisions of this kind the Prime Minister had a special knowledge not open to others.

Thursday 21 November
Lunch was followed by a meeting on the regional policy and the regional fund, which was in a sense the crunch meeting. I interrogated my officials about what had happened to sovereignty. Under the regional fund, you simply pay over the money and you get the same money back but when it comes back it is under the control of the Commission instead of Parliament. You're also committed not to reduce your own expenditure so that also acts as a control on the domestic economy.

So I proposed four alternative solutions:

1. The Commission should issue a self-denying ordinance, saying that it would not intervene.

2. The Council of Ministers should publish a statement that they would overturn the Commission if the Commission did intervene.

3. An amendment under the Treaty.

4. An amendment to the Common Market EEC Act, Section 2, making all regional and industrial policy subject to the British Parliament

Well, officials just sat there pointing out that none of these options would be acceptable. So I said that left us with one alternative and that was to give up the sovereignty of Parliament. To me, that also seemed unacceptable.

Part was really very cheeky and told me that the Manifesto had been badly written and was meaningless. I said that that may be so but it was what we had fought the Election on, and I knew exactly what I was doing when I wrote it.

So that was how it was. This is the crunch because I am saying the magic words – that Common Market policy is a plain breach of the Manifesto commitment.

Friday 22 November
I walked through St James' Park and got to Number 10 at 10.30, where the joint meeting of the Cabinet and NEC was taking place up in the State Dining Room.

Harold began by announcing that owing to the bombing in Birmingham last night,[1] he wouldn't play much of a part in the discussion but he hoped to look in and out. In fact, he disappeared altogether and except for one walk through the room later, he kept himself absolutely clear of the whole business.

The bombing story is absolutely dominant with anger rising, a petrol bomb thrown into a Catholic Church, some factories in Birmingham refusing to work with Irish workers. The damage done to Irish people here, even though they may be Protestants, is terrible, every one a victim of this same awful process of escalating violence.

The meeting began with Ron describing the Conference* arrangements. He added that there would almost certainly be emergency resolution at Conference on the subject of Simonstown.

---

* Because the second General Election of 1974 was held in October, the Labour Party Conference was curtailed to four days in Central Hall, Westminster, from 27–30 November.

By 10.45 we came to the 'Strengthening of liaison between the NEC, the Government and the PLP', and Ron Hayward described the liaison procedure.

Then there was a bit of a pause and nobody seemed to want to start. I thought the whole meeting was going to fold, till Frank Allaun spoke. He said that the Manifesto had been flouted by the Simonstown naval exercises and Ministers had been compelled to withdraw what they had said at the NEC. This had created cynicism and disillusionment and as there were fourteen Ministers who were also on the Executive, it posed a very serious danger. He therefore wanted to see two things done; he wanted the Prime Minister to indicate that members of the National Executive were not to be compelled to defend policy that was contrary to the Manifesto, and he wanted the PM to reaffirm that elected members of the NEC were responsible to the Conference for their behaviour.

Reg Prentice spoke up. He was worried by the fact that Frank Allaun was to address a Conference meeting on the subject of, 'Can we control the Labour Government?' He said that the whole concept of control of the Labour Government by the Party was contrary to parliamentary democracy, which rested on the collective responsibility of Ministers, the whole responsibility of the Government to Parliament, and the responsibility of Parliament to the people. He said that if there was a conflict between the constitution of the country and that of the Party, then the constitution of the country must come first.

Several other members spoke and then Bryan Stanley said that he greatly regretted that this had all blown up and of course we all wanted unity. But the movement had put us here to do a job, and if the Government broke the Manifesto, the Executive had to point it out to them.

Joan Maynard referred to the Simonstown exercises, and was really worried at how morale had fallen in the Party between 1966 and 1970. It was very important to avoid that happening again.

I said that during the period of minority Government from February, the Labour Manifesto had been implemented and that had won confidence. Now with the new Government elected in October, a good working relationship was essential to avoid the dangers of the past and build on the successes of our years in Opposition. There were of course inherent difficulties in this relationship because we all had a multiplicity of responsibilities. We were all individual members of unions or the Party, and as MPs we were also responsible to the local parties which had selected us.

I had news for Reg Prentice, which was that the problems were more complicated than he thought. For example, the Privy Councillor's Oath was completely incompatible with the principle of Cabinet collective responsibility. I had begun reading the Privy Councillor's Oath, when Jim said, 'Oh it's secret.'

I said, 'Well, I got it from the House of Commons Library. It says that we have a responsibility to be true and faithful servants of Her Majesty, to defend all her pre-eminences against foreign prelates, potentates and so on. When Clem got rid of the Indian Empire, he was in breach of his responsibilities.' There was laughter at this. 'Our commitment to the Manifesto doesn't come from the present Conference. Many of us, including myself, in our Election addresses, announced to our constituents what our politics were. We were committed to the Manifesto and this was the basis on which we were elected. It is all very complicated. All constitutions are unworkable if they're written – not just the Labour Party constitution.

'As to collective Cabinet responsibility, it's very difficult to define. I know, Jim, you won't allow me to refer to the correspondence that recently occurred with the Prime Minister – though much of it appeared in the press – but I've looked at collective Cabinet responsibility in Herbert Morrison's book *Government and Parliament*, and he says it is Ministers' responsibility to support decisions in the Cabinet. Well, there are many issues that never go to the Cabinet.

'The only way of solving this problem, in my opinion, is that we should all see ourselves committed both to the Manifesto and to the success of the Government. We have to assume each other's responsibilities. And we have to recognise that we are all committed to support the Government so that it can implement the Manifesto. We can't live in watertight compartments. The NEC cannot instruct the Government and I know nobody who thinks it can, but similarly the idea that Labour Ministers are turned into civil servants when they become Ministers is simply not acceptable. I am sure no one really wants that. The dividing line that I see is between what the Government has done in the past, which in a sense we all have to defend because it was done with our consent, and what it is going to do next – where we all have a right to advise, even if we come to the conclusion that it should act differently compared to last time. The past we must defend, the future we must shape together. On the Simonstown resolution to the Executive, by deploring what Ministers did, we were on the wrong side of that dividing line.'

Jim interrupted here but I got it on the record.

Monday 25 November

Walked across the park again this morning. The John Stonehouse drowning is a bit mysterious. Bob Mellish had dug out a Hansard text of the last written question John Stonehouse asked before he disappeared, requesting the statistics on death by drowning. It was a most extraordinary coincidence – or else very mysterious. People don't believe he's dead. They think that with the financial trouble that he's in, he's just disappeared. Coastguards on the Florida coast say that he certainly didn't swim out more than fifty yards because they monitor all swimmers who go out that distance. I can't bring myself to write to Barbara, I don't know what to say.

Cabinet met at 10.30 and the first item on the agenda was the report from the Home Secretary on Northern Ireland. His paper outlined the measures he proposed: to outlaw the IRA and other organisations, to provide for closer border checks with the Republic and to take powers to deport certain Irish people in Great Britain who had lived here for less than twenty years back to the Republic or Northern Ireland. The main provisions were to be temporary and would expire after six months unless continued in force by an order.

They were emergency powers of a pretty draconian kind, including the power to extend the detention period from forty-eight hours to seven days on the Home Secretary's instructions.

Harold Wilson asked, 'I take it we'll include other terrorist organisations' and Roy replied, 'Yes, but not the Palestine Liberation Organisation – or the NUM, no matter how difficult they get!'

Merlyn Rees said, 'Look, we've really got to integrate this with the Northern Ireland powers because my authority is quite different. I have the power to intern without trial and you don't in England, and you're just going to send all your IRA people back to Northern Ireland. The thing would be completely unbalanced as between one set of powers and the other.'

Then Sam Silkin, the Attorney-General, came in and said that these were more stringent than any powers ever introduced in peacetime. He said that they introduced a principle of banishment from Great Britain which had not existed since the Middle Ages. They would affect all citizens. Harold Wilson interrupted, 'Well, we *are* in the Middle Ages.' Sam went on to clarify where the banished people would go. Would they simply be sent to Northern Ireland?

Elwyn Jones said that there was a state of war and he accepted that. He said that he hoped Roy would not mention 'civil libertarian squeals' because it would be most inappropriate.

Roy interrupted and pointed out that his record on civil liberties was pretty well established and Elwyn replied that he knew that, but he would advise Roy not to use that phrase in the House of Commons. Then he said that the persons excluded from this country would be detained in Northern Ireland under internment powers.

Jim Callaghan supported Merlyn, saying he didn't think Roy should simply throw all the problems back on to Northern Ireland. Elwyn thought that there should be a tribunal to assess whether or not people could be banished. But Roy said he wouldn't accept a tribunal. Elwyn replied that the European Court of Human Rights would not accept the measures without this, and Roy said he couldn't help that.

Michael asked if the powers could be introduced for three months instead of six.

Denis Healey said that we really could not insulate Northern Ireland from Great Britain, to which the Lord Advocate Ronny King Murray replied that we were trying to isolate an alien inhumanity from coming into the country.

Bob Mellish was concerned that the death penalty pressure would build up. He was also afraid that the Republic of Ireland was doing nothing and attacked the Catholic hierarchy. Roy Jenkins said, 'I intend to be very tough today, but I shall be a bit more conciliatory when I introduce the Bill on Wednesday or Thursday.'

Having listened to the debate I added my thoughts, saying it would have an effect on the constitutional relations between Northern Ireland and the United Kingdom, it would affect civil liberties, it would introduce a new debate on capital punishment under most unfavourable cirumstances. Although I recognised that we must respond to public feeling – which I knew was very strong in Bristol so I hesitated to think what it must be like in Birmingham – people were really saying one of two things; hang them or get out of Northern Ireland. I had a very real fear that we might awaken deep sectarian feelings against the Irish and against the Catholics which had been quiescent for over a hundred years in England.

Later, I saw Don Ryder and I offered him the chairmanship of the NEB, which was a bit of a formality since he already knew about it through Harold. He is very managerial, rather conceited and he thinks he is the cat's whiskers. But he will carry a degree of confidence and that's about as far as I need to take it. I think if I give him a couple of strong union men he'll be under a bit more pressure than he might expect.

I talked to Frances about the whole impact of the civil war that has begun. Three postboxes were blown up at Victoria, King's Cross and Piccadilly today. It is very alarming and one doesn't know what's going to happen but I suppose we'll have to learn to live with it like the Irish do in Northern Ireland. There's no doubt in my mind that we shall have to get out.

Tuesday 26 November
I dashed to St Ermine's Hotel where the National Executive was meeting. After the meeting, I had a brief word with Michael who finally agreed I could send off the letter from Peter and myself to Harold asking for freedom during the entire Common Market argument.

Wednesday 27 November

Overslept and only just had time to get to the Labour Conference for 9.30, held at the Central Hall, Westminster. There were pretty tight security restrictions due to the IRA bombings.

After lunch I listened to the debate on whether parliamentary candidates and MPs should be eligible for reselection in between Elections. Jim Callaghan had played it disgracefully: he let the Conference get all muddled by darting about on different amendments; then he let the lunch break come; then he put the whole clause without the amendments. In fact, the change was defeated by 3,200,000 to 2,400,000 so that great chance to democratise the Labour Party has been lost. Mik speaking against it made a very big impact.

Thursday 28 November

Conference, and the elections to the Executive. Sam McCluskie of the National Union of Seamen, one of the 'tightly-knit group of politically motivated men' Wilson accused in 1966 was elected in Bill Simpson's vacated place; Rose de Giorgio, the Young Socialist, was replaced by Nick Bradley, one of the Militant group. So I reckon we now have a majority of 15–13 anti-Market left-wingers. It is a most interesting situation. My vote bumped up from last year's 367,000 to 466,000, overtaking Michael Foot, so I am for the first time top of the Executive; Denis Healey just clung on with a few thousand ahead of Eric Heffer; Shirley Williams plummeted from the top of the Women's Section to the bottom, no doubt because of her Common Market speech in the Election, leaving Judith Hart at the top. So, all in all, it was a most satisfactory result.

Then came Harold's speech. For the first time in years he did not get a standing ovation, so I was spared the agony of having to get on my feet out of loyalty. But at the centre of his speech were the NEB and planning agreements and he made a reference to me, the first time he has ever done so in a speech.

At the end of the morning the one resolution on South Africa which had been picked was from Liverpool Toxteth, congratulating the three NEC members who voted to censure the Government on Simonstown. So, in fact, the Conference had explicitly and specifically endorsed what I did and it wipes out the correspondence with Harold. No doubt it made him very angry.

Went back to the office where I found that the combination of my coming top in the Executive and of Harold Wilson fully endorsing the NEB and saying it was the most significant development in industrial policy for twenty-five years, had absolutely dazzled my Private Secretaries Roy Williams, Martin Vile and Peter Thompson. All of a sudden they realised that this enormous centre of power, namely the

Labour Conference at Central Hall, was dominating Parliament; it was much more important than Parliament. And there tucked away, modestly sitting amongst the delegates, were some of the most powerful men in Britain – Scanlon, Ray Buckton of ASLEF, David Basnett, Clive Jenkins, Joe Gormley, and so on. It has been, of course, a tremendous experience for me: I can't describe what an experience this week at Conference has been for me.

Friday 29 November
Still at the House of Commons at 3.30 am, so I went in to see Bob Mellish who was dozing in his room and said, 'Bob, since I have got to speak to the Conference tomorrow, and also British Leyland has gone bust, I wonder if you would let me go?' I got to bed at 4, was up again at 7, and at 9 I had the meeting about British Leyland. Broadly the position is that British Leyland have not just got an investment problem but a cash problem as well and they need something like £250–300 million. They export £500 million a year and employ 185,000 people so there is no question of it going bust. But the problem is how we handle it. The office want to put £100 million in, even though the shares on the Stock Exchange are only worth £43 million. I agree that the Stock Market has collapsed and we can't pay £100 million and still end up with less than 50 per cent equity. So I said to the officials, 'I want you to prepare a proposal that allows voluntary acquisition, that is to say a one-clause Bill.'

As I was leaving the Conference I saw the Meriden people, so I chatted with them and we had lunch together. They are absolutely desperate, so I asked, 'Could you get the three shop stewards from the plants together quickly, and make your unions work for you harder on this? And would you consider a contract for doing bike spare parts at the moment?' They were saying that the men simply hadn't enough to live on. John Grattan told me his child brought a friend home from school the other day and said, 'His daddy works – not like you. He works.' The whole thing is very sad.

Went over in the early evening to a party at Number 10, where we talked to Mary Wilson about how ghastly the press was: she commented on how awful they were being to Caroline. Mary said she didn't give interviews and Caroline replied that she didn't either.

We moved on to the AUEW party at County Hall where Hugh Scanlon and Tony Banks greeted us. Again, a whole host of shop stewards, many of whom I knew.

Saturday 30 November
Limped out of bed. Last day of Conference and there were a lot of debates: Jack Jones made a powerful speech on Chile; Lena Jeger on

Clay Cross; Bryan Stanley on the Shrewsbury Pickets.[2]

Then Chancellor Helmut Schmidt addressed the Conference as the fraternal delegate of the SPD. He gave a very witty and amusing speech. He is the German version of Denis Healey and I see it all absolutely clearly now; the argument that will be used for contributing to the Community Budget is that it saves jobs. Next it will be, we have got to *stay* in Europe to save jobs. You can just see the Schmidt/Healey line coming together. I have no doubt Healey thinks he will replace Harold Wilson and then it will be the Healey/Schmidt Anglo-German axis against Giscard d'Estaing – a most alarming prospect.

Sunday 1 December
The John Stonehouse disappearance has now brought the Mafia into some of the press reports. It is a remarkable story. Nobody knows whether he has been abducted, kidnapped, killed, drowned or simply disappeared. Astonishing.

This afternoon, Geoffrey Goodman rang up to say there were stirrings among the pro-Marketeers in Fleet Street to set up a massive propaganda campaign in anticipation of the Referendum and that they were searching for a big figure to take charge of it, money being no object. The three possibilities were Sir Hugh Cudlipp, Lord Hill, or Sir Hugh Carleton Greene.* He said that the campaign would be on a huge scale and we must be ready for it.

Monday 2 December
At 10.15 Harold began the Economic Strategy Committee on Europe by reporting informally on his talk with Helmut Schmidt who, he said, had been helpful and keen to help us. He had spoken of the needs of the member countries of the Six, and he thought renegotiation should be under greater political control. He expected that Harold would be ready to commend the renegotiation package to the British people.

In the evening I had a message to ring Roy Williams at home and he told me the Prime Minister had decided to confirm the appointment of Sir Don Ryder as industrial adviser to the Government working at the Cabinet Office. So I shall just have to let that go by the board, though I did put in a minute expressing my hope that he wouldn't do it in addition to the NEB.

Apparently, the *Daily Mirror* got hold of the fact that Ryder is also to be appointed Chairman of the NEB and Harold has asked me to undertake a leak procedure. This is absurd, of course, as I first heard

---

* Sir Hugh Cudlipp, see Principal Persons p. 698; Lord Hill of Luton, a former Conservative MP and erstwhile Chairman of both ITA and BBC; Sir Hugh Greene, Director-General of the BBC, 1960–69.

about his appointment from Frank McElhone, who is not even a member of the Government. Frank had been told by Harold at dinner.

Tuesday 3 December
Donald Stokes came to see me at my request to discuss British Leyland and we began to explore a number of options: liquidation, retrenchment, Government injection of capital, or public ownership. It was agreed that he would cost these alternatives.

Wednesday 4 December
At 1.45 we had an hour's discussion on the Scottish and Welsh Development Agencies. The civil servants are thoroughly worried that there is going to be a massive distribution of responsibilities, at the Scottish Office, the SDA and perhaps beyond that to a Scottish Assembly and Government. The whose vista of the disintegration of the United Kingdom opened up.

Dennis Johnson and the Meriden stewards were waiting at the office but I couldn't see them as I was seeing Frank McElhone. Frank wouldn't take off his overcoat, but he had two whiskies and sat slating me up hill and down dale. He said I didn't see enough of him and I didn't care about the PLP. He criticised Frances Morrell for being an 'intellectual influence', hates the Institute for Workers' Control, thinks I should sever my connection with Ken Coates, and so on. In the end, it turned out he didn't want to be my PPS any more. Well, I shouldn't have argued with him, but I did for an hour and a half.

Thursday 5 December
At 9.30 I went to the Ministerial Committee on Economic Strategy, where the first real item on the agenda was the miners' new wage claim. Michael reported that if the miners got their normal increase to maintain their living standards, it would mean £5 for a surface worker and £7 for a face worker. But Arthur Scargill was demanding £30, and even in order to maintain their position in the league table of wages at the end of the miners' strike in March they would need £15 per week.

I listened to all the comments, which were absolutely characteristic of Labour Cabinets over the years. Harold is beginning to emerge more strongly as an anti-union man. Jim, of course, has been anti-union for a long time, very frightened by their power. Eric Varley cannot keep off his dislike of Scargill and McGahey and says he wished he could work with Lawrence Daly instead. Harold, of course, sees it all in terms of politically motivated men.

The next item was a paper from the Think Tank, which they had put in to this committee without any ministerial sponsorship at all – not through Peter Shore who was the appropriate Minister, or the Treasury. It was simply a paper saying that the property market had collapsed and the only way to put some vitality into it was by ending the freeze on business rents so that the property market itself would be more profitable. The Think Tank warned that the property market supported the secondary banks, which were themselves supported by the clearing banks; pensions and insurance funds were also invested in property and now the whole thing might be at risk, particularly as the clearing banks in their turn were supported by the Bank of England.

Sir Kenneth Berrill introduced the paper exactly as if he were a Minister, so we have now found a way of getting Tories into the Government, regardless of whether or not they win an Election. Peter Shore and Denis supported the paper and Harold warned of the possibility of a real collapse. The clearing banks might actually not be able to meet their withdrawals, and we might be in the sort of situation that the Americans were in in 1933 of having to close the banks. Well, if that really is the position – and the Central Policy Review Staff may have done us a favour by drawing our attention to it – then we have an absolute choice as to whether to adopt Tory measures in order to prop up the old system or to go forward with something else. In effect, what they were saying was that the final collapse of capitalism might be a matter of weeks away.

Harold said, 'Of course, if we had the money, we would acquire all this land at the present low price and buy ourselves into the market, but we are prevented from doing that by the Public Sector Borrowing Requirement.'

So the Treasury concept – that the role of the public sector in our economy had got to be limited in some way – prevents us from doing what would otherwise be sensible, namely acquiring land and, for that matter, companies, at their present deflated prices, while socialism on the cheap is possible. I think this situation will test whether we do intend to go forward with socialist measures.

Friday 6 December
The papers this morning said 'Leyland goes to Benn', 'Benn to help Leyland'. The whole story got out and with not one word from me to anybody; I did discover later in the day that the Prime Minister had asked Sir Douglas Allen to investigate the leak.

Sunday 8 December
The Sunday papers were full of British Leyland, and Sir Don Ryder's appointment. Nora Beloff made a great deal of the fact that Harold

had appointed Ryder to control me. Eric Heffer rang to express his anxiety about Ryder.

Monday 9 December
Ryder came in at 9.30 and, just before Part and Williams joined us, said, 'Look, I want to tell you that I've only seen Harold Wilson once. I regard myself as working for you with this Department. I don't run with the hounds and chase with the hare. I'm going to be absolutely loyal to this Department and to you. I shall never say anything behind your back.'

'I very much appreciate your saying that,' I replied. 'I don't leak and I don't brief. I make speeches and we perhaps shan't always agree but that's the basis on which I do business. Some of my colleagues don't quite share this view, but it's the view I adopt.'

On that happy note, I gave him an inscribed copy of 'Labour's Programme for Britain', the two Manifestos that contain reference to our industrial policy, and the White Paper.

I had to dash off to the memorial service for Sir Frank Wood* at St Clement Danes, the RAF church in the Strand. Afterwards, I gave Charlie Hill (Lord Hill of Luton) a lift back to the House of Lords. He was friendly and asked me how I was surviving as the bogeyman: 'So long as you have a happy family circle and you don't discuss the press handling of yourself with them, therefore insulating them from it, all will be well.' I'm afraid that is advice that I'm not strong enough to take, because I need to be supported a bit more than that.

Geoffrey Goodman came in from 5.30 till 6.45. He said that he thought Lord Cudlipp was the most likely man to run the pro-Market campaign with millions of pounds behind it. They'd have to be a bit careful even so, in case the press overdid it.

Geoffrey told me he believed there was really a strategy to bring about a Government of national unity by having a statutory pay policy by, say, February. This would throw Michael into disarray because the Social Contract would have broken down, and it would be argued that the Common Market situation was so overshadowed by the economic crisis that there might have to be a national unity Government. If one could be established, it would get rid of Harold, perhaps have Jim as Prime Minister, or Denis, and then that Government would go to the country and be elected for a five-year term. It is a possible scenario and certainly something to watch.

Frank McElhone then arrived and I took him home for a meal. As he spoke to Caroline and me, it all came out again, his absolute

* Permanent Secretary at the Ministry of Posts and Telecommunications, 1975; formerly my father's Private Secretary at the Air Ministry, 1946.

disenchantment with my performance. He said that the Parliamentary Party remains Centre and Left, and that if I didn't give some attention to the Centre of the Party, I would never have any chance whatever. He still had great faith in me but he said I really did have to take this seriously now; even the Market was going to slip through, with only the Left voting against it.

Obviously, he was sick of the fact that I haven't made much use of him over the last seven months, haven't listened, and that there've been no perks of office. Then he said, 'Look, I've got ten premium bonds in the bank. I haven't got a penny behind me. I've just put a new loft in the house and I've told the children that if the Scottish Nationalist advance goes on, and I lose my seat, we're back to a council flat, in the ghetto. We'll just go back to where we started.'

He made it clear that his work with me made him hated both in the lobby and the PLP, and he now feels that this makes life too difficult. I think he suspects that his chances of becoming a Minister would be greater if he severed his link with me, and he needs the money as a Minister. I think that's it, and I've done nothing for him: it's very human and understandable. So, he actually wants to break the link. He says that we'll still be friends and that he'll do what he can for me, but he does not want that organic link.

He then gave me lots of sensible advice about how to launch the Referendum campaign but in his heart he's a very right-wing guy and he doesn't agree with what I'm saying. He may well be in the process of transferring his allegiance to Jim Callaghan, whom he thinks will possibly be the next Leader.

Tuesday 10 December
Caroline and I went off to the British Steel Corporation Christmas party at Grosvenor Place, where we met Monty Finniston and his wife and a lot of the executives and board members of the BSC. I must say they were Tory to a man. The whole atmosphere was Tory. You wouldn't believe it was a nationalised industry. There was no commitment to socialism or public ownership. I found it revolting, and I'm not surprised that workers feel that it has nothing whatever to do with socialism, because it hasn't.

There was a twitty little stockbroker who was complaining about the current level of wage demands: there were two workers from the steel unions there, so I said that I made a very simple rule never to discuss wages unless everybody in the room was prepared to state their own. I said that I earned £13,000 a year as a Cabinet Minister, and I asked him what he got. He said £30,000 a year. I told him that that ruled him out from commenting on what claims these lads put in, and that even though he may be an expert on gilts and the Stock Market, that didn't mean he could talk about this and neither could I. He was pretty angry.

Wednesday 11 December
In the morning's papers there was a story and picture of Don Ryder arriving early yesterday morning at his office, photographed in the dawn light in Whitehall and really looking quite silly. He had had a press call so every one knew he was going to be there.

At 3 we had a huge staff meeting of 800 people in Church House, with Sir Antony Part, Peter Carey and all the Ministers on the platform. I thanked them for their work, then said we weren't going to discuss staff matters. 'But I'd like to tell you personally about our policy and how serious the situation is, and then we'll have questions.'

Well, they began a wee bit slowly, but then they got cracking along, mainly asking about industrial democracy and participation and democractic self-management. Each of the Ministers gave replies and it was a most interesting exercise, if a little artificial, because you knew that you were their boss and their relationship with you was constrained by that. Also I feel strongly that the arguments we are putting across now have become sharpened by class, and they were an overwhelmingly Tory audience, I should think. But it was quite jolly.

At the end, Part thanked us and I said, 'I beg to move that Sir Antony Part be re-elected Permanent Secretary to the Department of Industry', just to give it a democratic flavour. This idea was discussed quite seriously in Eric Heffer's office afterwards.

On 9 and 10 December 1974 the nine heads of the enlarged Common Market met in Paris to consider a number of fundamental issues affecting the EEC, including Britain's demand for a recalculation of her contribution to the Community Budget as part of the renegotiation of terms of entry.

In preparation for this summit, Wilson had talks with Chancellor Schmidt and with President Giscard d'Estaing in the preceding weeks. A long communiqué was issued from Paris on 10 December setting out agreements and stating that a 'correcting mechanism' for Britain's contribution to the Community Budget had been agreed to meet one of Britain's basic objections to the terms.

At the summit itself, Wilson agreed that, subject to the British decision in the Referendum to remain in the EEC, he would accept the principle of direct elections to the European Parliament. Hitherto, members of the European Parliament had been nominated by each country. Wilson had no Cabinet authority for his pledge, but the British Government was bound by it and as a consequence had to introduce the necessary legislation.

Thursday 12 December
At Cabinet Harold reported on the EEC summit. He said that the

heads of government had reached sensible agreements on energy and the recycling of Arab dollars, and that the Germans were introducing a massive reflationary budget which would boost confidence. On some matters in the communiqué we had abstained. On re-negotiation, he had stuck rigidly to the Manifesto commitments, and on the Community budget the French had tried to veto what we had proposed. But they had been overcome, and he had made it clear that we should want freedom on regional aid.

It was a most unsatisfactory, devious report because the communiqué of course agreed to abandon the unanimity rule on major questions affecting the Nine, to go for a European directly-elected Parliament, that the heads of government were in favour of an economic and monetary union, and so on – all major developments of policy that had never been discussed by the Cabinet. I said, 'I don't accept this, I'm not committed to it, and we must all be free to discuss. This is a critical matter.'

Harold Wilson said, 'Well, when I stated at the summit that I would recommend the terms to the British people, it was deliberate, because there is a letter from Michael and some of his colleagues [me and Peter] asking for freedom to express their view, and I therefore thought the best thing for me to do was to put myself forward as offering to recommend the terms.'

I said, 'Is the communiqué the policy of Her Majesty's Government?'

'Oh, no,' said Harold, 'we don't agree with an economic and monetary union at all.' So I said, 'Well, as Michael said, the communiqué states that their [the heads of governments] "will is not weakened" on this.' He said that made no difference.

Then Peter made a tremendously strong statement, saying that he was deeply shocked by the comuniqué, that it destroyed our credibility, that the right of veto by member countries had been weakened, that power had been transferred to permanent officials, and that he was not having his permanent officials deciding things. It was unacceptable.

Harold responded, 'I strongly resent the idea that I was an innocent abroad, that I went there and was just swept along. I've been negotiating since some members of this Cabinet have been at school.' He was really het up. 'I've been standing absolutely firm on the Manifesto, more than other people.'

I came in, 'Couldn't we be a bit more relaxed about it? We all have different views, we're all standing on the Manifesto in our own way. I disagree with Harold Lever on the economic and monetary union and he knows I take a very strong view on the sovereignty/democracy argument, but it really is the time now when we ought to be free to speak our minds.'

Later, I went over to the House of Commons to the PLP meeting, where there was another row about the EEC regulations. Dennis Skinner said, 'Look, these are all meaningless because Parliament has no power. They should be put in a pigeonhole and everyone should be free to speak right up to Cabinet level.' So the argument for free speech is beginning to build and build and grow and grow. It is absolutely critical and at the Executive on Wednesday I shall certainly raise the question of a special conference on the Market.

Then Eric Heffer got up to raise the case of the Shrewsbury Pickets. We had been told there couldn't be a meeting on the Shrewsbury Pickets, it was in some way *sub judice*. Eric said, 'I don't know if I'm allowed to speak at a party meeting, but I'm speaking not as a Minister but as a member of UCATT, and I can imagine circumstances where, as the chief shop steward, I would have been in jail. These are good men and they shouldn't be in jail, and we must get them out before Christmas.'

It was agreed that there would be a Parliamentary Party meeting next week on the Shrewsbury case. It was an overwhelming vote, which is very encouraging. The pressure on the Government is now building up and Eric did well.

Friday 13 December
The papers this morning were full of reports of yesterday's trade figures. The situation is pretty grim.

Secretary came. We discussed Don Ryder and Leyland, and I told Part how shocked I had been at the way the Treasury – Henley, Leo Pliatzky and Dell – had come in almost as if to take over the Department.

To Bristol for a surgery. There were a wide range of cases – housing, tax, subsidence, a little pressure group trying to get a zebra crossing, a Pakistani wanting to be naturalised. Really, without constituency work a Member of Parliament simply wouldn't be in touch, particularly a Minister.

Saturday 14 December
Rang Joe Ashton and asked his advice on who I should appoint as my new PPS. He agreed to do it himself, saying, 'I wouldn't do it for anyone else, and I wouldn't do it for you for a long period, but at this particular moment you need your friends around you, so I'll help.'

That's settled then. I'm very pleased because I like Joe; he gets on well with the media people, he has a good solid trade union background, he's a journalist of note and linked very closely with the trade union movement, and as he is Chairman of the Industry Group of MPs we shall work very closely together.

Monday 16 December

It took me fifty-two minutes to walk across the park this morning, and it was rather pleasant. The papers were speculating whether John Stonehouse was a Russian agent or a CIA agent and mentioned that he had been under surveillance by M15.

Joe Ashton, Frances and I talked for about an hour in the office and then we went over to the House. Caroline joined us with Stephen for dinner. Joe's real concern was to get me into the Tribune Group, saying it was essential that I should join because of the polarisation that had occurred. There was no middle ground and people wouldn't understand why I wasn't in the Group. A new list of names was going to be issued tomorrow.

Tuesday 17 December

I went up to ASTMS for Christmas drinks with Clive Jenkins and John Garnett, the Director of the Industrial Society, who incidentally is the brother of Peggy Jay, Douglas Jay's former wife.

Lunch at Jack Straw's Castle on Hampstead Heath, and we talked about the idea of a whole-day meeting with the Industrial Society, discussing the industrial policy. Perhaps Clive Jenkins and an industrialist who was sympathetic – Geoffrey Robinson for example – could lead the debate.

John Garnett is one of those Christian do-gooders who has got into industrial policy by running this Society, but is quite ineffective because he hasn't got the power of the trade union movement behind him. Jack Jones gets on with him all right and the Duke of Edinburgh is on the fringe of this sort of stuff. But real strength lies in the trade union movement, that is what one discovers.

I went briefly to the Labour Party Christmas party, where there was a cabaret. I missed the funniest item, which was Harold depicted as a mafia boss with Haines as his henchman. Haines said, 'You made that guy, boss; with your little finger you could break him,' then the rest of the skit was about the attempt to break Tony the Wedge.

Went over to vote, and then I came home. Had a word with Douglas Jay's wife, Mary, about the Common Market arrangements. She said the 'Get Britain Out' campaign consisted of George Wigg, Powell and Christopher Frere-Smith. Douglas had formed a National Referendum Campaign and agreed tonight at a meeting that Neil Marten would be the Chairman. There is also the Common Market Safeguards Campaign, British Businessmen for World Markets, the Anti-Common Market League, and the National Council of Anti-Common Market Organisations. Mary said they were desperately trying to bring them all together for the campaign.

I must say it is going to be an awful rag-bag, and the only thing I

really want to have anything to do with, frankly, is the Labour Party.
I want to get the Labour Party to come out against Europe, that is the
key.

Wednesday 18 December

At 9.30, the Devolution Committee met at Number 10 to consider a
paper by Ted Short, in which he wanted a huge number of principles
agreed immediately so that he could get on with instant legislation.

On the timetable I said that I thought we couldn't make a decision
until after we knew whether or not we were going to remain in the
Common Market. 'Devolution is constitutional change and I think we
may have to have a referendum on that,' I commented.

'Oh, we don't want a referendum,' said Harold. 'This has been before
the people in the last Election.'

'It's a constitutional change, you know, a very important one, and
it affects the rights of the UK.'

Harold insisted, 'Well, we're not having one.'

I had to hurry over immediately after that to the accountants Touche
Ross in the City, where for two and threequarter hours I was grilled
by the three Court Line inspectors sitting behind beige tables piled
high with papers. It was like a court martial. The Treasury Solicitor
and Peter Carey sat beside me and I was pressed hard on general
matters, on the acquisition of Court Line Shipbuilders, on nationalisation, and was asked about the points that Heseltine had made.

I realised that it was just another Tory court, it wasn't a fair court
at all. They kept talking about the threat of nationalisation, wasn't it
'odd' that I had nationalized the profitable shipyards instead of the
unprofitable ones, as if the function of nationalisation was to pick up
the failures.

Then they questioned the statement on holiday-makers, using the
words 'safeguarding', 'stabilise', 'securing'. They tried to suggest that
people shouldn't believe what was said in Parliament. I said, 'No, not
at all, it's the opposite. I feel as let down as the holiday-makers, because
I was given false information.'

Finally they had a question about the feasibility of Court Line
carrying on, and I did as well as I could, trying to give them as little
ground to criticise me as possible.

Thursday 19 December

At Cabinet for a long struggle about top salaries. Michael Foot and I
were arguing that we should peg top salaries both for civil servants and
the nationalised industry chiefs. Harold Lever commented that 'I pay
my cooks more than some of these senior civil servants', and it got so
embarrassing that Harold sent the civil servants out. Jim Callaghan

strangely enough was in favour of deferrment. Roy Mason and Eric Varley were for paying.

Lunch with Donald Stokes and the Board of Leyland, all of whom seem very relaxed about the collapse. They were pretty angry that they had been caught by the Government because although Donald himself has been very cordial all along, it is a highly *private* enterprise firm. I talked a bit about the need to involve the trade unions and they described how difficult it was. I said, 'Well however difficult it is, we ought to find a way of giving the unions an opportunity to contribute to the solution of the firm's problems because frankly if there were no industrial disputes, you would be making hundreds of millions of pounds a year and wouldn't have any financial troubles at all.' They couldn't dissent from that. So the bigger the element of strikes in a company's financial position, the more incentive they have to let the trade unions help them out of their difficulties: this is the way one presents the socialist argument to people who are by no means socialist.

Friday 20 December

Michael told me today that Jack Jones was absolutely solidly against the Market and was in favour of Ministers being free to speak as the only way in which the Party could remain united. Jack was in favour of a special Party conference, although mentioning that the T & G would be campaigning against the Market in any case. Both he and Ron Hayward were going to say all this to Harold and that's extremely important news.

Then Caroline arrived and we went over to Australia House for Christmas drinks. Gough Whitlam, the Prime Minister – a great, tall, red-faced man with curly white hair – was just making a speech.

Sunday 22 December

My own Industrial Development Advisory Board criticised me last week on the grant of £4 million for KME* and today the BBC rang up at home to ask if I would give an interview on the affair. I thought Heseltine's charge that we were throwing away public money was so damaging that I agreed to do it.

In the evening we went to the Shores' house for dinner with Michael and Jill. We agreed that there should be a paper on economic strategy which we, as a threesome, would put in to the Cabinet when it met, and also that we would put in a paper on the Common Market.

Michael is disenchanted with Harold and he did threaten to resign

---

* The IPD (Fisher-Bendix) factory from which the cooperative was set up with funds from the Department of Industry was renamed Kirby Manufacturing and Engineering Company, KME.

last week over the top salaries issue. Today in the papers Walter Johnson, the very right-wing Labour MP for Derby, criticised the top salaries publicly. So collective responsibility is breaking down again, which is a good thing.

Monday 23 December

Frances Morrell helped me begin work on a letter on the Common Market Referendum campaign to my constituents, in which I hope to try to open up some of the really basic questions of sovereignty and parliamentary democracy.

Came back and began wrapping Christmas presents. I am really tired, and pleased the holiday has arrived.

Tuesday 24 December

Christmas Eve. I delayed a few things that were in my red box; one was a draft letter to Ford Motors thanking them for informing me that they were laying off thousands of people and saying I was sure they regretted it. Well, I'm not prepared to leave it at that. Next, a letter re-appointing the members of the Industrial Development Advisory Board which I am going to think about further. Third, an important document on NVT stating that it would cost £25–35 million to set up the British motorcycle industry which, again, I am not prepared to accept at this moment.

Wednesday 25 December

Christmas Day. A huge family lunch, with Caroline's brother Graydon, his wife Diane and their boy Dougie.

Thursday 26 December

Boxing Day. Continued the draft of my letter to my constituents on the Common Market. The argument hinges on five democratic rights which are at the heart of parliamentary democracy: the right to elect an MP who makes the laws and passes taxes; the right to elect an MP who changes the law and changes taxes; the right of MPs to see that the laws they pass are enforced by the Courts; the accountability of Ministers and Governments to Parliament and to the people; and finally, arising from all these things, the obligation that Ministers and MPs have to listen to people because they know they are capable of being dismissed in an Election. Thus I proposed a definition of sovereignty as the power belonging to the people and being lent to Members of Parliament to use.

I identified the five changes that would occur as a result of Common Market membership, stressing that I was writing as an MP and not as a Minister. I was not dealing with the arguments for or against entry.

I added that I was ready to accept the verdict of the Referendum but that we should respect each other's views, and so on.

Friday 27 December
Frances arrived and we worked from about 11 through till 8, going through the draft, cutting out chunks, compressing it, polishing it. We had a typist in who typed three drafts and then finally put it on stencils. I tried to get hold of Peter Shore but he was on his way to Cornwall, so by the time I did talk to him the whole thing was written and the stencil cut; but he did suggest that I delete one reference to the re-negotiation.

Saturday 28 December
Up early and stapled the copies together then sent them round to all nationals, to the Press Association, to the *Western Daily Press*, to the *Bristol Evening Post*, to Harold Wilson, to Joe Ashton, to the office, to Michael Foot and to Peter Shore. The copies went out at 12.30 and that was the die cast, though the release time is not until 1 pm on Sunday. I sat tight and waited to see what would happen. Sure enough, at 6.20, one of Wilson's Private Secretaries rang and said the Prime Minister had received the text of my letter and wanted to know whether the copies have already gone out to the press. So I said 'Yes, they have, but if you are speaking to him, you might draw his attention to the fact that I do not deal with the re-negotiation at all, simply the constitutional change that has occurred.' He told me that I would be receiving a personal message later tonight from the Prime Minister. Then I did begin to think that he was going to make this the occasion for firing me and I became slightly anxious.

On the other hand, the issue is so crucial that I couldn't possibly withdraw this one to please him. I rang Peter who asked if there was any reason why I shouldn't hold it back for a bit if the Prime Minister asked me to. It would be almost impossible to ring round all the papers and cancel it and I didn't intend to do that. But it would be very disappointing to be fired at this moment.

Left for Stansgate at 7.30, and within a few minutes of arriving, the phone rang and it was Roy Williams. He had had a telephone call from Stewart, one of the Prime Minister's Private Secretaries, with the following message:

'We spoke earlier this evening about a statement which your Secretary of State is releasing to the press tomorrow morning in the form of an open letter to his constituents about the Common Market. I understand that the text of this statement is already in the hands of the press with an embargo for midday tomorrow. The Prime Minister, who has seen a copy of the statement, has asked that what follows should be conveyed to your Secretary of State tonight as a matter of urgency:

'The Prime Minister considers that this statement contravenes the Cabinet decision of 12 December as minuted in the confidential annexe sent to all Cabinet Ministers immediately afterwards and summarised in the Prime Minister's letter to the Secretary of State for Employment and copied both to the Secretary of State for Trade and to your own Secretary of State in reply to their letter on the proposed agreement to differ.

'The Prime Minister trusts that your Secretary of State will recall that on the meeting on 12 December it was agreed that the Cabinet should meet early in the New Year to discuss all aspects of the handling of the problem, including the issues raised in the letter from the Secretary of State for Employment, and it was agreed that no one should be involved in private enterprise on these issues until the Cabinet had collectively discussed how the matter is to be handled.'

I said to Roy Williams that he should ring Stewart to say he had transmitted the message to me and that I did not believe that I had contravened the decision of 12 December; indeed, I did not recall having received the letter Harold referred to, responding to our joint request that Cabinet Ministers should be allowed to differ over the Common Market. Roy Williams couldn't recall having received it either. So if the Prime Minister has made an error and this letter did not reach me, that puts me in a slightly stronger position. But I emphasised he should say to Stewart that as the Prime Minister's message contains a reference to documents, I would have to wait until Monday until I could have access to those documents and then I would send a minute in reply. This means that on Monday, in a fairly leisurely way, I can get the documents and study them and compose a very short response. I am not going to get locked into a long correspondence with the PM. He's a very curious man; he simply won't talk to any of his colleagues, he has to communicate by correspondence which creates an arm's length relationship that is entirely artificial and unreal.

I read Roy the text of my letter to my constituents and he said, 'It's magnificent but, of course, it will be taken as an attack upon the re-negotiation and the way it's handled, upon the summit, and a comment on the Common Market.' So he felt he was being drawn into something that could be grim. As a matter of fact, my reaction on reading the Prime Minister's message was that it could have been a lot worse. If he had said to me, 'You must withdraw the copies by noon tomorrow and prevent them being issued', I would have been in real difficulty, because although it would have been theoretically possible I would not have felt morally able to do so.

Sunday 29 December
Very nice to be away from the rush and furore. Joshua was busy with his car.

Came upstairs and began listening anxiously to the 1 o'clock news which contained a reasonable summary of my letter. 'The Secretary of State for Industry has made an attack upon the Common Market and said the British people would be signing away their democratic rights if we remain in the Common Market.' They went on to list some of the democratic rights that I had said would be affected. There was no comment and there was an interview with Harold which had obviously been recorded before he went to the Scilly Isles. So it has got the best possible start and we shall just have to see what happens. Nothing further has come from Number 10. On Monday when I get the documents to which Harold referred in his message, I shall be able to consider my reply.

Monday 30 December
I did a very unusual thing for me: I got up early and drove to Southminster to buy all the morning papers. *The Times* made the letter their headline: 'Mr Benn makes a sweeping attack on the EEC'; the *Morning Star* had 'Benn's warning on the Common Market'. The *Daily Telegraph* compared it unfavourably to Burke's letter to his constituents and every other paper took it up.

Still nothing from Number 10.

Tuesday 31 December
I had a message from Herbert Rogers who told me that the Bristol Executive had met last night and had decided to distribute 30,000 copies of the letter. I said, 'Now whatever you do, you must not add a single word to the leaflet.' I was terrified he would put a heading like 'Benn attacks fascist Market' or something of that kind.

1975 is going to be a very dramatic year in the world economy and world politics, the British economy and British politics. Of that I have absolutely no doubt. However you look at it over-all, the nation has to reduce its living standards during 1975. Well, if that just means everybody takes two steps down the ladder, those at the bottom will be submerged below the water and drown. So it is going to raise, in the most acute form, the problem of the distribution of wealth and income in Britain. If we are not able to give people more money, how else do we cope with the situation? We can't go down the old track again with stop and go, a wage freeze and unemployment, because none of those things is acceptable under the Social Contract. My own guess is that this is the moment when the arguments about the distribution of wealth and power become critically relevant. Indeed, if we can't give people money, we can give them power – that is to say, erode the power of private management. We can give them more leisure, unpaid admittedly, but in effect sharing out work as an alternative to mass unemployment.

As far as I am concerned, the important thing is that we should stick with the trade union movement. That is our long-term strength and that is how we should fight the Market. I intend to campaign for the Referendum as though my life depended upon it because I think that the European unity idea – whatever its idealistic objectives – is in fact part of a long retreat from parliamentary democracy and is being forced on us. So 1975 will be a very difficult year.

Wednesday 1 January 1975
The 'Get Britain Out' campaign re-launched itself today, describing parliamentary sovereignty in exactly the same terms as my letter: 'Sovereignty belongs to the people, not to Parliament. It is lent to Parliament and has to be returned intact to the people to be used again.' Get Britain Out is a negative title, but more important is getting the Labour Party to come out against the Market at the special conference.

Sunday 5 January
Prominent stories in the papers today about Wilson's speech attacking the Left, saying that firms where workers strike mustn't expect public money, his old 'In Place of Strife' theme – anti-trade union and anti-worker – which he always comes back to when he is in a jam.

In the evening, we had this year's first meeting of the political triumvirate – the Benns, the Foots and the Shores. Caroline thinks that Harold will want to tie us, by a Cabinet minute, to an agreement to keep our ranks closed until the renegotiations are completely over, and thus silence us until it is almost too late to do anything.

The three of us have got to hang together now. Michael carries with him the tremendous authority of his office, his links with Len Murray and Jack Jones. Peter has a great Civil Service intellect, and the three of us know that we are all likely to get into trouble together. I don't think we can be fired, although it looks as if Harold might put Michael out on a limb by telling him there will have to be a statutory pay policy. Michael is going to see Harold tomorrow and he might make a little progress.

Monday 6 January
An astonishing day and I don't really know how to begin. *The Times* had a huge front-page story saying that I had ignored the advice of one of my senior officials, Peter Carey, on KME. It is the first time in

my life I remember a Minister's disagreement with officials being the subject of public comment. I asked for a report.

At 11.30, the CSEU representatives came to see me about British Leyland. I gave an account of the background and the circumstances under which we had decided to give support and asked what was the trade union analysis of the reasons for the difficulties confronting British Leyland? What proposals did they wish to make for the future of the company both in relations to the degree of public participation or ownership and in respect of the development of industrial democracy at all levels? We went round the table and got everyone's views. I believe that was the first time all those unions had met together.

At 5.05 I went over to Transport House for the Home Policy Committee, at which Ian Mikardo was going to nominate me for the chairmanship. I arrived early, and found Frank Allaun and Geoff Bish already there. Geoff said Denis Healey had been trying to block me and instead had suggested Bryan Stanley. When Denis, Shirley, Barbara and Bryan Stanley came in together, I thought I was sunk.

Anyway, in the end Frank Allaun nominated me, then Denis said, 'I want to say that I think it is most undesirable that a Minister should be Chairman of the Home Policy Committee because of the conflict of loyalty. Can I say that?'

Ron Hayward replied, 'Yes, you can say that, but Tony Benn has been nominated. What do you say, Tony?'

'It hasn't altered my acceptance of nomination.'

They tried everything. Denis having said the Chairman should not be a Minister, he could not nominate Shirley Williams or Barbara. So he suggested John Chalmers.

John Chalmers said, 'I'm seconding Tony Benn.'

'What about Sid Weighell?'

'I've got other things to do,' said Sid.

'What about Bryan Stanley?'

Bryan refused. 'This is my first meeting of the Home Policy Committee. I don't think I want to be made Chairman at the first meeting.'

Shirley Williams asked, 'What about John Cartwright?'

'He's in the Middle East,' said Ron Hayward. 'He can't do it.'

So in the end there were no other nominations. I took the chair, thanked them and went straight on with the agenda. Of course, it is an absolutely major appointment and I can't conceal my excitement when I think of the people who have been there before me: Herbert Morrison during the war and right up to 1948, maybe later; Jim Griffiths; Nye Bevan for a year; Harold Wilson; George Brown; Jim Callaghan; and Bill Simpson.

This evening I received a minute from Carey with a photocopy of the Accounting Officer's responsibilities attached. This pointed out two relevant paragraphs: Section 8 where, if the Accounting Officer advised that something was not a prudent use of public funds, he could, if questioned by the Public Accounts Committee, defend that expenditure on the grounds that it was a policy decision; and Section 9, whereby if the Accounting Officer felt an expenditure was really an abuse of a Minister's power, he could still defend himself but it was much more serious and he would have to report to the Comptroller and Auditor General and the Treasury.

Tuesday 7 January

At 5 Part came in. The first point was a letter to him yesterday from Robert Armstrong, saying that Harold wanted to know the details of Carey's written objection to my proposal for KME as he would be asked about it in the House. Roy Williams had warned me that Part appeared to be making difficulties; Part's approach towards me seems that of a Detective Chief Inspector trying to get me for murder.

As Part must be quite aware, if Harold can pick me up on a technicality like this, it could be very serious.

Part then raised an objection to an article by Michael Meacher on saving jobs, specifically to the phrase that the 'anarchy of capitalist markets had developed after 1970', which he said was a political phrase and inappropriate for use by a Government Minister.

I said, 'Well, what if he had made a speech on the same subject and used such a phrase, and *The Times* had reprinted it?'

'Oh well, that would be different.'

'What about a speech at Conference?'

'Oh, all Conference speeches are different.'

'What would you say if Michael Meacher had talked about the unacceptable face of capitalism?' I asked him.

'I am sure that Mr Heath's Cabinet would have agreed with a phrase like that!' he said.

'Well, Secretary,' I said, 'I think you put yourself in a very great difficulty if you try to interpret what the Cabinet would think of Michael Meacher's article. In the end we are all responsible for what we do and I have approved the article.'

He had with him the Procedure for Ministers and he said, 'I wanted to warn you.'

I asked him, 'Are you giving me an Accounting Officer's Minute about this too?' So he laughed and said, 'Well, I hope we don't have to do everything in writing.' But it may be we shall.

I have serious differencies with Part but as I see very little of him, it doesn't bother me very much. I see him once a week or once a fortnight, and the rest of the time I don't know what he does.

Wednesday 8 January

At today's NEDC meeting, I felt strongly that the CBI leadership had absolutely copped out, lost confidence. It is easy to blame individuals but I think they are trying to run a system that simply can't be made to work. They tried to get us to do three things: have a statutory pay policy; control the unions; and get into Europe. That they say would produce investment. Well, we fooled about with these three things when we were in Government before. We did have a statutory pay policy and dropped it; we produced 'In Place of Strife', which we withdrew; and we applied for Europe. It produced no effect. Then the Tories came in and did all three – passed the Industrial Relations Act; applied for Europe and negotiated the terms and took us in, and they had a statutory pay policy which ended in disaster.

So now the CBI is hoping that if all the politicians could get together and go into Europe, there would be a Government of national unity or a Government of European unity, if you like, which is in a sense what the Common Market is.

James Margach rang and tried to draw me out. He said, 'I have been asked to write a piece on Sunday about "Bennery", and the way I see it is this. In the 1945 Government, Attlee was Prime Minister and the link with the unions then was Ernie Bevin who kept his office at the Transport and General Workers Union, and that was the trade union base. There was Nye Bevan who was the hero of the constituency Left. Herbert Morrison was the machine man at Transport House. Now it looks as if you have got all three jobs and so of course you are frightening people.'

Thursday 9 January

On the way into the Ministerial Committee on Economic Strategy, Denis Healey and I had a chat about economic efficiency. 'You know,' he said, 'the French are much better than we are at spending money. When money is allocated to a French organisation, they spend it within the year. I remember when a French military delegation came across to discuss a joint project, I had them bugged in their hotel room.' The British Minister of Defence had the French military delegation bugged! 'We did it because we discovered four bugs in the British Embassy in Paris and we didn't feel morally obliged not to do so. I got very little of value except that the French delegation couldn't understand why the British were so inefficient, and couldn't spend the money that had been allocated.' An extraordinary story.

Friday 10 January

I had a letter recently from a Tory MP, on behalf of a constituent of his who had been rejected by the Civil Service and was querying it. As my Department was involved, I asked about it and I was given a note by my office saying the Security Services had an objection to her. Then I was handed a completely innocuous letter to sign to the MP, saying that her case had been considered but she had had not been found suitable. So I said, 'What is the actual security objection? I am not prepared to sign that letter until I know.'

A few days later a minute came back, filtered through the Security Services, to the effect that she had shown an interest in Communism; I was again given the letter to sign, saying I was satisfied that she wasn't suitable. I said, 'Well, I am not satisfied. I want to know more.'

Today, Roy Williams told me that when the Security Services were cross-examined about it by the Department at my request, it turned out that the only objection to her was that she read the *Morning Star*, and apparently her father read it too. Roy said this simply wouldn't stand up to examination and he has put it to Sir Antony Part. But if it really is true that the Security Services put an employment bar on anyone who reads the *Morning Star*, that is a serious situation. I think my little plunge into the unknown with a Tory MP about a constituent whom I didn't know throws an interesting light on the Security Services and their policy.

I remember a note coming to me in 1969 or 1970 about Jack Jones being a security risk, and if I send Harold a minute on Jack Jones and on this case, it might precipitate some examination of the procedures, though the Security Services would never forgive me for doing it.

Sunday 12 January
There was a most unlikely article today by Peregrine Worsthorne called 'Leyland: Benn or Bust', arguing that industrial democracy was now the only way of dealing with the Leyland crisis.

Caroline and I went for a long walk in the rain in Holland Park and then sat in St John's Church in Ladbroke Grove, listening to the organist practising.

Monday 13 January
At 11.45, Sir Antony Part and Peter Carey came in to talk about Part's reply to Robert Armstrong, in response to the PM's inquiry on the Accounting Officer's Minute.

Part had written a reply which I looked at over the weekend and frankly it was just unacceptable to me. He refered to KME and the warning notes I had received, he brought in Meriden and Scottish Newspapers, and the grant for the Welsh TUC. He described in detail what had happened, and then stated that an Accounting Officer's Minute was a very rare precedure; no other Departments had issued Accounting Officer's Minutes to their Ministers in this Government, and the Department of Trade and Industry had not issued an Accounting Officer's Minute to a Tory Minister in the previous administration.

I worked quite hard over the weekend providing an answer to this, so when Part and Carey arrived, I told them how I intended to deal with it. 'I'm going to say that I don't agree with your account of events. I'm going to go through each of the cases separately and describe what happened, drawing attention to the fact that Cabinet considered all these matters and I did not maintain any secrecy about them. I shall refer to the fact that you said that there had been no Accounting Officer's Minute in the last Government: nor were there any to me on projects that were clearly *not* viable like Concorde or the HS-146, and none under the previous Labour Government on Rolls Royce, Upper Clyde, Marathon oil rigs, and so on. I'm going to say that when I analyse it, the only Accounting Officer's Minutes I have had have been about grants for working people for the three cooperatives and the Welsh TUC. This is no coincidence, and in fact it is a matter of political judgment, not financial propriety.

'Then I shall insist that in future all Accounting Officer's Minutes take a special form, are explicitly numbered and circulated to everyone to discuss them. I've a mind to say that I'm not prepared to authorise the grant of any further money unless every single penny is covered by a certificate from you, as Accounting Officers, telling me that you're satisfied that it's right.'

Well, they both went as white as a sheet.

When they saw how I intended to fight back, I think they were shocked.

After they had gone, I dictated the letter to the Prime Minister to reach him tonight with Part's paper. I was pretty angry and I am determined not to let this go.

I had to go off to meet the CSEU at 3 in the Ambassador Hotel in Upper Woburn Place. Hugh Scanlon was in the chair and Danny McGarvey, Ken Gill and about thirty others were there. It was a tremendous meeting.

I went through a whole list of problems: relations with the shop stewards, relations with the Confederation, the possibility of an emergency panel for rescue cases, and the need for advice on appointments and for the possibility of continuing liaison.

Ken Gill said that these were very important matters to consider, and Danny McGarvey said that when they'd first heard of this idea of liaison, they had thought that I was asking for the minutes of the Confed to be disclosed to the Minister. But this put a different perspective on it and they'd consider it. The Confed Executive actually applauded me – I've never before attended a committee that applauds you.

I did say to them, 'Look, a Labour Minister cannot do this job properly unless he keeps in continual contact with the Confed because there's such an overlap of interest, so many problems. I need your advice, and you must be quite free to criticise the policy, but of course I may have to act without consultation because of the need for speed.'

All of the trade union movement's past suspicions are really beginning to melt.

At 6, Eric Heffer came to the office. We let our hair down and had a good old talk. Just as we began, Roy Williams put his head round the door and said that the Permanent Secretary wished to see me. I told him I was talking to the Minister of State, and we kept Part waiting for forty-five minutes. Then when he did come in he was white. He'd got the draft that I had written to the Prime Minister, and went through it trying to get me to change it.

He was acutely embarrassed at having mentioned that there were no Accounting Officer's Minutes under the previous administration in the Department of Trade and Industry. He said that he shouldn't have said it, that he should have simply stated that he understood that none came in, and if that was true then all these other projects must have gone through without them. At the end, I was blunt with him. I said, 'I think you set me up for a rebuke, and separated me from my colleagues in this Government and from Ministers in the previous Government. I'm fighting back, I'm very sorry but I'm not having it.'

He tried to be more friendly, 'Well, we understand that you're pressing the case and we don't want to have difficulties, we want to work with you.'

I said that I was sure he did, and I accepted that it was all an innovation.

He was livid at my point that all the Accounting Officer's Minutes had been about workers' cooperatives. 'I cannot accept that any civil servant is political,' he said.

'That's not a term of abuse in my book because politics is my profession, everything's political – not in a narrow Party sense, but in a broader sense, and this is a difference of judgment. You shouldn't have tried to dress it up as a matter of prudent financial administration.' Anyway, he went off and the minute was typed and I stayed late to sign it.

I finally got the full security report on the Civil Service applicant whose case had been brought to my attention. There was a letter – which has in fact been available since 18 October last year – to my departmental security officer.

18th October – Miss X

Please refer to the attached normal vetting inquiry.

There is some evidence that Miss X may be a fairly regular reader of the *Morning Star*, the newspaper of the Communist Party. Reliable sources informed us of this on several occasions since 1967, when she is known to have been interested in holidays arranged by the Young Communist League, and in a sea trip to the Soviet Union.

There was a reliable report in 1974 that her father, Mr X, also reads the *Morning Star*.

Though recent inquiries have provided no grounds for believing that she or her father are actively interested in supporting the Communist Party, it is a fact that it has not been possible to discover her views on extreme political matters. She works alone as a chiropodist, and the most that can be said is that there have been no complaints about her attitude from either patients or staff at the various clinics where she practised.

Reading a Communist newspaper does not in itself necessarily imply support for the Party, but we feel that to read it consistently over a long period (other than as an academic exercise or for research purposes) may well indicate an attitude of mind, which on a security annotation, may cause some unease. We would therefore prefer to err on the side of caution in this case.

The Security Service advises that the above information should not necessarily debar the candidate from access to information classified 'Confidential' or above, but you may prefer to make other arrangements especially if access to particularly delicate material is involved. May we please be informed of your decision in due course.

It was on that basis that this woman was refused security clearance. It is astonishing, and I shall have to consider whether to minute the PM. It is an outrage that the Security Services should be allowed to get away with something as remote as this.

Tuesday 14 January
At 9.30, we had the Legislation Committee to consider a huge programme. As I listened to it and got the mood and attitude of Ministers there, it became clear that legislative pressure is one of the methods by which the Labour Government postpones what it ought to do.

First of all, we were told that we were short of parliamentary draughtsmen and that it took fifteen years to train one. Well, that is rubbish. Shortage of parliamentary draughtsmen is a calculated self-inflicted wound which the Treasury go along with, because if there are no draughtsmen bills can't be introduced. It slows down the legislative programme and slows down the impetus of a Labour Government.

I raised some points. 'Look, there's Common Market legislation going through without Parliament having any right to say anything. There is a vast contrast between the handling of domestic and European legislation where, as far as I know, they haven't had to wait for fifteen years while they train their draughtsmen.' This was brushed aside as being unhelpful. On the Industry Bill, the NEB and planning agreements, I said that Ministers were deliberately holding up the policy and that I'd made such concessions as I could, but was not prepared to go beyond a certain point.

Cabinet at 11, and it began with Rhodesia,* Jim having just returned from a tour of southern Africa. The Africans would like us to take the lead, Vorster was anxious to reach an understanding with the Africans, Smith might accept majority rule later, and so on. Jim is anxious to get ahead with a constitutional conference, perhaps in London or in Gabarone, and this was to be his great initiative. However, as Barbara quite rightly warned him, we couldn't push Smith, and Willie Ross said that it would be better to let all these pressures develop and let Smith come to us for help.

I rather share that view, though I didn't say so, because there are real pressures on Smith: first, the guerrilla activity and the African determination – and Rhodesia is very vulnerable; second, the fact that Frelimo, the Mozambique Liberation Front, have taken over there; third, Vorster's desire not to be over-extended; and fourth, the sanctions, and these were producing results. We should let these pressures work their way through. If we come in with a host of compromises, we shall simply get the blame for failure. Jim agreed to play it a little bit cooler.

At this point Harold Wilson intervened. 'Now this is very, very secret, and I see some members of the Cabinet have been writing full notes. They're to leave them on the table.' Well, the only person writing notes was me, and they weren't about that. I was writing a note to Roy Williams about the Legislation Committee. So I scribbled a few points I *might* have made and I left them on the table. That is Wilson for you.

The other item was the Channel Tunnel. Tony Crosland had announced in effect that it was dead, and the whole thing would be abandoned. Very good news.

Wednesday 15 January
To the House at 3 for a meeting with Frank Beswick and officials in preparation for my aircraft statement to the House. In the Chamber I had my little dictating machine in my breast pocket, so I recorded something of the enormous row that developed.

---

* Since Prime Minister of Rhodesia, Ian Smith, declared 'independence' in 1965, ensuring continued white minority rule, no political solution had been found to secure a black majority government. Callaghan had talks during his tour with African leaders, and Dr Vorster, the South African Premier, but was prevented by the Rhodesians from meeting a delegation from the African National Council of Rhodesia.

After I had made my statement, Michael Heseltine attacked me, and I responded, 'It ill-befits the Government that first bankrupted and then nationalised the jewel of the British aero-engineering industry, Rolls Royce ...' I got no further because there were shrieks and shouts of 'Liar', and Heath rose. It was a marvellous start and I hadn't expected to cause such a row. Heath said that I never spoke the truth. He got up several times but I think I dealt with him quite effectively.

Thursday 16 January
The press went absolutely mad on my aircraft statement – the *Daily Mirror*: 'Wedgie swoops to rescue giant firms', the *Daily Mail*: 'Benn hijacks the plane-makers'.

At 9.30, Industrial Development Committee where I had a major counter-attack on the Industry Bill on my hands. Shirley, Eric Varley and a number of other Ministers, notably Harold Lever, had objected to giving the power to unions to demand disclosure of company information. I had prepared myself with all sorts of ammunition including an article by Eric Varley from 1963 on workers' control, in which he said that information was essential for industrial democracy. He capitulated so I didn't have to use it, though I told him afterwards that I had had it with me. 'You bastard!' was all he said.

Harold Lever attacked statutory instruments as a means of acquiring companies that might fall into foreign control, and I beat him off. He said, 'Why don't you just prevent them from being taken over by foreign companies?' So I got a new power added, the power to prevent take-over and the power to acquire.

At the end, Harold Wilson said, 'Well, that's the end of this Bill,' and Ted Short muttered, 'What this Committee has put together, let no man put asunder.'

I wound up. 'May I thank the Committee very much for their work over the last nine months. I wouldn't conceal from you that there have been many days when I've been up the wall with anger but I told myself that if I couldn't persuade my colleagues, then I'm unlikely to persuade the CBI and the TUC.'

'Can we have that in writing?' retorted Harold.

We'd gone on so long that by the time we came to a proposal for the nationalisation of the shipbuilding industry it was 10.29 and the Cabinet was due at 10.30. So Harold said, 'Shipbuilding?' and I replied, 'Well, Harold, I think it's been more or less agreed.' So nationalisation of shipbuilding went through in thirty seconds.

At Cabinet we had a brief report on John Stonehouse as to whether he should be unseated from the House of Commons and I asked, 'May I say something that I know won't be very popular. I think we've got to be very careful about this. I'm the only man sitting here who's been expelled from the House of Commons by a House of Commons committee, and that's wrong. The electors put us here, and once we start arranging that people can be dismissed by the House of Commons, that's a very dangerous precedent. Stonehouse hasn't been convicted of any offence, you can't pre-empt that. When Peter Baker, the Tory MP for Norfolk South, was in jail in 1954 for nine months awaiting trial, he didn't resign. You say Stonehouse has been absent from the House for two months, that's true, but Francis Noel-Baker was absent from his Swindon seat for *three years* after the 1966 Election. You say that he's let his electors down, but then Chris Mayhew changed parties. The Chiltern Hundreds is not for nothing because an MP *cannot* actually resign from Parliament.'

To my amazement I got a bit of support. Roy Jenkins and one or two others agreed. Bob Mellish just took the lynch mob's view, 'The Party's angry, we want to get him out.' So we agreed to set up a select committee.

At 3.30, there was a massive meeting in the Department about economic strategy. The origin of this goes back before Christmas when we had a meeting on the relations between the National Enterprise Board and Finance for Industry, and out of that came the first serious discussion about economic policy.

Eric had written a paper calling for the nationalisation of the banks and more public ownership; Michael Meacher had written a more cautious paper, and I had a paper which I had commissioned Francis and Frances to write. It had been to Michael Foot and Peter Shore already, so the officials arrived apprehensive of what we were going to discuss. I handed round my paper which had no classification or date or initials – nothing. It began by declaring that the present policy wasn't working and forecast a gloomy future; I didn't want any argument between the two strategies, broadly speaking the optimists and the pessimists, and thought we both had to take a grave view.

It described Strategy A which is the Government of national unity, the Tory strategy of a pay policy, higher taxes all round and deflation, with Britain staying in the Common Market. Then Strategy B which is the real Labour policy of saving jobs, a vigorous micro-investment programme, import control, control of the banks and insurance companies, control of export, of capital, higher taxation of the rich, and Britain leaving the Common Market.

Well, the officials were riveted – Strategy A was what they all wanted and Strategy B was what they knew we wanted. I said at the end after a long discussion that I would like the latter strategy prepared. No doubt word had already reached the Treasury that the Department of Industry was preparing an argument for import controls and various other things, and I expect Whitehall will be humming with this tomorrow morning, if not by tonight. I heard later that Part had summoned all his officials into his room to commission work on the paper.

Friday 17 January
The Devolution Committee was held all day at Chequers. Roy Jenkins gave an absolutely classic feudal definition of sovereignty which I wrote down because it threw such a lot of light on to his thinking.

'Sovereignty in Britain belonged to the Sovereign, whose power then went to the Cabinet to exercise, and the Cabinet has succeeded in exercising sovereignty to the extent that it has successfully manipulated Parliament and the electorate. Therefore, we do not want Westminster models, but we should study American and German written constitutions, and see what light that throws on other methods of devolution.'

Willie Ross said that Scottish Devolution was the most important decision since 1707, and we were not going to give up sovereignty but devolve power. Harold Wilson pointed out that sovereignty itself could be devolved but it could of course be brought back to the centre again.

I said, 'I am stirred to comment by Roy's definition of sovereignty. His presentation was of a feudal fiction under which parliamentary democracy simply meant an elected monarchy, in which MPs were elected to inherit the powers of commissioners to exercise the functions of the Crown.

'An elected monarchy has come to the end of the road because power really has fallen from Parliament; it was exercised first by the King against Parliament, then by the landowners, then by the industrialists in the City who dominated us in 1931, and has now moved to the trade union movement in England, to the Ulster Workers' Council in Northern Ireland, and indeed, to the nationalists in Scotland, because it is their sovereignty we are now trying to take on board. What we're talking about is not the dripping of the feudal sovereignty from the top downwards but democratic self-management coming up from underneath. Sovereignty really belongs with the people.'

Over lunch, I had a word with Elwyn Jones about the disturbing security case of the Civil Service candidate excluded because she read the *Morning Star*.

'Elwyn, I'm talking to you now as a great liberal Labour lawyer,' I started.

'Well,' he said, 'I'm Lord Chancellor now.'

'I know you've been corrupted by power like all of us but let me put the point.' He listened intently but he wasn't particularly disturbed by it and suggested I have a word with Roy.

Then he said, 'Of course, this security business is a problem. One of our ministerial colleagues in the last Government had his whole career ruined by security.'

'You mean Stephen Swingler?'

'No,' he said, 'Niall Macdermot.'

I asked what had happened.

'Niall Macdermot's Italian wife was investigated by the Security Services and was suspected of being a securitry risk. At the time she was working in the UN in Geneva and when they reported back, Niall left the Labour Government in disgust.'

That was the first time I'd ever heard that and I was so interested that Elwyn said, 'Oh, I shouldn't have told you that, you'd better forget I told you.' Well, I shall never forget it, it's just an amazing story.[3]

We resumed the Committee, wthout having had a walk in the gardens as we usually do. We began with a short discussion about the transfer of functions to a devolved Assembly; would some functions as had originally been proposed be transferred, some reserved, and some in the middle? Ted said they'd decided to transfer specified functions.

We came to a major section, the extent to which the House of Commons would retain the power to over-ride the Assembly and how it would be done – would it be for sins of omission, or sins of commission or both? There was the question of security, the unity of the UK, and anything that affected the well-being of the UK.

On elections to a Scottish Assembly, I was in favour of them being coterminous with the House of Commons, first because if the Assemblymen and MPs were elected at the same time, that would reflect the same political mood, and secondly, because having candidates for the Assembly running parallel with the House of Commons would guarantee that there were some correlation between the policies that were being advocated in Scotland or Wales and the UK Parliament. Thirdly, it would mean that national issues were always discussed at the same time as Scottish or Welsh issues.

When we came to trade and industry I said, 'The European Commission has all the power, and don't let's kid ourselves that there is any ministerial veto. If the Scottish Assembly wanted to do things that the UK Parliament didn't want it to do, but the Commission had authorised to be done, the Scots would say that if it is all right with the Commission, why should Westminster stop us?'

It is obvious that this whole area needs to be looked at again, and I suggested that there should be a study by the EEC European Unit and the Devolution Unit in the Cabinet Office to sort all this out.

Tuesday 21 January

Cabinet, where the entire morning was devoted to Europe.

First Harold said that he thought an agreement among Ministers to differ would be acceptable from the moment of the Cabinet decision. We would need guidelines to ensure that we all behaved in a comradely way, and there should be no personal attacks.

Michael Foot thought that freedom for Ministers followed from the Referendum. The only way to preserve the unity of the Government was by following Harold's method.

Roy Mason said that progress had been made in the renegotiations, the Foreign Secretary was likely to recommend that we stayed in, and he doubted the wisdom of giving freedom to Ministers. He said that after the Referendum, certainly some colleagues would not be able to stay in the Government, but the Cabinet had to recommend one way or the other.

Barbara Castle agreed with Michael that the freedom we were being invited to agree followed from the Referendum. Of course, in the end, the renegotiated terms we got would not necessarily meet with the requirements of the Manifesto. There would be a messy middle-of-the-road muddle.

'You talk about a messy middle-of-the-road muddle, but if the Cabinet understands what I mean, I'm at my best in a messy middle-of-the-road muddle,' said Harold.

Everybody hooted with laughter; it was a very revealing comment, and Harold is at his best in those circumstances, laughing at himself. Bob Mellish passed a note across to me; 'He's like a hippopotamus who likes flopping about in the mud.'

I said that the debate had already started between members of the Government and, on the whole, it had been a very high-level debate. There would be self-policing because the Party would never forgive anyone who attacked another member, knowing that the Party had got to come through this.

Jim said that the general agreement was realistic; he didn't share my views because I had unbounded optimism. 'Don't forget that in Norway, the Market Referendum wrecked the Labour Party', and Michael Foot said, 'Yes, that's because the Labour Government in Norway recommended entry.'

Willie Ross feared that the Cabinet and the Party would find themselves in opposition to each other.

Then Harold Wilson said, 'Well, as far as my constituency agent is concerned, when the Referendum campaign begins, he's going to lock up the canvassing records and go on holiday.' Typical of Harold, absolute cynicism about the great innovation he was just about to announce to the public.

Caroline came into the House where we had dinner together, then we went in to the bar where Frances Morrell was with a chap called Callaghan, Secretary of the TUC Economic Committee. Earlier Frances had told me that Callaghan had asked Alan Lord to come along and talk about planning agreements to research secretaries of all the unions. Frances had said to him that she'd like to go and Callaghan had said, 'You can't, you're too political, we don't want to be muddled up with politics.'

I bust a gut to get the Department of Industry to take notice of trade unions and when finally we get our policy, the trade unions only want to talk to civil servants, they don't want Ministers or political advisers! So I argued this out with Callaghan, and he said, 'Well, mindful of our need to remain above the party battle –'

I interrupted, 'Mindful of our need not to get muddled up with the trade union movement, I don't know whether I can really let an official like Lord come and talk to trade unions. This is too controversial.'

Wednesday 22 January

First engagement was the National Executive, where the main item, of course, was the paper from Ron Hayward on the handling of the Referendum.

The ultimate answer, I think, is to have a simple vote 'In or Out'. I said that I thought it was wrong to suggest, as Ron had done, that all the voters should be counted and declared nationally; it should be done on a constituency basis which was the view I had expressed in 1971 when I published my Referendum Bill: first, because we wanted to make it as much like a General Election as possible; second, the only motive for doing a national count would be to conceal regional variations; third, it wouldn't work because it would leak and there would be polls that gave alternative views; fourth, the impact of existing Common Market membership on the unity of the United Kingdom was a major issue anyway, and to try to deny the British people in Scotland and Wales the opportunity of assessing that impact would be quite wrong.

Thursday 23 January

At Cabinet at 10.30 Barbara was furious that George Cunningham [Labour MP for Islington South and Finsbury] had successfully moved an amendment in committee abolishing the 'earnings rule', and this would cost the Government £170 million, and she was angry that Lewis Carter-Jones [Labour MP for Eccles] had done something about disabled housewives that would cost her Department another £5 million. The idea of democracy actually breaking out, that Labour MPs should have any part in policy-making, just makes Cabinet Ministers wild. There was talk of a vote of confidence and a General Election if the House didn't reverse the measures – incredible.

But the main item again was the Government's EEC statement to be made later today. On the question of freedom for Ministers, Willie Ross asked, 'Will Ministers be allowed to vote freely in any House of Commons debate to consider the terms?'

Harold said that the *end* of the renegotiations would be the starting gun for freedom to speak.

'Well, when does the freedom begin?' I asked.

'After the Cabinet has made its decision.'

So Willie Ross said, 'The position of Ministers who are also on the Executive will be very difficult if the Executive discusses the EEC question before the Cabinet has decided.'

In the afternoon, I heard Harold make his historic statement, that there would be a Referendum and that Ministers would be free to speak and to vote – a notable constitutional change. I am intensely proud to have been associated with it.

Dashed over to the office where Gregor MacKenzie was giving a party for Burns night. He asked me to propose a little toast to the immortal memory of Robert Burns. I said my mother was a Scot and I therefore spanned the great border. I had as Postmaster General instituted a stamp for Robert Burns, though when I suggested it, my officials were very much against it. They warned me that Robert Burns's private life had fallen below the standard that would be accepted by Her Majesty for admission to the enclosure at Ascot. I played this up, and said I had decided to have a meeting with the Queen herself – 'For the full details you will have to wait for my memoirs and see if they are cleared by the Secretary of the Cabinet of the day and the mandarins.' I had pointed out to Her Majesty that Robert Burns had never been commemorated and I said, 'Ma'am, I must tell you that my officials feel that the private life of Robert Burns might not be entirely acceptable to have his head on the stamp next to yours.' The Queen looked at me, I looked at her and then she said, 'Postmaster General, it was a very long time ago.' And that, I said, was the basis of my toast to the immortal memory of Robert Burns; it was a very long time ago.

Later, I went over to the House and I saw Bill Hamling, Harold's PPS. 'Bill, I would like better relations with Harold, were that possible. I know I am an awkward character but I am not trying to undermine him, as he thinks I am. I am only interested in the right to speak freely because I think that is what politics is about.'

He said, 'Well, I keep saying to Harold, "Why don't you talk to Tony. He is your Secretary of State for Industry; when did you last see him, why don't you ask him over?"'

I told Bill, 'I loathe this exchange of angry minutes and I would like to see Harold very much. I think Joe Haines is the cause of the trouble.'

'Well, I hope you notice I didn't comment.' He obviously dislikes Joe Haines.

Friday 24 January

At 11.30 I dashed over to the BBC and they showed me the *Man Alive* programme on Meriden, which I had missed on TV. It was marvellous. It was so moving I actually had tears in my eyes which I had to brush away in the darkness. All the BBC top brass were there: Aubrey Singer, Desmond Wilcox, Alasdair Milne.

Saturday 25 January

To Bristol for a Labour Party social and at 9.45 Caroline and I got in the car and were driven to Coventry by my temporary driver, Barry, a young lad of about twenty-three. When Ron Vaughan is away, he takes over. He got hopelessly lost but we finally arrived in Coventry after midnight at the Meriden works. There they were around the brazier on the picket line and they were also working in the experimental shop on a new carburettor design. Went into the office and I told them candidly how things stood and the difficulties there would be. Then I went to the men around the brazier and said, 'It must seem awful to you being here night after night, but if this stopped, Meriden would be dead in twenty-four hours, so you must keep at it and I will do my best for you.' It did me a power of good.

Sunday 26 January

I had a note in my box repeating the fact that the woman disbarred from the Civil Service for reading the *Morning Star* could not be employed – it didn't give the criteria. It mentioned another case of a man who was a member of a radical Catholic organisation and had been referred to once in the *Morning Star* as a member of the British Peace Committee, which is Communist controlled. On those grounds, he was being refused. So I wrote a note out saying, 'Does the fact that you read Communist or fascist newspapers debar you: does membership of a left-wing religious organisation bar you; what are the criteria by which the Security Services operate; and are Ministers advised to accept the recommendations?' I am determined to get to the bottom of this.

Also there was a letter asking me to instruct our officials in Brussels to tell the Commission that the Industry Bill would never be used in defiance of the Treaty. I refused, replying that 'this is what we mean by saying that Parliament must retain the powers to pursue regional and industrial policy'. There will be a row, I expect.

Monday 27 January
Caroline held a press conference today to launch her pamphlet on the impossibility of coexistence between comprehensive and grammar schools. She was supported by Fred Jarvis, General Secretary of the NUT, and Dame Margaret Miles (the former headmistress of Mayfield Comprehensive). She said the press was hostile but it was very well attended.

Tuesday 28 January
At 10.30, before Cabinet, I had a word with Willie Ross and Elwyn Jones about Crossman's *Diaries*. They said how shocked they were that colleagues might be writing down what they were saying so as to make money from their memoirs and how it would ruin relations with civil servants. So I replied, 'Oh, come off it. A lot of Cabinet Ministers leak regularly to the press about their colleagues; the only difference is they do it straight away. As for civil servants, my civil servants' advice to me is regularly put into the press. There were two leading articles recently defending a civil servant, Peter Carey, over KME. Memoirs that throw any light on the frontiers of *secrecy* are considered a threat. That's what the opposition is about.'

Wednesday 29 January
I have been told that the Foreign Office will stop the Industry Bill if I don't give a pledge to the Commission that it will conform to Treaty obligations. I am bloody angry and this is the real crunch, revealing the Foreign Office at its weakest. All these promises that are given that you wouldn't have to bother about the Commission, that British interests would be safeguarded, are absolutely false, so tomorrow's Legislation Committee will be crucial.

Thursday 30 January
I went along to the Legislation Committee all geared up for a fight. I must say I was nervous, and Roy Jenkins, Shirley Williams and Bob Mellish were there. I went through the Bill, pointed out all the changes that had been made and then, at the end, the Lord Advocate, Ronny King Murray asked, 'What about our obligations under the Common Market?'

'I am sending a letter to Spinelli,' I said, and I read it out.

Dear Commissioner Spinelli,

I am writing to send you a copy of the Industry Bill which the British Government is publishing [today] and which will be debated in Parliament within the next few days. As you will see, it sets out the policy of the

Government along the lines forecast in the White Paper published last August which you have seen. It is a long time since we have met and I look forward to seeing you again either in London or Brussels.

With every good wish.

Well, this was so cheerful and friendly that they did not actually raise the problem of whether I should give an assurance that the Industry Bill would always be used with regard to our obligations under the Treaty of Rome. So, I was all ready for them but the opposition never appeared. I was staggered.

Friday 31 January

Watched the BBC news which was hideously biased, didn't describe what was in the Bill and simply mentioned 'this controversial Bill which will please the left wing with its planning agreements'. Then long quotes from Heseltine and Campbell Adamson of the CBI – nothing from the TUC.

Sunday 2 February

The *Observer* had a centre page piece called 'Mr Benn's New Britain', which began to take the whole industry policy seriously. But as I might have predicted, by the time the liberal centre gets hold of it, they see it in terms of it being the basis for the real reform of capitalism, and these are the warning signs. Thank God, Campbell Adamson attacked it so violently!

As far as the implementation is concerned, the trade union movement has got to play a key role and we have got to be careful to see this doesn't become a corporate instrument – that is to say, the NEB plus Sir Don Ryder does not equal socialism.

Called at the Arnold-Forsters. Mark hasn't been very well. We talked about the French Security Service and how, as part of their job of protecting the President, they have had to vet all his mistresses, including the youngest of fifteen. This all confirmed my suspicion that Mark Arnold-Forster is, in fact, a British Intelligence agent. He goes to all these trouble spots and no doubt reports everything back to the Security Services.

Monday 3 February

Dashed over to the House for Questions. One Tory MP asked if I would publish the advice of my Permanent Secretary. I said, 'Are you really saying that officials' advice should be published, which would suck them into controversy and at the same time allow Ministers to shield behind them?' Were they saying they had never done anything their civil servants had advised against? Another Tory MP asked wasn't it intolerable that I was consulting employees without the permission of their employers, implying that they were just serfs. The exchange pleased the Party, although the House was almost empty.

Tuesday 4 February

The great event today is the Tory leadership election and I heard Heath make what turned out to be his last intervention as Leader of the Opposition when he asked about the risk of a war in the Middle East. He was pretty confident against Mrs Thatcher.

Made my statement on steel and there was a bit of a hoo-ha in the middle of Questions and Answers because the result of the first ballot for the Tory leadership was spreading round the benches. It was Mrs Thatcher, 130; Heath, 119; and Hugh Fraser, 16. So Heath resigned and that's the end of him. Very sad in a way. Politics is a brutal business, and I think we would be foolish to suppose that Mrs Thatcher won't be a formidable leader; and Harold couldn't pour scorn on a woman because people wouldn't have it. I think the quality of the debate will be raised because the Tory Party will be driven to the Right and there will then be a real choice being offered to the electorate.

Wednesday 5 February

Willie Whitelaw, James Prior, John Peyton and Geoffrey Howe announced that they were standing against Mrs Thatcher in the second ballot.* But I guess that she will sweep the board, because the opposition has become a completely negative 'Stop Thatcher' campaign, which I think will bring her tremendous support.

Thursday 6 February

Antony Part is in Westminster Hospital after a heart attack, and I went to visit him.

Caught the train to Bristol for the General Management Committee. There were two resolutions, one from the Young Socialists calling for withdrawal from the Common Market and for a United Socialist States of Europe, and the other, written by Herbert Rogers, where I made only one amendment, was as follows:

This meeting of the General Management Committee of the South-East Bristol Labour Party expresses its complete opposition to the Common Market. We regard the Treaty of Rome which is the binding legislation on

* With Edward Heath's defeat in the first ballot, leading Heath supporters swiftly moved to stand against Margaret Thatcher. The results were: Margaret Thatcher, 146; Whitelaw, 79; Geoffrey Howe, 19; James Prior, 19; John Peyton, 11.

Daily Express, 10 February 1975

all member countries as inimical to the democratic principles which we hold, and has been instituted in the interests of big business which is fundamental to a corporate state. The Treaty of Accession which binds this country to Europe was passed by Parliament without the consent of the people and we pledge that we will use every legitimate means to enlighten the people of this constituency on the facts of the situation and work for an overwhelming vote in the Referendum to get Britain out.

Only two people voted against it in the end.

Saturday 8 February
I worked on my box and one thing I spotted was the Foreign Office briefs for Harold Wilson when he goes to Moscow. They presented the Common Market renegotiations as simply that we were trying to improve the terms of membership, and then put them to the British people, and pointed out that the world Communist movement, and the *Morning Star*, were opposed to us being in the Common Market because it would strengthen the Common Market against the Russian military ambitions. This wasn't even accurate because the Italian Communist Party and the Chinese Communist Party want us in.

There were long extracts from recent Radio Moscow broadcasts demonstrating how unpleasant they were about Britain. There was even a special brief on outstanding claims against Russia arising from the 1917 Revolution – £500 million belonging to the Tsarist regime which Harold was told he might have to raise. There was a defensive brief that a royal visit couldn't be organised because the Queen couldn't go until the General Secretary, Brezhnev, had come to Britain, and how keen the Russians were to have the Queen visit. There was another brief explaining why it was undesirable for us to recognise the Baltic States *de jure* even though we accepted them *de facto* and another saying that we didn't want to cooperate with the Russians in celebrating the thirtieth anniversary of the downfall of Nazi Germany because it would be used as propaganda against West Germany.

Those briefs, all written by officials, gave you an insight into the intensely reactionary nature of the Foreign Office.

Sunday 9 February

Today extracts from the third stage of Dick Crossman's diary were published in the *Sunday Times* – fascinating to read. Dick's diary is the most important contribution that he has made to the politics of his period, without a doubt. My diary, of course, records political life throughout all the years of Opposition and hopefully it will illustrate what needs to be done if Britain is ever to become socialist through parliamentary democracy. But it may be that parliamentary democracy has been something of a fraud and that, with Britain inside Europe, the strength of the British trade union movement would be harnessed to national indignation, if the Commission tried to take action or impose policies that were unacceptable. I say this with some reluctance.

The Civil Service doesn't care about the Market because as far as they're concerned, the Commission is just another version of the Treasury to which they have always bowed low. Labour Ministers, once they get into the Cabinet, don't particularly care about making a change because as far as they're concerned they've got where they want to be and there's no strong desire for change.

We really will have to use this crisis to break out of the circle of deception which lies at the heart of parliamentary labourism.

Monday 10 February

At 9.30, Peter Carey and Douglas Lovelock, the Establishment Officer, came to see me about the recent security cases.

I said, 'Look, I'm an old-fashioned liberal, I've never been in the Communist Party and I've never been tempted to join, but I want to know just what the rules are. Is it really true that if you read the *Morning Star*, or if you're a left-wing Catholic, you're not considered suitable for the Civil Service?'

'Oh no,' they said, 'such people can do ordinary jobs in the Civil Service but in the Department of Industry there are so many Private Office tasks, they're not considered suitable.'

I put it quite simply. 'If it were known that to read the *Morning Star*, or to be a radical Catholic precluded people from getting into the Civil Service, first of all there'd be an outcry, and secondly, people would warn their children not to read the *Morning Star* or be associated with left-wing Catholics if they want to get into the Civil Service. You'd breed a group of morons who didn't understand what was going on. I'd sack an official who hadn't ever read the *Morning Star* because I believe he wouldn't fully understand what was happening.'

'But it's different for the Civil Service,' they insisted.

'In America,' I went on, 'the CIA is being grilled by the Congress but in this country these things go on without anybody knowing.'

'You've got to keep negative vetting secret; positive vetting we admit to, but negative vetting is secret.'

'That's what I'm complaining about,' I said.

I felt that even raising this issue would probably get me in bad odour with the Secret Service, but I have no alternative, otherwise I'm simply copping out.

In the evening I went to the German Embassy for a reception. I saw Lord Gladwyn there, the old Sir Gladwyn Jebb,* who's very anti-Thatcher and pro-Whitelaw. I said, 'Well you know, what has happened is that the soggy Centre has failed, and we're going to have a bit more Left and Right.'

'Do you want a confrontation between Mikardo and Enoch Powell?'

'Not confrontation,' I said. 'Democracy is about choice.'

'Do you want the generals to come in, do you want a military coup against the strikers?'

'It isn't like that, it's a real choice, and this idea that you've got to fall between the *Daily Telegraph* and the *Guardian* to be respectable, is all rubbish. The consensus has broken down.'

Tuesday 11 February
At Cabinet we discussed the campaign by editors over the NUJ closed shop along the lines of it presenting a threat to the press. Roy Jenkins said that we had a marvellous press; perhaps the United States was freer, but we had the best press in the world. So Harold Wilson commented. 'Well, I really don't agree with that. When I think of what's been done to me, the lies that have been printed, the editorial influence that has been used to try to see that we lost the Election.'

Then Jim Callaghan said, 'I've just been to Portugal and the press

* Permanent Representaive to the United Nations, 1950–4 and Former Ambassador to France, Vice-Chairman of the European Movement.

there has fallen into the hands of the Communists;* what we must do is to see that Communists don't get control of the press here.'

This made my blood boil. The Tory majority in the Cabinet was trying to pretend that somehow the National Union of Journalists was a greater threat than the newspaper proprietors. Harold is wobbly, of course, because on the one hand he's sensitive to the proprietors, but on the other hand he's been badly treated by the press. Michael was good, calm and quiet, and Peter was reasonable though he said that he had doubts about the NUJ. The fact is that the NUJ is now trying to get a bit of industrial democracy in the press, which is quite right.

We came on to foreign affairs. Jim reported that in Portugal, the Communist Party had infiltrated the army and 200 officers met every Friday at 10 am and went on till late at night – I whispered to Michael that it sounded like the Putney debates of 1647.† Jim suggested that junior Ministers be sent to Portugal to sustain the new regime. Very interesting; obviously Portugal is now undergoing the same experience as we had during the English Civil War, and most of today's Cabinet would have been on the side of the King!

Wednesday 12 February

To Number 10 for the meeting with the CBI. Ralph Bateman opened by wishing the Prime Minister good luck on his Russian trip. He said that since the Election the CBI had worked hard to find common ground with the Government; after the October Election and the November Budget they felt that they had reached a closer accord, and they were grateful for the relaxations in taxation and the price code. Since then, however, the Government had embarked upon a course that threatened private industry, and the CBI wanted to put their worries and fears before the Prime Minister.

He then mentioned three issues. First, the Employment Protection Bill, which he said went into areas of negotiation which should be left to industry and threatened smaller companies; second, capital transfer tax was an enormous threat to smaller companies; and third, the Industry Bill which was the climax of this process of hostility. The Bill was worse than the White Paper, it was a prescription for the death of

---

* In April 1974, Dr Caetano, the right-wing Prime Minister of Portugal, was overthrown, and Western governments feared the possibility of a Communist regime; Dr Mario Soares, the Socialist Foreign Minister, was therefore supported and subsequently became premier in 1976.

† A remarkable series of debates in Putney Church in October/November 1647 held by the General Council of the New Model Army between the Levellers and Agitators, including Colonel Thomas Rainsborough, and the Grandees, including Cromwell himself, to consider the basis of a republican constitution.

the private sector. Assurances not put in the statute book would be hard to rely upon.

Then Campbell Adamson spoke. 'Let me start with the Bill. We in the CBI recognise that we must all work together, but basically our criticism is that this Bill is a charter for workers' control.'

He had five points of concern about the Bill. First, it gave wide interventionist powers to the Secretary of State, the power of Parliament was reduced: and the National Enterprise Board had got an actual requirement that it should 'extend public ownership into profitable manufacturing industries' and could 'do anything' in pursuit of its objectives. These powers given to the Secretary of State or the NEB were such that no company could feel safe, particularly when 30 per cent or £10 million worth of shares could be acquired without specific Government approval.

Second, it eroded the private sector. It might affect the capital market, particularly if there was no agreement required with the companies before acquisition. The provisions under the Tories' Industry Act, which they hadn't necessarily liked, had provided that the Government must rid itself of shareholdings when it didn't need them. Now it would appear that the shares could be held permanently.

Third, the disclosure of information powers were very far reaching. Key information could leak to anyone, consultation would be hindered, and this could be very damaging. He thought that information should be given only to the company's direct employees and not to the trade unions.

Fourth, the shareholders' interests were not even referred to in the Bill, and the emphasis was on creating employment instead of efficiency. Nor was there any reference to creditors or suppliers.

Fifth, where selective aid might be given, safeguards against unfair competition were inadequate.

Well, those were Campbell's five points, and it was useful to know them because they'll clearly be the basis of the attack upon the Bill.

Harold replied. 'The White Paper stands: what the White Paper said takes precedence over what is in the Industry Bill. The Bill does not herald the death of the private sector and the White Paper sets out the limits for the transfer from the private to the public sector. It is not a charter for workers' control, but a charter for worker participation. The Secretary of State is answerable to a committee of the Cabinet, and if there are problems raised by the CBI then of course amendments can be moved at the Committee stage of the Bill.'

Well, this was Harold beginning to cave in or, alternatively, which may be worse, giving the impression to the CBI that he was ready to cave in.

Denis Healey then came in, saying that the NEB only had permissive functions, except in the case of sudden risk of foreign take-over where it would have the power of acquisition. NEB actions would require the agreement of the Treasury, under the financial disciplines agreed with it, and there would be a strict limit on money. £1,000 million for five years was not very much.

We had to go off for a division at that stage, and when I returned, Harold asked me to speak. So I said, 'First of all, I'm very glad, Prime Minister, that you explained the way in which the Government works, because of course the Cabinet committee to which you referred and the Cabinet itself had approved the whole Bill as it stood. I personally am rather tired of getting the credit for this Bill because it was properly shared with a whole Cabinet committee and the full Cabinet. It is hard to get this across because we haven't exactly had a sympathetic press but we aim to work by consent, after the unhappy precedent of the Industrial Relations Act.

'I want consultation with the CBI. The problems of investment are deep-seated and we all realise that production could be raised by up to 40 per cent if we could somehow release the energy of people at work. The powers of intervention are no greater than have been envisaged under the Tory Counter-Inflation or Industry Acts. And the compulsory acquisition powers are very limited.

'On the disclosure of information, the CBI has understandably put the negative side but we are actually trying to be constructive here, to give greater certainty to industry, to get a more meaningful dialogue going, to get greater disclosure by Government. As to the disclosure by industry, there are difficulties and I recognise them, but in the Chrysler case, the Honeywell case, the Robertson's Jam case, the Singer case, people were simply not told anything whatever, and workers are no longer prepared to accept that.'

Then Bateman said that the CBI needed time to consider it, that they were not worried about the foreign take-over problem but they would like more express provisions in the Bill.

Harold, winding up, said that the capital market had collapsed. He was glad to hear what they said about foreign take-overs; some of their points might be considered at the Second Reading.

Harold had drinks brought in and I came away not deeply worried because I don't think for a moment that he could get away with major amendments. The TUC Economic Committee put out a strong statement in support of the Bill this morning, and if there is an attempt to move amendments, there will be a hell of a row.

Thursday 13 February
At the PLP meeting, we discussed the Shrewsbury Pickets. There had been a motion moved by Martin Flannery, the MP for Hillsborough,

raising again the case for a debate in the House on the issue. Cledwyn Hughes, Chairman of the PLP, gave the reasons against. He said that there was no time, it would divide the Party, it would be unhelpful.

There were some first-rate speeches made in favour of a debate by Jack Mendelson, Norman Atkinson, Joe Ashton, Martin Flannery, and Syd Bidwell. Some awful speeches against by Bruce Douglas-Mann [MP for Mitcham and Morden] and Arthur Palmer [Bristol North-East]. Roy Jenkins said it would put the Government in difficulty, as if somehow it was a Cabinet decision, which it is not. Also he said that he would be forced to present information that would be damaging, and he hoped to get the pickets out anyway.

At the end, I simply sat stolidly and didn't vote and the request for a debate was defeated by something like 63 votes to 25, so the Right really had mobilised. Michael Foot voted against, Eric Heffer for. I came away very sick about it and decided to write to the Prime Minister.

Just one final point today. I had mentioned that Jack Jones had been ruled out for membership of the NEB partly on the grounds that its members needed positive vetting because of the NEB's Rolls Royce defence connection, and partly because Jack Jones is seen as subversive. There had no doubt been a lot of discussion between the Security Services and the Department and I heard today finally that they had decided that positive vetting clearance was not after all necessary for the NEB and therefore their objections to Jack Jones had failed, or were not being sustained. The point is that they dare not put me in a position where I minute the Prime Minister saying that Jack Jones is regarded as a security risk. But I still intend this to be the basis of a re-examination of security procedures.

Friday 14 February

Caroline had taken Melissa and Joshua to Stansgate with my mother for the weekend so I was on my own at home.

I discovered one or two interesting things today. First of all, Harold Wilson sent a cable from Moscow saying there are to be only three speakers on the Industry Bill which means he doesn't want Michael Meacher. I shall fight that. But the thought of the Prime Minister sitting in Russia thinking of how to stop the Industry Bill looking radical in Parliament is in a way both tragic and comic.

Sunday 16 February

Spoke to Dave [Benn] on the phone who is anxious that the Americans may be trying to de-stabilise the European Left. Secretary of State Henry Kissinger had apparently told the Portuguese Foreign Minister, Mario Soares, how angry he was that the Communists had been brought into the Government in Portugal and there were rumours this week that the CIA had been responsible for a collision in the Thames which sunk a shipload of buses from Leyland going to Cuba. Of course, the Americans are very influential and powerful and it may be that they have decided to back the Centre.

I noticed today that Ivan Yates, an *Observer* correspondent and a contemporary of mine from Oxford, has died in a street accident, only a week after David Wilson, also an *Observer* correspondent and the son of Sir Duncan Wilson, the former Ambassador to the Soviet Union, died in a similar accident in London. I record it here only because later we may discover more than we now know: the Americans denied for years that they had done anything to destroy Allende in Chile and yet they have now had to admit under cross examination in Washington that they did spend a lot of money de-stabilising the Government, supporting the lorry drivers' strike and finally bringing Allende down.

Monday 17 February

I moved the Second Reading of the Industry Bill, a very dull speech as a matter of fact. There were a lot of interruptions from the Tories, and Heseltine made an enormously long speech in which he said the Tories would repeal the Bill. One forgets that our parliamentary majority is paper thin and of course if the Tories can defeat the Industry Bill, Mrs Thatcher would have a tremendous triumph and I don't know how the Cabinet would cope with it. I don't actually rule out the possibility that one or two Labour MPs might pull out and get the Bill defeated.

Michael Meacher did terribly well at the end of the debate. He is bright and able with lots of fight in him and a clear mind. I struggled hard to get him to speak, so I was glad he was a success.

Tuesday 18 February

I talked to Frances Morrell about all sorts of things. First of all, Maudling, who is anti-Europe, has been brought into the new Tory Front Bench (Mrs Thatcher is anti-Europe); Peter Walker who was very pro-Europe has been dropped; Robert Carr's been dropped; and Heath has gone. There is now a little group of experienced pro-European Ministers on the Back Benches and the Front Benches are Rag, Tag and Bobtail. Mrs Thatcher's attitude to Europe is, why should she bother to get Wilson off the hook? If Wilson wants to advocate membership, she'll let him do it and that will put him in difficulty.

Cledwyn Hughes told me today that he had seen Heath and said, 'I'm sorry, but you know that's politics.' Heath had replied, 'They are absolutely mad to get rid of me, absolutely mad.' He was furious. 'I'm in reserve,' he said. So we may be witnessing the break-up of the Tory Party.

Wednesday 19 February

Just before 12, Don Ryder arrived in a great state of excitement to discuss British Leyland. One episode from that long running story which deserves to be recorded relates to Geoffrey Robinson, the go-ahead Managing Director of Jaguar. Apparently Geoffrey has been trying for some time to get a new paint shop ordered and British Leyland board have been very difficult, but he succeeded in getting authority from them to order the long-lead items which would be necessary to make it possible for the paint shop to be built. On this basis there has been some most unfair criticism of him. To find an industrialist who is secretly investing is so attractive that I couldn't avoid a smile. Geoffrey is an active, energetic and sympathetic man – which is more than you can say for most of the directors in the British car industry. If only others would follow his lead.

Caroline, Melissa and Josh came to the House and we had a lovely dinner together. George Brown came up drunk and he said, 'Why don't we have a dinner party. I'll get the old people from the IRC and the new industrialists together to agree to the NEB, which I support.' Then he sat down at the next table with his two guests, and just shouted at them.

Thursday 20 February

Melissa is eighteen today.

Cabinet was devoted mainly to the Referendum. In the end we more or less settled, I think, for the question, 'Should the United Kingdom stay in the European Community Common Market. Yes/No?'

Then over to the House of Commons for a meeting on industrial strategy. It was really rather funny. The whole Department was there: Peter Carey, Richard Bullock, Alan Lord, Ieuan Maddock, Anne Mueller, masses of them, and Peter Carey began by saying, 'This country needs an industrial strategy, a thing it has never had for the last fifty years. It must be selective and accountable' – mouthing the language of officials. 'We must make industry efficient. We cannot spread our resources too thin.'

I listened very carefully and said, 'Let's agree to this. First, that we will go immediately for a major training scheme for 500,000 shop stewards, managers and civil servants on planning agreements. Second, we will identify the areas for planning agreements. Third, we will consider the possibility of launching planning dialogues in which the Government's role will simply be to provide the agenda. Fourth, we will consider our defensive strategy in terms of jobs, productive capacity, location and import controls.' I asked my officials to prepare brief papers on these things and they went away.

Friday 21 February

I found in my box a report on discussions that had taken place at the Foreign and Commonwealth Office on 17 February between Roy Hattersley and Herr Wischnewski, the West German Foreign Minister of State, about our entry into the Common Market. The report of the second session went like this:

1. Continuing the discussion of the coordination of regional aids, Mr Hattersley said that the evidence was that the Commission would produce a paper which would meet the needs of the UK regional policy.

2. The British Government had no wish to prevent the Commission from exercising its proper legal function. Hattersley had, however, told Mr Ortoli during his recent visit, that the British Government hoped the Commission would exercise caution during the period before the Referendum and not act in such a way as to lose favourable votes in the Referendum. Herr Wischnewski said that while the Commission was completely independent, they had fully understood Britain's situation and would behave accordingly. The two German Commissioners certainly understood that a forward position on the part of the Commission would not be helpful. Indeed, the Commission's proposals . . . showed that the goodwill was there even though, for some of the Commissioners, this might not have been easy. Precisely because of this, he hoped that the British Government would be prepared to handle the regional question with care. The difficulty could not be so serious as to become a sticking point.

My Private Secretary had added a note: 'This amounts to a calculated deception of everyone. You might draw it to the attention of the PM in a personal minute.' And so, indeed, I shall. The plain truth is that not only has no attempt been made to meet our renegotiation objective in the field of regional policy, but there is a deliberate attempt to conceal from the British people the significance of the betrayal that has taken place. There is also a deliberate conspiracy with the Commission to see that that betrayal does not become apparent until the votes for the Common Market are safely in the ballot box. It is an unspeakable example of the conduct of Hattersley, Callaghan and the Foreign Office.

Came back from a function in Leeds on the train with Ray Tuite. Ray is very amusing and has had long experience of Whitehall. He said that I was respected for not gossiping to journalists, and told me that my colleagues said the most malicious things about me. Apparently there was endless gossip about my being a teetotaller, about my private life, all sorts of things. I have to let all this wash over my head. I don't know whether it is right but that is what I have decided to do.

Saturday 22 February

Mrs Thatcher has been mobbed in Scotland. She's like the Queen really; she looks like her, talks like her and is of the same age. I don't know whether she will be able to survive after the honeymoon but she is a popular figure. Heath is being forgotten and is being sloughed off just as Eden, Macmillan and Home had been.

Had a long talk to Frances Morrell about Yorkshire and the trade union movement there, and the feeling we both have that the people who are running our regional offices are really District Commissioners. We are not at all a democratic society. All the top leadership comes from a particular class. Indeed, the more I think about it, the more the class interpretation of British politics becomes the only intelligible one. Of course, I was brought up with a particular framework in which to do my thinking, but events have driven me to a completely different perspective.

Sunday 23 February

One interesting little thing this morning to note. Clyde Chitty, who is the deputy head of a comprehensive school and on Caroline's Comprehensive Schools Committee, came to the house for a meeting. Clyde is the son of a well-known Scotland Yard detective who conducted an inquiry into sabotage at the Winfrith atomic energy station some years ago. He told me that when Reginald Maudling was appointed Shadow Foreign Minister by Mrs Thatcher, his father resigned from the Tory Party and said, 'I will never vote Tory again; that Shadow Cabinet is made up of fascists and crooks.'

Clyde said his father knew the Chief Inspector who was looking into the Poulson scandals. He deduced from what his father said that Maudling had been much more deeply involved in the Poulson business than had ever come to light and that his father thought that there had been a big cover-up over Maudling's role.

Eric Heffer rang me up. He's been unwell, I think the strain of office is heavy on him, all the tensions of the Industry Bill debate and the struggles he has in fighting to preserve jobs for people. As he said, 'When I see these people come, I see them as people, not just as workers and non-profitable enterprises. I think of their families and their wives; I have been through it myself and know how worrying it is.'

Frances Morrell told me that she had heard from the journalist Patrick Cosgrave that Tory Central Office had prepared a tremendous campaign in favour of Britain remaining in the Common Market and constituency parties were being asked to work flat out to get a 'Yes' in the Referendum. But when Mrs Thatcher was elected she told them to drop the whole thing – this was the price demanded for the support of the anti-Marketeers. So Tory Central Office has shelved it. It is a most interesting story.

Meanwhile, Heath is to head the pro-Market campaign around the country and if he becomes the hero of the Tory press, that will undermine the position of Mrs Thatcher. On the other hand, if Wilson is supporting Heath then it will do enormous damage to Wilson. Heath's support won't help anybody!

A telegram arrived last week from Bristol saying, 'Get out if you value your life.' It had been passed to the security people who sent it to Cannon Row Police Station where a Superintendent Harden had asked Mary Lou to go in and see him tomorrow to discuss it. It is slightly odd that they should take so much notice now. I have been getting letters every month saying, 'You have six more months to live,' '. . . five more months to live', '. . . four months', and so on, posted in the Reading area and nobody seems to have taken any notice of them. But this telegram apparently interests the police. I am surprised that the Post Office agreed to send such a telegram. Perhaps they reported it to the police in Bristol; perhaps they know who sent it. I am slightly irritated in fact that Bristol should be the source of the message because I have always rather prided myself on never getting any threatening letters from the city of my own seat.

Monday 24 February
A leak from the Department of Trade to the *Morning Star* about the Queen's private wealth was the big story today. Michael Heseltine was interviewed on the 8 o'clock programme this morning and he said, 'Well, this is the fourth serious leak from the Department of Industry.' (Of course, it's Trade and not Industry but I let that pass.) 'First of all, there was the Accounting Officer's Minute about the Kirkby cooperative. Next there was the leak on British Leyland. Next there was the publication by Anthony Wedgwood Benn of the letters to Arnold Hall. And now this. It shows how unwise it would be for information about commercial secrets to be revealed to the Government, because they would be splashed all over the place.'

In a flash, I saw that this could be a dirty tricks campaign to demonstrate that the Department of Industry was leaking, and in that way to win the battle against disclosure of industrial information through the implication that the Department of Industry couldn't be trusted. Notably, of course, it is a way of implying that the Labour Government, particularly me, gives information to the *Morning Star*; this would explain why only the *Morning Star* received the information, and it might possibly link with the fact that the Security Services are preparing a counter-attack on me for making waves over those recent security cases.

At 10.30 I went over to the House of Commons for the TUC-Labour Party Liaison Committee and Harold put me in the chair. The discussion revolved around the Social Contract. After Denis had welcomed the TUC's constructive role I said I would like to speak from the chair, then emphasised that the Social Contract was about more than wages. Rather, it was about jobs and we were faced with a planned reduction in investment, putting many jobs at risk, especially in the regions. We had an agreed framework, basically a voluntary system using disclosure, planning agreements and the NEB. I couldn't see why we shouldn't start straight away with planning dialogues across the board, identify firms in trouble, identify opportunities and see if investment couldn't be raised, and plan jobs, wages and productivity in the context of a single firm. This seemed to be the most valuable thing we could do.

At lunch, Eric came in very upset. He said to me, 'This is a most reactionary Government and I am living a lie by giving it credibility. I would like to get out.' When I showed him the Hattersley exchange with the German Foreign Minister, this further reinforced his gloom.

Tuesday 25 February
The Ministerial Committee on Economic Strategy this morning where we dealt with the economic paper I had submitted, called 'A Choice of Economic Policies', outlining Strategies A and B. I said this was 'an offering for the Chancellor for his Budget'. I took the view that the situation was very grave indeed and to that extent I agreed with Roy Jenkins who feared a collapse of confidence. My paper had been set out in draft before Christmas and although I had thought the trade figures might be worse, I felt we all ought to agree on the gravity of the situation. I said I therefore wanted to set out the options on a broader basis before things got tougher and we were suddenly faced with a huge package of cuts. The Government strategy was coming under pressure and Strategy A which I had identified was the strategy which had been discussed fully in the committee so far. It consisted of three aspects: tax increases and public spending cuts; some form of enforceable pay restraint; and further transfers of cash into the company sector. I thought it would be very serious to adopt this strategy, which I feared would lead to heavy deflation, rising unemployment, cuts in real wages and the withdrawal of support from the Government by the TUC and the Labour movement.

In outlining Strategy B, I favoured a twelve point approach:

1. A full explanation by the Government to the nation of the reason for the crisis – that is to say it is a world slump related to a failure to invest, and not just the fault of the unions.

2. Real discussions with the trade unions of the need for a new over-all economic strategy.

3. The maintenance of the price code.

4. Selective assistance to industry on a larger scale, intended to save jobs but also to avoid stock piling, and to encourage investment and help smaller firms.

5. Selective import restrictions.

6. Rationing and allocation of some imported materials.

7. Work sharing and, particularly, temporary employment subsidies.

8. Tax increases on the basis of greater egalitarianism.

9. Saving of foreign exchange by deeper cuts in overseas defence, control of capital outflows and levies on investment dollars.

10. Control of banks and other financial institutions to get the NEB going.

11. A further downward float of sterling.

12. The development of wider trading arrangements like OPEC or the Anglo-Soviet agreements.

On the last point I said that, like Roy, I thought that the EEC was a key player in this economic situation and we would have to make up our minds whether we saw the Common Market as a life-raft or whether we were being tossed into the deep in a straitjacket.

However, I warned that this strategy might strain international relations possibly including retaliatory measures, strengthen middle class opposition and impose some stress on relations between the Labour movement and the Government. Finally, if the Government continued on its present course, there might be severe confrontation which would merely deepen the existing social divisions. When I had finished, Denis came back, saying that we mustn't panic; that the situation wasn't anything like as bad as was suggested; and that we must switch to exports and investment. He was against import controls, because it would mean that we were failing to expose British industry to foreign competition.

Jim said, 'This business about export/import controls is like devaluation. It doesn't solve the problem. It was pushed on us ten years ago.'

'The key question is,' said Denis, 'can we go on borrowing? We are living 5 to 6 per cent above our earnings. It will be very much harder to borrow £3 billion this year; maybe we will have to go to the IMF or the OECD and suffer supervision. Tony's policy is a caricature; it oversimplifies to the point of distortion. It is not a strategy at all. It would produce a run on sterling, a cut of 6 per cent in our living standards, and he is trying to freeze the pattern of production.'

Harold summed up by saying, 'We endorse Paragraph 11 of Denis's paper, that is the tightening of the Social Contract. We are in favour of more training, and we confirm the need for the Export Committee to look at export activities. There is an official committee which will look at all the proposals.'

I asked, 'Can I be absolutely clear that any Minister can put in papers to that official committee?'

'Yes,' said Harold.

So I shall put Strategy B straight in to that.

I came away exhausted. It is getting awful tough now.

At 5.15, I had to go to the Industrial Development Committee and it was one of the most unpleasant meetings I have ever attended. They are all unpleasant, but this was bloody awful. First item was Meriden. I described the £8 million export credit which had been agreed and gave the background. I said we had to reverse the decline and then re-equip the factories and have a three-plant plan for Norton Villiers Triumph under public ownership.

'What is intolerable,' said Denis, 'is that assurances have been given to the trade union movement. We cannot have the Secretary of State for Industry talking to the trade unions. You know the Government's credit is at stake on this.'

Then Joel Barnett bemoaned the decision and said, 'The Japs are now well entrenched in motorbikes; we can't compete.'

Jim Callaghan didn't think we were committed at all. 'As far as Meriden is concerned, belligerency, militancy and tenacity have succeeded and it will simply spread to other places. We can't have it. Small Heath have learned the lesson. What we need is a proper survey of the industry.'

Harold Lever reminded us, 'I said months ago that this was most undesirable.' (Actually he had supported the cooperative.) 'All we've had is hot air and a recipe for the impoverishment of our economy.' That was Harold Lever's comment on the cooperative – 'hot air and a recipe for the impoverishment of our economy'.

Roy Jenkins asked me, 'Did you give assurances to the other NVT workers in Small Heath?'

'No. I have a tape-recording of everything I said, including what they said to me. I certainly did not. I have been very careful.'

Tony Crosland echoed Joel Barnett's view that the Japanese were in motorbikes, so Harold then said, 'Well, we agreed £4.95 million for Meriden and £8 million for the export credits but no more. Make it clear; we want a proper survey.'

I came over to the House in time for the vote at 10 and saw Bob Mellish. 'Look Bob, let me pour my heart out. I don't grumble often,' and I told him all the agony of this job, of being knifed by colleagues and briefed against. I said I was absolutely fed up with it.

'Well, don't worry. You have got the support of the movement. You will be next Leader of the Party.' He cheered me up a bit; mind you, Bob's a very clever politician.

One little titbit before I finish. One of my Ministers told me today quite definitely that three very senior officials in Whitehall were actually responsible for the leak of the Accounting Officer's Minute which led Number 10 to ask Part to give a report on what had happened.

Wednesday 26 February

I was just working on a speech when two minutes arrived, one from the Prime Minister and one from Edmund Dell, about the CBI demand that the NEB should not buy shares in a company without the consent of the board of directors. Harold's said he had considered this and he was prepared to offer to the CBI an amendment to the Bill, in which there would be a code of conduct or guidelines agreed with the Treasury. Well, this would greatly limit the powers of the NEB, though it wouldn't in fact debar it from buying shares. I arranged to see Harold later.

I went over to Number 10 where I found not only Harold, but also Robert Armstrong, Sir John Hunt, Denis Healey, and Don Ryder. Harold said, 'We were just discussing the CBI.'

'I very much hope, Prime Minister, that you won't make the concession you suggest,' I replied.

'Well, we have got to make some concession.'

'First of all, you can't limit the NEB's right to acquire shares by a directors' veto because they could "up" the price. Even the old IRC had the right to purchase without consent. There is company law and this would frustrate the whole purpose.'

'Well,' said Denis, 'we have to maintain the confidence of businessmen.'

'Why just the confidence of businessmen?' I asked.

'Because the whole of our future depends on the confidence of businessmen. And the speeches you keep making undermine confidence all the time.'

'I don't think you can make a change as big as that without going to the Industrial Development Committee. I only had the minute two hours ago.'

'I get your speeches two hours after you have made them,' commented Harold.

'This isn't a speech, it's a proposal for an amendment to a Bill. This is before the House of Commons has seen it and before the TUC has seen it,' I replied.

'Well, the TUC are coming to a meeting on Tuesday,' said Harold.

So obviously a telephone conversation I had earlier with Len Murray produced results and that gave me strength. I said, 'The TUC will be absolutely furious if there is any change in this because they attach a lot of importance to it.'

'Well, we have got to do something.'

'In that case, Prime Minister, perhaps you would excuse me from attending Tuesday's meeting because I think it would be more helpful to you if I wasn't present,' I said.

'Oh no, you have got to attend.'

'I'm afraid it would be very difficult.'

So Harold immediately said, 'All right, where my minute said we propose an amendment to the Bill, I won't push that. And I won't say that we have debarred the NEB from buying shares, I shall just talk about a "code of practice".'

I left it at that, not sure whether I had won or lost.

The CBI arrived and Campbell Adamson reiterated his worries that management will be less effective should disclosure be made mandatory.

Harold Wilson said, 'May I make it absolutely clear that these talks we are having are purely consultative. We shall have more meetings and we want to remove misunderstandings. We shall also be consulting with the TUC. I am not talking now about amendments.' (That was a real gain for me.)

Campbell Adamson then expressed his anxiety about profitable manufacturing industry.

I said, 'Look, I have always maintained that this will have to be done by consent. I think a code would be sensible, I think openess would be a good thing, and I can see no reason at all why we shouldn't consult the CBI and the TUC on those. As to disclosure, it is a reserved power but we would have to have it.'

When we came to the code of practice, Harold said, 'I must make it clear that we have not considered this collectively. I think you ought to tell the CBI Council and we shall tell the press, that we have been discussing the problems but whatever you do, don't mention amendments or the code because this talk has been very tentative.'

'We would be in serious trouble if it appeared that we had launched a new initiative with the CBI,' Denis warned.

I said, 'Of course, we would expect the Government to disclose a lot more too if we could get any information out of the Treasury. As far as the Treasury is concerned, as the Prime Minister said, it controls everything. I can't blow my nose without asking the Treasury.'

'But you can make speeches without asking it,' Denis said.

On the whole I don't think I did too badly, though no doubt it will appear rather differently in the press.

Joe Ashton and Frances and Francis came in later and we all went and had a meal in the cafeteria. We were talking about civil servants' obstruction and Joe said, 'There are only two sorts of people who can defeat the Civil Service; the public school boys and the Arthur Scargills.'

I don't think anybody can beat them. I have been awfully slow to see it, but the only way you can make sense of any of these problems is by realising that the Civil Service is defending the class interests of owners and professional people and the unions are pressing for a change in that. Industrialists don't worry about Government intervention, they are not a bit worried about it. What they are concerned about is the thought that the trade unions might be more powerful. Where they tried to clamp down on the unions, we are trying to liberate them. And in the Cabinet, it is the Tony Croslands, the Jim Callaghans, the Roy Jenkinses, the Denis Healeys and the Harold Wilsons who hate the idea of the unions having a say. What I am doing is working with and for the unions, and I don't have the same hesitations and doubts that I used to.

Thursday 27 February
This morning Jack Jones came to see me at my request. I told him everything was all right with Meriden, and then I asked him if he would like to serve on the NEB. 'No,' he said. 'I am a General Secretary of a major union and I can't do this too.'

'Could you be pressed?'

He said, 'No.'

Cabinet at 10.30 with a report by Harold on the Ministerial Committee on Economic Strategy, saying there should be no speculation by Ministers about the possibility of a statutory pay policy as a result of pressure on pay, or of import controls.

Michael said, 'Whatever you do, don't blame the unions.'

I agreed strongly; the unions are not responsible, frankly. We must get disclosure by firms themselves so that workers can see the relationship between wages and investment, and management can be put under pressure because there is an investment strike. I agreed we shouldn't say a word on import controls but, as Harold knows, I am very strongly in favour of them and I told him that we were surely going to have to have them.

Crosland said, 'I must say I am very cross that Tony Benn should criticise businessmen. You can't expect them to invest now.'

'Don't get yourself into a 1972 situation by threatening the statutory policy because then you make a voluntary one impossible,' Eric Varley said. 'The TUC is the key.' That was quite a useful little discussion.

The next main item of the Cabinet was regional aid and the steel proposals of the EEC Commission. This was my subject and I said, 'I don't expect to convince members of the Cabinet because I know most people have made up their minds. But we are, in fact, discussing industrial and regional policy and who controls it, and this is at the very heart of the Labour Party relationship with the unions. On the EEC Commission, unlike the Council of Ministers, there is no British veto at all. You don't elect these people, they are Commissioners, and they are not accountable.' I read out what Christopher Soames, Vice-President of the Commission, had said, that the Common Market is a capitalist club and those who enter do so because they believe capitalism is the best.

I went on, 'This re-opens very basic questions of Party democracy. It affects our right to make the laws through Parliament and it therefore raises the whole question of parliamentary democracy. It affects our right to take executive action as a Government. It affects our right to enforce the law.

'These are not theological, theoretical, academic or legalistic arguments. If I want to put it in a single phrase, the Commission's proposal in relation to our regional and industrial policy does not meet our Manifesto commitment, it re-opens Clause IV, re-opens the whole question of parliamentary democracy; the Commission will have powers that we would never tolerate from the House of Lords. It rolls back 120 years of parliamentary democracy. You would never get it through a Labour Conference.'

I must say, I did speak passionately.

Harold said, 'We have got to be practical.'

Jim warned, 'If we can't get this agreed, the Regional Fund will fail and I might as well pack up my bags.'

Roy Jenkins didn't think this was a genuine difficulty and Jim should carry on. He did see the problem about collective responsibility for those who felt that their position was being pre-empted. 'But sovereignty doesn't really exist,' he said.

'You have got to deal with the content of the law,' Reg Prentice said, 'and if you adopt the legalistic view then you must withdraw. Tony Benn's speech was a speech for withdrawal.'

Then Willie Ross spoke. 'For twenty years the Community has made no progress with its regional policy. The remote areas have most to lose in the loss of sovereignty because it is the poor who have the countervailing power. The Commission has the power here and the Hattersley discussions were simply a cosmetic arrangement to try to make it look good. The worse the regions are, the more important it is that the power of Government should be stronger.'

Harold Lever preferred pragmatism against the pedantic approach, which he called anarchic individualism. 'International disciplines must be enforced.' Of course, what he meant was international capitalist disciplines.

Crosland was alarmed at my phrase about rolling back democracy a hundred years and he hoped that if this was the type of language that was going to be used in the Referendum, guidance would be given by the Prime Minister to Ministers.

So I commented, 'Gaitskell said the Common Market would end a thousand years of British history.'

'I thought that was a pretty poor speech by Gaitskell,' Tony replied.

'I know you thought it was a poor speech. But that's what he said. If we are told to use moderate language, I hope Harold Lever will be told he can't describe parliamentary democracy as anarchic individualism.'

Harold Wilson was getting a bit worried then and said, 'Now, now, calm down.'

Feeling was running very high.

Then at 4.15 I went over to the Department for what I thought was a final round of talks with the Meriden people. I reported what had happened and said, 'We have cleared the sum for export with the Cabinet. Now I am hoping we can make progress. Are there any problems?'

So Poore said, 'There is a little problem. You want an annual review of the figure and I must have a guarantee for five years.'

I said, 'Look, the Cabinet wants this to come off. It must come off. We have got to find a way.' I banged the table and I was a bit rude.

He then added at the end, 'And I want an inflation guarantee.'

'Come off it,' I said. 'Well, that's it, you'll have to close your factories. Every time anything is agreed, you want something else.' He left the room at this point.

It is this kind of thing that makes me a socialist. If you take the Meriden situation, why should I have to deal with one man about the jobs of 2000? Caroline put that to me and she is absolutely right. It is an extremely primitive way of dealing with industry.

Later this evening I watched George Brown in an interview on *People and Politics*, Llew Gardner's programme. George was sober, which was a surprise. First of all he attacked the Referendum and then Llew Gardner asked him, 'You said there was an extremist in the Shadow Cabinet in 1972; that Shadow Cabinet is now the Cabinet. To whom were you referring?'

'Oh,' said George, 'I am not going to say.'

'Well, is Tony Benn an extremist? Is he an enemy of democracy?'

'Yes,' said George Brown, 'he is. He wants soviets, as in the Russian model.'

I sat there transfixed. I did find it a very unpleasant experience to be described as an enemy of democracy, even by such a tragic figure as George Brown.

Friday 28 February

I went off to record an interview in a video studio near Moorgate. I arrived there just as ambulances and fire engines were pouring by, within a few minutes of a crash at Moorgate tube station in which between fifteen and twenty people were killed, an appalling tragedy.

At 12 Alvin Toffler and his wife Heidi came to see me at the office. Toffler wrote a sensational book *Future Shock* in 1968 which grossed millions of dollars. I was a bit surprised to discover two things. One was that Nixon had invited him in to the White House, which made me wonder what his connections were. Secondly, in 1972 he had asked me to go to an Aspen Foundation conference in Colorado. I didn't go because it was the week I was defeated for the deputy-leadership of the Party by Roy Jenkins. I wondered who could afford to pay to bring people all the way across the Atlantic for a weekend of discussion. So I asked him, 'Was it CIA money?' He said, 'It might be.'

Given this, it is important to establish a good relationship with the US Ambassador Elliott Richardson. He is a decent, New England lawyer – no doubt conservative, but still a very straightforward man – and he may have some countervailing influence. I notice Cord Meyer, supposedly a CIA man, has been recalled and I think CIA activity must be under some sort of check following recent questions in America.

I wouldn't be at all surprised to find that there had been discussions between Callaghan and Kissinger as to American intelligence activity. Of course, the Americans could be doing a lot here that the British Government knows nothing about. Kissinger must have toyed with the idea of de-stabilising the British Government. I am putting all these thoughts down because, improbable though they may seem, at some stage one might be able to look back and make sense out of what they really mean.

Alvin and Heidi stayed for about an hour and at the end I said, 'There is one thing, Al, that I would like to say to you. You have heard what we are doing and what the issues are. There can't be many people in the United States who really understand it because it is a very complicated question. But if you can get a message through, don't let them de-stabilise us, if you know what I mean.'

'I know exactly what you mean,' he replied.

I continued, 'The reforms that we have to undertake are too significant to be disturbed in that way.' I hope the message does go back. I told him I was going to get in touch with Elliott Richardson.

At 2 Sir Douglas Allen, the head of the Civil Service, and Sir Douglas Henley, one of the Treasury knights, came to see me about the Accounting Officer's procedure and associated leaks. They handed me a document saying they had made a recommendation for a slight amendment to Chapter 8 of the procedure in a situation where officials disagree with their Minister's advice, but are not arguing that there is an impropriety.

I said, 'You should abolish Chapter 8. There is nothing in it. There is no distinction between official advice on financial matters and official advice on other matters, apart from impropriety which is quite a different thing.'

'Oh' they insisted, 'there is a difference.'

'What is it?'

They said, 'You have got to establish viability.'

'Who said you have got to? Certainly Ministers have agreed guidelines that have never been published. But the defence forces don't have to be viable. The Education Department doesn't have to be viable. Health and Social Security doesn't have to be viable. And in Industry, there were no Accounting Officer's Minutes about the viability of Rolls Royce, Concorde, UCS, Govan Shipbuilders, even Aston Martin. The only Minute I had ever had concerned the workers' cooperatives and the Welsh TUC research grant. These were innovations of policy; they were exceptional cases and there were differences with my officials. But they are nothing to do with financial prudence.'

'Well,' said Sir Douglas Henley, 'you are an exceptional Minister.'

'I am not an exceptional Minister at all. I am a Minster implementing Labour policy.'

They said, 'We feel we must do this to protect civil servants so that when they go the Public Accounts Committee, they can at a certain point say that this was a matter that their Minister had imposed on them.'

'In that case,' I asked, 'can I say the same to the House of Commons if I am asked whether I have had adverse advice from you?'

'No, you can't. That would reveal there is a difference between a Minister and civil servants.'

'Why should civil servants be able to reveal there was a difference with a Minister before the Public Accounts Committee and a Minister not be able to reveal that there was a difference with civil servants in the House of Commons?'

'It's different.'

I argued, 'It's not different, because the whole Accounting Officer procedure divides the interests of Ministers from civil servants.'

'Of course, everybody knows anyway that Ministers differ from civil servants,' they replied.

'Well, that's an invitation to leak because if you are saying that everyone knows, then it is implied that it is the duty of a Minister to let it be known. I won't do that. But I will have to answer any questions candidly. Why doesn't the Public Accounts Committee summon Ministers when an issue reaches a certain point?'

'They never have done.'

'Well, I think you should look at this again because I am not prepared to accept this proposal to amend the procedure.'

Sir Douglas Allen has got a nervous twitch and his eyes were opening and shutting all the time. Sir Douglas Henley is a bright but arrogant wooden fifty-five-year-old Treasury boy and I don't think he had ever been treated like this by a Minister.

'Quite frankly,' I commented, 'when the leak came out, it was done to damage me. I have been attacked as being mad, ambitious, a Communist, etc. But these leaks suggested I had behaved with impropriety.'

'Certainly not,' they said.

'Well, I am sorry but the whole affair changed gear when that happened – a leading article praising my Permanent Secretary for standing up against the Minister; a minute from the Prime Minister of quite a different tone from anything else; then my Permanent Secretary sends a minute reporting me like a teacher to a headmaster.'

They retorted, 'Well, we are not even sure you did have an Accounting Officer's Minute, except on the Welsh TUC grant matter.'

The discussion went on for about an hour and twenty minutes. The truth is that the Accounting Officer's Minute, as Roy Williams said – and he was present during the interview – probably hadn't been thought about for fifty years and when Part tried to shoot me with that rusty blunderbuss, it blew up in his face. So now they are trying to pick up the pieces and develop a more powerful line for dealing with a Minister in such cases. It was left with them agreeing to send me a draft report.

I was actually quite jolly and friendly, but I refused to be shifted. It gave me pleasure in a way because I am almost certain now that I can stand up to all officials from any Department. At the back of my mind has been the feeling that Treasury officials might be so brilliant, so bright, so clever that I couldn't out-argue them. But, in fact, I demolished them today and I am particularly glad I did it because as the *Economist* this week said, the Prime Minister was having to spend most of his time policing my activities (no doubt also a leak from Number 10, or from other Ministers).

Saturday 1 March

Today I got a letter, posted in London, written in purple felt pen to Mr Wedgewood (spelt wrongly) Benn, House of Commons. It read, 'You rotten traitor. Thank God you have only 7 more weeks.' I don't take much notice of death threats, I think because nobody has been murdered in the Palace of Westminster since Spencer Perceval, in 1812. But you never know, with George Brown's attack on me as an enemy of democracy, a good citizen might feel it is his public duty to polish me off. I will just have to take reasonable precautions.

Sunday 2 March
Michael Foot made a major attack on Reg Prentice this weekend. The background to this was that last night in a speech, Roy Jenkins said that inflation was the worst danger facing us since Hitler, then Reg Prentice spoke somewhere and made his familiar attack upon the Scargills and McGaheys, the Marxists hoping to undermine the economy for their own ends. He said the Government had fulfilled its part in the Social Contract, now it was for the trade unions not to 'welsh' on the decisions made in their names by their leaders. This was too much for Michael and last night he said that it was economic illiteracy to blame the trade unions who had an exceptionally difficult job to do, and he also hit out at the use of the term 'welsh' which is, of course, an insult to the Welsh people.

I had a telephone call from Allister Mackie of the *Scottish Daily News*. He told me that just before Bob Maxwell went to Moscow two days ago, he made a bid for the whole of the paper, insisting that in return for his £100,000 investment, he should be made Chairman and Chief Executive and the whole cooperative structure should be wound up, leaving him in charge. Allister said it was a terrible bombshell.

I said, 'Look, there are two points. First of all, remember that if Maxwell wants to take it over, it is the first real independent proof of viability because he wouldn't want to take over a dead duck. Secondly, call his bluff, don't change the prospectus because if you bring it back to Ministers, they will kill it. So issue the prospectus as far as you can, as it is.'

He said he had a telephone call through to Maxwell in Moscow. An hour later he called me back saying he had made it clear to Maxwell that they were not prepared to accept his conditions and Maxwell had backed down, so it looks as if they are safe. I was delighted.

I was on the telephone to Frances about my speech when Caroline came down and silently beckoned me away. So I went upstairs and discovered that Joshua was picking up my telephone call to Frances on his radio. So obviously there is a transmitter bug in my room, whether put here by the CIA, by MI5, by the Post Office or the KGB, I don't know. The portable radio wasn't even plugged in at all to his electrical system, so it is an absolute confirmation of what I have long suspected, that my conversations are recorded.

Tuesday 4 March
Frances Morrell had rewritten the text of a talk I am giving to American press correspondents, leaving out all the good bits. So I lost my temper and stamped and shouted. She said, 'Well, we have got to be careful.'

I said. 'Yes, but this won't help.' I cooled down and apologised. It is becoming clear that I can't make the speech I wanted to at all.

At 4.30 I went to Harold's office at the House for consultations on the Industry Bill with the TUC. Harold's opening speech was unbelievable, given his near concessions to the CBI last week. He began by saying, 'The CBI have a couple of queries on disclosure and acquisition' – (playing it all down), 'and the fact that there are some differences between the Bill and the White Paper.' He thought some guidelines issued by the Secretary of State with the support of the Treasury might be a good idea to reconcile the Bill with the White Paper.

Len Murray asked, 'Would the Government have to agree on purchases by the NEB of shares?'

'Well,' said Harold, 'in a crisis, of course, the Government or the NEB could act immediately.'

'What about asset stripping and conglomerates?' asked Jack Jones. 'Could you deal with them?'

'We would have to look at that.'

Then Len Murray said, 'The TUC attach great importance to the enterprise part of the NEB. We don't want the Government to be able to stop the NEB buying profitable companies.'

'Oh it would just be a matter of informing, that's all,' said Harold.

Hugh Scanlon said, 'We are very anxious about this; when I heard Heseltine attacking Tony Benn at the *Financial Times* conference last week, I realised they really hate this policy.'

'These attacks on Tony Benn are quite wrong,' responded Harold. 'But anyway, I am not bargaining with the Opposition. These guidelines, you know, could be statutory or non-statutory, and as for foreign control, we might have to extend it to include asset stripping.'

I said, 'Well now look, Harold, can I take a case in point. Take Johnson Firth Brown, the new steel company in Sheffield. Through BSC we wanted to buy the shares belonging to the owners Jessel Securities which were on the market, because Jessel Securities had gone bust, and the European Commission wouldn't let us.'

'Leave the European thing out of it,' Harold replied.

I went on, 'Let me finish. The Commission wouldn't let us, so we decided to buy the shares through the Appropriation Act, as the Government. But the board of Johnson Firth Brown objected, even thought Jessel Securities would sell them and now they have been placed with institutional investors.'

Harold said, 'Now look, on this question of take-overs we had better strengthen the clause to include a transfer of control over domestic take-overs, with a prohibition order to cover multinational take-overs.

In other undesirable cases the NEB could give a "cease and desist order".'

It really did prove that Harold hadn't read the Bill because what he was promising was the power to take over any company without problems. It was a measure of how far that man would go to buy peace, because he is now giving absolutely contrary pledges to the unions and industrialists.

David Basnett said the TUC General Council attached great importance to this Bill. 'We want to strengthen it. The NEB should be as free as private enterprise.'

Dick Briginshaw asked, 'Are all decisions on the Bill Cabinet decisions?'

Harold said, 'Yes, everything Tony Benn has done for the last year has been a Cabinet decision.'

I nearly said, 'Well, you might give me that in writing.'

So I came out of the meeting utterly dazed and I said to Peter Carey, 'What do you make of it?'

'I don't know,' he replied, 'because he has now given contrary pledges to the two bodies.'

Wednesday 5 March

At midnight a debate on Meriden began. Heseltine and the Tories shouted. It was extremely unpleasant. What really angers them is that workers have got away with a campaign against redundancy and have been supported. It has nothing to do with Government financial support because they gave tons of money to private industry. Anyway, I made my speech and some excellent contributions followed. At the end Eric Heffer, like a great tank, rolled over the Tories.

Got home at 4 am.

Thursday 6 March

The *Any Questions* programme was raised in Cabinet because I had asked the producer why Cabinet Ministers weren't asked on to it; as a result Number 10 had been consulted, and they said No.

So Harold said, 'Well, I am not obliged to ask Cabinet about this, but I put it to you as the point has been raised. I think Ministers shouldn't go on because they might be asked embarrassing questions.'

I disagreed with Harold.

He said, 'Well, 90 per cent of the requests for Ministers to speak are requests for *you*.'

'Leave me out if you like but it does seem silly that we spend half our time at Cabinet meetings saying we must get the Government case across and the rest of the time seeing that nobody ever broadcasts it.' But I lost and that was it.

Afterwards I was about to do a radio interview from the office when the division bell rang so I dashed to the car. It was pouring with rain and there was a bad traffic jam so when we got to Parliament Square I said to Ron, 'I'll run.' I jumped over the low wall, slipped and fell into a pool of water. I jumped up, ran across the grass into the Palace of Westminster and voted. Just got there in time, looking as though I had been pulled through a hedge backwards.

Monday 10 March
Parliamentary Questions at 2.30 where there was the usual knockabout. I was accused of being a Maoist, so I said, 'The last intervention by Mao in English politics was when he entertained the late Leader of the Opposition in Peking last May and indicated his strong support for British membership of the Common Market.' I left it at that.

At 10 pm I had a meeting in my room with Joe Ashton, Douglas Jay, [Michael English Chairman of the PLP Parliamentary Affairs Group], Dick Clements, Norman Atkinson, Audrey Wise, Nigel Spearing [Labour MP for Newham South], Frank Allaun and Syd Bidwell to discuss the action we should take after a Cabinet decision on the Referendum has been announced. We put together a statement:

> We who have signed this declaration welcome the Government's announcement of a Referendum to allow the people of the United Kingdom to decide for themselves whether we should be in the Common Market or withdraw from it; accept that that decision must be binding; believe that it is in the true interest of the people of the United Kingdom that we should retain for the British Parliament, which we elect, the sole power to make the laws and impose the taxes under which we are governed; desire to re-establish the power of the United Kingdom to trade freely, particularly in the case of food, with any nation and to restore our power to make policies of world-wide cooperation which are not possible under the European Treaty; declare our intention to campaign for the withdrawal of the United Kingdom from the Common Market and to vote No in the Referendum and invite our fellow citizens to do the same.

Tuesday 11 March
My first engagement this morning was at 9 in Peter Shore's office with Len Murray, David Lea, and Michael Foot to discuss industrial democracy. Peter, who wants a department inquiry, explained that this was a great revolution in the capitalist system and we had to go at it carefully. Fortunately Len Murray, though he doesn't favour experimentation and is a bit skeptical of some of the things I am doing, certainly doesn't want progress delayed by a departmental inquiry. So I found warm support from him and David Lea. Peter was isolated and

in the end Michael suggested we should produce a Green Paper in the summer describing everything we have done so far and that we should look at the concept of a two-tier board separately. I favoured this, namely that there is a special problem of formulating a new type of democratic company.

Husbands-and-wives' dinner. Barbara is organising what she calls the Cabinet against the Market (CAM). She produced a list of people who were anti-Market, which I managed to pinch from her. I did get everyone present to agree that we would launch a total list on Tuesday, immediately after Harold had made the announcement.

Wednesday 12 March
To the House of Commons, where Harold made his statement on the Dublin summit of the heads of the EEC Governments to finalise British terms. It was really rather sad to see the Tories waving their Order Papers and Labour people silent, except for the pro-Market group. It is all over bar the shouting. Shirley Williams reiterated on the radio today that she would resign from the Government if the country voted to leave the Common Market. So, in fact, she has now established freedom to dissent.

Caroline and I went to a party at the US Embassy. We talked to Elliott Richardson and I told him that his comments on the Common Market – reserving his position – had been much appreciated, even though he had admitted that all his officials were in favour. I tried to persuade a few of the Americans there that the Referendum would be a re-run of all the historic decisions in British political history.

Thursday 13 March
First item at Cabinet was Harold saying a word about the arrangements for the Market decision and announcement. There had been a request from junior Ministers for a meeting with non-Cabinet Ministers, which was being arranged for Monday evening.

I said, 'Harold, don't you think it would be sensible for members of the Cabinet to be free from now on because there is an air of unreality about the position. The view that you and the Foreign Secretary hold is in a sense obvious and people know what our views are. There are very few people here who haven't made up their mind.'

'I haven't,' interrupted Merlyn Rees.

I went on, 'Shirley Williams was on the *Jimmy Young Show* yesterday – and I didn't complain – saying that she would resign from the Government if the vote went against Europe. I think it would be better if we all had our freedom now and then we could all contribute to the PLP meeting.'

'Certainly not,' said Harold. 'The Cabinet has not yet decided whether to accept the terms. We must have a paper.'

So there was a bit of a discussion, and Harold accepted that we should decide on Tuesday.

I was hoping to go to Bristol today for the Annual General Meeting but I couldn't because of a three-line whip. So I rang Herbert Rogers, who told me that he was going to print some of Harold's speeches when Wilson was anti-Market, as well as some of Hugh Gaitskell's. He really is a marvellous guy. He knows what the score is.

Friday 14 March

There was a superb cartoon in the *New Statesman* this week of a football crowd and on the pitch a naked man – that was me – streaking across and being arrested by four policemen, Tony Crosland looking on disapprovingly, Denis Healey holding his helmet over my private parts amd Jim Callaghan and Roy Jenkins holding my arms. Harold was running up with a raincoat to cover me up. It was most amusing.

Saturday 15 March

I checked over with Mary Jay the list of people opposed to the Market and we now have 141 definite antis, including thirty-three Ministers and six Cabinet Ministers. Nine of the question marks have now been identified as anti. The declaration that I circulated is being signed and I think we shall be able to put 141 straight on to the Order Paper for Tuesday.

The first real target is to get over 50 per cent of the PLP; then to go for the Executive and get the declaration adopted as a resolution at the special Conference; to get constituency parties and trade unions committed; then to go back to the Cabinet and say, 'Look, Cabinet is not representative of the Labour movement, change your recommendation' (which will undoubtedly be in favour). That would certainly push Harold back into a corner. I think it is just conceivable that we might succeed.

Sunday 16 March

To the Castles' house where there was a huge gathering of people. We had drinks and then we went right through the list. There are now 232 firm antis.

We had a fairly rough and ready agenda. Mik, who is an excellent chairman, was immediately put in the chair. We discussed the NEC resolution first and a few modifications were made, then we agreed that everybody who supported it should have their name on it. Mik is going to canvass the Executive.

Barbara is still keen on getting a Cabinet anti list out on the first day after the Cabinet decision, Ministers on the second and Back Benchers on the third, but I said, 'No, we don't want that because we want to show mass strength immediately to save the wobblies.' That was more or less agreed.

I went on to say that Mrs Thatcher would be playing it softly so as not to contribute to a triumph for Harold, and Harold won't want to be more pro-Market than the Tories, so there could be quite a lot of constructive restraint.

Clive Jenkins had brought iced champagne, and he gave me a china plate commemorating the five Pentonville prisoners of 1972. I must say it is a lovely memento.

Monday 17 March

The first of two Cabinets to come to a decision on Europe. Harold said that he hoped we'd conduct the meeting with good will. He described the timetable: he had to make his judgment tomorrow and then announce it to the House. He would introduce guidelines and he hoped there would be no public debates between Ministers.

Jim made a few general points. There had been a substantial change in the Community since we first examined it, the Commission was now under tighter political control, the Economic and Monetary Union was now no more than a twinkle in the eyes of its advocates, and the federal idea was dead.

We came to the Community budget. Jim said that they had changed the method but not the taxes themselves. £125 million refund would be coming to us if we fell below 85 per cent of the average EEC Gross Domestic Product.

Harold said the Economic and Monetary Union was as dead as a dodo or, to quote the *Economist*, if it wasn't actually dead, it was on the list of species likely to become extinct. Michael disagreed, saying that in Paris it had been reaffirmed.

On regional policy, Jim believed we'd had a real success. I said, 'We haven't, you know. All that's happened is that we've been licensed to continue with our existing policy but there is no transfer whatever of powers back to us.'

Jim thought there was no problem with industrial policy. I intervened again: 'Nothing has been achieved on this at all. Articles 92 to 94 are exactly as stated, and as for the Industry Bill, of course its powers will all be checked.'

No queries were raised on fiscal policy, but on Value Added Tax we got some further information. Harold Wilson said that that was no threat and Denis added that we had total freedom to set VAT and we wouldn't harmonise.

Jim said that we'd done very well in the re-negotiations on trade and aid, and achieved our Manifesto. To that Barbara commented, 'I understand that Judith Hart has sent round a minute on this.' I volunteered to read it out. 'Speaking as a responsible Minister, we have not carried out our Manifesto objectives.' That was just brushed aside.

By then it was 1.30 so I left and went back to the office for the ministerial lunch where there was great gloom because Eric Heffer had announced that he was going to resign. 'It's too much,' he said, 'I can't stand it, I'm not accepting the guidelines, I'm going.'

After lunch, I took Eric aside for a private talk. 'You've got to make up your mind, Eric. I know, I feel the same, but we must stick together at this stage. You can always go after the Referendum if you want to.' He wouldn't accept that, so I told him to think about it and not to make up his mind immediately. I just can't spend any more time on it.

At 6.40 I went to the PLP, where Harold announced that the Cabinet had met this morning but it has not reached a decision. As to the agreement of Ministers to differ there would be guidelines issued and there were to be no attacks on each other.

During the meeting, Mik passed me a note saying that the NEC resolution that we had agreed last night had now been tried out on individual members of the Executive and he'd got fifteen out of twenty-eight people to sign it with four still to come, an absolute majority. I was thrilled.

Tuesday 18 March

A momentous day in the history of Britain – the day of the Cabinet decision on Europe, the day of the parliamentary decision, the day of the dissenting Ministers' declaration, and of the Early Day Motion on the Order Paper.

At Cabinet we had before us the papers detailing the renegotiation package, and for the first time the issue of sovereignty was discussed properly. The crucial question was whether the Community was to be a supranational structure or a community of sovereign states.

Crosland wasn't concerned with sovereignty because he thought sovereignty has passed anyway to the power workers and the hospital workers. He *was* concerned about the host of gratuitous harmonisations which he found he had to deal with. He said he would like this matter put to Ministers to try to stop it.

I said, 'Sovereignty is not the same as omnipotence – nobody is omnipotent. The Americans aren't omnipotent; they were beaten by the Vietcong, they couldn't do what they wanted. Sovereignty means democracy, in the sense of power to make your own laws.

'There are three options open to us. One is to protect our parliamentary democracy, which would offend the Community; the second is to abandon parliamentary democracy which would offend the Manifesto; the third option is to fudge it.

'This is the most important constitutional document ever put before a Labour Cabinet. Our whole political history is contained in this paper. It recommends a reversal of hundreds of years of history which have progressively widened the power of the people over their governors. Now great chunks are to be handed to the Commission. I can think of no body of men outside the Kremlin who have so much power without a shred of accountability for what they do.

'The Community will destroy the whole basis on which the labour movement was founded, and its commitment to democratic change. That's one of the reasons we have a small Communist Party, why the ultra-Left is so unimportant, because we can say to people "Change your MP and you can change the law". That's where the attack on democracy is coming from. If we accept this paper, we'd be betraying, in a very special sense, our whole history.'

Michael spoke. 'We're being asked to accept everything we opposed when we were in Opposition. Take tachographs as an example – we opposed them, but they have still been imposed on us. We are conniving at the dismemberment of Parliament. We are destroying the accountability of Ministers to Parliament, and if we elect a European Parliament by 1978, it will destroy our own Parliament. It will encourage Scottish and Welsh separation because they'll say, "If you can do *that*, what about helping us to govern ourselves?" People will think we're crazy to dismember our Parliament at the most dangerous moment in our history.'

Jim said that it was not the first time that a document of this importance had been before a Labour Cabinet. It was all set out in the 1967 White Paper. Sovereignty of Parliament was not an issue, it wasn't even in the Election Manifesto.

This led to a protest from Michael who said that what was at stake was a draconian curtailment of the powers of Parliament. Harold pointed out that Michael was quoting from the February Manifesto. So Michael said that the phrase 'authority of Parliament' was used in the October Manifesto. 'Well,' said Wilson, 'these are the differences between the old and the new testaments.'

Jim disagreed strongly with me when I said that there was more of a danger posed by the Commission than by Mick McGahey or even the International Socialists. He said, 'Well, the Communist Party may have gone over the top, but the International Socialists are penetrating the authority of Parliament.'

He too was worried about things like the standardisation of rear-view mirrors which he said was offensive; there may be too many Commissioners, but the time to study the Commission would be after the Referendum. 'We don't want to give Parliament the power to hold things up. Sovereignty was destroyed anyway by interdependence,' he said and he was confident in what Elwyn Jones had said, that the power was there if the people felt strongly enough.

Harold Lever commented, 'Tony Benn is a legal pedant,' and debates on whether this was irrevocable were silly. The decision to withdraw would be disastrous.

Harold Wilson said, 'The British Parliament has the power to come out at any time.'

I asked if he'd be prepared to say that publicly.

'We can discuss that later,' he replied, 'when we come to the handling of the statement.'

For Elwyn Jones, political sovereignty was the power to make our own laws and Parliament could repudiate the Treaty at any time. 'Parliament has handed over part of its law-making powers already. When we were in Opposition, it was the exercise of those powers which we had ceded that we criticised. British influence can be exercised in future by the Foreign Office. Government can continue to declare war, Parliament can continue to throw out the Governments that fail. We have given limited powers to the Commission, and Parliament can take them away again. A legal framework is difficult and disturbing. The practice is more important than the legal machinery.' This from the Lord Chancellor!

Reg Prentice accepted Paragraph 2b – the surrender of sovereignty and improved scrutiny. 'We need to strengthen the power of Parliament over the pressure groups at home, and we must institutionalise our external interdependence, but of course, the juggernaut lorries can and must be stopped. We mustn't be too neurotic about a seepage of powers away from Parliament.'

Barbara Castle said that the philosophy and theology of the Common Market were to remove the distortions to market competition – that was what the free movement of capital and labour was all about.

Peter accepted that there was anxiety, and he regretted there hadn't been earlier discussions. 'Sovereignty is the right to make your own laws, and the minutiae are not the real issue. Freedom of movement of labour is very important, and our Courts may enforce our law at the moment but they won't later.'

'The free movement of labour was never an issue,' Harold said.

Ted Short told us that one of the new Commissioners had cut down on attempts to harmonise. Parliament could not divest itself legally of its own sovereignty. We could only strengthen our parliamentary procedures, and he, therefore, favoured radical proposals for doing so.

That was the end of the discussion on sovereignty. But as is already evident, the referendum will produce some deep thinking about the nature of our Government. I've had so long to think about it, with the experience of the peerage battle and all that, that I feel I am one jump ahead of my colleagues.

Harold then brought us on to the main question. Should we accept the terms or not? 'I recommend that we should stay in and that is the view of the Foreign Secretary, though he will speak for himself. We have substantially achieved our objectives, the Community has changed *de facto* and *de jure*. The attitude of the Commonwealth has changed too. The Commonwealth wants us to stay in, and the Commonwealth trade patterns have regrettably changed. If we had a free trade area for the UK, the conditions upon us would be stiff or stiffer. I am only persuaded 51 per cent to 49 per cent, indeed I had anxieties right up to the last few days, but I now recommend that we stay in.'

Jim Callaghan followed, 'In supporting you, Harold, I would like to say something about the development of Europe. I am unashamedly an Atlanticist, but we are living in a regional world and we must use the regional organisations. The Soviet Union does not find our membership of the EEC a hindrance to detente. Indeed, I believe that secretly they might like us in, to control the Germans. The seventy-seven non-aligned countries which are now banded together at the United Nations have the potential to destroy the UN and we are better able to withstand them in a regional group. As to the prospects for democractic socialism in the Community, four of the countries are Labour, or have Labour representation in the Government: Holland, Denmark, Germany and the Republic of Ireland, and now Britain. The market economy as an idea is quite fly-blown, and the withdrawal of Britain would strain our relations with Ireland.

He quoted Benjamin Franklin: ' "When I first looked at the terms for this Constitution I was not persuaded of it. As wisdom came, I came to see that I was wrong." '

Willie Ross said, 'We cannot ignore the Manifesto. Parliament has lost its power, and the only power remaining would be the power to come out. Anything less than that the Courts would have to decide. We haven't changed the CAP. On fishery policy the anxiety in Scotland is that under the Common Market rules fishermen would be able to fish right up to the shore. Indeed, the Scottish National Party has won constituencies on the coast on these grounds.'

'Well, that point has never been raised at all in the last twelve months,' Harold Wilson pointed out.

On the terms, Willie quoted the Foreign Office paper. 'Regional policy is another problem. Once in, it will grow. A greater degree of oversight from Brussels is being urged.'

Ted Short wanted us to stay in. He said Jim Callaghan should be awarded a doctorate in re-negotiation. He would take advantage of the agreement to differ if Cabinet decided to *come out*.

'You know, this is not a great divide,' said Harold Lever. 'This is the beginning of a new relationship with Europe.' He favoured staying in.

Shirley Williams agreed. 'We could stop the Commission, and indeed we did when they tried to harmonise our milk and beer measures. On the market economy, they have gone much further on the Continent than we have, and in Germany industrial democracy is far ahead of us. Europe spends more on the public services than we do. France and Italy have a larger public sector than us and they see it not as an ideological matter but as a practical advantage to their country. On democracy, they're doing well too.'

Bob Mellish said that the Common Market was here to stay and we should stay in.

I made my final speech. 'Prime Minister, I fear that the Cabinet is about to make a tragic error, if it recommends that Britain stays in. I recognise that Jim has done his best and probably got the best terms that are compatible with continuing membership. But we have not achieved our Manifesto objectives and indeed we did not even try.

'We have deferred the real issues, like the authority of Parliament and regional and industrial policy, until after the re-negotiation was over. We have confused the real issue of parliamentary democracy, for already there has been a fundamental change. The power of electors over their law-makers has gone, the power of MPs over Ministers has gone, the role of Ministers has changed.

'The real case for entry has never been spelled out, which is that there should be a fully federal Europe in which we become a province. It hasn't been spelled out because people would never accept it. We are at the moment on a federal escalator, moving as we talk, going towards a federal objective we do not wish to reach.

'In practice, Britain will be governed by a European coalition government that we cannot change, dedicated to a capitalist or market economy theology. This policy is to be sold to us by projecting an unjustified optimism about the Community, and an unjustified pessimism about the United Kingdom, designed to frighten us in. Jim quoted Benjamin Franklin, so let me do the same: "He who would give up essential liberty for a little temporary safety deserves neither safety nor liberty." The Common Market will break up the UK because there will be no valid argument against an independent Scotland, with its own Ministers and Commissioner, enjoying Common Market membership. We shall be choosing between the unity of the UK and the unity of the EEC.'

'It will impose appalling strains on the Labour movement. No one in this whole discussion has mentioned the TUC with whom we signed the Social Contract, or the National Executive, or Conference who are joint partners in the Manifesto and to whom we should report back. I believe that we want independence and democratic self-government, and I hope the Cabinet in due course will think again.'

Michael took over, 'We're giving up so much. The Commonwealth view is not our view. We shall dismember Parliament and the UK. Western Europe is a coalition system and the British don't want coalitions. We must present this fundamentally. The cost of coming out is used, but it is a defeatist argument. Gaitskell said that we should make that clear.'

Denis Healey said that it would be a mistake to present the issue as Michael Foot and Tony Benn had suggested. The consequences outside would be serious, and economic problems were more important. He said this was a matter of judgment and a choice between evils. The Commission was set by the Treaty of Rome and it would have been better if we had been in there at the start. Leaving now would not end the matter and there would be pressure for reversal of the decision and for our continued entry later. That is why he approved the application. The decision to leave now would be more damaging than the decision not to join would have been. We would have no sympathy from the white Commonwealth if we left, we'd have no sympathy from the US which is turning inwards, and the idea of a North Atlantic Free Trade area was out. Europe was a bargaining counter with the US, and there would be a long period of uncertainty if we decided to leave, whereas industry needed certainty. It would not be a disaster if we left but it would be a risk, and he hoped we would not overplay the disaster aspect or we would have no credible posture with the British people if they did vote for withdrawal. He hoped the people would vote to stay in and improve the Market from the inside.

Tony Crosland agreed with Denis. He was an agnostic, skeptical about large markets but he thought there were strong arguments for staying in. If we did not go in, we would go back to a sort of Churchillian myth that we were the greatest and most important country in the world.

Reg Prentice said, 'I am a one-world man and regional groupings help the Third World. The EEC exists and we're in it. It would be a danger to detente if we came out. The Third World food crisis is our great problem and we would make a bigger effort to deal with it if we were in.'

Eric Varley said, 'We are being asked to take too much on trust. There have been no fundamental changes in the Common Agricultural Policy or the Economic and Monetary Union. I'm worried about Parliament, but my main worries are about energy and oil, because if the Treaty of Rome is applied to the Continental Shelf – and the Community is studying its application – then we'll be in difficulties. We *can* survive outside. I regret the long campaign which will strain the Party, but I am opposed to our remaining in.'

Peter Shore felt that the balance of advantages was unfavourable. 'Britain's relationship with the English-speaking Commonwealth was closer than that with the Continent. That is how the British people feel.' As to the regional and national argument, Peter said, 'The EEC disintegrates when it comes up against real issues like energy. Our base is not in Western Europe. It is too weak, too small and too old fashioned. In real instances it makes the problems worse. France is no friend. I do not think you can have this degree of intimacy without a real community. We are friends and allies with most neighbours on the Continent but we don't have that degree of intimacy with them. We can survive without them, and prosper and contribute more.'

Malcolm Shepherd the Lord Privy Seal said, 'It has been a privilege to listen to this debate and I hope the same spirit will illuminate the Referendum and the Government and the Party will come out of it stronger.'

Fred Peart's attitude of course was coloured by agricultural matters. We should stay in.

John Silkin believed that it was an irrevocable decision and to suggest we could change it would be like suggesting we could repeal the Treaty of Paris of 1789 and bring the United States into colonial status again under Britain. This was the last chance. A federated Europe would require a fundamental change in the Common Market and therefore he would vote against staying in.

Merlyn Rees said he was not a federalist but he had noticed that the French and Germans were working together and the youngsters today in Europe didn't think nationally at all. The Commission worried him a bit, and the Party and the Conference and the unions might take a different view, but he had read every paper he could find and he had come to the conclusion that we should stay in.

Roy Mason believed we had succeeded in getting substantial changes and these successes were well known. To unravel Europe, beginning with Denmark, would be terrible, it would mean the UK would wither on the vine. Our balance of payments would be badly affected. It would be traumatic for Britain, an embarrassment for the City. He was for staying in.

Barbara felt it was bad to ask people to stay in an organisation whose principles we did not share. We had accepted that we could not challenge the central theology, and so we had not tried hard on parliamentary control, on steel or the CAP. The power of the veto to safeguard national interests sounded attractive, but it was not as simple as that. The EEC worked by compromise. Everything was a bargain, and this was a charter for coalition which would destroy the Labour Party. The EEC was an institutionalised constitution.

Roy Jenkins said he had been wrong to underestimate the scope there had been for improving the terms. He was an Atlanticist too, more at home in America than on the Continent. But Europe was a pillar of Atlantic cooperation.

Willie Ross believed in the maximum strength for the UK to prevent its division.

John Morris said that on forms and principles, he thought the Common Market was frightening. In practice, it was more acceptable.

So, in the end, it was sixteen to seven for staying in. Harold then said, 'I hope that nobody will think the result has anything to do with the way I composed the Cabinet because when I formed it a year ago, there were eight for Europe, ten against and five wobblies. Now, of those who have expressed their view, who intends to take advantage of the agreement to differ?'

Six of us said Yes – myself, Barbara, Michael, Willie, Peter and Eric.

Thus it was that the Cabinet reached its view to stay in the Common Market.

The guidelines on the agreement to differ were passed round, strongly discouraging debates between Labour Ministers, or Members of the Government taking a different view without advance permission, or appearing on platforms with people from other parties.

Shirley asked, 'What about me appearing with Geoffrey Howe on the Tory side?'

Harold said he didn't want to discuss that until Thursday.

We finished and at 1.30 I walked through Downing Street, back to the office. After that, I just needed to unwind.

Wednesday 19 March
Harold's statement to the House of Commons yesterday got a rather bad press, partly because he did it poorly, partly because it had been predicted, and partly because though the Tories are pleased he has done it, they have no particular interest in him thereafter. He is simply performing their function and now they want to win without giving him any credit. Mrs Thatcher made it clear last night that this was going to be her approach.

Peter was over at Number 10 and he told me later that Harold was crabby and nervous.

Thursday 20 March
At 9.30 the Industrial Development Committee met. The first item was Triang Toys in Merthyr Tydfil, a firm owned by an Iranian. We had agreed to buy it if it went into receivership, but he was now trying to

blackmail us by saying he would close it down without going into receivership. I had put in for £5 million to save 500 jobs.

I was denounced by Joel Barnett, Harold Lever, Peter Shore by everybody except John Morris who wanted to save the jobs at Merthyr.

Harold Lever said the plan was outrageous. 'What we want is another firm to buy it, Mothercare would be perfect, they produce baby products. As a matter of fact, my wife Diane has a cousin who owns Mothercare – I'll ask her to do it.' Everybody laughed.

Malcolm Shepherd said, 'I used to represent Triang in the Far East years ago, and they're a lousy firm, not worth saving.'

I said, 'I accept that we can't get away with this scheme, but this is a problem because we have abandoned a solemn Manifesto commitment that we would take the power to bring firms into public ownership by statutory instrument where they had failed their workers. The fact that we have to depend on a member of the committee having a rich relative to buy the firm, or another member who happens to have worked in it to give us guidance is outrageous. This man is blackmailing us, and I recommend that we ask officials to look again at my paper calling for compulsory acquisition, and adopt a socialist solution.'

I hit them between the eyes, and it was agreed to look at it again.

Next was Bearbrand who produce tights in Liverpool. I was asking for £350,000 to save another 500 jobs. Having made such a tremendous fuss on the last one, I found the committee coming round in my favour, except for Harold Lever, who always says, 'I don't know why we should be doing this, it will never be viable.'

Shirley asked me, 'Have you done a market survey on tights?'

'I can't do a worldwide market survey on tights for a single firm that could go bust at twenty-four hours' notice. That's ridiculous.'

Harold Lever was opposed to the scheme and I said, 'Look, I put in a proposal last July for a temporary employment subsidy. Instead of paying to sack people, and then giving the unemployed the money, you could give it to the people and let them carry on with the firm.'

He went on to ask what I'd done about approaching Boots the Chemist, which was recommended in the report as a possible buyer.

'As a matter of fact,' I answered, 'Boots were approached, and when they were told Bearbrand was in trouble, they exploited their knowledge of Bearbrand's weakness to force them to make a price cut, which is why the firm has gone bankrupt. That is capitalism. Everybody is out for themselves and nobody gives a damn about people who lose their jobs.'

Cabinet at 10.30 – and it turned out to be most acrimonious and dramatic. Peter had told me that there had been a tremendous scene last night and when we got into Cabinet, Harold began to speak.

'I've pulled you in without officials because a very dangerous situation has developed. When I gave permission for an agreement to differ, I assumed that the anti-Market people would appoint a spokesman to speak for them. Instead I find that there has been a press conference, a statement by dissenting Ministers, an Early Day Motion, and an NEC resolution in circulation asking the special Conference to fight against a Government decision. I know one or two pro-Market MPs may be campaigning but this is an attempt to bounce the NEC and it's dangerous.

'I cannot lead a Cabinet when its members mobilise outside agencies including the NEC. It is impossible for me to keep the Cabinet together on this basis. One Minister offered to resign last night, but I don't want to lead a rump. It has been a field day for the Tories and I have got to face Parliamentary Questions today. We must face it, it could be 1931 all over again. If we get disorganised, there are members of the Party who would put the Common Market before the Party. What I'm afraid of from this polarisation is a pro-Market coalition, a Tory-dominated coalition with perhaps a titular Labour leader – and it would have much worse relations with the trade union movement than even Heath. Indeed, I doubt if democracy could survive, and I'm not going to play it this way. The Cabinet should discuss it and find a solution by 12.30 today.'

Shirley Williams said, 'I will never join a coalition. I had hoped that the Party would show the same charity towards dissenters as the Cabinet.'

Michael Foot, who had spoken to Harold about this last night, thought the problem was not insoluble but we couldn't have a cut-and-dried solution by 12.30. He said to Harold, 'It's no good saying you can't tolerate members of the Cabinet heading a campaign against the Market. We are entitled to head a campaign. We're not prepared to engage in a charade. We are going to make our view effective like you. It is the only dignified basis on which to proceed.'

'The most intolerable thing was the Early Day Motion, and the National Executive resolution,' Tony Crosland chipped in.

Michael went on, 'We in the Cabinet are entitled to lead the campaign – we'd be reduced to puppets otherwise. There is a problem with the special Conference, but the Party must have a right to a view. The NEC and the Conference must have a right to a view. The NEC and the Conference must have a vote. If the PM says we've abused our rights, well we may be wrong, but the EEC issue has cut deep. In the next two or three months there will be huge pro-Market allies, the Prime Minister, the Cabinet, the newspapers, and it is simply not fair to stop *us*. Indeed, at the last full Labour Conference in 1973, I spoke from the platform to try to persuade the Conference not to pass an anti-

Market resolution because I said the terms weren't through, and I secured a deferment. But I can't engage in a fake; the pro-Market people have a chance of winning the Referendum and so have we. But don't take it tragically. Last night, Harold, you said that if we resigned, you would resign too.'

'The Early Day Motion on the order paper was silly and sly,' replied Harold. 'A campaign by both sides may be inevitable but the NEC question is more serious. Are the PM and the Treasurer of the Party to have to ask for the right to dissent? Are we allowed to attend the Conference? I've been kicked around too much, and the NEC resolution was put out without even telling me. Am I to be absent at the Conference or just a spectator? Cabinet must think out what they want me to do. I object to Ministers on the NEC campaigning against Government recommendations. People cannot wear two hats, even though we have accepted an agreement to differ. There is a grave economic crisis. Am I in a credible position if hostile NEC action is taken by Ministers?'

Peter Shore said he wasn't on the NEC but he knew the NEC had agreed to meet a week after the Cabinet decision and to have the special Conference.

'That was done by members sitting round this table without even telling me,' said Harold.

'But they would have done it anyway,' said Peter. 'The Party wants a view, Labour can't abstain. You implied that to "differ" was passive. But if the Cabinet decision had gone the other way Roy and Shirley would have campaigned in favour of the Common Market. We're all bound to want to win the Referendum.'

Harold said that he objected to Cabinet Ministers leaving the Cabinet after a decision had been reached and then, like a lot of kids leaving school, throwing bricks at it.

'You asked us to indicate whether we wished to dissent,' said Peter.

Harold said, 'Well, it was cheap just to try and show how many boys you could collect on your list.'

Then Jim joined in. 'The campaign is not a problem, the problem is the NEC and the Party campaigning against the Government. *My* fear is that we'll end up in Europe with Labour out of office after a Referendum. The NEC do have the right to dissent, but is it right to exercise it, to precipitate a constitutional clash, pushing the Labour Government out of office? We've had intolerance in the House of Commons, blackmail, bandwagoning to get MPs to sign the resolution. The Party can't survive this as a Government. If the Party machine is used, we'll be split from top to bottom. I don't ever recall a round robin like this being signed before an Executive. Mikardo fixed it to stop the debate and Michael engaged in a fake when he sent me to Brussels to renegotiate. He didn't want renegotiation, he wanted to come out.'

Michael interrupted, 'Prime Minister, I hope you'll notice who is using the rough language first.'

'Well, you *were* engaged in a fake,' Jim insisted.

'We all are at one time or another,' said Harold.

Of course, what Harold meant was that we all sometimes say things we might not mean for the sake of the Party.

Denis tried to lower the temperature of the debate. 'The solidarity of the Cabinet is what matters and the Party must be as tolerant. The bulk of the activists don't even think the Common Market is important. Ministers on the NEC must not establish a collective decision, it would be damaging, it would go to the Party Conference, and therefore I want to ask those Ministers concerned to withhold their support for anti-Market campaigns. It would split us deeply, worse than it did when we were in opposition.'

Willie Ross added, 'We are all collectively responsible for the well-being of the labour movement. I opposed the Referendum but the Leader is now being tied. We have no one else to rely on but Harold Wilson. We must limit the damage and drop the campaign against the Leader because the logic of it is only too clear. Ministers ought to be a bit busier in their own offices.'

Barbara said, 'The accusation then is about the press conference and that it is intolerable to campaign against the Cabinet.'

'I never said that,' Harold interrupted. 'I shall apply for legal aid if this sort of thing is said.'

'Well,' said Barbara, 'if it had gone the other way, I'm sure the pro-Marketeers would have campaigned for the Market. I have followed the guidelines, I refused to debate with Shirley Williams on television. But you're also saying we shouldn't embroil the Party. That's naïve, and the guidelines didn't cover the Party anyway.'

'I sent *instructions*, not guidelines, to Ministers when they were appointed last year, that they were always Ministers first.'

'Yes,' argued Barbara, 'and I have always given Cabinet priority. I didn't go for cheap popularity on the South African arms deal last year. But now we have divested ourselves of collective Cabinet responsibility on this issue, you can't neutralise the Party. After all, the Executive is the co-custodian of the Manifesto on the EEC. Are we to be silent? We were warned and hence the NEC was arranged to pronounce on the matter. There was bound to be a motion. You were asking us to accept automatically the view of the Cabinet. Should Ministers vote against their own views on the Executive? I have long thought that the Cabinet would accept the new terms, I have long thought the Conference would oppose it, but can't the NEC convey its view to the Conference? It is built into the situation. If the motion is withdrawn at the NEC, another would be carried.'

Harold replied, 'Well, we must have the Government view presented on the NEC, you're making light of the problems of Conference. Am I to be silent? Am I to be in opposition, not to attend? That is the problem that the Cabinet has got to consider.'

Eric Varley supported Harold. 'What is the Leader to do? His position is intolerable, you can't go to the Conference and humiliate the Leader. I very much hope that Ministers on the NEC will not let that arise. It could destroy the Party and some will think the EEC transcends other issues. What about the National Enterprise Board that Tony Benn cares about so much? And the British National Oil Company? All these things will be killed off. It would be serious if the NEC passes this resolution.'

Reg Prentice intervened. 'Well, Harold, you did ask for our view, and I think you've overreacted. You wanted a vigorous debate and that won't destroy the Labour Party; the Referendum is bound to lead to this sort of thing. I would prefer that there be no Conference vote; I think Harold should go to the Conference and make a speech and be defeated, and then campaign for his view against the Conference view. But Ministers on the NEC should not use the Party machine or Transport House staff.'

Harold Lever turned to Reg. 'Are you really saying that the Leader can campaign against the Conference?'

'Well,' said Reg, 'I'd prefer there were no votes at the special Conference, then there would be no Labour Party campaign.'

During coffee break, Harold slipped away up to his study. We met again at noon, without Harold, and with Ted in the chair.

Bob Mellish began by saying, 'We have underestimated the strength of the anti-Market vote. There are about 160 pro- and about 140 anti-Market MPs, and a split would damage the movement. The London CLPs are broadly anti-Market but they don't really care. We could make the Prime Minister look a laughing stock. I plead with the Ministers on the NEC not to use their power. And as for Harold, I hope he will not overreact because this is a test of his leadership.'

Crosland thought we'd got off to a bad start. 'The people in Grimsby don't worry and I shall persuade them not to take a view.'

Roy Jenkins said this situation was endemic in a referendum, which is why he was against it, but he didn't want to make too much of that. He didn't think the press conference or the Early Day Motion were important, but freedom for campaigning must be absolute. Ministers on the NEC had not considered these matters. The Leader's position would be impossible and we must have symmetry all round.

Roy Mason argued that the PLP was bitter because of the acts of a minority. It was all planned before Tuesday – the Motion, the blackmailing of MPs to sign, and the NEC round robin. As for television, Michael, Peter and Tony Benn had all been on, and it was a devious and clever conspiracy. 'Our comrades have been dishonest, they have jumped the gun, they planned a coup of the Party machine against the Cabinet. It will mean civil war, a nasty campaign, and it will bring in the International Socialists and the Communist Party to smash the Party. If there were any goodwill, the NEC resolution would be withdrawn. Obviously the Prime Minister and the Foreign Secretary would be ready to attend a genuine discussion on the NEC because people would actually listen to the argument. After all, three to four Cabinet Ministers have shifted their views since we came to power because of the cost of withdrawal. The PM must explain all this to the NEC and issue the paper written by the Foreign Office in order to convince them. Colleagues must salvage what they can.'

I said, 'I think the difficulties are inherent in this situation. There is a real division with sincerely held views on either side and, on the whole, we've been quite generous to each other. We've all behaved perfectly properly, we mustn't overreact. There are two ways in which the Party could be damaged: one, it is argued, is by pitching the Party against the Government, and the other would be for the Cabinet to try to impose silence and inactivity on the Executive and Conference. That is not on.'

'We're on the brink,' said Elwyn, 'the Prime Minister's near to resignation. It could be a disaster for social democracy if he went. The NEC resolution will tear the Party apart. Other Ministers might resign.'

'Well, if the Prime Minister resigns, we'd all be out anyway,' said Jim.

'Withdraw the motion then,' said Elwyn.

Michael suggested that the matter be deferred. The talks should go on for the next day or two, maybe Ron should put up a statement to supersede the NEC resolution.

Jim endorsed Michael's proposal for more time, and Ted said that it looked as if we were going to have to rely on Harold to get us off the hook once again.

It was, without doubt, the most extraordinary Cabinet meeting I have ever attended. The comparisons with 1931 just stare you in the face – Harold Wilson trying to drive us into a coalition Government with the Tories, without actually resigning from the Labour Party and the Labour Government. But we have made a very big impact. Harold will now have to cool off, and then we'll have to help him to adjust his position on the Market because he's made a big boob, a very big boob.

Friday 21 March
To Meriden in the West Midlands. There was no one to meet us at first
because they were all so busy, which was good. There are about 170
people working there now, at a flat rate pay of £50 a week – a dream
for them after eighteen months of privation. They have 2000 applicants
to work at what is £20 below the going rate in Coventry. No supervision,
and no clocking in. They have elected organisers in each shop and
they've managed to cut out a lot of the paperwork.

Sunday 23 March
We had our first press conference of the 'Dissenting Ministers' at St
Ermine's, in a room crammed with lights and TV cameras. Peter read
our statement, and then there were twenty minutes of questions about
the Labour Party until I intervened. 'Look, we're trying to run a
campaign on the Market, not on the Labour Party.' So then we got
some good questions on the Market, and we were pleased with the way
it went.

Monday 24 March
Ron Vaughan, my driver, told me that tonight, Enoch Powell was
leaving the House of Commons by the Ministers' entrance where all
the Government cars are lined up. One of the Government drivers was
a black man, and as he saw Enoch he said, 'Please, keep us out, Mr
Powell,' Enoch put on a huge smile and walked into the darkness.

Tuesday 25 March
Cabinet, and Denis introduced a package of proposals for a £1,000
million cut in spending. He gave all sorts of reasons, wage inflation, the
economic situation, our ability to borrow, the need to switch into
exports, and so on. He said he had to have a decision today.

Tony Crosland said that this was the most important paper we had
had since we'd been in office. There was a smell of 1966 and the cuts
package. He was against a decision now, what was the object of it? It
couldn't improve the balance of payments this year, it couldn't moderate wage claims, there was enough slack in the economy to provide
the shift. The PSBR was muddled between capital expenditure and
resources, the political effects would be traumatic and half the Manifesto would go down the drain, including rent controls, transport
subsidies, land policy and pollution. The paper had been written by
Treasury officials, and Defence had got away with murder.

Peter thought the situation was worse than at any time since 1931
and that the painful decisions we would face were due to the OPEC
countries' increases. Denis's total sum was right, but the composition
of the cuts was a different matter.

I said that I appreciated that Denis had problems to deal with on our behalf but the way in which the issues had been presented to us was totally unacceptable. If we agreed, we'd be abandoning measures to which we were committed through the Social Contract. Secondly, it was a massive deflationary step and what Denis was saying was that we couldn't get back to full employment in the lifetime of this Parliament.

Thirdly, the package would force us to cut back productive capacity, having already lost 7 per cent in manufacturing over the last few years at great cost to the Exchequer. It would lead to a sharp fall in investment, and with a slump, this would worsen the investment blight leading to cutbacks in factory re-equipment. It would be political suicide.

Roy Jenkins saw no alternative to the strategy Denis had proposed. My strategy was, in Roy's view, a protectionist one. We had to face the wages issue and remove our Victorian inhibitions about it.

Jim agreed with Denis and Roy, it was a re-run of 1966, and he was therefore not surprised at the paper. He rejected a statutory income policy, but wages had broken through and they would have to be stopped elsewhere. No Government could get policies through with inflation at this level – 'be it a Labour Government, a Tory Government, a Maoist Government or a Benn Government'.

On the news tonight. Harold was reported to have sent a minute to all Ministers warning them against any activities on the NEC that were incompatible with their membership of the Cabinet.

One other interesting little tit-bit today. When Gvishiani, Deputy-Chairman of the Soviet Committee on Science and Technology, came here some time ago, among other things, he recommended me to read Engels's 'On Authority' which he promised to send to me. Well, this evening at a reception at Lancaster House a member of the Soviet Embassy gave me an envelope containing a copy of the article in English.

It was fascinating – it would have made Trotsky's hair stand on end. Engels argued that if you're a socialist you can't ally yourself with anarchists and others who are in favour of freedom in a capitalist context, because in a revolution you are seizing power, and when you've seized power you've got to prevent the old class getting it back again, which means even more authority than existed under capitalism. You've got to have authority in order to build and preserve socialism. With hardly any amendments, it could be printed in the *Daily Telegraph* today. It illustrated how establishments in all countries under all systems of Government have a similar view of authority.

Wednesday 26 March

The papers this morning were full of the great split on the NEC and
Wilson's intended minute to Ministers on the National Executive. This
is his war of nerves against us, or so he thinks.

The NEC was held at 10 and we devoted all morning to the special
Conference arrangements.

I said that I very much hoped we could make progress. We were
coming together, but I hoped we weren't going to be influenced by the
press which was universally hostile to us.

As I might have guessed, Harold's mind was already working on
how to present this in the most favourable light, and by the time the
evening papers came out, it was a great victory for Wilson. He'd
'halted the Market rot', he'd got campaigning deleted, he'd frightened
Ministers into doing what he wanted. Well, these paper victories are
useless to him because they only demonstrate his weakness.

Thursday 27 March

Don Ryder came at 9 with his report on British Leyland. He said there
would be no redundancies; the company would be turned into four
divisions; it would need £200 million Government equity (giving the
Government a 65 per cent holding) and £500 million worth of loans
(which I will query). The company will have to produce a new Mini
by 1980.

After that I had a runaround on the *Scottish Daily News*. I had told
my colleagues that the Action Committee were £40,000 short and
recommended that the Government put in the difference, but I had
had no favourable response at all. I asked Roy Williams to ring the
Prime Minister to fix for me to see him this afternoon to discuss the
NEB appointments and the *Scottish Daily News*. Roy set that up but
Harold later cancelled the meeting. So I was just about to send a bitter
minute around to the Prime Minister and everybody else saying, 'You
have now killed the *Scottish Daily News*, when I thought I had better
ring Allister Mackie first. I apologised for not succeeding and he said,
'I never thought you would. Maxwell is going to put up the extra
money.' I literally leapt for joy.

At 3.30 Bob Wright of the AUEW and Jack Service came to discuss
Ferranti. They said the Ferranti brothers, or Basil at least, had tried to
persude the unions to agree to just a 25 per cent Government holding
so that the family interests in the firm could be preserved. In fact, we
are going to have to go up to 75 per cent or 85 per cent holding as a
result of the need to put in large sums of money and to value the shares
correctly.

Friday 28 March

I dictated a few words of support for the SDN Action Committee for their mass meeting at 1 today. When my message was read out, apparently there was a standing ovation for it. I must say that brought tears to my eyes.

The North Vietnamese have captured Da Nang, are moving down towards Saigon, and Phnom Penh is about to fall. The whole of American policy in the Far East and in the Middle East appears to be in tatters.

Thursday 3 April

My fiftieth birthday. Quite a landmark. I have found the last three or four years very satisfying and I get a lot of pleasure out of getting older. I have got a marvellous job, I don't worry so much and I enjoy life.

Sunday 6 April

The *News of the World* carried extracts from John Stonehouse's memoirs. There were huge photographs of John and of me. John wrote: 'I was the fall guy for Wedgie Benn,' and described at length how he had had to cope with the awful mess I had left at the Post Office.

I have never really trusted him and I thought he was up to some funny business. After 1970, when he was not put on the Front Bench as a Shadow Minister, he went in for a lot of business deals which have been fully chronicled, and everybody who knew Stonehouse felt there was something suspect about him. Out of friendship I argued most strongly in Cabinet that we ought to send somebody to Australia to try to persuade him to come home. Now my desire to bring him home has somewhat diminished.

Monday 7 April

At 12 I saw Sir Antony Part who is back following his heart attack. He is doing a quiet day from 10 to 4 and then going off for a fortnight's holiday next month. I went over a few things – he was particularly anxious that I shouldn't use Department of Industry notepaper to write personal replies on the Common Market in response to letters addressed to the Department. It was a piffling point. I shall continue to use the stationery.

Then we went over the progress of the Industry Bill, aircraft and shipbuilding nationalisation, the Ryder Report on British Leyland, and the economic situation. He thought there would be a great crisis in July because although exports were holding up at the moment, when wage increases worked their way through, exports would be uncompetitive. He is preparing for the economic squeeze or statutory wages policy which he thinks Healey will have to introduce. I let it pass.

Harold opened the European debate and made a low-key speech.

At a dinner for industrialists, economists and trade unionists, Jack Jones told me, 'Don't bother about the House of Commons during the Common Market campaign, just campaign in the country.' Jack, Michael Foot, Harold and Ron Hayward make up the quadrumvirate that runs the Party.

It is interesting that Mrs Thatcher is doing the dirty work on Europe for big business in Britain, Harold is doing the dirty work for Mrs Thatcher and Michael Foot is doing the dirty work for Harold. So there is a complete conspiracy actually not to work hard to get us out, not to speak with passion or enthusiasm.

At dinner we discussed industrial democracy and management and there was a great passion for change and for the devolution of responsibility. What is clear is that people on the Left in the Party see all this as an instrument for socialism and jobs, while the technocrats see it as a way of improving efficiency and profitability. It was a better gathering than most IDV Committees – well worthwhile.

Afterwards Joe Ashton, Frances Morrell and I went back to my room at the House and had a brief word. Frances, who is thinking seriously about who is going to lead the Party in future, said it was essential that when people look back on this period, I shouldn't be seen to have rocked the boat.

Came home and Caroline took the same view as Frances. 'Don't get into a position of defiance. Don't give the press the chance to build your campaign up as an attack on Harold. Just organise.'

Tuesday 8 April

Cabinet had been hurriedly summoned to discuss the date of the Referendum. Just before I went in, Michael took me aside and told me that Harold had called him in yesterday to say he didn't want Ministers to vote at the end of the debate on the Common Market re-negotiation.

The 'Dissenting Ministers' were depleted because Barbara was in America and Peter was still in the Gulf. We spent half an hour discussing the date of the Referendum, and in the end it was agreed that Roy would ask the national returning officer to look at it.

'Well,' said Harold, 'there is one other matter that I must raise and I think perhaps the best thing is for me to quote from a letter from the Lord President [Ted Short] that it is "inconceivable that Ministers could vote against the Government in the House of Commons because the position of the Prime Minister would be impossible." I really felt I must bring this to the attention of the Cabinet.'

'You will put us in a very difficult position and create great animosity,' Michael told him.

Eric Varley supported Michael and said it would provoke a great crisis in the Party.

'There is a crisis' said Jim, 'and it is a crisis of miscalculation. I miscalculated the number of Dissenting Ministers. Apparently there are now thirty, forty or fifty. I assumed it would be much smaller. I don't think you can stop Ministers voting, but we should urge on them the wisdom of not voting.'

Harold responded, 'In the reshuffle after the Referendum, I shall judge people on the basis of whether they have behaved in a spirit of comradeship. I won't have frivolous voting – people who vote in a particular way because it's popular or because they're under pressure from local parties.'

'The Cabinet is agreed on the way we handle this situation,' I said. 'First, that there be a Referendum; second, that there be an agreement to differ; and third, that we all accept the Referendum decision. I agreed with Michael Foot that we must vote; we should now modify the guidelines to allow Ministers to speak in the House. There ought to be an absolute symmetry between the National Executive, the Conference, the Government and the House of Commons. We have already changed the guidelines to allow people to appear on platforms with others, and when Roy appeared with Reggie Maudling and Willie Whitelaw, which I strongly supported, I don't think it did us any harm.'

This caused an uproar.

'There is no parallel at all between the Conference and the House of Commons,' said Harold, 'and I should take very gravely a breach of the guidelines. It is quite unheard of for a Government not to have the majority support of its own party.'

John Silkin agreed. 'We can't have Ministers speaking against the Government in the House. It would be a shambles.' That was him climbing off the anti-Market bandwagon.

Bob Mellish said, 'Well, if you have a three-line whip on Wednesday, I can only tell you that four of my Whips would resign immediately.'

Harold told Bob that his great achievement was that he had led a Cabinet that was split down the middle. Everybody laughed, but it is true.

Roy said, 'I don't think you can stop a vote but I recall that during the Common Market debate in 1971* the people who advocated a three-line whip were Michael and Tony, and when I defied it, they both stood against me for the deputy-leadership.' But is was clear by the end that there will be a free vote despite a lot of arm twisting.

* This crucial episode in Labour's history is described in my diaries for 1968–72, *Office Without Power*.

Lunch with Dick Briginshaw, General Secretary of NATSOPA. He's taken on an air of respectability since Harold made him a peer. He told me that Harold had promised him a job at the NEB, and he described how he had foiled attempts by the *Daily Mail* and the *Daily Express* to print smear stories against Labour during the Election simply by threatening to stop the presses.

One last thing. I heard from Margaret Jackson, that John Harris – Lord Harris who is Minister of State in the Home Office – is actually going to Lincoln to speak for Dick Taverne's pro-Market organisation against Margaret herself. It is incredible, but I'm sure it won't appear in the papers.

Wednesday 9 April
Went into the House to hear Eric Heffer make his speech against the Common Market in defiance of Harold's guidelines to Ministers.

At 10 the Division bell rang and I went into the No Lobby. Later, I heard that there was an overwhelming majority for the negotiated terms. But the number of Labour MPs voting in the No Lobby exceeded Labour MPs (including Ministers) voting in the Aye Lobby.

Just as I left I heard that Eric Heffer had been sacked. Apparently Harold sent him a letter, without even seeing him first, saying he had informed the Queen that Eric was no longer a Minister. I issued a short statement which I cleared with Eric:

> I greatly regret the dismissal of Eric Heffer. He has worked hard and loyally for the Labour Government over this last year and his contribution as a Minister in the Department of Industry has been outstanding. He has served the Labour movement faithfully and well.

Friday 11 April
I went with Michael Meacher to the Free Trade Hall in Manchester for a public meeting on the Referendum. There were about 2500 people there and it was one of the best meetings I have ever attended. That great tide of opinion cannot be held back now, of that I am sure, because this time we have espoused the issue of our national identity. The Tories have thrown it away because they have lost confidence in Britain as an independent nation. But we have not, and our people have not.

The sleeper back to London was cancelled so I arranged to meet Michael at the Midland Hotel where a car had been laid on to bring us back, but Michael didn't turn up. We waited forty-five minutes, then left without him. On the motorway heading back, a police car flashed alongside and stopped us, and a burly sergeant got out and said, 'Mr Wedgwood Benn? There's a Mr Meacher in Manchester looking for you.' The police took us to a cafeteria on the motorway to wait for Michael; there were Hell's Angels and the motorbike brigade, and old men looking lost. Michael finally arrived in a police car and we got to London at 3.30 am.

Sunday 13 April
To Glasgow for a great gathering of the Scottish Anti-Market Movement at Norman Buchan's house, to discuss how to handle the campaign.

Frank McElhone took me to the *Scottish Daily News* works in Albion Street where we met Allister Mackie, Bob Maxwell, all the workers and their families and the press and television. Bob Maxwell said they needed Government advertising and some scoops to get them launched. The reception was quite overwhelming – it's impossible to convey the goodwill there.

Tuesday 15 April
Part told me that the Department had recommended Ralph Bateman, President of the CBI, for a knighthood, direct to Number 10, without going through me.

'Why?' I asked.

'We thought you might not like it and in any case Bateman has a statutory right to a knighthood after a year as President of the CBI.'

'Well, you should have put it to me first.'

'There is still time to complain to Number 10 if you don't like it, only do so quickly.'

They are so bloody cheeky. I have no intention of complaining to Number 10 but I shall certainly let word out – any discussion in advance of a knighthood kills it off.

I drove to see Claudia Flanders – I heard that Michael died today.

Thursday 17 April
At 7, we had the Dissenting Ministers' meeting. Barbara was in the chair, bossy but brilliant. John Silkin, Peter Shore, Tommy Balogh, Judith Hart and, what I would call our permanent officials, Dick Clements, Frances Morrell, Tony Banks and Jack Straw were present. Barbara began by coordinating all the meetings and issuing a list of who was speaking where.

We discussed organisation before coming to my paper, 'A Strategy for Withdrawal'. Peter had doubts about whether it was a practical proposal and wondered if it would confuse everything.

Barbara was marvellous. 'Look, this is a piece of black propaganda.

What we are doing is establishing the credibility of an alternative strategy.'

In the end, we overcame Peter's doubts and re-worded it slightly.

I had a letter today from the man who has been writing to me over the last eight months saying 'You have eight months to live' then 'You have seven months to live', and so on. Two weeks ago he told me I had seven weeks and today he asked if I had written my will, since I only had a few days left. Roy brought the letter in and said the matter had been handed over to the police.

Saturday 19 April

In my red box was a note from the Post Office, submitting next year's stamps for my approval. They did include trade union stamps which I had insisted on last year, after a hell of a row. But a request for a stamp celebrating the bicentenary of the American Declaration of Independence was turned down. The reasons were explained thus:

> Although the bicentenary of the Declaration of Independence by the thirteen American colonies has support from the Foreign and Commonwealth Office, it is our view that this subject is not suitable for inclusion in the special programme. However it might be approached in design terms, there would be a danger that ordinary people would criticise the issue as celebrating a defeat. Moreover, there could well be a feeling in those former British colonies which achieved independence later and without bloodshed that, whilst for instance we did not mark the centenary of the British North America Act of 1867, we should seem to honour those who rebelled.

Well, if that were published it would make a laughing stock of the Post Office. So I sent a letter back saying there *had* to be a commemorative stamp.

Also in my box was a note from the European Office of my Department advising me that, when putting the case for financial support for British Leyland to the Commission in Brussels, I should say it was only 'an act of public ownership' and the provision of ordinary loans to allow the company to proceed. This is simply not true. The purpose in this case is not acquisition. I sent a note back:

> I have read the proposal you make for notifying the Commission of the Government's decision – when it is reached – to support British Leyland. No doubt it is the best way of slipping this through with the minimum of fuss before the Referendum. But I fear that we shall not be telling the Commission the truth about our motives or methods. The Ryder report is intended (a) to subsidise a British motor manufacturer that would otherwise collapse in order to preserve jobs and capacity that would otherwise be replaced by imports from the EEC and elsewhere; (b) to provide long-term

loan capital at non-commercial rates in order to re-equip and improve capacity; (c) to make British Leyland Motor Company more competitive in the EEC with Fiat, Renault, Volkswagen, and other car manufacturers than would otherwise be the case if market forces operated; (d) to acquire public equity as a by-product of the above objectives.

Thus on my analysis, the support for BLMC will be a clear breach of Articles 92–94.

I am not suggesting that my statement should be sent to the Commission, but I want to put on record my view that membership of the EEC – with its unacceptable interference in our national interest – requires us to seek to mislead them. Please proceed as you propose.

In a speech to the Young Conservatives at the Central Hall, Westminster, Heath described me, Foot and Shore as 'the extremist witches in a coven in Transport House'.

Sunday 20 April
The Times had a leader a few days ago on sovereignty, in which it differentiated between sovereignty as influence for our leaders – which would be improved by our going into Europe – and sovereignty as the right to make our own laws by democratic means, which it identified as the Marxist position. So the instigators of the social revolution which begins to make an impact on the structure of power through strong trade union organisation and the ballot box are denounced as Marxists or Communists. There is a limit beyond which those in power will not accept real change.

How you cope with this, is difficult. If you come out of the Government, it may mean coming out of the Labour Party as well and trying to push ideas from the fringe. But then you are dismissed as a fringe politician without a platform. And why should you risk that for policies which the labour movement through its democratic organisations of the Conference and even the PLP, doesn't actually support?

I am sure the thing to do is to stay in, to argue the case inside, although at the same time argue it outside too, not by attacking individuals in the Cabinet but by launching clear alternative policies and maintaining a clear alternative analysis. Open politics is possible, but the pressures are phenomenal. When you look at the way the BBC handles all news in terms of Communists in Cambodia, Communists in Rhodesia and South Africa, Communists in Portugal and now Communists in Britain – everything is presented as a conspiracy.

The Tories now think that Wilson, Healey and Callaghan are doing their work so well that they don't want a coalition Government. Better to let the Labour Party do their work for them. But if the Labour Government needed support from the Opposition benches, which is what's happening on Europe and the Budget, they might be prepared to come in under Labour leadership. All these various processes may have to be gone through before any real and necessary changes can be made.

Willie Whitelaw has made a statement that the Tories would not feel bound by a negative Referendum vote and Frances advised me to involve Mrs Thatcher over this. So at 1.30 I rang the Press Association and dictated this letter, embargoed until 5 am.

Dear Mrs Thatcher,

Mr Whitelaw has predicted a constitutional crisis if the British people vote No in the Referendum.

As the Labour Party is pledged to accept the result, this could only happen if the Conservative Party in Parliament used their votes to block the people's decision.

Will you please – as Leader of the Conservative Party – say whether or not the Conservative Party in Parliament will consider itself bound by a majority vote for British withdrawal from the Common Market?

Everyone is entitled to have a clear – and immediate – answer to this question.

Yours,
Tony Benn

Monday 21 April
At 10.30 I went to Congress House for the meeting of the TUC-Labour Party Liason Committee. There were about a hundred media people there with TV cameras and microphones, jostling and pushing like a lot of vultures; they thought there was going to be a hell of a row between the Labour Party and the trade union representatives.

'Is the Social Contract dead? What will happen!' they shouted.

'We're old friends,' I said. 'It'll be a good meeting.' And so it was.

From there to the House at 2.30 for Questions. It was exciting and enjoyable with a lot of knockabout but I did deal with the Common Market questions. I said the Tories' noise was all just a cover-up for their failure to answer the simple question, 'would they abide by the result of the Referendum?'

Had a brief word with Michael Heseltine. 'Look, we want your help in getting the Industry Bill out of Committee by the middle of May. Can you do it?'

'It depends on what is said about disclosure in the light of the Prime Minister's statement recently.'

'I can't negotiate about the Bill.'

'Well, that worries us,' he said.

Tuesday 22 April

The papers this morning reported Mrs Thatcher's reply to my letter, saying that the Tories would not be bound by the Referendum, basing herself on what Harold Wilson had said about a Referendum not being binding on Parliament.

The only item on the Cabinet agenda was British Leyland. Denis used the Ryder report as a basis for the discussion. He said Stokes and John Barber, the Managing Director, had to go; market penetration especially in Western Europe was the key; the project would cost £2.8 billion by 1982, half of which would be generated internally; the profit estimates were uncertain and the scheme would involve £1.4 billion of public money; productivity was appalling and labour relations were bad, and there would have to be a reduction of overstaffing. Motorcars had an uncertain future but he thought this was the only feasible plan.

I endorsed Denis's comments. The Ryder Committee had done well. A million jobs were at stake and other industries were involved. We had to be cautious, get the cooperation of workers and have proper corporate planning, but the importance of it was that this was the first example of our industrial policy at work – it was Rolls Royce, without a collapse involved.

After Cabinet I heard that Thatcher and Wilson had had a huge clash over whether the Government should be bound by the result of the Referendum. Harold had insisted that the Government would accept the result, no matter how small the majority. Thatcher had said she wouldn't necessarily abide by the result.

I sat and talked to Joe Ashton. He told me that Dennis Skinner and others had asked when I was going to make my bid against Harold. Right-wingers were saying that I was so active that it must mean that I was going to challenge Harold.

'For God's sake, Joe, damp that down. I'm doing a marvellously interesting job and I've got the Referendum on my plate.'

'Well, don't forget that if you lose the Referendum and we stay in Europe and have a million unemployed in November, Harold will have some questions to answer.'

I said I knew that.

Mary Jay rang to discuss the follow-up to 'Labour Against the Market' which someone suggested should be given the acronym LAMB – Labour Against the Market Bastards. I said it should be BEEF – Britain for Exiting from this Execrable Federation, or MUTON – Millions Unwilling to Take away Our National Independence!

Wednesday 23 April
Ruth Khama, the wife of Seretse Khama, President of Botswana, came
to dinner at the House with her twin boys Tshekedi and Anthony who
is my godson. Stephen, June, Melissa and Caroline were there. I put
them in the Gallery for a while. The two boys, sixteen, are both six foot
three and Melissa got on with them well, though she found them very
reactionary.

Thursday 24 April
The most beautiful spring day and I walked through the park in the
sunshine. The tulips were out and the waters of the lake were perfectly
calm.

At Cabinet, Harold announced that he and Jim were going to be
away for a couple of weeks and he hoped nothing untoward would
happen. The Referendum campaign was going well and he hoped we
would attack the Tories rather than each other.

I walked out with Jim. He had read an article by Peter Jay* called
'Making Sense of Mr Benn' in which I had been described as speaking
for the Cambridge Group, notably Nicky Kaldor and Francis Cripps.
For the first time, Jim was showing signs of interest. 'Look, if you're
going to get all these investments, it's got to come from consumption.
How do you bring consumption down?'

Harold made a statement in the House about Leyland. It was quietly
received. Heath made formidable interventions, as did John Davies
and Peter Walker, and there is clearly a revolt in the Tory Party against
the Thatcher leadership. But somehow the whole thing left a sour taste
and Harold didn't know all the answers.

At 7 to the 'Dissenting Ministers' meeting. We considered the proposal that we should appeal to the Commonwealth Prime Ministers'
meeting in Jamaica not to join in any welcome of our continued
membership of the Common Market, on the grounds that the labour
movement which supported their fight for independence would expect
them not to interfere during the Referendum when we were were trying
to determine *our* future and trying to maintain *our* independence. As
Stephen said later, it was 'Britain as the last colony in the British
Empire' argument.

Friday 25 April
I learned from Ron Vaughan that Harold Wilson had arranged that
in future all former Prime Ministers were to have their own car and

---

* Son of Douglas Jay, married to James Callaghan's daughter, Margaret (marriage
later dissolved); economics editor of *The Times*, 1967–77, appointed Ambassador to
Washington, 1977.

chauffeur for life. That's never happened before and indeed until 1970 even the Leader of the Opposition didn't have a car and a chauffeur. It was Heath who agreed that for Harold. Of course now Harold has returned the favour, but he has also given a car and driver for life to Home and Macmillan. The drivers in the car pool are saying, 'The crafty bugger must be preparing to get out, and then *he'll* have a car for life.' That's the conclusion to be drawn, because when he does go, he'll never be made Leader of the Opposition again.

Caroline told me that she went with Ruth Khama to see Seretse at the Botswana High Commission. Seretse said that the Common Market was not in the interests of Botswana because they couldn't sell their beef to Britain as they used to, but he realised that the Foreign Office was putting tremendous pressure on the Commonwealth Prime Ministers to endorse Britain's membership of the EEC.

Saturday 26 April
To the Sobell Centre in Islington for the special Labour Party Conference on the Common Market.

Harold Wilson made a half hour speech, saying that he had never been a European, that he had always been a Commonwealth man, but he thought it was in our interests to stay in. It was a flat, dull speech which must have discouraged even the pro-Marketeers.

The speeches that did make an impact were by Roy Jenkins who blustered and bullied but was passionately pro, and by John Mackintosh [MP for Berwick and East Lothian] who made the only really good pro speech by lashing out all around him. He got a cheer as a result; if you are going to be in this game you've got to believe in it.

Clive Jenkins made a funny speech about the lack of crematoria in Luxembourg which means that bodies have to go to Belgium to be burned. They are counted as raw materials, so VAT is charged on them when they go to the crematorium. Then when the ashes are brought back there is a customs duty on imported manufactures!

Jim Callaghan made a mediocre speech. He was very testy and he shouted 'You clot' to somebody who interrupted him.

Michael Foot wound up with a brilliant speech. He really exceeded himself, quoting Aneurin Bevan, and Thomas Rainsborough at the Putney debates of 1647. He got a standing ovation from half the Conference and we won by almost two to one – 3.9 million to 1.7 million. We not only won the vote but we also won the argument.

Sunday 27 April
Heath had an article in the *Sunday Express* entitled, 'Are you voting for a Communist take-over?' supported by a column which reminded readers that when the Nazis threatened Britain, there were some in

Britain who supported them. 'Could anyone really be sure, if the Communists threatened Britain, whose side Anthony Wedgwood Benn would be on?' I should think this is probably libellous, but I shan't take any action.

Monday 28 April

The press are having a nervous breakdown over the Common Market. Anthony Shrimsley wrote in the *Daily Mail* that the right wing of the Cabinet is determined that I should be dismissed, and David Wood in *The Times* says, 'Mr Benn Tries on The Mantle of Leadership.'

Sir Monty Finniston, Chairman of British Steel Corporation, has described Government policy as an abortion. He believes that if we go into the Common Market without investment the Germans will knock hell out of us; but if we stay out the Japs will knock hell out of us. He said he could produce 37,000,000 tons of steel with 50,000 workers, which would mean 170,000 redundancies. He also feels it is quite wrong to give money to Meriden (which has nothing to do with him at all). There was going to be a crunch on wages and the crunch would come in steel. He wanted 20,000 redundancies by September – totally irresponsible, and I sent him a letter saying as much.

Bristol Channel Repairers, who have been running a £100,000 campaign against my nationalisation of ship repairing, have now taken to printing my private address in their advertisements suggesting people write to me or come and see me, and two people turned up today. The possibility that I will be shot or the family harmed can't be absolutely ruled out.

Tuesday 29 April

At 2.30 I had a meeting with the Department on planning agreements. For the first time, we really challenged the idea of the profitability principle for the NEB. I said that the whole market principle was becoming a nonsense; in some nationalised industries, the market principle was set aside to finance high technology; in other industries to finance low technology, that is to say steel closures; in others, employment or social considerations were paramount. Wouldn't it be better to adopt the principle of common sense?

The officials were completely taken aback but the truth is they can't defend the market economy any more – it does not produce the goods, or solve the problems or get investment, and this is what I am trying to get through to them, though as yet with no effect.

Wednesday 30 April

A journalist from the *Daily Mail* turned up at home and asked Caroline how Joshua was in hospital. She said, 'Joshua is not in hospital,' –

thank God, he was home at the time, so she knew nothing had happened to him at school.

Then the reporters went to the school and asked the same question. They went to Hilary's house, and even tried to get in touch with Stephen at Keele University. It was hysterical harassment.

I flew up to Newcastle with some members of the Private Office and we were met by one of the Boilermaker's Union executive, and taken to the Friends' Meeting House where about 100 full-time officials and shop stewards from the main shipbuilding areas were gathered.

Danny McGarvey, the President, presented me with a large scroll admitting me as Honorary Member of the Amalgamated Society of Boilermakers, Shipwrights, Blacksmiths, and Structural Workers, a very old craft union whose origins go back to 1839, and with the scroll, a leather-bound facsimile of the 1839 rule book. Danny said, 'Only given to those who have been thirty years in the union. I'm hoping to get mine next week!' I was very touched, and I replied, 'Mr President, fellow members of the Society, your predecessor Ted Hill began as a boilermaker and ended up in the Lords – I've done it the other way round.'

Thursday 1 May

Caught the end of the London May Day march, and came home to find that there had been further harassment of the family over the story of Joshua in hospital. I believe it is the eighth time the *Daily Mail* have said that one of our children was in hospital after an accident. So I rang the paper and spoke to the night News Editor. I complained about the harassment and told him none of my children were in hospital. I asked for the Editor's number but he refused, saying the Editor couldn't be disturbed in the night. I told him I had been disturbed in the night. He rang later and told me that the Editor had asked me to ring back in the morning, and refused to give me the Editor's number, and I told him I would call in the police if the harassment continued.

Saturday 3 May

Caroline and I got the train to Newcastle for a May Day meeting. I spoke for forty-five minutes and then a group played a calypso about the nationalisation of the shipbuilding industry, written by a worker at Swan Hunter's yard at Wallsend who is known as Ripyard Kuddling. It was wonderful. Afterwards, we talked to shipyard workers who gave me a copy of their plan for workers' control in the yards. They told me they were beginning to attract the interest of younger professional management whose future lay with the industry and they were frustrated at the possibility of a delay in implementing the Bill. I tried to reassure them.

At 10.30 the Special Branch drove us to the Swallow Hotel and they told us that the International Socialists brought an action in Sunderland Magistrates Court over the fact that they were prevented from selling their paper *Socialist Worker* in the streets, which meant that, as no newsagent would take the paper, they couldn't get their message across. Apparently they won their case. The Special Branch told us openly that they keep a close eye on political groups.

Sunday 4 May
Peter Walker attacked me today, saying I had the Prime Minister under my control and was the most dangerous man in Britain. I had taken Britain further towards socialism then anyone in the whole history of the Labour Party. Although I tend to brush these things off, it will make Harold hopping mad, which is a shame when I was making such progress.

Ted Heath and Reg Prentice appeared at a pro-EEC rally in Trafalgar Square today. Reg warmed up for Heath who went on to attack Michael Foot and Peter Shore in Reg Prentice's presence. Amazing!

Monday 5 May
At 7.30, I went to discuss the guillotine on the Industry Bill with Ted Short, Bob Mellish, Patricia Llewelyn-Davies who is Captain of the Gentlemen at Arms [Labour Chief Whip in the Lords] and others. She said if we guillotined this it would be harder to get it through the Lords and we mustn't hurry them. I said we must get the Bill through by the end of July but they argued that it was not necessary, since the session could be extended.

Here we are in 1975, contemplating the capacity of the House of Lords, which is full of hereditary or appointed peers, to stop us from implementing our policy. The thing is an absolute scandal. Bob Mellish saying, 'My beloved Tony, you have to understand . . .' None of them gives a damn whether the Bill goes through or not. They can get the Prevention of Terrorism Bill through in a day because it's 'urgent', but socialism is never urgent.

Wednesday 7 May
There was a lead story this morning in the *Daily Telegraph* by their political correspondent Harry Boyne, who is in Jamaica covering Harold Wilson at the Commonwealth heads of government meeting. The piece was called 'Wilson to Clip Benn's Wings,' and was clearly the result of an intimate talk to Harold. It said when the Prime Minister returned he was going to take over the NEB, impose guidelines, stop the Industry Bill from being effective, and so on.

Len Murray, Jack Jones and Hugh Scanlon were missing from the

NEDC – only Alf Allen, Sid Greene and David Basnett were there representing the TUC. We discussed a paper put in by NEDC dealing with investment: it called for phasing out price controls, higher dividends, more cash for the company sector, a more responsible role for the banks, wages to be kept down, and so on.

At the end I told them I thought the conclusions were very disappointing. A great deal of money had been put into the company sector in the last two Budgets but investment was still slumping; we had to help firms in trouble by channelling money from the pension funds. This was a deep crisis and the Government had to move towards an agreed policy.

Denis turned on me and got full support from the CBI, Dick Marsh saying, 'Pension funds have got to be put where they're most profitable.'

'Like works of art?' I said, which is what British Rail have invested in.

'Well, we live in a capitalist society,' said Dick, 'and if you get the best return on a work of art, that's where you should put your money.'

I said, 'I think that is completely irresponsible, unless we're aiming to be the Sothebys of the world and earn our living that way.'

Shirley Williams advocated a shift away from confrontational politics. We could never make up our minds for two years at a time; we had to agree on the nature of the mixed economy we wanted. We should not have to do this 'damned minuet' every two to three years. She was saying, in effect, that democracy is incompatible with successful industry. What we could do in terms of industrial policy would be limited to what the Opposition would let us do.

'I agree with Shirley,' said Denis. 'We want a broad consensus between political parties. There may be a role for the Opposition in the NEDC.'

As Denis was about to wind up, I said, 'Before what Shirley said, and what you have taken up, Chancellor, enters into the mythology of the NEDC, I would like to register the fact that I profoundly disagree with the idea that there should be some kind of agreement on industrial policy. To take industry out of politics would amount to a coalition and if you get all the top people together, all you would do is open up the divisions between the Establishment and the people as a whole.'

'I absolutely deny that I was calling for a coalition,' Shirley said.

Thursday 8 May

I went to the House and was just in time to hear a Question put on the 'row' between Shirley Williams and me at Neddy. I was sitting looking solemn and Ted Short replied, 'I can assure the House that there is no disagreement between my two Right Honourable friends.' Well, I couldn't help laughing and I tried to hide it but hundreds of

Daily Telegraph, 9 May 1975.

Tory fingers pointed at me. Ted looked round at me and I nodded my head, trying to keep a straight face. He went on, 'No disagreement about the undesirability of a coalition,' which was followed by loud laughter. Then he announced the guillotine on the Industry Bill and there was a predictable skirmish.

Friday 9 May
Don Ryder telephoned me to tell me that, at the last minute, the Ferranti brothers had asked for contracts: one at £25,000 a year for ten years, the others at £20,000 a year for ten years, and they wanted us to pay. I told Don that I wouldn't do it and that I wouldn't be having them as Chairman and Deputy-Chairman anyway. They would be ordinary executive directors.

Saturday 10 May
To Barnsley Civic Hall to address a thousand delegates representing 60,000 Yorkshire miners at an anti-Common Market rally. Arthur Scargill chaired the meeting and made a powerful speech – the first time I have heard him publicly. Douglas Jay was there making his first speech to a miners' meeting – incredible for a sixty-year-old Labour politician and former President of the Board of Trade.

I am getting a lot of interesting (and abusive) cards and letters at the moment. A Mr Steward wrote to me:

I am 67 years of age and I have witnessed during my lifetime all kinds of press propaganda against politicians who happen to be objectionable to the media. I remember the slanders against Keir Hardie, Ramsay MacDonald, A.J. Cook, Aneurin Bevan (they took photographs through his letter box); even Harold Wilson has been subjected to the same treatment. The current attitude by the media against you exceeds all previous records. I am writing to assure you that all decent-minded people are disgusted by the manner in which the press and TV have attacked you. An *Evening News* headline recently was surely libellous. Can this be submitted to the Press Council? I can assure you that you have the support of ordinary working people. We may not alway, have entirely agreed with your proposals, but by God, after this kind of treatment from the media, we will back you a hundred per cent in everything you are doing.

> With kind regards
> Yours sincerely,
> W. E. Steward

The press is contemplating my dismissal at the moment and hinting that I might be given the DHSS. Harold is evidently implying to Barbara that I am a competitor for her job, in the hope of neutralising her, as he has neutralised Peter.

Sunday 11 May

'Bye, Bye Benn' was the headline in the *Sunday Mirror*, followed by a nasty article by Woodrow Wyatt. The story was typical of today's press as a whole, and it is obvious that there has been heavy briefing by Number 10 that Wilson will remove me after the Referendum.

There were eight press cars outside the house, full of photographers and reporters who kept coming to the door. They've taken a flat opposite my house, so we are now under siege. I couldn't even go out for a walk because they would have followed me.

In effect, Wilson has destroyed my credibility as a Minister with my own officials and so for the next three and a half weeks until the Referendum, I will not be able to control the Department.

Whether I'm sacked, or kept in the Cabinet, or put in a different Department is of no consequence to this country, but what does matter is the freedom to govern ourselves, to get cheap food for our families, to have policies that will give us jobs. I think it might well be that I am coming to the end of my period as a Minister. If I am dismissed, I shall have to work within the labour movement in some other capacity, perhaps within the trade union movement.

Actually the Labour Government's days are numbered, and certainly the days of Wilson as Leader – his style and his politics – are numbered. A Labour Government that betrayed the people a second time would not survive for very long, but a coalition has been born without being formally declared: it is broadly the Tories and the Liberals throwing their weight behind Callaghan, I think. They won't touch Wilson. They'll get rid of him just as they got rid of Heath. Jenkins has no following in the Labour Party. Healey is not liked, even though his economic policies are now Treasury dominated, because he has been silent on Europe. So, Jim would be the one – trade-union backed, pro-Europe, very right-wing and ready to compromise. I wouldn't be surprised to find a Callaghan Government formed within the next couple of months.

In this maudlin mood, I rang Joe Ashton and told him I was going to clear the office and continue on a care and maintenance basis only. He said, 'Don't be a damned fool. The word will spread in Whitehall that you are about to resign. You must fight. You mustn't give up.' I must say he perked me up.

Monday 12 May
Had a chat to Frances who was very touchy – she kept going out and coming in until she finally explained that she didn't mean to be lacking in sympathy but she felt that I was responding too vigorously to Wilson. She's probably right – her advice is always good, and I shall keep it in mind.

At 12.45 Michael Meacher, Roy Williams and I had lunch at the American Embassy with Elliott Richardson. He's very highly thought of and has had a distinguished career – he is a former Secretary of Defence. He is an ambitious man and is allegedly after Kissinger's job as Secretary of State, and he may even want the presidency. He's a WASP – White Anglo-Saxon Protestant – from Boston where he was Lieutenant-Governor, and was also Governor of Massachusetts. He dresses in Abercrombie and Fitch outfits and spotless white shoes – and is quite humourless. He never smiled once.

He believes that political democracy is inseparable from capitalism because power is dispersed through capitalism. Government intervention is ill-founded because it does not have the technical management expertise to do the job properly. I argued that we were really thinking of de-centralisation, and at one stage I said, 'Your arguments against bureaucracy would have convinced me against the Market if I hadn't been against it already.'

I went on to press the argument. 'Now look. You are living in a fantasy world where you believe the Brezhnev or the Stalin nightmare is happening here. If that were the conclusion of the American Government, then America would move to de-stabilise us and that would be a very great mistake.'

The words 'de-stabilise' is the one that is used to describe what

America did in Chile, and I think he got the message.

Tuesday 13 May
The front page of the *Evening Standard* had a classic picture of Heath, Jenkins and Thorpe at their press conference with the heading 'The Euro-Coalition'. Roy had apparently sat there while Ted Heath attacked me, Michael and Peter. The Party is terribly upset about the way things are going and I honestly don't blame them.

I shall be removed from the Department of Industry, and the papers say that Edmund Dell will take my place. He is the most reactionary, obscurantist Treasury man you could find.

Wednesday 14 May
I did an hour-long *It's Your Line* for the BBC with Reginald Maudling on the Common Market. Very good questions with Robin Day in the chair and everybody being terribly careful. All Maudling said was 'Rubbish, nonsense. I agree with Shirley Williams' and 'I prefer the Foreign Office to Mr Benn' – he didn't put forward one single argument. I was probably the only anti-Marketeer in the studio, or rather in the whole control room, because the BBC is a hotbed of pro-Market people.

Thursday 15 May
At the Cabinet, we discussed arms for South Africa – or rather, the supply of spares which really means ammunition for the weapons we sent a long time ago, and also the supply of air-traffic control equipment and gas masks for the South African Navy.

Peter was in favour of stopping everything. He thought the items were trifling but we had to carry the burden – especially him.

Roy Mason and Eric Varley thought we should supply the spares. 'It will threaten our uranium supplies from the Rossing mine in South-West Africa if we don't go ahead,' said Eric. That was a scandalous comment. Of course, the Atomic Energy Authority deceived me in 1970 when I was at Mintech by not telling me they were getting their uranium from South-West Africa.

Roy Hattersley was for going ahead and Harold said, 'Spares are all right.'

Shirley didn't think we should press South Africa now because of the situation in Rhodesia – so much for her liberalism.

'Nothing should go,' I said. I asked, 'Are we sure that the gas masks are only for protection against chemical and biological weapons? Because the AEA never told me their supplies were from Rossing; so are we absolutely sure this information is correct?'

Roy Mason said, 'Yes.'

It is the most reactionary Cabinet.

Thursday 16 May

At 11.45 a Superintendent from the Special Branch came to see me about security because of all the death threats I've been getting. He told me that they had looked at the letters and they didn't think they were 'assassination-type letters'. I said I didn't either. He said, 'Your attitude is obviously quite right but there may be a risk of you getting biffed or attacked in some way.'

Anyone could kill anyone if they really wanted to. I had a nasty letter recently from Liverpool saying that a group of businessmen called Defenders of Private Enterprise had each put £20,000 into a pool and paid an assassin in America to murder me. Actually, it was addressed to Caroline, using her maiden name, and it said, 'Madam, We regret that your husband is going to be killed and that you will be a widow, but it is in the public interest.'

Monday 19 May

Eric Heffer's farewell party was held in the office.

Caroline told me that the school had received another call today saying that we had moved our children from the comprehensive school into a private school – another canard going round. Stephen came back from Stansgate and said the press were hanging around, repeating the story about a member of the family being in hospital. Caroline is beginning to see this as a threat – if you don't stop, one of your children *will* be in hospital.

Went over to the House for Questions. Tom King, the Conservative Industry Spokesman, asked if I thought it was right to take part in the steel demonstration today. 1500 steelworkers, mainly from Scotland, had come down by train to demonstrate on the 20,000 redundancies, and the papers this morning carried headlines, 'Benn To Join In Steel Demo.'

'The day Ministers are frightened of meeting their constituents is the day Parliament will perish and die,' I replied.

Then at 9.45 there was a bombshell. It was announced that Finniston had dropped the redundancies and that the BSC and TUC had reached an agreement on other ways of tackling the steel industry's problems. It was a complete victory and I don't think I've gone to bed happier for a very long time. It was the workers who had done it, not me.

Tuesday 20 May

Misc 83 Committee under Harold Lever to look at the textiles industry, and to cut a long story short, we are now committed to a strategy of unemployment. Anything that prevents unemployment is regarded as an attack on the macro-economic strategy.

Wednesday 21 May

Came back to the Cabinet Office and on the way I had a word with Michael Foot who told me he was seeing Harold tonight to try to put him off dismissing me. I said, 'That's very nice of you, Michael, but you don't have to bother. I have no idea what he will do but I feel quite free now that he's threatened it publicly. I've got a certain sense of relaxation and freedom.'

'Oh, we're not having it,' he said, and he did see Harold. I'll know later what the outcome was.

To the House of Commons to open the debate on British Leyland. Heseltine laid into me, but I actually fell asleep during his speech which annoyed him.

Thursday 22 May

In the *Socialist Worker* today was a piece saying that what really terrified the Establishment was that I was fighting for jobs, while they were trying to sack people and this was the real offence, together with workers' participation and public ownership.

So for the first time, the ultras have had to take on board my strategy and identify the divisions between Healey and Thatcher, who are the monetarists, Heath and Shirley Williams, who are corporatist coalitionists, and myself.

Cabinet at 10.30, possibly my last.

Denis Healey presented his paper showing his own forecast of the economic position. He said that he needed to get £2 to £3 billion out of the economy and for that purpose he wanted to get agreement on the £3 billion figure to give him room for manoeuvre.

Tony Crosland was against deciding today.

I was called next. 'I think the economic situation is much graver than the Chancellor supposes. The strategy is wrong because the diagnosis is wrong, and I want to say why. First of all, this strategy has got to be seen against a background first of rising unemployment – one million or higher this year and probably much higher next year – and growing redundancies. We are on the rim of the recession and haven't yet descended down into the centre; second, falling investment where, despite the £3 billion transfer in two Budgets to the company sector, and easements of the Price Code and company taxation, there has been a catastrophic drop in investment intentions; third, poor world trade, and I am more doubtful about an upturn towards the end of next year because that forecast is based upon the impact of the German and American reflationary packages of last year but there is more spare capacity in Germany, Japan and America than there is here, more competitive spare capacity, and therefore we may not get the business; finally, declining productive capacity, as we close down British manufacturing industry at a devastating rate; we cannot recover our position and we won't be ready for the upturn if it happens.

'The Chancellor has asked us to agree to this policy because he needs an earlier reduction in the balance of payments deficit and wants to cut it through the public sector. He aims at £3 billion cuts, half from formula percentage cuts, half from higher charges, lower subsidies and lower standards. But it won't work because of rising unemployment. The £3 billion cuts will mean more jobless, leading to a £1.2 billion loss in tax revenue, a £1 billion increase in social security payments for the unemployed, and I calculate it would only give him £800 million saving and only a £1 billion gain in the balance of payments at a cost of £4.6 billion sacrifices in national income.

'The standard of living of the unemployed is sustained by the state and unless we are prepared to cut the unemployment benefit, which is the next thing the Chancellor will come to, it will not help. Public expenditure has a low import content. I accept that public expenditure may need to be re-planned in the full employment context and even cut back, especially where high import content may be shown to exist, but the present strategy will cut back the real resources available for investment and it can't be done.

'It will destroy our Manifesto commitments because the macro-strategy will put our micro-strategy in a strait jacket. For example, when we were discussing textiles a couple of days ago at Harold Lever's committee, Sir Kenneth Berrill said, "You can't try to save jobs when your economic strategy is to have higher unemployment." But we have to save jobs if we want to save productive capacity.

'The strategy will not be acceptable to the labour movement because it means actual cuts in public expenditure as distinct from slowing down the rate of acceleration, and the unions will become the scapegoats. The parallel with 1931 is very obvious; the Cabinet resisted protection then but they had to do it. We shall have to have protection and reverse our policy on import controls within a year if we survive in office.

'As for the alternative, I put in a paper on 29 January calling for protection and import controls on consumer durables, textiles, clothing, furniture, cars, electrical and mechanical engineering, boilers, machinery, mechanical appliances, radio, TV and TV tubes. This is what we need. In the context of a return to full employment and protection, we should develop a strategy to double investment and to win the support of the trade unions.'

I think I made an impact, particularly with the reference to 1931 and I passed around a photocopy of the passage in G. D. H. Cole's book about the 1931 Cabinet.

Denis replied, 'First of all, as for what Tony Benn has said, this Budget is not a device for generating unemployment. Public sector employment is not productive and what we have to do is to shift more people from the public to the private sector. We do need a package in July on wages, investment and so on. I hope we're not going to have all this nonsense about half a million unemployed as a result of the Common Market – that's the economics of the mad house. Last year, the TUC agreed to guidelines but they haven't complied, and voluntary bargaining will not work. We cannot assume the promises of the trade unions will be kept. If we are going to change priorities, then some programmes will have to be reduced and everyone must be ready for a big cut in living standards.'

Harold Wilson chipped in, 'We'll have to resume this after the recess, consider inflation separately. We don't want any leaks from the Cabinet, no gossip to the press which does us a lot of damage.'

It made me laugh to hear Harold Wilson attacking gossip in the press.

The streaker: a naked man running across Twickenham during a rugby match provoked this cartoon in the *New Statesman*.

Friday 23 May
Harold was on television tonight. He was questioned about the econ-

omic situation and the Common Market. He just waffled. Then they asked him about me and he said, 'Oh well, Mr Benn is a bogeyman like Lloyd George and Churchill and Bevan.'

Robin Day said, 'But you've attacked him yourself, called him an Old Testament prophet.'

'Well, he dreams about the future but what he says isn't Government policy,' Harold said.

'Are you going to dismiss him?'

'When I make my ministerial dispositions, I shall see you get a copy.'

That was a clear indication that he intends to get rid of me; actually it gives me a marvellous feeling of liberation.

Sunday 25 May

The *Sunday Express* headline was 'Bosses win their battle against Benn' and said that Harold Wilson had written to the CBI to tell them that he would be disposing of me after the Referendum. The 'Crossbencher' column had a profile of Edmund Dell who is supposedly to succeed me, saying how modest he was and how good he would be at the job, having worked fifteen years in industry. The *Sunday Times* said, predictably, that I'd got my figures wrong on job losses caused by the Market,* which is exactly what they said last year about my figures for the coal stocks during the three-day week. In both cases the figures had come from Francis Cripps and in both cases were absolutely reliable.

Monday 26 May

The press this morning was astonishing. Denis Healey put out a statement last night from the Treasury that 'truth is the first casualty in war' which was a roundabout way of calling me a liar. The *Daily Mirror* also had a front-page article called 'Lies, Lies, More Lies, and Damned Statistics' and the *Sun* had a major front-page story about the Common Market and predicted a majority of eleven million for staying in. My feeling is that as the battle hots up, if we keep calm, we shall make an impact. The latest polls show that the majority of people think it was a mistake to enter the Common Market but feel that now we are in, we can't get out. So we have to give them the confidence to vote No.

Tuesday 27 May

The job losses point is being picked up by the papers. The Establishment is worried, particularly as white collar workers and professional and managerial staff are beginning to appreciate the likely effects of the

---

* At a press conference on 18 May 1975, I had announced that as a result of the trade deficit with the Common Market, half a million jobs had been lost in Britain. The figures were based on the Government's Overseas Trade Statistics.

Market. The fact is that the figures are Government figures and the half a million job losses was a breakdown by reputable economists: the argument is about interpretation.

Frances and Francis told me that a major industrial policy unit has been set up in the Treasury, under Sir Douglas Wass [Permanent Secretary to the Treasury], and this unit is engaged in planning industrial policy without reference to the Department of Industry. None of their papers are coming to me because they don't want me to be able to use them for political purposes. Francis Cripps says he knows somebody working in that unit and they are preparing for the Economic and Monetary Union to be brought forward as soon as the Referendum is out of the way – which is very significant.

Came home. Roy Jenkins attacked me by name today and it was on all the news programmes. On Radio 4 the political commentator Tony King, who is wildly pro-Market, said there had never been an attack like this by one Cabinet Minister on another since the eighteenth century, that the whole Government's credibility was at stake and that Jenkins had confirmed everything the press was saying about me. If there was a Yes vote, my position would be impossible, and if there was a No vote the Government couldn't survive.

I spoke to Ray Tuite who thought the violence of the language at this moment was unprecedented in political debate.

Wednesday 28 May
Caught the train to Wakefield for an ASTMS meeting and met Clive Jenkins so we talked all the way up, until he dozed off. He told me that when Vic Feather was General Secretary of the TUC, indeed also as Assistant Secretary of the TUC, he received a retainer from Cecil King at the *Daily Mirror*. Cecil King had also given a retainer to George Brown. This is how the press corrupts public figures.

Thursday 29 May
On the late news, Roy Jenkins was pontificating and warning us about joining the Soviet bloc – filthy anti-Communist stuff. But these are his views and at least he has been smoked out; we now know the character of the right-wing leadership of the Labour Party.

We have just got to stick to prices, jobs, and self-government. I said tonight that the only weapons that people have for survival are secure jobs and the vote. With jobs at risk and the vote devalued, things are tremendously difficult.

Monday 2 June
A couple of days ago the *Birmingham Post* reported that Eldon Griffiths had compared me to Goebbels, and the *Daily Mirror* challenged me on

their front page. 'Tell The Truth, Mr Benn'. So I rang the Editor and he agreed to give me 750 words for Wednesday which I will get Frances and Francis to write.

Melissa started her A levels today and Joshua starts his O Levels tomorrow.

Began preparing for the debate on *Panorama* with Roy Jenkins, which we are recording this afternoon. It is like preparing for a heavyweight championship because if he knocks me out on the number of jobs at stake, I really will be in trouble. Francis and Frances came in and we went over the arguments. Frances suggested I open the discussion on the right to self-government and the devaluation of the vote, leaving jobs until later in the debate.

A BBC car took us to the Lime Grove studios where we were met by Roger Bolton, the producer, and I discovered that questions about the coalition, about the Labour Party, and about the future of socialism were also going to be put to us.

'I came here to discuss the Common Market and I'm not discussing anything else,' I said. Then Roy arrived, all smiles, but looking slightly guilty, probably because he had made that personal attack on me.

We began, as I insisted, on the general question and the discussion went on from there. Dimbleby was thrust aside and said practically nothing. On the job loss figures I held my own and said that they had not been refuted. We went on to discuss the siege economy, and the great dream of Europe versus the defence of jobs. The discussion didn't deal with socialist questions; it was much more the constitutional and high-level macro-aspects which was probably right at this stage in the campaign.

Roy didn't accept the figures – based on his experience as Chancellor and so on. I kept recalling that we had worked together in Cabinets, we had introduced import surcharges, we had devalued the pound, we had controlled capital movements. We needed these powers. At the end, my impression was that it had been a worthwhile debate.

The big news today is that Edward Du Cann, the MP for Taunton, Chairman of the 1922 Committee and chief conspirator to replace Heath with Thatcher, has come out against the Market. It is a huge political event.

Tuesday 3 June

Neil Kinnock picked me up and drove me to Cardiff. He thought it was essential to keep together all the people who had come to work in the labour movement against the Market. Two thousand people were waiting, an enormous meeting. Michael Foot turned up, the first time I'd seen him since he had come back from Venice and he looked pretty old and tired.

There were a few 'Keep Britain In Europe' people waving their banners which helped to make it interesting. Michael made a speech and George Wright, Secretary of the Welsh TUC, and Dai Francis, President of the South Wales Miners, were on the platform with MPs, Caerwyn Roderick, Ioann Evans, Roy Hughes, Kinnock and Elystan Morgan who had been defeated in the February Election. It was a tremendous meeting in which I made an attack on Heath.

Wednesday 4 June
Eve of Referendum and I campaigned all day in the streets of Bristol. I had an article in the *Daily Express* and in the *Daily Mirror*. There was also a sympathetic piece by Peter Cole in the *Guardian*.

Jack Jones and Len Murray are going to see Harold on Tuesday to tell him he must not move me. No victimisation, Jack Jones says. So I

Evening Standard, 6 May 1975

feel the support of the great strength of the Labour movement.

Thursday 5 June
Up at 6 o'clock and back to London. Melissa and I walked to St Peter's

Church Hall, Portobello Road, where we cast our votes – the first time Melissa had voted.

Back to Bristol, where Caroline met me and we drove around in a lorry for four hours with the loudspeaker simply shouting, 'No to the Common Market.'

The ITN 10 o'clock news predicted a 69 per cent Yes vote and a 29 per cent No vote, so it looks like an enormous majority for staying in.

I rang Frances. She's realistic about it. 'Oh well, people are sick of elections, they are glad it is settled. Harold has scored a tremendous triumph, but it's over and done with now. The Left has played its trump card and been soundly defeated. This is the moment really to fade out.' If that is the case my inclination is to get out and work on the sidelines.

I worked out a draft statement on the Referendum. I would say that it had been a good debate and that I accepted the verdict. It is half past midnight, I am desperately tired. It looks as if in this great Referendum, the British people have overwhelmingly voted for Common Market membership, but it may be that even the leaders of the three Parties and the entire press have not been able to secure more than 50 per cent of the vote, and that is less than wholehearted consent. I must not be resentful but that might be worth pointing out.

There is a swing to the Right which I think one has to accept will continue for the remainder of the 1970s. The 1980s may be different but it is going to a long hard wait.

Friday 6 June

Got home from the POEU Conference at Blackpool to find a dozen journalists gathered in the front garden, plus a television unit. I said I would make a statement when I had seen the complete results.

Stephen and Hilary were in the house with Dick Clements, then Frances and Francis arrived, followed by Michael Meacher and Joe Ashton. It soon became clear that there was a Yes majority everywhere.

Jack Jones was on the television, saying that if Tony Benn was moved from the Department of Industry it would be a grave affront to the trade union movement. He was serious, strong and principled.

We sat down in the front room and hammered out the statement: that we accepted the verdict of the people; that we were glad there has been a Referendum; that we wanted to thank all those who had worked so hard; and that we needed our industrial policy and our Manifesto all the more now.

At 4 I went into the garden with Caroline and I made the statement. There were lots of questions, many of them, as I expected, about my own personal position and whether I would resign. By lecturing them on democracy and making it absolutely clear that I accepted the verdict and the right of the people to make their decision, I got through the interview.

To the House of Commons at 6.15 to the National Referendum Campaign party. Neil Marten was host, Douglas Jay, Enoch Powell and many more were there. Enoch came over to me; I don't think I've spoken to him properly since I attacked him in the Election for his racist views.

'Well, Enoch,' I said, 'you certainly got your case across clearly and concisely, and the great merit of it all was that it was good political education.'

'The great political education is only just beginning,' he replied.

'What do you mean?'

He told me that he'd just come from the ITN studios in a taxi, and the taxi driver had asked him, 'Are you Mr Powell?'

'Yes,' said Enoch.

'What attitude are you adopting towards the Common Market, Mr Powell?'

Enoch was much humbled by this and said to the taxi driver, 'Do you remember I used to be a member of the Conservative Party?'

'Yes,' the taxi driver said.

'Do you remember why I left the Conservative Party?'

The taxi driver said no, he had never heard the reason. So Enoch asked how he had voted in the Referendum.

'I voted No.'

'Oh, did you.' said Enoch. 'Why?'

'Well, I heard there was some talk of a European Parliament and I was not prepared to see the British Parliament put under a European Parliament.'

The point Enoch was making to me was that the campaign had not gone on long enough for people to understand exactly what everybody was saying, but they had picked up the gist of it.

At the end of the day, we heard that 17 million people had voted to stay in, and 8.5 million to come out, which was some achievement considering we had absolutely no real organisation, no newspapers, nothing.

Saturday 7 June

Went with Caroline to dinner with the Foots, the Baloghs, the Shores and the Harts.

Peter wanted us to go and see Harold and Judith agreed. 'Yes, we should tell Harold he mustn't now humiliate the Left.'

Michael said, 'I saw Harold after the last Cabinet before the Referendum, because I had heard all these reports that Tony was going to be sacked, and Harold told me he couldn't discuss the reshuffle with me but he wasn't planning to upset the balance between Left and Right in the Cabinet.' He said Harold was very cheerful, he had just made a speech against Mrs Thatcher and felt it had gone well. But I think Harold is planning to move me immediately.

We discussed whether Peter or Judith should go and see Harold over the weekend and I said, 'No, for heaven's sake, that would be crawling to him.'

'Why does he always work with his enemies, when we are his real friends?' Tommy Balogh said.

I told them I couldn't take any more. 'He betrays the Party and takes us into Europe working with the Right, and I would believe anything about him except that we are his true friends. Long may he prosper. He's the cleverest political leader we have had for a long time, but why should we believe all that nonsense?'

Tommy laughed but Peter got angry. 'I am not crawling to anybody – I am not being told I crawled.'

Sunday 8 June

I don't sleep well, I was too tired to sleep, and just tossed and turned all night. I thought very carefully about what I should do and I came to the conclusion that I shouldn't be on the sidelines – I have to do something. So I sent a telegram to Spinelli, the EEC Commissioner for Industry:

> Now that the British people have made their decision, I am sending you this personal message of goodwill and hope to renew our personal links perhaps when it is convenient for you to be in London.
>
> Best Wishes
> Tony Benn

That will arrive Monday morning and, no doubt, the word will go around Brussels.

I rang Jack Jones, thanked him for what he said on television and told him he did very well.

'You did all right yourself, mate,' he said.

Frances Morrell rang and said she was absolutely exhausted and wanted a week off, which I immediately gave her.

I'm pretty tired myself. Caroline and I went for a lovely walk in Holland Park before lunch and looked at the sculpture exhibition. It was a beautiful sunny day, with the temperature in the eighties.

Monday 9 June

Cabinet at 10.30. Harold began by saying we would have much tighter guidelines though he thought that the Referendum had gone reasonably well with one or two excesses.

He called the Lord President to discuss immediate questions and Ted Short described the Stonehouse problem, that he'd been arrested in Australia this morning while trying to get home and that he was being held until extradition papers could be arranged. The House was due to debate the case for his expulsion from Parliament this week.

Elwyn Jones said, 'This would be difficult because you would be expelling him while extradition proceedings are going on in Australia to bring him home for substantive charges.'

Michael recommended that Ted defer the debate. Barbara and Shirley were also for postponing the debate. Ted said, 'If we do defer it, he'll probably hang on for another year.'*

I was first for Questions in the House this afternoon, and it is the first day that Parliament is broadcast by the BBC. I announced that the Government would consider the publication of a further White Paper on the working of the proposed Industry Act.

Then Harold made his statement on the Referendum, and afterwards, in the Tea Room, I heard he wanted to see me at 6. I walked over to Number 10 and went into the Cabinet Room where Harold was waiting, looking very brown and relaxed. I sat some way from him and he said, 'I'll come straight to the point. I'd like you to take Energy.

'It is a very important Department, dealing with North Sea Oil; the negotiations with the oil companies are under way with Harold Lever and Edmund Dell. It involves the miners who you know very well, it involves nuclear power which you know inside out, and that's what I want you to take. You've got lots of energy, if you know what I mean,' he said smiling.

I didn't smile.

'You'd enjoy it,' he said. 'It's a very important job.'

I said nothing.

'Well, haven't you got any questions?'

'No,' I replied, 'except how long are you going to give me to think about it?'

'I must know soon. Two hours.'

'Overnight.'

'Oh no,' he said. 'Got to know by 9.45.'

'Well, my wife is away till 10 and I want to discuss it with her, so what about 10.15?'

'Nine forty-five,' he insisted.

'I'll see you in the lobby at 10. All right?'

---

*John Stonehouse did hang on, for over a year. He did not finally relinquish his seat, Walsall South, until August 1976, once he had been given a seven year sentence for fraud.

I picked up my coat and Ron drove me back to the House.

I said to Roy Williams, 'Clear up my office, remove my banner, take everything out as if I had never been here.' I invited Stephen and Hilary to come to the House because I wanted their advice. I rang Caroline but she was at a Governors' meeting at Holland Park School so Melissa, bless her heart, went all the way to the school and pulled Caroline out. Caroline's first thought was that I had been assassinated, which in a way I had.

She came to the House and the evening was spent in endless discussions with a succession of colleagues, with Joe bringing up trayloads of grub from the Dining Room (which I really must pay him for).

The general opinion is that I *should* take Energy, because there is no principle involved in being offered another job in Cabinet.

Ten o'clock came and went, and I heard Harold had called Michael in again before 10 and said he'd decided to postpone the whole matter. That was a good sign.

But after the division, Eric Varley rang and I went down and had a word with him. He is very close to Harold and he told me what had happened. 'I think Harold entered into some commitments with the City or somebody, and he has to get rid of you.'

NOTES
Chapter Three

1. (p. 270) On 21 November 1974, two pubs were bombed by the IRA: twenty-one people were killed, one hundred and sixty injured. The tragedy led to emergency legislation in the form of the Prevention of Terrorism Act by Home Secretary Roy Jenkins. Six Irishmen were convicted of the murders and in 1989 still are serving life sentences. But widespread belief in their innocence, and new forensic evidence, resulted in an as yet unsuccessful campaign led by Chris Mullin (MP for Sunderland South since 1987), for their release.

2. (p. 277) Des Warren and Ricky Tomlinson were jailed for three and two years respectively under conspiracy law for picketing offences during a bitter strike in the relatively un-unionised building industry in 1972. The sentences were seen by the Labour and trade union movement as part of the Conservative Government's over-all attack on unions and intense pressure was put on Roy Jenkins as Home Secretary, who however refused to release the men.

3. (p. 304) Niall Macdermot, MP for Derby North, 1964–70 (and Lewisham North, 1957–9) was Financial Secretary to the Treasury in the Labour Government of 1964. In 1968 he resigned in disgust after being told by Wilson that his wife was considered by security to be a 'suspect Soviet agent'. The reference to Stephen Swingler concerned smears by MI5 against Swingler, the MP

for Stafford, 1945–50 and Newcastle-under-Lyme, 1951–69. In 1968 Wilson refused to promote him to Transport Minister in Barbara Castle's vacated post because he might be a 'security risk'. The scurrilous role of the Security Services in both incidents is described in detail in *The Wilson Plot* by David Leigh (1988).

4
The Last Days of Harold Wilson
June 1975–March 1976

Tuesday 10 June

To the House of Commons at 11. Judith Hart told me that although she had been reinstated as Minister for Overseas Development by Harold, her office had been told that she would not be allowed to go abroad. Joe Ashton came in and said that there had been uproar in the Committee on the Industry Bill this morning because of my statement in the House yesterday that there would be a new White Paper on it. Michael Foot looked in to say he would be seeing Harold again today, and Peter Shore came over and reminded me that Energy was a very important job, and that the wealth of this country was in energy.

To the Café Royal for the Industrial Society lunch. I hadn't been in the office all day, and Roy Williams told me that my office had been completely cleared and the banner removed; but he felt he should still accompany me to the lunch. I spoke about industrial policy disclosure and answered questions, but the atmosphere was icy, and there is no doubt that the Referendum and the press attacks really made an impact on these middle class senior managers. They hated me and I felt I had reached the end of the road.

At 4 Joe Ashton and Michael Meacher brought me a letter which had been signed by all the members of the Industry Group of Labour MPs. It read:

Dear Tony,

We were really disturbed to hear that there may be a further White Paper in relation to the Industry Bill. This would seem to suggest that there could be fundamental changes to the Bill which is currently being discussed in Committee and which is under guillotine and in these circumstances, we would appreciate it if you could make a statement to the Committee this afternoon.

Yours,

Doug Hoyle, Audrey Wise, Eric Heffer, John Garrett, Brian Sedgemore, Mike Noble, Bob Bean, Giles Radice, John Horam, Caerwyn Roderick, Jeremy Bray, Max Madden and Ian Mikardo.

I told Michael, 'Say to them that you've passed on the message, and I am not able to be at the Committee.'

Michael Foot came in, having just spent forty minutes with Harold. He told Harold that he thought I wouldn't take Energy. Harold was very cross and said he was sick of personality politics and all that went with it. Michael said that Roy Jenkins had withdrawn his threat of

Daily Express, 12 June 1975

resignation which had only been made to protect Reg Prentice.

Harold had told Michael that Fred Mulley would be going to the Department of Education and that Judith had been offered Transport, outside the Cabinet. Reg Prentice was to have Overseas Development, in place of Judith, under the aegis of the Foreign Office.

At 5 Joe rang to say that when the Committee on the Industry Bill began, Eric Heffer opened by asking why Michael Meacher, and not Tony Benn, was giving the statement. Michael Heseltine apparently rushed in saying he couldn't believe that nobody knew where the Secretary of State for Industry was, given that the media had been with him at every moment. When Michael Meacher made a statement on my behalf, the Labour members simply walked out, followed by Heseltine, so that the Committee lost its quorum and had to adjourn. Presumably, Heseltine went to see Mrs Thatcher.

Walter Harrison, the Deputy Chief Whip, asked me why I wasn't at the Committee, and I told him I had been sacked. Ted Short phoned and also asked what had happened, so I told him. He didn't know and he said he was sorry.

Barbara Castle looked in at 5.15. I was absolutely exhausted, it was so hot in that room with the bright sun coming in. It was awful. She got me some tea.

Watched the BBC news and there was Michael Young, the new chairman of the Consumer Council appointed by Shirley Williams, giving the first major statement favouring a price freeze, subsidies running at £2500 million a year paid for by an increase of 11p in national insurance contributions (which is the most regressive form of poll tax there is). He also called for a statutory pay policy and a relativities board – in short, the Heath policy plus food subsidies. It was a scandal.

At 6.10 I was summoned to see Harold in his room in the House of Commons. I had to run the gauntlet of Bernard Donoughue and Joe Haines outside his room. Harold looked at me intently with his piggy little eyes.

'What is your answer?'

'Well Harold, I have been thinking very hard about it. I am concerned about two things. One, the possible humiliation or downgrading of dissenting Ministers, and two, the implementation of the Manifesto.'

'On the Manifesto,' said Harold, 'as far as industrial policy is concerned, you know I am as keen on it as you are.'

'Well, I don't accept that, but if you say so the Manifesto will go ahead.'

I continued, 'The third thing I'm concerned about is the Party. We've had two General Elections and a Referendum which has been a great strain. You yourself said we should all buckle down and you have now created this terrible uncertainty and alienated everybody. The Industry Bill is in chaos because you've taken me off it. With Eric Heffer and myself gone there is nobody to run it. What you are doing is simply capitulating to the CBI, to the Tory press and to the Tories themselves, all of whom have demanded my sacking.'

He said, 'Well, I am not taking Jenkins's advice.'

'I don't give a damn what Jenkins says, you are capitulating and if you think this is going to save you, you've made a great mistake because they'll be pleased for twenty-four hours and then they'll turn on you.'

'They'll turn on me anyway,' Harold said. 'I am just a captain of a cricket team wishing to make changes, and it has got nothing whatever to do with the Referendum. I am entitled to make changes.'

I said it was difficult to know when to go, and he had never understood me, always thinking that I was after his job when all I wanted was to see the policy implemented. 'Of course,' I went on, 'this now has to be seen against a much wider background. Michael Young is calling for a statutory pay policy and we are heading for a coalition.'

Harold insisted that that had nothing to do with him. I pointed out that the movement would interpret it that way.

'You don't speak for the movement,' he said. 'I know as much about the movement as you do.'

He pushed me for my decision about the job. Looking back on it, it is possible that if I had refused Energy, he might have kept me in Industry. But as he was going to see the Queen at 6.30, and I am sure she would have had to have had advance notice, perhaps he wouldn't have. Indeed, later tonight, I heard that he had said that if I had refused to go to Energy, he would have taken over the Department of Industry himself as he did in the 1964–70 Government with the Department of Economic Affairs.

Anyway, I accepted the job. I think he was quite surprised. I walked out and banged the door.

At 7.30 I went over to the Overseas Development Ministry where Judith was giving a party for her staff. She was almost in tears. I gave her all the arguments for not resigning and told her that we'd both been humiliated, but one couldn't resign because of personal pride. She refused to accept it, saying how close she had been to Harold, how she had helped him in the campaign to become Leader. Now she believed he hated her. She insisted she would not take Transport so I promised I'd support her in her decision and asked what she planned to do.

'Well, I'll go and remind him that I took the Pensions Department when Peggy Herbison left, I helped him when – '

I interrupted, 'Look don't plead with him. Go in strength and warn him about the consequences of what he is doing, and then at the end tell him you are not going to take Transport.' I suggested we get on to the Speaker and ask for her to make a statement in the House on Thursday. This seemed to cheer her up a bit, but later she telephoned to say she was definitely out.

Frances Morrell and Tony Banks were there and we all agreed that Wilson was a shit for what he was doing to Judith. She had been a very good Minister, she was known worldwide and had committed no offence. She was simply a dissenting Minister, and for that she was being victimised. I suddenly felt that we had to save her. I decided to ring Number 10 and ask Harold if Michael and I could see him. We went over to Harold's. Michael began, 'Now look Harold, we have come to see you because we want to be constructive. We are very concerned about Judith. It is quite reasonable to offer her Transport, it is a very important Department and Tony and I have urged her to take it. But it must be in the Cabinet.'

'Oh,' said Harold, 'we can't do that. We would have to introduce a Bill to increase the size of the Cabinet.'

'You've done it before, you can do it again,' said Michael.

'I can't have people arguing, we don't change the Cabinet to fit people.'

Michael was warning Harold of the unsettling effect all this was having on the Party, when I came in. 'Now look, Harold, let us be quite plain about this. It is victimisation, either because of the Referendum – '

'It is nothing to do with the Referendum – ' Harold interrupted.

'You now offer her a Minister of State's job, Number Three in the Department of Environment, with the first two – Crosland and Silkin – in the Cabinet.'

Harold said he couldn't discuss it but I added that he appeared to be making a clean sweep of everyone who had ever had anything to do with industrial policy. Judith had gone, Eric had been sacked, I had been moved, Michael is being moved – '

'Who told you that?'

'That's what Barbara told me,' I said, realising I shouldn't have.

Harold insisted that Judith's had been a sideways move, and that, in fact, I had accepted a bigger demotion than her because of my attachment to the Industry Bill.

'Don't re-open that, I've said what I have to say.'

'Judith would not take the job, unlike you Tony. You very bravely did.'

'Look Harold, you say it is suicide but there is no doubt that you gave her the knife.'

'Well,' he said, 'she shouldn't have taken that attitude. We can't have prima donnas.'

Then Barbara turned up. I do admire her for that, it was nearing midnight and she had got dressed again after a heavy day, jumped in a taxi and come all the way to the House to save Judith. She fought her corner and even said she would accept being replaced by Judith at the DHSS.

By now it must have been becoming clear to Harold that we were not prepared to serve if Judith was not put in the Cabinet. He said that he had made his position clear. 'I've got to do this,' and looking directly at me he said, 'when you have my job, you'll have to do it.' That was intended to annoy Michael and Barbara.

Barbara described Judith's contributions with great affection, and Michael was very courteous. But it was left to me to say time and again, 'It is a basic trade union principle that you do not victimise people after a strike; we will not have it.'

At this point, he began to realise how serious it was and looked a bit shaken. We left saying that we'd be back tomorrow morning to give Harold some time to reconsider.

We went upstairs to Room 18, which was crowded with people – Barbara and Ted, Tony Banks, Frances Morrell, Norman Buchan, Neil Carmichael, Judith and Tony Hart, Margaret Jackson, and John Grant, [Under-Secretary of State, Overseas Development Ministry] whom I don't trust. I described what had happened and said that Barbara was great and Michael was courteous. Later Joe said, 'Tony, if you are going to become Leader of the Party, and you now stand well above anyone facing Harold, you have to fight that man, get into the ring like Cassius Clay and knock him out or be knocked out. The Party and the Tribune Group think that you should have held out longer on Energy.'

I took his point. I will have to fight but it will be at a moment of my own choosing, on the cuts or the statutory pay policy, or the reactionary economic policy.

Came home to find the house besieged with photographers. They flashed their cameras and two photographers blocked the way through the front gate. I looked up and put on my tough and determined face.

I talked to Caroline, Stephen and Josh until nearly 1 am. Then I rang Clive Jenkins and told him that Harold had made a clean sweep of the Industry Bill Ministers and it was the beginning of a massive swing to the Right. Clive agreed and promised to stir things up. He had, in fact, said on the 10 o'clock news that sacking me was like sacking Aneurin Bevan during the Committee Stage of the National Health Service Bill, a point Caroline had made to me and I, in turn, had made to Harold.

A memorable day, and I have a reasonably accurate record of it for those who want to study how the Labour Government betrayed itself. I think there will be a major revolt because Labour MPs on both sides simply will not accept the amendments to the Industry Bill.

If Harold goes, I should think Denis Healey would take over as the strong man in a crisis, or perhaps Jim. Roy would not get it and I certainly would not because the PLP would be too nervous that I would lose them the Election. I suppose I have a vague interest in Wilson going on, but what we have seen today is a completely new procedure for dealing with reshuffles. The Left must organise and advise those people offered a job or pressured to move out of a job as to what they should do. Wilson has made a fatal error and he will not be Leader of the Labour Party by the end of the year.

Stephen says that spending an hour in the middle of the night putting all this down for the record is probably my most useful service to the Labour movement, and he is right.

Wednesday 11 June

The press were outside our house again by 7, three cars filled with reporters, poised with telescopic lenses. Ron Vaughan turned up at 7.30 with all the morning papers. The *Guardian* had it right: 'Wilson gives Benn's head to the City'. By the time Josh left for school, there were about fifty journalists, two television units and three or four radio interviewers with microphones standing outside. We had decided not to say anything at all to the press, so when they confronted Josh, he ignored them. One of them shouted, 'You fucking well answer my questions.' Josh took no notice so they said, 'You push off, you little shit.'

Now Josh, at sixteen, is perfectly capable of exchanging harsh words with anybody of his own age, but when two or three grown men who, in a sense, are symbols of authority, swore at him like that, it really worried him. Melissa was followed as she went off to do her exam and she too refused to answer any questions. 'Thank you very much indeed for nothing,' they said sarcastically.

Ray Tuite rang home to say how sorry he was. It reminded him of the Berlin Blockade, and, indeed, he said earlier this week that the two great moments of his life had been the Berlin Blockade and working in the Department of Industry!

Jack Spriggs from the Kirkby Cooperative also rang and said, 'We have passed a resolution of support. Is there anything we can do, Tony? Can we see you and Eric Heffer to discuss things?' I said I'd do what I could.

I had a call from Bernard Ingham, my new Press Officer at the Department of Energy, and I left at 11.45 for the House of Commons. The press corps were outside. I must confess that, despite my experience in these matters, I did feel nervous. I took my jacket off, Ron walked ahead of me with my bag and Caroline, Stephen and Hilary watched me as I left. I walked out slowly and as I opened the front gate, the television cameras turned, the flashbulbs popped and the mikes were pushed menacingly at me. 'Do you regard your job as a promotion or demotion?' 'What do you think of Mrs Hart?' and so on.

I just walked through them as if they weren't there and that made them wild. They had dehumanised me in the press, now I was dehumanising them by not acknowledging their existence.

Joe told me that Bill Rodgers was now making an approach on behalf of the Manifesto Group to ditch Wilson and to set up a coalition between the Manifesto Group and the Tribune Group: if the Left were to abandon its pressure for defence cuts, the Right would agree to nationalisation and workers' control; and if the Left would let the Manifesto Group have the Foreign Office and the Treasury, they would allow the Trade and Industry Departments to go to the Left.

Michael Foot turned up at 12.30. He had tried to see Harold again about Judith but Harold said that he was too busy and could not see him until this afternoon. 'Well, Judith is making a statement this afternoon,' I said. 'Look, let's simply say to Harold that you and I will both resign unless Judith is put in the Cabinet.'

'Oh we can't do that,' Michael said, 'that is no use.' I have no doubt that even Michael and I alone could have saved Judith, but Michael did not want to. It's clear now that I must not rely on Michael for anything more than cover.

At 6 I went over to the Palace to exchange my Seals of Office and there was the Privy Council with Ted Short, Fred Mulley and Eric Varley. I looked a bit of a mess, wearing a blue shirt with a frayed collar and my Labour Party tie. I had lost a button on my suit and it was all crumpled. We all had to get down on one knee on a footstool and have the Oath administered to us. I was affirmed as Energy Secretary and I said to the Queen, 'My old Seals of Office have been used. My son melted down some sealing wax and we made quite a number of lovely impressions. Is that legal?'

'Oh' said the Queen, 'I think the impression ought to have been defaced by putting a hair across it.'

'Well, good heavens,' I said, 'I know it is an offence to reproduce stamps, but I have not attached the wax seal *to* anything, I have not given myself authority to do anything.'

She was slightly shirty about it. It was quite funny.

I went back to the Department of Industry with Ron Vaughan for my farewell party.

Thursday 12 June

Cabinet began with Ted Short in the chair because Harold was on his way from Chequers. The first item was how we should handle the American bicentennial celebrations. Apparently Ted Heath set up a commission a couple of years ago to look into it. One idea was that there should be a joint meeting between both Houses of Parliament and Congress at Westminster Hall and a facsimile of Magna Carta should be presented.

Willie Ross was against that because Magna Carta had no connection whatever with Scotland.

I suggested finding out whether any of the 1776 legislation on the tea tax or the British colonies was still on the statute book and we could have a ceremonial session of each House in which we will repeal these Acts and legitimise the American revolution. That was half taken seriously. I told the story of the bicentenary stamp and how the Post Office had said it would be most inappropriate because American freedom had been won by violence.

Harold arrived and we came on to discuss the economic situation. 'Whatever we do,' Harold said, 'we must not make speeches on the economic situation without checking it first with the Chancellor.' Thus the restraint on Ministers is tightened again.

The final item was the bill to lift the penalties from the Clay Cross councillors in accordance with our Manifesto pledge.

I said, 'We had a clear statement of policy in advance of the General Election from Ted Short and we discharged that obligation by bringing forward a bill. The Party feels strongly about it, or did at the time of the Conference resolution. Whatever you may think about the Clay Cross councillors, their campaign against the Housing Finance Bill emphasised the basically undemocratic nature of the Government measures and the way in which local democracy was being undermined, in exactly the same way as the campaign against the Industrial Relations Act highlighted the attack upon the democratic rights of trade unionists.'

Later in the evening Alex Eadie* told me there had been a disaster at Houghton Main pit near Barnsley and that he was flying up in the morning. I arranged to go with him.

Friday 13 June

Left home at 7 and drove to Northolt with Alex and the assistant inspector of mines. We flew to RAF Finningley. Alex told me his father had been killed in the pit at the age of sixty-two and how distressing it was when there were relatives at the pithead. We were met there by John Mills, a member of the National Coal Board, who told us that a massive explosion had killed five people, by blast and by gas. We arrived at the pithead to find press and television reporters. The only time working-class people are allowed to become heroes is when they are trapped, dying or dead.

Arthur Scargill, President of the Yorkshire Miners, was there and he had been down the pit with two NUM mining engineers. Arthur wanted a public inquiry.

Saturday 14 June

Lunch at ASTMS. Clive Jenkins had invited me, and Judith (and Tony) Hart, as the two victimised Ministers. I said how much I appreciated the tremendous leadership ASTMS had given during the Referendum campaign and its support for the industrial policy.

'But,' I said, 'we really must ask ourselves a much more fundamental question. Why is it that when we get the right policy, we sweat it out

---

* See Principal Persons for biographical notes of the Ministers and officials at the Department of Energy.

and then it doesn't get implemented? The reason is that when we're in office, we are not wired in to the Labour movement. When the Tories are in office, they are automatically wired into the City, to the big companies. When we get in we are actually tied to the Tory pressure groups, so we go on pumping out Tory explanations for everything.

'Today is the Trooping of the Colour and exactly forty-five years ago, when I was five, I went to Number 10 with my Dad to watch it. He was Secretary of State for India in Ramsay MacDonald's Cabinet and to the day he died, he always regretted not standing up to Mac-Donald. I told Harold this when I saw him this week and said that the position now was at least as serious as it was in 1931. We stand on the rim of depression but we dare not let the movement fail a third time – 1931, 1969, and 1975 – we cannot do it. It is no good meeting afterwards to try and give the kiss of life to a Government that has failed. Why are we giving it the kiss of death before we fail?'

Monday 16 June
The main news today is that the revelation that the CIA contemplated joining with French dissident groups to assassinate General de Gaulle. They planned to have one of their agents wear a poisoned ring and shake him by the hand, piercing his skin, and then to slip away before he collapsed. Fidel Castro was another target. They were also considering making sex films with an actor impersonating the former President of Indonesia, Sukarno, to discredit him, and then claiming the KGB had made them.

Ron drove me to Chequers where we had a meeting of the Devolution Committee. We began by circulating press cuttings from the Scottish papers, suggesting that the Cabinet was pulling back from the Scottish Assembly.

Denis Healey had put in a paper. 'I am not speaking against the principle of Devolution but I am urging caution on speed and content because of the danger of separatism. Therefore, I don't want legislation in the next session.'

Roy Jenkins agreed. He was worried that the magnitude of the changes and the consequences might lead to the break-up of the United Kingdom, and he felt that there had been inadequate discussion in England.

Ted Short disagreed. The matter had been fully considered by Ministers and officials and if we were to hold back, it would lose us our parliamentary majority. Nationalism was not the same as separatism, but it could be if we handled it wrongly.

Willie Ross said the leaks to the press did not surprise him. Healey was obviously against separatism, we all were. But if the Healey-

Lever-Jenkins line went ahead, it would destroy the credibility of the Government.

John Morris, the Secretary for Wales, endorsed what Ted Short had said. The movement for Devolution was old. The nationalist vote in Wales was 10.5 per cent but it could grow.

I said, 'I want to talk not about the oil side, which is obvious to everyone, but about the political side. I am strongly in favour of the principle of Devolution, as I said in 1968 when I first raised the question of the Referendum. We have a clear Election commitment which we must honour.

'The main argument for Devolution is that Government in Whitehall is too centralised, too bureaucratic, too secretive and too out of touch. I share that view and the situation's getting worse. We are the last of the colonial administrations, perhaps particularly so in Scotland, but in England too. I believe that 1776 to 1976 would be an appropriate two-hundred-year span to de-colonise all that was in the British Empire.

'We have to give people time to get used to change because the implications are slow to come home to them. We may even have to consider English devolution though there isn't the same pressure for it in the regions because there isn't the same cultural identity, though I'm sure Bristol would want to be a city state.

'Therefore, we should publish all these papers for discussion, possibly hold constitutional conferences where we could get people together informally to formulate their demands. And finally, whether you like it or not, you will have to have specific endorsement for it, through a Referendum. I still believe that the only way you can ever persuade a minority to accept a majority view is if you ask them. I would never have accepted the Common Market without the Referendum.'

I finished by suggesting we get an Assembly or constitutional convention set up as quickly as possible with which we could negotiate. At the moment we had nobody to negotiate with.

Over a pleasant lunch of salmon, salad, strawberries and cream, cheese and coffee, we talked about diaries. Barbara Castle thought that Dick Crossman emerged as a lesser person through his diaries than he was to those who knew him.

Incidentally, I heard this morning that the Attorney-General, Sam Silkin, is going to ask for an injunction against Dick Crossman's literary executors to prevent the book being published. That's worrying because if the Labour Party, which is in favour of open government, acts to prevent a dead colleague from having his memoirs published, it would be a most disturbing development. Of course, the theory is that it does damage to Government, but that's nothing compared to the damage done week after week by briefings and leaks from Ministers. The undermining of my authority at the Department of Industry was a result of

Harold Wilson's press briefing in Jamaica that he was going to clip my wings.

Tuesday 17 June

At 3.30 Sir Derek Ezra and two Deputy-Chairmen of the NCB came to see me. Although the Coal Board is nationalised, it is the usual set-up, like the Steel Corporation. There has been no real shift of power towards working people. It is still the same old gang that ever there was, and I can only deal with it through strengthening the unions. I shall have to spend hours on this question because the Coal Board is very important and the NUM is the key to the whole future of the coal industry.

Wednesday 18 June

To Tower Pier on the Thames with Caroline for the first landing of North Sea Oil. We met Ronnie Custis, my new Private Secretary, and boarded the hydrofoil for the Isle of Grain. On board we found a complete cross-section of the international capitalist and British Tory Establishment and their wives – Fred Hamilton of Hamilton Oil, Sir Mark Turner, Deputy-Chairman of RTZ, Elliott Richardson, Ronny Spiers, the American Minister and Vere Harmsworth from the filthy *Daily Mail*. I was so glad Caroline was there to talk to.

At the Isle of Grain, Hamilton and I went on deck, turned the valve and the oil allegedly went on shore. I find it just as unattractive when the press are treating me as some sort of celebrity as when they are making me into a bogeyman. It was a bright, hot day and even the Isle of Grain, the most ravaged, desolate, industrial landscape in the Medway, looked quite beautiful.

From there to the Gay Hussar where Caroline and I had dinner with the Silkins, the Foots, the Shores, the Baloghs and Barbara Castle; it cost £10 for the two of us. We discussed the economic situation. The real purpose of the dinner was to get support for Michael Foot's proposal – which had been put up by Jack Jones – for a flat rate 15 per cent increase, which is about £9 a week across the board, to be endorsed by the TUC and to replace the first mark of the Social Contract.

After they'd all said their piece, I said that this was a political problem. We had to see it against a background of a massive onslaught on the trade union movement. Nobody else got the blame for anything. Most of the Cabinet didn't really believe in the trade union link, and if you tried to do something, the PLP as a whole would not support you. Mrs Thatcher would join the Right in the Lobby in support of tough measures against the Left, and the Party would slip into a coalition. Harold would be replaced by somebody who favoured a coalition – Roy Jenkins or Jim Callaghan – with Heath and Thorpe in the Cabinet.

I tried to argue that this was the moment when you simply couldn't go round the course any more with public expenditure cuts, mass unemployment or a statutory incomes policy. We had to recognise that democracy was incompatible with the generation of capital through inequality in our economic system. We had to shift power very substantially and that was the only way to cope with the wage problem.

Friday 20 June
Ron Vaughan picked me up at 9 on an absolutely perfect summer's day and we drove to Chequers for an all-day Cabinet on the inflation and incomes situation. Harold announced that this would be one of three Cabinets to discuss pay and prices; the medium term assessment would be discussed on 14 July, and public expenditure priorities on 25 July.

Michael Foot introduced his paper and said there were broadly three choices before the Cabinet: we could go for the Social Contract, with the CBI and the Government brought in; for voluntary policy with or without guidelines; or for statutory policy. Michael favoured the first course.

Denis Healey thought the situation was more urgent than the Cabinet realised and the alternatives had to be seen against that background. Anything could trigger off a run on sterling, which had already cost us \$500 million to support. The rail strike could, or indeed a rail settlement. Unless we could get inflation down to OECD levels, public expenditure cuts of £1 billion this year might be necessary. In those circumstances, unemployment would go from one to two million, there would be a big cut in real incomes and investment would virtually cease. None of these measures would actually help inflation and they would require a statutory incomes policy. Therefore, we had to have a credible policy by the end of July. A wage freeze all year would be ideal and this would reduce inflation by 7 per cent. By September 1976 inflation had to be down to 10 per cent a year. Ten per cent wage rises or £5 per week flat rate was the absolute maximum we could afford.

Roy Jenkins argued that a statutory pay policy had worked very well from 1968–70. We face an unparalleled crisis and he favoured sanctions because non-compliance would be substantial.

Michael interrupted, 'Are you suggesting putting people into prison?'

'We'll have to face that,' said Roy, 'but we must also have cuts in public expenditure because of the Public Sector borrowing Requirement.'

I said, 'These policies are politically impossible for the Labour Government. They brought us down in 1970 and they brought the

Tories down in 1974. They are economic nonsense because they would cut back on our productive capacity and ratchet us down. The crisis is mounting. We have to face the fact that power has shifted in our society and the ballot box is now incompatible with the market economy as it operates. Power has shifted to people on the shop floor. The TUC can agree to things, they are members of the Establishment, but there are 5000 shop stewards who play a leading part in running British industry and they have to be won over too. You can call it capitulation to this power, or institutionalisation of it, but what people want in industry is not just wages, but truth, perspective, leisure, equality, power, and reform.

'I want a coalition with the trade union movement. The Cabinet and the General Council should meet. After all, the TUC asked for import controls, the price freeze and the industrial policy – these were the things we had to respond to. Nothing else would work with us in the short term, not even the Tories could make it work, and nor could a coalition in the long term. We must come to terms with reality.'

But mine was the only voice raised all day along these lines.

Denis wound up. 'We should announce a credible policy soon because the Arabs and the shop stewards are both threatening us. We must have the acquiescence of the unions. The Government must tell the TUC that 10 per cent is the maximum for pay increases and formula agreements must not be more than 12.5 per cent in total. There must be a monitoring body. The voluntary versus statutory choice is false because we want specific sanctions, a wages fund for the public sector that would cut off *jobs* if the increases were too high but not *investment*, because that would be burning our seed corn.' This was one point on which he disagreed with Harold.

Harold asked us to leave behind the key Treasury document, so there would be no leaks. He said we had reached a consensus: it was 10 per cent maximum pay increases to be voluntary with monitoring, a tight timetable for a statutory policy if the voluntary approach failed, and an early announcement and a Government decision.

Afterwards Peter asked me what I thought of it. 'I think we have seen the end of the Government.'

As I went down the stairs with John Silkin, I just pointed my finger at Ramsay MacDonald. That was my feeling as I left Chequers. It was an absolute disaster and I could see no real prospect for success.

Saturday 21 June
I met up with Frances and Francis, Bob Harrison of the TGWU and Larry Whitty of the GMWU in the little garden between Westminster Hospital and the nurses' home, which used to be an old graveyard. We pulled up two wooden benches and I gave them the outlines of the

Government's strategy. I said, 'This is 1931 all over again. It means wage cuts, public expenditure cuts and rising unemployment, and you will have to see that the TUC responds.'

They took it very seriously and asked what to do.

I said, 'I don't want to tell you exactly what happens in Cabinet but you must interrogate the Government on public expenditure policy, on unemployment, the industrial policy, casual or 'lump' labour, disclosure, import controls, price freezes – on all the things that concern you.'

The meeting had a slightly conspiratorial air about it and maybe it would have been better to do it through Frances and Francis, but it was a first-rate communication system through to the labour movement. We walked back to Westminster and bought ice creams, and I caught the tube home.

Sunday 22 June
Sat down with the hundreds of supportive letters that had come in during the Referendum, and I scribbled about 250 replies by hand. That gave me a boost.

Monday 23 June
At 9.30 Brian Tucker, Deputy Secretary of Energy, and my officials came in about the coal industry. The wages problem is the key question and Brian Tucker said the NUM was ruining the industry because of its militancy, and the leadership was out of touch with the rank and file. It was the usual Whitehall self-deception.

Tuesday 24 June
The first item at the Energy Committee was the terrorist threat to nuclear stations, that is to say Dounreay, Windscale, Harwell, and Winfrith. The position is that the police are unarmed not only when guarding the stations, but also when plutonium and enriched uranium are transported by road. The potential for terrorist attacks or even theft represents a very serious danger.

The Special Air Service unit in Hereford is available, but it would take five hours to get up to Dounreay, so it was agreed that we would arm the Atomic Energy Authority police with sidearms and automatic weapons, and they would be trained for protection against terrorists by the Ministry of Defence police. The Department of Energy would be responsible for security, so I now have an extra burden on my shoulder, and a very grave one.

Joe Ashton rang in the evening and he thought I should deal with the miners' issue by calling for workers' control in the pits. I think this would be the most important thing that could possibly be done.

Wednesday 25 June

To Transport House at 10 for the NEC meeting. There is that air of disillusionment within the Party which I feel everywhere, deriving from the exhaustion after the Referendum, from the severe defeat imposed upon the Party during the campaign, and the fact that the Right of the Party have now emerged from the shadows and are making progress on every front. It is very much in line with my general feeling about the political situation, namely that support has melted away.

To Hastings for the CSEU conference. It was a beautiful, dreamy summer afternoon, almost like pictures of the beaches in August 1914 or 1939 except there was hardly anyone on them (no doubt because there isn't the money for holidays at the moment).

I made my speech which lasted half an hour and it was quietly received. I got the same feeling of the conference in retreat in confusion, in disarray, defeated, tired. Maybe it is the way *I* feel. There was polite applause at the end, nothing like the thrilling meetings during the Referendum campaign with that eve of poll atmosphere everywhere.

Flew over in a Hawker Siddeley 125 to Luxembourg where Sir Michael Palliser, our Permanent Representative to the European Communities, met me. The more I think about the Commission, the more utterly depressed I become. Here is a great bureaucratic network with Ministers and civil servants and grand buildings and long conferences, while all political initiative drains away from those who have been elected to the unelected officials. I have to accept the Referendum result, but I have such a feeling of gloom as if somehow I have been taken back in time to before the French Revolution and into the *ancien regime*.

Dinner with Henri Simonet (Vice-President of the Commission), Sir Michael Palliser, the Energy Commissioner Guido Brunner, and the two Cabinet Ministers from Simonet's office. We got into a discussion about the Community and their dream of a European Federation. I told them they'd do better to consider people's desires and try to respond to the common interest that is there, rather than cram solutions that they had developed down everybody's throats. I talked about the role of the politician as preacher rather than as bureaucrat. It was interesting and I think I identified my feelings about the Community without being offensive. In fact I thought I was quite agreeable.

Thursday 26 June

Michael Palliser greeted me at 8 and we went to the British Delegation office in the Community building to look through the brief. At 9.20 we went down to the conference chamber where there was a BBC television crew all the way from London just to photograph this anti-Marketeer taking his seat with the Council of Ministers.

It was a very glossy building, more like the UN than the House of Commons, which is tremendously old fashioned. We were seated at a huge square table and I couldn't make out the features of the people at the far end. There was simultaneous translation, of course, and each of the nine Ministers had three or four advisors with him so there were sixty or seventy around the table, and possibly another couple of hundred behind us.

The Council is really a parliament because it is a legislative body, but it poses as a cabinet. I felt, as a Minister and an elected representative, that I was among a tiny group of fellow Ministers, all burdened down with briefs prepared by officials to submit to the Commission, also made up of officials. The political impulse has been completely overcome and the system is so cumbersome and so secret that there is no real feeling of being engaged in a democratic process at all. It is the board of directors of a huge multi-national company. Not a single working person or the needs of working people are brought anywhere near this centre of power. It depresses me beyond words.

Although I'm here to discuss energy I know that the Commission is really plotting the enlargement of its own area of responsibility and moving nearer and nearer to supranationalism. Everything I said in the Referendum campaign seems to be borne out by what I witnessed here today.

The other thing that is so unpleasant is that even when you do not agree with something, there is a continual temptation to compromise and not be difficult, to agree to something in principle and get the experts to look at it, instead of standing firm for what you want and forcing them to take notice. This slithering along towards compromise and concession is something I find awfully hard to accept.

At lunch I spoke to Justin Keating from the Irish Labour Party who is anti-Market, but he said, 'Well, what does membership really matter? There is so little democracy in our societies that this is not much of a change.' In a sense, he is right. On the other hand, the power of the ballot box in Britain is still very strong and, at this moment, it is frustrating the capacity of capitalism to work effectively.

Flew back to London and it is now just after midnight. I am exhausted.

Friday 27 June

Michael Kerry, a lawyer from the Department of Industry, came to go over the Department's response to the draft report written by the Department of Trade inspectors on the Court Line affair. They have blamed me for what happened and so has the Parliamentary Commissioner, Sir Alan Marre, whose report was issued at about the same

time. So I am for the chopper, but I did stiffen up the response a little
and that is going in.

Had a word with Peter Lovell-Davis who is a good personal friend,
and he feels the media have overdone the attacks. He told me, 'Harold
is very fond of you really and Marcia thinks highly of you.'

'But Harold thinks that I am undermining him all the time.'

'Oh no, I don't think so,' said Peter.

I said that the atmosphere with Harold recently had been cold and
I suggested he might do something to improve it.

'You ought to go and see Marcia,' he said. I might invite her to tea.

Sunday 29 June

It is such a relief to be out of the newspapers. It looks as if the main
battles at the moment are on the housing front where Tony Crosland
has finally been caught out as a totally inadequate Minister. He has no
real policy and the impending public expenditure cuts are bound to
affect housing adversely. Well, that's his problem.

The Attorney-General is continuing to battle it out with the *Sunday
Times* to prevent the publication of the Crossman *Diaries*, and that too
is extremely encouraging because it shows up the Right in their most
unfavourable light. Crossman's *Diaries* have become a sort of Watergate – for heaven's sake, if Nixon's private discussions with all his
civil servants were obliged to be published in America, why on earth
shouldn't Dick Crossman's reflections on his experience as a Minister
ten years ago see the light of day?

Monday 30 June

When I got home I found in my box a farewell letter from Sir Antony
Part. It read:

Personal, 29 June

Dear Secretary of State,

It was sad that, for whatever reason and perhaps due to a misunderstanding,
we did not say goodbye to each other when you left the Department. At
any rate I want to write now on behalf of the staff of the Department as
well as myself, to thank you for all the many courtesies you displayed
towards your civil servants, and so far as I am concerned, the sympathetic
consideration you showed to me during my recent illness.

It was especially kind of you to find the time to come and visit me in the
hospital and write as you did to my wife with your programme of radical
change. Granted the political balance within the Cabinet, you were bound

to face your senior advisors with some difficult problems, but whatever our professional anxieties were from time to time, we enjoyed the challenges and the stimulation, and you were generous in your appreciation of the support that you received on such key subjects as the Industry Bill and the Post Office.

We admired your outstanding skill in communication (even when, occasionally, we were worried about what you were communicating!) and the deftness of your drafting. But, important though these are, they are less significant than the general thrust of your philosophy, so clearly illustrated in its many facets in the book of speeches* (and it is characteristic I know that they were speeches and not private memoranda) that you kindly gave me.

In our different careers we have both sailed through rough waters and, indeed, I expect we should each be surprised if the waters were ever to become smooth, and possibly not know what to do with ourselves if that were to happen! For the marriage of ideas and reality is unending and fascinating, and the responsibility for the fate of others is an unremitting burden for people who are in positions of leadership.

But where would either of us be without such challenges – and how would either of us fare without the imperturbable and invaluable help of such people as Roy Williams?

I send you from myself, Peter Carey and all those who served you in this Department, the most sincere salutations together with my own warm thanks for your personal kindness.

Yours sincerely,
Antony Part

No one can resent a warm letter; in the end I sent the following reply:

Dear Sir Antony,

It was very good of you to write and I appreciated it. I well realise that my brief period in the Department of Industry imposed a heavy strain on you and your officials arising from new policies and initiatives which in turn aroused a major public debate.

Throughout all this I received every possible personal help and I hope you will convey my gratitude to all those involved at various levels, from your own throughout the Department, and including the Private Office.

I am sorry that the pace of the reshuffle made personal farewells imposs-

* *Speeches by Tony Benn*, Spokesman Books, 1974.

ible, but that is one of the hazards of political life. I do hope you are completely fit again and that the anxieties of the winter will never recur.

With kind regards,
Tony Benn.

Tuesday 1 July

Cabinet at 9.30. Harold said that the economic crisis had become very serious and a statement would have to be made outlining the Government's approach to the situation. A White Paper would need to be published containing the pay norm, though we were not to refer to it as such, and there would have to be a two-day debate in July followed by legislation. He called on Denis to explain.

'The pound is crumbling,' said Denis, 'and we must announce measures today. Nigeria, Kuwait and Saudi Arabia have given notice that they will withdraw their money if it falls below a certain level. For the Kuwaitis that level has already been reached and the Nigerian figure was just .004 below that. If we do not make a statement today we shall have to slash public expenditure which will not help us at all.'

He described the progress with the TUC and said that Len Murray and Jack Jones had accepted an inflation target of 10 per cent by September 1976 and single figures by the end of that year. Jack agreed that this would, in effect, suspend all collective bargaining for a year, but the AUEW and the Scottish and Yorkshire miners were against the Social Contract and therefore non-compliance would be a problem. What sanctions could we have, Denis asked. On the nationalised industries we would have to fix a total limit and see that no further subsidies of any kind were provided beyond it. It must be made an offence for an employer in the private sector to pay any settlement above the norm. The TUC could not openly approve such a policy and Jack Jones would criticise it but they would have to accept it.

Harold said that the sterling collapse was the problem and he thought that a viable policy would be acceptable to the TUC. He felt we should rule out criminal sanctions against workers; we should go for a wage fund in the public sector, where people would have a choice between jobs or pay, but even this might require statutory backing; and in the private sector, there should be statutory price controls, possibly threatening a freeze for offenders. There would have to be legislation against employers and he thought the CBI would support us on this.

He said that, as in 1966, we might take the precedent of general powers, but only implement them if necessary. In the case of British Leyland and those firms that had public money, these could be forced to comply, and we could have an insurance scheme to finance firms faced by strikes (that's to say, an insurance scheme for strike-breakers) but there would be no sanctions against the workers.

Michael Foot recognised Denis's difficulties but he did not think this would work.

Roy Jenkins said he had some sympathy with Michael Foot's complaint that we were taking a risk by adopting a new policy within twenty-four hours. He thought that a general, tough statement could do more harm than good. The TUC and the militants were out of touch with public opinion, and the statement alone would not help, especially if the onus was put on prices. He favoured a total wage and price freeze for three months.

Denis said the Governor of the Bank of England had told him that he thought an incomes statement today would stop the rot, that public expenditure would have to be firmly held and a separate statement on the Public Sector Borrowing Requirement would be needed.

Peter Shore recognised the danger, a floating rate had attractions because it was self-containing, but a sterling guarantee with Nigeria, Kuwait and Saudi Arabia might be worth looking at. We needed more time, there was a danger of a breach in the movement that would be of historical importance, and what we were desperately fighting for was authority in the United Kingdom. We needed the help of the TUC.

I asked some practical questions. 'What is the size of the wage cut that is to be imposed?' I estimate that the service sector or local government workers who came in at the beginning of the round, will have suffered a 25 per cent erosion of their living standards in the last year through inflation, and they will then be asked to accept a 10 per cent ceiling on wage increases which will mean that in the year following September 1975, with inflation at 12.5 per cent they will suffer a cut of nearly one third of their income.

'What is the estimated effect of this package, particularly in relation to wage restraint, on unemployment due to a falling off in the domestic market? What are our intentions on public expenditure and do we still adhere to the £2–3 billion? Finally, what is our response to the TUC requests on prices, rents, import controls, investment support, etc? Because it looks as if we are being even less forthcoming than Heath.'

Harold replied, 'The Tories will go along with our measures, they have to; and if the Left of the Party votes against us, we therefore can rely on Tory support, but if the Tories move a motion of No Confidence, then of course the Labour Party would no doubt unite to defend the Government.' A tactical device typical of Harold.

I wanted to speak again but Harold said I had left it a bit late so I made it clear that I was opposed to a statement today.

Wednesday 2 July

At 9.15 I saw Bernard Ingham who asked me about my personal position. I told him I was strongly opposed to the proposed economic package and that there were four options: to put up with it, to oppose it from the inside, to come out and oppose it constructively, or to come out and oppose it destructively. I thought opposing it from the inside was perhaps the best thing to do.

He asked if it would be a good idea to brief Ian Aitken of the *Guardian*. I arranged for this to be done later.

Thursday 3 July
At 7.30 a group of Ministers gathered in my room – Peter Shore, Michael Foot, Stan Orme, Albert Booth, Joan Lestor, Michael Meacher and Barbara Castle. Frances Morrell joined us. At the prospect of resignations by the Left, Barbara began shouting, 'The Left, it is always the Left, you always lose. Why don't you fight? Why don't you put up an alternative?' Shirley Williams has the room next door and the walls are so thin, she probably heard every word.

I said, 'I put up an alternative months ago on import controls.'

'Oh that's no good,' she said. Barbara thinks socialism is about the social wage, which of course is based on the expenditure of her own Department. Although she argues against a statutory policy, she would accept it if it would prevent public expenditure cuts in the DHSS. Actually she's not on our side at all, she's on the other side.

Boy, was she shrieking, throwing her arms in the air. 'All right, you say I am not fair, but nobody has ever been fair to me.' That revealed the burning sense of personal injustice which makes Barbara tick. She is a tough woman and she certainly fights for what she gets, but she is very cynical, and she hates my guts. One thing's for sure, all of this will get back to Harold. If Barbara tells him we are thinking of resigning, that will really worry him.

Sunday 6 July
The *Observer* had a huge two-page spread on the Government U-turn. It included a leading article praising Wilson for adopting the Heath policy, and a piece on Jack Jones describing him as the Godfather, privy to everything that was going on and supported by Michael Foot. It was also reported, and I'm sure it's true, that Michael thinks Denis Healey would make a very good leader. It was confirmation that the Foot-Healey-Jones-Wilson group is running the Government, and that explains why I am on the outside. Of course, the question is will they succeed?

Melissa told me that a woman from the *Daily Mail* had come to the house to ask whether one of the children was in hospital. That's about the fourteenth time that the *Mail* has made that inquiry.

Wednesday 9 July
The *Guardian* had a report about an international mercenary called Carlos who murdered a French spy in Paris recently and has since disappeared. He was living in Bayswater and a cache of arms was found there, along with a 'hit-list' with my name on it, between Vera Lynn and David Jacobs!

To the NEC for a meeting on the economic situation.

Thursday 10 July
Bernard Ingham said the press would be interested today in whether or not I would resign. I told him I wasn't sure what to do but the movement wanted us to stay in. He thought I might have to explain to my constituents the agonising choice I'd had to make.

Cabinet, and the first item was the White Paper, 'The Attack on Inflation'. Harold assumed we'd all read it and wanted to move on to specific amendments.

'Half a minute,' I said. 'I've only just seen it. Can I ask some general questions? Can we have a report on what has happened because apart from what has been in the papers none of us really know?'

Harold was very crabby and called on Denis, who told us 'The TUC have agreed to sanctions against employers through the price code.'

'What is their attitude towards reserve legal powers to enforce the pay limit, or punish those who break it?' I asked. 'Because the TUC statement said that they were in favour of voluntary application of the policy at all stages.'

'Well,' Denis said, 'there is no TUC objection to the White Paper. As to the reserve powers, they haven't really discussed them.' Well, I know for a fact that Len Murray said he was inflexibly opposed to reserve powers. Denis said, 'Len has been told by the Government that it has the right to make decisions for itself after taking account of TUC views.'

We went through the paper and came on to Paragraphs 38 to 47. I said that these paragraphs were immensely important because they represented a completely different economic strategy from the one on which we had fought the Election. They had been imposed on the Cabinet by the Treasury, as a byproduct of the run on the pound. We were elected on the basis of the Social Contract, full employment and an interventionist industrial policy to which the movement is deeply committed. Now we were being told not only to accept real pay cuts, rising unemployment and public expenditure cuts of £2–3 billion, but also to push for higher profits in the hope that this will lead to investment through the market mechanism. This was pre-Keynesian and a recipe for a major slump. I was totally opposed to the strategy and suggested that the paragraphs be removed.

Harold put it to the Cabinet but I was the only one who supported the omission.

We adjourned for tea and Harold brought out my blue and white mug. I always get my special large mug of tea when things are difficult, and I should think there'll be quite a lot of blue and white mug days in the coming weeks.

The meeting resumed and we came on to the reserve powers. Harold opened, saying these would involve fines against employers who broke the pay limit. There would be a change in the law so that there would be no conspiracy charge brought against workers who struck against employers, and he felt this was necessary.

Michael thought Denis had understated the attitude of the TUC, and the Cabinet could destroy the Government if it went ahead with this.

Denis replied, 'I take this very seriously and I feel emotional about it. Michael and I have worked together to achieve some successes for the Government and I recognise the heroic work of the TUC. But it is my duty to recommend reserve powers to the Cabinet because last year's Congress guidelines were not carried out.'

I said that in a democracy only the nation could fight inflation and we had three great assets on our side – public opinion, which wanted inflation reduced, the Party which wanted to maintain the Government, and the unions which wanted to maintain the Government. There was no short cut to fighting inflation other than through general support.

Harold asked Denis to wind up, and Denis said, 'If we refuse to accept the reserve powers it puts me in a personal difficulty. I shall have to consider my own position. If we dodge this, it means that we will have to have a full statutory incomes policy later. The CBI have actually *asked* the Government to legislate against employers. We have a battery of weapons.

'As for Tony Benn, it is easy to be wrong about the Party and the trade unions, and public opinion – as the Referendum proved. I *would* be prepared to announce that legislation has been drawn up to deal with non-compliance which would not constitute reserve powers, only a threat to take powers if necessary.' He was just playing with words.

'Let's be clear on this,' said Michael. 'We are removing from the White Paper all reference to the reserve powers and simply saying that "legislation has been prepared?"'

'Yes,' said Denis. 'I might just get away with that because some of our creditors don't actually believe in incomes policy – they want cuts in public expenditure.'

Harold said it was crucial that there be no leaks and Denis warned that we would have to be a lot tougher on public expenditure. We may have to meet tomorrow or Saturday if there is a further run on the pound.

We left at 3 and I drove to the House, after shaking off a few journalists anxious to know whether I was going to resign. Michael, Barbara, Peter and I went over it all and we wondered whether it had all been fixed from the beginning. But Michael thought that Harold had actually agreed to go along with Denis and was surprised at the way the Cabinet reacted.

Well, today has been a success in the sense that we fought off the complete abandonment of our policy. That's not to say we have won, because the White Paper is still very grim. I despair of the Labour Government as a force for transformation.

I am exhausted and I desperately need a holiday.

Friday 11 July

The papers this morning were full of yesterday's Cabinet discussions. There were one or two pictures of me entering Number 10 with the Manifesto under my arm, which was intended as a tremendous message to the movement, done without any breach of Cabinet loyalty.

The *Financial Times* had a full briefing of my position, according to 'political friends of Mr Benn'. When I went into the office, Bernard Ingham told me he had been talking to John Bourne of the *FT* about how I thought the policy was bound to fail, and how I was anxious about wage cuts and public expenditure cuts and rising unemployment and so on. I was slightly nervous, as I think was Bernard, that they had printed it so fully.

At 11 I went to the House and sat on the Front Bench while Harold made his statement on the situation. It sounded very urgent and tough and he spoke in a staccato way, helped by the fact that Margaret Thatcher completely failed to rise to the occasion. Ted Heath looked incredibly smug.

I went to Otto Clarke's memorial service at St Margaret's, Westminster. Sir Douglas Allen, Head of the Home Civil Service, made the first of two addresses. The whole massed ranks of the Whitehall mandarins were there.

Just before the service began, Roy Jenkins came in larger than life and went straight to the front and sat down. He, of course, is their political leader. They represent the great colonial administration which has run Britain for years and seeing them there confirmed my feeling that Britain is the last colony in the British Empire. These men and their fellow administrators from the India Office and the Colonial Office and no doubt the Irish Office and all these other Offices, governed the world before they were driven out from colony after colony. Now a little group of them meet to bury their dead heroes.

Otto was such a man, though rather exceptional in that he began as a journalist, a marvellous writer, and a Thirties Fabian before going into the Civil Service. During the war he went into the Treasury and that's where he lost his pre-war radicalism, turning his mind instead to the art of decision-making and the satisfaction of having power without the agony of election. He came into Mintech, abrasive and brilliant and, in retrospect, I have more affection for him now than I had when I was there. He was fun to work with and I am somewhat influenced by the knowledge that he liked me.

Saturday 12 July

I had a word with Ken Coates this evening and he advised me to get out. He said if I stayed in, I'd be tarred with the same brush and the movement would never respond to me in the same way.

I said, 'Well, if I had come out on Chile, Simonstown, or the Common Market, I wouldn't have been there to do anything. There will be a dozen events over the next twelve months where I will find myself in a minority, but I just have to survive.'

I thought about it. If you come out, you're accused of rocking the boat and the movement doesn't want to endanger the Government; but then you have a vested interest in the failure of the Government because you have left it, and everybody disregards what you are doing on the grounds that you are trying to bring the Government down. If you leave the Cabinet but vote with the Government right through, then you are sustaining a Government you have left. The whole thing is so complicated, and I believe the best strategy is to develop the campaign for Labour policy from inside the Government.

Tuesday 15 July

To the North Sea Re-negotiation Committee at 9, with Harold Lever, Edmund Dell, Tommy Balogh, John Smith, Jack Rampton, Leo Pliatzky, Kenneth Berrill, John Liverman and other officials. All the papers had been written by officials, and the first suggested that we bring Shell and Exxon in for a further presentation, and that a presentation be given to the banks and finance houses. Harold Lever was in favour of reassuring the banks. Edmund Dell said the cost of participation to the Public Sector Borrowing Requirement would be such that he was in no hurry to move. 'Shell and Exxon will resist.'

The next paper related to buy-back – the proposal that we should offer to sell back participation oil – our share – to the oil companies. Harold Lever thought the idea was ridiculous. We should simply ask the companies what they want and tailor our policy to meet their needs.

Edmund Dell agreed. 'We don't want to pay for what we don't need.

How much oil does the British National Oil Company really need? Where is it to be refined? And at what balance of payments cost? What is the target? We must make it clear that we are not going to insist on getting two-thirds of the oil, otherwise we'll frighten the oil companies.'

Fred Atkinson, the Department's Chief Economic Adviser, asked, 'In that case, why are we having participation at all?'

Leo Pliatzky said, 'There is no financial gain in this either way. We want control, especially in an emergency, a public sector capability and a seat on the operating consortium. How much oil do we need for that?'

Tommy Balogh believed we *could* avow our real reason which was control of exports to the EEC. We needed control to deal with emergencies, and to help in the refinery decisions.

'But it will cost money to erode their right to the oil and it will take time,' said Harold Lever.

Sir Kenneth Berrill said the central question was whether you could keep the oil in the UK, and if the EEC prevented you from keeping it here, could you offer a buy-back in perpetuity.

I said, 'I know I'm a newcomer to this but the whole thing looks as if it's being done with mirrors. There's nothing in it at all.'

'Whatever you do,' Harold Lever repeated, 'don't frighten the oil companies. They think you're after them, Tony. You mustn't frighten them.'

It was agreed finally that we would offer buy-back contracts without specifying a date and see what the response was.

Harold Lever is uncompromisingly pro-oil companies. When I argued that they were sophisticated, experienced people, used to dealing with Governments, and they would expect us to defend our national interest, he wouldn't hear of it.

As for Edmund Dell, he wants to frustrate public ownership of any kind, partly because he doesn't believe in it, partly because he has now got the petroleum revenue tax and he doesn't think it helps very much, and partly because of the PSBR and the economic situation.

Cabinet at 10.30. Harold announced that we would be meeting on Friday to consider the Chancellor's statement on public expenditure cuts. We were discussing next week's business when all of a sudden Harold or Denis exclaimed, 'When are we going to publish the Reserve Powers Bill?'

We had specifically agreed that we would not mention reserve powers in the White Paper, only that 'legislation was being prepared'. Without telling anyone, it appears that Harold has announced that a Reserve Powers Bill would be published. In the end, after discussion, he agreed not to publish before the TUC Congress in September.

There followed a tremendous discussion on MPs' pay which is now

£4,500 pa. The report recommended £8,000 and we finally agreed on £5,750, plus full allowances of £1,250. It is an improvement but the rise still covers only half of the rise in the cost of living since the last wage settlement. On Cabinet Ministers' pay, I voted for the renunciation of the increase in MPs' salaries. Of course democracy is about narrowing differentials and although it is painful, you can't lecture people for earning too much when you're highly paid yourself. But a lot of MPs will think we've let them down.

At 3.30 Sir Eric Drake of British Petroleum came to see me and I went out of my way to be charming. He said that Government holdings of British Petroleum shares must be kept below 50 per cent because it would destroy the credibility of the company in the United States, in New Zealand and elsewhere – BP operates in eighty countries. Therefore, he wanted the BP Burmah shares sold off in the open market but not to foreign Governments. Well, I'm not accepting that.

I had contemplated giving Drake the chairmanship of BNOC but he was so negative and hostile that I changed my mind. I'm glad I saw him and it is probably a good thing to be on reasonably good terms with him, though he is the most Tory of Tories.

Spent most of the afternoon on the Petroleum Bill Committee.

Spoke to Gerald Kaufman who told me that, at a meeting in Oxford, a man had got up and said, 'The only reason that Tony Benn didn't nationalise Westland is that he has shares in it.'

Well, that's an extraordinary story. I was grateful for him telling me.

Wednesday 16 July

Took the HS-125 to Aberdeen with Ronnie Custis, Bernard Ingham and representatives of British Petroleum. We were then flown in a Bristow helicopter down to the Graythorpe I platform.

The little community on the platform has its own satellite communication network, a heliport and all the necessary equipment. Ten magawatts of electricity are needed for the pumping of the oil which goes 120 miles to Cruden Bay and then right down to Grangemouth.

In the middle of winter when the conditions are exceptionally rough, it must be absolute hell to work there. It is a complete science fiction world and it is a sobering thought that our future as a nation depends upon the Forties Field and others like it in the North Sea, and how vulnerable they are to foreign attack.

At the Station Hotel in Aberdeen I met the inter-union Oil Committee and the North Sea Action Committee and they raised a number of important points, mainly about unionisation on the rigs. They cannot get union representatives on to the rigs and they are very anxious about safety. They say that if they can't make progress, they are determined to black the rigs. So I offered to write around and try to get things moving. Dinner with Sandy Mutch, who is Chairman of the Grampian Regional Council and used to be President of the Scottish Conservative Party. He is a friend of Ted Heath's and he told me that there was a feeling at the grass roots of the Conservative Party that they would never win another Election with Heath as Leader, so he had to go. But he doubted that Mrs Thatcher would ever be Prime Minister. 'Even if she wins an Election, there will be a coup d'état between the Election and the formation of the Government and someone else will be Prime Minister.' He wouldn't say who. He didn't think much of Howe, Joseph, Soames, Whitelaw or Du Cann.

Thursday 17 July

The papers over the last couple of days have reported the news from New York that Exxon has openly admitted to paying $51 million (£20 million) to Italian politicians and political parties over the last nine years. That's over £2 million a year flowing from a single oil company into Italian political funds. The number of people who could be bought, corrupted, suborned, diverted, blackmailed and assassinated with £20 million defies the imagination. One shouldn't be in any doubt at all as to what we're up against and I shall use this if necessary to defend the development of BNOC.

Friday 18 July

Went to the Atomic Energy Authority reception at Banqueting House in Whitehall to celebrate the twenty-first anniversary of its formation. I hadn't wanted to go, though I'm glad I did because I met lots of old friends. Ieuan Maddock, my scientific adviser at Mintech, was there.

I met a few trade union people, including Sir Harry Crane of the GMWU, who chaired the Conference Arrangements Committee of the Labour Party for years. I had always seen him as a right-wing trade unionist and what he told me was amazing.

'You have got to watch it. I used to have regular contact with the Security Services when I was in the Labour movement and whenever I got information about anybody from them, I would pass it on to Sara Barker. You have got to watch the Communist Party all the time.'

Here was a senior Labour trade unionist admitting that the Intelligence Services were passing information about Labour MPs and trade union officials to Harry Crane so he could then pass it on the National Agent of the Labour Party, who no doubt got them expelled. Utterly offensive.

I said, 'The main thing is that we maintain good relations with the trade union movement.'

'Nonsense,' he said. 'I told Attlee and Gaitskell that the sooner they broke away from the trade union movement, the better. Gaitskell said the money was the problem but I told him, "You're the Government; you've got to govern the trade union movement. What right have they to tell you what to do?"'

It was like being with one of Madame Tussauds wax models but listening to him, I realised that it was a taste of what's to come: this is the way the wind is blowing.

I had lunch with Audrey Wise, Dennis Skinner, Bob Cryer and Brian Sedgemore. Dennis shrewdly said, 'You realise that with the miners and the GMWU and the TGWU voting the way they will, the Conference will support the £6 pay restraint. That will put you in a difficult position.'

'That would be the least of my difficulties, Dennis.' He too has anticipated the swing to the Right in the Labour Party but the policy won't work, and I think there will be revolt in the course of the winter when the unemployment figures rise.

Saturday 19 July
Went shopping with Melissa and we walked up Kensington High Street. We went into Biba's store which really is the end of a dream. You can see why it failed really because it was the final fling for the excrescences of Sixties' fashion, now all gone bust.

Tuesday 22 July
I heard today that the problem of what we would do with oil off the Falkland Islands has been settled by the Foreign Office. They have insisted that we agree to discuss with Argentina joint exploration of the South Atlantic, and this is intended to get us off the hook.

Lunch with Frank Kearton at Courtaulds headquarters in Calenese House. I have known Frank now for nine years and he is resigning tomorrow as Chairman of Courtaulds. He told me about his wartime experiences and how he had known Klaus Fuchs* very well. Fuchs had often come to stay with him. Then the news broke that secrets had been leaked and the Security Services came to see Frank, saying, 'Secret papers available only to you and Klaus Fuchs have leaked, and it's either you or him. We've gone through your records and they seem all right, so it must be Fuchs.' Frank had been shocked.

We talked about Harold Wilson and he said he had met Harold recently and Harold had told him, 'In politics, timing is everything,' and compared himself to Stanley Baldwin. Harold has compared himself to all sorts of people in his Walter Mitty life. He was the Kennedy figure in 1962 with 'Let's get Britain moving again'. Then he

* Klaus Fuchs, a German-born nuclear scientist working in Britain, was jailed for fourteen years in 1950 for passing information on atomic weapons to the Soviet Union.

became a bit of a Macmillan figure. Then he and Lyndon Johnson were the greatest pals. Now he's Baldwin. That just about sums him up.

We discussed Jack Jones for whom Frank has enormous respect because he's a great statesman. We talked about worker participation and economic policy and I mentioned the cooperatives. I said that the Treasury was now running things.

'I don't think the Treasury has a policy,' he said. 'They stumble along from day to day. When William Armstrong resigned from the Civil Service, he had a little dinner party at Sunningdale and I was invited. He just kept saying that all was lost, and there was no hope for the country and he couldn't see his way forward at all. I have never seen a man so utterly defeated.'

I said, 'That's because he was the one who persuaded Heath to drop the Party's objections to the prices and incomes policy, and then he saw the policy crumble in the face of the miners and I think he was utterly demoralised.'

Melissa came into the House and everyone admired her out on the terrace, saying she looked like an actress from a television programme, *The Main Chance*. She was shy as the MPs came up to speak to her but I was so proud of her.

Wednesday 23 July

NEC at 10 and the first item was a motion by Renée Short on abortion, welcoming the evidence of the National Women's Advisory Committee and attacking the James White Bill.* Walter Padley, Bob Mellish and Shirley Williams launched into an attack and said it would lose us votes. In the end, after Judith Hart had moved an amendment to add the words 'fully recognising the right of individual conscience in this matter', the Executive passed the motion with only four votes against.

At 4.45 I went to the Industrial Development Committee where there was a discussion about Court Line. On 14 July the inspectors will report that I was responsible for giving holiday-makers the idea that there was a Government guarantee against any loss. The Ombudsman is going to say the same thing. Peter Shore thought we should compensate. Sam Silkin said it was basically a legal decision and we weren't legally liable, but we might be morally liable.

I said it was difficult for me because I had taken personal responsibility even though it was a Government decision.

---

* The Abortion Amendment Bill, sponsored by James White, Labour MP for Glasgow Pollock, aimed to amend the 1967 Act so as to severely restrict access to abortion. Risk to the woman's life had to be 'grave' and a twenty-week limit was proposed, raised to twenty-four weeks where a consultant diagnosed handicap.

The next item was Meriden. I had written a paper but it was so obvious that they had decided to destroy the British motorcycle industry that I left before it was discussed. Peter told me later that I was severely and personally criticised, and I said, 'That's why they moved me because I wanted to save jobs and that's no longer acceptable.' But they underestimate the strength of the argument if they let that cooperative go down the drain.

Thursday 24 July

The main news this morning was that Reg Prentice was rejected by the Newham North-East party by 29 votes to 19. The interesting thing is that the minority who supported him did not echo his complaint that the Party had been infiltrated by Marxists.

Cabinet at 10 and Jim Callaghan reported on Portugal saying they had no Government and Soares, leader of the Portuguese Socialist Party, feared assassination. The Communist Party and the armed forces were worried that the NATO exercises being carried out in the area might possibly be part of an interventionist strategy. He also told us that this was very secret, and Schmidt, Giscard and Wilson would be discussing with Brezhnev next week the extent of Soviet commitments there, with a view to trying to get them scaled down. The Socialist International was at work and the armed forces were split between those who wanted the overthrow of the Communists and those who were working with them.

Friday 25 July

We had an all-night sitting on the Remuneration, Charges and Grants Bill and I didn't dare sleep in my room in case I missed the division bell. On one vote we had a majority of only one. I managed to sleep on the Front Bench for a couple of hours but the trouble is, if you put your legs out people trip over them, and if you put your legs back then people bump into your knees. Every time there was a division somebody shook me but I have no recollection of how many times I voted or on what.

I had a word with Judith Hart. She and Tony are going to Portugal for their holidays and we talked about the CIA and our suspicions that they were involved in skulduggery there. Kissinger must be busy de-stabilising the regime because if it continues for much longer, it may bring Spain into open conflict. The Americans have to avoid that because of their dependence on Spain for their NATO bases.

Sunday 27 July

In my red box today were a number of papers for the Energy Committee on international research and development, on the fast breeder reactor and on the need for a tripartite examination of the coal industry. This will come up tomorrow and it is not made easier by Arthur Scargill writing in the *Sunday Express* that he would like to see me as Leader of the Labour Party.

Still, if the Tories in Newham North-East have decided to support Reg Prentice and if Ted Heath has called upon the Tories to give unequivocal support to the Government's anti-inflation policy, I suppose it is not unreasonable that Arthur Scargill should give some support to me. Incidentally, Arthur also wrote that the Leader of the Party should be elected at Conference.

Tuesday 29 July
Caroline had a letter from her brother today with a surprising second chapter to the death threat against me which she received a while ago. Someone using her own surname, De Camp, wrote 'on behalf of' a group of ten businessmen in Britain who planned to assassinate me. I handed this to the Private Office and heard nothing more. But it appears that the UK got on to the FBI and the FBI began watching people with this surname in the USA. This came out when Caroline's brother, who is a journalist, finally confronted the agent watching him and asked what was going on. He laughed when he heard, because, he said, he was hardly likely to write threatening letters to his own sister, of whom he was very fond. The FBI were completely unaware they were watching Caroline's brother, which shows how inept the Security Services are.*

Melissa told me an interesting story today. Two or three days ago, she spoke to her friend Gina on the office phone. Then she picked up the home phone to make another call, and her previous conversation was played back. This confirms categorically that both phones are wired through a recording room where they are tapped. The conversations must be recorded and then someone plays back what was said. That was what Melissa heard when she picked up the other phone.

Yet more strange goings on with our rubbish. For some time it has been collected very early each morning, whereas before, Kensington Borough Council only collected it once a week. We wondered who was taking it and, as we read recently in the paper that someone had bribed the trashmen in Washington to give them all the rubbish from Kissinger's house, it occurred to me that this might be happening to me. So I decided to buy a shredding machine and also Joshua fitted

---

* No explanation was forthcoming for this extraordinary episode but later there were some press reports of a 'Club of Ten', said to be South African agents operating against the Left in the UK; no connection was definitely established.

up a wire leading from the rubbish area at the front of the house to a bell in the house.*

Talked to Bernard Donoughue who was interested in the fact that officials were mainly concerned to protect the confidentiality of official advice to Ministers, which is why the Crossman *Diaries* worried them so much.

At Cabinet we talked about Meriden and the future of the cooperatives, and the discussion threw light on a number of things. First of all, it was absolutely clear that both Court Line, and Meriden, which is Eric Varley's razor job, are being used to discredit my period at the Department of Industry. They are trying to make out that it was incompetence on my part, and linking it with Rolls Royce, Upper Clyde Shipbuilders and Concorde.

Secondly, Harold's strategy in moving me from Industry is not only to reverse the policy, but also to ensure that I get the blame for the troubles that come when the policy *is* reversed. He is hoping to chip away at my standing within the movement at the same time as the new policy is being prepared – a Treasury policy under which people will not be able to go to the Industry Department for money because there will be no money, no help, no tea and no sympathy. Gerald Kaufman is certainly in there digging around seeing what he can find that might be damaging to me.

Ron picked me up after Cabinet and took me to the ASTMS office for lunch with Clive Jenkins. He was in his shirtsleeves tossing the salad, a marvellous spectacle, and we sat down to a very fancy lunch.

Elliott Richardson had invited him to dinner the other night and Clive had apparently pointed to various people there and said, 'He's on the right-wing of the CIA and you're on the left-wing of the CIA.' Elliott is now rumoured as its possible future head.

Clive told me (saying he was simply acting as a 'conduit', which I think may be a technical security phrase), that Gordon McLennan, the new General Secretary of the Communist Party, had been to dinner with him last night. McLennan said, 'Clive, I have come to ask you what you think the Communist Party should now do because it is re-thinking its position. We have been considering the future of the Labour Party and we have come to the conclusion that the only credible alternative Leader is Tony Benn and the only credible rival for him is Denis Healey.'

Clive told me that when he tried to join the Communist Party just after the war, he went to see Jim Cattermole, the Regional Organiser

* On one occasion, the bell rang in the early hours of the morning and Joshua saw from his bedroom window someone removing the rubbish into a private car which then drove away.

in the Midlands. Jim said, 'Don't do that. You're just the sort of chap we want in Parliament. I'll arrange for you to have a seat.'

Had a long talk to Neil Kinnock later who told me to beware of the Communists.

Wednesday 30 July

Went over to the House and missed the PLP but was delighted to hear that the meeting voted by 75 to 50 in favour of voting again for the lifting of the disqualification of the Clay Cross councillors. The debate was largely carried by a speech from Lena Jeger who said it was no longer just a matter of Clay Cross to which we were committed by Conference, but whether the Commons would accept a defeat in the Lords on a commitment in our Manifesto.

Thursday 31 July

The newspaper exploded with Court Line. It was exactly as I had predicted, namely an excuse for a major attack on me and the policies with which I was associated at the Department of Industry. 'Benn: the day of reckoning' in the *Daily Express*; 'Guilty Benn' in the *Mail*. There was fury at the Government's rejection of the Ombudsman's report and the report of the Department of Trade inspectors.

Friday 1 August

At 11.30 Elliott Richardson came to see me with Miller, the Minister from the US Embassy, to discuss the North Sea Oil policy. This is the third time that a foreign Ambassador has been to see me to complain about Government policy. The first two occasions were when I was Minister of Technology and I appeared to be favouring British firms at the expense of foreign firms: the Japanese Ambassador for giving preference to Marconi in the establishment of an earth-tracking station in Hong Kong, and the Swedish Ambassador about the build-up of the British ball-bearing industry at the expense of a Swedish company. Well, the Japanese and Swedes are one thing but the Americans are quite another.

In walked Elliott, smooth and sleek, an Eastern Republican lawyer who acquired a world-wide reputation when he resigned as Attorney-General after Nixon dismissed the special Watergate prosecutor. He has got a huge record of service in the United States – Under-Secretary of State for Health, Education and Welfare under Eisenhower, Secretary of Defence briefly, as well as Attorney-General. Elliott has made a special effort to acquaint himself with British trade union leaders. He's had Jack Jones, Hugh Scanlon and Clive Jenkins in to see him.

He sat down, opened his polished leather briefcase and handed to us copies of a note addressed to the Secretary of State for Foreign Affairs and dated today. It read:

The Ambassador of the United States of America presents his compliments to His Excellency, the Secretary of State for Foreign and Commonwealth Affairs, and has the honour to refer to the Petroleum and Submarine Pipelines Bill now being considered by Parliament. The Ambassador wishes to bring the following comments to Her Majesty's Government.

The Petroleum and Submarine Pipelines Bill has given rise to considerable concern among American companies engaged in North Sea Oil development. The United States Government shares many of these concerns regarding the potential effects of this legislation.

The points raised were: the changing of existing licences; control of exploration or development; the possibility that these powers might impose a financial loss or the penalty of loss of licence; there was no provision for compensation; the companies involved believed the Bill would further reduce the speed of development of North Sea Oil resources – a very threatening point – at a time when the US Government believes that the development of new sources of energy is of common interest to the United States and Britain; the Bill raised the question of its compatibility with international law regarding the regulation and taking of foreign property and contractual rights.

It was recognised that there had been some amendments to the Bill and the assurances given by Eric Varley were quoted. It ended, 'The United States Government expresses the hope and expectation that Her Majesty's Government will continue to take account of the concerns of licensees and that the Bill, when it becomes law, will be administered in such a way that the pace of development of the North Sea will not be diminished.'

I said, 'Ambassador, I am not familiar with diplomatic niceties and I notice that you presented a formal note addressed to my colleague, the Secretary of State for Foreign Affairs, so in a sense, I am a spectator in this exchange.'

'Oh no, it's about you that I have written,' he told me.

I went on, 'Constitutionally, all Secretaries of State are indivisible in English law. There are about twenty of us but we can sign each other's documents, so to that extent it is addressed to me at least in one-twentieth of my role. I recognise that you will probably require a written response which would be forthcoming from the Secretary of State for Foreign Affairs but perhaps you would allow me to comment informally upon the points that you have made.'

I gave the background to the policy, saying that I was not the Minister at the time it was devised but I felt that I could explain it best from a detached point of view. The Bill gave us powers which we thought necessary since we now had these vast natural resources to develop. For example, the requirement for licensees to undertake exploratory work had been met by an amendment saying we would only ask them to undertake work that it would be reasonable for a licensee to undertake if he had adequate resources and with a reasonable commercial expectation of return. He accepted that but argued that development was different.

I went on to the question of international law and told him that after looking into this most carefully, we had concluded that questions of international law did not arise because every nation state had the right to change the environment in which companies operated in that country.

I finished, 'I must ask you to treat my legal views with circumspection since my doctorate in civil law is an honorary one but I imagine that when the United States Congress passed the prohibition law, the long-term contracts of Scottish whisky manufacturers were adversely affected. In the Emission Control and Safety Regulations which the American Government passed, long-term contracts by British firms were affected and, indeed, all budgetary changes and environmental controls on the depletion or use of natural resources would come into the same category. There was absolutely no discrimination in this regard.'

The Ambassador said, 'We only said that this "raised" a question of international law – not that the matter was settled.'

I said I was relieved to hear that. In any case there had been full consultation and I had given many assurances in the Committee that there were reserve powers. They were not retrospective in the ordinary sense, they did not make illegal what had been legal at the time, but they introduced new criteria.

'However,' I said, 'the basis of the relationship between states, particularly parliamentary democracies like our own which have always observed most scrupulously the principles of international law, is bound to be one of confidence.' He accepted that, and that there had been consultation between the oil companies and the Department.

I went on, 'I notice that in your final paragraph, you refer to the administration of the law. We would seek to administer the law in the same spirit in which we conducted the consultations.'

We moved on to the supply of equipment and he hoped there would be no arm-twisting in the case of the purchase of oil equipment by American firms.

'No,' I said. 'There will be a bit of elbow-jogging but no arm-twisting.'

'I hope it doesn't go as far as blackmailing the companies into buying British equipment.'

I said No, but we were anxious that more British equipment be used by the American firms. I told him that I had heard of hand tools for use in the North Sea being imported all the way from Texas. He insisted that it must be on the basis of full and free opportunity and Miller intervened to underline that point.

'Are you suggesting that it should be on the basis of reciprocity?' I asked.

'What do you mean?' Miller said.

'Well, I have had many complaints from British firms in the States that under the Jones Act, it was illegal for any but American ships to operate around the United States, and that our own ships which were being built for the North Sea, where 60 per cent of those operational were of foreign construction, could not then be used in the United States.'

They obviously didn't know that and were somewhat taken aback. It was a friendly discussion but having the American Ambassador come to me on behalf of the oil companies was a tremendous and vivid reminder of the power of the American Government and its prime concern – namely to defend its own giant multinationals. This was a warning shot across my bows – and across the Government's bows. I felt a bit like a Latin American leader who had got a bit out of tune with the requirements of American international commercial policy. I realise that my position here may be harder than I had imagined.

Wednesday 6 August
To the Commons for the Court Line debate. Peter opened with a marvellous, fighting speech, in which he attacked Heseltine and defended the Government's record. Heseltine came back with a pathetic speech after all his arrogant posturing over the affair, and was totally crushed. Whitelaw's contribution was very woolly, saying a mistake had been made and a ministerial apology would be in order.

The House filled up and there was going to be a vote with a two-line whip. I had had a final appeal from Bob Mellish to apologise and yesterday Humphrey Atkins, the Conservative Chief Whip, had assured Bob that if I apologised, they wouldn't go to a vote.

I spoke for twenty minutes using notes and documents, giving way only once to Whitelaw. I got the political and industrial policy implications of Court Line across and it is now on record. Although I didn't feel it was a triumph, which it couldn't be really, it was a defence of the position.

We got a majority of 24. A lot of Labour MPs stayed on to vote and I was touched by their warm support. Harold sat beside me and Michael Foot, bless his heart, always supports me.

Sunday 17 August
Stansgate. Cycled to Southminster, up Steeple Hill which nearly killed me. In the evening I rowed to Osea, so my exercise is reaching a peak.

Not much in the papers and I certainly do notice, when I am separated from day-to-day politics, how wildly hostile the press is to everything to do with working people, trade unions and young people. It is an extremely dangerous tendency which I have noticed building up over the last few years. Whether it is a move towards fascism is perhaps too early to say.

Wednesday 20 August
Harold Wilson was on television tonight appealing to the nation on the counter-inflation policy. Huge advertisements have been organised by Geoffrey Goodman in the Counter-Inflation Unit at the Treasury, and booklets are going to be put through every door in Britain, all in anticipation of the TUC Conference. Wilson looked tough and piggy-eyed, and although the message sounded reasonable, it was the Ramsay MacDonald line all over again.

Thursday 21 August
Tonight Willie Whitelaw appeared on television supporting Harold Wilson, so that is the National Government being formed under our very eyes. How on earth the Labour Cabinet can get satisfaction out of national support for a policy of this kind I don't know, because there is no foundation for support, or at least there shouldn't be. We want to change society, we want public expenditure to continue, and yet somehow we have got ourselves into a position where all national differences have been sunk in a survival policy for Britain, based on making working people pay the price for resuscitating the capitalist system.

Friday 29 August
A bomb exploded opposite the post office in Kensington Church Street just a few minutes' walk from where we live, destroying a shoe shop and killing the bomb-disposal man.

At a reception for the Qataris in the evening, we talked to the PLO representatives who are here for the Inter-Parliamentary Union Conference tomorrow. I said that if there were some solution which did not absolutely destroy the State of Israel, it would help strengthen the PLO case within the Labour Party.

We had had special instructions from Harold Wilson about tomorrow's IPU Conference, in which he said that Ministers were not, under any circumstances, to be friendly towards the PLO representatives, and they were only to speak to them if they were approached at parties.

That instruction, had it been known, would have confirmed the very worst of the PLO's fears, that the Labour Party was not even sympathetic to the Palestinian cause.

Friday 5 September
Got to the House of Commons at 12.10 and missed the bomb at the Hilton Hotel by about ten minutes. It killed two people and wounded sixty-nine.

Saturday 6 September
Ken Coates rang to say that Lord Chalfont* had asked the Institute for Workers' Control to participate in an Anglia Television programme based on the article by Tom Stacey called 'The Road to Communism'. Ken Coates refused and the company offered £2000 to the Bertrand Russell Press which prints IWC publications if they could film them at work. £2000 is an enormous amount of money and it makes me wonder whether British Intelligence is involved in an attempt to make it a big exposé of revolutionaries in Britain.

Monday 8 September
Caroline, Stephen and I went to dinner with Elliott Richardson at Parks Restaurant in Beauchamp Place. He is an Anglophile, Establishment figure and mixes with the Ascot set, but still he's making a better job of it than his predecessor, Walter Annenberg.

'The trouble with you is you don't believe in profits,' he said.

I told him I believed in Old Testament prophets.

The CIA was mentioned and I said I'd heard he was tipped as next head.

'Anyone in the White House would say we have to have a lawyer,' he said, 'someone with experience and so on, and my name would be bound to be among the top two or three. I would like to do it except it might interfere with my political ambitions.'

It was clear he was thinking of running for the presidency though I don't know if he has enough public support. He seemed to think that if Ford lost next time, he might be the candidate. 'But you see I'm fifty-five and I might be too old. I won't conceal from you that if I am not able to get the presidency, the Secretary of State's job would be the next best thing.'

Towards the end, I said, 'Stephen is doing a PhD on advisers in the White House.' He was very interested in that and they had a long talk.

* Alun Gwynne Jones, former Defence Correspondent of *The Times*, created a peer in 1964 and appointed Minister of State at the Foreign and Commonwealth Office by Harold Wilson in the 1964–70 Labour Governments.

'You forget that these men don't have power. They just do a regular job, they're just advisers,' Richardson said.

Stephen commented on Nixon's working methods and Richardson told us how tough Ike was as President and, though he might look friendly to the crowds, he was really a bastard and had everything under his control. Nixon too made all the decisions.

Wednesday 10 September

Chequers for the talks on devolution. Harold explained that we were here only to look at papers and no decisions would be made today. Ted Short reminded us that we were committed to introducing legislation this session. There was growing support in the SNP for devolution but we were not devolving sovereignty. We were preserving economic and political unity, national security, international relations, regional management and balance, social security and electoral law.

Willie Ross said, 'We're committed by the Queen's Speech and it was scrutinised by everyone. We must trust a Scottish Assembly as law-makers.'

'Wales only wants executive devolution, not legislative devolution,' said John Morris.

Roy Jenkins thought we should discuss such a fundamental issue with the Opposition. There was no ideological conflict here. We and the Tories had been forced into it and there were legislative risks.

Harold agreed with Roy and said that we would have talks with Mrs Thatcher. Ted Short said he had already had courtesy talks with Whitelaw.

At lunch, Harold came up for a talk and I mentioned a hoax bomb alert on the North Sea oil rigs which I had to deal with in August.

So he said, 'I carry my walkie-talkie with me at all times to receive messages quickly.' He told me that the Russians always have a submarine or trawler off the Scillies when he is there and they can even pick up the walkie-talkie. 'Last summer, the zip on my trousers broke and I told my inspector to radio back to the police at the house to tell them. I thought that might be misunderstood by the Russian captain so I just said into the walkie-talkie, "British Prime Minister to Russian trawler. When I saw my zip is broken, I mean that my trouser button has come off. There are no flies on the British Prime Minister."'

He went over all his experiences and told me that no one in the Shadow Cabinet had voted for him when he became Leader in 1963.

I said, 'I heard you got a letter from one person congratulating you and then received a copy of a letter the same man had written to George Brown saying he had voted for him!'

'Yes,' said Harold, 'and that man is here today.' I concluded that it must have been Jim Callaghan.

Thursday 11 September

I received in yesterday's post a photocopy of a letter allegedly from Dick Taverne to William Rees-Mogg, the editor of *The Times*. 'Taverne' had been written in brackets after the signature by whoever sent it to me. Whether authentic or not it was fascinating.

Dear William,

I shall be away in Scotland for the next few days. I did want a brief chat but it may be just as well to write rather than telephone.

The Prentice meeting, at which Roy and Shirley are speaking, seems to me a vitally important one. Harold has rather got away with things for the time being but I believe all that he has done is postpone the moment of truth, and the sharper the clash between the Left and Right in the Labour Party, the better for the future of our politics. What worries me slightly is that the meeting on the 11th has not, as far as I have seen, had much recent publicity and may therefore not be quite as large or provocative as it might be. Would it not rate a leader on Thursday?

If by any chance you thought it did, could you not also commend the attitude of the Vice-Chairman of the local Conservatives who admires Reg greatly and he has stated that Conservatives should not oppose him if he should take his fight further. I believe that, while I was away, this produced a strong reaction from the Conservative Right and I am told by the Social Democratic Alliance people that public support from *The Times* and elsewhere would be very helpful at his stage.

It is just a thought, but I felt it was worth passing on.

Yours ever,
Dick

PS – My address until Wednesday night is Gleneagles Hotel, 0764 62236.

My first reaction was that this was dynamite, and if I circulated it widely it would do a great deal of damage by linking Reg Prentice to Dick Taverne. But then I wondered whether it might be a forgery. I decided to show it to Frances Morrell before taking it any further.

It may even be the press attempting to draw me into the discussion on Reg Prentice's position in order to associate me with the so-called extremists who are trying to prevent Reg from continuing his parliamentary work. In any case, all this discussion of Reg Prentice is irrelevant when the real issue is unemployment. In the end, I decided not to do anything about it.

Roy Jenkins, Shirley Williams and Tom Jackson duly went to speak for Reg Prentice in Newham. The National Front threw a bag of flour and he was heckled a lot by the International Socialists. Of course it had nothing to do with the Labour Party, Left or Right, but it will be used to build up the idea that extremists are trying to take things over.

Sure enough, the coverage which Dick Taverne had requested did appear in *The Times* today in the form of pieces by Ronald Butt and George Clark. The meeting had been provocative and therefore did help Prentice.

Sunday 14 September
Both the *Observer* and the *Sunday Times* specifically dismissed the National Front attack on the Jenkins–Prentice meeting, while the *Sunday Times* warned that the Labour Party would fall into the hands of left-wing thugs and fascists which was an incredible – and contradictory – statement. But it does indicate the strengthening of the Right in the Labour Party.

Frank McElhone rang to tell me that last Thursday he had been summoned to Number 10 and had been made Under-Secretary of State in the Scottish Office. He was absolutely delighted and was most grateful to me for speaking to Bob Mellish. On Wednesday at Chequers I had talked to Harold about the intrusions that the Scottish Nationalists were making into the Catholic vote in West Central Scotland, and it was the following morning that Frank was summoned. It is little enough, in return for all he has done for me.

Monday 15 September
Flew to Paris for the start of the tour of EEC capitals with Bernard Ingham, Frances Morrell and Gill Brown, seconded to Energy from the Foreign Office. We were taken to the Embassy Residence and went up to my room, and who should be next door but Barbara Castle. She's here for a dinner with Simone Veil, the French Minister for Women.

Went downstairs and found Sir John Hunt with the Ambassador, Sir Edward and Lady Tomkins. Barbara had told me Sir John Hunt was here about oil so I said to him, 'I hear you're here to discuss oil.' He denied it but I think he probably was.

Then I asked him about the Crossman *Diaries* and I said I sympathised with his difficulties. He said, 'I'm trying to apply the rules; but do you think it would be possible to have an absolutely open system? Would it be safe?'

'I think it's malice towards colleagues, not information, which is the problem,' I replied.

'What about civil servants?' he asked. 'Could they reply to allegations or stories?'

I said, 'I wouldn't mind.' I described Peter Carey and the Accounting Officer's Minute.

We came on to collective responsibility and I said the principle was very simple. 'What happened up to five minutes ago you're all responsible for; what happens five minutes from now is an open argument. I don't see any reason why people shouldn't know what the Cabinet arguments are. After all most arguments in Cabinet come from departmental interests. Everyone knows that Roy will take one view and Michael another, and so on. I don't think it does any damage to publicise it if there's no malice expressed.'

Tuesday 16 September

At the Residence this morning I met Robert Pontillon, the International Secretary of the French Socialist Party, and Michel Rocard, the Party's economic adviser. They said that unemployment in France was 1,000,000. If production were to rise again and qualified people got the benefit, there would be very high social tensions probably towards the end of 1976. They also had some external trade anxieties.

I asked if they would have the capacity to meet the upturn when it comes.

Rocard said, 'Remember we had our industrial revolution a century after the UK and we have a savage form of capitalism at the moment. If the French do decide to go for growth, they could do it with 20 per cent inflation. An alternative strategy would be to go for 2 per cent growth and higher inflation or to opt for a slump but this could lead to a popular front, when voters will change their leaders after the crisis. It is when the problems are not solved that opposition is heard.'

Pontillon said, most affectionately, 'We very much welcome our talk with you because discussion is too narrow at the moment. We would like more contact with the British Labour Party.

Seeing Pontillon was most useful and I told him I'd like to talk to Mitterand [Secretary of the French Socialist Party] if I could: he assured me that it could be arranged.

We flew from Paris to Rome and were taken by the Ambassador, Guy Millard, to the Residence – the Villa Wolkonsky, built in 1890 by the son of one of the mistresses of Tsar Alexander I. It served as the German Embassy and the Gestapo Headquarters during the war; Hitler no doubt slept here during the war. Many people had been tortured in the basement; indeed a skeleton was discovered in the garden in 1954.

We had dinner and walked around the garden, and Frances went for a swim in the pool. In 1938, the German Ambassador had been told he was to stay in Rome throughout the hot summer. Since the Ambassador had children and was unable to take them away for a holiday, Hitler authorised the building of the pool as a compensation. It must have been used by Hitler, Himmler, Goebbels and Goering, a historic place.

Before going to bed, I read some of Clem Attlee's book, *The Labour Party in Perspective*, published by the Left Book Club in 1936–7. This was Clem in the Thirties with a very critical analysis of capitalism and how a Labour Government could never support it. Clem didn't believe in running capitalism, he didn't believe in profits, he wanted the extension of public ownership. I shall make good use of this in the weeks leading up to the Party Conference.

Wednesday 17 September
Up at 7 and had a bath. They had unpacked everything from my suitcase and I had to search every drawer and cupboard to find my possessions and put them back in the case. After a lovely breakfast, Frances and I arrived at 9 at Pietro Nenni's apartment, which was very modest, a sort of working office full of files and press cuttings and books. It was the office of a real working politician. We were greeted by Finocchiaro, Nenni's political secretary, from the Italian Socialist party – the PSI – of which Nenni is President.

Nenni was in slacks and an open-necked white shirt. He is now eighty-four, and was in the Socialist Party with Mussolini before the first World War. Once he was imprisoned in the same cell as Mussolini, who later spared his life because of their association. An extraordinary career.

I thanked him for seeing me and, with the help of a Sicilian interpreter, said I wanted to hear his analysis of what was happening in Italy, the economic and political situation and what socialists in the world, particularly in Western Europe, should be doing.

Nenni said, 'In Italy, it is the most serious situation we've had for many years. We have exorbitant wage demands, wild-cat strikes called by the autonomous unions and, in parallel, a strike of capital by Confindustria' [the Italian CBI].

I said we were beginning to wonder whether capitalism and democracy and full employment were compatible.

Nenni said, 'My greatest regret is that we revitalised capitalism at the end of the war when it was beaten; a decision for which I bear personal responsibility in 1947 and 1954, and against which we now have to fight because it is collapsing again. Now is the time to make major strides towards socialism. The difficulty is that the Labour Party is the main instrument in England but here we have the Communist Party as the main instrument. As for the Socialist International, it's merely talk at the top with no depth.'

It was a riveting discussion. Nenni radiated sincerity and goodness, his mind was sharp and he was very modest. I really enjoyed it.

We went from there by car to see Guiseppe Saragat, President of the Italian Social Democratic Party, who had broken away with three other members from Nenni's Italian Socialist Party when Nenni suggested fusion with the Communists after the war. Although there had been attempts to re-unify the Party, they had failed, and the Parti Socialiste Democratico Italiano – the PSDI – was back in business.

The two men could hardly have been more different. Saragat is a former President of the Republic, properly to be called Mr President, now living in a comfortable villa in a very swish part of Rome. He looked very solemn, rather pompous – a Herbert Morrison-cum-Jim Callaghan figure. He made it clear that he was a friend of Denis Healey and Lord Robens.

I asked him if British and Italian socialists might cooperate economically and politically.

'Well,' he said, 'there are very substantial differences between the two systems. Britain is a unified country, no one has been able to get into Britain without a visa since 1066; in the 17th century, while Milton was advocating free speech, Galileo was being tried in Rome for heresy. The Anglo-Saxons have been absorbed and have themselves absorbed the various races. Italy is a cocktail that the bartender has forgotten to mix, as Winston Churchill said during the war. We stretch from a Swedish society in the North to a Tunisian society in the South. Marsala is named after Marshall Ali and we only have a hundred years behind us. Freedom is in intensive care and has been since the war, and we don't know yet if it will survive.

'We experienced rapid industrialisation and the Communist Party is the party of protest. The public services have been ignored and they have to be dealt with. The CP of course works for the Eastern Bloc; you only have to look in the faces of Brezhnev and Lenin to see the Mongol influence. The CP has unlimited money from the Russians to finance its activities but at least they spend it on their work, which is more than you can say for the Christian Democrats and the Social Democrats, who simply are corrupt.

'There is also a crisis in the Catholic church since in Italy many priests are working-class people and not middle class as in the North and therefore some of them are, as in South America, committed to the Communist Party. This is a problem.

'I cannot see a basis for cooperation between Italy and Britain because the differences are too great. The Germans have got a brilliantly organised party, the French have got Giscard with his reforms which are a problem for the French Socialist Party, but Britain is different again. In London, people take their children to Hyde Park Corner to hear Communists speak as a curiosity. As for the Socialist International, it exists only on paper, it is not a reality.'

Reading Attlee, listening to Pietro Nenni, hearing the anxieties in Germany, seeing the problems in the French Socialist Party and knowing what struggles there will be at the Party Conference, I am certain that a strong, radical, left-wing, democratic socialist posture based on trade union and Labour Party links is the only future for Britain.

Thursday 18 September

Bonn. Today was a day of extraordinary activity, beginning with a visit with Frances to Willy Brandt at the Bundestag. We had heard a lot about Willy Brandt's gloominess, and I had met him on occasions when he had been pretty miserable, but today he was very charming to both of us. He had a close-circuit TV set on in the room showing the debate in the German Parliament on the Government's economic measures, and although the sound was turned down I found it slightly distracting.

I explained that I was on an official tour to discuss energy matters, but that I was also trying to make contact with the parties on the Continent. I told him about my talks with Pontillon and Rocard in Paris, and Nenni and Saragat in Rome.

Brandt was smoking and looking thoughtful and it seemed that since he ceased to be Chancellor and became Chairman of the SPD, where he is a hero, he has found a new enjoyment in life, free from the detail of domestic policy about which he wasn't very knowledgable and which he found boring.

I said, 'I have one point to put to you – if the economic situation is desperately difficult and if we are heading for a slump of 1930s proportions, then what effect will it have on the politics of Western Europe, the industrialised world, how do we avoid the mistakes of the pre-war years? After all, Mussolini began as a socialist and turned fascist. We had a man called Oswald Mosley who was a member of the Labour Government, and then formed the British Fascist Party. And of course the Germans had National Socialism which went wrong. So how do we avoid it? What is your feeling about the role of the socialist parties in dealing with this. Does it interest you?'

'Of course, of course,' he said, 'it interests me very much. The Socialist International is not working well, and we need to think of it as various layers of activity.'

For about thirty minutes he analysed these three layers: the layer linking European democratic socialists with all those in other countries with whom we are broadly sympathetic, such as Hubert Humphrey in America, or Julius Nyerere in Tanzania. We couldn't limit ourselves to the American Socialist Party – charming though they are – or the smaller groups in each country. We must try to have some influence on the shaping of – he didn't say it, but he meant it – liberal opinion.

The second layer of activity was in establishing links with other

European countries outside the Community, such as the Swedes and the Austrians.

'Including Eastern Europe?' I asked.

'No, we can discuss that in a minute,' he said.

'A penumbra of democratic socialists around the Community?'

'Yes,' he said, 'and here we should go into intimate detail – not only discussion on the Party net but consultation at Government level to see if we can't bring them in.'

Thirdly we had to consider the problem of the Mediterranean countries in the southern part of Europe – Portugal, Spain, Italy.

'What about the Ostpolitik?' I asked. 'What about underpinning that with some form of dialogue?'

'Well, I go to Moscow and Eastern Europe and I'm able to talk to Brezhnev and Kosygin and so on.'

'What about the Young Left which is not Communist but more often Trotskyist, or outside Left? I find that they challenge the fundamentals of society while we simply seem to say, don't worry, we'll raise pensions by 10 per cent.'

He believed we needed a layer of thought – perhaps a journal or a socialist organisation with maybe a quarterly socialist review. We could build our organisation up a bit more around that.

I mentioned the growing radicalism of the Catholic Church, particularly in South America, and he seemed keen to forge links with progressive movements around the world.

Then we shook hands – I think he called me Tony – and I left with Frances.

Friday 19 September

Up at 7 and had breakfast at the Europa Hotel. Michael Palliser arrived to take me back to the British Delegation office. When the history comes to be written, the quiet work of Michael Palliser in winning Harold Wilson over to Common Market membership will turn out to be very significant indeed. He came to Brussels at the end of the Conservatives' negotiations undertaken by Geoffrey Rippon as Chancellor of the Duchy of Lancaster, with responsibility for Europe, and stayed right through the entry, the Election of the Labour Government, and re-negotiation and the Referendum. Harold is obviously pleased with his work.

As we walked over to the Commission building and went up to the top floor which the Commissioners occupy, that feeling of total oppression overcame me – the thought that these men should have impregnable positions of power when they haven't even been elected.

I went in to see Spinelli and there he was with his white hair, red-faced and smiling. One cannot but admire a man who spent sixteen years in jail from his early twenties to his late thirties for his political beliefs. On the other hand he did transfer his idealism from Communism to federalism and is, to put it crudely, a silly old fool.

Then we saw Henri Simonet, the Belgian politician, in one of the conference rooms. He was with Guido Brunner, a Free Democrat recently appointed as a Commissioner. Brunner was modest and likeable but immensely bureaucratic. We were asked to give our impressions.

I argued that we should build on national interests and Simonet said, 'I have no objection to that but how do you reconcile differences between member states, and do you see intergovernmental links as precluding the role for the Commission and excluding the sense of a political community?'

I said, 'I don't know that that is really a different question. After all, I've spent all my life as a politician in a federal state if you like – England, Wales and Scotland – and we have had to reconcile our differences. We also have to see the role of the politician as offering a service to people. So I don't see any problem there.'

At lunch, Simonet became very jolly and began to tell funny stories – one about when Franco put his toe in the water at Lourdes and died, and his officials cried, 'Ah, a miracle!'

Then he said, 'What about Mrs Thatcher? What is she like?'

I said, 'She is a serious, intellectual woman trying to build up the Conservative Party on a narrower class basis. But she is certainly to be taken seriously.'

'She seems to me to be a bit of a fascist,' he said.

Gill Brown from the Foreign Office was horrified at this so I said, 'Well, Poujadist perhaps.' We had quite an amusing discussion about politics and I warmed to him.

Came home and was greeted by Caroline and Josh. Josh is working on a huge dossier of press cuttings and he discovered from the electoral register that the flat opposite us is occupied by someone on the *Daily Express*. He found out the phone number and rang up the flat, and a voice answered 'Foreign Desk'.

Saturday 20 September
London, and a very late lie in after the European trip.

Eric Heffer rang and I told him about my meeting with Nenni. He said that the trouble with the Italian Socialist Party was that it was led entirely by middle-class lawyers, journalists and administrators, and the only party in Italy which had real working-class leadership was the Communist Party. Of course, many Italian Communists could so easily fit into the Labour Party and vice versa.

That is, of course, the weakness. The bourgeois liberal movements have adopted socialist language as part of their stock in trade but wanted to fall short not only of socialist action but of allowing the working class to break through and act on its own. That's why the whole problem is the relationship between the unions and the Government and the degree of political education within the trade union movement. I think I see it clearly now.

Thursday 25 September

There were more reports in the press on the hearings in Washington which have revealed that the CIA was opening the mail of senior politicians, including Nixon before he was elected. One really is indebted to the American investigative process for bringing things to light. No doubt similar things have happened here and exactly on the same basis, but they are kept completely secret.

Caught the train to Blackpool and checked into the Imperial Hotel.

Labour Party Conference, Blackpool
Friday 26 September

The papers today reported the admission by the FBI that they had engaged in over 250 domestic burglaries for political and other purposes. There was also a report in the *New York Times* that the CIA was again giving money to West European socialist parties to intervene in Portugal.

Just before the Executive at 10 I had a word with Bryan Stanley and I mentioned my concern about telephone tapping.

'Oh yes,' he said, 'there's no question about it. I believe that the Tories were engaged in a widespread surveillance campaign involving the telephone tapping of activists in the trade union movement and the Labour Party, as well as in the Communist Party. The aim was to prepare a general dossier so that, in the run-up to an Election, he could blacken the character of his political opponents and get public opinion on his side.

'Whenever I tried to find out anything about it from my own members, I discovered that this telephone tapping is done by specially recruited people who, though they may be members of my union, are not prepared to say a word about it. There is tight security amongst them. It goes on on a more limited scale now, but during the Referendum campaign, for example, people in the anti-Common Market groups on one or two occasions picked up their telephones and found recordings of what they'd just said coming back to them.'

Saturday 27 September

At dinner I saw Denis Healey sitting alone so I went over and joined him. It was the first time in years that I'd spoken to him privately. I was friendly and I told him I'd seen Saragat, and asked him what he thought about Brandt and Helmut Schmidt and Conference and so on. He told me that it was at Blackpool, thirty years ago, that he had made his first speech.

Sunday 28 September

When we were last at the Imperial Hotel two years ago, Tony Wilson, a seventeen-year-old who worked in the hotel as a sort of page boy, told us that he earned only £14 for an eighty-hour week. I suggested he form a union. Well, he knocked on the bedroom door and there he was with his little spectacles and his cheeky manner, and he said, 'Oh, Mr Benn, I formed that union. When they heard that Mr Benn had suggested it, it spread like wildfire. We've got the TGWU here – and we're 60 per cent unionised – and we've now got £20 for a forty-hour week.'

At the UCATT party this evening, Roddy Connolly, President of the Irish Labour Party, came up. He is the son of James Connolly, the Socialist and Republican who was executed by a British firing squad after his part in the Easter Rising in 1916.

I was invited to the POEU/UPW dinner and was asked to speak. Afterwards Bryan Stanley paid a tribute to Roy, Denis and Jim, and said, 'I want to say a word about Tony Benn. I'm very sorry that he was moved from the Department of Industry and from Tele-communications. It's not for me to comment on the circumstances but he was the best Minister the Post Office has ever had because he identified himself with our members. We were very sad to see him go.'

It was a courageous speech and Jim and Denis looked absolutely sick. I wish Harold had been there but he arrived later, just as we were thanking and leaving. I tried to avoid him but he saw me through the door.

Monday 29 September

First day of Conference and a debate on housing. Frank Allaun had refused to speak because the Executive wouldn't accept his composite.

The afternoon session was a replay of the TUC Conference debate on incomes policy, with David Basnett supporting and Tom Jackson frightening us all with the problems of inflation. Hugh Scanlon made a powerful speech and Michael Foot wound up with a magnificent performance. There was this great figure with his white hair swept back, almost leonine, defending with a gale of oratory and eloquence the like of which I have not heard for a long time, a policy which is basically wrong and which I would like to say he doesn't believe in, but he does. He misled the Conference, told them the Cabinet was united in wanting reflation, which isn't true.

Jack Jones led the standing ovation and it reached Jim Callaghan at the far right of the platform but I didn't stand and neither did Frank Allaun and others to my left.

To the AUEW party, where Johnnie Boyd, the right-wing Salvationist, was greeting the guests and checking the tickets. I said, 'Johnnie, I've brought the whole family but we won't drink anything. We're all like you, blue ribbon boys.'

I saw Bryan Stanley today and thanked him for the friendly reference he made at the POEU/UPW dinner last night.

'I had to,' he said, 'because when you were moved, there were branches up and down the country threatening to disaffiliate from the Labour Party, and some were even considering industrial action, so I had to speak on their behalf.' He said it with such genuine feeling that I think it must have been true.

Tuesday 30 September

The first item today was the National Executive elections and I came top again with 523,000 – more than last year – and Michael Foot rose to 501,000. Eric Heffer jumped up and pushed Denis Healey off, which was a shattering blow for Denis. Jim became Treasurer with a slightly narrower margin than last year.

Harold made his usual contemptible speech, ploughing through the implementation of the Manifesto in such a way as to denigrate the achievements we had made. He mocked the critics of Labour's foreign policy and challenged them to find any past Government with a comparable record. He talked about Mrs Thatcher before coming on to what was intended to be the guts of his speech, a warning against extremists, a rap over the knuckles for Reg Prentice, and an attack on the Social Democratic Alliance. But the crux of the speech was the attack on extremists taking over local parties. It was awful but I did stand at the end because he *is* the Prime Minister.

Next there was a debate on the economy with a motion favouring import controls moved by Clive Jenkins. Denis Healey wound up and I sat behind him because I couldn't bear the thought of sitting beside him throughout his speech. He referred to his own defeat on the NEC which he obviously felt keenly, but as a result he made a rather more fighting speech. He tends to bully people, and Clive Jenkins was his victim today. He got a standing ovation in which I did not join.

Wednesday 1 October

I worked till 3 in the morning on my speech for the industrial policy debate today. Judith presented the industrial policy statement in a very academic way. There were various other speakers. A Young Socialist from West Stirlingshire made a marvellous speech. It was the youngsters in many ways who stole the limelight. One man got up and said, 'I cannot let this occasion go by without saying plainly that the removal of Tony Benn from the Department of Industry simply for implementing our policies has created a deep mood of cynicism and despair.'

I spoke for about fifteen minutes and it was very effective. I got a rather different sort of standing ovation from Michael, Denis and Harold, in that it began on the fringes and moved into the middle. I don't think Jack Jones stood up and I know he was reading his newspaper throughout my speech, as he had through Eric Heffer's and Judith Hart's.

I had been asked to go with Jack Jones to see a delegation from the TGWU about offshore oil workers, so I left the platform and Jack walked out with me. Well, he turned on me and I hope I can be forgiven for repeating what he said.

'What's the fucking use of talking about redundancies in that general way when I've got these fucking workers and you have done fuck all about them?'

'The offshore oil workers?' I asked.

'Yes, these people at Graythorpe. I don't suppose you've ever been there.'

'Not only have I been there, Jack, but I've been trying to get new orders for them from the oil companies for the last two months. Indeed, yours is the one union that hasn't taken any interest whatever in this issue.'

He said, 'Well, what about getting union recognition on the rigs?'

'I'm working on that too.'

'The National Union of Seamen have done a deal on their own in which the men on the rigs are members of the NUS, not the TGWU.'

I said, 'You've been slow off the mark. They've done it and it's nothing to do with me. I'm not in charge of the National Union of Seamen.'

He was boiling with rage. 'Who do they think they are, all this criticism of the Government?' and he referred to the Tribune Group. I told him I wasn't even a member of the Tribune Group.

We arrived at the Planet Room where all these awfully nice guys – shop stewards and one full-time official – were waiting in the hallway. I shook hands with them and in Jack's presence I told them what I had done.

'I've been up to Scotland. I've been to Graythorpe and Nigg, and I've seen the union committee and the Scottish TUC. I've written to the oil companies, and the OPEC oil prices will help. I've also arranged a new licensing round. I'll continue to help in any way I can. I'll keep in touch with Jack Jones. If you want to come to London you can see me. Jack has been pressing me on this.' This was quite untrue and he knew it, and when I said that I think he felt guilty.

Dick Clements drove me to the *Tribune* rally in the Spanish Hall which was crammed with people. Dick Clements took the chair. Eric made a strong speech warning us that we could end up like Chile. I developed the argument about democracy and its relationship with capitalism. Neil Kinnock did a brilliantly funny collection. Then Mik began to speak and I could see he was using a press release. He said, 'I make a very serious charge against the trade union movement, that they did not ask for enough from the Government. They accepted a £6 limit without bargaining on full employment or on the Industry Bill.'

He then revealed in detail the watering down of the Industry Bill and how it had been completely changed in the Committee Stage. He said it was the only Bill where all the responsible Ministers had been dropped before it completed the Committee Stage and that merited a place in the *Guinness Book of Records*.

As he spoke, I heard shouting and I thought it was a heckler. Then I saw Jack Jones, who hadn't been invited to address the meeting, stride up on to the platform waving the press release of Mik's speech that had obviously just been given to him by Geoffrey Goodman. 'I'm not sitting here to hear the trade unions being attacked,' he bellowed. He was white with rage, waving his fist and it was clear he wasn't going to sit down. Poor old Dick Clements was terrified. Not only is Jack an old friend of his but the TGWU orders 12,000 copies of *Tribune* every year I didn't know whether there was going to be any physical violence but Mik would look neither left nor right and resumed his seat until Jack had calmed down. Mik did finish his speech and got tremendous applause.

Thursday 2 October
Everyone is discussing the Jones-Mikardo clash last night. Joe Ashton thinks it is a tragedy because it will discourage and confuse everybody. My own feeling is that it has brought into focus the real balance of forces in the Government and ended the pretence of a Left fighting a Right. The Healey-Jones-Foot triumvirate is now apparent, with Wilson on the sidelines.

In the afternoon, Mario Soares gave a great speech about Portugal, but one only had to look at him to see he had nothing to do with working-class socialism – he was a well-dressed lawyer who had suffered a bit but had been out of the country part of the time. I don't suppose these ultra-left groups with their dreams of workers' democracies and neighbourhood councils make a lot of sense in terms of providing a real alternative workers' structure to the bourgeois capitalist system, but that is the way the thing will have to go because nobody will accept

Stalinism again; social democracy isn't attractive either, if it means rigid control of the country by a marginally left-of-centre leadership.

Went to the Mayor's reception. Talked to Mik and told him what I thought about his contribution. 'You lifted the lid, Mik, you did it too crudely, but you lifted it and it's all got to cool off now.'

Joan Lestor said Mik had thought he might be knocked off the Executive and that was why he had made the speech last night. He is now the elder statesman of the Left.

Friday 3 October

Filthy piece in the *Mirror* by Terry Lancaster which clearly represented Harold Wilson's view, crowing at his great Election victory and saying that now the Conference had swung to the Right there was no possibility that I might be elected, even if Conference were to elect the Leader.

Friday 10 October

I had a dream that Harold had called me in and said, 'I want you to be Vice-Chamberlain of the Royal Household with a seat in the House of Lords in charge of boxing under the Minister of Sport.' He told me this in the great Cabinet Room which was full of people. 'I'm afraid this doesn't mean a place in the Cabinet for you,' he said. I replied, 'Harold, I must think about it,' and Sir John Hunt said, 'Boxing is very important. We must preserve the quality and excellence of the Lonsdale Belt.'

Frances Morrell came to see me. She had been giving a great deal of attention to the question of agents, MI6 and CIA, and she said, 'You are a prime target. There is a real chance you might be Leader of the Labour Party and they'll put their top people on to you.'

Saturday 11 October

Caroline went to her conference at Islington Green School to form the new organisation, Programme for Reform in Secondary Education, PRISE.

Tuesday 14 October

Yesterday Robert Kilroy-Silk, Labour MP for Ormskirk, told me that £2 million had been left unspent by the pro-Market lobby and it was in a fund of which the trustees were Heath, Thorpe and Jenkins. They were trying to find out whether they could use it for other purposes and their legal advisers had told them they could. He said the rumour was that if Wilson moved too far to the Left, they would use the money to set up a new Party.

Wednesday 15 October
At 9.30 the North Sea Re-negotiation Committee met and I got Frank Kearton to come because we were discussing the interests of BNOC, of which he is Chairman designate. Harold Lever, predictably, objected.

Afterwards, I took Frank Kearton up to my room for a talk and he said, 'The North Sea is the richest oil field in the world and the oil companies just don't believe that the British Government can be so moderate in its demands. They are uncertain because they fear that when the Government discovers how rich the oil fields are, we'll confiscate it all.'

He felt as I do that we need to make the structure stand up and that's where the BP link would be helpful. Also he said, 'You should go for the really big companies, Exxon, Shell and BP.' He thought with Shell and Exxon we could get 25 per cent participation in the whole operation.

Tuesday 21 October
The *Daily Mirror* ran a story under the heading, 'Britain to become the nuclear dustbin of the world', by a Stanley Bonnet. In fact, the man behind it was Bryn Jones from Friends of the Earth who is the industrial correspondent on the *Mirror*. It was about the BNFL contract under which we would reprocess 4,000 tons of irradiated fuel from Japan and would then have the problem of disposing of the toxic waste. I decided to go on the *World at One* so a chap came along to interview me. I think I put the case across and I told the Department to put out a background note.

I rang Marcia and invited her for a sandwich lunch. She came in Harold's car and gave me a message from Harold, 'Tell him to keep cheerful.' I asked how it was going at Number 10 and she said it was awful. 'In the old days I had Gerald Kaufman to work with but now it's Haines who's the official man and Bernard Donoughue,' whom Marcia thought was just feeding Harold's insecurities.

'I have good personal relations with Harold but I'm shut out completely.'

She said that Harold sometimes nearly gives up and she was sure that one day he'd resign.

Well, that's a load of rubbish! She asked what I thought about being moved. I said, 'It was like moving Nye Bevan from the Health Service. It was a complete capitulation.'

'Harold was under heavy pressure,' she said, 'not just from outside but from inside too.' Well to hell with that. 'Harold reported that you had lectured him more than he had ever been lectured before. He does have a difficult time and he thought it best to move you, and he found a way which both met the criticism and annoyed the others.'

I said we should keep in touch because I like Marcia. If she went it would be awful.

Thursday 23 October

At 8.50 this morning, just before I went off to work, Caroline and I were in the bedroom and there was the most enormous explosion. I thought it was a bomb in Roy Jenkins's house nearby. So I dashed down the stairs and opened the front door and I saw there were a lot of people about 150 yards down the street. Then, through the trees in Campden Hill Square, I saw flames licking up twenty-five to thirty feet and realised that the explosion was over by Hugh Fraser's house. Indeed, it turned out that someone had put a thirty-pound bomb near his Jaguar.

The street was in a tremendous state of uproar with police cars and fire engines all over the place. There had been a bomb just up the road at Notting Hill when the Jordanian Ambassador was hurt, but this was the closest to home and it absolutely shook us. A friend of Josh's, who comes up the hill every day to meet Josh, said the boy just in front of him had been blown off his bicycle. Some of the windows in the house next to ours had been blown out.

The press turned up in their hundreds and Caroline went down and asked whether any schoolchildren had been injured and when they said no, she went up to the school and told the Headmaster, so that when anxious parents rang up, he was able to tell them that everything was all right.

One thing I should record for my own Intelligence purposes: the press kept going in and out of the flat opposite us, and journalists also went into the basement next door.

Crosland was burgled this morning – a regular burglary they say, without political significance, though that may or may not be the case.

Cabinet at 11. We came on to the Queen's Speech and it was clear that the Treasury absolutely dominates the argument about the economic policy now, saying that the main priority is the fight against inflation. Michael Foot tried to get unemployment put on an equal footing with inflation instead of the present wording lower down – 'and we express our concern about unemployment'. He managed to get the balance of the words changed, but it is a true indication of the policy of the Government and nobody should be under any illusion about that.

At 2.30 Frank Kearton came and we had half an hour going over our proposals for the BP/BNOC link before the 'Misc 103' Committee at 4.30. Frank said quite plainly that the oil companies were insisting that BNOC was a dead duck, that we'd never get it off the ground, and that we might as well pack it in.

At the Committee I was asked to comment on the official paper submitted by the officials. I said they had written the most violent attack on the BP/BNOC proposal. Parts of the report read like a Tory manifesto, saying that relations between Government and industry had improved greatly in recent weeks, and that this would create a new crisis of confidence, and so on. I thought we should have a look at the difficulties that have been raised and go through it again.

Denis said that Kearton had frightened everybody off by talking about it in the City.

Edmund Dell rejected the proposals. We dare not damage BP, we had to rule it out. The City was anxious, the Government couldn't consider it and we must rule out all these schemes. The Coal Board and the Gas Corporation might be involved and we should ask BP to help, perhaps by secondment. But we had to rule out the break-up of BP.

Callaghan had received a letter from Sir David Steel, Chairman designate of BP, warning that participation must be got through and the Burmah Oil shares sold. Then they'd agree to help.

Here we have a company where the Government holds 68 per cent of the shares and still they refuse to cooperate with us. A public ownership majority does not even give us the capacity to get them to agree to sit down with us and work out how we are going to solve the problem of BNOC. It is an absolute disgrace.

Eric Varley said Kearton was looking for a short cut and there wasn't one. Why the hell shouldn't he look for a short cut? The Government policy is to look for a short cut towards establishing our own oil company.

Denis Healey warned of the risk of losing BP International which had always resented Government interference, and BP was a great international asset. BNOC must not destroy it, any more than the Department of Energy, and we should bring in BP at an early stage.

Harold suggested a mixed committee of officials with Lord Balogh, Harold Lever, Edmund Dell, and so on.

'No,' I said, 'I'm very sorry but as the departmental Minister, I have not had the opportunity to put in a paper on how we might overcome these difficulties. I must ask that I be allowed to put in a paper, and that we have a committee to examine it. All these interdepartmental committees should not come in at an early stage.'

Harold said they had been operating like that since 1950, but I insisted on the right to report on participation talks, to comment on the official paper, to make proposals for interdepartmental consideration, and there should be no approach to BP for a decision on their shares. Kearton would now work with us on this matter.

I left it there. It was a very tense and difficult meeting.

Monday 27 October

The front page of the *Daily Mail* had a nasty story that Barbara Castle's officials were disgusted by her behaviour, once again proving that the Civil Service is in no way non-political. It is exactly the treatment I had when the Department of Industry officials were fed up with me, and Barbara is under heavy pressure at the moment. Harold Lever will no doubt be put in charge of pay beds.[1] Barbara will be edged out, moved or made a peer. The repudiation of Ministers who fight for the Manifesto is a regular occurrence now.

At 9.30 Frank Kearton came to see me privately about BNOC. I reported to him what had happened at the Committee last Thursday.

He apparently went to see Harold Lever and Edmund Dell when he was first appointed because the Prime Minister had led him to believe it was a real job. They said, 'Oh the petroleum revenue tax is getting us all we need, you don't really need to bother.' Harold Lever more or less indicated that he shouldn't take the job too seriously.

Then Frank went round and talked to the oil companies and they said exactly the same thing. He said that the participation arrangements that had previously been reached gave all the oil back to the oil companies for seven to ten years and we would only get the residual oil. The whole participation business was a charade. Even the oil companies were suspicious about it, and they wanted something real.

Elliott Richardson had told him that if the oil companies were asked to explain the participation arrangements to the British Government they would simply not be able to do so, and this is what is worrying them.

I said, 'Look Frank, I support you of course, and I have the right to put in a paper to this committee. I want you to help me write this paper based on the following: a report on participation, the problem for BNOC if it is asked to grow the slower way, and an alternative oil policy.

'I want to examine the proposal that you put forward for the 25 per cent total participation of Shell, Exxon and BP, but with no pledge on petroleum revenue tax or future policy. I also want you to join the participation team and take on the Chief Executive's role in the North Sea. Finally, we should appoint a BNOC Organising Committee with Tommy Balogh, perhaps, and Lord Briginshaw and some bright young men, and start work on it right away.'

He was happy with that and I suggested he see the Prime Minister this evening and then we'll see whether we can knock this paper into shape by next week.

I spoke to Ivor Manley, my Establishment Officer, who I've known since Mintech days, and I told him I wanted a proper Private Secretary, I wasn't satisfied with Ronnie Custis who I felt was unsympathetic. I'd never complained about my Private Secretaries before but this time I had to make a change.

Then Ivor told me that I had changed a lot. I denied that and insisted that as a Minister I was entitled to enough loyalty to allow me to do my job.

I felt I couldn't speak to my own Private Secretary, and if the situation wasn't changed, I would do things privately from now on.

He asked if I'd spoken to Jack Rampton about it and I said I hadn't because I wasn't making a formal complaint, I just wanted a different Secretary.

He suggested it was because I didn't agree with the majority of the Government and I told him that the Prime Minister appointed me because of my views, not in spite of them.

'But,' he said, 'other Departments are involved in what you are doing,' and I said that was fine and if other Departments wanted to comment on my papers, they could do so, but I would not have opposition stirred up in other Departments by my officials before I'd had a chance to work things out myself.

He was a bit shaken by all this. I have a very good relationship with Ivor and we'll move on from there. He said he'd send me a list of people of the right degree of seniority who would help.

Tuesday 28 October

I'm enjoying life now, and I'm feeling quite cheerful, particularly if I get my Cabinet paper in on the economic situation because that will put the argument for new policies on the record. Although I don't expect support, I can argue that there is a new national consensus to be built, but around *our* policy instead of around the policy that the Treasury is trying to foist upon us. Theirs is a phoney consensus with the Tories which they haven't the guts to push through.

Wednesday 29 October

Lunch with Frances. She had a talk with Jack Straw who told her how Harold Lever had intervened on the pay beds. Apparently, Lever is in continual touch with the President of the Royal College of Physicians and he tells them everything that is going on so they can bring pressure to bear on the Government. Then he gets Harold Wilson to urge Sir John Hunt to persuade the DHSS to set up an inquiry into pay beds, despite the opposition from the officials. So Barbara, who has also been opposing an inquiry, finds herself isolated, goes to the Cabinet and it is all agreed. Then there will be pressure to defer the whole issue of pay beds.

This evening Judith Hart, Eric Heffer, Michael Meacher, Norman Atkinson, Joan Lestor, Frances Morrell and I had our first informal talk. Norman believes that there will have to be alternative leadership to rally the Party.

Joan Lestor still feels that if we stay in the Government we're going to be compromised up to the hilt and she expects that Harold Wilson will put further pressure on most of us in the Executive.

Judith Hart recognised that the TUC-Labour Party Liaison Committee was crucial and as Harold no longer had a majority on the Executive, he would try to shift the emphasis to the Liaison Committee where Jack Jones and Len Murray would back him up.

I said we mustn't give up because there were important developments. First of all, the movement knew what the industrial policy was about and wanted it. Secondly, the Industry Bill with all its weaknesses could be used by a determined Government and events were such that we would be forced to use it.

We agreed to meet again whenever there was a three-line whip.

Thursday 30 October

Bernard Ingham came to see me. He's a very difficult man, an old *Guardian* reporter, and I think when Eric Varley was at Energy, he and Ronnie Custis did exactly what they liked. Eric is entirely guided by his civil servants. I think part of my problem has been trying to get control of those two.

Friday 31 October

At 9.45 I had a meeting with three of my officials – Jasper Cross, in charge of coal, Philip Jones, electricity, and Chris Herzig, nuclear power. Brian Tucker, the Deputy-Secretary for all three areas, was also there. Custis had set up this meeting because the senior officials were worried that I was neglecting them.

Brian Tucker said, 'We don't see enough of you and we've noticed from some of your comments on our papers that there is some uneasiness on your part about what we are saying, so we thought it would be useful to have a talk.'

I said, 'I don't want you to think of me as a hostile Minister just sitting in my office, but my feeling is this. First of all, any new Minister is ignorant and I have to be careful not to approve accidently something I don't quite understand. So I tend to stop things until I am sure I understand what they mean. That's not directed against you.

'Secondly, I have noticed a tremendous change since I left office in 1970. In those days a Minister was in charge of his Department. He and his officials put in papers to colleagues and if colleagues didn't like them, they got an interdepartmental committee to look at them. Now I feel that officials are working direct to some interdepartmental group and their loyalty no longer rests with Ministers. If a Minister turns up at a meeting of Ministers and finds there's already a report from an interdepartmental committee of officials, then he hasn't really got a role.

'Thirdly, the Treasury is much more important now. In the old days, we had the Department of Economic Affairs, then the Ministry of Technology, then the Department of Trade and Industry which were counterweights to the Treasury. Now the Treasury pulls the strings. That's my feeling.'

Monday 3 November

Arrived at Aberdeen at 8.30 for the landing of the first oil from the Forties Field. After breakfast at the Skeandhu Hotel, a film was shown of the Forties Field and then Harold Wilson arrived with Jim Callaghan, Sir Eric Drake of BP and a lot of others, and we all drove to BP's headquarters at Dyce.

The first thing I noticed was that the workers who actually bring the oil ashore were kept behind a barbed wire fence and just allowed to wave to us as we drove by. We arrived at a huge tent, constructed at a cost of £40,000, and laid with an extravagant red carpet. The tent was about the size of two football pitches and held 1000 people, most of whom had been brought up from London. We were given a cup of coffee as we waited for the Queen to arrive.

Eventually we were taken out on the dais to watch the Queen's Rolls Royce approaching. Out came the Queen in a green dress, followed by the Duke of Edinburgh and Prince Andrew. She shook hands with all of us, and we went back into the tent and had drinks, and the Queen circulated. Then she went into the computer control room and we followed. She pressed a few buttons I believe before going outside for her walkabout. There, behind another fence, were about 500 Aberdonians waving Union Jacks, and the Queen and the Duke of Edinburgh walked in front of them as if they were animals in a zoo.

At lunch I sat next to Mrs Steel the wife of David Steel, who is to succeed Drake as Chairman of BP. Jim was on her other side and he said how much he enjoyed the Foreign Office and it wasn't like the Treasury. 'You know, you would enjoy the Foreign Office, Tony.'

I said, 'Well, Jim, perhaps in your second administration that will be possible.' He laughed.

To be frank, the day was a complete waste of time and money, and when you see the Queen in action, everything else is just absorbed into this frozen feudal hierarchy. All the old big-wigs are brought out into the open as if they were somehow responsible for a great industrial achievement, while the workers are presented as natives and barbarians who can be greeted but have to be kept at a distance. It is a disgrace that a Labour Government should allow this to continue. I know there is a security problem but there was no need for this. I also felt that this great Scottish occasion was just an opportunity for the London Establishment to come up and lord it over the Scots.

Tuesday 4 November
Frances told me that the Prime Minister had sent a minute to all Ministers with political advisers, banning them from attending a meeting organised by Geoff Bish at Transport House. I haven't had such a minute but if it is true, then what are advisers supposed to do? They can't go to meetings called by Ministers, they can't go to meetings called by officials – their whole purpose is to keep in touch with Transport House.

To Number 10 for a cabinet committee and outside, waiting to go in for Item 2, was Bernard Donoughue. He asked if I had seen the piece in the *Economist* about the Central Policy Review Staff. I said I had seen it but hadn't read it very carefully.

'The Think Tank's very powerful,' he said, 'and it's being used now not just to provide briefs but also to undermine policy commitments.'

'I agree. It's all part of the centralisation of Government. What about *your* think tank?' I hadn't any idea what he had been doing over the past eighteen months.

'Ah,' he said, 'we report to the Prime Minister.'

I said, 'I suppose Kenneth Berrill reports to the PM too.' It was a bit unfair to equate him with Sir Kenneth Berrill but when I thought of all the briefing Bernard Donoughue has done against me and the Department of Industry in the press, I didn't see any reason why I should join him in his little power game against the CPRS. I don't like the Think Tank at all but Bernard Donoughue is power mad and he just wants to establish a dominant position for himself in Whitehall.

Overseas and Defence Policy Committee, where I had put in a paper. GEC had been asked by the South African Atomic Energy Board to help them build a plant to construct radio isotopes mainly for biological, medical and industrial purposes. GEC want the Atomic Energy Authority here to act as consultants for them. It was put to me and I refused. My paper included an appendix from 'Labour's Programme for Britain' in which it set out quite clearly what we said two years ago about an unhealthy involvement in apartheid. It was rather nice to see a Cabinet paper with 'Labour's Programme for Britain' attached to it and marked Confidential.

Jim got angry and said he had looked into it very carefully and there were no military implications. I daresay that's true because radio isotopes can't easily be used for military purposes. Denis said, 'Can't we get over this irrational trauma about all things nuclear?'

Roy Mason suggested that it could affect our defence sales, which was quite untrue. Harold Lever and Reg Prentice were in favour.

I said, 'I begin to wonder whether we take a political view about anything at all. Our whole movement is against apartheid, it is a burning issue. I try not to be a departmental Minister but to look at these things politically. There is no advantage to us in this and we have said we won't do it.'

Peter and Ted Short gave me a bit of support but we were outvoted by 5 to 3 and Harold stood back. I think one of the reasons they pushed it ahead was that they thought it would be fun to implicate me. I came away feeling absolutely sick because there is no common thinking at all. They don't believe in any of the ideas which inspire the movement.

Wednesday 5 November

Drove to Chequers on Guy Fawkes Day, a day when the Labour Government, having abandoned its Manifesto, sought to get consent from Neddy to a policy so weak and watery as to be a mere cover for Tory measures. Sir Ralph Bateman, Campbell Adamson of the CBI, Len Murray, Hugh Scanlon, Jack Jones and Danny McGarvey from the TUC were there, as well as the independents – Dick Lloyd of Grindlays Bank, and Michael Young, the groaning right-wing consumer representative. The whole object of the meeting was to get a national approach to the problems facing us – an approach devoid of any political content or change.

Harold called us to order and welcomed us, particularly Danny McGarvey, the new union representative, and called on Denis Healey to introduce his paper.

Denis said he wanted to set the paper in the broadest context. It was about fundamentals. He had come very early to the conclusion that there was a risk of serious deterioration in the size and efficiency of our manufacturing industry, and it was harder for the United Kingdom to reflate because, with the weakness of manufacture, we had a lot of imports coming in. What had happened to the motorcycle industry was a good example.

He said we must make a better use of capital and manpower, that was the quickest way forward. Shedding labour was only acceptable if investment is on its way and we needed an industry-by-industry, firm-by-firm, and plant-by-plant approach. We must raise the efficiency of the average to the level of the best and the Government must provide money for investment and restructuring. The NEB guidelines had been discussed and the criteria had been laid down. We must choose priorities; we were not picking winners but turning round key industries and we needed an analytical framework and an early warning system.

Of course, this is pure 1966 Mintech thinking.

He said a national plan on the Soviet model wouldn't work because we didn't have a command economy. Macmillan and George Brown had ignored industrial realities. We were building a Government-management-union consensus on how to solve our problems, as they had in Sweden, France, Japan and Germany (again, all 1964 thinking), and the Treasury and the micro-departments, Industry, Trade and Labour, were all involved.

Eric Varley joined with Denis in rejecting the national plan on the Soviet model. Prospects and problems in key areas needed to be looked at. There was a lack of industrial effort – look at motorbikes. The pace of advance was slower and we were falling behind in the international tables. We should look forward five years and be flexible and have a process of discussion as important as the plan itself, as in the French case. We needed three levels – national, sectoral and firm – for tripartite discussions which fitted the Government financial and economic calendar. Our central objective was international competitiveness and an increasing share of world trade for Britain.

Ronnie McIntosh, Director-General of the National Economic Development Office, said there was a lot of common ground though there had been no collusion. The main danger was the acute contraction of the manufacturing base which was rapidly accelerating. This was exactly what I had been saying for eighteen months at the Department of Industry, and was the basis of the ten-year industrial strategy.

Len's contribution was very poor stuff – detached, cynical and quite angry – with a complete absence of analysis or thought.

Harold Watkinson, the Deputy President of the CBI and chairman of the Tory Party, said, 'I want to speak bluntly. The CBI could be unhelpful. The business world expects a lot from Chequers and I hope we are all agreed that Neddy [the NEDC] is the chosen instrument for this purpose and not the NEB.' (In effect, he was saying there was no consensus in the Government.) 'We must rebuild industrial confidence and businessmen will go along with the NEDC as the coordinator.' He was clearly bullying us into adopting a coalition policy, with the NEDC replacing the Government.

Danny McGarvey's was by far the best speech of the day. He said, 'There's a complete lack of realism among Ministers and the NEDC; the papers before us say we are going to have to increase unemployment because of overstaffing. But high unemployment will increase restrictive practices and steel won't have an easy ride. There will be more Jarrows to come.' He objected to the phraseology of 'winners and losers', which he said was the language of the market place.

Harold wound up the morning meeting by saying he didn't want to introduce a note of piety or he would get a blast from the Bishop of Southwark – a reference to Mervyn Stockwood's recent article in the

Morning Star about the Archbishop of Canterbury's appeal for moral values.

Looking back on that meeting, it was the third stage in the fake coalition consensus. The first stage was the Common Market, the second was the £6 limit, the third is the abandonment of Labour's policy. The so-called consensus is a front for a monetarist, lame-duck policy.

Thursday 6 November

A devastating article by Peter Jay in *The Times*, ending up with a comment on the Chequers statement: 'Never since Ramsay MacDonald said we should get on and on and on and up and up and up, has such nonsense been published and there isn't a sentence in the statement that couldn't have had "or not, as the case may be" added to it without altering the meaning.'

At Cabinet Merlyn Rees said the Northern Ireland convention would be reporting tomorrow and then it would be dissolved. He wanted to play it with no sense of crisis. Although the cease-fire hadn't been entirely effective, there was no major war imminent and there were splits. 'The English disease is looking for a constitutional solution to the Irish problem.' A shrewd remark. I am persuaded we should get out of Northern Ireland, but it is not the moment to say it.

We came onto the major discussion on the economy. Harold snapped, 'These forecasts are very, very secret and nobody is to make any notes.' That made it difficult for me to record the discussion.

Harold called me to speak on my paper. I recognised that the statements made by the Chancellor were major policy statements and that we were now at a turning point in the policy of the Government. 'But before we endorse the present strategy, we must have answers to some questions. The situation is far more serious than the Cabinet yet realises. The present policy is failing, not on the £6 limit as such, not on wages, but the strategy and its acceptance are failing.

'The £6 limit was sold as a substitute for higher unemployment and public expenditure cuts and was to be accompanied by strict price control. In fact, we are getting the £6-limit policy plus rising unemployment, plus public expenditure cuts and Shirley is planning a transfer of between £1 billion and £1.8 billion to the company sector by relaxations in the price code.

'Investment is collapsing and is unlikely to recover. There is no sure way of restoring jobs and a loan would only postpone the crisis or trap the Government into international control. There is no national consensus for our policy. It is a policy of deflation. The unions are committed to the £6 limit but are not committed to deflation. The Tories don't believe in wage restraint but they are going along because they think that by doing so they can weaken the links between the

Government and the unions. When those links are weaker, the Tories will be ready to strike and we won't be strong enough to resist. The public are worried about inflation but they don't know the real nature of the policy we're pursuing.

'There are two options: one is devaluation to hold wages and boost profits. It is hoped that this will benefit the UK in the upturn but it has four fatal defects: it will import inflation; it will alter the £6 limit conditions; it will lead to a statutory wages policy; and it will produce higher prices with no guarantee of investment.

'The second policy is to rebuild behind a wall of protection. We are faced with a grave and accelerating collapse of industry – in motorbikes, textiles, cars, machine tools, footware, ships, aircraft, television tubes, and so on. As the Cabinet knows, I have urged protection in one form or another for eighteen months: first, a policy of rescuing firms in 1974, then temporary employment subsidies and selective import controls. But I am now convinced that to protect the balance of payments and protect jobs we need a major wall of protection around us because senile industries, like infant industries, must be protected.

'The trade union movement and the Labour Party have been moving slowly towards and arguing for policies which are right – import controls, a target rate for reducing unemployment, a big investment programme announced now not just through reflation but through the NEB and real planning agreements, channelling pension and insurance funds, control of investment abroad, maintenance of public services; and lastly for keeping our freedom of action. There could be real popular consensus for a national recovery plan of that kind but it would involve much closer links with the trade union movement which is the only source of our political strength. We must reject the deflationary and monetarist policies we are now pursuing.'

I spoke very quietly and it did make an impression on the Cabinet. I think they know well enough what is happening.

Michael Foot didn't share my gloom but he was anxious about unemployment and said we must watch public expenditure. Fred Mulley said, 'Tony Benn is right on the gravity of the crisis. But how can you tell the people how grave the crisis is without accelerating the collapse of confidence?' and Tony Crosland suggested that unemployment was producing much less of a public reaction than it used to but its social effects were still serious.

Eric Varley warned of a collapse of confidence if my proposals were accepted. He said the TUC were simply sloganising about planning agreements and whenever he asked for their help, they didn't know what they were about. As for the NEB, he endorsed the Labour Party policy that it should not be used for lame ducks.

Roy Jenkins agreed with me on the gravity of the crisis. He thought our survival depended on keeping the tightest control over the PSBR because of business confidence. He was afraid of import controls because they would push up the cost of living. 'Foreign goods are better and cheaper and we have to accept that.'

Barbara Castle said, 'The link with the trade union movement is vital. As to import controls, they are very badly needed for textiles.'

After all that, the Cabinet didn't really decide anything but it will be reported as having endorsed Denis Healey's strategy. That means that we will ask for a loan which he said he was going to announce tomorrow.

Tea in the Tea Room, where Dennis Skinner advised me to resign and so did Audrey Wise, though in the nicest way. Joan Lestor was sitting there listening. I said that the only time it would make sense would be if one decided that the Government was doing more damage than good, and that was not the case yet.

Saturday 8 November

On the train back from Bristol, a nervous, rather weedy-looking buffet car attendant came round with coffee. He told me he served in the army but after four or five stints in Northern Ireland, he had a nervous breakdown. 'It was terrible,' he said. 'The children spit at you, the grown-ups throw stones at you and shield behind the children. My friends were blown up, but what really upset me was that I used to go out with a Catholic girl who was going to be a teacher. Her brothers found out and shot her through the knee caps as a punishment for going out with a British soldier. She had to have both legs amputated.'

It was a most brutal story. My God, we have to get out of Ireland.

There was a programme last night about the Orange Order in Glasgow marching through Catholic areas to provoke them. We will have to get out because the English cannot solve the Irish problem.

Tuesday 11 November

The *Scottish Daily News* died yesterday.

The big story this morning is that the Governor-General of Australia has dismissed the Prime Minister, Gough Whitlam, on the grounds that he would not agree to a General Election after being unable to get his Budget through the Senate because of obstruction. This will have two effects. First of all, it will identify the undemocratic role of the Monarch, even though her functions are carried out by a Governor-General, appointed by the Australian Prime Minister, who advises the Queen. Secondly, it will probably weaken the link between Australia and Britain.

Cabinet at 10 and there was an oral report on Chrysler. I had stayed up till 3 am going through all my papers on this. Eric Varley told us that American-owned Chrysler had been in difficulties earlier this year and that 25,000 jobs would be directly affected. Chrysler have said that if the UK took it over, it would have losses of £55 million and another £80 million would be needed for investment. The alternative would be to let it go into liquidation in three months.

I said, 'Prime Minister, this is the biggest collapse in the industrial history of this country, twice the size of UCS, involving perhaps 67,000 people at a cost in unemployment pay of about £70 million. It is a disaster. This is a repeat of the motorbike industry, and it is happening year after year.' Harold Wilson said it wasn't a lame duck, it was a dead duck. '138,000 working days have been lost in disputes in the motor industry this year and the report must go forward and be agreed.'

That was the end of that discussion and we went on to Devolution. Had a most fitful night just lying on the couch with the light on and my door open so people could see me. Every time the division bell rang I went to vote – I have no idea how many times.

Wednesday 12 November

After lunch I dictated my ministerial broadcast on the North Sea and Petroleum and Submarine Pipeline Act. Bernard Ingham and Ronnie Custis had advised against it on the grounds that it would not be interesting enough, but I had insisted they ask Number 10 and to my amazement Number 10 agreed. So Ingham and Custis put a note in my box last night saying, 'We take it you'll only want to do a radio broadcast?' I told them I would also do a television broadcast since the authority covered both. So I found myself talking to the nation for five minutes on an issue that is non-political, in the national interest and is good news.

At 2.30 I went to meet the NUM at the House of Commons – Joe Gormley, Arthur Scargill, Mick McGahey, Dai Francis and others. Joe outlined the anxieties and uncertainties, especially the statements that had been made. 'We want the Government and the Board and the union to make commitments', he said, 'and we are very worried about power stations.'

Then a number of them expressed their anxiety in tremendously powerful language. I said, 'I'll deal with the individual points but the key point is that this country has not got an energy policy.'

My officials went white when they realised I wasn't following the innocuous briefs they'd given me. I went on, 'We have to bring into the public arena the discussion between the unions and management throughout nationalised industry, on all those issues that are of real concern to us: plant closures, coal burn, the possible conversion of oil to coal, nuclear power and the annual reports of the nationalised industries. We need a forum where these things can be discussed and I shall use it for EEC energy policy. I need your support.'

Thursday 13 November
Cabinet at 10 and the much delayed discussion on public expenditure. Harold opened by saying this was the hardest of all decisions for any Government to make and he hoped there would be no recriminations.

Denis Healey began, 'We are talking about the period when we are returning to full employment. Output will be rising from 1977 to 1979. There will be a shortage of resources and money. We must make room for investment and exports. A 10 per cent increase in investment is expected in 1977–9. We must aim at a balance of payments surplus in 1978–9 or else the debt repayment will burden us and mortgage the North Sea oil. The Crosland proposals for lower cuts would pre-empt resources and would be a recipe for disaster. We cannot escape these cuts. We cannot borrow unless we make the cuts now or within the next six months. We are already borrowing 20 pence in every pound. The only alternatives to public expenditure cuts is to print money or raise interest rates and a quarter of the PSBR is now due to the recession.

'As for taxation, some increases are inevitable which will undermine the £6 pay limit policy. If company tax is raised it will either cut jobs, investment or prices; on income tax you might go up by between 5p and 9p in the pound, which will cut take-home pay and the unions will then start bargaining on post-tax income.

'At the Labour clubs you'll find there's an awful lot of support for this policy of cutting public expenditure. They will all tell you about Paddy Murphy up the street who's got eighteen children, has not worked for years, lives on unemployment benefit, has a colour television and goes to Majorca for his holidays.' If that's the case, I'd be interested to know how many people who frequent the Labour clubs actually vote Labour.

Sunday 16 November
Peregrine Worsthorne in the *Daily Telegraph* stated that now that the trade unions were so strong, the Establishment would have to prepare the army to fight the unions in order to retain power – the most explicit fascist argument I've heard for some time.

Today a taxi driver asked me, 'How do you stand up to all these personal attacks?' I told him I didn't take much notice of them. He said, 'I don't read the papers because they are all against socialism. Anyway, you keep at it.'

There was more in the paper about the bomb at Hugh Fraser's house, saying that armed attachments from Notting Hill police station went immediately to the houses of Mr Jenkins and Mr Benn to guard them. The trouble is you don't know whether you're being protected, surveyed, monitored or what!

Monday 17 November
Fifteen years ago today, Father died in Westminster Hospital. I sat beside his bed and he told me about his early life. On top of the terrible bereavement I suffered, it was of course the day I was expelled from Parliament.

Caroline and I went to the National Film Theatre to see *Winstanley*, a film about the life of Gerrard Winstanley made by the British Film Institute, on a very low budget. It was the story of the Diggers and Levellers movement of the spring of 1649 when Gerrard Winstanley set up a commune in Surrey to demonstrate his genuine theories of political equality and the cultivation of the land. It was very interesting because this is a part of our history which has been forgotten.

But it also revealed in startling form the difference between the sort of early socialism that had emerged out of the seventeenth century when people were moving towards the idea of equality but were still in the grip of the idea of an objective truth laid down by God, and the later nineteenth-century socialist ideas influenced by Karl Marx's theory of historical materialism, where history was seen as the history of the class struggle and 'truth' as reflecting that struggle as it developed.

Watching the film I felt that this was a part of the secret history of working people from Wat Tyler and the Peasants' Revolt through to the seventeenth-century Levellers and Diggers, the Tolpuddle Martyrs and the Peterloo Massacre of the early nineteenth century, and the Pentonville Five and the Shrewsbury Pickets of our own time.

Tuesday 18 November
At Cabinet we had the first major paper on direct elections to the European Assembly. There has been talk about the introduction of direct elections in Europe since 1957, and before the Referendum Harold Wilson had reserved our position on them. The Common Market countries want direct elections by 1978, so the United Kingdom has got to move and the Cabinet should steer Harold as to the desired size of the Assembly, whether there should be one election day throughout Europe, or many, and how many national representatives we should send.

Harold Wilson said, 'Once an Assembly has been elected, there will of course be pressure for it to be given powers.'

Jim Callaghan said, 'The European Commission is weakening while the Council of Ministers will be getting stronger and fighting the Commission.'

I said direct elections would establish a new centre of electoral legitimacy which would eventually challenge the authority of the House of Commons. I could see circumstances where the SNP were in power in the Scottish Assembly, the Tories were in power in Strasbourg when the Government's popularity was low, and Lord Goodman, as ever, was in power in the House of Lords. This would mean the erosion of parliamentary democracy. Different national and European results would pose serious problems. What was particularly fishy about it was that all previous democratic advances had been demanded by the people but this was being demanded by the federalists. It would re-open the controversy within the Labour Party recently quietened by the Referendum. Taken with Devolution, it would undermine 150 years of struggle by the British people to get democratic control through the House of Commons and would add nothing whatever to the demo-cratisation of the EEC because the Commission would use an elected Parliament to fight the Council of Ministers. We had reached a stage where voting was becoming a substitute for democracy.

On the way out, I talked to Joe Haines about Bernard Ingham. He said Bernard didn't like the Number 10 set-up, he didn't behave like a political press officer and was capable of creating terrible trouble if I got rid of him.

Wednesday 19 November

Lunch with the Japanese Ambassador, Mr Kato. His wife was most amusing, very beautiful, and had been brought up in America. We had a long talk about acupuncture – the Ambassador has arthritis and he has had fifteen injections at £20 each which have done him no good at all. Madame Kato said, 'I could have bought a new outfit with that.'

I said, 'Look, I have some acupuncture needles and I'll come and stick them into him any time you like. Then you can have a new outfit.'

Madame Kato asked me if I had heard of pressure points. I said I hadn't and the Ambassador told me that it was part of Zen Buddhism. Madame Kato began to press my hand and pull my fingers, saying, 'This will help your heart, this will help your stomach, this will improve your eyesight,' and we had a good old laugh. It was most unusual because the Japanese are generally rather formal.

Jack Rampton came to see me and we had a helpful talk. I said, 'While we're on staff matters, I'm a bit worried about Bernard Ingham.' He told me Bernard had gone to see him, saying he feared that he'd lost the confidence of Ministers. I said, 'I think that's true but it's a much deeper problem. He doesn't seem to take an interest and isn't very helpful.'

'He's an energetic chap,' Jack said. 'He has an idea of what a Minister should do and he bullies him until he does it.'

I said, 'On the principle that everybody does best what they most enjoy doing, wouldn't it be a good idea to give him a full-time job on energy conservation?'

'That might be one way of doing it or else I could have a word with Douglas Allen of the Civil Service Department and see what can be done.'

Thursday 20 November

At 9.45 the Foreign Editor of *Pravda* came to interview me. He asked about the economic situation, about my assessment of the slump and the policies we were pursuing.

I said, 'Like Malenkov, I am in a power station in Siberia.'

He laughed and I told him a bit about the debate that was going on. At the end he asked about Michael Foot and why *Tribune* spoke so critically of him. I said, 'The only interesting debate going on in Britain is the debate in the Labour Party and the most important debate within the Labour Party is on the Left. You will know that at the Labour Party Conference these matters were discussed and feelings were very strong.'

Had a drink with Peter Jay, Frances and Francis. Peter's analysis was that the present situation would go on for eighteen months, culminating in a massive crisis. Then a proposal would be made that this be dealt with by sound financial and monetary policies involving massive slashes in public expenditure. After that, there would be a coalition which Harold probably wouldn't join, an Election which the Tories would win, the whole Labour movement would come out against the Tory Government and law and order would break down, leading to domination by an authoritarian figure of the Left or Right.

I agreed with him that ballot box democracy was becoming incompatible with the capitalist market economy and the inequalities inherent in capitalism. 'But we are not just spectators. We are here to influence events, and if that awful scenario is what you see – anarchy leading to authoritarianism (which I don't see at all), – let's find a better way. Our policy of protection and reinvestment is, after all, a better deal than that.'

He returned to the anarchy theme and I said, 'It may look like anarchy to the middle classes if the workers get greater control, but for the people who are unemployed, it must feel like anarchy now.'

He said, 'If only you could get away from this corporate state image of being in favour of the Don Ryders and the NEBs and so on, there would be a lot of support – from myself and others – for a kind of market socialism.'

'I understand what you mean,' I replied. 'I want industrial democracy. I don't believe in these great corporate figures any more than you do – Finniston, Ezra, Ryder, and so on – but I lost that battle.'

'If you could show that you really care about industrial democracy within a market economy, I am sure you'd have a lot of support.'

'I doubt it,' I said, 'because my scheme is really based on the trade union movement, since they are the only people strong enough to achieve it.'

'But the trade union leaders are corporate state people. You'll never get them to support you on this.'

I said, 'I know, but at the shop floor level there is quite a different constituency and they ought to be given a chance. You find the only way that wage levels can be controlled is by people fixing their own wages in the light of their own circumstances.'

Went to see the Swedish delegation and sat opposite the Swedish Minister of Industry. The Minister told a lovely joke about a man who sent his mother a $10,000 parrot which sang *Rigoletto* in English, French and German, and she wrote back and said the bird tasted good but it was very hard to pluck.

Saturday 22 November
Herbert Rogers rang to read to me an absolutely devastating letter he has written to Harold Wilson about the decision to send Malcolm Shepherd to represent the Cabinet at the funeral of Franco. It was marvellous – and so strong that even Herbert is not going to release it to the press, but he is going to give me a copy.

Monday 24 November
At 12.15 to the first press conference since the Referendum of the Labour Common Market Safeguards Committee to launch their new magazine, *The Bulletin*.

Alan Phillips from my Private Office rushed in and gave me a note from Ronnie Custis:

Ken Stowe [a Number 10 Private Secretary] rang to give me a message from the Prime Minister for you. Any Minister attending the press conference of the Labour Common Market Safeguards Committee *must not* make any statement which is inconsistent with Government policy or inconsistent with the fact that the agreement to differ ended on 6 June.

Peter came in and he had had a similar note.

The Chairman of the Common Market Safeguards Committee, Ron Leighton, introduced the programme and said they had a number of demands: no direct elections, no European Monetary Union, reform of the CAP, better control over the budget, no free movement of capital, improved overseas aid and no VAT harmonisation.

I said that we were not re-fighting the Referendum. We accepted the verdict and we wanted to be constructive in safeguarding the national interest but there were various questions for discussion. I mentioned the federal versus democratic question, and the link between the EEC and Devolution. I talked about energy policy and the Coal Board being hauled before the European Court, and the separate seat at the Energy Conference. I compared it with Château Rambouillet where de Gaulle vetoed British entry to Europe, when the governments had been represented as nation states. I told them that the Executive would be producing a future policy document for next year's Conference.

Ronnie Custis later told me that Harold wants to see me, so I may read in the papers tomorrow that I'm to be carpeted for my speech.

Tuesday 25 November
Two things I should mention on the surveillance/harassment side. The area around the house is still under surveillance – the numberplates tend to begin with ML which denotes police.

Secondly Melissa rang home today and a woman answered, 'Inspector's Office.' 'What do you mean, Inspector's Office?' Liss demanded. 'What number are you?' 'What number do you want?' the woman asked. Melissa gave the number and the woman became flustered and rang off. Melissa dialled again and in fact her previous call had rung at home but nobody had had time to answer. So it seems as if the bugging office got confused.

To Energy Committee where the first item was security of nuclear materials from terrorist threats. Malcolm Shepherd reported how far the training of AEA guards in pistols and automatic weapons had progressed. Willie Ross said Scottish Chief constables were keen to prevent automatic weapons from being used off site. We did need to have automatic weapons available for the AEA guards and as nuclear materials in transit were the most vulnerable, we ought to consider protection for them.

The main item was Chrysler where Eric Varley recommended we let the company go bust. He gave the history and the alternatives and then said, 'The NEB don't want it. Leyland don't want it. Vauxhall are afraid we might help Chrysler. Ford don't want it. Industrial Development Advisory Board is split 4 to 4, not on the viability question – only Wilfred Brown thought it was viable – but on the question of whether we should help it, which was not within their terms of reference anyway.'

I was called and I said this would be the biggest single immediate industrial collapse, involving possibly 60,000 men and the repercussions were absolutely unpredictable. Denis had implied that the Government could get away with what it liked now – since there hadn't been a row on the rate support grant or on the increase in prescription charges – and I thought this was a dangerous doctrine, bringing to mind the story of the straw and the camel's back. I was against it on merit and thought it was a massive further step towards industrial suicide. We would never make sense of these issues if we insisted on confusing company viability with national viability; you could have a narrowing manufacturing base and a slump and still have some companies manufacturing that were profitable and until this basic fallacy was removed I said we would make no progress.

Lunch with Paul Martin, the former Canadian Foreign Minister who is now High Commissioner in London, a very friendly man. He is full of words of encouragement. He told me that when McKenzie King was making speeches similar to the ones I am making, he was the most hated man in Canada and after that became the Prime Minister with the longest service in the whole British Commonwealth.

At 9 pm I went to see Harold Wilson. All he wanted to tell me was that he was going to take away Tommy Balogh as my Minister of State and that he would promote John Smith to that post, would give me Peter Lovell-Davis as one Parliamentary Secretary and another one if I could justify it. I went through a list of people. If I can't have Michael Meacher, my choice would be Joe Ashton, Norman Atkinson, John Ellis, Margaret Jackson, Neil Kinnock, John Prescott or Brian Sedgemore. I tried to discuss other things but he wasn't interested: he is too busy reshuffling.

Had a chat to Neil Kinnock who told me of a producer on the BBC *Today* programme with whom he had had lunch and who thought I was an 'able extremist': Neil said, 'You must make more of these contacts.'

Wednesday 26 November
Hilary's twenty-second birthday.

The *Western Daily Press* had a marvellous headline, 'Benn and Son Lead New Market Attack' and said, 'Mr Tony Benn, Energy Secretary, and his son Hilary, together with other Cabinet Ministers . . .' It was because Hilary was on the list of sponsors of the Common Market Safeguards Committee. I was really pleased.

When I got to the office, I asked Ronnie Custis to get on to Special Branch to check the ML cars. I had a note back later saying, 'Special Branch cannot identify the cars from the data provided; they need full registration, make, colour. It does not follow that failure to identify the cars as OK means they are suspect, but care should be taken.'

At 9 the Shop Stewards' Liaison Committee came along representing all the rig sites around the country, expressing their concern at the lack of orders and complaining about lower standards abroad. We agreed we might have tripartite discussions, that they needed to develop a shop stewards' strategy. They were pleased. It was the second or third meeting with shop stewards and as Secretary of State for Energy I'm getting back into the same relations with the rank-and-file of the unions as I had at Industry.

National Executive at 10.30 at Transport House. From the Organisation Sub-Committee we had the question of the Militant 'entryists'. Shirley said, 'We should look at it and get the regional organisers to advise.' Frank Allaun warned against proscription and Eric Heffer advised, 'Don't stir the pot. Remember that one of the leading Young Socialists who was expelled before the war from the League of Youth, Ted Willis, is now in the House of Lords.' Bob Mellish said there were thirty Militant organisers according to this report and we ought to examine it. I said, 'Hell, the Labour Committee for Europe have got organisers. We don't want to follow that route.' Nick Bradley said, 'Why don't we have an inquiry into the activities of the CIA? Last year a report was written on the subject which Harold Evans refused to publish in the *Sunday Times*.'

Harold Wilson went on and on and on, saying he remembered the famous occasion when the Party had tried to get rid of Bertrand Russell and he himself had never favoured the withdrawal of the whip in the Lords. It was clear that he was reading from a text from under the table. He said something like, 'People seem to forget that I decide who goes in the Cabinet, not the Newham North-East Party' and 'Every paying member of the Party should be able to vote on who their candidate should be', and that he would regret it if the PLP put up their own Parliamentary Labour candidates. He hopes it would never come to that but he put in our minds the possibility that if a Labour MP had his nomination withdrawn by the local Party, the PLP might sponsor that person against an official Labour candidate. An incredible doctrine.

So that brought us to the Reg Prentice question. Reg had sent a letter to everybody on the NEC demanding the right to be heard personally and saying that his removal by the local Party was a constitutional outrage that threatened parliamentary democracy.

Walter Padley said, 'We must hear him at the NEC because the lawyers have decided that if there is, in the constitution of an organisation, the right of appeal, then the man must be heard personally.'

This opened up two enormous issues. One, is a parliamentary nomination a legal right which a man is entitled to hold even if he is not wanted? And two, if we uphold Reg Prentice's right to appeal, do we have to do it for everybody? We agreed that there would be one last attempt at conciliation between Reg and his CLP but Reg has in effect lost his appeal.

Then there was a vote on 'entryism' and by 16 to 12 it was agreed that the Organisation Sub-Committee paper lie on the table with no further action.

Judith came back to Harold's statement and said, 'Harold must recognise that the role of the NEC is to represent the movement and the idea of PLP candidates against Labour candidates would be very serious indeed.'

I triggered off Joan Lestor to say, 'Look, if you have Parliamentary Labour candidates, under the Party's constitution they would all be expelled if they stood against official candidates.'

Anyway, it was all referred to the Org Sub. I said nothing of any significance.

Then there was an emergency resolution on Spain, deploring the decision to send Lord Shepherd to Franco's funeral, which was carried unanimously.

There was a resolution on the cod war with Iceland and Sam McCluskie of the National Union of Seamen told us he was against the present gun-boat diplomacy on the part of the Government and navy. There was only six million pounds worth of fish involved a year and the experts had confirmed that the Icelandic Government were absolutely correct to go for conservation, that the UK was wrong and that the Law of the Sea Conference was in the process of favouring the 200-mile limit.

I was called out for a moment because the board of Burmah Oil Company met today and had decided that in the absence of a financial guarantee by Friday, they would seek other financial support or go into liquidation. This is an absolutely massive development, and it may be that this is what the Treasury wants. It is going to be difficult.

Thursday 27 November
The press reported that Reg Prentice had been rejected by the NEC on his appeal but that some attempt at conciliation was going to be made; Reg has now said there are a number of Trotskyite Labour MPs in the House of Commons. He is doing himself terrible damage and I think his prospect of recovery is slight.

Cabinet, and the first item was the problem of pay beds in the NHS. Barbara Castle said she was faced with militancy by the consultants and the unions and she wanted the Cabinet to agree that she could legislate to phase out pay beds and establish control herself over all private hospitals with more than seventy-five beds in case there was a flood into private hospitals.

Harold Wilson said he didn't mind that (though he had doubts about it) but there would have to be real consultation and there were some things he couldn't say now because they would leak. I guessed that, for the first time, he was talking about Harold Lever leaking to the doctors. On every issue Harold Lever always supports the Right, the rich and the powerful against the Labour Party and all it stands for.

Harold Lever himself said he was against a general holding power, and he thought there was great danger in putting such power in the hands of a Minister. There was a risk of bringing the Government down because there would be a Labour revolt in the House cf Commons on private pay beds, and he said there was a lot of Trotskyite pressure on the Health Service.

At the end, Harold Wilson said, 'Don't let's decide anything today. Just empower Barbara and me to see the doctors and we'll have a little miscellaneous committee of Ministers to consider it.'

Listening to the discussion, which could in a way herald the end of the Health Service, I was reminded that the key question is, whose interests are you looking after? As a Cabinet it is our job to look after the 90 per cent of the population who use the Health Service and not to worry about the 10 per cent who don't.

Friday 28 November
Up at 6.30 and with Caroline to visit the Bedwas Colliery.

Ken Jones, Secretary of the Bedwas Lodge of the South Wales Miners, met us – it was he who organised all the canvassing help by the miners in Bristol last year. I went there really to say thank you to them. It was a foggy rainswept morning when we arrived at the colliery and at the bottom of some tall steps were three women standing in the pouring rain with placards, back to front. The manager of the colliery was waiting to greet me at the bottom of the steps, and I asked if the women had come to meet me and what they wanted to say. At that point they turned their placards round and on them were written 'Rosedale Industries Thank You for Your Help.' They handed me a letter which moved me so much that I have put it in my diary.

Dear Sir

I am asked by the workforce at Rosedale Industries Limited to convey to you our sincere appreciation of the efforts you made initially on our behalf. We are satisfied that Operation Survival Rosedale would not have been a success without the active participation by yourself in the problems we faced. Your intervention and policies advocated laid the foundation by which a continuation of employment for almost one thousand people became possible. We, realistically, and only after careful perusal, state that we will prove by future successes that your confidence and support were justifiable.

Yours sincerely
D E Davies
Secretary of the Shop Stewards Committee

After lunch we headed off down the pit. There had been a great fuss about whether Caroline could come. Ronnie Custis had told us that superstition prevented women being allowed down the pits. So I made the most scrupulous inquiries and could find no trace of this.

Anyway, they decided to send a young nurse from the pit hospital down with Caroline and a party of about twelve of us set off in all the gear – woolly underpants, a blue shirt, a great orange boiler suit, a donkey jacket, socks, boots and a scarf. It was an old pit opened about 1912. We went down about 2500 yards into the roadway below and sat in a little train which took us up the roadway. Then we walked in the dark with the lamps on our helmets to guide us. We had to crawl about 300 yards along the coalface to see the coal cutting machine in action.

One of the dangers pointed out to me by the manager was a break in the chain pulling the machine along, and in fact it did break. We could hear a lot of talking and shouting over the loudspeaker system but they were all very polite. Later I realised the reason they didn't want Caroline to come down was because they were afraid of the bad language. In the social club later in the evening, I said, 'That explains why when the chain broke, I could hear the miners up and down saying, "Oh bother it, dash it, golly, it's broken!" '. The miners roared with laughter.

We were underground for about two and a half hours. Then we came up and had a shower and a cup of tea. The characteristics of the mining industry that make it so remarkable are that most of the colliery managers, under managers, overmen, deputies and shot-firers all started at the pit and worked their way up and therefore there is no management brought in from the outside. There is no real parallel with the rest of British Industry in that sense.

The nation is not remotely interested in the mining industry. If there is a pit disaster, they are heroes; if there is a wage claim, they are militants, but as to the rest they simply don't want to know.

Afterwards at the social club we met Neil Kinnock and his wife Glenys, a sweet woman. Arthur Hayward, the chairman of the Lodge, welcomed us. 'Tony, we greet you as a friend. Many of us came over to help you last year because we felt you were a good man and we wanted to assist you during the Election; and we want to make a presentation to you. We want to make you an honorary member of our Lodge in the NUM.'

Arthur went on to say, 'We recognise the work you have done and the attacks on you in the press which may affect unthinking people but it certainly hasn't affected our miners who know your value.' Then they called on Dai Francis, Secretary of the South Wales Miners, who had come specially across the valleys for the occasion, who said, 'Now

I am going to present you with Volume II of *The History of the South Wales Miners*. It is the first time I have ever presented Volume II to a Cabinet Minister in the Bedwas Miners' club but Volume III will be better because my son Hywell Francis is working on that!' He gave me a remarkable book by Robin Page-Arnot. The first chapter is called 'The Miners Refuse Coal for the Navy in 1914' and the reason they refused was because they felt the British Government should not intervene in the war between Austria and Serbia. So you had the incredible combination of strong, powerful and active trade unionism against the accepted world view – marvellous stuff!

Dai said, 'This is the greatest and most powerful union and the South Wales area is the best of the NUM. We didn't take on the Heath Government but the Heath Government took us on and Tony wouldn't be there if it weren't for us' (which is true). 'We must support Tony if we want a proper energy policy.' I was a bit overcome truthfully.

Caroline was presented with a brooch and a bouquet and I with a miner's lamp. I made a little speech. 'Comrades, thank you very much. The first reason for being here is to thank you for having come to Bristol last year to help in the Election but, of course, that only consolidated a relationship which I deeply value with the South Wales miners. I came here five years ago to speak for Neil Kinnock as a young member, and I came to speak for Harold Finch when he was an MP and I have been elected to come next year to your Gala. Dai Francis came over to the Bristol Trades Council during the miners' dispute and what an impression he made! This relationship is the key relationship, indeed my local Party is run by Welshmen brought up in this tradition. The mining industry has now got a real chance and we must work together to make it succeed.'

Afterwards, I was given an overman's stick and all the miners signed it for me – a lovely reminder of the day.

Tuesday 2 December

While we were driving to work, Ron Vaughan told me that last night after he had dropped me off, five separate ML cars picked him up at various stages on his journey back and one of them, with a little aerial, which was unmistakably a Special Branch car, followed him all the way home. The whole thing is so cloak and dagger!*

At 10 Frank Kearton came in to discuss BNOC appointments. He

---

* Eventually it was discovered that these particular vehicles were on surveillance of the traffic leaving the Soviet Embassy from Kensington Palace Gardens.

was very demoralised, and said, 'Quite frankly, wherever I go, I find BNOC completely undermined. Sir Eric Drake, the outgoing Chairman of BP, made no secret of his hostility to the British National Oil Corporation.'

Frank offered to resign and I said, 'Certainly not. I've no intention of letting you resign. I am going to fight this to win. We have got to see all the oil companies together, and we might mobilise the support of the TUC Economic Committee. We must make public speeches.' I hope it cheered him up. I said, 'As you know, I am not a particularly left-wing person by ideological standards, but I am serious and I am not interested in being a Minister just to fool about and get public relations successes every morning in the press.'

On the 9 o'clock news, three revolting items were reported from the European Summit. One is that we have abandoned our national determination to have a separate seat at the Energy conference. Harold was repulsed by an attack by Schmidt and the Italians: in fact the whole eight turned on him and he ran away. Secondly – and this made my stomach turn – we have agreed to abandon the navy blue British passport in favour of a European passport which will say 'European Community' with the words United Kingdom passport underneath. I had an absolute gut reaction that this was selling our birthright for a mess of unemployment. Third, we have agreed to direct elections to the European Parliament although it is recognised that Britain may not be able to go along with it. That means we'll have a second legitimate elected parliament in opposition to the House of Commons. I'm so bloody angry about it.

Thursday 4 December
Roy Jenkins reported to Cabinet on the release of prisoners detained under Internment laws in Northern Ireland. 'Next week we've got a debate in the House on capital punishment for terrorist acts and there's a minor disagreement between Merlyn and myself because he wants to let the detainees out of prison now and I feel it might be awkward and counterproductive just before the debate. So I would be grateful if I could just take the mood of the Cabinet about that.'

Merlyn explained his view. 'I have let ten detainees a week out of prison and now we've reached the final few, having promised I would let everybody out by Christmas: I have only got forty-six people left. But my Intelligence reports say that the Provos are very divided. On the one hand they are determined to stop detention from being ended because detention contributes to their capacity to get the civilian population on their side. On the other hand, I am afraid that if I *do* postpone the release of these detainees, there may be some massive sectarian murders just before the debate – and that will make things worse for Roy.'

We went round the table and Denis Healey, John Morris, Bob Mellish, Fred Mulley, Michael Foot, Jim, Malcolm Shepherd and I supported Merlyn. Reg Prentice, I think, supported Roy, as did Peter Shore, Elwyn, Willie Ross, Fred Peart and Harold Lever. There was a majority for Merlyn. It was most interesting and I was surprised.

When we came to Foreign Affairs and the EEC, I said, 'Can I ask one question about passports? On television I saw a picture of our blue British passport disappearing and a purple European Community passport being substituted. That really hit me in the guts. It is quite unnecessary. Everybody knows that Britain is in the Common Market. You could put European Community on the back of the existing passport, you could stamp on page 3, "This man is a European whether he likes it or not." But we have got to be careful: like metrication and decimalisation, this really strikes at our national identity and I don't like it.'

Harold Wilson said, 'I don't need to be lectured on Kipling.'*

I said, 'Well, Harold, if you can talk to the Commission and keep the common touch, I shan't worry.' Everybody laughed but it is a serious concern.

Sheikh Yamani, the Saudi Oil Minister who is in London for talks with Esso, came to see me. He is an absolutely charming man. He talked about our oil policy and gave advice on Government participation and said the important thing is not the cash but to be in on the act. I asked about a permanent energy forum and he thought I was trying to get away from the producer-consumer dialogue. I said, 'Not at all. But I want a place where we can talk about energy.'

I was late to see Garvin and Tin Pearce of Exxon. Garvin is an American Republican oil man with red hair, a real tough cookie. After the courtesies I said, 'I want to do a partnership arrangement with you – good faith and good will – but we want it and we're going to push for it.' He replied, 'If it's *voluntary*, we won't have anything to do with it. If it's mandatory, then of course I'll do it tomorrow.'

'That's a funny way of doing business,' I said. 'Why should things only be done if they are statutory? We don't believe in doing things like that; let's discuss it.'

He said, 'If I'm drawn in and then it fails, I'll be in real difficulty.'

I said, 'What's the real problem?'

'It's ideological,' he said. 'There's a great ideological gulf between us.'

---

* Harold Wilson had the Rudyard Kipling poem 'If' on the wall of his office.

'That's ridiculous. Have I got to change my political opinions or you yours before we can meet, or has there got to be a change of Government? What are you saying?'

He was somewhat taken aback. 'You're putting pressure on me,' he said.

'Not at all. Maybe you're putting pressure on *me*.'

He replied, 'We've no power at all in this.'

'Well, I haven't got much power either. I have to get elected which is a difficult thing to do. In fact, you have arrived on my twenty-fifth anniversary in Parliament!'

Saturday 6 December

There was a very funny item in the *Guardian* this morning called 'What Makes Tony Benn Run?' by Martin Walker. It estimated that on my eighteen pints of tea a day for forty years, I would have drunk 29,000 gallons, used 20,000 KW hours of electricity and a ton and a quarter of tea, etc. It quoted what doctors said, what the Tea Council said: that the Jockey club would argue that this was a higher rate of caffeine addiction than was permitted for race horses.

Tuesday 9 December

Since I made enquiries about the number of cars that have been doing counter-espionage surveillance around our house, they have disappeared!

Cabinet at 9.30 and I could tell from the beginning that it was going to be a difficult Cabinet because tea was brought in at about 11.30 with my special blue and white mug on the tray.

As I went in to the Cabinet, Jim Callaghan said to me, 'Now we know your secret, you're always drunk on tea.'

Harold said he hoped there would be no tetchiness and that nobody would appeal to members of the Cabinet 'using socialism or democracy' to support their arguments on public expenditure.

Denis Healey began. 'We must get £3.75 billion cuts for 1977–8. If we don't it means that taxes will rise so high that it would rule out cooperation with the unions.' He said he had tried to discuss the problem with the Neddy Six trade union representatives but they would not discuss priorities on cuts because they didn't accept the need for them. He concluded by saying that the Ministry of Defence campaign against the defence cuts had been counter-productive, that Helmut Schmidt had rung him yesterday and said that defence cuts would make Britain unpopular with NATO, and when Denis had told him what he meant to do Schmidt had understood it completely.

Barbara pointed out that as a result of demographic changes which meant more old people and children, the proposed cuts would mean an absolute reduction in the NHS standards for the first time ever, and it would be unacceptable to her, to the Party and to the Health Service. We would be closing hospitals and even accident wards. 5,000 jobs would have to go on the basis of the cuts suggested. It would mean a moratorium on new buildings and she was only asking that the rot be stopped. On pensions, she said she was prepared to go along with a part of the estimate on a forecasting basis.

Harold Wilson mentioned the sale of council houses. 'My staff are working out a plan which would produce huge savings and a reduction in maintenance costs.'

When we came to education Fred Mulley said he had never expected to be in a Labour Cabinet and hear education demeaned as it had been. He said, 'Education covers 40 per cent of our people. Each child only has one chance: the Open University would have to be cut.' He said his Permanent Secretary had told him that it was impossible to go further without desperate damage and demoralisation to the education service. 'If this is the way it's got to be, let the Treasury and the Think Tank run the country.'

'We might consider that,' Harold Wilson said.

Fred went on to say that cuts would involve cutting schools for the handicapped and that the nursery schools programme would go.

Roy Mason said he couldn't accept the defence cuts, it would appal the Germans and the Americans, break up NATO, breach the Brussels Treaty and lose the confidence of the Shah. We were now completely withdrawing from abroad, leaving only our role in NATO. The aircraft and shipbuilding industries would be affected, the multi-role combat aircraft would be cut and possibly cancelled.

Harold Wilson said that Schmidt had attacked the British Government in the EEC and NATO on the defence cuts.

Jim said, 'Denis is right in general and if we were to cut defence, it would have a very serious effect on international confidence in Britain.'

Fred Peart said that the manpower implications of defence cuts had to be taken into account, and what frightened him was that there were ultra-leftists in the Party who will defend the Red Army but not the British Army.

Michael Foot pointed out that member states of NATO spend 3.9 per cent of their GNP on defence and we would be spending 5 per cent after the cuts.

'Yes,' said Roy Mason, 'but if you take total expenditure or expenditure per capita, Britain is doing less well than France or Germany. The formula cuts would require the loss of thirty-two ships, 32,000 sailors, 40,000 soldiers, 122 aircraft and 10,000 airmen.'

Harold Wilson then suggested defence cuts of £275 million against £450 million which the Treasury wanted.

The Cabinet broke up after four hours of discussion without reaching final agreements.

Lunch with Elliott Richardson and two Embassy people, Spiers and Miller. To begin, I handed him the letter of February 1975 from the Post Office, giving reasons why there couldn't be a commemorative stamp for the bicentennial, mentioning rebels and bloodshed and how it would give offence and rub in the British defeat. I said to Elliott, 'You see you are really a militant and this is the way the British Establishment views you!'

We sat down to lunch and he said he was interested in industrial democracy but he felt that the Labour Party wasn't very democratic.

I said, 'The trade union movement created the Labour Party to be their peaceful instrument for change and if you created a Liberal party again by separating us from the trade unions, then all that would happen would be that the trade unions would set up a new party. You simply couldn't put them down.' As to the trade unions, I was strongly in favour of union democracy but they were at least more democratic than business organisations.

'I don't deny that,' he said. 'A business isn't democratic.'

We pursued this and then I talked about democracy, the cooperative movement and profit sharing. Elliott has been appointed Secretary of Commerce and may well end up in the White House.

Went back to the Department to meet representatives of TASS. They told me the most hair-raising accounts of the struggles to organise the union in Highland Fabricators and about victimisation, beatings up, falsification of records. I said I would write to the companies concerned and see if we could set up a Memorandum of Association on good labour practice.

Ron Vaughan told me this evening that Government drivers had been told to take Ministers a different route home tonight because with the Irish terrorists holding two hostages in Marylebone [the Balcombe Street siege], there is a real fear that the IRA might try to kidnap Ministers to trade them off. I spoke to Stan Orme who said that his Government detective is desperately worried. I rang Caroline to tell her to bolt the front door and close the shutters and not let anyone in. What an extraordinary time.

Wednesday 10 December

The papers this morning apparently contained a very full account of the Chrysler crisis. To recap, under pressure from his Department officials – Part and the others – and with the full support of the Think Tank, Eric Varley has recommended to the Cabinet that we simply let Chrysler go bust. There has been much opposition to this. Willie Ross wanted Scheme B which would let the Chrysler works at Linwood survive. I wanted the total nationalisation of Chrysler plus car import controls, forcing the company to open its books. The majority of the Cabinet undoubtedly supported Eric Varley but Harold Wilson was worried about it and after a great deal of effort and struggle, Harold Lever suggested he could save some babies from being thrown out with the bath water. In my opinion, his real reason was not to save Chrysler, but to make it impossible for the Cabinet to go for import controls on cars. There have been various discussions going on and a scheme has evidently been hatched which we will be told about in Cabinet tomorrow. Joined in a marvellous Christmas drink with the canteen staff at the Department.

Thursday 11 December
As we drove past the Department of Industry at 8.25 am I saw lots of cars already outside, so obviously the Chrysler business is boiling and there is going to be a massive rescue operation.

Cabinet and a long and complicated discussion. Shirley Williams said she was worried by what she read in the press about Chrysler. It was agreed that we would discuss it tomorrow, if need be, because there were currently further negotiations going on.

Harold said, 'We need guidance now from Ministers without large spending budgets. I did say earlier that there was going to be no reshuffle of major Cabinet posts over Christmas but I may have to clear this by putting Barbara at the Treasury and Tony Crosland in Health and Social Services, etc, etc,' which was quite a good joke.

Joel Barnett said, 'The Treasury have now found over £3 billion in cuts and we need a little more.'

Harold Wilson came back to the possible sale of council houses.

Ted Short said, 'We have overmanning in Whitehall,' to which Malcolm Shepherd added, 'We have increased the number of civil servants by 40,000 since we came to power and we are planning to add another 40,000.'

Denis Healey thought that one way of saving money would be by not having the wealth tax, which required an enormous number of civil servants to collect it.

I said, 'Well, Prime Minister, I'm in a bit of a difficulty because, as you know, I don't accept the strategy. I think it's a disaster which will deepen and prolong the slump and I think the fluctuations and forecasts make it all unreal. For example, the Treasury only wanted £2 billion in May, now they want £3.75 billion and that assumes 600,000 unemployed in 1978 which I don't believe. It seems to me there are four things we could do: either press the cuts home by surgery which would inflict terrible damage; or reduce the demand from £3.75 billion to what we have now reached on the grounds that the forecasts change; or publish the £3.75 billion without specifying beyond £3.5 billion where it would be spent, having a negative contingency fund; or fill the gap by tax reliefs or tax changes because the Chancellor has offered us nothing. If you look at it in terms of merit, savings can be made. What about removing the subsidy of £2 million a year from the Foreign Office, or the £15 million a year from the Ministry of Defence which goes towards public school fees?' My contribution was completely disregarded by Harold who read the papers all the time I talked but still I got it on the record.

Harold Wilson said, '700,000 civil servants cost £2.8 billion a year. If we got a 5 per cent cut, that would give us £140 million. Why can't we do that?'

We adjourned for a bit. When we came back we had another final haggle and Barbara stuck out and made some gains and Fred Mulley stuck out and fended off some of his cuts.

Went over to the House and voted against the re-introduction of capital punishment for terrorists – we defeated it by 360 to 220.

Friday 12 December
The *Daily Mail* and the *Sun* predicted that Eric Varley would quit over Chrysler; it certainly created a very exciting background for the 9.15 Cabinet.

Harold Wilson said that the Misc 50 Committee had met yesterday, and that a majority of Ministers had been in favour of the rescue proposals that had been put forward.

Then Eric Varley said that the total contingent commitment in supporting the Chrysler operation up to 1979 could be £184.5 million but that the Government would only lose the total amount if Chrysler UK and, I think, Chrysler US were to fold. He told the Cabinet that he had never favoured support, it was an open-ended commitment and, in his judgment, a rotten deal. He thought it would make a mockery of some of the painful public expenditure cuts which the Cabinet had authorised yesterday.

Denis Healey said that Chrysler had done a complete U-turn – they had agreed to retain 100 per cent control of Chrysler UK. They would cover all losses after 1976. He thought the whole Cabinet should work together to make a success of it. There were three factors that had influenced him: the Finance Minister of Iran had evidently told our Ambassador in Tehran that if we let Chrysler go it would destroy our credibility in Iran and would therefore have a profound impact on our defence sales to all OPEC countries. Second, it was clear that the British Government would not get agreement on import controls on cars either from the commission or from the USA. Third, giving extra redundancy pay to Chrysler workers would be disastrous because it would establish a principle across the board.

I said I'd taken the view from the beginning that, first, Chrysler should be forced to pay its full liabilities for what it owed to workers and to the Community. Second, that we should nationalise it at a valuation that took account of these liabilities, and third we should have import controls which were needed not only to help Chrysler survive with support but also the other manufacturers – Ford, Vauxhall and British Leyland. Above all, this case did prove the need for a fundamental re-examination of our industrial strategy.

I might just make a note at this stage that I predicted that when the full logic of the monetarist policy became apparent and it was clear that lots of jobs were going to be scrapped as a result, Harold Wilson would begin to pull back a bit from it. At this Cabinet, Denis was pulling back, he maintains, because of import controls. This is separating Harold and Denis from the real Right which consists of Roy Jenkins, Shirley Williams, Reg Prentice, Fred Mulley, Roy Mason and Eric Varley. Therefore when it comes to the crunch I don't rule out the possibility that this process will go further. I don't think Denis will be able to abandon his policy so easily but I wouldn't rule it out because he is entirely without principle. But as Harold pulls back the real attack on him will come from the Right. They'll try to get rid of him. Then there will come a moment when Harold will be looking to the Left to save him and help him. I have no doubt of that.

But it was clear that there was a majority for the Healey plan and at that moment, Harold had to go, to be made a Freeman of the City of London. I thought that it was somehow appropriate that he should be honoured in this way for getting rid of the Manifesto policy and putting in the new tough Chequers strategy, and that he should receive the honour at the moment when even that strategy had been abandoned.

I left at about 12.15. Had a quick word with Frances and then caught the train to Bristol for a marvellous celebration of Fred Phillips' twenty-five years as Agent.

It was a lovely evening and I couldn't have enjoyed it more. Fred is a remarkable man. He was born in the Austrian Empire in 1914 before Czechoslovakia came into being. He came here as an illegal immigrant with the help of the socialists at the time of the German occupation of Czechoslovakia, met his wife at an Independent Labour Party function and served in the British Army. In 1950, they came to Bridgwater.

I read out a message from Harold Wilson then said, 'Fred, I was asked to go to an EEC Energy Council meeting of Ministers today but I said I couldn't because of the presentation to you.'

Saturday 13 December

When I got back to London there was a message from Number 10. *The Times* contained a report, 'Benn Delays Energy Talks – Mr Benn said today that he had deliberately delayed talks on energy in Europe to attend a Labour Party meeting in Bridgwater.' The Prime Minister said he wanted to know the truth by Monday. It was ridiculous. I mention it because this is the sort of harassment you get from Number 10.

Tuesday 16 December

Office lunch with John Smith, Alex Eadie, Joe Ashton, Frances and Francis and we asked Nicky Kaldor over. Nicky thinks the economic situation is serious and nothing can be done. He thought it would be different if I were PM, and I said, 'I don't rule out the possibility that we might get a shift of policy – after all Harold will do anything. The question is can we push hard enough?'

Nicky takes the view that a long period of protection is necessary and the sooner the Government is out the better – to leave it to the Tories. John Smith thought the Party would never forgive us for quitting and running away, they would never elect us again. He is right really. But it is interesting that Peter Jay and Nicky Kaldor, the sort of liberal Labour-sympathising intellectual Establishment, should see the problems not in terms of power but of getting shot of a difficult situation. It is a sign of weakness although there is a part of me that feels the same.

At 4, Arthur Hetherington and Denis Rooke, the Chairman and Deputy Chairman of the British Gas Corporation, came about appointments to the Gas Board and I agreed to Don Ryder and the three industrialists they wanted. Of the trade unionists, I wanted Hugh Scanlon and Terry Parry of the Fire Brigades Union. Hetherington said, 'Well, as far as Scanlon is concerned, I want to be sure that the man we have is loyal to the country.'

The background to this is that Rampton has written a note that security would not allow Hugh Scanlon to see any documents that are confidential or above – in effect saying he's a security risk. I had this with Jack Jones and the NEB last year. So I insisted that I see the security report which led Rampton to write that minute because unless good evidence is produced, I'm not prepared to rule that he's ineligible. But I've no doubt that Number 10 will ban him anyway.

The truth is that Hetherington just does not want Hugh Scanlon appointed to the Gas Board at all.

We came on to the appointment of a woman member. I said I wanted Marjorie Proops from the *Mirror*, a very tough, down-to-earth woman.

'Oh,' they said, 'let's have … let's have the Duchess of Kent.' That really summed it up. They wanted the Duchess of Kent, a Tory industrialist, and two right-wing trade unionists. I wasn't having it, but was good natured about it all.

Wednesday 17 December

I had a letter from Mervyn Stockwood, Bishop of Southwark, saying that Gordon McLennan, the General Secretary of the Communist Party, would like to meet me, and would Caroline and I go and have dinner with the McLennans and Mervyn at the Bishop's Palace.

I'd like to meet Gordon McLennan but Mervyn Stockwood is such an old gossip that he'd tell everybody that he'd had a dinner party for the Secretary of the Communist Party and myself, so I don't really think I can accept.

Lunch with Frank Chapple whom I like, in a curious way, though he's a thug. He told me the TUC General Council this morning had been bitter as hell about Chrysler. Len Murray said he'd been told absolutely nothing – less than his wife tells him about what she's buying him for Christmas. In fact, Frank said, they had accepted very reluctantly the Government's Chrysler package out of loyalty but he thought the trade unions would take a much tougher line with the Government from now on.

Frank said that Jack Jones was one of the old 'religionists' who thought of nothing but the Spanish Civil War and pensions, and wasn't really concerned with the role of the trade unions in the future. Frank is a right-wing toughy in the trade union movement but he does have a certain candour which I admire.

Joe Ashton told me that Jeremy Thorpe is being blackmailed by a male model. It's all gossip of course.

Friday 19 December

To BP at Britannic House for an hour and a quarter's briefing from their top people. They talked about BP as a British international company – there were 650 companies in seventy countries with 170,000 employees, 15,000 of them in the UK. They dealt with 165 million tons of crude oil every year and the value of capital employed was £4,300 million. They went through all the figures.

We got on to BP-Government relations and BNOC and in effect they repeated what they had said before that they couldn't possibly cooperate with the Government until we'd sold off the shares that the Bank of England held. They argued that Government ownership was a great handicap to them. I've got to take that seriously but I don't think we can drop below 51 per cent and I did make that clear.

Sunday 21 December

A day given over entirely to leisure. In the evening, I sat down for five or six hours of continuous television. Richard Burton was in *Anne of the Thousand Days*, a film about Henry VIII's tempestuous love affair with Anne Boleyn, depicting the clash between him and the Pope which had important parallels with the clash between a future British Government and the Commission in Brussels. The issues were the same, basically – who rules Britain? – though in that case it was a matter of wedding the British state to the definition of faith as laid down by the Cardinals. Now it is the wedding of the British state to a definition of what is right and proper economic policy, namely the worship of the market economy embedded in the Treaty of Rome. The idea of England breaking with Europe was an exciting one.

The other interesting aspect was that it showed the brutality of the Tudors, and when one thinks of Saudi Arabia today, it is really at its Tudor stage.

Then we saw the end of the *St Valentine's Day Massacre*, an American film about Al Capone and the Chicago gangland massacres in 1928–9. It was followed by a news bulletin showing the latest murders in Northern Ireland and the hijacking in Austria of eleven OPEC Ministers attending the talks in Vienna, including Sheikh Yamani. Finally, there was the *London Programme* showing black violence in South London. At the moment 38 per cent of black school leavers are unemployed, and 4 per cent of black youngsters are criminals, but whenever the police try to arrest them, the whole black community rally round the ones that are arrested. The police are trying to enforce law and order in a pretty aggressive way and this is creating a lot of trouble. By then it was midnight and I had seen enough to set my mind racing.

Monday 22 December

I had a brief word with Rampton, cleared the BNOC appointments, agreed to put Brian Tucker on the board of the AEA, then we went on to the Gas Board appointments. Rampton told me that I couldn't see the Security Services report on Scanlon and it would have to go through Number 10. Well, this is the first time I have ever been denied information from the Security Services. I am now (and perhaps all Ministers are) in a category that is not allowed to see security reports. Since Committees of Privy Councillors are supposed to be able to interrogate security officers about these matters, it is an astonishing drift away from accountability. Anyway, I sent a minute to Harold setting out the details and said that, subject to his approval, I thought Scanlon should be appointed.

When I think of all those bloody businessmen on nationalised industry boards who hate nationalisation and, if they are merchant bankers, invest their money abroad, and these guys have the cheek to say that because Scanlon is a bit left-wing, or for all I know he may have been a Communist at one stage of his life, that his loyalty is in some way suspect, it makes my blood boil. What they are really saying is that Scanlon might convey information to enemy forces; of course there is nothing secret in the Gas Corporation except the laying of pipe lines and the idea that Scanlon is a sort of prewar traitor with blueprints is ludicrous.

A few days ago, I had a note saying that the British Nuclear Fuel Corporation wished to renew an option which expires on 31 December for another 1,100 tons of uranium for Britain from the Rossing mine in Namibia and would I approve it. I shall put in a minute suggesting we do not take up this option until we have clarified the position. Of course that will be overturned by Ministers and the contract will be signed. Here is a case where I simply don't trust the BNFL, Rio Tinto-Zinc who own the mine or the Department – they have no sympathy with what we, as a movement, are trying to do, and I have no confidence in their informing me accurately about the position after 1970, when the contract would have cost £6 million to cancel.[2]

Tuesday 23 December

The real event of today was my extraordinary success in getting the uranium contract option postponed. I had rung Eddie Shackleton, who was just off to the Falkland Islands, but he agreed to see Sir Mark Turner, Chairman of RTZ (Sir Val Duncan having died a day or two ago). Then Mark Turner himself told me he had contacted Windhoek in Namibia and told the company that the British Government required another month so as to decide whether to take up the option. So at least I can get it considered collectively.

Thursday 25 December

Stephen and June, Hilary and Rosalind and their sheepdog, Wellington, came round and we all exchanged presents. Our home is a great family centre and it is all a result of Caroline's love, her care, her attention to detail. She is a remarkable woman. No man is more fortunate than I.

Friday 26 December

Giorgio Fanti, the Paris correspondent of the *Paese Sera*, the Communist evening paper in Italy, came to see me; I have known him for many years and he is a friend of Peter Shore and Dick Clements. He is staying with Eric Hobsbawm, one of the leading Marxist historians who teaches at Birkbeck.

First of all, he brought me up to date with developments in Italy where one effect of the proposal for the '*historico compromiso*' between the Italian Communist Party and the Christian Democrats has been to stimulate Nenni's socialists and the PSDI to think out the implications of this coalition.

It would establish the CP in Italy tactically in a formidable position via a black-red coalition but it would certainly not be in the long-term interests of the reunification of the Left in Italy. One effect of the activities of the socialists had been to make the Communists think twice about the whole position. They had clearly not thought out the long-term consequences of such a move.

Enrico Berlinguer and Georges Marchais, the Secretaries-General of the Italian and French Communist Parties, had met with the Secretary-General of the Spanish CP and were trying to hammer out a joint position which would involve them in making a clear stand on personal liberty and democratic reform. They had indeed issued a statement recently severely criticising the Russian Communist Party for the labour camps and their attitude towards dissent.

Meantime, Mitterand had called a meeting of the democratic socialists from Southern Europe in Paris on 24 January, to prepare the way for a meeting of socialist and Communist leaders in Western Europe to begin moving towards the idea of some form of joint association without actually losing their identities. Georgio also told me that the German SPD with, he suspected, the support of Harold Wilson and certainly with the support of the Americans, was trying to drive a wedge between the Communist and socialist parties in Europe.

It would seem to me that the line-up is likely to be Portugal, Spain, Italy and France on the one hand moving towards a grand popular front, and on the other hand the West German SPD and Harold Wilson with American backing attempting to isolate the Communists and drive the democratic socialists back towards a right-wing position.

Wednesday 31 December
Well, looking back on the year the following points stick in my mind.

First, the Referendum campaign and the defeat on 5 June was a far bigger defeat for the Left – and for me in particular – than I had realised. Like bereavement, it hits you but at first you don't really take it on board.

Second, the Department of Energy is really a side Department. It is very important – energy couldn't be more important – but compared to Industry, at any rate as I had hoped to run it, or the Treasury or the Foreign Office or the Home Office, it is a side Department and although I can be competent and good at it, it is not going to be central.

Third, and this is the first time I have really appreciated it, I see that the power of a Prime Minister is such that it is not possible to do anything to change British society unless one is Prime Minister. Up to now I have always rather brushed aside ambition, but now I realise that that is the only base in Britain from which one can really change our society and realise political aspirations. If I want to do anything other than frolic around on the margins of British politics, I must be Leader of the Labour Party and Prime Minister: therefore I must do something about it.

I think I have managed to come through this year without dishonoring myself, people know that I mean what I say, and somehow I am not implicated in the Government's present economic policy. So the pilot light is burning and people do want to hear what I think, particularly media people who in a way realise now how badly the dissenting Ministers were treated. From that, I might be able to build up some sort of support and undo the real damage done by the media and the Establishment to me earlier this year.

On a more pessimistic note, there is the possibility that Wilson, Healey, Shore, Foot, Callaghan and Jack Jones are right in their strategy. Perhaps the situation will be such that after an awful year the economy will pick up in 1977, unemployment will peak in March and then fall off, and the recovery will begin. By then oil will be half ashore, half our needs will be met and there might be just a dash for the polls and possibly a Labour victory. Maybe Wilson will pull it off, which would leave me in a minority of one.

Perhaps my approach is too strained, and it will take time for my scenarios to play themselves out. Frances said she thought I must aim to be the man in the middle – I must not be the person who articulates the anger of the extreme Left so that I get in the way of the Party and the movement fighting for what it wants. Perhaps a period of silence, or rather acquiescence, would give the Party a chance to assert itself.

I should give serious and thoughtful lectures and try to get my message across that way. This is the Colombey-les-deux-Eglises strategy of waiting and arguing because the media have made me out to be destructive and fanatical, just as they did Enoch Powell. Yet I have slogged it out and soldiered on. I am not what they make me out to be and truth will out.

I must also slightly reduce the pace of life because it is killing – all the late nights. I also have to confront the genuine fear that state socialism, run by the shop stewards, will destroy individual liberty. I don't think there is anything in it, but people are afraid of it and I have to ensure that my socialism is lubricated with the old democratic ideals. There is a deep suspicion of power at the heart of the British.

It is midnight on 31 December 1975 at Stansgate, which I love so much, with the family I love even more.

Sunday 4 January 1976

The *Sunday Telegraph* this morning reported that Harold Wilson was cracking down on the work of political advisers, notably Frances Morrell, Francis Cripps and Jack Straw – that is just another attack by the press on the Left, using advisers as a weapon; they never take any interest in Denis Healey's adviser, Adrian Ham, or Tony Crosland's adviser, David Lipsey, or Ted Short's adviser, Vicky Kidd.

I worked at home and wrote a very strong argument against taking up the option of uranium from the Rossing mine in Namibia.

At the end of last year, I said that the only direction Britain could change was from the top down and I made explicit, in a way that I hadn't done before, that I should go for the top. Honesty prevents me from removing the admission but I've been slightly concerned about it. If you do set yourself that target, it is bound to begin the process of corruption. If you can't say what you think for fear that it might prejudice that goal, I think is it very difficult, and if you are clear in your mind that that is your objective, then everything else takes second place. I'm so confused in my mind about it because I have never previously set myself that objective and I'm not sure that I want it now.

At the moment, a number of thoughts spring to mind. The Tories are happy to have Harold Wilson in power. They couldn't possibly – with Mrs Thatcher as Prime Minister – do to the British economy in terms of wages and the trade unions what the Labour Government can get away with because of its close links with the unions. So actually they want the Labour Government to continue for a while.

On the other hand because of his enormous experience and his national standing, which is now quite unrivalled, Harold Wilson is a formidable figure. He wouldn't be easy to beat. Mrs Thatcher must recognise that, at a certain stage, she will want to fight an Election and her prospects of beating Wilson are pretty limited because of her lack of experience. She would find it difficult to make her campaign to run Britain better than Harold credible.

So I think there are now the beginnings of a campaign to get rid of Harold Wilson and the Tory strategy runs roughly along these lines: they are saying they want the Labour Government to do at least another year's work because only they can do it; they think that in the process the break between the left-wing and the unions, and the Government, will widen, at any rate at rank-and-file level, so that if there were an Election, the Labour Party might well be defeated through general disillusionment. They know that in order to win they have to get rid of Wilson and therefore they are beginning to look for their ideal Labour candidate to replace Wilson.

Jim Callaghan – Uncle Jim – would in my opinion win overwhelmingly in the present PLP. He is older, he has a lot of experience and he is thought to have a feeling for the Party. The Tories don't want Jim because they think he might be too popular with the country and partly because I think they are not absolutely sure about his role vis à vis Europe. They want Denis Healey and they are going to start building up Denis as the tough man. That is my guess. I think Harold Wilson has done all that's required for the Tory Party and they'll try to get rid of him this year.

Monday 5 January

We left this morning for Teheran and in the party were Peter Le Cheminant, my new Private Secretary, Frances Morrell and Bryan Emmett.

The visit is becoming an interesting one because the Shah is in financial difficulties as a result of the liftings of oil having fallen, so he's now pushing us to increase our purchases.

I talked to Peter in the plane about his time at Number 10 and how the power of the PM had increased. The PM now has at his disposal his Private Office, the Cabinet Office, the Think Tank and Bernard Donoughue's own policy unit, and in this way power is moving further towards the Centre. It is evident that Dick Crossman's theory of prime ministerial government is turning out to be correct. I don't know why I doubted it at the time.

We were met at Teheran Airport by Iraj Vahidi who is a relatively young Minister of Energy, with the British chargé d'affaires, George Chalmers, and lots of photographers.

Tuesday 6 January

At 10 I went to see Dr Eqbal, who is the Chairman of the National Iranian Oil Corporation, and Parviz Mina, the brilliant Director of International Relations for NIOC. I put my oar in straight away and said that Iran was a developing country producing oil, and moving towards industrialisation, and we were an industrialised country discovering our own oil and therefore each of us were in a sense rather unique in the producer–consumer dialogue.

All in all, it was a relaxed meeting and I can't believe that the problem of falling oil production was anything like as serious as had been made out.

At 10.50, I went and met the directors of the NIOC. Parviz Mina described how NIOC had been conceived in 1951 and how from 1954 the Consortium had been set up with NIOC as the sole agent. It was free to operate in partnership and to act commercially. The Prime Minister was the Chairman of the shareholders' committee, which could only approve the plans and programmes and look at the financial accounts. The Chairman and Chief Executive of NIOC were appointed by the Shah but the directors were approved by the Council of Ministers.

I asked about the trade unions and he said they had none, they had labour syndicates which were organised to reach collective agreements on wages, and disagreements were arbitrated by the Ministry of Labour.

Lunch with Dr Akbar Etemad, the President of the Atomic Energy of Iran, AEOI. He had some doubts about the size and scale of economic planning and, in his view, Iran was too centralised. People had had their expectations raised too high and if cuts became necessary to curb an ever-rising rate of growth, he thought there could be serious trouble in the country. He was really a Manchester School liberal breaking out and I found him a thoughtful, philosophical man. In the light of what I heard later, what he said was really of considerable interest.

Came back to tea at the Residence and at 4 I went to see Jamshid Amouzegar, the Minister of the Interior. He was involved in the hijacking by Carlos of the OPEC Ministers in Vienna. He said that Kreisky was weak and that Carlos had boasted that Kreisky would certainly concede to the demands of the hijackers, which he did of course.

Carlos had apparently talked completely openly and indeed boasted his view. He had broken with Arafat and had expressed his hatred for Yamani who he claimed had sold the Arabs down the river. He had remained calm and collected throughout, although for forty-four hours he didn't sleep at all. Carlos said that sometimes he had gone for seven days without sleep. Amouzegar asked him how he managed it and Carlos said he had ski-ing holidays and that he only did a job like this every six months.

Amouzegar said some of the young terrorists who were with Carlos were very nervous and their hands were shaking. They sat facing the Ministers, with machine guns in their shaking hands. He thought Carlos was a split personality, a Jekyll and Hyde. He gave autographs, asked the Venezuelan Minister to post a letter to his mother, waved to the crowd, and when I suggested that he was a bit of a Robin Hood, Amouzegar agreed that was a fair description. He wanted to be loved, and he felt that he was doing it for the poor.

Back to George Chalmers's house in the Embassy compound and within a few moments of my finishing my diary in the bedroom, there was a tap on the door and Chalmers came in looking very white. He had something he wanted to say to me privately. He had had a secret message from London to the effect that the Shah was worried that if his development programme was affected in any way by a fall in revenues, this could undermine his whole personal position and prestige and open the way for critics in Iran inside and outside the Cabinet.

Chalmers had not been told this in Teheran but the Foreign Office had taken it so seriously that they had sent it through Number 10.

Now the pieces of the jigsaw are beginning to fall into place. Having arrived in Teheran with the normal briefing that here is one of the strongest and most powerful regimes in the world, with a formidable Shah developing his own programme, you find that with the slightest hiccup, the whole set-up is in danger of being undermined.

Frances said she'd had a discussion with Parviz Mina and the First Secretary at the Embassy. She picked up a rumour that we had murdered the two American Air Force officers attached to the US Military Mission last year out of envy of American military power. Frances said she raised the CIA question and everybody froze!

Wednesday 7 January

Chalmers took me in his car to see the Shah and on the way he said to me, 'I suppose the Shah is really like Mussolini in his early days – with a vision and an idea – before he became involved with Hitler.' He also said the previous Empress had been completely corrupt, she'd had affairs with young men and with women. She'd done terrible damage but the Shah had been infatuated with her. He said the new Empress was liberal and popular and one had to take this into account.

We were met at the Palace by Vahidi and Etemad, and shown to a waiting room lined with photographs of Podgorny, Brezhnev, Mao, the Queen with Prince Philip behind, and various other heads of state – almost all of them signed to His Imperial Majesty. Then at 11.30 we were shown into a beautiful room with marvellous arms and glittering crystal decorating the walls, and an exquisite view of the snow-covered mountains. There was the Shah looking neat and well groomed. He is fit and well preserved but of course he does look older than he appears in photographs. Every office has an oil painting or a photograph of him and the Empress. He beckoned me towards him and someone with a movie camera took pictures. George Chalmers, Peter Le Cheminant and Bryan Emmett were all present, Bryan sitting writing notes.

The Shah greeted me and said that Britain was learning what Iran had learned about oil in the past, and that Iran was playing a world role and had to consider the developing world and the maintenance of the Iranian way of life. He said there were two countries in the world that had to maintain their own standards, Iran and possibly the UK. There were dangers but we had to succeed. We needed each other, we had a common philosophy and a common interest in the Persian Gulf. He said our boys in Oman were fighting 'side by side'.*

---

* The Iranian and British Governments both provided the Sultan of Oman with military support during the 1970s against the People's Front for the Liberation of Oman and the Arabian Gulf, the PFLOAG, which became the PFLO in 1975.

He talked about the oil companies who were trying to get a few cents off the barrel and said that if Iran collapsed, they wouldn't be able to get the oil out and the companies must understand that. He thought some oil should be used for exchange and some sold on the market, but for exchanged goods Iran needed other revenues. He had said earlier that they had to replace their oil revenues with other revenues and were concerned that food producing countries shouldn't raise food prices.

Then he described the Iranian nuclear power programme and he said he was getting the technology from the French and the Germans, and he might even take it from the Soviets – why not? But he was happy to cooperate with everyone. I described our programme and said we had made a lot of mistakes and we were happy to make our knowledge available.

Then he went on to talk about other sources of energy – solar energy in the South, geo-thermal, electric battery cars. He told me he would be ready to contribute immediately to this latter development because he saw a time when every family in Iran would have two cars – an electric car for the town and an automobile for getting about. The country's annual per capita income had risen from 200 dollars to 1500 dollars so they could well afford this. I said Walter Marshall, the Department's Chief Scientist, might come to Iran to discuss these matters with him.

He asked about the North Sea and I described how profitable the BP Forties Field was. He said that the North Sea would transform our prospects if we were not imprudent. It depended on our not sitting back and assuming it would solve our problems. I mentioned NIOC and he said the oil companies must learn the lesson that capital could not interfere with the national interest.

Then I asked him about the 'white revolution' of 1963 when he introduced his reform programme, and he was most interesting. He told me that during the War Iran had fallen very low, and even as a boy in Switzerland he was already 'thinking about the peasants'. During the war Iran was, of course, a victim and all the people could do was hold together. They had very serious problems with their oil and after the war, a madman (that was a reference to the Prime Minister Mossadeq) did them great damage. Khrushchev had believed that Iran would fall like a ripe plum into his lap but he had been proved wrong. He said that another country (meaning the US) had thought it could control Iran and that too was a problem. All these factors led to the white revolution – Iran had to be free of foreign influence and modernise but maintain its independence, its national identity and cultural heritage.

In fact, he said, there were so many reforms over the years that they didn't have much to destroy – just 'landowners and priests'. There was no great gap between rich and poor and even in the old days, when Persepolis was built, Persia had no class system and tolerated different religions. Persepolis he told me was built by paid labour.

I said this was an interesting period for the UK; we now had strength in energy and we were going for industrial re-equipment and basic social reforms. I told the Shah that he'd live to see the century out and that he'd still be younger than many world rulers today, pointing out that he was the senior reigning monarch in the world.

He intends to retire by 1989 in favour of the Crown Prince, after the present Five Year Plan, and the next two Plans had been completed and the preparation of the third is well advanced. By then he would be seventy.

I left after an hour and a quarter. What was my impression of him? He is a man with an idea – a Mussolini without doubt, a man who thinks it can all be settled at the top. But maybe in this stage of Iran's development he is right. He must feel uneasy about the situation in his country – obviously very uncomfortable about Russia on the border. He is a man for whom it would be impossible to have affection but who would count historically as having been a 'good king'.

Afterwards, Frances and Peter and I talked about security and bugging in Britain and Peter said he was sure it didn't go as far as it did in America. Frances said that Nixon had apparently had the most salacious bugging reports gathered by the FBI and the CIA put before him every night to read in bed. Frances was very shocked that the internal phones in Brussels were bugged by British officials. Le Cheminant said the French certainly bugged politicians in Brussels and we bug everywhere.

By then it was 6 and we went off in the Rolls Royce again with the officer in charge of security sitting by the driver and two motorcycle police escorts, plus armed guards behind us – because the British and Americans are given fantastic security in Teheran – to Prime Minister Hoveyda's office. Hoveyda was very amusing.

We discussed the Common Market and he said it was a very uncommon market. National interests would always predominate because people were mainly interested in jobs and the ideals of cooperation didn't affect over much. He was keen to get markets in the EEC now they had the trump card of oil.

We talked generally about international affairs and he said he distrusted expertise because all decisions were political decisions. He never could understand why the Western world was fussing over financial crises: money should be made to have a passport in the way individuals were, so that you couldn't move it without it. I said that was why we were opposed to the Common Market and he understood that.

On Eastern Europe, he said that people were living within the Communist world because they had to, as they had had to accept British rule in Iran. Marxism was the East European myth, just as the Bible was the myth in the West and the Koran in Iran.

I asked him his opinion of different political leaders and he liked Chirac of France, and he admired Indira Gandhi and said she should follow the Chinese example. Then he said you couldn't run countries in the world today to please the *Observer* and the *Sunday Times*, with all these Fabian ideas. They didn't know anything about real life – and the press generally did a lot of damage, turning from one scandal to the next.

I asked him whether he thought Nixon had been unfairly treated by the American media and he said yes, but Nixon should have apologised and got rid of Haldeman and Ehrlichman. He said that the incredible thing was that here was a man who bugged himself – that was a reference to the Watergate tapes. It was incredible.

Friday 9 January
Flew to Ahwaz, where we were taken straight to see the Governor-General of Khuzistan Province, a young man who comes from a rich family in the north.

We went out and visited a production well and it showed how simple the oil business was here as compared to the complexity of North Sea operations. This little place, manned by one supervisor and three manual workers, was producing about 750,000 barrels of oil a day.

Lunch with George Link, the Chairman of the Oil Service Company, in his beautiful house overlooking the water, with a swimming pool around which a soldier, armed with a Sten gun, was patrolling.

I talked to the Governor-General's wife about Kissinger and she didn't like him. 'He's just a fixer. He just fixes things by himself, but he doesn't really analyse the reasons for conflict.' I said, 'I sympathise with you about that but then whenever there's a crisis, we always want it fixed to give us more time to settle it.'

She asked me what I though of Iranian politics. 'I find them very competent,' I replied, 'but when I see the great investment going on in Iran, this indicates great political change.'

'But the Shah is wonderful,' she said.

'Yes, but politics is not made up of the intentions of political leaders,' was my answer.

Then we flew down to Abadan where we were met by our host, Mr Razmjoo. He took us to the guest house on Shatt-el-Arab, not much broader than the Thames, the other side of which lay Iraq. We went out for a walk in the town and one Iranian official walked beside me and said, 'You understand how the regime works in Iran? You realise there is no criticism. We have decided we must set out on a determined course of action. To maintain the policy which is so important to us, we have to suppress all criticism and control the army. We have a very powerful Security Service.'

I said, 'Yes, I understand that.'

'You realise that Iranian Students abroad will not be allowed back, that if the Security Services have to interrogate people, it can be very savage.'

I nodded.

Saturday 10 January

Finally left for the airport and we began the long flight home. I did a lengthy TV interview at London airport, arriving home absolutely exhausted with a hacking cough and bronchitis after a most thrilling week in Iran. The regime is hateful and I can dictate this openly now on to my diary tape; in Iran I always feared my rooms were bugged. It is the most royalist, repressive, absolutist National Socialist regime, but that isn't to say it isn't going to grow and be important, so we have to have some relations with it.

One of the most unattractive aspects about politics is that whatever your own aspirations may be, you have to work with others who are repressive. That is certainly true of the Soviet Union and now we know more about America, it is certainly true of the US. But our own record in Northern Ireland, and in bolstering up the Sultan of Oman's corrupt regime, is also quite appalling.

Tuesday 13 January

Ministers' lunch, where we spent our time discussing Jim Sillars and the Scottish situation. Joe Ashton thought Sillars would win in South Ayrshire if the SNP didn't put up a candidate, Alex Eadie said he wouldn't.* Frances was in favour of the Scots being a bit more independent. I said the collapse of the English ruling class and their failure to deal with problems had precipitated a lot of this. Then we got on to the possibility that there might be violence in Scotland, like Northern Ireland, with the Catholics isolated and repressed by the Orangemen.

Tommy Balogh, who is a Hungarian pessimist, took the same view that when the English did turn nasty, they would go anti-Catholic, anti-Irish, anti-Scot and anti-foreigner.

---

* In January 1976 Jim Sillars and others formed the short-lived Scottish Labour Party, committed to Devolution; he resigned the Labour whip and sat as an SLP Member 1976–9. Subsequently elected for Glasgow, Govan, 1988 as Scottish National Party MP. Margo MacDonald, whom Jim Sillars later married, held the same seat for the SNP, Nov 1973–Feb 1974.

After that, I had a meeting on coal imports: I had asked for import control and Jack Rampton recommended against. So I said, 'I'll settle for two things. First of all, the cancellation of all the oustanding contracts after this year by the CEGB; and secondly the transfer of responsibility for importing coal from the CEGB to the Coal Board.'

This was more or less agreed, although there'll be a row about it; it is very important for the miners that we make this change.

Had dinner at Locket's with Michael Foot, Peter Shore and John Silkin. John said we should pull out of Northern Ireland and Michael launched into a tremendous attack on him. 'Let down our friends in Ireland, the people who stood up for us, Gerry Fitt, Conor Cruise O'Brien?' To make it worse, he said, 'Look what happened in Cyprus, when we got out of Palestine, when we got out of India.' Retrospectively, Michael appears to have been a great imperialist though I know he doesn't mean it. Peter supported him because Peter is very pro-Protestant on Northern Ireland.

Wednesday 14 January

To Number 10 for a meeting of OPD, where I presented in detail my Rossing uranium contract paper. I said that this was a major political issue and should certainly go to the full Cabinet. It was a tight timetable; I had been told last December that the contract expired on 31 December, I got the option deferred and we now had until 31 January to decide. I said, 'There is a long history to the matter and it's not a simple choice between necessity and principle. I am advised that the uranium is all for civil purposes here and the departmental view is that the contract should go ahead.'

Then I came on to my *own* views and gave the history of 1968–70, when we were misled. My view was definite – we should not proceed with the contract. I referred to UN resolutions. On the security of uranium, there was a great risk. There was SWAPO and Angola to consider. I thought there should be further talks with the Americans, the Australians, the Canadians and the UN and SWAPO. I invited colleagues not to agree to the taking of the option and to agree to an inquiry to examine the possibility of terminating the Rossing contract.

It developed into the most highly charged and unpleasant discussion that I have ever taken part in. Jim said, 'Tony Benn has changed his mind since 1970 when he put before the Cabinet proposals that we should accept this.' I interrupted to say that I was misled at that time.

'You may say you were misled but it is still embarrassing for you to change your mind. I've looked through all the papers from 1968 to 1970 and I know you have changed your mind. It's just embarrassing for you, that's your problem. It was not put in the 1973 'Programme for Britain.'

Harold interrupted. 'And that programme was not put to Conference or accepted by Conference.'

Jim continued, 'We don't recognise the Council of Namibia and SWAPO don't mind – there is a difference between their private and public attitude.' And while I was speaking earlier, Jim had interrupted me, saying, 'I wish you wouldn't refer to the Foreign Office.'

'Very well, Foreign Secretary,' I said, 'but I have a letter here from David Ennals Minister of State at the Foreign Office in which he writes to Jenny Little of the International Department at Transport House saying it's for the benefit of Namibia that this contract should go ahead.' Jim said, 'I agree with that entirely but that's not the Foreign Secretary speaking, it's the Ministers of the Foreign Office.'

Then Harold said, 'I will not accept Ministers taking part in NEC discussions and using those documents to put pressure on the Government. I will not have it.' This was because yesterday I circulated the paper on this matter which had been prepared by the International Committee. So I interrupted, 'Prime Minister, if you are referring to me, I have never until this year been a member of the International Committee of the NEC. My first meeting took place yesterday morning. I claim no part whatever in drafting the document. I have not discussed the matter with the International Committee and I have not met the SWAPO representative: I want this absolutely clearly understood.'

So Jim Callaghan said, 'I accept entirely what you have said but it is widely thought you have been stirring up the NEC in order to bring pressure to bear on the Government and that you triggered this off. But I accept that you didn't draft it.'

The only other person to speak was Peter Shore who supported me. The argument went back and forth and Harold was boiling with rage, as indeed I was. Jim said, 'Why should Tony Benn behave as if he were Foreign Secretary?'

'I don't,' I replied, 'but since my Department did not draw my attention to the UN resolutions, I put them before the Committee.'

Then the question of Angola arose. What did it have to do with Angola?

I said, 'Prime Minister, I have explained that on the Namibian-Angolan border there is a hydro-electric plant on the river whose future will be linked in some way with the further extension of the Rossing mine.'

I finally got Harold to agree that I could see all the papers relating to this during Eric Varley's period at Energy and I've got to work like a beaver on this. But I'm not going to be put in a position where the Foreign Office brief publicly about my attitude. The burning hatred directed at me in that room is still as evident as it was when I was

Secretary for Industry. As we left, Peter Shore said, 'That really was charged with emotion.'

Thursday 15 January
Ron Vaughan's father died of bronchial pneumonia during the night. Ron was very fond of his father, who had been a Civil Service messenger, and he was really knocked sideways by it.

At Cabinet, ministerial memoirs came up and Harold suggested that we accept the Radcliffe Inquiry.[3] Michael Foot said he hadn't read it but Harold went on, 'Well, if anyone has any queries – '

I intervened, 'Half a minute, Harold. This does raise very important questions. You can't just brush it aside like that. It touches on the central questions of our democracy and the relations between Government and governed. The report is a bit narrow. How do you balance the right of the public to know, against the necessities of good government? What is the relationship between the national interest and the convenience of Ministers? What about access to information on policy options? What about malicious gossip?' So Harold suggested I write a memorandum about it and I will.

Friday 16 January
Went to the Cabinet Office where we had a meeting of the Ministerial Committee on Energy. Jim Callaghan was in the chair and was unusually crabby. A paper was presented by Sir Kenneth Berrill who is allowed to operate exactly as a Minister, to put in papers under his own name for consideration at these meetings – it is really sub-contracting the thinking process of Government to a Civil Service department. He is a Minister in all but name. His Think Tank members are civil servants, and I don't know whether they include anyone sympathetic to us. It is most unsatisfactory.

At 10.45 I had a deputation from a variety of social service pressure groups about fuel poverty: the National Council of Social Services, Avon Community Council, Child Poverty Action Group, etc. One of the representatives launched into an attack straight away. 'If I ask you to put your political reputation at risk by attacking the Government for their energy policy and fuel tariffs and you don't, you personally will be responsible for the deaths of hundreds of old people and babies this winter.' They handed me seven action points.

I said I would be quite happy to consider joint discussions with the energy industries, and I reported to them that the DHSS was going to publish a new leaflet with advice to people in hardship.

Saturday 17 January

There was a report in the *Guardian* that over the years the CIA have been financing a news agency in Latin America which works very closely with Reuters, confirming the suspicion I have long had that Reuters has an Intelligence function.

To Bristol for a four-hour surgery. A man came about his payments from the DHSS; another man had a caravan which was being rated; a divorcee wanted help to visit her son who had been abducted by her Tunisian ex-husband and taken back to Tunisia; a couple who had borrowed £4500 for a little business and had paid off £78 a month for twenty-five months, reducing the loan to £3900, had been told that in order to discharge the debt they had to pay £5500.

Sunday 18 January

Caroline and I went to dinner with the Foots, the Shores and the Baloghs. We began in quite a jolly way discussing the CIA which none of them really takes seriously but when I told them that Jack Jones had been banned from serving on the NEB and Hugh Scanlon from the Gas Corporation on security grounds, I think they were a bit shaken. Then we talked about diary-keeping and it turned out that Peter had been on the committee which had approved the Radcliffe Report. Michael and I are going to put in memoranda about it, though Michael isn't very much in favour, on principle, of diaries coming out.

Michael and Peter have been to see Harold to argue for import controls. They are seeing Denis next week but I'm not hopeful. I put the case to them for general import controls, investment-led reflation, equity stakes for Government, control of capital movements and industrial democracy. Michael said that was completely unrealistic, given the present Cabinet and when I said I thought his plan was too, he replied, 'Yes, but it has a better chance.'

I attacked the complete abandonment of industrial policy and Peter said, 'If you feel that, you should leave the Government. Don't you realise there has been a big crisis since the Manifesto was written?'

I said, 'I am going to be perfectly loyal to the Government to try to make it succeed; but I think the present course will lead to our defeat and within the movement we must be big enough to argue the case out.'

Monday 19 January

Yesterday I had a talk to Jack Spriggs who is trying to get another £2 million from the Industry Department for KME and he told me that they recognized that he'd made great progress up in Kirkby, and that KME had a strong case, but they were unable to help because 'Tony Benn had said when he gave the money that it was a once-and-for-all

POLLING STATION

REFERENDUM

5TH DAY OF JUNE 1975

LONDON BOROUGH OF ISLINGTON
Central Electoral Area

Notice of Poll

Above: Day of reckoning:
the Referendum on
Britain's continued
membership of the
Common Market, 5 June
1975.

Keep Britain in Europe

Above: The Prime
Minister and his
principal Dissenting
Minister: after the
Referendum Wilson
dismissed me as
Industry Secretary.

Left: The coalition for
Europe: Heath at a
pro-Market rally,
1975, supported by
(left) Jeremy Thorpe
(right) Denis Howell
and Roy Jenkins. A
number of sports
personalities can be
seen on the platform.

Keep Britain in Europe

Labour men and women.
Right: Neil Kinnock;
Middle: (left to right)
Denis Healey and Shirley
Williams sounding the
retreat in July 1975; Roy
Hattersley; *Bottom:*
Judith Hart, one of the
architects of the '25
companies' plan; Eric
Heffer who was sacked
as an Industry Minister
for outspoken opposition
to the EEC; Joan
Maynard, the MP for
Sheffield Brightside, an
outstanding socialist.

Above: Trade (Peter Shore) and Industry against the Market.

Left: Britain's liquid gold: the first North Sea oil to be landed, June 1975. The opportunity to transform Britain's economic life was squandered by successive governments.

Below: Jam tomorrow: talking to workers at Robertson's factory in Bristol, 1974.

Top: Three Premiers: Anthony Eden and Ted Heath flank Macmillan at the Churchill centenary luncheon, 1973.

Left: The two Tory Parties. Whitelaw stood against Margaret Thatcher for the leadership after Heath was beaten in the first ballot, February 1975.

Below: Vanquished and victor at the Conservative Party Conference, 1976, Willie Whitelaw and Lord Hewlett separating the two.

Right: Michael Foot studies the small print, Conference, 1976.

Below: Emperor Jack: Jack Jones who as General Secretary of the TGWU was one of the Labour movement's most powerful men.

Bottom: Comrades in arms: Michael Foot, Ian Mikardo, Barbara Castle and Harold Wilson sing 'Auld Lang Syne' with other members of the NEC, Blackpool, 1975.

Gets to the heart of matters that matter

Dropping the Pilot

Top: Wilson faces the press after his surprise resignation announcement, 17 March 1976.

Above: It's all over.

Left: A Knight of the Garter, Windsor Castle, June 1976.

Top Left: A Whitehall Mandarin – Sir Antony Part, Permanent Secretary at the Department of Industry.

Top Right: Bernard Ingham, Director of Information at Energy – in training for Number 10.

Above: Francis Cripps (right) my economic adviser 1974-9, with John Smith, Minister of State at Energy.

Left: Frances Morrell, my political adviser 1974-9.

The secretary of State for Industry's office, 1974.

grant.' Gregor MacKenzie had made a great deal of the fact that he would like to help but 'Tony Benn wouldn't let him.'

Well, I had such a struggle to get any support for them at all that the fact that the Department should use me as a way of covering their own right-wing policies really annoyed me. I told him, 'Take no notice of it. It isn't true. The Government can support you any time they like.' He was pleased about that, but what a dirty crowd!

Had a good lunch at the Gay Hussar with Peter Sissons, Howard Green and Giles Smith, the ITN industrial correspondents. I described the labour movement's option of import controls, forced investment and industrial democracy. They said, 'In the past, you stirred up the management by your work with the shop stewards; that's what other Ministers said, you were stirring up the shop stewards.'

I told them, 'You've got to have confidence in the trade union movement before you can do a damned thing and anyway I think this is the only way forward.' Anyway, I took Caroline's advice not to try to argue with them but simply to analyse in an objective way.

Tuesday 20 January

I saw John Biffen today and congratulated him on his appointment as Opposition Spokesman on Energy and Industry. I admire him and I told him how much I looked forward to working with him, with no Benn-bashing, and exploring complicated energy questions.

Ministers' lunch and Tommy Balogh was very amusing. There had been a jibe in the press about BNOC being a geriatric ward and Tommy had put out a statement to the Sunday papers that he was of biblical age with biblical vitality, he was fond of fencing and his favourite weapon was the dagger. He told us over lunch that as a young man, he fought a duel and cut off the lobe of man's ear with a sabre. We didn't believe it.

'Yes,' he said, 'when I was in Budapest a man boasted that he had kissed my cousin's daughter on the fortress walls and, since my cousin was too old to fight him, I took up the charge of honour and challenged him to a duel – not for kissing my cousin's daughter but for boasting about it. I cut off the lobe of his ear and it bled so much that they thought it was his jugular, but when he discovered it was only the lobe of his ear he shook me by the hand and that settled it. The Germans, of course, padded up all their vulnerable spots but in Hungary we fought bare to the waist.' An amazing if slightly spurious story!

To the Energy Committee under Roy Jenkins's chairmanship in the large Ministerial Conference Room in the House of Commons. As Roy was a bit late, I told Edmund Dell about a dream Melissa had last week. 'She dreamed that I was freezing to death in a block of ice and she could see me there unable to escape and gradually being frozen to death, while Edmund Dell was weeping by the block of ice.' I said to him. 'I don't think Melissa has ever met you, but your name and face are familiar to her.'

The agenda was interesting. I had asked for a special study to be made of the terrorism risk to nuclear power stations after we had agreed to arm police at power stations dealing with radioactive substances. Malcolm Shepherd was anxious about the delay in implementing the decisions but said the security report suggested that nuclear power stations were not much of a target. Bill Rodgers said that Pagoda, which is the name of the Special Air Service unit in Hereford, was the right way of handling it. I accepted the conclusions that we didn't want to do much about nuclear power stations and thought we should simply have clear instructions in the event of a crisis.

The next discussion was on the disposal of nuclear waste – an interesting story. A note had been prepared by an interdepartmental official committee that we had a lot of radio-active waste including plutonium to dispose of. We had been disposing of it in consultation with the OECD's Nuclear Energy Agency based in Paris, but there was too much and therefore it was recommended that we should dump the waste on our own under the London Convention but notify the NEA privately.

This note had been sent round Whitehall and no Minister objected, having all been briefed to support it. So I raised an objection and they said, 'This was all agreed in correspondence in the Departments.'

I said, 'No, I want it to go to Ministers.'

'But Ministers have all agreed it.'

I said, 'It's important enough to be discussed collectively now.'

So they suggested I put in a paper but I said, 'No. Anything I have to say, I'll say it now to the Committee. I am being invited by this Committee to start notifying the NEA that we are going to dump radio-active waste without making it public, and, to put it at its lowest, we'll be caught out. Someone will leak it abroad and then what should I say?'

Roy disagreed. 'The question is do we go for the cheaper method of dumping on our own under the London Convention, or the more expensive method through the NEA?'

I replied, 'It is a matter of openness. I think we had better face this one squarely. We were open about Windscale and we gained by it, but I can't consult abroad without telling people at home. I must be authorised to describe what the problems are.'

John Morris said, 'We are dealing with the frontiers of science and we must share the problems and get advice.'

'Putting it in the sea is, after all, irreversible,' Bruce Millan warned.

Gavin Strang [Labour MP for Edinburgh East] said, 'The sea is safer than the land because the containers are deteriorating.' That wasn't very comforting.

Albert Booth was for going public. 'It will become known anyway and dumping at sea is a problem at Windscale because of the marine environment. I am told that if you are stuck in the mud off Windscale for more than an hour or two, you run a serious health hazard.'

Sir Kenneth Berrill said that a debate would defuse the issue and gradually the whole Committee came round. So it was agreed I could publicise it.

After the meeting, I asked Roy Jenkins what he thought of the Radcliffe Report on ministerial memoirs, which we're discussing in Cabinet tomorrow. Roy said, 'I think Radcliffe's got it about right. I don't keep a diary but I was on the committee which considered it.' I asked if Michael Foot was on it and Roy didn't think he was. I said I thought he should have been.

Roy said, 'I didn't know if you've read Dick Crossman yet, but I think he was surprisingly accurate.'

'Yes, but how he managed to get everything down at the end of each week, I just don't know, looking back on a whole week's events.'

Roy wasn't prepared to sign any undertaking on the publication of memoirs at the Cabinet and nor was I. I said, 'I remember when you and I were in the Shadow Cabinet and Harold Wilson wanted us to agree that every statement should be made only after it was passed by him. You and I refused. It seems to me the principle is between malice and information. You could write something malicious without information, and you could write something about political disagreements that wasn't malicious.'

'Yes,' said Roy. 'I could give an assessment of my colleagues without breaching a single confidence.' So it was a friendly talk.

In the evening, I watched Lord Chalfont's programme called *It Must Not Happen Here*, which purported to show how the *Communist Manifesto* was being implemented bit by bit in Britain. Bert Ramelson, Stuart Holland, Ken Gill and others were named and then Frank Chapple, Reg Prentice, Lord Hailsham, Brian Crozier of the Institute for the Study of Conflict, Woodrow Wyatt and Chalfont himself all spoke in support of this view. At the end, Chalfont produced a check sheet to show that out of the ten points of the *Communist Manifesto*, we had already met seven. It was frightening because you were looking at the faces of the Junta. Woodrow Wyatt referred to me by name. It was awful, the right wing of the Labour Party and the extreme right of the Tory Party uniting.

Wednesday 21 January

The press gave the latest unemployment figures – 1.4 million – and Mrs Thatcher is now referring to us as the natural party of unemployment.

Cabinet at 10.30 and Harold began by telling us that Radcliffe was 'very, very high powered', that some Ministers had given evidence and he certainly had. He said it was a useful historical summary, it set out the case for collective responsibility and the report's recommendations seemed broadly right. There was the question of ministerial relations with civil servants, of the discretion of Ministers, the problem of a Minister who kept diaries dying unexpectedly, like Dick Crossman, and the testamentary disposition of his diaries. I was particularly interested in this in case anything happens to me and there is an attempt to confiscate my diaries. Harold said, 'My advice to Ministers is don't keep a diary, and if you do keep a diary, don't die. The Government must have a view.' He therefore hoped we would accept the report.

Michael Foot said it was a great pity that we should be discussing ministerial diaries when unemployment was so high – and he hoped that wouldn't leak. He had been put in a difficult position because, as Dick Crossman's executor, he had to discharge his wishes. He felt that if he had resigned as executor, he would have been betraying Dick but he didn't really agree with memoirs. 'Churchill's use of diaries in the war was outrageous, particularly his attack on Auchinleck.'

Roy Jenkins thought Radcliffe was a good report but it was an unimportant subject and he never could see the difference between diaries in wartime and peacetime; he inclined towards a ten-year rather than a fifteen-year lapse before publication, but he wouldn't argue it.

Barbara said that in her opinion anyone who made their diaries too personal would be doing terrible damage to themselves.

Reg Prentice wanted to make one point that, as Ministers, we all had to accept that we were going to be attacked but civil servants must be protected – their confidential relationship with us simply had to be protected.

This was exactly the opening that I wanted. I said I thought it was an intensely interesting subject. 'However, when I read the report and looked at its membership, I understood why Harold called it "very, very high powered". It was stratospheric. Only one member was an MP and might have to consider the electorate; the rest only had to worry about the historians and were not the best people to think about the problem. Also we have to remember that what we say about each other is pretty well known, speaking as an Old Testament prophet,' I said smiling. 'If all the Tories of the 1970–4 period suddenly decided to publish their recollections of Tory Cabinets, we could not but be delighted at their breach of confidence.

'This question of civil servants, however, is important and we ought to get it right. I have a couple of examples which might amuse colleagues. I quoted from the *Sun* of 7 January 1975: "The *Sun* salutes the courage of civil servant, Peter Carey, the man who has thrown a spanner in the works of Industry Secretary, Wedgie Benn." I don't know how that got out but it wasn't from me.

'Next, my former Permanent Secretary, Sir Antony Part, contributed to a television programme on 13 November 1975 and I sent for the transcript; page 13 reads like this:

Vincent Hanna: Another quotation that has been made about Permanent Secretaries is this, they cannot make an unlikely policy become certain but they certainly can make an unlikely policy become impossible.

Sir Antony: Yes, I think a number of my colleagues have had considerable skills at blocking tackles and leg-byes, and I suppose it is always possible to put things in the way to the extent that the policy becomes unworkable.

'Vincent Hanna, the interviewer, asked Part about me and he replied that I drank a lot of tea and talked too much.

Vincent Hanna: And did this offend, upset or worry you?

Sir Antony: No, it didn't upset me as a technique at all. Some of the policies he was suggesting were pretty radical but we slogged it out between us.

Vincent Hanna: Now you say you slogged it out. In what way did you slog it out with the Minister? What's your style of slogging?

Sir Antony: Well, I would first of all try and persuade him that he was wrong and if I thought I wasn't getting anywhere, I would try something harder and we would really start hitting each other verbally across the table.

Vincent Hanna: How hard did you hit him?

Sir Antony: Quite hard, quite hard; you know I would say to him, that's bloody nonsense and so on.

'Now I don't mind that a bit,' I said, 'but in my memoirs I must be able to produce some evidence to show that Sir Antony was right.' They all laughed at this, and were really enjoying themselves.

'It isn't really about diaries,' I went on. 'It's about malice. You can have malice without information, and information without malice and you have to leave it to good sense.'

A few more people spoke and it was agreed that we would publish the report and come out in favour of it.

Thursday 22 January

Francis came in to lunch with his colleague Wynne Godley. I had never met him before: he's about fifty, with a tortured, ascetic face – the son of some Lord. He was at New College a year after me and has worked at the Treasury on and off since the 1964 Labour Government and, according to Francis Cripps, his great dream was to be a senior Treasury adviser. In 1971, he and Francis set up the Cambridge Policy Group and came to the conclusion that Britain was rapidly bleeding to death and it needed to adopt a policy of protection which is what Francis has been putting to me over the last couple of years. They are both terribly proud of their achievements and I am certainly glad to have contact with them, though my intellectual level is well below theirs and they make me feel a bit inadequate.

Went to the reception at Lancaster House to mark the inaugural commercial flight of Concorde, where I talked to the Chinese and Roumanian representatives for a moment. 'Look around this reception. It is really typical of Britain that there is not a single worker here, not a single man who made the plane, who got his fingernails dirty building the Concorde.'

George Edwards, who has just retired as Chairman of BAC, declared that I should have been on the first commercial flight because I 'saved the plane'.

Friday 23 January

Lakhdar Brahimi, the Algerian Ambassador whom I like very much, rang yesterday and said he would like to see me alone today. He told me that the British Gas Corporation had been buying liquefied gas from Algeria since the early Sixties on contracts to run to 1979 and had agreed to open negotiations about what would happen after that date four years before the agreement expired. The Algerian Oil Minister, had telephoned Brahimi yesterday to ask if the UK could make a gesture by agreeing to pay a higher price for the rest of the present contract. If that was impossible, could we reduce our quantity so that Algeria could sell the rest at a higher price.

After that we talked about Angola, and Cuba and he said, 'You know, the Americans forced the Cubans to go Communist – Fidel Castro wasn't a Communist – it was his brother, Raoul, who persuaded Fidel to say he was a Marxist after the Bay of Pigs incident. Khrushchev had been very angry with Castro for saying this because the Soviet Union didn't really think the Cubans were Communists. The Russians never had a lot of time for the opportunists in Cuba.' Brahimi told me that he and Raoul Castro and Khrushchev had spent two days in a boat in the Black Sea discussing it all. It was a fascinating insight into history.

The Lucas Aerospace shop stewards held a press conference yesterday in which they launched their corporate plan, which I had encouraged them to do.[4] I was very impressed by Mike Cooley and Ernie Scarbrow. I think Mike Cooley is an International Socialist and Ernie is a Communist and by God they have produced some excellent stuff – it just shows what the shop floor is capable of.

Saturday 24 January

A man called Robert Jenkins came to see me about a book he wants to write on the development of my political and economic ideas. I had resisted this at first but he is a nice young guy. He was at Lincoln College, Oxford, and told me that the Rector, Burke Trend [former Cabinet Secretary], had given a number of lectures which he had attended. Trend had said that politicians produced manifestos that couldn't be implemented and therefore they always relied upon mainstream Civil Service policies. This confirms my general view about the Civil Service which is that, if incoming Ministers drop their manifesto pledges and adopt departmental policies, the Civil Service will offer three things in return: they will work with the Minister; they will say what a good Minister he is; and they will help him to pretend that he is following manifesto policies.

I asked him at the end what his political sympathies were and he said, 'I am a disillusioned Young Conservative. I was very pro-Heath but I became disillusioned and I think that what you are saying is relevant and interesting, it's been misrepresented and it needs to be explained.' He is going to write three chapters of the book and then take it to a publisher in March, hopefully completing the book by September.*

Sunday 25 January

To Chequers in the evening for a meeting with BP about their relationship with BNOC. We had drinks in the Great Hall with a huge log fire. The place does look lovely. Harold asked endless questions about Alaska, Iran, Canada, and David Steel of BP was uneasy because he didn't really know the figures. Monty Pennell, the Deputy-Chairman of BP, was full of facts and Frank Kearton didn't say a word.

Harold talked about Oman and how the old Sultan had been removed from office in 1970 in favour of his pro-British son, in effect boasting about the British CIA-type operation against him. Then he said that all the organisations, and the American Government, were inefficient because there were so many agencies. He had heard a rumour that Kissinger would be out in three weeks. Ford did not like

* *Tony Benn: A Political Biography* by Robert Jenkins (1980). Writers and Readers.

Elliott Richardson and had originally offered him the job of Treasurer of the Campaign to re-elect Ford, which Richardson had refused. Elliott only agreed to take over Commerce when he was told he was going to be in charge of Energy.

Monty Pennell spoke about the Shah and described how the CIA had advised him to leave in 1953 and put him back on the throne in 1954.

Harold talked about being an Elder Brother of Trinity House and said that at a recent gathering, Prince Charles made a speech in the presence of the Duke of Edinburgh, President of the Elder Brethren, and Lord Louis Mountbatten, also an Elder. Prince Charles had said he never understood the 'Trinity' of Trinity House until his visit, when he had found God the Father, God the Son, and God the Holy Ghost!

Over dinner we discussed statistics. Harold said he had invented the concept of output per man-shift and even the concept of productivity which had been a theoretical concept before but he had got it extended over all industry. A terrible thing to have on his conscience. I asked him how he thought China had done so well without statistics. He said China was a dictatorship.

Afterwards Harold showed everyone round. He took us to Churchill's room which has been left untouched, and pointed out the little mouse which Churchill had added to a picture. We went into the Long Gallery and he showed us Elizabeth I's ring, with its little cameo of Anne Boleyn, which on Elizabeth's death had been carried all the way to her successor, James VI, in Scotland. James rewarded the courier of the ring by making him the Earl of Home. He showed us Cromwell's death mask lying on silk and his swords on the mantelpiece, Napoleon's red despatch case and the records made by the British soldiers who guarded him on St Helena.

Harold described how the swimming pool at Chequers had been built by Walter Annenberg, the former US Ambassador, to commemorate President Nixon's visit to Chequers and I suggested the pool should be renamed 'the Watergate'.

Then we sat round the log fire with coffee, brandy and cigars and Harold Wilson said, 'We take no decisions at Chequers. This meeting didn't take place. Tony has explained your position but I didn't understand a word; will you tell me.'

David Steel then launched into BP's objectives: independence; cash flow from the Forties Field; North Sea operations and international operations to be preserved. He said, 'The BP shares owned by the Bank of England are a problem. We can offer you help but no more.'

When the question of independence came up, Harold got into a long, rambling metaphor about the virginity of BP, how the original marriage had not been consummated because the bride was frigid and how rape was involved – how would they cope with a more randy customer, in the person of Frank Kearton? It was vulgar and thoroughly embarrassing.

Once we got beyond the preliminary chat, Steel said they'd offer BNOC some people and some consultation in an arm's length relationship, but Monty Pennell stressed, 'We must be given our head, commercially, that's absolutely crucial.' Then there was some discussion about participation.

Frank Kearton had been silent all the time, and then he said, 'If you go the long route for BNOC, it will take ten or fifteen years to build up and it's no good. We want a partnership and the participation talks have not really led to the sort of cooperation we need. We want a partnership in exploration and some downstream cooperation.'

Harold Wilson said, 'Why don't you set up a new subsidiary called, for example, BP Dogger Bank which might meet the needs?' They were doubtful. Then he said, 'Tony, you have been very silent.'

I said, 'There are several options. We can do nothing; or have a BNOC take-over, which I think we should rule out; we can go for minimum consultation; a middle way in which we could set up a subsidiary; or we could set up a partnership between BP UK and BNOC which I think is the best option. I think we should talk again after David Steel and Frank Kearton have discussed it further.'

Harold showed them out at about 10.30 and I waited up in the library to see him. Ken Stowe told me to go into the study and there was Harold, reading. He didn't even ask me to sit down. I thanked him and he said, 'The magic of Chequers worked.'

His performance tonight was pretty disrespectful, slighting and crude. Harold never rises to the occasion but he was very relaxed. Steel was friendly but difficult. Pennell is a Tory industrialist and basically hostile. Frank seemed rather less than full-sized because BNOC is so weak and there was no indication of support from the PM.

Monday 26 January

The newspapers are still reporting the repercussions of Mrs Thatcher's attack on the Russians last week,* and their retaliation, describing her as the Iron Lady or Iron Maiden, has absolutely delighted the Tory Party.

At 10.30 the TUC–Labour Liaison Committee marked one further steady step towards the ultimate re-examination of Government policy under trade union pressure.

Len Murray said, 'There is a loss of output; the TUC–Labour Party

---

* In a speech on 19 January 1976 Margaret Thatcher said that the Soviet Union was 'bent on world domination' and she accused the Labour Government of lowering the UK's defences in their public expenditure cuts.

relationship is constrained, which affects wages policy and industrial strategy and our support for both.'

'We must bring the number of jobless down,' said Jack Jones. 'The NEB should support firms for stockbuilding. We need the NEB to be used more firmly, with £1000 million to spend in a year, knowing that a boom would follow.'

David Basnett said, 'We all recognise that this is a task we must solve together. The media are trying to build up tension on the Social Contract which is not really at risk, but our credibility is. Industry is bleeding to death.'

Alf Allen of USDAW agreed that the credibility of the TUC, the Government, the Social Contract, and indeed of this Committee was at stake.

Denis welcomed the tone of the meeting and said we must face the Conservative Party which was reactionary and divided. We must talk privately inside the movement. This was a test of nerve, wisdom and common sense. When we came to public expenditure he said that there were difficult choices ahead: we could directly increase demand, we could raise tax thresholds, we could increase pensions.

The discussion went round the table and then, while we were waiting for a joint statement to be drawn up, Ted Short mentioned devolution. 'We can't explain the upsurge of nationalism, it may be a reaction to Europe and, in Scotland, to oil, but there has been a tremendous increase in the SNP vote and eleven Labour seats in Scotland would fall with a 5 per cent swing to the SNP. There are thirty-five SNP candidates who were in second place at the Election so the SNP could win thirty to forty seats.'

He went on to say that the unions in Scotland were pressing for greater devolution, the GMWU in Scotland were calling for socialist policies and a greater degree of devolution. There was a danger of polarisation. The political situation meant we devolved now to avoid *separation* in 1980.

Well, eventually the joint statement was proposed and Barbara was furious because Denis Healey appeared as the great hero who was going to save jobs. 'He wants to be God,' she said to me.

Tuesday 27 January

At 10.30 Frances and Francis saw Jack Rampton about energy policy and showed him a paper for the National Executive Energy Policy Committee. Rampton didn't like the paper because it was anti-nuclear and he said, 'You realise the Department may have to brief other Labour Ministers who attend the NEC against the paper.' If you try to make political choices then the Civil Service comes out of its corner. It recognises a new power centre and prepares itself to win the battle.

In a way, it is satisfying because the Civil Service is realistic and it shows that the Party matters, that there really is a new centre of discussion outside the Official Secrets Act, if you like. At the same time, it is an astonishing confession.

OPD, to go over Namibia and the supply of uranium. Sir Kenneth Berrill introduced the interdepartmental official committee paper which went through all the arguments I had used, identified the need for uranium and recommended that the Rossing contract go ahead. I was called on to speak and I said, 'My conclusions are that this should go to a full Cabinet because of its political importance; the option should not be taken up; discussions with Sean McBride, the UN Commissioner for Namibia, following the 1975 decision should include the question of uranium and SWAPO; and if we can't agree we should cancel the contract and seek supplies elsewhere.'

Ted Short, Roy Jenkins and Roy Mason agreed with the Foreign Office view expressed by Jim that it should go ahead. Peter Shore said, 'We ought to look at this again. The Angola situation has changed since last year.'

So I was defeated but before I left Harold said, 'Tony is right, it should go to Cabinet on Thursday, though it's too late to put in a paper.' I asked if I could put in an aide-mémoire and he agreed, so I went away and wrote it straightaway.

Thursday 29 January

The Rossing mine was on the Cabinet agenda, as Harold had promised. I said that it had been presented as an argument between toughness and realism on the one hand, because we needed the uranium, and political doubts on the other hand. But it was not as simple as that. I explained the background and my conclusions.

Harold called Jim to reply and Jim said, 'I don't see why I should answer. I don't see why for the benefit of future memoir writers I should always be the man who puts the other point of view. Tony is the Energy Minister, he needs the uranium; let him make the case. You're Prime Minister, Harold, you report what the Overseas and Defence Policy Committee thought.'

'All right,' Harold answered. 'I'm grateful to Tony for putting his case so briefly. OPD considered it and came to the conclusion that on the basis of official recommendations made by the Energy Department and by an interdepartmental committee, we should agree the contract.'

Denis Healey, Harold Lever and Roy Jenkins agreed with that recommendation. Then Jim said, 'There is a lot of nonsense talked about this,' and he went on to argue his case. Eric Varley was for going ahead. Peter agreed with me that we should look somewhere else, see what we can do and discuss it with the UN. Michael Foot also supported me. Elwyn Jones took a strictly legalistic view and said there was no obligation to cancel.

'Anyone else agree with Tony?' asked Harold. Barbara and Shirley said, 'Yes.' Before the vote, I said, 'Can we minimise the risk by discussing it with Sean McBride?' They didn't want that. So I lost and Harold announced the Cabinet decision.

Got back to the Department and there was Robert Neild who I used to find rather charming and engaging. I don't think he liked having Frances present and she certainly didn't like him, saying he was arrogant and discourteous to her.

He told me a good story. During the 1966 Election, when he was Economic Adviser to the Treasury, a group of Permanent Secretaries and top officials – Sir William Armstrong, Alec Cairncross, Tommy Balogh, Robert Neild, and Peter Jay, I think, were involved – wrote a paper saying that as soon as the Election was over, the Government should devalue. It leaked to Harold (everyone thinks through Tommy Balogh) and Harold had all the copies collected up and burned. 'It was quite medieval,' Robert Neild said, 'to actually have your advice burned so that no one would know the paper existed.'

Went over to the House for the big debate on unemployment and I heard Michael Foot speak – very poor stuff – and the Tories were shouting 'Resign', but they all want unemployment – such hypocrisy.

Came home. The hot water tank burst and forty-five gallons of water spread through the house. Caroline was marvellous about it.

Saturday 31 January
At 1 Caroline and I went to lunch with Nikolai Lunkov, the Russian Ambassador, and his wife at Kensington Palace Gardens. They had asked us through the Private Office and the four of us lunched alone at his flat. He has been here two and a half years. He's a fifty-five year old, rather dull, ponderous Russian bureaucrat and his wife is a nice middle-aged mum type. He had invited me because he liked to maintain contact with people and he had only met me previously on official occasions. I was a bit nervous because if you have a Foreign Office man there, at least you can be sure there's a check on what you have said; no doubt it was all bugged up so I was cautious, but in the event he did most of the talking.

He told us how upset he was that when he had written to object to Margaret Thatcher's speech, the press here had called it 'an outburst from Moscow'. The 'Iron Lady' tag, which appeared in the Red Army paper *The Red Star*, contrasted sharply with what Mrs Thatcher had said to him personally. 'When you meet her she's so charming, she wants better relations with the Soviet Union.'

'Her aggressive stand is just for internal consumption,' I told him, 'for her own rank and file.'

He said, 'Julian Amery was even worse. Do you think we should have responded?'

'It's pleased the Conservatives very much,' I said and left it at that. I didn't want to be drawn into discussions about Mrs Thatcher with the Russian Ambassador.

He was a tremendous name dropper I might add, mentioning Lord Mountbatten, Rab Butler, Sir Arnold Weinstock, the Prime Minister, Sir Alec Douglas-Home, his conversation was peppered with all the important Establishment people he had met. Caroline said afterwards, and I rather agreed with her, that this was the ultimate end of the Revolution, when you just had a great Russian Establishment interacting with the British Establishment, not that the Russian people haven't done better by having a change.

He said that Rab Butler had called him in and told him he hoped Anglo-Soviet relations might improve, that Heath had been quite friendly and had apparently congratulated him, or so he thought, on what *The Red Star* had said about Mrs Thatcher. He told me that her PPS, Adam Butler, who is Rab's son, is Mrs Thatcher's link man with the Soviet Embassy. Did I know anything about that? I said 'I don't know anything about the Conservative Party, Ambassador, but I am very grateful to you for briefing me.'

I asked him how he saw the general situation. He said, 'There are conservative forces at work in Germany and America and I think the business-military-industrial complex is afraid that detente may encourage the spread of ideas that would be damaging to them. Therefore they want to build up investment to deal with the slump by military rearmament.' He said the Soviet Union was anxious about the possible reunification of Germany and he also said, *en passant*, how difficult the Foreign Office was to deal with. I wasn't going to rise to that bait.

I asked him what attitude the Soviet Communist Party took towards the French and Italian parties. He said, 'I think if they want power they have got to adopt a tactical position.'

'I understand that but the statement by Georges Marchais, the French Communist Party leader, that the French CP had abandoned the dictatorship of the proletariat, was important.'

He replied, 'Well, it's part of the cornerstone of the Communist philosophy and I think their statement is probably tactical, they want support.' Whether he was quite as unworried as that, I don't know.

I said, 'Ideological discussions in the Communist world are important and they are taken seriously – what will the reaction be?' He rather wanted to play it down.

Then he said, 'How do you advise us to handle the question of foreign policy at the Party Congress?'

I replied, 'That's a terrible responsibility to be asked to advise Mr Brezhnev on what he should say at your Party Congress! But I think people would like to know what the Soviet analysis of the situation is. I think everyone is confused at the moment, particularly socialists. They would like to feel that you had looked at the state of development in various countries and had shown some sort of perspective so we could understand your position more clearly.'

He said, 'We don't want any aggressive statements of the kind that are made by Peking.'

I said, 'Certainly not. We just want analysis. That's what would be most helpful.'

He asked me, 'Why is the trade union movement so very non-political? I keep asking Len Murray why they seem so concerned with the narrow interests of their own members instead of broadening that out.' Len Murray apparently agreed with him.

I said, 'Yes, I understand that but don't forget, Ambassador, that in the Thirties, when we last had a slump, the Labour Government broke up and the Left disaffiliated and Mosley, the fascist leader, came from the Labour Party. The people are determined that it shouldn't happen again. You must understand that is our background, our history and that is shaping our thinking at this particular moment.'

Monday 2 February

The papers are full of Jeremy Thorpe who is in real trouble over this man Scott who has claimed a sexual relationship with him: it looks as though he's on his way out.

I talked to Frances and Francis about how we should cope with the mounting press campaign on fuel bills and hypothermia in the elderly.

Today Cliff Garvin, the head of Esso, gave a press conference saying that Esso refuse to cooperate with the Government in the participation policy. Well I am due to have lunch with him and Tin Pearce, the head of Esso in the UK and Campbell, the world deputy president of Exxon, its US name, today, so I had a long discussion with Bernard Ingham and Frances about whether to cancel the lunch or put out a statement. In the end I agreed to go and decided to be absolutely charming but not to make any reference to oil policy at all.

To the Esso Building in Victoria Street with Frances, Bryan Emmett, John Liverman and Jack Rampton. When we arrived there was no one waiting downstairs to receive us and when I was told by a commissionaire to give my name to the girl on the desk to see if we had an appointment, I must say I took it as a bit of a slight.

Went to the eighteenth floor and Pearce was extremely sorry. He is a nice decent guy with big ears, and I know he has been acutely embarrassed by the behaviour of Garvin. Anyway I was friendly, sat next to Garvin, and talked about Iran, the Shah, OPEC, and about Nixon, anything but oil!

Pearce said, 'We gave a long press conference about energy planning but only one element appeared in the paper today.' I said, 'Well that's the way it always is,' and brushed it aside.

We showed no sign of being worried by what they had said, so long as they don't think they are going to get away with it. I have got to assess how to fight the psychological warfare with Exxon.

I went to hear George Thomas elected as Speaker in succession to Selwyn-Lloyd. There were long tributes to Selwyn from Harold and Mrs Thatcher who made a very good speech, and by Jeremy Thorpe who in the circumstances carried it off with great courage.

Thursday 5 February

In my box I came across a minute from Harold Wilson saying that he had heard that I had suggested that the Home Policy Committee conduct an investigation into the honours system. As I must be aware it was his responsibility to advise the Queen on Honours, that he had continually reminded Ministers of collective Cabinet responsibility, and that I had given an assurance that I would follow this and the decisions that would flow from it, etc, he therefore wanted me to confirm that I would not initiate any inquiry into honours.

It is just another of Wilson's persecution campaigns and I thought about it and drafted a very simple reply:

> Thank you for your note. The press reports are inaccurate. When the subject came up I reminded the Executive of a paper I had written which had been published and was still available and I was following the precedent of Ministers in previous Labour Governments who had held the same position. The job was to provide an overview of future policy and it involved no breach of collective responsibility.

At Cabinet there was a proposal by Joel Barnett to get us to accept that students should be taken out of the unemployment figures immediately. Then he had the effrontery to suggest that we should remove the right of students to claim unemployment benefit and that holidays should be covered by student grants.

Friday 6 February

Meeting in the office on fuel disconnections, and I have decided to suspend disconnections of pensioner households temporarily and set up an inquiry under Peter Lovell-Davis to consider problems of payment and collection.

Sent my letter to Harold about honours with a copy to Mik.

Saturday 7 February
To Bristol for a surgery and then on to the Council House for the procession into the Cathedral for the enthronement of John Tinsley, Professor of Theology at Leeds, who has just been made Bishop of Bristol in succession to Oliver Tomkins.

There were eight policemen in nineteenth century uniforms with gold maces, coachmen in cocked hats and kneebreeches, and aldermen and councillors in robes and tricorn hats; the whole thing was like Ruritania. It is astonishing that seventy years after the Labour Party was founded this sort of thing should still be going on, other than at a folk festival. Anyway, as the senior member for Bristol, I marched opposite the Lord Mayor.

The Archdeacon of Canterbury came in to read the Archbishop's mandate, and the full weight of the Reformation and the Church Establishment came out clearly. The priestly craft is authority conveyed from above to below with the pretence that the congregation, or diocese, welcome the choice of the man appointed. The new bishop banged on the cathedral door three times with his crook, marched in with his huge procession and the Bishop of Malmesbury said a few words and he was enthroned.

Sunday 8 February
At 2.30 I went to a special meeting of my GMC in Bristol. Herbert Rogers said that as soon as the Tories see that Wilson has lost his credibility with the trade unions they will force an Election and win. On the Common Market he asked, can the workers of Europe take it over? It was a marvellous speech.

Jack Watson from the TGWU believed that the credibility of the Government was going. 'You, Tony, were a victim,' he said, 'we recognise that now. The CBI and the business community demanded your removal and you were removed, and we didn't stick up for you.' It was most moving. He asked why they didn't see me on the box and I said, 'Well, I'm not allowed to appear without the Prime Minister's permission, and he doesn't give it.' They were horrified and wanted to know why that never came out. I said, 'Well, it is not in my interests for it to come out because it looks as if I am having a row with Wilson.'

Alan Green then asked, 'Why don't you get out of the Cabinet?' and Brian Beckingham said, 'More than accountability, we want Members of Parliament to have the same lifestyle as working people, the same average wage.' I said that would be very difficult to visualise because it would take me a week to do a day's work if I didn't have tremendous support services, a car, secretaries, and so on.

Ros Flynn said at the end, 'Is the Cabinet important any more? Wouldn't it be better if we went for open Government? Isn't that the key?' The discussion went on in this vein from 2.30 till 6, most well-informed and educated.

Tuesday 10 February

The papers had reports of the TUC asking for £2 billion reflation, import controls, and further investment.

To the Electricity Council for a meeting with the Deputy-Chairman and the twelve area board chairmen. I thanked them for their help and said I wanted their cooperation on pensioners' disconnections; it was a difficult issue, I understood the problems and I didn't want to open the floodgates. But ending disconnection for pensioners over this winter on a temporary suspension basis would be helpful.

Glyn England of the South-Western Board said, 'We prefer to act quietly, we can quickly identify hardship and my worry is that a public statement might make things more difficult. On 30 January there were only five disconnected pensioners in the South-West.'

Southern Electricity said they had three disconnected and twenty-five hardship cases out of 1.5 million. Manweb (Manchester and North Western Electricity Board) said they had six pensioners cut off, and their chairman also feared the impact of a statement. East Midlands said they had none disconnected and Mr Wood of Eastern Region was very sympathetic and said they were not disconnecting pensioners knowingly. They were passionately in favour of delaying the statement so in the end I compromised and agreed to not making a statement until the end of May.

Arthur Hetherington came in late, simmering like an old kettle at the decision. He said it meant free fuel, it would open the floodgates, it would cost millions of pounds, it would be a disaster – 'I know a lot of wealthy old pensioners who will never pay a bill again.' I quietened him down gradually and although he didn't like it, he will go along with issuing the statement.

Wednesday 11 February

A meeting on the fifth round of oil licenses and three issues of significance came up. The Treaty of Accession prohibits us from specifying in the licenses for North Sea Oil that the companies applying should be made up of UK nationals or residents of the UK. I never spotted that during the Referendum campaign and it means that the Germans and Italians are free to develop the North Sea if they get the licences from Italy or Germany. We will have to get round this by making it a condition that they have an office in London and invest in Britain.

Moreover, we wanted to insist that the decision-making centre should be in Britain, to prevent the North Sea from being run from Texas, but this too would be a breach of EEC rules. A misty look came over officials as if to say, 'Well, you can talk as much as you like but it won't make any difference because this can't be changed.' It makes me increasingly angry that anything is decided in Brussels.

The third issue which worried officials was that we would make recognition of the unions one of the criteria for new licenses. I said I cared a lot about this and we had better talk to the TUC.

Thursday 12 February

John Biffen, the new Tory Energy spokesman, came at 10 and I had literally five minutes with him. I said perhaps we could establish what the options were so that our discussions in the House would be more sensible. He said he would like that. I commented that I didn't enjoy the bashing by Heseltine particularly, though I did admire him for making the headlines in Opposition which is a very difficult thing to do. I have high regard for John.

Several items came up at Cabinet, including the Falkland Islands. Jim said we had to face the fact that we may have a terrible national humiliation imposed upon us without the power to put it right.

When we came to fuel bills I introduced my paper and proposed that we suspend disconnection for pensioners and ask Lord Lovell-Davis to look at methods of payment and collection. It was quite different from Barbara's proposals for extra money (which I strongly favoured). This was extremely modest and everybody knew the problems of the old this winter: economic pricing, the OPEC increase, miners' wages had doubled fuel bills in two years. Pensioners were different from most because of the danger of hypothermia, they were proud and independent but they were afraid of being cut off; the 'Save It' advertisement campaign to conserve energy made some of them think they had a duty to freeze to death.

People would understand the difference between the old and other cases. The board chairmen rarely disconnected and there were less than fifty pensioners knowingly disconnected in the country. The chairmen were hiding their lights under a bushel. Anway it was agreed.

Then we came to the direct elections to the European Assembly, and Jim said we must make some response to the proposal that had come from the Council of Ministers. We were committed to the principle. Barbara advised us not to rush it, it was going to be very complicated and if we made a big thing about it it would stimulate nationalism. Roy thought we shouldn't drag our feet or we would be unpopular with our partners.

I repeated my strong views against an elected assembly. People fought for the vote because it was a route to political power, and we had one comprehensive House of Commons with only the House of Lords clinging round our neck. But now we were going to have assemblies claiming to speak for Scotland and Wales, and next we'd have a European Assembly. It was not the point that it had no power because it would create a rival domestic mandate.

Supposing the European Assembly elections were coming this week and the Tories won? It wasn't what they would say in Strasbourg that would matter, but that they would claim they were speaking for the British people. But in the end it went through.

Friday 13 February
I found that my office had circulated my announcement on disconnections without even letting me check it, and when I did, they had deleted bits that were crucial and added bits I had never agreed to, such as, 'I must stress that the scope of this relief cannot be extended' instead of my original reference, 'this limited scheme'. They wanted to tie me down. So I changed everything back again. Alan Phillips, the cheeky man, said, 'Are you sure your colleagues will agree?'

I said, 'Well, if the statement that I had drafted had been sent round, there wouldn't be any question of them knowing any different, and if officials think they are going to ring around Whitehall and stir up a hornet's nest, I'm not having it.'

The impertinence and arrogance of the Civil Service really sticks in my gullet. Frances blew her top at the thought of this well-paid young man of twenty-five thinking he knew how to handle matters affecting old people. She was really upset.

Jimmy Reid left the Communist Party yesterday and said he wasn't joining any other Party. He said he had withdrawn on philosophical grounds and it had been very difficult. His greatest anxiety was that he might damage the interests or the morale of those who worked in the Communist Party.

Today, there was a long centre-page article, 'Jimmy Reid talks to the *Daily Mail*'; he's been giving press and radio interviews all over the show, and I hope to goodness it isn't one of those betrayals, moving to the Right. Knowing Jimmy Reid, I don't think it will be, and I think he just doesn't want to join the Labour Party too soon. He wants to see how it goes. I hope he doesn't join Jim Sillars in the Scottish Labour Party.

Sunday 15 February
Had dinner tonight with the Baloghs, the Shores and the Foots. A very jolly evening. After dinner we sat down and had a semi-serious

discussion on the medium- to long-term issues. Thomas said that fundamental change was inevitable because our crisis was the crisis of capitalism but also the crisis of industrial weakness that had been growing since 1890.

Peter said that the Establishment had lost confidence in itself and all power rested with the unions. In one sense I agree that the Establishment has lost confidence in itself but it is still powerful despite that and it is coalescing. Although the trade unions are more powerful and more sophisticated than they were, they have been weakened and frightened by the slump, and monetarist ideas have become embedded in the heart of the Government. I said this, but Michael disagreed and said we'd carry out our policies when we had a working majority.

I said, 'Look, it isn't because we haven't got a majority, Michael. You know that as well as I do. It's because the Cabinet doesn't believe in the policy. If we had a majority of a hundred we wouldn't implement it. We're massaging capitalism back to life and keeping it in the intensive care unit. No wonder the City of London loves Harold – he's presiding over things we should never accept. The position is really this. We can't expose our strategy fully because in fact our strategy is to fight inflation by increasing unemployment, to pretend that we're keeping prices down when we're really trying to get prices and profits up, to pretend we're defending the public sector when we're really trying to cut it back.'

Michael said he'd like import controls but everything must not hinge on them because we probably wouldn't get them through the Cabinet.

Monday 16 February
Got up early, packed my bags, and flew to America with John Liverman, Bernard Ingham and Brian Emmett, to be met by Gordon Booth, the British Consul-General in New York.

I haven't been to America for five years, the longest time that I've been away. When I came in 1970 and 1971, I had the feeling that America was over the edge of its imperial greatness because the Vietnam War was bleeding the US to death and there were all sorts of anxieties. But it is stronger now, especially in New York. I love America and I much prefer it to France or Germany. But New York is a sick city, on its beam ends financially, the rubbish piled up in the streets in the rain, and quite deserted. Gosh, it was depressing.

Tuesday 17 February
To Washington where we were met by Lord Bridges, the Commercial Minister and the Counsellor (Energy), and taken to the Embassy Residence where I was put in the suite being prepared for the Queen's visit to celebrate the bicentennial – most luxurious – overlooking the garden.

I went almost immediately for a briefing meeting with senior members of the Embassy staff. The general view in Washington is that Wilson has swung to the Right and all is well in the world. I tried to explain that there was a real debate going on.

I must say, looking round, there might have been one or two there out of forty who would have voted Labour but just as the Church of England was the Tory Party at prayer, so any British Embassy is the Tory Party abroad.

The main purpose of the visit was goodwill and establishing confidence. Then we must get on with the oil policy as quickly as we possibly can because I can't make progress unless we can bring these oil participation talks to a successful conclusion.

Wednesday 18 February

Today has been an extraordinary day. It was 80 degrees Fahrenheit in Washington. I think the trip has been successful and a lot of uncertainties have been eased. If the Ambassador gives me a good report it will be valuable back in Whitehall. Looking back on my talks, one or two things strike me.

First of all, Congressmen are really engaged in a serious battle to reduce the power of the Executive – as very often happens, things occur in America before they strike Europe. I think this battle for democracy, accountability, publicity and openness in Government is something that will be a feature of our lives. The United States is ahead of us on this.

Going round America, of course, it is very easy to make fun of the confusion of their Government machine – it is even more confused than our own. On the other hand they are governing part of a continent and we're governing a country. If I compare the efficiency of the United States administration in tackling its problems, with, say, the efficiency of the Common Market, which is a comparable federation, I think the US shows up very much better. But I think, in time, they'll have to copy our Energy Department and hammer out a policy that makes sense.

When we got back to New York, a succession of detectives was attached to us because of the IRA threat to kill Cabinet Ministers. One of them was very candid and said that his job was Intelligence and security work, keeping an eye on radicals, labour disputes, etc.

The dinner at the Salomon Brothers offices in New York Plaza was a fantastic gathering of all the great money houses in America, the banks, the oil companies, the merchant bankers, the brokers, and so on. I suppose if you took the annual turnover of all the people there, you'd probably be running into billions of dollars. They were hard, tough men. One of the senior partners of the firm took me down to the office afterwards and showed me the floor where he operates, with a huge number of desks and phones, regular video communication with all the banks and other stock market outlets in New York and ten other cities in the US. It was like a vast cathedral. Something like 800 million dollars a day is traded there.

The market economy is now so complex and interconnected that everybody is reacting within a fraction of a second to what everybody else does. If one is serious as a socialist and one wants to get some control of this system, one has to see it against a background of a whole investment industry with its own interests.

Friday 20 February

Arrived home in time to wish Melissa a happy nineteenth birthday.

To the office and found that the new miners' banner with a plaque presented by Arthur Scargill had already been screwed up on the wall next to my desk. It is a most beautiful banner, a gift unlike the other one which is only on loan.

Saturday 21 February

Joan Lestor resigned as Under-Secretary in the Department of Education and Science because of the cuts in education, but the most exciting news is that Hugh Scanlon's appointment to the Gas Corporation has been accepted by the Prime Minister – so that tremendous battle has been won.

Sunday 22 February

There was a very revealing account in the *Sunday Times* of the fall of the Heath Government, which described Heath's way of working and in particular the extent to which he made his civil servants into politicians. That explains the behaviour of Sir William Armstrong, Sir Antony Part, Sir Jack Rampton and other Permanent Secretaries I've dealt with, in that Heath brought them into his Inner Cabinet and set up mixed committees with Cabinet Ministers and officials to discuss issues. This blurred the role between the two, and the same tradition has continued under Harold Wilson.

The article also made clear that in January 1974 the Tories and the whole Establishment thought that the revolution was about to happen. The miners bringing down the Government was a symbol of that revolution and explains the complete paralysis of Part and other officials in the Department of Industry when I turned up and announced that we were going to implement our socialist policy. It also explains why civil servants felt entirely entitled to fight the policy and why my time at the Department of Industry so antagonised members of the Establishment: they thought that in that Department the revolutionary impact of the Manifesto would be felt most strongly. The Establishment is of course tremendously relieved that the Government is moving to the Right.

Robert Taussig, a friend of Stephen's, turned up and had obtained the uncut tape which the BBC had recorded of Harold Wilson's famous row with David Dimbleby after the 1970 Election in the programme called *Yesterday's Men*. Harold was asked by Dimbleby how much he'd earned from his memoirs and he refused to answer. Dimbleby pressed it and Harold lost his temper and asked for the film to be stopped and the interview restarted. It is typically malicious of the BBC to make a tape of it and leak it.

We had a lovely birthday party for Melissa. Then at 6 Ken Coates, Joan Lestor, Judith Hart, Tony Banks, Michael Meacher, Dick Clements and Frances Morrell arrived. We discussed the present economic situation and Ken came back to his theory that I should resign. Judith said, 'Why keep the Government going?' and Tony asked why I didn't vote against the Government as a Minister.

We had to dispose of this argument not because it wasn't a good argument – it is a good argument – but only when you hear it deployed can you give the proper counter-argument which is that the movement wants three things. It wants the Government sustained; it wants loyalty to the Prime Minister and Ministers; and it wants a different policy to be pursued. If you resign, you'd get the blame for undermining the Government. If you attack the Prime Minister or other Ministers, you simply get into a position where you are deflecting people from real issues on to personalities.

At the end of the evening, Joan asked me what she should say about her resignation and I suggested she make a speech in the House of Commons. I found Nye Bevan's and Harold Wilson's resignation speeches and we read them. I told her I'd see her tomorrow and advise her. When I sat down, I realised that here was a priceless chance for Joan to get across what the whole problem was. So I wrote a resignation speech for her and she can do what she likes with it. It is an attempt to try to get the argument aired in the Commons in a way that would be hard to contradict: it would hoist up a real flag.

Monday 23 February
Lots of photographers outside Congress House for the TUC-Labour Party Liaison Committee, just waiting for the Party to collapse.

Denis began by describing the cuts and the Government's economic strategy. The Government had a majority of one, Denis said – we still had John Stonehouse – but if we lost control over the Commons the power of the Tories who were right-wing and anti-union, would prevail. 'Judith had said the real debate is in the Labour Party but anyone who says that must have been out of their tiny Chinese minds.' The real struggle was our people against the ruling class and to talk otherwise was sabotage.

It was the most violent and unpleasant speech I've heard Denis make. The whole economic argument was Tory and then it ended up with an appeal to class without any regard to ideology.

Len Murray said that we took sticking together for granted. The trade unions were prepared to take responsibility on issues on which we have reached agreement. But he had some stark points. The Government can't adopt a take-it-or-leave-it attitude to public expenditure, first because the figures will be different later and second, because public expenditure depends on the level of growth.

Jack Jones said that if this was a new strategy we could fall flat on our faces. Public expenditure should be reorganised to save waste, e.g. in local government. But we were concerned mostly with essentials and the main ground of our approach was being removed.

The TUC appreciated the consultations, said David Basnett. It had exercised responsibility for example over the £6 pay policy but he wanted to emphasise the need for a solution. We couldn't look at the White Paper without expressing fears.

Mik said he couldn't recall a case where any representations by the Party had had less effect on Government policy than in the field of industrial policy. We all knew the disaster in store if the Tories were to win but at the moment we have the Labour Government following Tory policies.

Michael Foot said he wouldn't answer everything that Mik and Judith had said. The movement did feel strongly and no one should be surprised at that. Indeed Ministers felt it too.

Hugh Scanlon pointed out that the trade union movement had accepted policies they would never have accepted from the Tories because they wanted the Government to succeed and wanted to influence the Government. So it went on.

I had a word with Hugh Scanlon afterwards and asked him to join the Gas Board. I left the meeting frightfully depressed. There is an absolute terror which even Hugh Scanlon feels about rocking the boat, weakening the Government and letting Mrs Thatcher in, but this loyalty unfortunately is being turned into a vote of confidence whereby you simply accept everything that is done. I think they really ought to argue their policy more strongly within a framework of loyalty. As somebody said, when you have the Government and the City and the TUC all supporting the policy for different reasons, it is difficult for the Left to be heard.

Tuesday 24 February

At 1.45 Arthur Scargill turned up. Arthur of course is the whole symbol of the Tories' defeat in 1972 and 1974. It was a bit like Ho Chi Minh being invited to the US State Department at the end of the Vietnam War! We talked about the Heath Government revelations in the *Sunday Times* and the most interesting thing from Arthur's point of view was that Joe Gormley had been to see Heath privately, without telling the NUM Executive, and had offered Heath a way out by agreeing that bathing time and waiting time and winding time would be included in working hours.

The truth is of course that Joe Gormley is a very cunning guy, he didn't want a strike. He wanted Heath off the hook as much as Heath wanted it. He didn't want to tell the Executive because he knew that he wouldn't get away with it and he was furious when Harold heard this was a possible answer and advocated it publicly. Scargill felt absolutely betrayed and there were demands for Joe Gormley's resignation.

We went on to discuss the tremendous reserves of coal in Yorkshire, seven-foot thick seams, the finest in the world. Arthur is a very fluent guy. I have a lot of time for McGahey, the Scottish miners' leader, but Arthur really is of a different order.

Wednesday 25 February

The *Daily Express* had a banner headline today, 'On the Rack: Left Wing Tries to Oust Benn from Cabinet', with my picture and a story that no other paper was carrying. I wondered whether this had come from Sunday night when the *Daily Express* flat across the road was occupied and they saw Judith and Joan come to dinner.

The NEC was held at 10 and, looking back on it, one or two things are clear: the link between the Left and the TUC has in effect been broken – what I feared would happen at the last Party Conference – and this is very significant. The trade union leaders do not want to be exposed by their rank and file, or by members of the Government, or the Party; second, people in power, whether they be trade union leaders or Labour leaders, don't trust the rank and file. This is the key to the whole business. Third, now that Harold does dominate the NEC he is completely unchallenged. The Tory press support him, the City of London has made him a Freeman, the General Council of the TUC supports him, the NEC supports him, the Cabinet supports him, the PLP supports him. He is unchallengably powerful and I wonder what he'll do next.

At 6 I went to the Grand Committee room at the House of Commons to address the Socialist and Environmental Resources Association. I spoke on energy policy and there were some shrewd comments made about the quality of energy. The participants were very anti-nuclear, as I had expected, including Walter Patterson from Friends of the Earth. A nice guy. I respect him very much.

Caroline and I went to a party hosted by the Kuwaiti Embassy, and chatted to the Chinese chargé d'affaires about Nixon's visit and how popular Nixon was because of his work in bringing about a detente.

We asked about the new attacks on revisionism and he said Mao believed in a cultural revolution from time to time and this was the moment. The 'big character' posters were going up again – mainly on education, bringing theory and practice together.

B. K. Nehru, the Indian High Commissioner, a very friendly man whom I like enormously, came up. 'Come and have a gas with me sometime,' he said. I agreed that would be nice and then he told me that at Chatham House recently Helmut Schmidt had attacked me in a lecture, saying that Britain had to accept she was a member of Europe – you couldn't alter the facts of geography 'even if you hang your maps of Great Britain upside down.'

Thursday 26 February

At the PLP meeting yesterday on public expenditure cuts, Denis Healey attacked the Left, called them 'silly billies' and so on – he is most offensive. It was all reported today.

Cabinet at 11.30, and outside was a TV unit filming Ted Short for a programme called *A Week in the Life of Ted Short* with other Cabinet Ministers and bright lights. I whipped out my little camera and took some snaps myself.

At 6.15 I had everyone in to brief me on the AEA Constables Bill and discussed in great detail the risks associated with nuclear energy – plutonium, toxic materials, explosion, ransom, blackmail, etc – then I introduced the Bill in the House. There were a number of Questions I couldn't answer, and all my civil liberties anxieties were alerted. This is the case for open government within Parliament; a lot of what was said on the other side I agreed with.

I was so tired I dozed off on the Front Bench. A number of people spoke, including John Biffen who made an excellent contribution. I really like that man.

Sunday 29 February

Peter Shore, the Foots and Thomas Balogh turned up, and Stephen joined us. He is getting a unique view of what is going on in the Government.

At dinner I raised the question of the excessive power of the Prime Minister – patronage, control over the Lords, nationalised industries, personal advisers, use of official committees – a general erosion of democratic strength. Peter came in saying that in fact since 1964 individual Cabinet Ministers had become much stronger – nobody used to argue with the PM then, Harold, George Brown and Jim Callaghan were a triumvirate; now things were much more open.

That is true. Of course, I was in the Inner Cabinet in 1969–70 and I am now in outer darkness. After dinner I came back to it. 'Look, the plain truth is that we are a more right-wing Government than we were from 1964 to 1970.'

'That's simply not true,' said Michael. 'The trade unions are brought into consultations and discussions.'

I asked them, 'How can one maintain loyalty and also take the view, as I do, that the policy is entirely misdirected?'

Jill said that there were two or three people in the Ebbw Vale Party who thought Michael should resign from the Government but none had the courage to tell him. Thomas Balogh gave his usual explanation, that the problems arose from Harold appointing the wrong advisers.

I said 'I cannot accept, Thomas, that democracy is all about appointing the right advisers. It is about the structure of accountability and whether you even want to implement the Manifesto. The Cabinet doesn't believe in the policy because it is a right-wing Cabinet.' I am afraid I went further than I had ever done before. I can't believe it's just me who believes this.

Peter commented. 'Of course, you are a very unloved member of the Cabinet. Harold puts you at the extreme end of the people he hates. Where once you were in the inner circle and he was wary of you, now he just loathes you.'

Monday 1 March
Went to the House and couldn't decide whether to vote for compulsory seat belts. I thought it was a form of tyranny that would make me look a Stalinist. But I rang Caroline and she said, 'Think of the babies, the children would all want you to, and lives might be saved.' So I voted in favour and it was carried by a huge majority.

Tuesday 2 March
The only really good news today is that George Brown resigned from the Labour Party. Most people thought he had left years ago but he finally resigned and was on the radio tonight – drunk as ever, giving the most muddled reason why he resigned. But there will be real pleasure inside the Party. If the right-wingers would slip off one by one, that really would be a gain.

Wednesday 3 March

George Brown claimed in the *Daily Mail* today that his resignation had been triggered off by listening to Alexander Solzhenitsyn. There were some sad, indeed absolutely tragic, pictures of him, falling over by his Jaguar car and being helped to his feet by journalists. One is torn between pity and loathing for a man who is ruined. I can't put it differently – for someone who has played such a savagely right-wing role in the Labour Party. He began to come to prominence with his attack on Cripps and his motion to get him expelled from the Labour Party; then he tried to get Bertrand Russell expelled and generally speaking he pursued all the wrong courses on everything, trampling on everybody who got in his path.

NEDC at 10.30. I hadn't been for months and I don't really know why I went because it depresses me so much.

Dinner at the London Graduate School of Business Studies in Regents Park, where I gave a speech. They were monetarists to a man, senior management, mainly accountants and marketing people in their early forties on £11,000–£12,000 a year. It was a tough, hard gathering and they were obsessed with the worker cooperatives I had established; I think that does indicate that the co-ops were considered revolutionary. My hosts believed they undermined industrial discipline.

Thursday 4 March

At Cabinet we discussed Northern Ireland and Merlyn Rees said that Sunningdale – Heath's conference – had been a piece of British suburban illusion, a sort of *Guardian* solution which was no solution, that the level of Irish politicians was very low, that we had worked very hard to get them to be constructive but to no avail. We must end the Constitutional Convention (elected last May) tonight or tomorrow and direct rule must go on. Harold Wilson said he had talked to Enoch Powell who supported direct rule.

Caroline and I went to Thomas Balogh's for dinner and found it was a party for Pierre Mendes France, radical socialist Prime Minister of France in 1954–5, now aged sixty-nine. I last saw him sixteen years ago when Nye Bevan asked me to lunch with him. Nye had said on that day how he didn't believe that affluence would in any way weaken or change the conflict in society between those who owned the wealth and those who worked. At the time, I thought he was wrong. Mendes France remembered the lunch very well.

He is a rather frail man. I think he has dyed hair, and he has a mournful look but he is very thoughtful, quiet and modest.

I also had a word with Marcia Williams, who was depressed. She said the power of the Civil Service was appalling, that Harold could settle it, but won't. She said he was bored and wanted to give up.

I've heard it all before. Indeed Nicky Kaldor said Harold's only power was to reshuffle. They were all saying he would give up but I don't believe that for a moment. I described my troubles with my own officials and Marcia said that this was what she tried to get through to Harold but she couldn't interest him. I said I was sorry my relations with him were so bad and that I wasn't consulted any more.

Saturday 6 March
Went for a long walk with Melissa and we visited Westminster Abbey, the first time Melissa had been inside. Of course the whole of Westminster is my village. That's where I was born, went to school, where Father and Mother were married, where Father died and where his memorial service was held, and where I work. It is a strange place, Westminster, very dull in the sense that there are no natural centres or shopping areas but I've been around there for fifty years.

Sunday 7 March
Dinner at the Foots. There is a very strong rumour that Harold Wilson is about to retire. Nobody knows where it comes from except some funny things have evidently been happening. There is a possibility that some papers which were stolen from Harold's desk may envelop him in some way in a scandal. Jill is very much in favour of Harold going and I have little doubt that she, Michael and Peter would all support Denis as leader. But if Roy stood, as I think he would have to, and Denis, Jim and Tony Crosland, but Michael *didn't* stand, then it would be a very curious line-up. Whether I stood would depend on whether I was nominated and by whom.

Monday 8 March
At 10 John Smith, Thomas Balogh and officials came in to talk about how we would organise oil prices. Would we have an administered price overall, which might raise problems with the US tax authorities, or would we have an administered price only with an arm's length relationship? We agreed we would get Edmund Dell and John Smith to have a look at it together.

At 4.55, as I was going into a meeting I had a letter handed to me containing a minute from Number 10 and a covering letter that Harold had heard that I had been asked to do a broadcast tonight on the House of Lords, after the Home Policy Committee was held. Actually, I had refused. The minute from Harold said, 'You're not to brief the press after today's meeting.' I can't accept that I am not allowed to be a human being and meet the press, but I'm going to be cautious.

At the end of the Home Policy meeting, I invited the press in and when I came out, there was a message from Number 10 asking me if I had given a briefing. I presume this will come up at Cabinet and I would have to report to the NEC that I was prohibited from speaking to the press about NEC business. I suppose I could make a speech saying that the policy is coming through the Executive and we shouldn't forget the role of the Party. He simply couldn't stop me doing it. But it is a form of harassment and very depressing actually – like living under the Shah and worrying when you're going to have your head chopped off.

Tuesday 9 March
Ministerial lunch with Alex, John Smith, Peter Lovell-Davis, Frances and Francis. I must say I do enjoy those lunches. We sit around the table with beer and Coke and a plate of sandwiches for an hour. It is clear that the Bank of England is deliberately allowing the pound to fall as part of the economic strategy being pursued, which means, having negotiated a wage cut last July allegedly to avoid public expenditure cuts and to help with unemployment, the Government have now got the wage cut *and* the public expenditure cut *and* continuing unemployment; on top of that they are getting another across-the-board wage cut as a preparation for negotiating a third wage cut in July, with a view to a fourth next year. This won't solve the problem, it is just bleeding the country to death. The theory is that the tremendous increase in profits resulting from devaluation will produce investment and Britain will recover by this particular form of surgery. Thomas and Francis are now absolutely certain that import controls are right and they are going to help me to draft a statement for the Cabinet on Friday.

Wednesday 10 March
Harold Wilson is reported as saying that he believes the South Africans were in some way involved in discrediting Jeremy Thorpe. You can see why Harold said it. First of all, his interest in trying to boost the Liberals lies in the fact that their lost votes would go to the Tories. Secondly from a PM's point of view, to be generous to a man who is down might get him some credit. But thirdly, it does take me back to Sunday's discussion at Michael Foot's house, which makes me wonder whether Harold is himself vulnerable and wants to establish the principle that the South Africans are trying to destroy British political leaders.

At 4 Abba Eban, the former Israeli Foreign Minister, came to see me. He said, 'Things are very difficult. Henry Kissinger is a friend but diplomacy can't be conducted in the open way in which they do it in Washington. It's very dangerous. Only Henry could do what he did because he had to be able to offer us something to compensate for the negotiating loss.' He said they had got disengagement with Egypt and President Sadat was bitterly anti-Russian.

Caroline and I had dinner in the House with Joe Ashton. Today is the great debate in the Commons on the White Paper on inflation and public expenditure. Joe didn't know whether to abstain or not. I was anxious to tell him not to abstain myself but Caroline was strongly in favour of it. He said, 'I don't want to abstain if it's just half a dozen nuts but if it's a solid group, then I think I will.' They are all voting against the Tory amendment and then abstaining on the White Paper.

The division bell rang and I was just behind Geoffrey Rippon and I heard him saying, 'Of course this will establish the Conservative Party as a credible opposition.' I voted against the Tory amendment where we had a majority of 30, then I voted for the White Paper and went up to my room to wait for the result. In fact, thirty-five Labour MPs abstained and the Government was defeated by 28 votes. Joe Ashton came up and reported that there had been a tremendous explosion in the House with Tories cheering and Labour Members shouting at the Tribune Group.

Eric Heffer was interviewed on television and he said, 'Let's be absolutely clear. We voted down the Tory amendment, but we couldn't support the White Paper. The cuts don't come into effect for a year. We've got a year to campaign against the cuts. Anyway, you may not realise that Labour MPs are not consulted. The Cabinet decides and then tells us. Of course if it comes to a motion of censure, we'll vote for the Government.'

The interviewer said, 'Won't this be very upsetting for the Government?'

'It's very upsetting for all of us,' said Eric. 'We don't like doing it.' He was good. He didn't mention the Tribune Group but spoke about the Party and that is what it is all about.

When asked, I will say, 'This is very serious, but the Party has been asked to put up with a lot over the past year and they want to keep the Government in power.' Then I'll list all the issues they have put up with: the EEC, Eric Heffer's dismissal, unemployment, high prices, devaluation, divergence from the Manifesto, Chrysler, the TUC, corporatism. I shall say our task must be to restore the position by getting our majority firmly re-established in the House and trying to introduce some perspective into our policies.

Thursday 11 March

Frances is thrilled by what Joe has done. The defeat last night has transformed the situation; it has ended the phoney peace and people see now that the Government is supported by the right-wing forces in society, that they can't carry the Labour Party in the way they have and Jack Jones can't blank out all criticism.

Cabinet and Harold said, 'We must have a motion of confidence in the Government today.' Roy Jenkins agreed, 'We must have a motion. An Election would not solve our problems because we would get the same gang back again.'

I stress the word 'gang' because the way the rebels were spoken about throughout was as if they were criminal thugs.

Roy went on, 'It would be nice if we could get the constituencies not to re-adopt the MPs concerned but we couldn't do that with Transport House in its present state. This is a very serious danger. We must make them vote for the very opposite of what they voted for last night. That's why we need a motion. They must vote for a motion explicitly in support of the financial and economic policies of the Government.'

Jim Callaghan said that a motion of confidence would not be enough, and Michael Foot replied, 'We must recognise that the Cabinet did not consult the PLP. The way to avoid this in future is to make all votes a vote of confidence.'

Then Jim Callaghan commented, 'There are some people who abstained last night who wouldn't mind a Tory Government.' He added, 'If Labour MPs won't support us, then let's have the Tories in,' to which Michael Foot replied, 'You know, trying to make people eat humble pie isn't any good.'

Bob Mellish thought the Tribune Group were outright thugs and four of them had said they wouldn't vote for the Government while Des Warren, the Shrewsbury Picket, remained in prison. He said six members of the NEC and two PPSs, one of whom was Joe Ashton, had abstained. He assumed their Ministers would do the honourable thing and sack them today. Of course, in the case of Jim Sillars and John Robertson, [Labour MP for Paisley] they had actually voted with the Tories but the Whip couldn't be withdrawn because it would affect the balance in the House.

Shirley suggested that we ought to have two votes of confidence; one today and another on Monday.

'We have got to think of sterling,' said Denis. 'That's the case for having one early.'

Jim Callaghan suggested we appeal to Mrs Thatcher to help sterling because she wouldn't want to see it damaged.

Roy Mason disagreed. 'There is great bitterness in the centre of the Party and it's no use making an approach to Thatcher. She won't support you. This is the moment when she sees her prospects improving.'

At one stage Bob Mellish had been calling to me, 'Tony, when are you going to sack Joe Ashton?' and he raised the question, 'What about sacking the rebel PPSs? When is that going to be done? Who's going to do it?'

So Harold said, 'It could be done at once but I think we might wait until after the vote of confidence.'

Tea was brought in, which always happens when there's trouble and Shirley began singing 'Happy Birthday' to Harold which was odious.

Then we came to the medium-term assessment and Denis said, 'We are going to publish the new public expenditure forecast in November.' I said that I thought that the Cambridge Group were going to publish forecasts soon which more or less revealed that if we opted for monetarist policies – Thatcher's policies – we would have 2 million unemployed in 1980 and real wages would be 4 per cent below what they were in 1975.

If we went for devaluation by a substantial amount, we might have 1.5 million unemployed by 1980 and wages about the same. If we went for protection, i.e. cutting back 30 per cent on our manufactured imports, though it would be difficult in the first year, we could get unemployment down quite quickly after that and raise real wages.

I said I personally favoured this course. The TUC view argued strongly for import controls and David Basnett said at the NEDC that this was absolutely essential to get unemployment down.

Denis replied to this. 'The Cambridge Group were wrong last year, they will be wrong this year and I think Tony should be a bit skeptical.' As to Basnett, he was out on his own and when he, Denis, had raised it with other TUC people, they had just smirked.

Went over to Locket's and had lunch with Mike Molloy, the Editor of the *Daily Mirror*. He told me something very interesting. A year ago he had been invited to dinner by Sir Val Duncan, head of RTZ, together with Bill Deedes, Editor of the *Daily Telegraph* and Bruce Page of the *Sunday Times*, Alf Robens and a man with a name like 'haricot bean' from the BBC. There were also a couple of staff officers who had worked with Field Marshal Montgomery. Val Duncan had called them in to head off the revolution. He said, 'When anarchy comes, we are going to provide a lot of essential generators to keep electricity going, and we have invited you, the Editors, to tell us if you can maintain communications to people, then the army will play its proper role.'

Mike Molloy said he had been absolutely bemused by this. I said it sounded like something written in *Workers' Press*. But it is interesting that that meeting took place just before the Referendum, and that the Establishment was so frightened.

Went back to the office and Frances Morrell had left on her desk a piece of paper listing six jobs, one of which was, 'Tony's problem of credibility with the Left of the Party' and another, 'How to organise the campaign against Treasury strategy'. I left her a note, 'Is it wise to leave these open on the desk?' and I covered the list up.

Caroline and I went to the reception for Anne Armstrong, the new

American Ambassador, and her husband. Caroline had known her at school. Caroline and I went over to meet Cord Meyer, who's been here since 1973. 'The Tories were in power then and we were just trying to get rid of Nixon,' he said.

'You know, I met Nixon in 1969 when he came to London and I liked him very much,' I told him. 'He made a tremendously favourable impression. His politics weren't exactly mine as you know, but I wondered whether the media had been unfair to him. He sat round the Cabinet table and couldn't have been more charming.'

Meyer said, 'He was a terrible man. He did a lot of damage to us.'

'I don't know. When I look at the chronicle of human error that goes to make up political experience, I would have thought that bugging your opponent wasn't so bad.'

He said, 'He shouldn't have done that. It was very serious.'

I said, 'The tapes will form a most fascinating record of the administration when all the fuss has subsided and Nixon is forgotten. There will be a completely chronicled record.'

'You mean like the Crossman *Diaries*?'

'No,' I said, 'like the Dead Sea Scrolls. We really will discover what the President thought when the Italian lira was devalued, with or without the "expletives" '.

I'm glad I met him. At least in America, they tell you who the head of the CIA is. In Britain, when Sir Denis Greenhill was allegedly in charge of MI6, nobody was supposed to know.

Returned to the House and had a cup of tea with Eric Heffer, Joe Ashton and Neil Kinnock. I thought it was a night to show myself with the Left in the Tea Room. Norman Atkinson came up and said, 'I wrote a piece in *Tribune* and referred to you and Michael in it and what you should do now. You should stay unless you are forced to be silent.' He's a nice guy, although a bit muddled really.

I replied, 'There is a big difference between Michael and me. Michael is the architect of the present policy and I am not. Harold is now trying to harass me on the Home Policy Committee.'

He described to me in detail what was going to happen in the unions, at the special congress of the TUC, etc, etc. 'It's nice to keep in touch,' he said. 'The Left is leaderless and we have been having meetings about who would we think should take over. We think Michael has given up and if Harold went, it would have to be you, but we would like to know what sort of basis you would do it on.'

'It doesn't matter who is Leader,' I said. 'The important thing is to get the argument across. What we need are socialist speeches.'

'Yes, but it's a matter of more than ideas. There's got to be an absolutely key lead to the Party at certain moments.'

Well, I went through the Division Lobby in this great vote of confidence.

Joan Lestor came and had a word. 'Did you see that Harold has appointed Margaret Jackson, a Tribunite, to succeed me at the Department of Education?'

I said, 'He's no fool. If I went, he'd put Stan Orme or someone in.'

After 10, Joe Ashton was dismissed.* What a bloody awful man Wilson is, cheap and nasty.

Friday 12 March

Maureen Colquhoun [Labour MP for Northampton], has apparently written to Cledwyn Hughes complaining about the language used against Party members. For example, Healey was very abusive last night and referred to Eric Heffer as a lapdog.

Went to University College Hospital where a professor had a look at me and told me I have a disease of the gums which means all my teeth will fall out – a nuisance really.

I had a brief word with Chris Herzig about fast breeder reactors because I am not in a great hurry to proceed at the moment. Then Jack Rampton came in and good old Bryan Emmett had prepared a whole list of questions for me to raise. I told Rampton I wanted to be a bit better informed in line with this minute. I thought I would be friendly because I have had a rather sharp relationship with him recently.

Saturday 13 March

The Thorpe story is moving to its climax. On the news tonight, it was reported that he had made a statement to the *Sunday Times* denying seven allegations made by this decrepit, sad, blackmailing, former male model, Norman Scott. I think that the press have decided to destroy the Liberal Party because it is now an embarrassment to the cause of building up Mrs Thatcher as an alternative to Wilson, and they are doing it by releasing information about Thorpe which they have had for years. Some Liberal MPs, like Steel and Richard Wainwright, are concerned about this, and then there are some inconsequential ones like Pardoe and Cyril Smith – absolute cynics and opportunists – who are trying to seize the leadership; the Young Liberals are trying to get rid of Thorpe because they think he is not left-wing enough. So we are witnessing the crumbling away of the Liberal Party but it will recover when the Tories come back to power and people don't want to vote Labour. It is going to be round the mulberry bush as with everything in British politics.

*Joe Ashton continued to act as my PPS until November 1976.

Sunday 14 March

Quite a chilly day, and Caroline and I went for a lovely walk in the park, round all the places we used to take the children. We felt like an elderly couple, which I suppose is what we are at fifty.

Monday 15 March

It was Ron Vaughan's birthday yesterday and we gave him a suitcase. I am trying to help him with his housing situation because even though he has lived in the same house for forty years, now his father has died the council are turning him out.

I went to see John Biffen to say we were accepting his amendment for the EEC energy debate tomorrow. I said to him, 'My speech is being looked at by the Foreign Office and the Cabinet Office but I hope we can bring out the nature of the derogation of sovereignty that is taking place as a result of our membership.'

He said, ' We have got a few mad federalists on our side but by using my language carefully, I seem to be getting away with it.'

Went back to the office and Geoffrey Goodman came to see me. He has decided to give up the Counter-Inflation Unit and go back to the *Mirror*. He told me that Heath went to Nuffield College a couple of weeks ago to address David Butler's seminar and he was asked what mistakes he thought he had made. He said, 'Two. First I never had a machine at Number 10 executing the decisions the Cabinet made in the way the Cabinet wished them executed. That was one area where I absolutely failed to get my way.' Secondly, he said he had only been at Number 10 a short while when all the newspaper proprietors came to see him and told him they were thoroughly dissatisfied with the press set-up under Joe Haines and Trevor Lloyd-Hughes. Heath said, 'I thought it was a bit much that they should tell me how to run the press side but anyway I appointed Donald Maitland whom I had known during my EEC negotiating time in Brussels.'

I asked Geoffrey about his work at Number 10. 'Something strange is going on,' he said. 'I believe that Bernard Donoughue and Joe Haines prevent me seeing really sensitive documents. The security officer comes and pokes around my office from time to time and asks questions that could only have come from Joe Haines. I know my phone is tapped.'

Geoffrey said he thought Joe was jealous of his role. 'Let me give you an example of what goes on. I was invited to a meeting at Number 10 with Joe Haines to discuss the future of the Counter-Inflation Unit and Joe made it clear he wanted the whole thing wound up. Later that night Harold Wilson rang me and said, "Will you come and see me at my home, 5 Lord North Street: Joe Haines won't be present. I understand you were a bit uneasy and I thought you would like to come and see me." So I went along and Harold said, "You carry on with your unit," then added, "I won't tell Joe Haines you have been here." '

What in heaven's name is going on when a Prime Minister has to operate almost conspiratorially against Joe Haines!

Tuesday 16 March

A day of such momentous news that it is difficult to know how to start.

After a meeting with Frances and Francis, I went to Cabinet at 11. Harold said, 'Before we come to the business, I want to make a statement.' Then he read us an eight-page statement, in which he said that he had irrevocably decided that he was going to resign the premiership and would stay just long enough for the Labour Party to elect a new Leader. People were stunned but in a curious way, without emotion. Harold is not a man who arouses affection in most people. I sat there listening quite impassively and although other people were shocked and surprised because nobody knew it was coming, there was still a remarkable sort of lack of reaction. But when he had finished speaking and thanked us all, Ted Short said, with visible sorrow – his eyes were filled with tears and his face was red – 'I think this a deplorable event and I don't know what to say except to thank you.'

Bob Mellish said, 'I take it we'll proceed straight away to the election of a new Leader.'

Jim Callaghan, who found it hard to conceal his excitement, said, 'Harold, we shall never be able to thank you for your services to the movement.'

Then Harold got up to go, because he had to see Len Murray and Cledwyn Hughes to tell them. He walked out of the Cabinet and that was it.

When he had gone, Shirley said, 'Don't you think we ought to formalise our thanks.' Barbara agreed, so the two of them began to draft something.

After a rather odd Cabinet, I left Downing Street at about 1. By then there was a huge crowd of people, hundreds of television cameras. Over my ministerial lunch, we discussed why Harold had done it. Alex Eadie said the movement would be shaken and we had to protect against fears of a coalition. Then the question of who would stand for Leader arose. Everyone had left except Frances, Francis and Joe and Joe said, 'You must stand. You'll get a lot of votes.' Frances and Francis agreed.

I called Bryan Emmett in and I said, 'Now look, you mustn't say to anybody that I'm standing because I haven't made up my mind yet but I want the decks completely cleared of all engagements. Just tell Bernard Ingham that you don't know what I'm doing.'

Went over to the House and into the Chamber. I sat on the Front Bench and Harold came in at 3.15 for Prime Minister's Questions and a Question on the Royal Commission on the press provided an opportunity for everyone to pay tribute to Harold. Margaret Thatcher wished him well and suggested a General Election. Jeremy Thorpe joked, most inappropriately, how nice it was to hear Harold was going on the Back Benches because it was such a comfort for a Leader to have his predecessor beside him. Heath congratulated Harold on joining the fastest growing political 'party' in the House of Commons. Enoch Powell congratulated him for bringing peace to Ireland in contrast to the appalling policies of the previous Government, which was an absolute hammer blow.

Had a cup of tea and saw Stan Orme who said, 'Tony, you shouldn't stand. I'm a friend and I admire you very much but Michael Foot has got the best chance – Eric Heffer and Dennis Skinner feel the same.' I said, 'Thank you. I fully appreciate it. There's a big difference in policy between Michael and myself and I think if I stood it would have to be on that.'

Ernie Fernyhough [Labour MP for Jarrow] came up and said 'Tony, you know how I feel about you but I am supporting Michael Foot and I have told my local paper.'

I said, 'It's entirely up to you. I'm not campaigning or canvassing in any way but I should be fighting for policy changes.'

Frank McElhone told me that the Scottish Members were divided between Jim Callaghan and Michael Foot, and therefore I hadn't any support whatever from them.

Then I saw Mik and he said, 'I argued on the radio that I would support you. I don't think you'd win, and I'd support you against Michael if the two of you ran together. But I think Michael has the better chance.'

I said, 'Look Mik, there's only one case for standing and that is to campaign for a change of policy.'

Went back to my room and Joe and Maggie Ashton came up, then Barbara Castle followed by Ted. Barbara had come in to say how we must get a 'Stop Jim' movement going – a typical defeatest view – how she thought Denis was good and how Michael should stand. I said I was going to see Michael so I didn't let her guess anything. She began by saying 'Wedgie, we all agree the future is yours.' That's a load of nonsense really, the question is what does the Party do *now* to avoid a collapse?

Michael Meacher came to see me and asked if he could help in any way. I said, 'Yes, take soundings and help me draft a statement saying we should campaign for a change of policy.'

At about 8 Joe and Maggie came home with me, where Stephen and June, Hilary, Mary Lou, Frances, Francis and Melissa and Caroline were all waiting. Almost everyone there thought I should stand. Frances had her doubts. 'You might be badly defeated and humiliated,' and Francis (who takes his lead from Frances) then added, 'Yes, it might damage the policy if you didn't get any support.' Joe Ashton said, 'You could always withdraw if you aren't getting the support.' Well you can't do that.

Hilary thought I should throw my hat into the ring first because 'if Michael comes in later, he is theoretically splitting the Left vote, not you.'

I listened and set all the arguments down on paper. The case for standing is winning, or to win next time, to get an alternative policy across, to influence other candidates, to establish a power base. The case against, is that people will say you're frightened that you might be humiliated, attacked by the trade union leadership, massacred by the press.

In the end I decided I would stand.

Wednesday 17 March

I didn't get to bed until 2 and I was up at 6.50. Joshua went out and bought every newspaper which reported in full Harold Wilson's resignation statement and a list of possible candidates. It confirmed my view that I must move very quickly indeed to implement my decision to stand. I rang Michael Foot and told him, and he said he might stand, and would like to see me this morning at 11. I then rang Herbert Rogers to tell him I had decided to stand on policy and asked him to arrange a special meeting of the GMC for 7.30 on Friday.

Stephen picked me up at 8 and took some equipment to the House of Commons for Mary Lou who is going to set up her office in Room 18 on the minsterial corridor for the duration of the leadership election. From 9.15 until 11.15 Frances and Francis, Joe and I hammered out my initial statement, explaining why I was standing; I had three points: industrial policy; open government and parliamentary democracy; and industrial democracy. I heard that Jim Callaghan had declared and Michael had indicated that he would stand. At 11.15 I went to Room 18 and was told Michael had been in several times but I decided not to go to see him until after my press conference because I didn't want any one to be able to ask me if Michael Foot had requested me to stand down. At 11.30 I met the press, and then had an interview with ITN and the BBC. At 12.15 I heard that Crosland had indicated he would stand. Crosland said on the news that he was a radical moderate who stood on his record.

I had a pre-arranged lunch at Locket's with Danny McGarvey and I went back to the House at 2.40 and saw Michael Foot and said, 'I'm fighting purely on the issues,' and he said, 'I think you are wrong to campaign in the open, for a new policy.'

'Michael, I think the moment has come. You know my views, you have heard me in the Cabinet and I have told you privately. I think I must do it this way and, as you know, I will support you in the second ballot if I drop out as I probably will.'

He said, 'Well, we have been friends for many years and we always will be.'

Caroline arrived at 4 to give advice and help. Then Judith Hart turned up and I took her into the office next door, which was empty, and she put her hand on my arm and said, 'Tony, I love you dearly. I greatly admire you. You must be the Leader of the Party one day but not now.' I took her hand gently off my arm and said, 'Judith, no emotion and no feeling. You must do what you think is right. I am fighting on a policy and I have no option. I am doing what you did last summer – and I supported you – because I must now bring out the truth.' She agreed with everything I said and at the end she said, 'I hope you know I'm very fond of you.' I gave her a big kiss.

Frances and Francis said to me, 'Look, you are not going to get many votes' – I agreed with that – 'so you ought not to be saying you are going to win.' I said, 'I understand that, and I'm not fighting to win anyway. But I don't want to give the impression that I'm a minority, that I'm a loner, because, after all, I am carrying the banner for the TUC Economic Review.' We had a lot of strategic discussions about all this and Joe Ashton kept popping in and out. He was marvellous.

At 6.15 the Tribune Group of Labour MPs met and Joe Ashton told me what happened. 'The Foot gang' as he called them are voting on his record and on grounds of tactics. Of the 37 who were at tonight's Tribune Group, he thought there was a majority for Foot but that we would get the following MPs: John Garrett, Audrey Wise, Tom Litterick, Dennis Skinner, Brian Sedgemore, Stan Thorne, Jimmy Lamond, Norman Atkinson and Ron Atkins.

At 7.30 the *World This Weekend* wanted to interview me. I said 'Look, if this is a programme about my background, a political profile, if you want to have me washing up, like Mrs Thatcher, No. If it's policy, Yes. That's the only reason I am standing and I fully understand if you don't want me on the programme.'

Then my Tribune supporters came in. I asked them what they thought. Dennis Skinner said, 'First of all, have you got a way back?' I said, 'If you mean am I going to withdraw my candidature, I am not. I am fighting this on policy.' I went over all the ground very clearly with them and Dennis said, 'Right, we'll fight for you.' They were all thrilled. We agreed to meet every day and see how things were going. Audrey said she would send my statement out to all of the Tribune Group with an accompanying note.

Went back to my room and Joan Lestor was using the typewriter.

She didn't know I was standing. I told her, 'It's like your resignation. I have got no choice. I have got to do it.'

She asked if it would damage me personally, and I answered, 'Nothing could damage me or humiliate me save something dishonourable. I must put this forward. I am not going to ask you to vote for me because I am not asking anyone. But this is what I am doing and why.'

Ron Vaughan drove me to Television Centre and there were Neil Kinnock and Pat Duffy [Labour MP for Sheffield, Attecliffe] to discuss the leadership after I had been interviewed. The interviewer, Bob McKenzie put it to me, 'Only 7 per cent of the public want you, only 7 per cent of Labour MPs want you. What do you think?' I said, 'I am not surprised', and I opened up in a way that I think has never been done before in the history of British politics. I said, 'This is what I am campaigning for and this is what I believe.'

McKenzie said, 'Surely what you believe is contrary to the Chancellor's policy.'

'I am collectively responsible for everything, but the public is entitled to know my view.' I jumped through the burning hoop and I came out the other side. It was amazing. I am a free man and I don't know what the Cabinet will say tomorrow but this is a completely new development. Besides, Harold can't do anything to me now.

Interviewed afterwards, Pat Duffy said he thought Jim was marvellous, had the confidence of the international community. Neil Kinnock said Michael had a marvellous record, and absolute integrity.

Caroline was pleased with the TV interview. Hilary rang and said it was good. Stephen rang and said it was fantastic. Joe Ashton couldn't believe it.

Thursday 18 March

At 10.30 Stephen drove me to Cabinet. Jim Callaghan reported on Angola. The Russian Ambassador, Lunkov, had been to see him to say that Brezhnev wanted the British Government to convey to the South African Government a message suggesting a way out of the Angola situation that would allow the South Africans to withdraw completely from Angola over the border into Namibia, evacuating the dam stations on the river.

Jim said he was in favour of it because the Russians were showing signs of detente and it would be ghastly if the forthcoming American presidential election became the excuse for another Cold War.

Then Harold said, 'I would like to ask a word about arrangements. Should we cancel the Cabinet and the NEC meeting on Tuesday?' Jim and Shirley thought we should go on. Denis Healey said, 'Perhaps half a day would be sufficient.' Then Harold said, 'On a domestic matter,

I am going to give my dinner for the Cabinet on Monday night because I don't know how many ballots there will be and I don't want to have to give it in a fish and chip shop. It will be informal dress.'

Then we discussed the Falkland Islands, a paper from Jim pointing out that there were thirty-seven marines there and 2000 islanders and the Argentinians were being very difficult. There was possibly some oil there and we couldn't hold the islands against an attack. He had two suggestions, one of which, rather tougher than the other, was to consider a condominium or to let sovereignty pass to the Argentinians and lease the islands back and develop the oil jointly.

I had a short nap in the afternoon and at 3.15 I went into the Chamber where Harold Wilson was doing his last Questions. He was very relaxed. Peter Shore sat next to me and he said, 'By the way, I'm backing Michael Foot.'

'I knew that. That's why I didn't tell you I was going to stand.'

'I hope one day I can vote for you,' he added.

Went up to my room and dictated a letter to all Labour MPs. I decided to make it short, simply setting out what I'll call the catechism of the Labour Leader:

> I believe in the Manifesto. I believe in the links with the TUC. I believe in the Party Constitution. I believe we must sustain the Government. I believe we are a coalition. I believe in free speech. I believe in Party democracy. Like all Members of the Government, I accept collective responsibility for everything that has been done but I feel it right to put my views forward.

Finally I affirmed that I would accept the Leader the Party chooses and would campaign to keep the Government in power and get it re-elected. Just ritual, but I felt I had to say it.

In the afternoon Bob Maclennan approached me. 'If you were Leader – ' I interrupted, 'I don't want to answer any question that begins with that preface.' He went on, 'Would you put your own supporters in the Cabinet?' I said, 'Any Labour Leader's first job is Party unity. We are a coalition. Healing the wounds would be the most important thing. Of course you have got to have a balanced Cabinet.' He was a bit surprised.

I heard in the course of the afternoon that Arthur Bottomley is supporting me. He is the MP for Middlesborough, used to sit for Chatham and when he was defeated in 1959 my father sent him a letter saying, 'Dear Arthur, The best is yet to come. Yours, Wedgie.' He has never forgotten that.

Went to the PLP meeting at 6 and first Cledwyn reported on the procedure for the leadership election. Then Stan Newens and Eric Heffer and one or two others raised the issue of metrication and were angry at it being pushed through. Shirley said casually, 'We have to fulfil our requirements under international and EEC law,' and the plain truth is we have no choice. Whatever Parliament did, an EEC requirement would become law.

In the lobby Eric Heffer came up to me and said, 'I think it's a pity you're standing.' I said, 'I know you're voting for Michael and there's nothing else to say.'

I should think, now, I have probably got thirty votes.

Friday 19 March

To Bristol by helicopter for the special General Management Committee and rang London to see what was cooking. Frances Morrell passed me on to Michael Meacher who said, 'I think you have made your point. You should perhaps now stand down in favour of Michael Foot. You'd get a lot of credit for it.' I said, 'No, Michael, I won't and I'll tell you why. There are two points here. One is, don't feel you have to vote for me.' He interjected, 'Oh I will, even if it's only you and me left.' 'Second,' I went on, 'if Michael Foot will endorse my policy statement or issue one of his own, that would change the situation.' Michael replied, 'He won't.' 'So it's not my problem,' I said.

Frances came on the phone and said, 'Have you thought about it? Don't you think you should stand down now?'

I said, 'I won't discuss it, Frances.'

'No, Your Majesty.'

I said, 'It's no good saying that. It's no good saying to a candidate in the middle of a campaign, "Won't you withdraw?" I won't withdraw.'

The GMC was held in the very room in which I was selected twenty-six years ago. It was crowded. I said, 'I'm going to be rather formal', and I read them the three statements I had issued: on why I was standing; on Parliamentary reform; and the text of my letter to MPs. It was a highly principled, intelligent meeting. They accepted the resolution after a long discussion about whether other candidates should be asked to announce their adherence to the policies adopted by the Labour Party Conference. Then there was a debate on the proposal by the YS delegate that there should be a special conference to elect the Leader and deal with unemployment. That was actually defeated on the grounds that you couldn't change the Party rules in the middle of a term. It was really touching and I enjoyed it.

Saturday 20 March

There has been a note circulated from Harold Wilson saying political advisers are not to be active in the leadership campaign. This will be the last rebuking message from him.

Sunday 21 March
The *Sunday Times* showed I was the second most popular choice for Prime Minister by Labour voters after Callaghan, ahead of Healey, Jenkins and Foot. That was interesting.

Monday 22 March
To Number 10 for Harold's Cabinet dinner and arrived to find a tremendous gathering of cameras in the State Drawing Room. Harold had organised the dinner so that we would all be sitting in our usual Cabinet places around the big table, so I was between Michael and Peter. We had a marvellous meal. During the second course, of poached salmon, the hollandaise sauce slipped off the tray, dropped on to Denis's plate and splattered him: he was in a very jolly mood and laughed loudly.

I said to Michael, 'Do you ever regret not having been in the 1964-70 Government.' He said, 'Yes, in a way I do.' So that was the old rebel shedding his rebel's robes retrospectively. He said how difficult it had been for him to write the book about Nye, not having himself served in earlier Governments. Then I showed him the transcript of the obituary I had recorded of Harold with Kenneth Harris in 1965. He asked me why Harold disliked me so much. I said I didn't know.

At the end of the meal, Ted Short got up and he made a boring speech, followed by Harold who was even more boring, describing how he had avoided giving any indication of whom he would vote for, that he knew how every Member of the PLP would vote, and so on. As Harold sat down, Michael said across the table, 'Harold, Tony wrote an obituary of you ten years ago and I think you ought to hear it.'

So I got up and said, 'I foolishly told Michael about this obituary, but as a matter of fact, I happen to have it with me! When I was young and naïve many years ago, I asked you, Harold, at Chequers what we should do if you were run over by a bus and you said, "Find out who was driving the bus,"' so Harold interrupted and said, 'What do you mean *when* you were young!' and we all laughed. I said, 'This was in the good old days before you had to ask Joe Haines's permission to broadcast and what Joe would have said if he had had a request from the Secretary of State for Energy to do an obituary of the PM, I don't know! Anyway, I won't embarrass you by reading it though I wouldn't change a word of it all these years later and it was very nice. But I will read you the last question Kenneth Harris asked me. "Mr Benn, you have said some very nice things about the Prime Minister. Have you any criticisms?" I said, "Yes, he was never a Back Bencher."

'Harold, the Party, if the press is to be believed, is about to elect a very senior politician to be its new Leader and in a few years' time there will no doubt be a demand for a younger man. All I hope is that when you stand again, you won't split the left-wing vote.'

Jim was friendly to me, and cheerful. He said, 'I had given up ambition years ago but when the opportunity to become Leader comes your heart is bound to quicken and I am really fighting to win.' I said, 'I know that.' Of course he wants my vote in the second ballot. I can get on well with Jim Callaghan though he is a tough politician and wouldn't let you get away with much, probably less than Harold.

Michael Foot said he didn't think Harold was going to retire at all. He said he thought in a few years' time there would be a national clamour for him to come back and take charge again.

Spoke to Marcia who said she couldn't understand it and that Harold had said the other day, 'I suppose Paddy,' (that's his labrador) 'is going to be replaced by an older dog.' So there is no doubt who he thinks is going to win and who he wants to win – Jim Callaghan.

'By the way, Harold, I'll tell you who knew your secret before anyone else,' I said.

Harold had been boasting how it had been a well-kept secret, and he said, 'Who?'

'The Government Car Service.'

'What do you mean?'

I said, 'As far as I remember, Ted Heath provided you with a car when you were Leader of the Opposition, the first time that had ever happened, and you gave him a car when you won in 1974. But last year when Ted Heath gave up the leadership of the Tory Party, you made a ruling that *all ex-Prime Ministers* would have a car. I gather you foisted a car on to Sir Alec Douglas-Home who didn't want one, and Lord Avon who didn't want one. Well, the word went round the Government Car Service that the reason you'd done this was because you were going to retire.'

I said this jokingly, but Harold began looking very sick. He said, 'Not at all, it's for security reasons.'

Marcia was just smirking and it was obvious Harold didn't like it. She said to me, 'You are a naughty man – of course that's right!'

So Ron Vaughan had been absolutely bang on.

Harold said, 'Well, you'll be here one day.' There is no doubt that Harold has a deep personal dislike of me and I don't know what it is. The pathetic thing about tonight was that nobody was sad that he was going. He hasn't inspired any affection, he's just done his job like a Civil Service Prime Minister for years, fudged every issue, dodged every difficulty, but kept us in power, kept us together, ground out the administrative decisions. It is difficult to feel warmth for him though, as a matter of fact, I get quite soft when I think of his kindness.

Tuesday 23 March

During the course of the morning I sent across to Harold some photographs I had taken in February when Ted Short was being filmed. I thought I would keep on being friendly this week, partly to neutralise the malice of the man and partly to bury the hatchet.

At 4.10 my campaign committee met – Ron Thomas, Stan Thorne, Jimmy Lamond, Audrey Wise, Joe Ashton, Brian Sedgemore and Syd Bidwell with Frances and Francis also there. The figures were 35 definite and 10 possible and by late night it had gone up to 37 definites.

Wednesday 24 March

NEC at 10, where we discussed Harold's retirement. Tom Bradley spoke and then Harold said he had been on the Executive twenty-four years and for the first eight years and last eight years, he'd been in a minority. It was quite an amusing comment because for the first eight years the Executive was right wing and he was left wing, for the next eight years the Executive was central and so was he, and for the last eight years, he was right wing and the Executive was left wing.

Nobody else said a thing! No party leader could ever have gone with so few expressed feelings of regret or emotion. Amazing!

Thursday 25 March

A remarkable and dramatic day. Today was the first ballot in the leadership. Caroline, Josh and Stephen came over to the House of Commons. Mary Lou and Joe were there, then Frances, Francis and Mik arrived. He is a scrutineer and I told him I had decided to announce my withdrawal immediately from the second ballot at the Party meeting even if I had got through to the second ballot. Mik said, 'I think that is right.' I asked if I was in the second ballot and he said 'Yes', and then I asked if I was ahead of Healey and he said, 'You are, quite clearly, though you haven't got as many votes as I would have liked.'

I had a tremendous row with Frances who has changed her view, and Caroline was on her side, saying that I shouldn't withdraw immediately but should think about it.

Then I went to the committee room where the PLP was gathered for the result, and sat on the back row just behind Cledwyn Hughes. The results were announced by George Strauss [MP for Vauxhall], the chief scrutineer. Foot 90, Callaghan 84, Jenkins 56, Benn 37, Healey 30, Crosland 17. Foot did extremely well, Jim less well than he expected, Roy Jenkins got twenty less than he expected, I got twenty more than many people thought, Healey did very badly and Crosland did marginally better than the disastrous result that had been forecast. When Cledwyn announced, 'In the second ballot Crosland goes out

"Don't let's celebrate too soon, Mary! If none of the candidates gets a thumping majority, I may have to stay here indefinitely!"

Daily Express, 24 March 1976

and the candidates are –' I got up and said, 'Cledwyn, I have decided to withdraw my name from the second ballot in favour of Michael Foot.' However, the Party was so stunned by the surprise result, that they didn't really notice what I had done.

As I was walking down the corridor I passed Michael Foot's room and it was jammed with people including Neil Kinnock, Judith Hart,

John Silkin and I said, 'Good luck'. They said come in and I said, 'No, I just want to wish Michael luck.' I went to the lavatory and when I got back to my room Neil Kinnock and Judith were there, both feeling guilty, I think. They again asked me to go to Michael's room and join the campaign. I said, 'I am going to support Michael, you needn't worry about that. But I am not going to sit in as a sort of Back Bench member of Michael Foot's campaign committee. I'll talk to Michael privately.'

Did several TV and radio interviews and came back and talked to Joe. I must say a word about Joe. Not only was he my PPS for just over a year but he has been my friend and as campaign manager has been absolutely brilliant. Every time he is on television, his whole presentation has a completely different flavour from that of the other po-faced campaign managers. He says, 'Now look, Tony Benn has issued a policy statement. The others haven't. He speaks for the grass roots, and has had tremendous support from the country. He wants open government, more influence for Back Benchers, and is in favour of import controls.' Joe is marvellous. He is so obviously down-to-earth and practical and I can never thank him enough for what he has done.

Caroline, Stephen, and I went off to dinner and I felt most relaxed.

The big news, apart from my own immediate withdrawal at the Party meeting, is that Roy Jenkins has also withdrawn and the Jenkins camp is in disarray. It was a terribly disappointing result for Roy. When I think of the fantastic press that man has had year in year out, and all the banging I've had, it is gratifying that he should have only got eighteen votes more than me and that Denis Healey should have got seven less. That is amazing. I think Jim will romp home on the next ballot.

Came home and it is now 2.45. It has been a marvellous campaign. It has focused on the most important questions of all: open government, less secrecy; the control of the Executive by the legislature; the alternative economic strategy. The Wilson era is over, that is absolutely clear.

I haven't replied to Harold's minute of 8 March and so I wrote a letter tonight saying:

Dear Harold,

Thank you for your minute of 8 March. I am enclosing a minute I sent to Industry Ministers soon after the Government was formed giving a rather different view and I adhere to that view. I hope you will agree that the greater freedom of Ministers in the Referendum and the leadership election hasn't damaged the Government. It has strengthened it.

Friday 26 March
Cabinet at 10.30 and as I sat waiting with Michael outside the Cabinet Room Jim came up and he said, 'Well, Michael, I just want to tell you that if you win on the next ballot, I shall have twenty-four hours of disappointment but after that I shall be completely all right.' Jim was trying to be friendly but it wasn't terribly convincing.

Saturday 27 March
Slept until midday, then Caroline and I went to the Holland Park School Fair and had a lovely day. Gradually began sorting out the backlog of work.

Monday 29 March
Michael Foot asked if I would have dinner with him on Sunday. Then he said, 'What are you doing on Friday?' because the next ballot ends on Thursday lunchtime. I said, 'I am going to be in Scotland on Wednesday, Thursday and Friday. Perhaps I should come back?' He said, 'You must leave a note about where you will be because I am sure if Jim Callaghan wins, he will call me in to discuss appointments. What do you want to do?' I said, 'I've done twelve years of industrial work, as PMG, Minister of Technology, Minister of Power, Secretary for Industry, Secretary for Energy and I think I'd like a break, partly because I have been dropped off all economic committees and partly because I am a critic of Government policy, as you know. What I would really like to do would be Leader of the House with responsibility for parliamentary reform, Back Benches, Devolution. This seems to me to be a useful job, that's unless you want it, Michael.' He said, 'No. I think I'll stay at Employment and finish my job this year on that.'

Went to the Tea Room and spoke to Joe Slater* and he told me that when the CBI was trying to get rid of me from the Department of Industry last year, he had been to see Harold and said, 'Don't get rid of him, Harold. I just want to tell you, don't move him.' Harold had said, 'I have to because of all his Trotskyite connections.' Now that is something I have never heard before. Joe Slater said, 'That's what he was fed with.' What on earth could this mean, other than that Harold is probably so stick-in-the-mud that he thinks if you have contact with Ken Coates, this is a Trotskyite connection. He had probably been told that I read *Workers' Press* and *Red Weekly* and *Socialist Worker*. I confirms my theory that my phone has been bugged and has been fed through to Harold. This is the only time I have ever been given an explanation

---

* Assistant Postmaster General 1964–9 and a former PPS to Harold Wilson. Created a life peer in 1970.

as to why I was moved. I'll raise that with Harold in some way and find out.

Had lunch with Joe Gormley who said I had been absolutely right to stand for the leadership and put my marker down – he was rather friendly considering he didn't agree with me politically. But he said, 'You must stay at Energy because you are the best Minister of Energy we have ever had and what you are doing should have been done years ago,' namely consulting the industry.

Went over to Number 10 for Harold Wilson's farewell party. I thought it would be for Transport House people but when I got there I found it was a typical Harold party with all sorts, including the two policemen from Number 10, with their wives, Wilfred Brown and his wife, the Baloghs, David Frost and his latest actress girlfriend, Morecambe and Wise, the Judds, Ron Hayward, Marcia.

It was rather sad. Talked to Bill and Bob the policemen, who have been there for twenty odd years and are just about to retire at the age of fifty-one and fifty-two. Also had a chat to David Frost and told him I had first been in this room forty-six years ago as a four-year-old watching the Trooping of the Colour when Ramsay MacDonald was Prime Minister. Marcia was very miserable. I saw Mary Wilson and said she would be able to have a quiet life now. 'I have done my best,' she said, 'but I now just want to slip back into obscurity again.' I asked Ron Hayward, 'Why do you think Harold has retired?' He said, 'Things got too much for him, and he's lost his nerve.' I don't think that's true, but it is an interesting thought.

Just before I left, I went over and thanked Harold for inviting me and he said, 'I invited you because you were a committee chairman and we were inviting all the chairmen of committees.' What a bureaucratic thing to say! He might have said because I was an old friend or he had known me for a long time or something, but to say I had been asked because I was a chairman seemed to be a final comment on Harold.

Tuesday 30 March

Caroline gave her press conference today on the extent of public subsidy to private education which her committee estimated must run to between £50 million and £100 million a year. She is a most modest person who never wants to push herself, but really is making a substantial personal impact on British education policy.

I heard an interesting thing: when Harold Wilson's minute about political advisers not being involved in the leadership campaign was sent out, the Private Secretary at the Treasury said to Adrian Ham, Denis's adviser, 'This means you must go.'

That was how his post was terminated.

So that is the end of an uneasy relationship.

The results of the second ballot were Jim Callaghan 141, Michael Foot 133, Denis Healey 38. I must say the fact that Denis only got one more vote in the second ballot than I got in the first gave me great pleasure; he was utterly rejected really. It looks as if Jim is going to make it, but there are still uncertainties one way and the other.

At 10.15 I went and voted for Michael Foot in the final ballot.

NOTES
Chapter Four

1. (p. 450) The 1974 Manifestos committed the Labour Government to the phasing out of private pay beds from NHS hospitals in order to deal with the different levels in the standard of care within the service based on the ability to pay. Barbara Castle, strongly wedded to this policy, was faced with such vigorous opposition from the hierarchy of the medical profession that she was forced to amend the legislation. Private pay beds would only be phased out where sufficient facilities existed in the area for the reasonable operation of private medicine. At the same time as the pay beds issue, Barbara Castle was grappling with industrial action by junior doctors and health workers over pay and conditions.

2. (p. 484) The purchase of uranium from the Rossing mine in Namibia has a long and chequered history. In the late 1960s the Cabinet approved a purchase of uranium from Canada but it was indicated that it might be necessary to shift it to South Africa, and the impression had been given that such a shift would require a second Cabinet authorisation. In the event, in early 1970, I was notified that the AEA had actually signed a contract with RTZ for uranium from Namibia, which was controlled by South Africa, contrary to UN resolutions. I was also told that it would cost £6 million to cancel that contract and the Cabinet, on my recommendation, decided not to do so. Subsequently, when we were in Opposition, the Party pledged itself to cancel the contract.

3. (p. 497) In January 1976 Lord Radcliffe's 'Report of the Committee of Privy Councillors on Ministerial Memoirs' was published. Commissioned by Harold Wilson in the wake of the publication of Richard Crossman's *Cabinet Diaries*, it recommended a code of conduct including an undertaking by Ministers to submit works intended for publication for prior approval by the Cabinet secretary. Neither Roy Jenkins, Harold Wilson nor I signed it.

4. (p. 505) The Lucas Plan was designed by a committee of shop stewards to prevent redundancies in the aerospace components industry, of which Lucas was a major supplier, by converting resources mainly used in defence production to the development of socially useful products. Prototypes ranged from

medical equipment to alternative transport technologies. The Flan involved a reassessment of the production process based on social needs and on employees' development within the industry.

5
The Death of Consensus
April–December 1976

*Jim Callaghan took over as Leader of the Labour Party and Prime Minister at
a time of rapid international change, particularly in the USA, which was important
for Britain given American domination in world economic matters. Gerald Ford
had assumed the presidency from Richard Nixon following the latter's resignation
in August 1974 over the Watergate scandal, and was now, in the summer of
1976, facing an unexpectedly successful Democrat challenge in the run-up to the
Presidential elections from Jimmy Carter, a relative outsider from Georgia.*

*During the economic crisis that beset the Labour Government that summer,
culminating in the IMF loan, Callaghan claimed to be in touch with Ford and
Chancellor Schmidt of West Germany, supposedly to ease the bankers' pressure on
us. But since Ford was a right-wing republican and Schmidt an unrepentant
monetarist, Callaghan's hopes were more optimistic than real. The Cabinet having
abandoned the vigorous and interventionist policies on which Labour was elected,
the City of London, world bankers (the IMF) and the Treasury now took the
opportunity of the impending economic crisis to force the Government to make cuts
in public expenditure.*

*The choice open to us was either to accept these international pressures for cuts
by adopting monetarist policies, or to resist them using a clutch of defensive
measures – the Alternative Economic Strategy – including tighter exchange controls,
import restrictions and the use of our imminently available North Sea oil reserves
as a bargaining counter against those attacking the pound sterling. Our oil was a
powerful economic and political weapon. I suspected then, and believe more strongly
now, that this was a 'try-on' by international capital to attack a Government it
did not like. The Alternative Economic Strategy, which had its origins in our 1973
programme, was rejected by the 'IMF Cabinets' in December 1976, leaving us no
choice but to accede to the bankers' demands – an act of unilateral economic
disarmament from which the Government never recovered.*

*At the Department of Energy, a central concern was the future of the nuclear
power industry. In 1973 the Central Electricity Generating Board had proposed to
abandon the British-designed Advanced Gas-Cooled Reactor (AGR) in favour of
the American-designed Pressure Water Reactor (PWR), and also argued for a*

move towards the Fast-Breeder Reactor (FBR) of which a demonstration model had been built at Dounreay. Under my predecessor, Eric Varley, the Department prepared – and the Cabinet accepted – an alternative plan, the adoption of another British-designed reactor, the Steam-Generated Heavy Water Reactor (SGHWR). However, so hostile was the CEGB to this that they argued that there was no urgency for the reactor programme at all, and tried to stave off the SGHWR development. This was the situation I had inherited.

From 1976–8, the arguments flared about which system should replace the abandoned AGRs and the unpopular and expensive SGHWRs. Underlying these negotiations was the nuclear lobby's pressure, strongly supported by the Ministry of Defence, which needed plutonium, the by-product of nuclear energy generation, for its military programme, and by the Foreign Office on behalf of the US Government which also wanted plutonium for its defence requirements.

Thursday 1 April

The HS-125 was waiting at Prestwick Airport with my old friend Captain Dan Thomas, and I flew with John Hill, Bryan Emmett, and Bernard Ingham to Dounreay where Dr Blumfield, the Director, met us. I had a chance to look at the new security fence and perimeter track. I pursued with John Hill and with the Deputy-Director exactly what the fast breeder hazards were and the answer is simple: if the sodium pool in which the reactor is situated ran dry or if the control rods could not be inserted and the reactor went critical, then you could get a melt-out through the metal chamber and possibly, though John Hill denied this could happen, through the concrete emplacement: you would have what is called the China syndrome – where the thing would simply burn its way down through the earth and come out in China. (That's a ludicrously extreme reaction).

In Dounreay, the scientific élite have assumed the role of the lairds and treat the local people as the hoi-polloi, although their high level of skill means there is an element of mutual respect.

Monday 5 April

The speculation today was that Jim would be the next Prime Minister.

Went off at 11 to the Budget Cabinet – Harold's last – and my briefcase was stuffed with cameras. Standing outside in the hallway we saw Harold come in and everybody was looking very solemn. Barbara was morose because she thinks she will be chopped, as does Ted Short. As we were sitting down, I pulled out my camera and said, 'Can I, Harold?' and he said, 'No, not in here,' so I put it away, and somehow it didn't seem appropriate. I would have loved to take a picture today but it wasn't quite right.

Hugh Scanlon came in to see me at 3. He was very friendly, and said, 'I want to congratulate you on your magnificent campaign.' He emphasised that he would stick by me and there would be no question of Callaghan getting rid of me because of the leadership contest. I don't think Jim will, but I can't make up my mind whether I want to stay or not.

The PLP at 6 was crowed, I was behind Cledwyn Hughes, and the chief scrutineer, George Strauss, announced that 315 ballot papers were issued and 312 were returned, of which Callaghan got 176 and Michael Foot got 137.

It was a bit of a disappointment. Michael had only received four of the Healey votes. There was a lot of wooden applause from the Callaghanites – bang, bang, bang – totally without spontaneity or feeling. The Footites, including myself, were sitting pretty quietly and applauding a bit – that was the least one could do.

Cledwyn got up and asked us to make it unanimous and pledge our support, and so on, then made a long speech about Jim's and Harold's qualities. Then Jim made a very emotional speech – to become Leader and Prime Minister together must be an overwhelming experience, and Jim is a human guy. Then he got tough and said politics wasn't all about economics, or the NEB, important as they may be. Politics was about life, about human values. It was the older man speaking, the Party fixer with the block vote and the praetorian guard of the trade unions behind him.

Then Cledwyn called Roy Jenkins to speak and he stood there with notes and made a most ponderous, rather Victorian speech. He looked shattered – this contest has been as much of a death for him as Herbert Morrison's execution at the hands of Gaitskell in 1955. I think Roy does now realise he can't ever be Leader of the Labour Party.

Harold spoke and quoted at length from the statement he had made at Cabinet, 'I can't do it like Frank Sinatra because that would be stealing a phrase already used by a former Deputy-Leader of the Party,' [George Brown]. Then he slipped out and went to Chequers for the night and cleared up there.

Why has he suddenly gone? What is it all about? There will be a great deal of speculation about this in the months and years ahead. It is mysterious. The Wilson era has ended and the Callaghan era has begun. I would say that Jim will prolong this Parliament as long as he can because it may be his only period as Prime Minister. If he loses the next Election, in due time he too, will go.

Tuesday 6 April
The papers were full of Jim's victory, lots of pictures and illustrations from his family albums.

Today, I received an historic letter.

5 April 1976

Dear Tony

I have today submitted my resignation to the Queen; and, as you will know, this carries the resignation of the whole of the present administration. This does not require other Ministers to tender their individual resignations to Her Majesty; but they should of course regard their offices as at the disposal of my successor. Meanwhile, I ask all Ministers to carry on the necessary administration of their Departments until a new Government is formed. I am arranging for the Ministers who are not members of the Cabinet to be similarly informed.

Yours,
Harold

Now the interest of that letter is that it was signed after he had resigned, so he was not entitled to Number 10 notepaper, he was a Back Bencher, he was no longer Leader of the Party. What right had *he* to ask me to carry on?

I went into the House for lunch and who should wander in but Harold himself, puffing his pipe and looking frightfully well. So I produced the letter, and said, 'This really is a most extraordinary document.'

'Well, of course I signed it last week.'

'I know,' I replied, 'but still, a Back Bencher is asking me to be a Minister. That is unprecedented!'

So Hugh Jenkins said, 'Well, setting precedents is what you've always done, Harold.'

Harold told us that, walking his dog at Chequers last night, he had decided he was going to sit on the Front Bench and listen to the Budget debate. I must say, my heart warmed to him a bit.

I am going to have a talk to him once the tumult has died down. There are a lot of things I'd like to know – particularly about the Security Services and I am sure he would be prepared to talk to me.

I sat through Jim's first Prime Minister's Questions and Number 1 led to twelve minutes of congratulations. The second was directed at me. 'Did the statement made by the Secretary of State for Energy about import controls represent the policy of the Government?'

Jim replied, 'No, Sir. My Rt Hon friend was giving reasons why he was putting himself forward as candidate for the leadership of the Labour Party.'

Then Norman Tebbitt got up and asked, 'Is it right for the PM to keep in his Cabinet somebody who hates the policies of the entire Government?'

Jim replied, 'I read my Rt Hon friend's statement carefully and if there hadn't been a better candidate standing, I might even have voted for him myself,' at which the whole House broke out in laughter.

Wednesday 7 April

Had a long talk to Francis Cripps. I don't know if I will ever be Leader of the Labour Party but I don't fit the specification for the job as it now is. If I were Prime Minister I would divide the job into three: there would be the Leader of the Party in the Cabinet, with the power of appointment. Then I would have a Chairman of the Cabinet to see that Government business was carried on in an orderly way. And I would have a leader of business whose job it was to turn the Manifesto into the statute book.

It may be that after five years of Tory Government we come back in the Eighties. I am sure that the time for all this is the Eighties. It is not now.

Thursday 8 April

Bryan Emmett and Bernard said they would like to take me to lunch. So Francis and I went with them to the Pimlico Bistro and had a meal. At ten to two Bryan was called away by the waiter. When he came back he said, 'The Prime Minister wants you to phone. There's no security problem about ringing from the restaurant.' So I went downstairs in this little cubby hole of an office, surrounded by dirty cups and bills, I phoned back and was put through to Number 10. Jim came on the phone. 'I want you to stay at Energy.'

I said, 'I think I have more to offer in terms of democracy and Devolution and Parliament, so I'd like to be Leader of the House.' I said I would phone back with my answer but I would also like to see him.

We jumped into the car and I went to see Michael Foot. 'Michael, what's going to happen to you?'

'I am going to be Leader of the House.'

'Well, in that case, I would like the Department of Employment.' Michael said Albert Booth had been offered it and accepted.

'Well,' I said, 'he could change. He would be a marvellous Secretary of State for Energy but on merit, seniority and capacity to pull the trade union movement together, I would do a better job at Employment. You know I could, it would be difficult but I would pledge my support. I could do it.'

'Well, I am afraid Albert has already accepted.'

Of course, the truth is that there has been a double deal – that Jim would block Roy Jenkins from going to the Foreign Office by putting Crosland there, on condition that Michael would not press for me to get Employment.

At 3.30 I went to see Jim in his room. 'Jim, I have thought about what you told me but I want to be Secretary of State for Employment. I will pledge you my support – I want you to succeed and be Prime Minister at the end of this Parliament. You will need me.'

'Well,' he said, 'I am afraid I have already offered it to Albert Booth and he has accepted it. As a matter of fact I suggested in 1974 to Harold Wilson that you should be made Secretary for Employment but he wanted Michael Foot.'

'But Albert would do Energy brilliantly, he is one of the most able guys.'

'Well, I can't be seen to be pushed around, I am afraid it is too late. It may be a mistake but it is not the last reshuffle. We shall have another one in a few months' time.'

I said, 'I want to be absolutely straight with you Jim, and I resent the fact that I am the only candidate in the leadership election who has not been brought in, not been consulted. Indeed you had fixed the whole thing before you asked me in.'

Jim said, 'Now look, I want to make use of your abilities, to harness them. There was an attempt to get you out of the Cabinet in the past, but I would like some way of using you.'

'Well, you know my views. I do not go in for leaks, I just make speeches and put out press releases. I was continually harassed by Harold about every minor thing and I know you will be different. You will call me in, you will bang the table, you will threaten to sack me. But no more needling, please.'

I rang Caroline to say I was coming home and had a long talk to her. She is so sweet.

Friday 9 April
The Roy Jenkins faction are hysterical that Roy hasn't been given the Foreign Office in the reshuffle.

Monday 12 April
I had a message to go over to see Jim Callaghan and he said, 'I will tell you frankly, they say you don't take an interest in Energy.' This is interesting because this must have come from Sir Jack Rampton straight to Sir John Hunt – the network at work.

We came on to my chairmanship of the Home Policy Committee and I said, 'All I ask, Jim, is that you think very carefully before you make a decision. It is important that we have a perspective. You once said I had "launched a little rubber dinghy" and I think I have got some more. If you want to know what my view of a Minister's responsibility is I will give you a minute which I sent out two years ago.'

'Well,' said Jim, 'I would like to integrate you into Government but you are critical of Government policy – people think you are waiting for it to collapse and then you are going to march in with the shop stewards.'

'That honestly shows how little the Establishment understands the British people, or me for that matter,' I said. 'It is true that, looking back at the fall of the Heath Government, they did think if there was a revolution, that Harold Wilson would march in after a General Strike, and I would meanwhile be stirring up the shop stewards. But it isn't quite as simple as that. On the question of my loyalty to the parliamentary system – for God's sake it couldn't be questioned. I differ from you in believing that conscience is above the law, but that is an old Liberal dissenting objection.'

'You have great ability,' said Jim. 'I think you could be one of the greatest leaders this country has ever had but I am not sure that you are not aiming to go out and be the darling of the Left. Well, I can be a very hard man and I shall call you in one day if it goes wrong and maybe I shall sack you.'

Jim is handling me skilfully because I am somebody who needs to be at least thought of as not destructive, if not appreciated. I assured him, 'I am not sitting waiting for the revolution to march on London, I live in the naïve hope that one day you will accept the policies that I advocate.'

'When they make sense, I will,' he replied.

'That's fine, that's all I ask. Incidentally,' I said, 'I won't resign unless I think the Government is destroying the movement, and I can't see that happening.'

'Not under me,' he said.

I saw Harold tonight wandering round the House and he has absolutely shrunk; it shows that office is something that builds up a man only if he is somebody in his own right. And Wilson isn't.

Tuesday 13 April

Jim's first Cabinet. The order of seating was changed. Jim opened by saying, 'I would like to thank formally the retiring members – Barbara Castle, Willie Ross, Ted Short, and Bob Mellish. I would like to welcome the new Members. I have changed the seating and perhaps you ought to look where everybody is. I hope you will look at my Minute on Procedure very carefully and ensure that your junior Ministers get it.'

When Foreign Affairs came up, Tony Crosland just said, 'Nil.' His idea of being clever is to pretend there is nothing that should be brought to the Cabinet. He once boasted he had had no debates in the Cabinet about Education, but he's not going to get away with it on Foreign Affairs.

In a moment of undue goodwill today, I decided to send a letter to Jim with my book of speeches, so I wrote him a note in my own hand saying:

> Dear Jim,
>
> This is strictly for your bookshelf and not for the Prime Ministerial reading list. These speeches chart a sort of Pilgrim's Progress which may be a better guide to what your Secretary of State for Energy really thinks than can be gleaned from Lobby or Whitehall gossip. It comes inscribed with genuine affection and respect, deepened by your personal kindness over these last few days and combined with heartfelt good wishes.
>
> Yours, Tony.

I inscribed the book, 'To Jim, with affection and respect, Tony Benn.'

Wednesday 14 April

As I walked along the corridor with Denis Healey today, he said 'You were very good when you were interviewed on television after you had withdrawn from the leadership. Very good indeed.'

I said, 'You know, I don't think the leadership election did us any damage. In fact, it did us a bit of good.'

'I agree.'

'I hope you noticed that I said I would like to be Leader of the Labour Party rather than Prime Minister.'

He said, 'I certainly did.'

'Perhaps we could do a deal on that,' I suggested and he laughed.

Came back to the office and Jim Callaghan phoned. 'Tony, you raised some points with me. First of all, thanks for your book. It was nice of you to send it, we've made a good start and I think we'll get on all right.' So the peace offerings have been exchanged now. 'On the practical things, I am putting you on the Economic Strategy Committee, EY.' Jim went on, 'There's one chap you recommended to me for a job in Energy, I won't mention his name on the phone, but there's a security risk involved. I can't put him in your Department but I'm offering him a non-sensitive job. You'll know who I mean when the list is published tomorrow.'

I said, 'On security, you know much more than I do because you have been at the Home Office but remember Jack Jones was ruled out as a security risk for the NEB.'

It's getting very near to Easter now and I'm looking forward to a holiday.

Thursday 15 April
At the Energy Committee (now renamed ENM), we had a discussion at my request on the bribes paid abroad by BP, which had been described in the *Sunday Times* and in *World in Action* on Monday. I had wanted an inquiry although the official Whitehall view was that we should lie low.

Joel Barnett asked, 'What sort of inquiry? There are real dangers in going too deeply into this.'

Roy Hattersley said he wondered whether national morale would stand for an inquiry but, on balance, he thought it would be better to have one and he quoted Kennedy's words after the assassination of Martin Luther King, 'If there are difficulties in both courses but one seems to be morally right and the other morally wrong, I incline to the view that we should do what is morally right.'

Edmund Dell asked, 'Where do we stop? If we start inquiring into BP, what about other companies? What about our regular practices in the Middle East generally? Wouldn't it be better to have inter-governmental discussion between different countries to see if we can stamp all this out?'

Harold Lever protested, 'We cannot have an inquisition of BP on this sort of thing. National morale would not stand it.'

But Jim agreed with me. 'I think Tony was absolutely right to raise it. It had been suggested that there should be a report from officials recommending alternative courses of action and perhaps we should proceed on that basis.'

Wednesday 21 April
A box was delivered this evening and there were one or two interesting things in it, including a most friendly note from Jim.

'My Dear Tony,

I did appreciate your letter and the inscription in your book.

And I want to say your good wishes are totally reciprocated – and don't let either of us believe all we read about the other in the newspapers!

Audrey has brought the speeches to the farm to read this weekend – despite my remonstrations!

Let us meet after Easter and have a talk about the way you see things going, not just in your Department but more generally in the Party. Please ring my office.

> Yours ever,
> Jim C.

I haven't had a letter like that from Harold Wilson in the whole of my life, and it really helps.

Friday 23 April
Harold Wilson has been made a Knight of the Garter. Ridiculous!

Tuesday 27 April
Caught the train back from the NUM Conference with Bernard Ingham and Bryan Emmett. Every time I talk to them they tell me something interesting about the last Government. This time they said how disgraceful William Armstrong's role had been under Heath where he had become, in effect, Deputy Prime Minister; how the mixed committees of Ministers and civil servants put the Civil Service in a dangerous position; how Heath's 'Switch Off Something' advertising campaign had been purely political, designed to prolong the community's capacity to beat the miners; and how many Tories had actually thought the 1974 Election was a revolution. This explains the way in which I was treated by Part and I told them what had happened in the Department of Industry. Gradually they are beginning to understand what it is all about. I like them both.

Wednesday 28 April
Went over to the Charing Cross Hotel for the farewell lunch for Harold Wilson. On the menu was written, 'Lunch by the National Executive in honour of the retirement of the Rt Hon Sir Harold Wilson KG FRS OBE MP . . .' It was awful. Had a word with Mary, such a nice woman.

Over to Number 10 for the discussion about BP corruption. Joel Barnett introduced the discussion, said we couldn't have a tribunal, we couldn't have a select committee, we couldn't have this or that. In the end, the officials under Sir Douglas Wass had absolutely ruled out any inquiry because it would hurt the industry, damage the reputation of BP, and so on – a classic Whitehall cover-up.

Thursday 29 April
Quite a day! At 7 the door bell rang and it was a journalist. Then when the papers arrived, the *Daily Telegraph* had a heading, 'Benn Set on Collision Course'. This referred to my abstaining at the NEC on a motion of censure attacking the public expenditure cuts instead of

voting against the motion. The *Daily Express* had a huge banner headline, 'Benn Rats on the Cabinet', and I must admit it worried me because I thought it was an awful start with Jim, with whom I was establishing a good relationship.

My pamphlet 'New Course for Labour' was published by Ken Coates today and he sent me thirty copies, and some to the press, embargoed until Friday.

On the way to Cabinet I asked Crosland how he was enjoying the Foreign Office and he said it was boring, which is typical of Tony. I said, 'I presume you are thinking about nothing but the Treasury.'

I had a message from the PM's office that he wanted to see me this afternoon so I went into Jim's office and he said, 'I had a question in the House today about collective responsibility and I gave the only answer I could, that collective responsibility includes all Ministers, who must be expected to defend Government decisions at all times. I don't want to be emotional but we can't have this. If somebody wants to take over this job and do it better than me, I am happy to give up but while I am in, you've either got to be with the Executive or the Government. You may have to choose. There are five Ministers who are also on the Executive and I think we should meet.'

'That's fine. I'll write a paper for it if you like,' I told him.

'No, don't do that. It must be absolutely secret.'

So Fred Mulley, Shirley Williams, Jim Callaghan, Michael Foot and I are going to meet for a discussion and I think that's very important.

I commented, 'There were more Ministers on the Executive at one time.'

'Yes, well, some went, some Harold got rid of, and I had to end Barbara's career. Harold used to keep a big majority in order to have a tame vote there and I haven't got it now.'

'I know, but I think we had better discuss it because I don't like hearing the Executive attacking the Government, or the Cabinet speaking with contempt about the Executive. Actually, I think the NEC wants to make a go of it.'

Jim said, 'I don't know. There are certainly three of them in continual contact with Communists. It's not "reds under the bed" or that sort of stuff' (which of course it was) 'but I know that everything that goes on in that Executive goes straight back to King Street. I have ways of knowing.'

'I suppose as Home Secretary you know how these things work, but I don't actually see it that way.' I presume he was saying that the telephones at the Communist Party HQ are tapped.

Then he said, 'You have got to accept our policy. You have a lot of ability. You are a young man.'

'I'm not a young man,' I said. 'I'm fifty-one. I've been here twenty-six years and the NEC wants to make a go of it. But I appreciate the way you have handled the situation, the problem created by my views.'

Friday 30 April
To Bristol for my surgery and one man told me, 'I'm retired, not very good at speaking, have done manual work all my life but what made me political was Winston Churchill.' I asked what he meant and he said, 'During the General Strike when I was eighteen, Churchill made a speech saying, "Give us enough troops and we'll force them back to work." That opened my eyes and I've understood politics ever since. Do you know, Mr Benn, what we need is another Oliver Cromwell and some heads will have to roll before we get this right.' This was a quiet, neat man of over seventy, most amazing. But what interested me was that the name of Oliver Cromwell should have survived over 300 years.

Sunday 2 May
'Benn May Be Dismissed – Callaghan to Assert His Authority,' said the *Sunday Telegraph*. The *Sunday Times*, said, 'Callaghan to deal with the Benn problem.' I was very gloomy about it. Then the phone rang and it was the Prime Minister. 'I've been reading the Sunday papers. There's nothing new in this is there?'

'It's nothing to do with me at all,' I told him. 'I deeply appreciate your ringing because this happened every week during the Wilson era and it all *originated* from Number 10. There are problems obviously, problems about the policy which we will sort out – and there are an awful lot of people who are anxious to make problems between you and me. But if we keep in touch I don't think it will happen.'

Caroline and I went to Michael and Jill Foot's. Michael is a most scholarly man and it is sometimes easy to forget that. He and Albert Booth had been summoned to Number 11 for another round on the pay talks and they turned up late. Denis foolishly went out for his 3 per cent ceiling without consulting the Cabinet, precipitating a head-on collision with the TUC, and the TUC can't deliver because the membership won't have it. It would have been much better to have said, 'What I can offer in tax relief will depend on the pay settlement and I am going to enter into discussions to find out what can be done.' As a Cabinet Minister I've had no part in this.

At dinner we were arguing about how to deal with prime ministerial patronage and I put forward the argument that we have turned democracy into an elected monarchy. Harold Wilson must have given ministerial office personally to an enormous number, I suppose 200 or 250 MPs, and created about 100 peers, between 1964 and 1976: this is a complete denial of parliamentary democracy.

Barbara believed that Harold got his way in Cabinet by knowing more than any Minister, and never going in without being sure of what he wanted.

I said, 'I don't think a PM needs to bother about that because there are other ways of taking control.'

She snapped, 'Well, you think of another way. Jim won't do his homework. Jim won't work as hard as Harold. You can catch him out.'

I said, 'Jim controls by picking the Cabinet he wants and that gives the result he wants, which is exactly what Harold did.'

'Ah, but Harold was very clever,' said Barbara. 'Look at the way he demoted you from Industry to Energy.'

I said, 'It wasn't very clever. If you're the PM with the power of patronage, you can do whatever you like.'

'Well, I believe in patronage,' Barbara declared. 'I've no time for the PLP. I don't think having Leaders elected is a sensible idea at all.'

Peter agreed. So I do think now the time has come to launch a major battle on behalf of parliamentary democracy as it ought to be, that is to restore the power of Parliament over the Executive and of the PLP over the parliamentary leadership. It doesn't seem particularly radical, but if it were done it would be revolutionary.

Wednesday 5 May

To Buckingham Palace with Jack Rampton and others to meet President Geisel of Brazil. At lunch I was between the President's wife and Senora Silveira, Minister for External Relations. Senora Silveira told me she went shopping this morning and when she was asked where to deliver the goods, she had the fun of saying, 'To Buckingham Palace'.

'Did they believe you?' I asked.

'Yes, I had someone from Buckingham Palace with me.' They had stayed in Versailles which she said was a beautiful palace, but you knew you were staying in a museum, whereas when you came to Buckingham Palace, it was reality, not history.

I replied, 'It is actual, but the question is, is it real?'

'But the Queen must have enormous power in England.'

I said, 'She has no political power but she does have enormous influence just being there.'

Thursday 6 May

Went over to the House and had lunch with Pat Duffy and Roy Mason, who said something interesting. 'I got to the office this morning at 7.30 and they were rehearsing the Trooping of the Colour; I stood at my window and I saw my troops and they made a lot of mistakes, but they'll get it right on the day.' The thought of the Secretary of State for Defence reviewing *his* troops was very significant.

Duffy, who has just been appointed Minister for the Navy, said he had been down to Portsmouth on an inspection and had visited the very dockyard where he himself had been as an Able Seaman and Roy said to him, 'Think of it, an Able Seaman now a Minister for the Navy.' One can see the tremendous excitement of an Able Seaman getting to the top and that is fantastic. But one also saw that for them socialism *was* people like them getting to the top, not actually changing the top, just getting there.

I am going to Burford on Saturday to a festival held every year to commemorate the Levellers, whose army was routed there in 1647 by Cromwell, and I rang the Chairman of the Roundheads Association, who lives in York and is a young freelance historian at the University. He told me that the Roundheads Association was a breakaway movement from the Sealed Knot, which had been set up to re-enact civil war battles. The Roundheads Association wants to study history more deeply. He told me that up to a thousand men are involved in these battles and they got very excited and feel the tingle of the old war hostility. He himself was passionately anti-royalist and anti-Common Market and was a Cromwellian, very much opposed to the Levellers. He thought more should have been shot because they were mutineers. Absolutely fascinating.

I heard that Douglas Hurd, Heath's former PPS, and Conservative MP for Mid Oxon, had written to Fred Mulley complaining that the Workers' Educational Association in his constituency were using a Government grant to finance a political speech by a Labour Minister (my forthcoming speech at Burford). So I wrote a courtesy note to Hurd, saying I would be lecturing in his constituency and that I had the goodwill of the Bishop of Oxford.

Monday 10 May
At 11 I went over to Number 10 for the meeting of the five Cabinet Ministers from the Executive – Jim, Michael, Shirley, Fred and myself. We went into the Prime Minister's sitting room on the first floor. Jim started by saying, 'This is difficult and we have got to see how to handle it.' He was quite sensible about it but Fred Mulley griped and said it was all impossible.

I said, 'I would like to express my appreciation at the way this meeting is being held. It has never happened before. First of all, there is the short-term difficulty of a censure motion – the Executive wants to censure current Government policy. We ought to have Ministers to the NEC Home Policy and International Committee so they can talk about it. Where the National Executive is worried, it is often over the same issues that worry Ministers. There is something manifestly absurd about Fred Mulley fighting like a tiger about his education budget when the Cabinet cuts it, and then implying it's disloyal when someone else on the Executive argues his case. It isn't disloyal. We are all concerned. We don't like doing these things but we don't want to condemn and deplore and protest. What we want to do is to find a way of expressing our concern as an Executive and put it down on the agenda for the next meeting of the Cabinet and the NEC.

'On the question of future policy, there should be discussion between the Party, the TUC and the Government. Of course, Parliament is going to have the last word. But Ministers feel their noses are put out of joint when Len Murray knows more about what's going on in the Treasury than they do, and we have got to find a way of bringing them in.'

On the whole, I felt I had made some progress. Jim took up some of the points I made, and did invite me to write a paper about it.

To the Energy Committee which really was interesting. Frances and Francis had written an excellent official paper on the fast breeder reactor under my direction. I said that Sir Brian Flowers [Chairman of the Royal Commission on Environmental Pollution] had stated that he wasn't yet persuaded that nuclear power should be expanded, there were fundamental difficulties of safety and stability in the processing of plutonium, of sabotage and theft, and he was afraid that the thing was going forward inevitably. I was afraid it might deflect resources from other forms of energy and I thought there should be a public debate and recommended we have a survey. Meanwhile, I wanted another £10 million to maintain Dounreay.

Jim said, 'You're a bit late with this. You were asked to do it last summer.'

'There is a change,' I said. 'Last summer they were just holding on in the hope of getting the fast breeder authorised. They didn't want a decision taken too soon. Now, I must be clear, I am really trying to delay it.'

Afterwards, I said to Harold Lever, 'I am not saying that the nuclear emperor has no clothing but I am asking a bystander if I could have the name of his tailor,' which made him laugh.

The big news is that Norman Scott, that awful male model, has finally succeeded in dislodging Jeremy Thorpe who resigned today as Leader of the Liberal Party. It is terribly sad for Jeremy. Maybe this is a great victory for the South African security police against whom Harold Wilson railed again yesterday. It makes you wonder whether he is the next one for some scandal of a financial kind, linked to the burglary of his papers. Very strange, I must say. I still can't understand why he has gone.

Tuesday 11 May

Today Alan Phillips gave me a note saying the following:

> Barry Penrose of the BBC rang about an anonymous undated letter from South Africa delivered to Harold Wilson last week about South African/Anglo-American company interference in British domestic politics. He thinks it may have been copied to you inter-alia as you are mentioned as one of their targets. If you want to talk to him about it, his number is . . .

I presume, if this story is true, I would be a target. I have never doubted that. But if I pursue it with Penrose, it will be 'Mr Benn, talking to the BBC today, made a statement . . .' I think I'll leave it. The dirty tricks department could be turned on me too.

A bit of good news today – George Davis of 'George Davis is innocent' fame was released from prison. That is another great working-class victory. Here is an innocent guy picked up and jailed for seventeen years and Roy Jenkins has released him after a huge East End campaign against his wrongful conviction. There is another guy serving eighteen months in jail for having wrecked the Headingley Test Wicket last summer to draw attention to Davis's case, and he ought to be let out too.

Wednesday 12 May

The first big meeting of the Executive to consider 'Labour's Programme for Britain 1976'. Jim stayed for almost the whole day which shows what a proper sense of priorities he has, unlike Harold who would have dodged it. Jim suggested I take the chair and I was able to get it through in a spirit of goodwill. At the beginning, I read out the statement I had prepared and sent over to Jim yesterday. Jim made a statement and in fact they married up quite well, though he wanted to make it quite clear that the policy statement did not, of itself, change existing Government policy.

Ron Hayward said, 'I think it would be a good idea if Tony Benn's and the PM's statements were issued to the press.' So they were both put out and we'll see what they make of it.

Jim kept passing little notes to me. One said, 'I'm very glad you are in the chair or we would never get anywhere. Don't be discouraged. Press on.' And, 'Art thou weary, art though languid, art though longing to break free? Don't give up. You're doing very well.' I sent him a note saying, 'Jim, what you are doing is rebuilding confidence between the Party and the Government.' I had another note from Joan Maynard and Nick Bradley saying, 'Tony, isn't the whole programme unobtainable under capitalism?' I nodded. But it was very good-natured, lots of laughter, lots of jokes and except for a few sections, we got through it all and referred the rest to the Drafting Committee.

Merlyn Rees told me a funny story today. 'During the first ballot of the leadership election, Roy Hattersley went to see Roy Jenkins and he looked very embarrassed and said, "Roy, we've been friends for a long time and I want you to know that I am going to vote for Jim. We've fought many battles together and I hope it won't destroy our relations." Roy got up and held his hands and said, "Roy, how nice of you to tell me. I very much appreciate it and although I am naturally disappointed, it certainly won't affect our relations." Roy Hattersley left the office and went along the corridor to Tony Crosland's room and he said, "Tony, we've been friends for a long time and I want you to know that for reasons which you will probably understand, I am going to vote for Jim. We've fought many battles together and I hope it won't destroy our relations." Tony said, "Thank you for telling me, now *fuck* off!" '

Saturday 15 May

At 9.45 we arrived at Burford Church where the Revd Gilbert Parsons was waiting, and as we approached we saw two elderly church wardens with paraffin and wire brushes wiping off a slogan on the wall 'Bollocks to Benn' – a piece of graffiti that embarrassed the vicar but not me.

We walked round the church and then got a lift up to the school where the film on Gerrard Winstanley was being shown which was quite moving. Members of the Roundheads Association were there in the uniforms of the New Model Army, with wives and children dressed up. It was lovely. Transport House Research Department had come in a coach and they had put out the whole text of my speech as a press release – nineteen pages of it!

Then we went to the Royal Oak pub where Morris men and others were dancing. The Morris Dancers go right back, I think to the Peasants' Revolt, and they wear white outfits with hats and ribbons, and carry sticks and bells and they dance and clap and drink and collect money. Apparently, many of them are closely connected with the Labour movement. Some of the New Model Army soldiers were sitting in the corner drinking their beer, like soldiers in any army, and since the pub was an old one with scrubbed wooden tables and floorboards, you might have seen the Levellers there the night before they were captured by Cromwell.

We walked to the High Street and there were people streaming up with their banners – the POEU, the Pressed Steel Branch from Cowley, the YS from Acton, people from all over the place. Outside The Bull, one man came up and said, 'We're drunk enough to ask you to come and be photographed with us. We are the TUC Research Department.' So I wandered over and there were all these young men, and they said,

'We wrote the Economic Review, at least the best parts of it.' I asked which of them wrote about import controls and one man put his hand up. Another said, 'I'm De-industrialisation of Britain.' I asked, 'Who's Compulsory Planning Agreements?' We laughed and watched the dancing a bit longer.

We walked on to the recreation ground where there was a huge crowd of 3,000, and all the Roundheads marched on to the field and did their drill and fired their muskets – an amazing sight. Then in the usual human and haphazard way, the banners were held up and people organised themselves.

When we got back to the church, the vicar, with the Parochial Church Council and a few Tory Burfordians, sat right up next to the altar. They wouldn't let me speak from the pulpit. As the church filled, there was a tremendous crowd, with about a thousand in the church house and many more outside. The vicar gave a little speech with some of the Roundheads Association standing around in their New Model Army uniforms just as they must have done before. The singer Roy Bailey sang some beautiful Leveller and Digger songs with tremendously powerful political messages. Then I got up to speak. The loudspeaker didn't work properly and the microphone wasn't right, so I had to shout. Then there were questions and discussion. A woman got up and said, 'I am a teacher. Surely what we want is people to be kind and love each other and socialism is unnecessary.' Then a Communist from Lucas Aerospace said it was not enough to talk about history, you must change it. It was one of the most thrilling days I have had.

I should mention that some people put out a little sheet saying the Levellers really believed in private property, were bourgeois, wouldn't have agreed with socialism and the interference of the state.

I came away understanding England much more, understanding the radicalism of the Peasants' Revolt and the Levellers, and the very early birth of English radicalism, why our history wasn't taught, and how rich we were in our own tradition. It is our own home-grown socialism.

Sunday 16 May
Went to see Kirillin, the Soviet Chairman of the State Committee for Science and Technology at the Embassy in Kensington Palace Gardens. We got on to the question of nuclear safety and he said, 'Some scientists say there is no risk, some say there could be. The Central Committee has taken the latter view.' When I pressed him, he said, 'We would much rather do without nuclear power but we have to have it because coal and nuclear is the baseload for the 1990s.'

Monday 17 May
Picked up Mother and we went to see Mr Cobb and Mr Ellison at the Parliamentary Records Office to look at Father's papers. They have done a fantastic job. They have started to laminate and bind them in volumes, beautifully done. There are still a lot more to do. In the same room were the Beaverbrook and Lloyd George papers. It certainly gave me ideas for organising mine, although my problem is I need more space.

Thursday 20 May
At Cabinet Michael Foot pushed a note across saying that when the pressure mounted to sign the Radcliffe statement on ministerial memoirs he would go and see Jim or suggest that Roy, himself, me and Jim should meet. When I spoke to Roy later, he said, 'Well, I'm leaving the Government soon and I'm not signing before I go.' So that's organised. I just won't do it.

The final item was on 'programme analysis review schemes'. It is just a bonanza for mini Royal Commissions whose findings are never published and whose academic value is very limited anyway.

I said, 'I met a woman recently, paid by the Home Office to study poverty in Lambeth. It would have been better to give the money direct to the poor in Lambeth – they would have made greater use of it. We ought just to abandon these studies. They are not worth doing.'

At this point, Jim said, 'It's funny you should say that because when I was reading all this in the early hours of the morning, I wondered whether we needed all these extra reviews, but I just assumed I was a senile old reactionary ...'

'Oh, I'm not challenging you on that,' I replied to huge laughter.

We more or less killed it.

To lunch with Norman Willis, Assistant General Secretary of the TUC. He's from Staines, I think, and his position at the TUC is not really taken seriously because Len Murray works with David Lea and Willis is simply like the Vice-President of an American Government. He joined the TGWU in 1949, at the age of fourteen, when Arthur Deakin was still General Secretary and his first job was to remove all evidence of Communist officials in the TGWU after Deakin had got a rule passed at their conference that all Communists, whether they be officials or members of the Council, should be declared ineligible for service in the union. They'd all been booted out and every member had to sign a loyalty oath that they were neither Communist nor fascist. Many members refused to sign and lost their jobs. I'd forgotten all this. That was Deakin – leader of the kind of 'moderate' unions that we want to get back to, so we are told.

Sunday 23 May

The scandal of Harold Wilson's resignation honours list* is still exercising the press. The whole thing is utterly corrupt. What we need at the moment is a great attack on the power of patronage that is given to the Prime Minister. It is much too much for any one man to have. We would never give a king the power to do all that a Prime Minister can do – far more than an American President, and far more than is desirable.

Monday 24 May

There were two very important items concerning nuclear power in the papers today. From Vienna there was a story that nuclear power industries had received a report that people who were anti-nuclear power were really subversives trying to deny the Western world necessary energy in the face of the Russians. Once it is accepted that if you're against peaceful nuclear power you must be a dangerous red, that is very serious indeed. We must watch that development carefully.

Second, Walter Marshall has now declared that the Westinghouse PWR is absolutely safe, part of Marshall's long-term aim to get us to buy American and drop SGHWR while at the same time demanding that we have a British fast breeder reactor. So the nuclear lobby rolls on.

Had dinner with Frances and Judith and we talked about how to deal with Thatcher's private argument, which is that the Labour Government are doing to the trade union movement what the Tories could never do; that in doing it the Government are getting profits up and holding prices down and therefore restoring vitality to the capitalist mechanism; and that by doing so they will disillusion their own supporters and make it possible for the Tories to return. Hence when the Tories do return they will find the Labour movement broken and divided and demoralised, with capitalism booming.

Wednesday 26 May

Talked to Michael Meacher who recounted the meeting on Monday at which the PM met junior Ministers. He told them he didn't want to talk about Elections, economic policy or anything that involved money, he wanted them to go round mentioning the things that don't cost money – social values, vandalism, why the comprehensive schools are not meeting needs, crime in the street, etc. Old Father Jim giving a

---

* The list was subject to a great deal of cross-party criticism for bringing the honours system into disrepute as a result of doubts as to the propriety of some of those rewarded, including a number of capitalist entrepreneurs.

right-wing law-and-order lecture to MPs. Of course there are non-economic things you can talk about which can also be socialist things, like reforming the Civil Service, ending patronage, democratising the Party, dealing with the House of Lords, ending the honours list. That of course is not at all what Jim means!

I went back to the office for a meeting with BP: Jack Rampton, Bryan Emmett and myself on our side and David Steel and Monty Pennell for BP. I told them that their proposals were simply not on, saying I wasn't going to pay a premium to get an option on oil – no Government would pay. Second, they were not giving us a real place on the operating committee with a seat, a voice and a vote. I said this was Government policy and I must have these. David Steel said it wasn't in the commercial interests of the company and I said that we owned 80 per cent of the company and we wouldn't do anything that would cause damage but this was the key, and they had to shift on it. They had shifted with every other Government in the world and they had to shift for us. I was not prepared to be frustrated by BP.

Thursday 27 May

Harold Wilson's honours list is still the big news item today. It is unsavoury, disreputable and just told the whole Wilson story in a single episode. That he should pick inadequate, buccaneering, sharp shysters for his honours was disgusting. It has always been a grubby scheme but the Establishment never reveal the grubbiness of their own peerages and honours. Still, we've never had anything quite like this in the Labour Party and it has caused an outcry. It will clearly help to get rid of the honours system.

To Locket's for lunch with Roy Hattersley. We had sort of committed ourselves to having a meal together and I enjoyed it. He is an attractive guy and we talked about Tony Crosland and Jim; he prefers Tony. He thought Tony trusted him more whereas Jim wanted to run everything himself. He found Crosland amusing and civilised and of all the people in the Labour Party, Crosland was the one whose views he shared most completely.

I said how pleasant life was without Harold and Roy said, 'Yes, but it is an appallingly pedestrian Government under Jim.' He described the junior Ministers' meeting on Monday. 'Of course,' said Roy, 'I take the view, as you know, that freedom is what matters. I've never been a member of any group.' I pursued that with him and we talked about education. He takes an absolutely hard line about banning all private education. On health, he's in favour of banning all private health provisions because it will destroy the Health Service. I said from these issues which he cared passionately about – and I didn't blame him – it could be inferred that he *wasn't* in favour of freedom. He said he knew that, but we had to carry out these policies.

I went further and asked him what he thought about jailing people who were against blacks. He thought you had to do it, you couldn't have the public exposed to that sort of racial hatred.

I told Roy that I was in favour of, say, the IRA having their own TV programme so they could make their case publicly because if they did that they wouldn't go on shooting people. But he disagreed. 'No, there would be absolute bloodshed if we did that because it would look as if the terrorists were being given recognition. We have to split the terrorists from the rest.'

Roy also said that when he had stayed in the Shadow Cabinet in 1972 after Roy Jenkins and David Owen had resigned, all his friends had cut him off – Bill Rodgers, David, John Harris – and he was absolutely isolated and pilloried and was always described as 'that rat' by Bernard Levin.

It was a very enjoyable talk.

I was told to go on the bench and hear Michael Foot winding up the enormous row over the Aircraft and Shipbuilding Nationalisation Bill. There had been scenes of disorder and shouting and Michael's speech was not wildly successful but he held his corner. Then came the vote on Mrs Thatcher's amendment which would have classified the Bill as a 'hybrid' bill, thus requiring special procedure and therefore delaying it. The Speaker had ruled that it was a hybrid bill and the vote was 303 to 303, so George Thomas then read out Speaker Denison's ruling on how Speakers should vote on a tie, i.e., to give the House another chance, and accordingly voted for the Government.

Then we had our main motion which was to go on with the Bill and on this we won by 304 to 303. Word spread like wildfire that the Chief Whip, Mike Cocks, had allowed one of our MPs, who had paired with a Tory, to vote, thus breaking a pair, to which he had been strictly tied, without warning. I was outside the Chamber when the result was announced but everybody knew what had happened. Heseltine picked up the mace and our people began singing the Red Flag and the Speaker suspended the session for twenty minutes. When the House resumed, the Speaker said that in view of the gross disorder, he would suspend till tomorrow morning.

I don't know how we'll cope with it. The fact is we cheated. The Speaker should never have ruled that it was a hybrid bill. The Bill had been cleared as a general bill and his ruling was wrong. He was bending over backwards to please the Tories and we responded by cheating. So now we are in a hell of a mess.

Sunday 30 May

Stephen came in tonight and he thought I'd have to consider my position if the Government decided to make cuts. That's true. If there is a break with the TUC that would clear the way but I don't know whether a resignation is right or whether I'd say to Jim that I could do a more useful job working with the Party than in working with the Government, and simply be transferred from one job to another – retaining a good relationship with the Government but being free to speak and identify issues. If I did go it wouldn't be a resignation on a particular issue, it would be a letter to Jim asking to be released for Party work. I have felt this for a very long time. It keeps coming back to me in waves.

Thursday 3 June

Jack Rampton came in and told me that Sir John Hill wanted to see me today to tell me he wanted to cancel the steam-generated heavy water reactor. An absolute bombshell. So Hill and Walter Marshall came to see me, with Chris Herzig, Rampton and Alan Phillips present. John Hill sat looking shifty, watching Rampton most of the time, and said, 'I have been in Russia and in Finland [or Sweden] and I've been thinking; I have come to the conclusion that we should cancel the SGHWR.' He then gave all sorts of reasons – it was expensive, there was a small market, the customer didn't want it, the American light water reactor (PWR) had been proved safe – and it turned out that he wanted the development of the fast breeder to be accelerated.

I let him finish and then I asked, 'What view did you take two years ago?'

'I was in favour of the advanced gas-cooled reactor,' he said. 'The customer has to decide.' He couldn't really give me a clear answer.

So I asked Walter Marshall what his view was two years ago. He said, 'I had only just joined the board. I didn't know much about it but I had doubts.'

I think there is now a plot to kill it off. They see it slipping, costs escalating, they want to save money and get on with the fast breeder without delay.

I said, 'This news is tremendously important. It's the AEA deserting its own child. We developed the Magnox and the AGR ourselves and we are proud of it. This will come as a real shock. Moreover, it is bound to throw doubt on the fast breeder because if you are not going to build the system, the SGHWR, which you designed, people will say, Why not buy the fast breeder from abroad?'

As a matter of fact, I am not sorry. I personally don't want the SGHWR but I shall fight like a tiger against the American light water reactor.

Marshall was very uncomfortable, even though for him it was a triumph. Rampton was looking quizzical because he never liked the SGHWR. I think they all reckon on my going quickly and then they'll get the American reactor. But I'll be absolutely opposed to that and I might have some influence over the decision wherever I am in Whitehall.

Sunday 6 June

There is a rumour that Powell may be offering to help the Government out in some way and the Liberals are also prepared to help if the Government drops the Aircraft and Shipbuilding Bill. There was a report of my speech 'Tories are the real saboteurs' in the *Sunday Telegraph* and a most revealing article by Peregrine Worsthorne ending 'Please, Oh God, break up the Labour Party now' because the unity and strength of the Labour Party is the main barrier to the application of coalition government based on Tory, monetarist policies.

This evening, the Foots, the Baloghs and Peter Shore came to dinner. Caroline says that whenever Michael comes, he has some package he wants to sell to us and, now I come to think of it, he did ring two or three times this week to say how keen he was to have the meeting. Just before he arrived, Number 10 rang to say the PM wanted to have a word with him.

What Michael wanted to tell us, though I didn't spot it at once because I am not as suspicious of him as I should be, was that in view of the parliamentary situation, the Aircraft and Shipbuilding Bill should not be proceeded with on Tuesday but should be deferred until we had a majority. So his strategy is clearly to postpone the Bill, the pound would then leap up to about $1.80, the Liberals would be cock-a-hoop, the Tories will regard it as a victory, and our people will be demoralised and disillusioned.

I do see in Michael the collapse of the Labour Government because he is totally out of touch. If this comes up tomorrow, I might make the point that, if we don't want to ask for a vote of confidence, we should challenge the Tories to put down a Motion of Censure and then see what happens. Powell is trying to do a deal with the Government for more Ulster Unionist MPs as part of the Devolution package; the Liberals haven't got a Leader and couldn't fight an Election; and the Tories are ambivalent about whether they could carry through their policy, though Peter Shore believes they have found a way of dealing with the trade unions in future just by creating unemployment and turning off their finance tap.

Monday 7 June

Members of Economic Strategy Committee gathered, officially to discuss the Chancellor's statement on sterling this afternoon. But before we heard the statement, Michael was asked to describe business for the House and he put to the Committee the postponement he had suggested to me last night.

Denis presented his statement and he said there had been a run on sterling which had been beyond our capacity to control through the reserves. He had arranged stand-by credit of $5 billion, $2 billion from America and $3 billion from the central banks which would be available for three months and should see us through to the autumn. If any of that was called upon, either to reinforce the reserves or to sustain the rate, we had given an undertaking that we would go to the IMF.

I said I wanted to concentrate on the tactics we should adopt in a Parliament, where we had lost our majority. Denis's statement this afternoon would be reassuring. We should make the Opposition take responsibility for their own actions against our legislation and we should challenge them to put down a Motion of Censure in the light of all they had said during the last ten days.

I also raised the possibility of an alternative policy if we were going to make tighter restrictions on public expenditure later this year. Denis said we might need to announce them in July. I wouldn't go into detail about the alternative measures but everybody knew what I meant. I said we should look at the options more closely. On the politics of it, I felt that a beleaguered Government facing aggressive Tories and Liberals should really strike back. The Tories were in a terrible mess, Heath and Peter Walker were not even on the Tory Front Bench. The Liberals couldn't have an Election without a Leader and the SNP must be wondering whether a Thatcher Government would ever proceed with Devolution. Therefore we must prepare *now* for an Election because when exactly it would take place might not be within our control.

Jim came in to say he had never heard a middle-aged man be so defeatist. I said, 'I am not at all defeatist. We are much stronger than we think.' But I was in a minority of one.

Went over to Transport House and confided to Ron Hayward my anxieties that we might be drifting towards a tacit coalition, where the Government didn't put forward things that it couldn't carry through.

At the PLP, Michael Foot announced the postponement of the Bill. Denis repeated his statement about the stand-by arrangements. Two remarks he made caught my attention. One was that we would have to trim back public expenditure to make room for the boom if it got underway at really high speed. Secondly, when he was pressed by Dennis Skinner as to what he was doing about speculation, he said the Treasury had examined the position and was considering its defence including the possibility of some tighter exchange control measures.

The remark about further public expenditure cuts aroused some immediate flutters of anxiety, and Neil Kinnock questioned it. I left at 6.30 but I am told that at the end, Jim Callaghan said this was the greatest opportunity that Britain had had since the war. Exports were booming and investment would pour in, we must cut back on spending and the people would understand.

Tuesday 8 June
Didn't get to bed until 4 am, up at 7.30 and another all-night sitting tonight. I brought my car in so Ron Vaughan doesn't have to wait up again.

Wednesday 9 June
Had lunch at the Foreign Office with Tony Crosland. He was in that great room overlooking the park. Anyone working there would be quite paralysed and incapable of challenging the existing authority in any way. He had his jacket off and was in his blue-and-white-striped shirt with his shoes off, his specs on his nose and a cigar. For him, informality is a sort of substitute for radicalism and it amuses him. He brought with him to the Foreign Office his diary secretary from the Department of the Enviroment and she obviously acts as his personal friend. I took some photographs of him. He is enjoying it enormously though he says it is a bore having to go abroad so much.

We gossiped about Roy Hattersley. Tony said that although Roy was very able, he was unsuccessful politically because he angered people. He had angered the Jenkinsites and the Left and generally speaking had isolated himself. Tony does love gossip – mind you so do we all.

He said Jim was jealous of him for having got on well with Kissinger, and also for having succeeded in abolishing the wearing of white ties at diplomatic functions. He said the problem arose on his trip to America with the Queen for the bicentennial. 'I settled it through the Vassar College circuit,' he explained. 'I got Susan to ring up Anne Armstrong who was at Vassar with her.' Anne rang President Ford and he agreed that at the dinner at the White House, though it would be white tie, the Foreign Secretary could come in a black tie. Then Tony had got his Private Secretary to ring Sir Martin Charteris at Buckingham Palace who asked the Queen if she would mind if the Foreign Secretary came in a black tie at the British Embassy dinner in Washington. The Queen had said she didn't mind.

Thursday 10 June

Jim announced at Cabinet that he was not in favour of guillotines on Aircraft and Shipbuilding, Education, Land Tax, and Dock regulation.

Then Fred Mulley announced that he was going to make a statement about Thameside Education Authority, which was defying Government policy on comprehensive schools. Michael Foot thought it would stir up the Tories, and Elwyn Jones said, 'I don't know anything about this but remembering how a previous Education Secretary, Patrick Gordon Walker, got into difficulties with the courts over enforcement, I would like to look at this first.' There is a complete collapse of will. In any case, Jim doesn't really believe in comprehensive schools.

Then Jim asked, 'Anything on Foreign Affairs?'

'Nothing,' replied Crosland.

'Lebanon?'

'I can't give a report until I see the Ambassadors.' So that was Foreign Affairs polished off.

Denis reported on the economic situation briefly. 'We've got to have public expenditure cuts for next year identified and published by July.'

Jim added, 'We might have to take even more extreme measures: but I'm sure the British people would take it from us.'

I felt I must chip in. 'On the energy side, our oil is worth an enormous amount – £200 billion – and we've got twice as much gas. I am trying to bring out monthly energy statistics. This is very important. Jim, you are going to speak at the Energy Conference with all the Ambassadors there, and it would be a great opportunity to get this across. The Americans, the Japanese, the Iranians, everybody will recognise the importance of it. Tony Crosland has said that the importance of this was recognised even in China. We must get it across.' I think Jim may see that I have given him a little political platform.

We came on to discuss the Charter of Human Rights document which Jim had brought before the Cabinet – the Shirley Williams–Sam Silkin concept. Roy thought it was good. Elwyn had reservations about asking judges to safeguard human rights and Peter Shore attacked it, saying it was transferring power from Parliament to the courts.

Shirley disagreed, and argued that 'minority' groups like women felt they were not properly looked after.

I said it was a great leap backwards and that the whole purpose of democracy was to maintain the tenuous thread that enabled us to say to people, 'Vote for us and we will change the law.' What are we to say to people? That their rights will be looked after by Lord Donaldson?

Jim said, 'I don't want to discuss it. I just want to know how people will feel about publishing it.'

I added, 'I am strongly in favour of publishing and having a big debate. But I think it's a ghastly thing and I would certainly oppose it.'

Friday 11 June
Cabinet at 10.30 where we had a long session on different aspects of Europe: papers on the Tindemans Report on Economic and Monetary Union, on the enlargement of the Community, on the method of fixing the CAP prices, on direct elections and on the new passport.

Tony Crosland said that the most important items in the short term were the fisheries policy – 'particularly for me in Grimsby after the Cod War settlement' – the Budget, the nuclear fusion scheme, the CAP and community procedures.

'On mid-term questions, there are direct elections, and on long-term, the future of the Community as envisaged by Leo Tindemans [Prime Minister of Belgium] whose report is not actually federalist in its proposals but does suggest we move towards an Economic and Monetary Union through the Snake.' He thought that enlargement of the EEC might be a way of strengthening democracy in the new member countries and fighting off Communism.

Denis Healey thought we ought to go very slowly on enlargement; even in the Community itself, standards varied and there was a difference between North and South. 'For example,' he said, 'Marseilles in France is really run by the Mafia under a very good socialist friend of mine called Deferre.'

I added, 'You mean like Grimsby!'

I said I had an announcement to make, that after a year of mourning after the Referendum, I had now taken off my black armband. Our objectives in the Community ought to be to approach all these issues in an open, free and cheerful way, to try to restore democratic control, to cut through the bureaucratic tangle. Talking to the Council of Ministers is like trying to get a conversation going at the Cabinet table in Madame Tussauds. I am afraid that if we don't assert democracy there, bureaucracy will eat us up.

'If you take energy, my real resentment is that the Commissioner doesn't seem to be interested in energy but is using it to advance the control by the Community over our resources. When we take the presidency of the Councils next year, we can campaign for a British approach.' Finally, I talked about the need to extend the Community to Eastern Europe so that we could build democracy and socialism together.

Roy Jenkins wanted to look at the realpolitik. He was not an idealist but he thought we should aim to exercise similar influence to that exercised by Germany and France. 'We must talk the language of the EEC. We mustn't try to change it too quickly during our period as

President. We have to enlarge but we must recognise that there will then be a two-tier Community and the question is, will the UK be in the top tier or the bottom tier?'

We had an amusing lunch in the State Drawing Room. Peter said that in 1968, presumably when he was Secretary of State for Economic Affairs, he had attended a dinner at the Royal Academy and sat next to Mrs Thatcher when she was Opposition spokesman on Economic Affairs, and he had tried very hard and very non-politically to get on with her (he said she was the most unpleasant woman he had ever met) but she had an absolute thrusting ambition and reflected the most odious values, of everyone doing well for themselves. Shirley Williams recalled sitting next to Ted Heath at a dinner and when she tried to speak to him, he declined to answer – simply didn't reply. She had turned to the man on her left and asked, 'Does Ted Heath not speak to women?' and he had answered, 'He doesn't speak to many people at all.'

Shirley thought Mrs Thatcher would be out by the end of the year, that the Tories simply would not accept her. That is interesting, but I find it difficult to imagine.

After lunch we came on to the EEC passport and a number of maroon passports had been handed round with the British crest and the words 'European Community' on the front. Peter jumped in, 'We don't have to have these passports, do we? Surely we can keep our British ones if we want.' It emerged that this was another deal Wilson had done and Peter could not keep his old one. He was boiling with rage. 'My children and grandchildren *forced* to abandon the old British passport!'

I joined him. I feel inordinately angry about this. Bruce Millan said most people in his constituency didn't have passports and it was just a middle-class sentiment. In the end it went through, so in due course we are going to have a flimsy maroon passport. I shall renew mine before then.

Saturday 12 June
To Bristol Polytechnic for a crowded Tribune Group meeting. Afterwards Bryan Beckingham came up to me and said a letter to him had been delivered in with a bundle to the Communist Party Headquarters in Bristol, which proved it had been opened and accidentally put back in the wrong pile. The Communists had sent it on to him and he had written to *Militant* about it. So we do live in a police state to the extent that they do open letters to people.

Tuesday 15 June
To Economic Strategy Committee for a very important meeting. A paper had been commissioned by Peter Shore to consider a limited

scheme of import restraints but officials had torn it to bits. Jim Callaghan said, 'I don't understand why there is so much anxiety about the IMF. After all, they ask reasonable things and I don't think we should make them into bogeymen. That's what the IMF are for.'

I was afraid the IMF would check our recovery and that we must have bargaining power. 'I do think there should be adequate preparation so that when the choice comes to be made we will have the option. I am in favour of being ready with a plan to freeze sterling balances, to control financial transactions, to control imports and to link it all to planning agreements and I think we should have it ready now.'

Denis Healey, who is obsessed with Francis Cripps, said, 'Tony Benn comes out with the Cambridge School theory which Francis Cripps advocates, but they want a much bigger cut in public expenditure than I want. I was talking to Arnold Weinstock the other day and he thinks we're pursuing a jolly good policy, but we will have to have further cuts in public expenditure and my plan is to make them before I go to the IMF.'

Jim Callaghan had seen Henry Ford, who also thought it was a marvellous policy, and had great confidence in Ford of Britain because there were no strikes now, and so on. I must say, if Arnold Weinstock, Henry Ford and Harold Lever think it is a marvellous policy, it won't last long with the movement, because we aren't in power to please them.

As I left Jim asked me, 'How do you like being on the Economic Strategy Committee?'

'Very much, though I know my view is a minority view.'

'You notice I didn't crush it,' he said.

'Yes, of course, but I feel I must argue my case.'

Went back to the office and commissioned from Francis a major economic strategy paper outlining the three alternatives; what we are doing, what Denis wants to do and what I think should be done.

At 3 we had a meeting on the fast breeder – Arthur Hawkins and Robert Peddie of the CEGB, Frank Tombs of the South of Scotland Electricity Board, Peter Menzies, Brian Tucker, Alex Eadie and Rampton. I began by saying, 'I am committed to looking at this again and there are a lot of general questions – safety, time scale, methods. Will you give me your comments.'

They told me that the fast breeder just wasn't safe. I think the phrase was that it was in some way 'physically unstable'.

'You mean because of the problem of the China syndrome?'

'Yes,' they said. 'The core might melt through the container and go right through the earth.'

'Well, if it's unstable at present, what about the reactor at Dounreay?' I asked.

Peddie said, 'Don't ask me about safety at Dounreay,' and everybody laughed.

I said, 'I have to ask.'

They told me that in fact the AEA have different safety standards to the Nuclear Inspectorate because they are doing research and development. I suppose the plain truth is that Dounreay isn't safe and that's why it was originally situated there.

Thursday 17 June

New Society published an article called, 'The Cabinet versus the Children' about the abandonment of the child benefit which Cabinet recently discussed.

This was raised at this morning's Cabinet, and Jim, who was sitting there looking relaxed, said, 'There is no doubt that this story is based on a study of confidential documents.' I think he said there were three Cabinet papers quoted directly and precisely, and the minutes of two Cabinet committees which had been given restricted circulation. 'This is a very serious matter. I will be under heavy fire in the House and leak inquiries have not proved satisfactory. I am thinking of calling in the police and I wanted to know the Cabinet's view.'

Peter Shore said he took a grave view of it and he supported the Prime Minister. Denis believed it had done enormous damage because it not only revealed Cabinet discussions but it also referred to his discussions with the Neddy Six about the matter.

I asked if the police had ever been brought in before and Jim said they had, once, on a Department of Trade inquiry. I went on, 'What would the exact status of the police be in this capacity? The Ombudsman, who has the duty of reporting on maladministration, is not allowed to see Cabinet papers.'

Jim said, 'I don't know the answer to that.'

'Furthermore,' I said, 'as we all know, Cabinet Ministers do canvass on behalf of each other or canvass each other for support. Are we to disclose to the police the nature of these contacts?'

Jim interrupted me rather brusquely, 'This is about the theft of a document.'

I said, 'Yes, but the question is how far can one discuss the fabric of communication that goes on between Ministers and others in the context of a police inquiry?'

Roy supported me on this. He though it was difficult and dangerous to have the police in because, apart from anything else, the police themselves were leaky. If the police thought they could do some damage to the Government as a result of interrogating Ministers, it is quite likely to appear in an article by Chapman Pincher in the *Daily Express*.

Harold Lever was against. Someone raised the question as to whether we were the right people to discuss a police inquiry because that would be a matter for the Attorney-General acting as such, and not under Cabinet instructions.

Michael Foot said that a prosecution under the Official Secrets Act against *New Society* would be inadvisable because there would be a lot of public support for them. I said I was strongly in favour of open Government and Jim interrupted me to say that my belief in open Government was not the same as this sort of leaking. But it is interesting that on this particular issue there is no clear or identifiable public interest involved, just the embarrassment of Ministers.

David Ennals arrived late because the PM had told him to ask the nine or so people in the DHSS who had seen the document if they handed it over to *New Society* journalists. Jim said he thought that it was likely to have been done by a politically motivated person and that he or she should have the decency to resign. The DHSS has close links with the press and many of these stories seem to appear after discussions with the committee civil servants, or more likely the committee of Ministers.

Friday 18 June

The front page of the *Daily Express* pointed the finger at Michael Meacher who was at the DHSS and whose wife, Molly, is a member of the Child Poverty Action Group. It is a most interesting case because whereas, on the one hand, the actual leak of physical documents is a very serious offence and would make government extremely difficult, on the other hand, there was no reason whatsoever, other than the convenience of Ministers, why the re-examination of the child benefit scheme should have been kept secret at all. Indeed, at the Cabinet, I did suggest that we consult the TUC quite openly about it but Denis Healey said we must not say a word until we were absolutely clear what we wanted to do.

I think public sympathy will lie with the Editor or rather with Frank Field, the Director of CPAG, who admits to having received the documents and written the article. He was quite happy to take the consequences for what he did.

Monday 21 June

The Energy Committee of the Cabinet met at 3, and after it Jim said, 'Come up to my room for a talk.' So I went and he said, 'Tony, I have a real problem on public expenditure. I am sure, indeed I know, that Denis is going to have to ask for huge public expenditure cuts next month – £1 billion, £2 billion, I don't know. How are we going to handle this in a way that doesn't damage the Party? You were very helpful this morning on consultation and so on. We mustn't let it damage the Party.'

I said, 'You may have noticed that in the leadership campaign I didn't criticise the public expenditure cuts, I simply said there should have been consultation, and there should be. But I think if you consult the TUC, you will also have to consult the Executive and the PLP.'

'But it's very difficult to consult the Executive because it's so leaky.'

'Well,' I said, 'tell everybody what you are thinking and then consult whom you like but you will *have* to have a meeting between the NEC and the Cabinet on this. Remember, if you do it, this is what will happen. Some people will say you shouldn't cut at all, others will say you should cut different things, some will say you should raise taxation and others, myself included, will say that you should have a different economic strategy. After that last meeting when I asked for your permission to put in a paper, I commissioned one from Francis Cripps and the draft is brilliant, setting out the arguments.'

'Will you send a personal copy to me?' asked Jim.

I said, 'I know that view won't get through because the Chancellor always wins in the Cabinet.'

'Well, that's not enough for me, I want the Party to come through properly,' Jim replied.

Tuesday 22 June

Big Energy Conference today at Church House and I introduced Jim to Francis Cripps. Jim made a speech which I had written with a couple of paragraphs from Tommy Balogh. I decided to have all the chairmen of the state industries speak first, starting with Arthur Hetherington, then Hawkins, Ezra, John Hill and Hedley Greenborough of the Petroleum Industry Advisory Committee, followed by Frank Chapple of the ETU and then Watkinson of the CBI. The speeches were serious, all the real arguments came out and people sat solidly throughout the day. I played it absolutely cool as a working chairman. Jack Jones made a marvellous speech, indeed the trade union leaders were better than the industrialists and managers – because they go to conferences to persuade people, whereas managers simply do PR exercises or read out papers.

The afternoon session began with fuel poverty. The consumer interest merged into conversation, and at the end Sir Brian Flowers made a most significant statement, saying that a plutonium society and the fast breeder reactor were very serious dangers – that will certainly get world-wide coverage.

Enoch Powell opened the last discussion with a marvellously didactic speech attacking the whole idea of an 'energy policy' and arguing that

Adam Smith would solve all our problems for us. He ended, 'Next, I suppose, we'll have an international Common Market energy policy, though at least, Mr Chairman, you and I could not be held responsible for that!' The speech was of dazzling clarity and force, but although it warned people off bureaucratic sub-committees of sub-committees, it had no relevance.

Today unemployment figures reached a postwar peak.

Wednesday 23 June

I could hardly believe my eyes when I saw in *The Times* 'Acclaim for Benn Move' and in the *FT*, 'Callaghan Opens Benn's Exercise in Open Government'. Marvellous press coverage.

Sir Douglas Allen, the Permanent Secretary at the Civil Service Department, came to see me about the leak inquiry on the child benefit scheme. I said, 'You remember the last time you came to do a leak inquiry was when Harold Wilson asked you to find out how the appointment of Don Ryder as Chairman of the NEB got out. In fact Harold Wilson had told my PPS who was a Back Bencher, Frank McElhone, before he told me.'

He looked a bit shamefaced and said, 'I am trying to piece it together. I have looked at the references in the article and they are taken from Cabinet documents.'

I told him, 'I haven't read the article, to be perfectly honest, and I was only marginally involved.' He showed me bits and related them to the Cabinet papers but they weren't direct quotes. 'I think what has happened is that somebody went through the file and jotted a few things down and then pieced it together for his article.'

I had wondered whether the whole file had been handed over which would be a very serious thing. He said, 'Oh no, I think that's what happened. For example, they made a mistake about a Cabinet meeting on 4 May when in fact it met on 6 May and that rather implies that somebody had just written the dates down wrongly.'

He went on, 'There are a number of possible suspects: somebody who is politically motivated; somebody who cares about child poverty; somebody who wants to wreck the Government, which I doubt; somebody who believes in open government.'

On this last part, I said 'Just think for a moment. If someone believes in open government, they would be unlikely to encourage a clamp down by leaking information.'

Then he said to me, 'I have got to ask you some questions. Did you hand it over?'

'No.'

'What about your advisers?'

'There is very tight security in my office because there was a loss of some Cabinet papers last summer, I think. Besides, anyone who looks at confidential annexes is immediately checked out. My advisers didn't see it and I didn't read the papers very carefully. I joined in the discussion because I was interested in the politics of it but I can't say I took a lot of interest in the scheme.'

'There is another possibility, if you don't think it cheeky of me to ask. Some people keep diaries and we wondered whether anyone had written down notes and handed these over.'

I said, 'I do keep notes and I write a diary of sorts but I do not hand over information nor do I write things down from documents.' He knew perfectly well that it wasn't me but I said, 'You had better talk to my advisers if you have any doubts or anxieties.'

Sunday 27 June

Still boiling hot, I think 95 degrees yesterday. The *Observer* had a piece on the Energy Conference, the first time they've seen any merit in what I have been doing since about 1970.

Went with Bryan Emmett to the Civil Service College at Sunningdale for the BP discussions. It is too complicated to go into detail but I will try and give an impression. The Civil Service College itself, the old Sunningdale Lodge, Ascot, is a great big house with fantastic conference facilities, low buildings with connecting corridors. I was in Room 14, I think, in Bridges House; all the buildings were named after civil servants. We gathered in a spacious, airy conference room with great sliding glass windows looking over to Sunningdale House, and there were the Thames Police walking by making you feel for a moment as if you were a member of the Central Committee of the Communist Party.

I wasn't absolutely sure how to go about such a big negotiation. A marvellous brief had been prepared by my own office covering every possible angle and I decided to talk it through initially. I thanked BP for coming, said I wanted to reach an agreement today, explained our interest which was to get oil in order to get knowledge and to have influence. I understood their difficulties and they were sensitive about the Government relationship.

Monday 28 June

Up at 8, to start at 9.30. We were almost there because the documents had been retyped to take account of what we had said. We almost had a protocol then, near the end, they raised the BP shares issue again and the independence of the company, so I drafted two notes for the record: what they had said to us about the independence and that they want to get rid of the shares, and what I said to them. David Steel said he couldn't even initial the protocol unless there was a reference to these two matters. Frank Kearton said I had actually shaken their confidence by what I had said and I think it is true that I was not going to yield one inch on independence, nor did I intend to give an inch on the shares. In the end they accepted that. By 1.30 it was over, twenty-seven hours of negotiation broken by six hours of sleep.

Tuesday 29 June

At 4.45 I had an interesting meeting on reactors with Sir John Hill, Lord Aldington of the National Nuclear Corporation, Walter Marshall and Norman Franklin of the AEA. They said, 'We want you to announce in September that you are going to go ahead with the fast breeder reactor in two and a half years time and that will give the industry security, and we'll get on with the reference design.'

I asked, 'What's your argument against doing it a bit more slowly? We don't need it in such a hurry.'

Franklin didn't think that would be credible and Walter Marshall said, 'What about the industry? It's the industry that matters.'

I said, 'Quite honestly, Walter, the industry has made no point at all about this. What they would like to know about is the SGHWR which you want to cancel.'

Aldington insisted that the industry would come forward to urge this. 'I saw Weinstock three days ago and his view on all this is changing.'

Hill pointed out that we were going to have the SGHWR three years ago and nothing had really changed. I reminded John Hill that three weeks ago he had told me that, in relation to the SGHWR, everything had changed in the last two years. Now he was saying the opposite. Marshall prattled on about the industry. It was all a load of rubbish.

I felt today, for the first time, that I had interrogated the nuclear lobby to the point where they simply crumbled and couldn't answer the questions, and all this in the presence of officials who are pro-nuclear and pretty sceptical of it all.

Wednesday 30 June

The big news at the moment is the cuts. Albert Booth is worried, so is Peter Shore and the general situation is very gloomy. The Government have got no fight. We are just lying down and letting the Tories walk all over us.

Today a message came through pointing out that I hadn't signed the undertaking on ministerial memoirs. So I drafted a little letter from my PS to go to Number 10 saying, 'I have informed the Secretary of State, who is not ready to sign the declaration ...' and I'll see what happens. I am not going to state that I will not at some future time give an account of my experiences without checking it with the Cabinet

Secretariat; it is absolute hypocrisy. You read in the papers every day what the public expenditure cuts are going to be, leaked by the Treasury, and then I'm told I can't describe my own experiences.

Thursday 1 July

Cabinet at 10.30 and Jim started off. 'I think I should report that with regard to the leak, Sir Douglas Allen, as you might expect, has not found the culprit. He thinks it possible that the documents themselves were not leaked but that somebody wrote down points from them and gave them to Frank Field. The Attorney-General has told me he has decided not to prosecute Frank Field or *New Society* and I have decided to call the police in.'

There was some discussion about this and Peter Shore queried why *New Society* was given immunity. But I plucked up courage and said, 'Look, if it's true that no documents were passed, that's one thing, and means we're back to the old routine about information passing. But as far as the police are concerned, I really must raise the point again that if the police come and interview Cabinet Ministers, what are we to say? We are bound by our Privy Councillors' Oath not to repeat anything that happens in Cabinet and presumably the police won't see Cabinet documents. I don't want to be put in the position of having to say I won't answer a question, but there are circumstances in which I think it would be wrong to answer. In America during the McCarthy period people declared, under the Fifth Amendment, "We are not required to answer that question" and they were described as Fifth Amendment Communists. We can't get into that position. As Jim and Roy Jenkins said last week, the police themselves are very leaky and it would come out that a certain Minister refused to answer questions. I am sorry but this seems to me to be a very important constitutional principle.'

'Tony can surround himself with a battery of lawyers if he likes,' said Jim.

I added, 'I hope nobody thinks that as I have raised this I am involved, because I am not.'

Elwyn Jones said, half jokingly, 'I assume that Tony Benn is raising it as a matter of high principle.' But though there were one or two nods, nobody spoke in my support. Still, I have registered it and if it goes wrong, as I think it will, it is on the record.

I had a quick word with Roy Jenkins and Michael Foot and said we were under pressure again about memoirs. Roy suggested leaving it over the weekend until the week had subsided and Michael agreed, so I pulled back the note I had drafted.

Lunch with John Boyd, General Secretary of the AUEW. We talked about Scottish nationalism and racialism. He said, 'Our people are very worried. There is no doubt the Labour Party in the Commons hasn't got its feet on the ground. We have *got* to limit the number of immigrants, partly because of employment and partly because of colour.'

'That worries me a bit,' I said, 'because I remember Mosley before the war, and with him it was the Jews, the Irish, the Catholics you know.'

'Ah, yes, but this is colour. I go to coloured people's houses and the smell is terrible. I don't like comparing the situation to the Jews.' He proceeded to tell a horrible anti-semitic joke. I got the measure of Johnny Boyd. He told me how he was controlling the research department, taking control of the union's journal, tightening up on cash and of course entirely pro-Treasury. Entirely right wing on race. Very unattractive.

Friday 2 July

Economic Strategy Committee at Number 10 to consider the economic situation. Denis had not put a paper in and Jim asked him to talk through the matter. Frances and Francis had written a paper in consultation with me so I was in the curious position of having pre-empted the Treasury, though actually the Treasury had leaked the whole thing in Monday's *Evening Standard*.

Denis gave his introduction and in the present situation I didn't feel I could take notes. He gave a general review about confidence and how the pound could drop, all the usual arguments that are used to persuade you to give up what you want.

Jim said to me, 'I have read your paper in which you say we should try to agree financial and monetary targets with the IMF. What does that really mean? I think they would demand things that we wouldn't be prepared to yield to them. Also, I don't like the use of the word "panic". There will be no panic cuts.'

I looked through my paper and there was no reference to panic cuts so I said, 'First of all, PM, I don't think the word panic is there because I wouldn't have put it in. The paper is bound to be cock-shy because a Secretary of State without resources can't easily move with confidence into this area of economic policy; I recognise there is a real problem and I want to break that problem down. There is tremendous political pressure to force us to cut. The Shadow Chancellor, Geoffrey Howe and the market are working together to force us to do it.

'There is also the other side of the political problem. There is the support we have in the Party and in the TUC who are told that wages are the cause of our problems, and who have held down wages and cut living standards. Then it was all supposedly due to strikes so the strikes have gone. Then we say all the awful things we did last year were intended to save jobs, but unemployment has risen. Or they were to save public expenditure but that's been cut. I think the important thing about public expenditure, apart from what we do, is our attitude to it. If we lend ourselves to the argument that public expenditure is undesirable, it will have a bad psychological effect.

'The argument on the PSBR simply isn't valid because the way to reduce the PSBR, perhaps even eliminate it, is to get economic growth. If these cuts increase unemployment, they will limit growth and in turn slow down any reduction in the PSBR. Those cash limits do involve putting a noose around our necks, particularly the big spenders, and when we kick the ladder away these guys will really be left in difficulties.

'Finally, there is the industrial argument. It is not credible to say that a great boom is raging in our society. We are at the bottom of a slump. The idea that you have got to cut to make room is incredible. As far as confidence is concerned, it is a very subtle thing; the monetary system doesn't want to see our pound attacked because it will weaken the whole system. On the other hand it is a threat. The three issues set out in my paper are: is there room for manoeuvre? What is our own judgment? What other remedies are there? The real solution should be to go to the IMF and to sell them the validity of our policy, get them to agree.'

Crosland said we were stronger than we thought, the pound was undervalued, we had the Social Contract and the alternative was deflation.

Then Roy Jenkins spoke. 'I must say one thing about Tony Benn's paper. When I read it, I didn't notice it was a Department of Energy paper or that it had AWB at the end, and I thought what a beautifully written paper it was, setting out the choices so clearly. I thought it was the Chancellor's paper. Then I decided I didn't agree with it and I realised it was from Tony and not from Denis.'

Harold supported Denis and Michael Foot warned about unemployment and its impact. Not a very deep speech but helpful.

I told the meeting that my paper emphasised that the survival of the Government depended on the maintenance of a relationship of confidence both with the TUC and the IMF. Whether we talked to the IMF or not, we still had to enjoy their confidence. We were talking about a tripartite relationship in which the task of statesmanship was to bring the TUC and the IMF together.

It was a very good day really. I felt I was big enough to be Chancellor of the Exchequer. I don't know why because I have never wanted the job and I don't want it now, but hearing all these wise people didn't impress me.

Went back to the office and signed a few papers. Talked to Bryan Emmett about the police investigation of the leak. Had they come in and asked for Cabinet papers? Had they asked for my fingerprints? It was impossible to work if one was under suspicion. He said he would not allow them to see Cabinet papers but assumed he would get guidance from the Cabinet Office about what they could and couldn't see.

Monday 5 July

To see Elwyn Jones, the Lord Chancellor, at 11.15. I told him that I believed a most dangerous precedent was being created. Yesterday, the *Sunday Express* said that MI5 was being brought in to look at the whole question of leaks from Government. I told Elwyn I had seriously contemplated inviting Hailsham to come and sit with me, as a constitutional lawyer, not because I was guilty or responsible for what had happened but, being one of only seven Ministers interviewed by Sir Douglas Allen, I felt I was suspected. I had discovered this by getting Bryan Emmett to ring up the Civil Service Department. Stan Orme, who is Minister of State at the DHSS, had not himself been interviewed.

Elwyn said there was nothing in it at all, it was just a discreet inquiry and I was 'creating tigers in the path'.

I said the question was whether I was a suspect, in which case I should be suspended from duty, or whether I was a witness in which case I would be expected to give the police information about everything, who talks to whom, fingerprints checks, etc. I wasn't prepared to tell the police what went on at Cabinet or show them any documents or notes that I may have made. I said I did write a diary – lots of people did – but I didn't intend to publish it. The police themselves were very leaky.

Elwyn agreed with that because a judge friend of his was breathalysed in Hyde Park and it was in the papers the following day. 'That's what would happen,' I said. 'They'll come in and find that not everyone will answer questions and then there'll be leaks that the police couldn't get on with the job because Ministers were not prepared to disclose what went on.' He agreed to have a word with the Attorney-General about it and I said if he were to conduct the inquiry I'd have no objections, but if the police were called in, we wouldn't control the ground rules. He said he'd possibly have a word with Jim and find out whether MI5 had been brought in.

I told him I had nothing to hide, but I cared very much about the principles of preserving the confidentiality and trust that existed within the Cabinet. I may have overdone it to Elwyn but I think I'm right.

Frances and Francis are worried but they think Jim Callaghan is stopping leaks by terrorising people, and that is true. It is effective in the sense that it makes everybody much more careful, but at a very high price.

Tuesday 6 July

Cabinet spent three hours or more discussing the papers that had been submitted by Denis Healey and Joel Barnett calling for a cut of £1.25 billion in public expenditure to produce a cut in the PSBR to £11 billion; and secondly, calling for the abolition of the contingency fund by reabsorbing all the extra bids back into the main programme and making cuts elsewhere.

I had two briefs with me, one from the Department resisting what was being suggested, and the other – an excellent paper from Francis Cripps arguing his case even more strongly and effectively on general economic grounds – linked to the paper at last Friday's Committee. I was therefore in the formidable position of being the only other Cabinet Minister with a view to put before the Cabinet.

We sat round the table in our shirtsleeves on a very hot July day and it reminded me of my first meeting as a full Cabinet Minister ten years ago when we were in exactly the same position.

Jim began by saying that it was a very difficult decision that we were called upon to take. Fortunately, he said, there had been no leaks (which was untrue because the Treasury had been pumping out briefings for two or three weeks, and even Jim himself had been broadly hinting at it).

Denis presented his paper, describing the problem of confidence, playing down the resource argument a little, still making a strong case. He said that it would be fatal to go to the IMF unless we had decided what we wanted to do in advance, which would have to be what they wanted us to do.

I said that it was very difficult for a non-Treasury Minister to write an economic policy paper. I hadn't had the thinking of the Treasury at my disposal, and only had the *Evening Standard* for last Monday which said that the Chancellor was asking for £1 billion cuts, which by a fortunate coincidence turned out to be right.

I made it absolutely clear that I was strongly opposed to the cuts proposed, and to the methods adopted to secure them, namely by briefing the press. I did not agree with the reasons advanced for the cuts, and I opposed the pressure which would guarantee that the Chancellor would win, because once his reputation was linked to a particular demand for cuts when the pound was weak, it would inflict the maximum damage on confidence if he didn't get everything he'd asked for.

I pointed out that the size of the cuts demanded was much bigger than it appeared – £1.25 billion, plus £1.6 billion that would flow from absorbing the claims on the contingency fund into the main programme – nearly £3 billion of cuts. I didn't want to worry the Cabinet at the moment with my departmental arguments but the damage would be irreparable to our policy on oil and other areas. If we did have to make economies, they should be done on a different basis.

My alternative was as follows: there should be a normal timetable for public expenditure surveys, preliminary discussion now and the rest in November; that we should prepare contingency plans to restrict imports to allow us to re-equip our industrial capacity but not import masses of consumer goods; that we should increase the tax on imported goods, such as oil, alcohol and tobacco; that we should provide a means by which the investment generated by higher profits could be got back selectively into manufacturing industry, which had never happened before and for which there was currently no guarantee that it would happen in the future.

I concluded that we were in a much stronger position than we realised. The IMF did not want speculation against the pound. They did not want to see the Social Contract break down because they knew that if we were replaced by a Government that couldn't handle the trade union movement then Britain would become a serious threat to the international monetary system.

Roy Jenkins said he had read my paper with great care and though it was well argued, he didn't agree with the conclusions. He thought it would be fatal if we drifted through into the autumn with the possibility of a sterling crisis and panic action. He agreed with Jim.

Denis said that the IMF would never agree to discuss things unless we settled our view. Harold Lever strongly supported him.

Michael Foot came out against the cuts but didn't agree with me that we should go to the IMF. He was in favour of a mix of packages.

After everyone had contributed, Jim summed up by saying there was a majority for the cuts. So he suggested bilateral talks between various Ministers to sort it all out, and we would consult with the Neddy Six and the PLP.

Wednesday 7 July

To see Elwyn Jones at his request. He said he had spoken to the Attorney-General and the police had been given strict instructions. Commissioner Habershon of the anti-terrorist squad had been put in charge of the investigation and he didn't think there'd be any difficulty. He didn't think I should have anyone with me. They know how strongly I feel at least.

One final note. Cyril Plant [Chairman of the TUC] told me at a dinner last night that a few weeks ago, Mrs Thatcher had asked him to dinner with Jim Prior. In the course of the dinner, Mrs Thatcher had said to him, 'You don't like me, do you?' Cyril Plant said, 'No, I don't.' So she asked him why and he said he didn't know what she was going to do if she won the Election. So she said they hadn't made up their minds yet, they were still thinking about it.

Thursday 8 July

This afternoon, Jim Callaghan was asked in the Chamber by Margaret Thatcher whether in order to prove his commitment to the profit motive and free enterprise, he would drop his Secretary of State for Energy who within a few hours of the NEDC meeting yesterday had made a speech calling for the extension of public ownership. Jim said he had not read the speech but he was sure that his Right Honourable friend had made a speech with his usual common sense.

Friday 9 July

Had lunch at St Stephen's Restaurant with Leo Pliatzky, who is now the Deputy-Secretary at the Treasury in charge of public expenditure. He's a contemporary of Tony Crosland and Roy Jenkins.

We talked about public expenditure and he sees himself as one of the really tough officials who keeps Ministers on the straight and narrow. The factors which had influenced the Treasury to go for public expenditure cuts were first that the Governor of the Bank of England had been in two or three times in June and demanded £3 billion's worth of cuts immediately, and second, that the Treasury was deeply wounded by the general charge that public expenditure was out of control. It was probably true when Tony Barber was there but certainly not now, because the cash limits are a noose round everybody's neck.

These two factors had burned very much into his mind and he had concluded that it was necessary to make the cuts. He was satisfied with the way in which Ministers were approaching their task as laid down by the Treasury. He said the whole Establishment in Britain realised that the maintenance in power of a Labour Government was the only hope, by which he meant that only a Labour Government could implement Tory policies.

Saturday 10 July

To Stansgate. Still unbelievably hot. It's been in the eighties or nineties for about a month now and the grass is absolutely brown, like Cincinnati grass.

Monday 12 July

Lunch at 12.45 with Norman Atkinson, Alan Fisher and Bernard Dix of NUPE and Reg Race whom I knew years ago as a student. We talked about the cuts and I encouraged NUPE not to fight as a poor public sector union but to point out to the production unions – the TGWU and the AUEW – that any cuts in the public sector would be bound to affect them. I think they took it on board.

Wednesday 14 July

My first appointment was with Dunster and Gausden, the Nuclear Inspectors from the HSE, about the fast breeder. They told me that past experience was no help in considering the safety aspects of the fast breeder. Sodium cooled systems were different from gas cooled ones, and plutonium, which was dependent on sodium cooled systems, raised special problems. There were two basic safety issues. One was the mechanism of a whole core accident which might derive from an escalating sub-assembly accident, perhaps a local blockage of fuel, though the Americans and the French were less concerned about this. As to a whole core accident itself, the core would disintegrate, melt and vaporise or collapse and perhaps explode the reactor, and the whole core would be released into the containment which could fracture; there was no agreement about the extent of the release of energy into the atmosphere, nobody could calculate it. I asked why they hadn't tested it at a nuclear testing ground. They said, 'The United States was to have tested the energy release but they found it too expensive, and then their fast breeder programmes were set back.'

'How many people would die?'

'Thousands would die over ten to twenty years, as well as those killed in the explosion.' They did say, however, that the commercial fast breeder reactor is licensable subject to conditions. After a long discussion I came up with the idea I would send them questions and publish their replies, and they were quite taken with that.

Went to the PLP meeting where Barbara made a marvellous speech. She said there was no fat left in public expenditure, they had got to the bottom of the barrel. The alternative to capitulating was import controls, temporary mobilisation of overseas assets and a fundamental change of policy.

Eric Heffer welcomed Barbara's conversion to Party policy and said that 'some of us' had felt it even before they were reshuffled out of the Government (a cruel jibe at Barbara).

Thursday 15 July

Cabinet at 9.30. On public expenditure, the main item on the agenda, Jim said, 'We have got to decide today what to do.' Denis then outlined his objective, to reduce the PSBR to £9 billion by 1977/8, to reduce money supply by 10 per cent and the domestic credit expansion to £8 billion.

There were two general papers, one from Peter Shore and one from me. Peter was called first and he said tax was the right solution, and he warned of the terrible dangers of making cuts in his particular field.

He rambled a bit. I must say I am lucky in having Frances and Francis, I do sound more coherent when I am called.

I said, 'I take it I am allowed to speak my mind; I don't want to put a departmental view. I welcome the discussion we have had for two reasons. First of all, it has brought the arguments out into the open before the decision has been made, and if the Cabinet insists on cuts you could argue that it has also prepared the public for what is to be done. The real argument is about foreign confidence. That is extremely dangerous because it is open ended. The IMF is in a position to press anything on us once we accept the confidence argument and there will be no end to it. It's the psychology of capitulation, that when you are faced with pressure, you capitulate. This is going to have very important effects because what we are saying to the British public is that it's all their fault.

'I adhere to my own view that we should fight for our own people. We have a very powerful position with the IMF. We should seek all practicable savings or tax additions that would help us with the current position. We should adopt import controls because what is happening is that our manufacturing base has shrunk and there is nothing in this which will allow it to grow as it should behind a wall of protection. And we should have compulsory planning agreements to see that investment occurs.

'Prime Minister, I think the Treasury have won the battle and lost the war because they will never ever be able to come back and argue this again; the Cabinet won't have it, the movement won't have it, the Party won't have it, the unions won't have it and the public won't have it. Can I finish with one point which I put without offence or discourtesy. I think that the British Establishment is now infected with the same spirit which afflicted France in 1940, the Vichy spirit of complete capitulation and defeatism. It is that which is going finally to destroy us. I hope nobody will take this as being offensive but my Privy Councillor's oath requires me to disclose my opinions in the Council and this is what I have done.'

Denis sat there scarlet. He always blushes when he is in difficulty and the argument is gaining force. A year ago, I was alone and now I am in a minority of five or six.

Michael Foot thought we should work it out with the TUC, that we should not accept the cuts, that the Government was now compounding the offence of the NEC which had ruptured the Social Contract and therefore, just as the TUC leaders before had been angry with the Executive, so they would now be angry with the Government. He was against going to the IMF and he warned the Cabinet not to strain the loyalty of the movement.

Jim Callaghan said, 'May I say one word about the alternative strategy? In my opinion, it would have the same public expenditure implications and therefore there would be nothing in it from a public expenditure point of view. Things have gone too far. I hope that Tony will stay with us but that is a matter for him, and if there is a later change of policy, then at least he can say "I told you so".'

After further discussion Jim Callaghan said, 'We must now move to a decision. Is it agreed that we exclude making cuts in social security benefits – because I think that would be impossible.' That was agreed. 'Is is agreed that we exclude cuts in overseas aid – because I think that would be very unpopular.' I think the report in the *Observer* that Reg Prentice might resign over such cuts had influenced him. So that went through, 'Right, let's take them section by section.'

During the ensuing allocation of cuts, Jim passed me a note asking me to see him this evening about the NEC and other things. I went over at 5.15.

'I understand you were quite helpful on the NEC,' he said.

I thought the right thing was to hold a joint NEC-Cabinet meeting. Jim said, 'The time is difficult. I want to announce these cuts on Wednesday before the TUC-Labour Party Liaison Committee meets. Otherwise you are asking them to buy a pig in a poke and then later they discover what you are doing. To come to the main point, at the NEC meeting on Wednesday week there will be a resolution criticising the Government for its policy and I am afraid that if you vote against the Government, you will have to leave the Government.'

I said, 'I appreciate that and I shan't go by accident from this Government – I would come and talk to you about it very carefully. There are two things I must make clear; one is that, just as Denis Healey anticipated a Cabinet decision and went out and campaigned for a particular solution – the £1 billion cuts – and has won, those who fought against it and lost but are prepared to accept it, must be allowed to make it clear that they have lost. I don't want to be a man on a white horse having fought bravely, but I think it must be an open discussion retrospectively and that must be made clear at the Executive.

'Secondly, my local Party who have been in favour of my staying in the Government and slogging it out have passed a resolution calling on me to criticise and attack the cuts. I have asked for a special meeting next Friday and I must be free to tell them frankly what has happened. If they do decide that I should leave the Cabinet, that would weigh heavily with me because quite frankly the only way I can square my continued membership in the Cabinet and support of this Government is the belief that opinion is shifting and that there will be a change in the policy.'

'You have been most constructive and most helpful and I appreciate it,' said Jim.

'It has been a pleasure to work with you, Jim, I won't deny it.'

Had a talk to Peter Shore, who said to me, 'Do you know, I would either like to be entirely free of responsibilities or Prime Minister.'

'I feel rather the same,' I replied, 'but as my ambition is to be Leader of the Party, it is not incompatible with your being Prime Minister!'

He said, 'I would also like to be Foreign Secretary because so much could be done. If only this country would mobilise all its assets, its defence assets, its oil assets which you are trying to get hold of, its goodwill assets, it could do so much.' I agree. I get crabby with Peter in my diary from time to time but I like him enormously.

Sunday 18 July

Frances rang me up to discuss today's *Observer*'s absolutely accurate account of my position leading the fight against the Treasury policy. The *Sunday Telegraph* says, 'Callaghan May Let Shore and Benn Quit' and then the old story about how I couldn't wear two hats at once, and so on.

Herbert Rogers rang to say that the local Party will want me to speak out against the cuts; but if I were to attack a Cabinet decision I would be fired and I have to decide whether it is helpful to be fired. The case for staying in is threefold: the unity of the Government; not getting the responsibility for the defeat of the Government; not paving the way for a coalition Government. Why should one want to stay in the Government? Because it is opening the way to trade union power, because the argument is being won and because the future policy is good. The case for coming out is that one would be able to mobilise some of the support for a change in policy.

Watched the Peter Jay interview with Professor Milton Friedman of the University of Chicago explaining monetarism, capitalism and the market economy. I listened intently because he is the main guru of the Right and I did find his arguments, the theory he had developed of a society free of coercion (when it is absolutely coercive in its character), surprisingly easy to counter. I felt as if one was living in a completely pre-socialist age; the contribution that Karl Marx has made to our thinking does enable one to see through that sort of argument very simply.

Monday 19 July

Went over to the Treasury at 6 for the meeting that had been arranged between the Home Policy Committee and the Chancellor. There had been various rumours that I wouldn't go. I was a little nervous. I led the way into the Chancellor's office, sat at the opposite end of the table and said, 'First of all, I would like to thank you very much for receiving us, Denis, and we would appreciate it very much if you would make an opening statement.'

'Well,' said Denis, 'you gave me a paper: I think you should introduce it.' That was a paper Geoff Bish had prepared for Home Policy, and it would be very embarrassing for me to introduce a critical paper, as Denis well knew. So I said, 'I think the paper speaks for itself and perhaps we could just ask questions. The paper was agreed by the Home Policy Committee as a basis for discussion.'

After a lot of questions, Barbara Castle asked, 'What has changed since February to justify a £1 billion cut now? We don't think you are being honest with us, Denis. Michael Stewart, the economist, estimates that the PSBR will fall.'

'I would not recommend this package if I thought it would create more unemployment than the alternative. The Cabinet and the NEC had a long discussion about import controls quite recently,' said Denis. He had to leave at 7 so after about fifty minutes I thanked him and said it was unprecedented for a Cabinet Minister to receive a Committee in advance of a decision being made by the Cabinet, and I thought everybody would recognise the value of that.

Wednesday 21 July

I didn't get to sleep till 4 am and woke up two minutes before 10, when the Cabinet was due to start. When I got to Number 10, they were already on public expenditure; I gave no apology or explanation. It was an awful thing to do.

There was a further trawl for cuts and Tony Crosland said he thought there should be more cuts in education. I said the people in the education world were very angry and worried that £25 million a year was spent by the Foreign Office and the Ministry of Defence on financing public school places for diplomats' and army officers' children; and local authorities spend another £25 million sending them to public schools.

Fred Mulley passed me a little note saying my counter-attack on the FO would have commanded the admiration of Cromwell's Levellers, which was nice of him. I felt I had done it for Caroline.

Crosland then launched into a great attack on how many long-haired social workers there were. It was disgusting.

We sat till nearly 1. At the end the Prime Minister said, 'Though I have supported the Chancellor all along, I feel we shouldn't go above £954 million.' He said we'd have a paper at this afternoon's session from the Chancellor containing something which he thought was attractive and colleagues might like to look at. I knew what that was — a national insurance contribution by employers.

At 3.20 Frances and Francis came in; they'd read the Chancellor paper and drafted a response. Denis wants another £1 billion on the national insurance contribution. I looked at the draft and, taking their arguments, I rewrote it.

Cabinet again at 5.30 and I had dropped off my paper into Jim's room to give him a chance to read it. He opened, 'I think we ought to look at Denis's paper, and Tony has circulated another paper.'

I said, 'Not without your permission – but may I circulate it?' He said Yes and I passed it around the table.

Denis said we had to do yet more. We didn't want to come back and he couldn't even guarantee this would work.

When Jim introduced my paper he said, 'I must say that it appears to me to go over old ground – a complete alternative strategy which is quite unacceptable to us. It can't be discussed. I don't see why you wrote it.'

He was implying that it was my resignation speech, so I said, 'Well PM, the Chancellor's paper only came in over lunch. I wrote this in a hurry and had it typed up. I won't go on to the alternatives but just analyse Denis's new paper. The object is to warn the Cabinet that we're taking on something of enormous magnitude without any discussion. The new £1 billion will have a double deflationary effect. It will be £2 billion of deflation. It involves a new undiscussed strategy which pre-empts many policy issues that would arise between now and the end of the Parliament. There's no assurance that it will succeed. It came at the last moment and there was no warning.

'Before agreeing, the Cabinet should consider the effect on the TUC and the Party of getting this with no warning, and within forty-eight hours of the announcement of the highest unemployment figures since the war. The Chancellor is creating a siege economy which will mean a semi-permanent slump with 1.5 to 2 million unemployed, and no hope of changing it before the Election.

'It runs absolutely counter to the Manifesto policy, counter to the diluted industrial policy put to Chequers and endorsed at NEDC. I won't argue the alternatives set out here, but the harder the present policy gets, the more attractive the alternative becomes. It's a very tough choice, we're adopting a defensive posture, we're sending people out to find those to whom we could surrender.'

Jim was very crabby about it all, repeating that I ought to be glad if it went wrong because it would prove me right.

I came upstairs absolutely dazed and stunned by the magnitude of the deflation that had been undertaken. There was a vote at 7.30 and just as I was going into the Lobby about ten minutes after the Cabinet had adjourned, I saw Jim and went up to him.

'Jim, I was going to write you a note because I am thinking a lot about you. The Treasury wrecked your reputation in 1964–7 and then

Harold threw you into a war with the unions on "In Place of Strife".'

'And you think they are doing it again?'

'Yes,' I said, 'I honestly do, but I feel very much for you and shall not do anything without telling you first.'

'Well, I have great confidence in you. The Treasury are angry about your Energy Commission but I have told them that I have great confidence in Mr Benn's common sense. He must be supported.'

Thursday 22 July

I went over and heard Denis's statement. Jim told me I was to sit on the Front Bench, so I did. I suppose it looked as if I was sunk in gloom but, in fact, I was sound asleep and I didn't hear any of the Questions or Answers.

But the statement was apparently received in the House without any explosions of rage. The Left had been hypnotised by the discussion and the Tories congratulated Denis warmly on what he'd done.

Friday 23 July

Overslept again this morning and I must say unless I get more rest, I shall be no use to anybody over the coming weeks.

Ron Vaughan drove me to the Administrative Staff College at Henley and at 11.15 I went in to address their course on the relations between government and industry. At about 12, just as I was answering questions, a man came in and told me the Prime Minister was on the phone. I asked to be excused and went to the office. Jim said, 'Tony, I have been reading your statement to your local General Management Committee tomorrow night and I am taking a much harder line than I did yesterday. I had only had a quick chance to look at it.'

'Well,' I said, 'I have made all the amendments you suggested.'

'Yes, but you must no longer assume even if you put out the amended statement that I am prepared to keep you in the Government. I shall be very sorry, but . . .'

I said, 'If you decide to do that, it is a matter entirely for you and I shall continue to give you support. Thank you very much for telling me.' And I rang off.

I went straight back to the meeting and managed to continue the discussion. Then I was taken to Reading and all the way in the train from Reading to Bristol I thought about what Jim had said. There could not be a more reasonable statement than the one I had made after including the amendments he had suggested. If he fired me on that basis, at least I would be on the strongest possible grounds of having offered to stay in the Government and support it provided the debate continued. It would be a powerful position to be in.

The other thing I realised is that although you can go along with

Jim so far, and I have tried very hard to go along with him, he is in fact a hard-line right winger, which I have always known, and will not tolerate dissent. It was better to know how things stood and be thrown out.

My surgery was in an old rambling vicarage in Windmill Hill with a succession of tragic cases, all of which could only be helped with higher public expenditure and I felt, as I always do, very exposed to the reality of life as compared to sitting in the Cabinet and trading off cuts to please the bankers. It really is no basis whatever for a Labour Government. Finally I met the Windmill Ward Party who have been brought together by this young couple, Mike and Dawn Primarolo* who are real fireballs.

I was taken from there to the GMC and Cyril Langham was in the chair. Herbert Rogers, quite wrongly, had invited other friends from the area to come in. I always feel suspicious when there are people from outside the Bristol Party, partly because I suspect that Herbert is stacking the cards in his favour, and partly because I'm never absolutely sure that some police spy won't have entered.

I reported what had happened and I went back to the Manifesto and the shift in 1974–5 after the Referendum. I described the cuts and the fight in the Cabinet and said that I had been defeated but that I felt it was right to stay in and fight.

When I sat down there was universal criticism of the cuts. Bryan Beckingham said what was needed was leadership. A young shop steward representing the dustmen in Bristol said that people were asking, 'Where's your Tony Benn now? What sort of a battle is there now?' Bob Glendinning, an old right-wing doctor, who is pro-Common Market, slightly shocked me when he said, 'I am not in the Labour Party to see the whole thing destroyed.' It was a tremendous attack. Nobody had a good word to say for the Government.

At about 9.15, Cyril suggested I sum up but they all wanted more discussion and I was quite happy to go on. At the end, I suggested another meeting next Friday and I shall bring Caroline down and consider very carefully what to do then.

Sunday 25 July

David Owen, Minister of Health in David Ennals's department, said to me that he had been to the *Guardian* to meet the staff, as I had, and they had been struck by the similarity between what he said to them and what I had said. I'd be surprised by that because he is a pro-

---

* Subsequently elected Labour MP for Bristol South, June 1987.

Marketeer and considered a moderate, but it was an indication of his desire to be friendly.

Monday 26 July

My first engagement was with the TUC-Labour Party Liaison Committee at Transport House at 10.30. As I went in, I had a word with Len Murray, who looks much better now, after his heart attack. The full phalanx of people were assembled: the TUC General Council, the Neddy Six, the relevant Ministers – Jim, Denis, Michael, Albert, myself and Edmund – and the Executive figures: Judith, Barbara and Mikardo. A formidable group, but not a peep of protest whatever from the TUC about the cuts, and that indicated the true political position. Jim scored his triumph.

At 6.45 I went to see Jim and I spent an hour with him. He asked me how I got on in Bristol.

'I'll tell you quite honestly,' I replied. 'Last year, when I went down, all but two members of the GMC thought I should stay in and slog it out, and last Friday, all but about two thought I should come out. I've never seen them so angry. A pro-Market, right-wing doctor, for example, who is on the education committee, was extremely bitter and said this wasn't what he joined the Labour Party for.'

I said I didn't put out the statement because I couldn't have carried the local Party on a proposal that I stay in. I said I was staying because I wanted the Government to survive; and I was assuming that he didn't want to get rid of me and that we understood each other's position. The problem of survival over the next few months was a very serious one but I was encouraged by what he said about never again conceding to the bankers. I hoped there would be a change.

'You mean you're hoping that the present policy will fail?' Jim said.

'No,' I replied, 'but I'm hoping you will decide to change it. My paper is really a political paper setting out my assessment of the risks and what we might do.'

He said, 'I am looking at the four points you have made very carefully, and I have asked Denis to look at import controls and deposits. I want you to keep this absolutely to yourself, I don't even want you to tell your advisers, but I have told you this because we must be ready for next time if it happens. I ask you only to be patient.'

We came on to the National Executive and I said that there would be a motion from Eric Heffer calling on the Government to adopt the alternative strategy, saying the cuts will not bring about a transfer of resources or boost confidence, but will alienate the Party and produce unemployment. I said I fully accepted that I couldn't support it but nor did I want to vote against it since it was the view that I had been urging in the Cabinet over the last three weeks. So I'd like to abstain.

Jim refused, saying I had to vote against it. I said that in that case I might not go to the Executive. He then recommended I say that the rules of collective responsibility required me to vote against it, thus providing me with a way back from the edge. But I can't say I didn't worry myself sick over the wretched thing for the rest of the day.

'You know, Jim, the Party is going to go to the Left now. In a slump, the Government holds the line, the TUC defends its membership, and defends the Government, and the Party has the job of looking ahead and going back to fundamentals and trying to get them changed.'

He replied, 'What I object to is the Party trying to tell the Government what to do. Perhaps you disagree?'

'May I give you my view?'

'Please do.'

'I think one of the problems is that the Treasury is much too powerful. It is a giant Department and it has gobbled up every chairmanship and function. It is monetarist in its thinking and it is surrounded by pygmy Departments – not pygmy Ministers. Employment is nothing now the Advisory, Conciliation and Arbitration Service ACAS has gone, Trade is nothing because of the Common Market, Industry is a nuts-and-bolts Department, Energy is important but it hasn't anything like enough strength, Prices and Consumer Protection is too narrow. You really must have a much more powerful industrial Department.'

Jim said he didn't believe in changing Departments, and I agreed but I said at least he should have a Cabinet committee – not under Treasury chairmanship – to look at industrial policy.

Had dinner with Stan Orme and he said, 'You know, you're destroying your credibility by trying to wear two hats at once.' Very blunt. 'You're painting yourself into a corner just like Denis did over the cuts. But don't resign.'

Dick Mabon came in to my room and said, 'I hope you'll still be Secretary for Energy on Wednesday.' Then Ted Fletcher, the MP for Darlington, came up to me in the lobby. He held me by the arm and said, 'Don't forget there are people who are not in the Tribune Group ...' I said I wasn't in it myself. He told me I had a lot to offer and I should not quit.

I came home and talked to Ron Vaughan. I tell him everything. It is a day when politics was perfectly bloody and I have a thumping headache.

Tuesday 27 July

Working at home. I decided to ring Herbert Rogers and Cyril Langham. Cyril said it would be very difficult to explain if I voted for the cuts, but if I abstained or kept away from the NEC it would be understood, and he said he would defend me. I must say, listening to

Herbert Rogers, who is over eighty, and Cyril Langham, a seventy-year-old retired head postman, was very comforting. I've never actually consulted as closely as that. It settled my mind.

I told Joan Lestor, Joan Maynard, Eric Heffer, Ian Mikardo, Norman Atkinson and Stan Orme my decision, and when I found Michael Foot in the lobby, said, 'Michael, it's either vote for the cuts or leave the Government, so I have decided not to attend tomorrow.'

It's now 12.30. Looking back on the day, I see that I am a collective animal and I mustn't operate on my own. I need time to think and consult and talk to people.

Wednesday 28 July

I left home at about 9.40, having rung Ron Hayward to make my apologies for the NEC. I got to the Department just after 10 and the phone began ringing almost at once with lobby correspondents who had heard I wasn't attending the Executive. I called Bernard in and told him the story.

In fact the Executive met from 10 till nearly 2. Frank Allaun moved a motion to reject the Social Contract and then he withdrew it. Mikardo moved a motion noting certain divergences between the Social Contract and Labour's Programme. This was defeated 13 to 11. The Social Contract itself was approved by 13 to 7, with four abstentions. The Heffer motion followed and was carried by 13 to 7 after some Ministers had left. The motion to nationalise the banks was carried by 17 to 3.

I had a report from Bryan Emmett saying that a low level lobby source had suggested that the PM had not taken my absence as defiance.

I went for a meal with Joe Ashton who is very uneasy at the moment. I think he thinks I should have resigned, that I made a cock-up of it. He's hearing all the criticisms of the Left, and Heffer is criticising me, according to Peter Shore. But the more I think about it, the more I realise that if you are to go on living with yourself, you can't go round feeling guilty all the time. Eric Heffer will be voting for the cuts in the Lobby next month, and that's no different from my not attending the NEC.

Thursday 29 July

'Wedgie Dives Clear', 'Tony Nosedives to Safety': the papers were awful but I'll have to live with it.

I visited three desperately sick MPs who had been brought in for the vote on the Aircraft and Shipbuilding Bill. Alex Lyon, the MP for York, looked as if he was about to die – old, thin and weak; Frank McElhone was flat on his back on a stretcher in a massive spinal carriage with Helen beside him; and Alec Jones from Rhondda was recovering from a serious coronary. Sir Alfred Broughton from Batley and Morley was brought in on a respirator. It is quite criminal but we needed those votes to win.

Michael Meacher told me that he had been interviewed by the police on the child benefit leak and not only that but the police had gone to his home to interview his wife, Molly. Then, horror of horrors, some Cabinet Ministers were apparently fingerprinted by the police.

Yesterday at a meeting, David Owen, for a joke, said he was responsible and he felt the time had come to own up; this was reported to Pat Healy of *The Times* and she was just ringing *The Times* from the House of Commons when a voice broke in, 'You must not print that.' Pat Healy's line to *The Times* was being bugged! This confirms everything I said about bringing the police in on the leak inquiry – I think even MI5 are involved. I'm certainly going to raise it with the Cabinet.

By train to Bristol and the GMC. About forty-five delegates turned up and I reported on the events of the week. I gave them my assessment of the Government and I discussed whether or not I should resign.

Jack Watson of the TGWU said there had been no disagreement in criticising the Government, the question now was what Tony Benn should do. He has an obligation to stay in and accept collective responsibility.

Bryan Beckingham said the leadership was in cloud cuckoo land and completely out of touch. Labour were carrying out Tory policies and there was confusion and despair among the rank and file which would strengthen the National Front. There was no chance of winning the next Election at present, we had to campaign, socialism would be discredited if we didn't. We should urge Tony, by resolution, to withdraw from the Government.

John McLaren referred to the effect of public expenditure cuts in Bristol and said the alternative was the Tory Party with even greater cuts, and a vote against the cuts by Tony Benn would be a vote for Tory cuts. I should stay.

Other people gave their views and then Cyril Langham read out two resolutions, the first from Bryan Beckingham that I should have voted against the Government on the cuts, and the second moved by Herbert Rogers as an amendment saying that the cuts were wrong, but supporting me and expressing confidence in me.

Cyril Langham said, 'I must tell the meeting that I did consult with Tony and I agreed that he should abstain. Herbert did the same.'

There was then a vote as to whether I should have abstained and it was endorsed by 19 to 11. All the young people voted against me and wanted me to resign. One way of looking at it would be Reg Prentice's way, that the local Party had been infected by Trots. The other way is to say that these are youngsters and they're impatient; and my God they are right. We have to have them and if they went we'd just be an ageing Party with no meaning. I don't disagree with their criticism; it is a tactical question.

Monday 2 August
The main news today is that the five law lords in the House of Lords have turned down the Department of Education's appeal that Thameside Council should not be allowed to select for grammar schools. This puts the spanner in the works of the development of comprehensives, and it is an example of the reactionary nature of the courts.

Wednesday 4 August
Went into the office to meet Peter Hennessy from the *Financial Times*, who is becoming the Whitehall correspondent of *The Times*. He asked me a lot of questions about Government and political advisers. He was particularly interested in collective Cabinet responsibility and asked if what I said could all go on the record. He told me that people were saying that my memoirs were going to be the most interesting of political books, first of all because I keep good records, secondly because I keep a diary and thirdly because I always photograph my officials.

Thursday 5 August
At 11 Ashley Jackson and Arthur Scargill from the Yorkshire miners came to present me with a picture of Woollacombe Colliery, and I had a private talk to Arthur. He is coming out strongly against nuclear power, partly in defence of coal and partly on safety grounds, but also because the Left is always more sensitive about these things while the Right tends to be technocratic. He is going to write a pamphlet on it and he said he thought the NUM would turn against nuclear power quite quickly. I'll have to watch that.

He thought I had been absolutely right not to attend the NEC last week, and he said when the ultra Left criticised me to him for not voting against the cuts, he said, 'What do you want him to do, do you want to cut off his legs and leave him with no trade union support?'

Arthur said that if it were up to the Conference, I'd be elected Leader of the Party (but of course Arthur would have to be President of the NUM!).

At lunch, Francis Cripps came in and, at my request, he had written a new paper showing how a change of policy might be effected. I liked it so much that I am going to send it to Jim Callaghan to read in the summer holidays.

That was my last day at work and my holiday really began today.

Friday 6 August
John Stonehouse was convicted yesterday of fraud and sentenced today to seven years in jail.

Thursday 12 August
Stansgate. I'm reading a remarkable book by Milan Machovec called *A Marxist Looks at Jesus* which the magazine *Theology* has asked me to review. It is a translation of the German book, *Jesus für Atheisten* and it is fascinating.

Tuesday 17 August
Hilary and Rosalind arrived a couple of days ago with the dogs, Wellington and Hazel, and six cats – Blackberry, Cyclops, Hisser and three kittens. Today Ron Vaughan drove Senator Tom Eagleton, accompanied by his political adviser and Stephen, down here for a talk and lunch. Tom Eagleton is a real Mid-Western lawyer, saying he is more liberal than he should be for the state of Missouri.

I asked him about Carter, who is the Democrats presidential candidate and what his economic policy would be. He said, 'He's neither a Friedmanite nor a Galbraithite, he's somewhere in the middle. He's pro-Israel because you've got no choice in American politics. Nobody knows what he's going to do on health and social welfare.' He went on to say that the Southern Baptists were very conservative, which they are, and Carter had no experience of Washington. 'One term as Governor of Georgia and he's capturing Washington from the South.' An extraordinary situation.

I can't claim that I learned anything about Carter, but Eagleton was friendly, called the children by name and was pleasant to Mother and to Ron. As he left I said it was nice of him to come, and asked why he had chosen to see me. He answered, 'I have a girl working in my office this summer who is from the CIA English desk and I asked her who I should see in England. She gave me six names – you, Enoch Powell, Mrs Thatcher, Denis Healey, Len Murray and Jack Jones.' I made a joke of it: 'That's something – getting CIA endorsement. When is the funding coming?' It was an expression of his naïvete that he should tell me that.

Stephen told me later that, in the car, Eagleton had said that the general opinion in Washington was that Britain was zooming to the bottom economically. Americans couldn't understand why the working class was trying to 'claw down the aristocracy'; also the present Government was stifling initiative. These are the standard Middle-Western, Republican views that emerge from their press coverage of the political scene.

Thursday 19 August

Caroline and I went to Bradwell for Tom Driberg's burial – he died last week at the age of seventy. Canon Burling, who had buried Father's ashes at St Lawrence, had come out of retirement to do this and was waiting for the hearse to arrive from London where the memorial service had been held. The hearse could be seen from the church, moving slowly along the road, followed by a crowd of people. At the graveside a High Churchman swung his censer which I found rather weird, though moving.

It is difficult to assess Tom Driberg.* I can't say he was an agreeable man, in fact he was very rude to waiters and railway porters, and so on. I think deep down he was an unhappy man, very dissatisfied with himself.

In his old age, he became sad and ill. Lena Jeger used to see him and told me a bit about his autobiography which is now going to be published and is totally candid and frank about his homosexual activities. I only hope he hasn't named names and involved people in his affairs, even though they may now be dead.

Wednesday 25 August

In my box was a reply from Jim Callaghan about Francis Cripps's memorandum, saying if we followed the course he suggested it would be a disaster.

Wednesday 1 September

Senator Eagleton phoned and said, 'I haven't had a reply to my telegram to Stephen.' I asked him what was in it, and he said, 'I have offered him a job in my office as one of my advisers, at £200 a month, though he would have to pay his own fare. He could watch the presidential elections and generally help around.'

So I rang Stephen and he just couldn't believe it; that lunch turned out to be a dream come true for Stephen.

Wednesday 8 September

Went to the dentist who has just moved into a new surgery in Westbourne Grove. All his new equipment is imported – Italian X-ray machine, Japanese light, German drill, and so on. This is what one sees

---

* Driberg was Labour MP for Maldon 1945–55 (Independent 1942–45) and for Barking 1959–74. He was the *Daily Express* gossip columnist, 'William Hickey' in the Thirties and Forties. Created a peer, Lord Bradwell, in January 1976. His book *Ruling Passions* was published in 1977.

everywhere, the decline of our manufacturing industry and floods of imports.

Thursday 9 September

First Cabinet since the summer recess. Tony Crosland said, 'I expect you have heard, Chairman Mao is dead.' In fact, I hadn't heard it on the news. He didn't say much about it. 'I don't suppose there's much point in my trying to assess Mao Tse Tung's role in the world,' and he just passed over the event. Somehow I did feel that Mao merited a moment of reflection in the British Cabinet. In my opinion, he will undoubtedly be regarded as one of the greatest – if not the greatest – figures of the twentieth century: a schoolteacher who transformed China, released it from civil war and foreign attack and constructed a new society there. His influence throughout the world has been immense, based to some extent on power I suppose, but also on his tremendous achievements. Whether history will just put him among the emperors or whether he will be seen as having a quality distinct from them, I do not know, but he certainly towers above any other twentieth century figure I can think of in his philosophical contribution and his military genius.

Friday 10 September

There is going to be a reshuffle triggered off by Roy Jenkins who has finally left the Government. Merlyn Rees becomes Home Secretary; Shirley is diverted into Education where she will have to carry the can on all the public expenditure cuts (although she does fully support them); John Silkin has been kept in, which surprised me, to become Minister of Agriculture, and there are three new members of the Cabinet* – Roy Hattersley, Stan Orme and Bill Rodgers. Fred Peart is now Leader of the Lords – how he survives, I don't know.

Roy Jenkins came into politics on the coat tails of Attlee, as the son of Attlee's PPS, and never shone individually while Gaitskell was alive because he was one of his principal lieutenants. When Gaitskell died, he emerged with full force as the leader of the liberal Right of the Party who believed more in Europe than in the Party, ultimately sacrificing the deputy-leadership in 1972 over the Referendum. He came back into the Government in 1974 as Home Secretary, desperately wanting to be Foreign Secretary. He has now accepted the Presidency of the European Commission as a way of getting out of British politics and can never return except possibly in a coalition government. He is a

---

* See Appendix II p. 721, for details of the ministerial changes made on 10 September 1976.

charming man really, an Asquithian Liberal I suppose – not Labour in any significant sense.

Saturday 11 September

One thing is crystal clear in my judgment, that the trade unions will push and press the Government but will not, under any circumstances, rock the boat. If the Left is going to be effective, it has got to argue for a change of policy without appearing to weaken or defeat or divide the Government – it has to attack capitalism without attacking the Government. I think this would be welcomed by the movement, including the trade union movement, because they want some real light at the end of the tunnel.

Thursday 16 September

The *Guardian* and *The Times* this morning, in effect, both said that there wouldn't be any trouble for me at Conference, which pleased me. The *Express* had an extraordinary piece: 'Healey to Fight All Out War Against his Rival Benn'.

Friday 17 September

My first appointment was at the American Embassy to talk to a number of senior political officers. I described our oil policy, how it was preferred by the oil companies to confiscation in OPEC or divestiture, and I joked about Henry VIII taking a 51 per cent participation in the Vatican and setting up the British Episcopal Corporation which became the Church of England. They laughed at that.

I said we were trying to look more fundamentally at our society and its twin problems of a weak economy, due to lack of investment, and inadequate industrial democracy, due in part to our feudal type of capitalism, and that we were now struggling to create a new consensus.

For an hour I was questioned on the difference between the British and the Americans, American democracy, stop-go, and relations with the unions. I said there was no more point in drawing a comparison between the US and Britain than there was between Britain and Russia because we were quite unlike them both. I don't think it was a great success but I did them the honour of saying to them what I would say at any Labour meeting. I don't suppose they've heard such a left-wing argument before.

Saturday 18 September

David Steel, the new Liberal Party Leader, has come out in favour of coalition in order to get proportional representation, and this has led to a great revolt by the Young Liberals.

Sunday 19 September
Thought about my Conference speech today. The real puzzle is why did the Labour Party, which was socialist before the war, abandon its socialism? If you look at the arguments before the war, they weren't policy arguments really, they were arguments about the popular front, about relations with the Communist Party, the role of the unemployed, and so on, and there was a Marxist stream and a social democratic stream, but there was no impression of a great bitterness between Left and Right at that time. We came into office in 1945 as a socialist party and we left office in 1970 with little socialism left. This is the problem that we really have to address.

Tuesday 21 September
At 9.30 Michael, Ron Hayward and I saw Jim at Number 10 to discuss some of the conflicts between the Government and the Party which will arise at Conference. He was really worried about the bank and insurance nationalisation demands and he read out letters that he had received from the clearing banks and the insurance associations asking for a view. He said he and Denis agreed that if it were passed at the Conference the pound would fall: it would be a disastrous policy, though he had no theological objection to nationalisation, indeed he served on the Italian nationalised bank as a director.

Ron Hayward said we should persuade Mik, who will chair the Conference, not to press the vote.

I said, 'Look, if you tell the Conference they can't vote on the issue, you are inviting a rebuff.'

But Jim was absolutely convinced that if it was passed it would be disastrous.

Ron immediately backed off and Michael, who looks more and more like a moth-eaten suit on a coathanger, was very worried. But, listening to Jim, I realised that if the crisis is so great that you have to postpone socialism, and that even mentioning socialism brings down such a bitter attack on you, you really are up against powerful forces that you don't control; if anything, that makes you more of a socialist. Jim says we'll be defeated by the banks and the insurance companies, but if that is the case, all the more reason why we must tackle them.

At 10.15 I left and Bryan, Chris Herzig and I flew from Northolt to Bonn Airport where we were met by Sir Oliver Wright, the Ambassador. The Embassy Residence in Bonn is a beautiful place overlooking the river, with servants and butlers and a brand new Rolls Royce that must have cost about £18,000. The luxury in which these diplomats live is incredible, so remote from the lives of the people at home: how they can claim to represent the British people in any sense I just don't know.

Before lunch, Chris told me that a high-powered working party was looking at Anglo-French nuclear cooperation and that this was likely to come up at the Paris meeting on 12 November when Jim, Denis and Tony Crosland and I are going over for talks with Giscard and his Ministers. I had never heard anything about this but of course it bears on the heart of Anglo-French relations.

During the war, Frenchmen were involved in the Chalk River atomic project in America, but then the Americans broke off all links with the French in favour of the special relationship with the British, the heart of which was nuclear. The French were as bitter as hell and when de Gaulle proposed a troika to run NATO, the Americans didn't want it and we just went along with the US.

This all became linked with British entry into the Common Market. When Macmillan visited de Gaulle at Chateau Rambouillet in 1961, it looked as if entry to the Market was agreed. Shortly afterwards, Macmillan went to Nassau, without telling de Gaulle, and negotiated a deal to buy Polaris submarines to replace the cancelled Blue Streak nuclear missile. De Gaulle was furious and saw it as another Anglo-American deal at the expense of France, which was by then working on its own nuclear 'force de frappe'.

That explained the French veto on our entry into the Common Market and the breakdown of the talks in 1963. It also explained why Heath was so keen, when in Opposition in 1964, to have an Anglo-French nuclear force, because the Anglo-French relationship had to be re-oriented around nuclear cooperation and that meant breaking with America. When Pompidou later asked Heath, 'Is Britain prepared to anchor itself to Europe?', he was really referring to the possibility of Anglo-French military cooperation.

Then the Almelo Treaty, which I signed in 1970, was designed to prevent the Germans having their own nuclear technology of enriched uranium by committing them to cooperation with Holland and Britain, again separating us further from the French because they wanted us to come in with them on nuclear technology.

The ultimate situation was therefore that we were kept at arms' length from the French, working with the Germans in order to prevent them from developing nuclear power independently.

Now it appears that Germany, Holland and Britain are going to do a deal with the French. A very close Anglo-French arrangement on nuclear effort, with the Americans accepting it, moves us towards an Anglo-German-French nuclear programme, which would be the beginning of the Western European nuclear superstate.

I also learned that Callaghan and Giscard have in effect agreed that there should be joint meetings between key Ministers and the British and French Cabinets twice a year, just as there are joint meetings between the German and French cabinets. Were the three Cabinets to meet together, it would upset the little countries in Europe, so the French have cleverly suggested that they should meet with the Germans and with us, but that we and the Germans should be a bit more discreet.

God, the French are clever diplomats and we are very foolish in allowing them to dominate the Common Market in this way. The Germans have the economic and industrial strength, the French have industrial strength and diplomatic leadership, and we are the poor relation of the big three; Italy and the smaller countries, Spain, Portugal, Greece and Turkey if they join, will be on the bottom rung. Of course nobody is chronicling these developments any more, but it is worth noting in my diary.

I went across at 3.30 to the Science Ministry, a monstrous office block, into a long room with a modern painting of blue and white slashes hanging on the wall and venetian blinds. The German delegation had just come in from an Election meeting, and Matthöfer, the German Minister of Research and Technology, insisted that we be photographed together to help him with his campaign. He said there had been some delay in our meeting because of the stoppage in the German nuclear energy programme for a couple of years due to the slump, but the demand was still there and we must keep it up.

We put out a little communiqué and we agreed that we'd have further discussions and meet again at ministerial level.

Back in London I came across a marvellous speech made by Gaitskell in the House of Commons on 5 December 1945. He said, 'Capitalism is inefficient, it creates insecurity, it is unjust, and the Labour Party is united by a single philosophy.' It will be really effective to be able to say, 'Many delegates quote Nye Bevan, let me quote this by Hugh Gaitskell as a reminder of what the Party is all about.'

Wednesday 22 September
Denis is now saying that we have to have import deposits but he rules out major restrictions on imports. Frances and Francis looked at the figures and came to the conclusion that Britain is bankrupt. They say the Treasury measures are quite inadequate, we haven't discussed alternatives, etc. Their paper in response is clear and sharp and they have been dashing around Whitehall discussing it with other political advisers.

But Jim has pretty clearly indicated that he is not prepared to go over to Left policies, so we're locked into a grinding period of further deflation, rising unemployment and a clash with the unions, all of which was predicted in the twin strategy approach which Francis wrote for the Economic Strategy Committee last year.

Thursday 23 September
Cabinet at 10 and Jim welcomed the new members – Stan Orme, Bill Rodgers and Roy Hattersley. He said he wanted to urge on us the critical importance of secrecy in all our proceedings. He wanted everyone to maintain close links with the Party, particularly the trade union movement, and he said he had looked carefully to see which of us would do that. He couldn't say when the next Election would be but he didn't have one in mind at the moment.

Rhodesia was a very interesting item of discussion. We had the papers of the Kissinger mission before us. He has been dashing off to Pretoria, and to see Smith in Rhodesia, Nyerere in Tanzania and Kaunda in Zambia, and his plan is to have an interim Government in Salisbury under a Council of State which would be in effect white-dominated with a black First Minister. Then there would be a proposal for majority rule in eighteen months to two years, when the British Government would provide some cover by legislative change.

I quietly asked how we could avoid legitimising the Smith regime in the interim. 'If we change the legislation, surely every one of Smith's white soldiers would become a soldier of the Queen and every civil servant would become a member of the FO. Then we would really be in the deep end.'

Crosland couldn't answer. The FO have an official, attached to Kissinger, who is receiving the British Ambassadors everywhere. Of course, this is Kissinger's great gimmick.

In the end, Jim said, 'Well, Kissinger is coming tonight and I think we'd better convey this view to him by having a group of Ministers to meet him – Elwyn and Michael, Denis and Tony Crosland.' It was interesting to see the Cabinet assert a bit of collective leadership. I think Jim is worried and rightly so.

Labour Party Conference, Blackpool
Friday 24 September
NEC, where we had a long discussion about BBC bias in giving a lot of coverage to Mrs Thatcher in Australia but none to Jim Callaghan in Canada.

Saturday 25 September
Difficult to get the feeling of Conference but obviously the unity theme is going to be very strongly expressed. The rank and file do not like to feel that the leadership is split and therefore one has to be constructive and identify the role and the future of the Party in a way that can't be taken as an attack upon the present leadership.

Tuesday 28 September

I retained my place at the top of the NEC, picking up 4000 more votes, with Michael in second place. Norman Atkinson became Treasurer, knocking out Eric Varley. Joan Maynard told me that Jack Jones had been trying to get her knocked off the NEC and have Margaret Jackson elected instead. Moss Evans [National Organiser of the TGWU] and Alex Kitson simply wouldn't go along with it so he dropped it. But that is where the trade union power will be exercised, getting right-wingers on the National Executive who will vote the right way. To that extent we are back to the situation of the early Fifties.

Next was Jim Callaghan's speech and it was an experience to listen to it. He began by paying tribute to Harold Wilson which was fine, that Harold had been brilliant and amusing and Jim couldn't be that but he hoped to emulate Harold's record of fighting five Elections and winning four of them. 'I hope aspirants for the leadership note that.'

He went on to give the most patronising lecture about our economic problems and how all Governments had dodged them, how we were living beyond our means and paying ourselves more than we could afford. He went on to use a phrase – a Freudian slip which must have been in his text, a printed, circulated, press released Freudian slip. '*I* don't *care* what economic system you live under, you can't pay yourself more than you earn.'

A reaction of horror came from the hall and he said, 'Of course I don't mean that, I mean under *any* economic system you can't pay yourself more than you earn.' Jack sat there looking pretty glum, Hugh Scanlon pretty impassive, David Basnett flushed. Jim was basically saying the main cause of our trouble was that we were living on borrowed money, borrowed time and borrowed ideas. He did mention racialism and local government reforms which got cheers but at the end he didn't get a standing ovation.

Then, there was a debate on Devolution, and Neil Kinnock made a speech attacking the statement, to which Michael replied. Neil Kinnock is not a substantial person. He is a media figure really; I have suspected it for some time and he knows I know it.

Joe Ashton told me there was a resolution calling for a working party to examine new methods of electing the Leader. This had been tabled by Ken Coates, seconded by Joan Maynard's constituency, Sheffield Brightside, and accepted. So that is a historical event.

The pound has dropped to $1.63.

Wednesday 29 September

On the way to Conference a delegate came up to me and said, 'Have you heard about the loan? I hope you're not going to guarantee it and accept it.' It was the first I had heard but apparently Denis had gone to the IMF and borrowed £2.5 billion and the conditions won't come out until after the Conference.

Went over to the *Mirror* party with Frances, and Jack Jones said amiably, 'You know, young man, you'll be Prime Minister next.'

I said, 'I have no ambition and I've seen too many who have.'

'I'm not talking about that sort of ambition. You will be if you play it right.' A bit patronising. He said Jim was out of his depth and didn't know what was going on, and he made a very offensive remark about Denis Healey.

Then Joe and Maggie Ashton, Frances, Caroline and I went over to the *Tribune* meeting where Eric Heffer made a most principled attack on Callaghan for his speech, and Neil Kinnock did a brilliant bit of fund-raising.

Thursday 30 September

News of the loan filled the papers and there is much confusion. The smell of 1931 is very strong in my nostrils.

We went over to the Conference and the first item was on education. Caroline's name was mentioned several times by one speaker who kept quoting 'Benn and Simon', ie the book Caroline co-authored *Halfway There*. The Socialist Education Association delegate spoke and attacked the quality of comprehensive education, which is part of the ultra-left campaign, and will be used by the *Daily Mail* no doubt.

In the afternoon, Mik, who had taken an entirely uncompromising line, made an absolutely brilliant speech on the nationalisation of the banks and very nearly got a standing ovation. There was an overwhelming two-thirds majority, although I think the TGWU and the GMWU abstained.

Denis had arrived during the banks and insurance companies debate with a terrific flurry of cameras. There were hisses and boos when he came forward to speak and he said, 'I have come from the battlefront.' He then went on to shout and bully and rule out all alternative policies, saying this was the only way forward.

Jones, Scanlon and Basnett looked very uncomfortable. The Conference was pretty hostile but when he finished, it having been such a bold and vigorous speech, parts of the Conference cheered him – the PLP, the Post Office Engineers, I think. I couldn't even clap him, his speech was so vulgar and abusive.

Denis went back to his seat and held up his hands in a sort of Mohammed Ali victory salute, suggesting it was a great triumph. Tonight the media presented it as Denis having won over the Conference to these tough new measures, and so on.

Summing up, the Conference has performed a valuable function by meeting during a sterling crisis. The union leaders are now anxious about Denis and uneasy about Jim who is playing it cool, but must be worried. The Party expressed, with total clarity and almost unanimity, its desire for a more socialist policy; at the same time it ratified the relations with the trade union movement which it wants to develop; and it decided it would support the Government. I think the Left has every reason to be highly delighted with the Conference but the Right is demoralised by it because all they have got is critical loyalty, no support for their policies. The trade union leaders are therefore not able to blame the Left for rocking the boat and they have got to confront the reality of the policy too.

I think we'll probably have import controls by the end of the year.

Friday 1 October

Joe Haines wrote a piece in the *Mirror* about the bully boys and the Trotskyites in the Party and how we must clean it up. It reflected the pit of Security Service paranoia that was epitomised by Wilson's kitchen cabinet in its later years. Thank God that man has gone, and Haines with him.

Sunday 3 October

Stephen rang from America. He told us he was taken on to the floor of the Senate and two extracts of speeches he had written for Eagleton went into the Senate record. Then he described this fantastic visit he made to see Alice Roosevelt Longworth, the daughter of President Theodore Roosevelt, and the Alice of 'The Girl in the Alice Blue Gown'. He and this ninety-five-year-old lady sat together in her darkened Edwardian room in Washington and he actually asked her whether she had been Joe Graydon's* lover. She answered, 'Not quite,' and winked.

I received a letter from Sir John Hunt at the Cabinet Office, 'Private and Confidential', written before the Conference, asking if the Cabinet Office could approach Francis Cripps to discuss the alternative strategy. Francis said yes.

Monday 4 October

An important meeting this morning on how to handle the Shell-Exxon participation talks. I toughened the officials with Frank Kearton's full but silent support. I said, 'I am not prepared to budge on the principle. We rest on the national interest and we interpret the national interest. We do it through title and participation and they have got to accept that that is the arrangement.' That is my starting point and I'll escalate it up to the top level with Garvin and Wagner of Shell.

* Caroline Benn's grandfather.

After they had gone I had a word with Frank Kearton and I said to him, 'You're an industrialist, what do you really think about the economic position? It would seem to me the policy is failing and we must do something else.' He said, 'I agree with you. Incidentally, I don't know how you can stand the bogeyman treatment and all that and be so patient. But there is a minority in the CBI and a growing minority in favour of protection. We have got to protect the country.' I said, 'I would like to meet some of them to talk.' He replied, 'There is one problem. Upper management have suffered a 30 per cent fall in their standard of living and they are worried. If you could get management with you then you could ignore the shareholders. As for the City of London, they are rolling in money and doing absolutely nothing about it.'

Tuesday 5 October

Had a brief talk to Frances about Enoch Powell's speech yesterday on repatriation in which he suggested that £1 billion be spent to send home one million immigrants with £1000 a piece in their pocket. It developed into a tremendous argument. Frances said, 'Of course it would help unemployment.' I said, 'That is a fascist argument.' 'You're saying the working class are fascist,' she said. 'I am not saying that. I am saying that is a fascist argument which, if it were accepted, would divert them from the real issue, which is how to get full employment, and so on, to the idea that the blacks are responsible for unemployment, and because workers are divided, one among another, the Tories would go in and clobber them.'

William Rees-Mogg came to lunch. I have known him since 1947 when he came back from the army as Sergeant Rees-Mogg. He was then a pompous young man with a gold watch and rather fancy waistcoat. He writes the great leaders warning about freedom and the corporate state and lets Bernard Levin savage me and Lord Chalfont suggest I'm a Communist and all that. I had an 'executive lunch' brought up from the canteen and he drank tonic water. There he was, surrounded by my trade union banners; he looked neither to right nor left and expressed no interest in the decoration or my statue beautifully carved out of coal or anything.

He told me he thought the Government would go on for some time, perhaps a couple of years. 'It will be more monetarist in its approach but not sufficient to deal with the basic problems. Unemployment will stay roughly where it is. Inflation will not get below 10 per cent. There will then be an Election.' He thought in Scotland the SNP would come first and would nudge a lot of Labour people out of their seats and the Tories, although recovering in Scotland, wouldn't be sufficiently strong to have any effect. In England the Liberal vote would drop to, say, 3.5

million and therefore Mrs Thatcher would get in – with a narrow majority.

I asked what policies she would pursue. 'She believes really, and so do I, in a monetary stabilisation. That is to say you would have a sudden attack on money supply and it would be like Schacht in Germany or Poincaré in France after the First World War or de Gaulle and Erhardt after the Second World War; this would lead to a temporary substantial increase in unemployment but then it would settle down, confidence would return, people would wake up and find they had a hard currency instead of a soft currency in their hands, though less of it of course. That, I think, is the right policy.'

Then we talked about the collapse of Keynesianism, the collapse of the Beveridge idea and when the consensus died: was it during the Wilson or the Heath Government? In fact we both agreed that the centre had collapsed under us and that there was now a pretty basic choice to be made.

After lunch we sat in armchairs and he said, 'Let me ask you one thing. I can never understand how the Left of the Labour Party, which is always talking about democracy, reconciles this with state centralisation. I said, 'I agree with you. I'm part of the democratic Left. I believe in dispersing power and my answer is that you have got to get investment into industry somehow, which will require state planning, but then you have got to break down the great big state bureaucracies.'

Then he said, 'Have you seen the figures we published in today's *Times* showing the decline in the rate of profit?' The profit at replacement cost had shrunk from 18 per cent in 1960 to 4 per cent in 1975. 'Those figures are awful and maybe Marx was right in saying there will be a historic decline in the rate of return on capital,' he said.

I asked him, 'To what do you attribute that? To Keynesianism, to trade unions, to socialism, or to the ballot box?'

He said, 'I don't know.'

'I wonder whether the capacity of poor people to buy hospitals and schools and pensions using the ballot paper when they haven't got any money doesn't put a spanner in the works,' and I quoted Bagehot.* 'What I feel is that we have got to find a way of getting investment, preserving democracy and maintaining liberty and it is in this area that we are really discussing what the new consensus is to be because you can't have a society without consensus.'

---

* 'I can conceive of nothing more corrupting or worse for a set of poor ignorant people than that two combinations of well-taught and rich men should constantly offer to defer to their decision. *Vox populi* will be *vox diaboli* ...'. *The English Constitution* (1869).

Wednesday 6 October
Today I circulated a list of stinging questions about the safety of the fast breeder reactor.

Then I had Jack Rampton, Walter Marshall, Brian Tucker, Peter Le Cheminant and others in to talk about my ideas on energy policy and my idea is broadly that you stick to the SGHWR but let the timetable slip, that you have a complete moratorium on fast breeder reactors, that you advance the Drax-B coal-fired power station order to keep the industry going and that you divert scientists to renewable and benign sources of energy.

Walter Marshall, who is a most conceited scientist, kept speaking to me as if I were a child and saying, 'Your logic is at fault, Minister.' But I got my view across and I think broadly they will go along with it, although it will be a bit of a struggle in Whitehall. We haven't got the money to have the fast breeder and the safety of the American reactor system in place of the SGHWR is not established.

Thursday 7 October
The item which occupied most of the Cabinet's time was the economic situation and it was one of the most interesting Cabinet discussions we have had. Denis began by saying that the rhetoric at Conference had made things worse and that today the Bank of England was announcing a 2 per cent increase in special deposits and a 2 per cent increase in the minimum lending rate, from 13 per cent to 15 per cent. So we now have a 15 per cent bank rate which is the highest there has ever been in the history of the Bank of England. These are crisis measures of tremendous moment. He went on to quote me on the question of the need for agreeing domestic credit expansion and so on with the IMF.

Jim said, 'This is a very difficult time for all of us. If you will forgive a little homily, we have got to stick together now. I know it is very difficult for people who disagree but if any impression gets about that there is disagreement in the Cabinet, then it does weaken our intent, people don't know where they are. Therefore, I must ask people to think very carefully about what they feel they should do.'

Peter Shore said, 'I don't mind sticking with the policy if it is working but this one has failed.' He made a powerful speech and a strong case for import controls, import planning.

After John Morris, I spoke. 'Well, PM, this is a grave crisis and one which has hit us after doing everything that the Treasury have asked us to do for the last two and a half years. I agree with you that it is a question of confidence, a political problem. Abroad, there are people who don't like us and although we may get the support of President Ford and Helmut Schmidt, they don't actually fix the exchange rate of sterling, others do that. At home, the Tories want to get rid of us. You ask about uncertainty and, if I may say so, the problem of uncertainty is a complex problem because there is a school of thought – what I call "the end of the road" school – which is saying we are living beyond our means. Once you say that and people have absorbed it, they say, "All right, if we have come to the end of the road, what are we going to do?" and uncertainty follows from these realistic speeches that we are hearing. I don't mean to give offence but if rhetoric at Conference is going to be referred to, I think speeches about rioting in the streets if the Treasury policy isn't followed are unwise. My anxiety is simple, it is that we are falling between two stools. Our policy has, in effect, failed. I welcomed what you said, PM, about our being able to express our views in Cabinet. There are broadly two courses open to us: the monetarist course which the Treasury recommend, and the protectionist course which is the one I have consistently recommended for two and a half years. If you compare them, protectionism is a perfectly respectable course of action. It is compatible with our strategy. You withdraw behind walls and reconstruct and re-emerge. We have also got to look at it from a political point of view, to consider the electoral consequences. Nobody pretends you can get a socialist millennium but even with the defensive posture that we are now in, the question of who pays the price is a crucial question and we are going to be asked to pay for it in jobs, prices and in social provision. I think we should change course and I recommend it to colleagues.'

'I would like to put a question to Tony,' said Jim, 'because I am not entirely persuaded of this. If you did adopt your course, and there is nothing particularly socialist about protectionism against monetarism, can you answer what would be the price you would have to pay for your policy?'

I replied, 'I haven't got the resources of an economic Ministry behind me. I don't conceal the fact that if you are going to do it this way, there would be hardship. I think both solutions introduce a siege economy. Denis is going for a siege economy and if you like, for the sake of argument, so would I. The difference is in his siege, you will have the bankers with you and the British people, the trade unions, outside the citadel storming you; with mine it will be the other way round. The psychology of this is so different, and I quote Derek Ezra who has said that you couldn't "get people to make sacrifices to propitiate those who are gambling with your currency, but you could get people to make sacrifices if they felt they were building up their economy again". Here is where the politics come in, pride of country, not chauvinism, not xenophobia but pride. This is the way you could sell that. I don't know about public expenditure, I can't give any answer to that but we would probably have to reduce borrowing, maybe by increases in taxation, I don't know. I am not putting my course forward as an easy one.'

After others had contributed, Jim said, 'It has been an excellent discussion, providing we can keep it to ourselves, and we have got to think further about it. The longer I am Prime Minister, the less sure I am that I know what is right and what is wrong,' a very open-minded thing to say.

At 5.30 I went over to Number 10 for the meeting with the miners. Joe Gormley introduced it and said, 'We've got a tight resolution calling for us to take industrial action if we don't get immediate earlier retirement from January; we are not expecting that but we could do it through the Redundant Miners' Payment Scheme.' This would cost about £10 million whereas the NUM resolution would cost £290 million.

Jim Callaghan said, 'We're in a bit of a difficulty because this is outside pay policy.' Albert Booth agreed.

It got pretty rough and Joe said, 'You're not helping me at all. You're saying nothing. Will you agree in principle?'

'We're sympathetic to the idea of earlier retirement,' Jim said, 'but I don't see what we can do. We can't have forward commitments, as Albert said.'

Joe suggested, 'What about us taking it out of our pay so that instead of getting a 4.5 per cent rise this year, we take 4 per cent and take the rest in earlier retirement.'

Albert said, 'That would be a new dimension.'

I sat tight, then Jim said, 'Perhaps we had better tell your chaps not to press for it, and rely on their loyalty to carry the ballot against.'

Joe said, 'It was a very narrow ballot last year.'

Jim said, 'Perhaps you're going to bring a third Government down, you nearly brought one down in 1972 and you brought it down in 1974, perhaps you'll bring us down.'

'We're politicians, we don't want to do that. But in general, you know, we are a long way apart,' replied Joe, to which Jim said, 'There you are, that's it, no move.'

So they went off, Jim having deliberately rebuffed them. I think it was a great mistake. I should have thought he would want to help Joe Gormley but Jim has got an absolute obsession with the unions and I think they knew the score. They said they would go and talk to the Coal Board.

Afterwards Jim said, 'Joe's a very skilful negotiator, much better to appear to give him nothing at this stage.' Jim's a pretty dab hand at negotiation too! I had asked for five minutes with him, so we sat in the Cabinet Room for an hour and a quarter and had a lovely talk.

'Well, what do you want to talk about?' asked Jim.

'First of all, I appreciate the very open discussion in Cabinet this morning. I want to make three concrete and helpful suggestions. One is that we might consider having a committee of Ministers responsible for the industrial strategy, that is to say Industry, Trade, Energy, Employment, to monitor the industrial strategy, checking how we are getting on, but it must be under non-Treasury chairmanship.'

'Denis won't like that,' he interjected.

'I am simply saying that industrial strategy ought not to be under the Treasury. Next, on the City side, I have been giving consideration as to whether we shouldn't have the Governor of the Bank of England attending the Economic Strategy Committee, just like the Chiefs of Staff attend the Overseas and Defence Policy Committee.'

Jim replied, 'Oh no, that's the Chancellor's job to represent the Governor's view, the Governor is just an instrument of Government policy and it would weaken the Chancellor.'

I said, 'I'm not so sure that is a bad thing because at the moment, we don't consult the Governor. The Governor ought to be able to convey to us the reality as he sees it and hear our argument.'

'Before the First World War, of course,' said Jim, 'the Chiefs of Staff were Members of the Cabinet, the First Lord of the Admiralty sat with the First Sea Lord, and so on. You probably know that as you are a historian. That's why they still come to the Overseas and Defence Policy Committee.'

He didn't like the idea.

Then we came on to Conference and he said, 'I though it was awful, sour, bitter and I had a lot of letters about your behaviour, which was seen on television, sitting there grimly during my speech. I've had the letters set aside and I'm going to read them later.'

I said, 'Well Jim, it would be very nice if every morning I woke up and found that everything I did was sweet and reasonable and sensible like Shirley Williams but it isn't like that. It is pretty rough you know, when even the *Financial Times* prints a picture of Michael and me side by side looking glum with the caption "Two unenthusiastic members of the Cabinet during the PM's speech", when we weren't even sitting together during your speech.' He hadn't seen it and I told him there was an apology in today's *FT*. 'Now look, Jim, you know that in every article about you that has appeared since you became Leader I have stressed how well I get on with you. And there's not a morning I don't wake up and thank God that you are Leader and Harold Wilson is gone.'

Then he said, 'There is another thing about the Conference. What about all these Trotskyites – and I get my information from a source I can't disclose.'

I said, 'I presume it's the Intelligence Services.'

He said, '57,000 votes were cast for Troskyite candidates for the

NEC. That must be a substantial number of constituencies under Trotskyite influence.'

'Jim, I only hope the Intelligence Services understand all this. I read all the Left press. Trotskyites are youngsters and if we get them into the Party, we'll win them over.'

'You're too optimistic about it. I think Conference lost us the Election. When do you think they will wish to have an Election?'

'I haven't thought about it very much but I presume that you want to leave it a bit. We must win the next Election, and I think we can.'

'As to you,' he said, 'I can see you as Leader of the Party in Opposition and ten years in Opposition you will be.'

'I will never be Leader of the Party.'

'Yes, you might and I'm trying to give you a fair do.'

I said, 'I know that the PLP as it is presently constituted will go for somebody else. I am not going to wreck my life by ambition.'

'Now, about this alternative strategy of yours, you were very honest this morning in saying it would involve sacrifices, but could we sell it to people?'

I said, 'Yes Jim, I'm sure we could.'

He replied, 'I think more public expenditure cuts are coming. Denis hasn't told me but I think it is going to happen.'

'I should think there are because that is the policy and we'll just have to stay glued together. That's all.'

Then he said, 'You know I mentioned that Helmut Schmidt was coming to Chequers this weekend.'

I said, 'Yes, I heard it from my office.'

'What do you mean? Nobody but Helmut and I knew.'

'I heard it from my driver who heard from the car pool that there was a meeting at Chequers and he wondered if I was going. The car pool is the source of all information.' I told him how Ron Vaughan had heard that Harold had introduced the rule that all former Prime Ministers should have a car and that was how we knew Harold was going. Jim laughed.

He went on, 'Helmut Schmidt and I are going to have a long, comprehensive financial talk with nobody present from the Foreign Office, nobody from the Treasury, they'll wreck it. But Helmut Schmidt has got $32 billion dollars in reserves. They could fund the entire sterling balances. He's from Hamburg and they all like the English.'

We had got down to gossiping by this stage and he said, 'I'll tell you a thing about Harold. When we were at a summit just before Harold retired, Aldo Moro [the Italian Prime Minister] was delivering a seventeen-page written speech on the international monetary system, and Harold took one earphone off and I took the one off my good ear, and Harold leaned over and said, "When I go, Jim, shall I take the

Garter, the OM, or go to the Lords?" So I said what I always say in those circumstances – "What would you like for yourself?" – and Harold said, "I think I'll take the Garter", which he did.'

I said, 'Well old Clem took all three – a Garter, the OM, and the earldom.'

'Yes, I remember in 1955 when Clem went to the Shadow Cabinet and said, "Just to let you know, I'm resigning and shall I take an earldom?" Edith Summerskill said, "Of course you must take it Clem", and he took it.'

I came home scribbling all the time in my notebook so that I didn't forget a word.

Friday 8 October
The last day of the Tory Conference. The Tories are beginning to beat the patriotic drum which they dropped when they became Europeans. Even after the Labour Government has adopted such right-wing policies, Mrs Thatcher was still able to say to her Conference, with a shred of credibility from the point of view of the audience, that it was becoming harder and harder to draw the distinctive line between Communism and Labour Party policy.

Sunday 10 October
Caroline and I went to dinner with Sir Brian Flowers, Rector of Imperial College, and Lady Flowers. They live in a fantastic house just on the corner of Queen's Gate with huge state apartments which have just been redecorated at endless cost. Later I talked to Brian Flowers about his report on Environmental Pollution which was published a couple of weeks ago and which has had a tremendous impact in the nuclear world. He is a nuclear physicist who has now decided that the fast breeder programme is not safe and wants it held back, and is being violently attacked by the nuclear lobby. He also thought Hill should go because he was quite indecisive and gave poor advice, and Marshall was a menace because he was so naïve and clever at the same time, as I well know from experience.

Monday 11 October
I went to hear Thatcher in the Commons. Her speeches are solidly argued, like an *FT* article, but don't carry conviction, have no depth, don't look into the roots of the problem. Jim made a bold and human speech which went down well and had more substance to it.

Tuesday 12 October
It is 2 am and today is Caroline's birthday. We have had such a marvellous life together and her radicalism and support and deter-

mination have really kept me going. I couldn't have managed without her.

Wednesday 13 October

Lunch with Anne Armstrong and Ronny Spiers the American Minister, a very active, decent, liberal democrat. During lunch they asked what was really wrong in Britain. I said, 'Two things are wrong, the education system and the class system.' We went right through lunch talking very seriously. Anne thought Carter would now win because he had mobilised the Democratic machine. Of course, she will be replaced if Carter wins.

Had my final round of negotiations with Occidental. Everyone from the various oil companies involved – Getty Oil and so on – was there, including Armand Hammer who is a most remarkable old boy. He went to Russia after the Revolution, when he was twenty-three, and personally negotiated a deal with Lenin to buy and sell asbestos. He used the earnings to buy works of art, set up the Hammer Gallery, then made a fortune selling pencils to the Soviet Union, went into the construction industry, picked up Occidental for $50,000 and made it into a major company. He bought up Roosevelt's home, gave it to the nation, and let Eleanor Roosevelt live there (she was subsequently a character witness when he was involved in a tax case). The only real problem we stuck on was the price and in the end I produced a form of words about how the price of the oil was to be settled. Dick Mabon is very good at all this.

Thursday 14 October

Cabinet at 10. I asked Shirley about the reports that Jim is going to make a major education speech and she passed me a note saying, 'Tony, no question of any change in emphasis on comprehensives. It's mainly on maths, why not enough kids are doing engineering, etc. A bit about standards. Curriculum will be the main row.' Caroline thinks it is to root out the 'lefties' who are teaching the social sciences, and all that. Shirley must be a bit worried, when the PM makes a speech on her subject.

Crosland reported on Rhodesia and told a story about Kissinger. Crosland said Kissinger was sending his man, Rogers, I think, over to London and Kissinger asked Tony, 'Would it be a good idea if Rogers went to see Thatcher?' Tony Crosland said No, it would not. So Rogers arrived in his office yesterday and told him he had had a very good meeting with Mrs Thatcher. Crosland blew his top and rang up Kissinger who apologised. Jim said, 'That's the way he behaves. The trouble with Kissinger is that he doesn't say the same thing to everybody and people don't know where they are.'

Sunday 17 October

In the papers there was an extract from Hugh Cudlipp's memoirs headed 'Citizen King's Fantasies', in which Hugh described in detail the Cecil King plot to try to bring about a coalition Government; and Cecil King's relationship with Harold Wilson from 1964 onwards. The climax of the story is that, on 8 May 1968, Cecil King went to see Lord Mountbatten, taking with him Hugh Cudlipp and Solly Zuckerman [senior Government scientist] and, according to the report, he said that the crisis he foresaw was round the corner, the Government would disintegrate, there would be bloodshed in the street, the armed forces would be involved, the people would be looking to somebody like Lord Mountbatten as the leader of men who would be backed by the best brains and administrators of the land to restore public confidence. He ended with a question to Mountbatten – would he agree to be titular head of a new administration in such circumstances? Mountbatten turned to his friend Solly who hadn't said a word and said, 'What do you think of all this?' Solly rose, walked to the door, opened it, and then made this statement, 'This is rank treachery. All this talk of machineguns and street corners is appalling. I am a public servant and will have nothing to do with it, nor should you, Dicky.' Mountbatten agreed and Solly departed. Lord Mountbatten was courteous but firm. He said briefly that he entirely agreed with Solly and that this sort of thing, so far as he was concerned, was simply not on. Later, Cecil King made his famous 'Enough is Enough' headline attack in the *Mirror* to try to get rid of Wilson.

I was so tickled by this story that I rang up Solly and he said, 'It's absolutely true. It was amazing.'

Monday 18 October

Jim Callaghan's speech on education is all over the news. It has opened up the debate on the future of education in a way most damaging to the cause of comprehensive education, and the Tory papers have gone to town over it. After years of inactive Education Secretaries, we now have in Shirley Williams a right-wing one working with a Prime Minister who has allowed himself to be briefed by Department of Education officials who themselves don't use the state system and who are hostile to it.

Harold Lever came to lunch. His relations with Jim are much less close than they were with Harold. We discussed the reasons why Wilson resigned. Mary wanted him to go. Marcia wanted him to stay and used to bully him. Harold Lever seemed to think that in future years more light would be shed on it. Maybe he couldn't stand the strain.

That's the first serious confirmation I have had of this theory; he had looked like a broken man since the spring. Meanwhile he goes on making ridiculous statements, such as the one in the press today on how his weekly audiences with the Queen were therapeutic.

Last week the *Economist* talked about a 'Bennite' party fighting the Government on cuts and that this party would be Marxist. This is the way the Establishment is driven to make Marx seem interesting.

Thursday 21 October

Last night Macmillan was interviewed by Robin Day and called for a government of national unity.

I have been trying to get hold of the memorandum prepared by Department of Education and Science officials for the PM in connection with his speech on education. It was leaked to *The Times Educational Supplement*. Jim, in fairness, just suggested that we should have a national debate but he and Shirley are working hand-in-glove to introduce reactionary education policies. My office rang Shirley's office, but they wouldn't send it to me. In Cabinet Shirley said to me, 'I'll let you have it, it was Number 10 that was the trouble.'

I said, 'If it can be leaked to the press, I think another Cabinet Minister is entitled to see it.'

She is worried because she knows she is engaged in some shifty change of policy and she has got all the teachers up in arms. Ironically, the press is building her up as the best Education Secretary, saying that she has inherited Roy Jenkins's mantle, etc.

Friday 22 October

Dr Edward Teller, the so-called father of the H-bomb, came to see me at Brian Flowers's suggestion. He is sixty-eight now. He was late, having got lost and had hurried through the rain and, like many Germans – of whom it is said they are either at your throat or at your feet – he was anxious not to appear discourteous. He thought the price of oil would create starvation and catastrophe in the developing world and therefore the West had a moral obligation to go flat out for nuclear power which would keep the price of oil down and help the developing world to survive. For him nuclear power was everything and it was vital we pushed ahead with it, and was extremely worried about the campaign against nuclear power in America and in Austria. He said Kreisky was faced with huge anti-nuclear pressure and was bending to it.

'I understand it really,' I said.

'But the fears are all overcome. Take vitrification of waste – you keep it a few years to get the heat out of it and then you find it will only have half a life of 300 years', and so on, a sort of Dr Strangelove figure.

The danger of the intellectual scientific élite distorting the whole pattern of society really does begin to worry me. He said fusion was so important because it will allow space travel, and so on. But this is a diversion of man's effort from his basic task.

Monday 25 October

During the TUC-Labour Party Liaison Committee, Jim said, 'I will just briefly report on my education speech. We may need a core curriculum; to talk about the three Rs can't be reactionary. We should be thinking about education and employment in engineering, about exams, and possibly publish a Green Paper.'

Len Murray welcomed the PM's speech, but said that education was not training. We could look at the curriculum but perhaps we should be looking at higher education, which had unfilled vacancies. We needed to attract more mature students.

I welcomed the fact that the debate had been opened by the Prime Minister because there was a massive attack on our comprehensive schools and we had to reject it. 'There are certain dangers to face: the danger of divisiveness engendered by the 1944 Education Act with all its nonsense about different types of minds requiring different types of schools, resurrected by Sir Cyril Burt who has, incidentally, been accused in *The Sunday Times* of doing fraudulent research into intelligence.

'The second danger is the binary system of higher education and the third is exams which we have talked about for ten years, whereby working-class kids get CSEs and the others get GCEs. We must turn away completely from the idea that working class kids should be given technical training and shunted into industry. We have to deal with the massive subsidies to private education, and we must end the stranglehold of universities over the school exam.'

I had prepared this little speech with Caroline's help, and Shirley sat there blushing, pink as anything, and I think I scored a lot of direct hits on what she would like to bring forward.

Shirley then warned against a backlash. There were genuine concerns about teaching methods: fashions in teaching had changed and hadn't always been thought through. We must look at the basics again and at the big comprehensives and avoid the mistakes of the past. In the sixteen to nineteen age groups there was duplication of provision which we couldn't afford. We could save hundreds of thousands of pounds. On higher education, we needed a gap between school and university. The polytechnics were dropping their part-timers, and student grants might perhaps only be payable to those who had previously worked.

Tuesday 26 October

Sat and talked to Frances. I am utterly depressed and dejected. I have absolutely failed to persuade the Government not to do what it is about to do. It would be better if we were defeated now, I am persuaded of that, but I mustn't bring the Government down because if I do the responsibility will be put upon the Left, rather than on the Right where it really belongs. Somehow the whole world is whirling and it is having a physical effect on me. I actually feel physically ill.

Had a meal in the Tea Room and Trevor Skeet, the Tory MP for Bedford, came up and said, 'How are you feeling?'

'Fine.'

'What do you think about the pound?' he asked, then for about ten minutes, with a lot of people listening in, he tried to get me interested in a coalition. He is a Friedmanite.

I told him, 'It's simply not on, you don't understand us. We'll have nothing to do with you.'

He replied, 'You are too preoccupied with 1931.'

'We are not going to do it.'

Then I asked him, 'Who would be Prime Minister?'

'Callaghan,' he replied.

'Who would be Chancellor?'

'Mrs Thatcher.'

'Foreign Secretary?'

'Ted Heath.'

'Who would get Industry?'

'Varley.'

I said, 'If the word gets about that you're forming a Government I don't know what would happen to the pound.'

But he went on and on and said, 'You won't compromise.'

I said, 'Either it would achieve nothing because it was deadlocked or it would do what half the Cabinet thought was disastrously wrong for Britain.'

'The crisis is very serious.'

'All you want is a one-party state to shut out the electors from having any say.'

'Only until 1979,' he said, 'then we would have an Election.'

I said, 'It's absurd.'

Wednesday 27 October

Had David Owen to lunch in the office. I don't really know him well: he worked with Barbara when she was at Social Services and she had great admiration for him, and he for her, and he is trying to be friendly. I asked him about his family and one of his grandfathers had been a clergyman, the other a miner. His clergyman grandfather had originally been a Methodist but as he was blind he couldn't go round the circuit so he transferred to the Church of Wales and David has been brought up in that tradition. He felt it was getting weaker in the labour movement.

He was tremendously critical of the Treasury which he feels is determined to encourage the IMF to demand cuts from the economy. They are just out for our blood, and were furious with Jim for trying to negotiate with Helmut Schmidt for a Common Market loan to fund our sterling balances over a long term to avoid the rigours of the cuts. He said Jim was saying nothing to the FO or the Treasury and was engaged in private negotiations of this kind. David himself was pressing the same course in the FO but the FO and the Treasury were out of touch with Jim's line. Jim really distrusted the Treasury, a feeling which was reciprocated. Then he said, 'Now on your alternative strategy, I can't go along with you on import controls.'

I countered, 'I recognise that the full alternative strategy is unlikely to be adopted by the Cabinet and even if it was, they wouldn't do it with any conviction but at least we should be standing up in a John Bullish way for the national interest and threatening the alternative strategy.'

I asked him about the threat Jim had made on television about withdrawing from NATO and whether this had been cleared with the Foreign Office. He said they knew nothing about it. I commented, 'I wonder whether the Americans took it seriously, because if they just thought that Callaghan was threatening to withdraw, they might decide that Jim was under such heavy pressure from the Left that he couldn't do anything.' It may be that Jim thought this was one up on his own without consultation and put it out to disarm the Left, but had created a false impression and had really started to shake American and German confidence in the British Government. The Americans are so suspicious of the Labour Party they might believe almost anything of Jim.

David Owen was one hundred per cent in support of planning agreements and particularly of the NEB and industrial democracy.

I said, 'Of course, it has all now been dropped really.'

He said, 'I am sure industrial democracy is right.'

Then, indicating his personal support, he said, 'You have more influence in the Labour movement than any other man at this moment and we have got to fight for these things.'

We got on to a curious discussion about élites. He said, 'I believe in élites, that élites have to lead and that you have got to have men of intellect and ability.'

'I agree you have got to have ability', I said, 'but I believe that it is *will* that really matters, a power of concentration and determination.'

That more or less wound up the discussion.

Thursday 28 October
At Cabinet Elwyn Jones said he wished to object to a phrase Eric Varley had used about the Lords being 'criminally responsible', or something similar, in blocking our legislation. Fred supported him and thought it was most unwise tactically to attack the Lords at this moment. I said, 'This is rubbish. We have got to mobilise our own people. I was up in Newcastle last night where shipbuilding is everything and if the Lords throw out the Aircraft and Shipbuilding Bill, it means the loss of thousands of jobs.'

Denis Healey came to lunch and I jotted down all the points he made. He told me that studies of the alternative strategy had been undertaken at his request in the Treasury from February 1975 onwards, which was when I put in my Strategy A and Strategy B paper. There was really no agreement on strategy in the Treasury and there were different views on policy. 'I am the only monetarist in the Treasury, and I am a monetarist by insisting on cash limits.' He would change the strategy only if the results of not changing it were worse, i.e., it risked the withdrawal of the TUC support for the Government or the withdrawal of support by the rank-and-file members for the TUC leadership. He said it would take a year for the alternative strategy to work and therefore you couldn't base an Election on it; all macro remedies such as import controls or devaluation are ineffective because British industry reacts so sluggishly to change in the environment, as depreciation has proved.

He was disappointed at the lack of detail in the alternative strategy. The IMF would be tough but manageable and he had privately threatened Simonet with the possibility that there might be a Cabinet majority for import controls if the EEC were to be tough on loans. He told me Jim had cleared his comment on *Panorama* about NATO with the Treasury but it was intended as a warning and not as a threat.

Denis said that if you asked the monetarists exactly what their strategy would mean in terms of unemployment they were on the defensive because it wouldn't be below millions for some years. He thought Labour would win the next Election because Thatcher was such a repugnant figure, less popular than Jim, and the public opinion polls showed us in a much stronger position than in 1968. He thought the balance of payments would be in balance by 1978, unemployment would be below 1 million, with inflation falling, and that retaliation against us on import controls might be severe if the world thought it had to teach us a lesson.

Confirming what Jim is up to, he said the IMF loan would not be enough and therefore there would have to be some additional EEC arrangements: the National Executive Committee meeting had cost us 2 cents to the pound. When I said, 'I was told by a Tory, Trevor Skeet, that Michael Foot being elected Deputy-Leader of the Party explained the fall,' he said that was rubbish. So you choose your own mythology.

It was my first lunch alone with Denis and for the first time I felt a meeting of minds and discovered a great deal more about what he thought. Clearly he is taking a political judgment which I think from his point of view is right, and it may be that his assessment of the reaction of the unions and the Party is better than mine. But I wouldn't be too sure about it. I have now got to argue the case for the alternative strategy politically, not as an economic case, because I recognise the real difficulties.

Went to the dinner which the Soviet Ambassador, Lunkov, was giving for Boris Ponamarev, the head of the Soviet Communist Party's International Committee. There have been Jewish demonstrations against him, a bomb scare, and apparently he had a bottle thrown at his car today. The hysteria the press are building up now is quite frightening, like Germany was before 1933. I had met Ponamarev in 1959. He's seventy-one now, an ideologue, an elderly academic-looking man, and quite harmless. He thought capitalism was weaker now, so I responded with 'The Labour movement is certainly stronger.' 'But,' he said, 'look at the position in Parliament, what good does that do?' It irritated me somehow. To be lectured by the Russians is more than I can stand.

At dinner I sat between the Party Secretary, a woman from Leningrad, and the Ambassador, opposite Norman Atkinson. We talked about China and Ponamarev said he had known Liu Shao-ch'i, 'the capitalist roader', and Chou En-lai. He told us that in 1968 the Russians had had a six-and-a-half-hour dinner at which the Chinese had asked for nuclear weapons and they had said to the Chinese 'They are very expensive. You don't need them and anyway under the Chinese-Soviet friendship pact, if China is attacked, we will defend you with our weapons.'

Stephen rang home tonight from Washington. He wanted to know how to brief Senator Eagleton to deal with the situation in Britain. The American papers, which ignored the British scene most of the time, had suddenly come to the conclusion that we were on the edge of bankruptcy and it had become, in a vague sort of way, an issue in the American elections, because Ford was warning that if Carter was elected, it might lead to the same sort of Welfare State in the US that has brought Britain to ruin. Stephen is out of touch because he can't get hold of any British papers. I felt I had to be extremely circumspect on the telephone, knowing that it was likely to be bugged. I said, 'First of all, the Labour Government and the Labour Party won't split. Second, the situation is not as bad as it would appear from the point of view of the social fabric, indeed there is nothing breaking at all. Thirdly, the coalition attempts will fail.'

But I did think that the propaganda put out by conservative and international banking circles had been effective. Jim encouraged it by saying that if the Labour Government failed, there would be totalitarianism of the Left or Right and so had Denis when he said that if the policy was changed, there would be rioting in the streets. This is the danger of bluffing when you are pursuing a right-wing policy.

Friday 29 October

Up at 6.30, and Caroline and I flew to a little airport and were driven to Selby for the opening of the new coal mine. There was the Lord Lieutenant, the Marquis of Normanby and the High Sheriff of the County who was a landowner owning 10,000 acres on the Selby coalfield. Derek Ezra and Joe Gormley and others represented the Yorkshire mining Establishment.

At about 11.45, the Duchess of Kent arrived wearing a red dress and a hat with a big tassel on. She had boned up and she said to me, 'How nice to meet you. I don't think we've met before.' Then we went across to a huge pink-and-white striped tent for the ceremony of drilling the first hole with the rig. First Derek Ezra made a speech, then the Duchess of Kent pulled a lever which revealed a plaque. The Bishop of Selby, in purple cassock, read out some prayers which confirmed everything the Marxists have said about religion being the opium of the people: 'At the end of each short prayer, I shall ask you to say Amen. Oh Lord, teach us to use the earth wisely for all mankind. Amen. Oh Lord, teach us not to make wage claims in excess of what we can produce. Amen. Oh Lord, teach us not to be envious of what others have. Amen.' Just a little catechism of reaction.

I was called to make a speech and I had little formally left to say since Derek Ezra's and the Duchess of Kent's speeches had been written by the Coal Board and had dealt with all the major points. I simply said how important it was to know the miners had been right, how Joe Gormely had argued with the Labour Government ten years ago about the policy of colliery closures and how King Coal had been restored to his throne!

Joe was called and he had a few notes and he began in a measured way and then somehow he forgot that he wasn't at a pithead meeting and started to talk about productivity and the role of the miners – he appeared to be rebuking the Duchess for implying the miners were barbarians being brought into these villages. It was a marvellous speech, absolutely political, and might have been made at a miners' rally. As Caroline said afterwards, the two Establishments were there, the old feudal establishment – the Duchess, the Bishop and the Coal Board –

and Joe, me and the miners representing the new Establishment, with so much more confidence than the old. Amazing that the old feudalism still survives.

Lunch was hilarious. The Duchess sat next to me and Joe leaned across and said, 'What's your name, love?'

She said, 'Katharine.'

He said, 'I'm Joe.' Then he held up his glass and said, 'If you can't be good, be careful.'

Then Arthur Scargill came up and had a word with Caroline and I took him over and introduced him to the Duchess. It must have been an extraordinary experience for her, meeting this guy who is regarded as the most revolutionary miners' leader in Britain.

Monday 1 November

Peter Jay came at 6 and stayed until nearly 9. We had a long talk about his idea of workers' control and laissez-faire, what he calls market socialism. I pursued in detail with him how it would work and he said you wouldn't need a Government, it would all be automatic, and you wouldn't need trade unions, the workers must elect directly without the trade unions. It became clear that his solution would involve dismantling the trade unions and reducing Parliament to a cipher on the basis that it would all be self-regulating.

Tuesday 2 November

Went off to Carlisle feeling pretty unwell. I think my cold has gone to my chest and I have a pain in my back. There were the working men with their raincoats and cloth caps and the women in scarves, just like the Thirties. They gave me a tremendous welcome and I took them back to 1945 and the pledge that we would never have unemployment again. Somehow although I was stirred by the absolutely basic, solid loyalty of it, I thought, 'My God, they're going to be dropped into it again.'

Dale Campbell-Savours is the Labour candidate for the by-election here, a tall, rather elegant mixture, I thought, between Bob Maxwell and John Lindsay, the Mayor of New York. Afterwards I had a cup of tea in a little hotel then went to the Labour Club. It might have been from that programme *Days of Hope*, and a real 1930s working-class club. The warmth, friendship and loyalty were there but it made you realise how little the postwar capitalist recovery in Britain had reached beyond the South and the Midlands.

Wednesday 3 November

It was clear that Jimmy Carter had won the American elections though it wasn't confirmed until later. I felt absolutely uncommitted and neutral about it. Better the Democrats than the Republicans, better maybe for the economy, better in some ways because of the forces on each side, but I felt no sense of excitement after a campaign which had so lacked any fundamental examination of the problems facing America or the West. It was a campaign just full of language about peace, prosperity, justice, brotherhood and love, while the American Government, through the support of the big multinationals, continued to crush the little regimes on its doorstep that are trying to survive.

Economic Strategy Committee at 4 and Michael Foot was back, first time I had seen him since he developed eye trouble. Denis Healey presented his paper of forecasts, which he said were very uncertain, the drought and depreciation having made the situation worse. The central forecast was 10 per cent wage claims. The key was industrial performance. The CBI and the TUC had to help, especially the TUC on pay and strikes. We were facing a formidable task and we must reach a conclusion this month. We must show the IMF the forecasts and head them off from wishing to disrupt the industrial strategy or the Social Contract and he would report back to the committee about the IMF's view.

Michael Foot said the gravest situation faced us and, although Denis's paper urged that we shouldn't, since we were obliged to publish the forecasts of the dire economic situation, we must.

Denis said, 'We can postpone the publication.'

Michael said, 'The unemployment level is unacceptable and we will have to have import controls put on the agenda again.'

I spoke next. I said it was an exceptionally grave paper and the forecasts meant that we would have unemployment of 1.75 million, lower growth, inflation at 16 per cent and wages rising at 10 per cent, which meant a cut in living standards of 6 per cent, while the PSBR was at £11 billion – i.e., it was getting worse. Secondly, we were advised to conceal the true position from Parliament, the public and the Party, but it had already leaked to the *Financial Times* as Peter Jenkins pointed out in the *Guardian* today.'

Denis butted in, 'It's quite untrue.'

'Well, it's there.'

'It's speculation,' he said.

I went on, 'What should we do? We should move step-by-step towards the alternative strategy. We should restore planning agreements for a central role in our industrial strategy, using statutory powers only if voluntary agreements fail. We should have control on the disposal of funds by financial institutions. We should have immediate quotas on imports for cars, electronic goods, consumer durables and textiles. We should increase the funds for the NEB and development agencies without countervailing cuts.'

Peter Shore said, 'All our targets have collapsed at the same time. We do have a PSBR problem but though important, it's secondary.' He wanted controls on a massive scale.

Shirley rejected dealing with the situation by public expenditure cuts, rejected import controls and favoured a huge loan. Then she said Jeremy Bray wanted to go to talk to Carter's team in the States and we should let him because although Carter's team is very theoretical, our contacts with him are few and far between. We were hamstrung by past commitments such as public sector pensions and local government reorganisation and we ought to toughen up on supplementary benefits, because there were people who were resentful that those on supplementary benefits had more money than those at work. There were no soft options. She asked Peter, 'Do you think you could carry international opinion with import controls?'

Peter said, 'Yes, I think we could.'

Then we came to Roy Hattersley who said, 'The forecasts are not even a survival strategy. They are not acceptable to the TUC and they would end their cooperation with us. We have got to tell the public the truth about the incompatability of our social and industrial goals. We cannot do it with import restraint. We have got to abandon a part of our social strategy. Selling the Burmah shares and import deposits are only a palliative.' He agreed with Eric Varley in giving industry precedence and that would involve cuts; our social goals, or some of them, must be sacrified because unemployment was the main cause of poverty. We must sacrifice our fight against inflation and abandon some of our social priorities to get employment.

Harold Lever said, 'I am the most optimistic member of this committee. This reminds me of 1968 and 1969 when we were very pessimistic. All we have to do is to manage our debt properly.'

Merlyn Rees thought the lack of confidence was not based on facts, a package wouldn't solve it at once, we shouldn't go to the IMF in a spirit of humility. He wasn't in favour of import controls except perhaps for textiles, he favoured tax increases and was against deflation.

Edmund Dell said Denis had a difficult problem. There was no escape except for major cuts which would be a main condition of the loan.

Then Denis spoke. We must fortify confidence and we could do that by reshaping the PSBR; for example, cuts in public expenditure would be very welcome and the supplementary benefit and unemployment pay are factors here: they are a cause of resentment and if we are going to cut those or reduce them we could reduce the rates of tax on higher incomes. We must have more incentives for our managers.

Well, it would be *hair-raising* to cut the supplementary benefit and then increase tax allowances for the wealthy managers.

He went on to say the IMF loan was not enough, therefore we shall have to fund the sterling balances. 'The strategy is right, but,' he said, 'the foreign exchange market has unfortunately influenced home confidence and we must put our arguments to the IMF.'

Jim summed up. 'A new political factor is needed; perhaps we should call it a national recovery programme.'

I left the meeting almost sick with anxiety and disgrace to hear people who were elected with the support of Labour people talking in that way. But by the end of the month, it will be public and explicit.

On the way out, I had a word with Michael about memoirs. We are both still being pressed by Jim Callaghan, and Michael said he would speak to Jim and suggest that we all had a word about it. Apparently Number 10 only want to know the reasons why we won't sign and Michael thought a talk would dispose of the matter.

To the House of Commons and Joe Ashton was there. Joe knew nothing of our latest financial problems and I couldn't say anything at all. He has been invited to be a Whip and he is accepting it so he will be within the Official Secrets Act and that will help a bit. He told me that a hundred people would sign an Early Day Motion supporting the alternative strategy. It was funny that he, as a Whip-to-be, was collecting secret signatures for a motion calling for an alternative strategy.

After he had gone, I went over everything that had happened with Frances and Francis. He was white, almost sick with anger, shaking with emotion and Frances was almost in tears. I really do wonder now whether I can possibly stay in a Government that does this. But this morning they had said I must stay in because the alternative strategy was winning. I do think the demand for a change of policy is going to grow and grow but whether I can be party to this, I just don't know. Came home and Caroline gave me a warm welcome, bless her heart.

She told me that Argentinian bishops had been in conclave for two or three days to discuss whether they would allow Portuguese and Spanish translations of the Bible to be published in the Argentine. She said that these particular translations had been done under the Allende Government which had begun to release the Bible in Latin America. Fascinating – a seventeenth-century situation with the Bible just about to be released in the vernacular, just like the age of the Levellers all over again. The mixture between the Bible, Catholicism, Marxism and Communism is an explosive force in that continent.

Sunday 7 November
Crossman's *Diaries* are dominating the newspapers. They throw a light on politics as it really is and say nothing malicious that hasn't appeared in every newspaper journalist's articles about the Cabinet for years. But coming from Dick it all has a certain authenticity. He once said to

me that he had never been able to write a book about socialism because if he did he thought he would discover he wasn't a socialist. Of course in a theoretical sense, it is a very difficult concept to define, but like an elephant, you know it when you see it. So Dick may have contributed rather more than he intended.

Monday 8 November

In the evening I went to Michael's room with Stan, Albert, John Silkin and Peter for a talk. Michael is still not well after his shingles. It was the very room where I used to go and talk to Dick Crossman; somehow history repeats itself. I had read the Economic Strategy Committee paper which none of the others had done. I said, 'I have a single simple point to make really. The CPRS paper for Wednesday's committee is just the strategy for a coalition Government – a national recovery programme, hard times and all that – and I think the time has come when we have got to be much more candid with the TUC and discuss together how we handle the options. We ought to have links between Left Ministers and Jack Jones and Hugh Scanlon and maybe even Len Murray, in addition to the ones through which the union chiefs get all their news via Denis Healey.'

Michael said he had spoken to Jack Jones and that the unemployment forecasts had risen to 1.75 million and were likely to stay stable at that level. Jack was pretty worried.

Joe Ashton was appointed a Whip today, one of my best people going; I think I'll appoint Brian Sedgemore in his place.

Tuesday 9 November

Brian Sedgemore agreed today to be my PPS. I went to Jim's room to tell him and he was having a sandwich with his PPS Roger Stott so I put my head round the door and said, 'Only thirty seconds. You took away my PPS and I'd like to appoint a new one, Brian Sedgemore.'

He asked Roger Stott to leave the room and said, 'I think you have made a great mistake. He is very uncouth with Mrs Thatcher. You ought to have somebody else more in the Centre of the Party.'

I told him, 'I think I ought to pick from one of the thirty-seven who voted for me. There weren't many of them.'

'Will he support us on the IMF?' he asked. I didn't know so he followed, 'You had better ask him. I can't have you appoint him now and then find he resigns in six weeks.'

'I'll put that to him if you like.'

He said, 'If you insist on him, I'll accept it.'

Wednesday 10 November

Economic Strategy at 11 and Jim opened, 'We are not here to discuss the IMF loans or anything of that kind but the perspective.' We had before us Jim's 'National Reconstruction Programme' drafted by the CPRS and a paper by Bernard Donoughue's unit, the first time that's been circulated to Ministers.

Kenneth Berrill was asked to introduce the CPRS document and he said there were two tough years ahead. The question was whether we should tell the people the position. There were some very austere sections that had to be included and there would be a fall in real take-home pay. One, we must raise the level of efficiency. Two, North Sea Oil alone wouldn't solve the problem. Three, we must maintain the mixed economy. Four, we must re-orient public expenditure. Five, we must reshape public attitudes to profits. Six, there will have to be a very long-term pay norm. Seven, there could be no increase in social expenditure but some re-allocation of it. This was a very unpleasant message to get across.

Crosland said, 'The CPRS document simply won't do. I am in favour of industrial democracy, not because I believe in democracy, but because I believe it will improve productivity. But this is a coalitionist manifesto. It will be praised in *The Times* as being courageous but will be quite unacceptable to the public as well as the Party.'

'The CPRS is a start,' replied Jim, 'but what worries me is that we might do as they say and then lose the Election. Bernard, what do you think?'

'I can't dissent from the CPRS analysis. The question is, how do we act, apart from projecting this awful message. We need more participation by arguing and persuading our way through.'

Denis Healey thought it was a useful framework but it was not inspiring and he wondered what could be added without compromising the austere message. 'The Cabinet and Ministers must ask themselves this question: is it right to let non-workers' incomes rise, that is those on supplementary benefit, the unemployed, and those who have retired, at the expense of those who are at work? We have got to ask ourselves what is the acceptable level of unemployment' – (implying it should be higher) – 'and what is the acceptable level of supplementary benefit?'

Michael Foot thought it would be disastrous to publish it. This was a coalition document. 'The TUC's support would go if they knew what the figures were.'

Denis interrupted, 'We needn't publish these figures at all,' and Jim commented, 'Forecasts are always wrong, and we mustn't assume these forecasts will materialise.'

I welcomed the idea of a national recovery programme, but I thought the paper had five defects. Its analysis was superficial. It was an amalgam of *Daily Mail* editorials over twenty years. It was riddled with scapegoats of lazy workers and incompetent managers. I said, 'I've heard of the people changing their Government but never the Government announcing it is going to change the people and their attitudes.' It was a coalition strategy calling for sacrifices but from whom? 'There is one point I want to make in general. There is always a choice in what you do, however tough the situation is. If you are in a lifeboat with one loaf of bread, you can either auction it or ration it.'

Jim said, 'I would have thought you should eat it.'

'What therefore is the alternative? First of all, in my scenario, there are no villains and no heroes. The real problem is that the market economy is incompatible with strong trade unions and the ballot box because of the pressure on profits. The market is the big spanner in the works and we have got to find a way of getting it out. Second, we must express confidence in our people. This theory that we are all to blame is incompatible with leadership. Third, we must take people into our confidence and tell them the facts. You have to have a trade-off of wealth and power and that is what industrial democracy and the Social Contract are about. It is a question of political reform, like 1832, 1867, 1906, 1945. We have to get a new settlement based upon the fact that the electors are more informed and the unions are more powerful, and win the argument. There really isn't a middle ground because Keynesianism with its inflationary remedies has failed.'

Shirley Williams said, 'The Germans and the Swedes do better. Our trouble is we are ambivalent about the mixed economy. Nationalised industry must be allowed to make a profit, and private industry must make a profit. We need continuity of policy.'

Then Jim asked me, 'Why *have* they done better in Sweden and Germany?'

'Well, first of all, we are the most civilised country in the world and we believe in the quality of life and have high standards. From the Luddites to the Club of Rome, the British people have always believed in quality and if you look back fifty years and say it's a package deal, I would rather have Britain than Germany or Sweden. Sweden was neutral and we know what happened to Germany. We must have faith in our own people.'

'I find that entirely unconvincing,' said Jim.

I continued. 'Bagehot got it right. He said the vote would be a disaster because the working class might combine and he was right. That has happened. I wish we could discuss it at a weekend meeting.'

'We might,' replied Jim, but he summed up absolutely against me.

Came back to the office at 12.30 and Gordon Richardson, Governor of the Bank of England, came to lunch. I think he was in the Treasury at one time. It was his first visit to the Department and he arrived in his green Rolls Royce.

I asked him whether he was a City spokesman or a Government agent.

'I am really both,' he said. 'The City come to me and if I think they have got a case I put it forward but I also have a responsibility to the Government. There's lots of money. I've got lots of control.' He then asked what 'this bank nationalisation' was all about.

I said, 'Well, I think if you are going to ask workers to make sacrifices now in the interest of the future, you may have to ask investors to sacrifice something in the interest of the future. Nothing has been asked of them yet.'

He said, 'But we have to get profits up.'

'I have never known anyone opposed to profits,' I replied. 'The question is what you do with them.'

'This coming year will be difficult, won't it? How would you deal with it?'

'I am for import controls. I came to that conclusion slowly and reluctantly as I realised we were bleeding to death and we would have to have them. I think Mrs Thatcher will see it too. I think if she were in power, the CBI would press it on her and after all it would be easier for her because nobody would link it to the Stalinist siege economy, the Common Market would know she was sympathetic to them and the international community would trust her.' He took that on board.

Thursday 11 November

Before Cabinet, I talked to Merlyn Rees who said, 'I have never seen the Party in such despair. People think the Government might fall by tonight, the Opposition may defeat the Aircraft and Shipbuilding Bill.'

In the meeting, Jim said, 'It is going to be extremely tough from now until Christmas and I don't want to carry on leading a Government that is divided. I don't want to give up, or anything of that kind, but we have got to be united. We have got to make that clear.'

We went on to the Queen's Speech which is to be delivered on 24 November. There was a reference to the 'unacceptable level of unemployment' and the point was made that we couldn't go on talking about it as unacceptable, so that was deleted. The reference to replacing the Official Secrets Act by some new legislation was omitted and the general point was made that the less Parliament did this coming year the better.

Jim said, 'We have just got to axe some Bills,' and he went through the list trying to get some of them chopped. Stan Orme suggested that the European direct elections might be deferred. Stan said, 'It looks as if the only Bills we can bring forward are those the Tories and the

Liberals will accept.' I was nodding in agreement and Jim said, 'It's no good Stan saying that. It's no good Tony Benn nodding sagely. We have got to face the fact we are a minority Government.' In the end, nothing in terms of legislation was actually cut.

Dashed over to the House and then went to see Jack Jones at Transport House with Stan Orme. We were shown into the Bevin Room overlooking St John's in Smith Square. I told Jack that I'd asked to see him because Stan and I were very worried about the situation.

'Well, don't resign,' said Jack.

'That's not the issue,' I replied, 'We are now facing very bad forecasts, as Michael has told you, and we have a big decision to make.'

'Well,' said Jack sullenly, 'they're only forecasts, and if unemployment is threatening to rise we shall have to take measures to deal with it.'

Stan intervened, 'You know the measures proposed by the Treasury involve very substantial cuts in pensions and supplementary and unemployment benefit?'

'Oh, the trade union movement wouldn't have that,' said Jack angrily.

Stan said, 'I am not talking about Cabinet decisions or Healey. I am talking about what the Treasury's talking about – which is cuts.'

Jack was extremely gloomy. 'There will have to be some cuts but we are waiting for some results. Anyway, what's the alternative?'

'Look, that's not the point,' said Stan. 'We are trying to put the position to you.'

'Jim is fine,' I said. 'He allows a very open debate in the Cabinet. And Denis is fine too.'

'I don't know about that,' Jack grumbled, 'and as for Jim having been in the Treasury, he doesn't really understand and he is not up to the job.'

He came to life at the thought of fighting an Election against the bankers and in defence of the Labour Government. Stan kept on, cheerful, smiling, tough – it was the occasion when working-class leaders should speak to each other. It was not the occasion for me to say very much at all.

I decided to let Stan carry the weight of it and just looked out of the window.

At 3.45 I went to see Merlyn Rees who is in the office Thatcher had occupied until this summer. I hadn't been in there since March 1974. I told Merlyn what the tactics were and gave him the 1931 Manifesto which I am sure he will pass on to Jim.

'You know,' he said to me, 'I don't feel I am in charge of the Home Office at all. In Northern Ireland I used to have meetings with my people late into the night, and Stan Orme and I worked out what we

644 THE DEATH OF CONSENSUS: NOVEMBER 1976

would do. But in this job, I am the ritual Home Secretary and I don't feel they take any notice of me.'

I told him he was in one of the three great unreformed Departments – the Home Office, the Foreign Office and the Treasury.

Had a cup of tea in the Tea Room and talked to Norman Atkinson who is a very thoughtful guy. We talked about Scanlon. I said the trouble with Hugh was that he lived in two watertight compartments – the compartment of his dream socialist world and the compartment of daily life and in the latter, he was always 'on a hiding for nothing'. He never relates his real life to his socialist perspective.

Norman said, 'I must tell you, Tony, at the moment there is no industrial support for the Left and we are powerless until it picks up again.'

I went up to my room and there was a message from Caroline telling me the house had been burgled; Joshua had come in, banged the door and switched on the television. He heard someone moving upstairs and thought it was Caroline and this chap must have crept downstairs through the front door and disappeared. Caroline came in a few minutes later, went up and worked in her room and she didn't realise what had happened, because although one of the drawers had been tipped over the bed probably in the hope of finding money, she didn't notice. Joshua came up and asked how long she'd been home and they went downstairs and found this bloke had kicked in the basement door with his boot, cutting his leg on the glass. He had come upstairs and started in Caroline's room. Josh was worried and Caroline was upset but it wasn't as bad as it might have been.

Friday 12 November
Stayed at home all day. Julie Clements, my new secretary, came in, a very nice woman. I like her very much.

Sunday 14 November
Up at 7, got Caroline breakfast in bed, and went to Bristol for the Remembrance Day Service at the Bristol Cenotaph – the first time I have been in twenty-six years. Right bang opposite the Cenotaph was a building which had been taken over by Chicago Bank with a big blue and white glass neon sign, *Chicago Bank Ltd* and the Esso building, and so you had the big multinationals as a backdrop to the layer of pageantry that went back to the seventeeth century.

I thought of Milton Friedman and the Chicago School, and Chile, and the alliance between modern industrialists and international financiers and the old British Establishment which is now so pathetically weak that it relies upon international companies to keep it in power. We have moved from being an imperial state with all the imperial splendour with those vulgar business people making money on the peripheries of our Empire to the point where we are now a nation governed by royal ritual, a client state of big business dominated by the United States.

Up to the Mansion House for lunch with about fifty people. Women in white gloves served roast beef, and rum baba and we had a loyal toast and speeches: the Establishment gorging itself on the occasion of Armistice Day.

Monday 15 November

At 12.30 Paul Routledge of *The Times* came to lunch. He told me that there was a rethink at the paper, that they were beginning to regard Mrs Thatcher more highly, although at the Tory Conference she had said that she might come to some arrangement with Jim Callaghan. I find that hard to believe, but that's what he said.

Tuesday 16 November

Late this evening, Ken Coates rang to ask if I could do anything about the deportation orders being served today on Mark Hosenball, of the *Standard*, and Philip Agee.* The Home Office say that Agee has been in touch with foreign Intelligence services. I don't know if that is true but I am sure they will be bugging his phone.

Wednesday 17 November

Tonight I began reading *Mein Kampf*, which was written by Hitler in the 1920s, long before he came to power. It contains statements that regularly appear in right-wing journals – about the Marxist state, trade unionism, corrupt bourgeois democracy, and so on.

I talked a bit to Michael Meacher who said that Frank Field had told him that the report by Inspector Habershon into the child benefit leak contained five suspects, of whom Meacher was one. Michael denied having leaked the document and I believe him implicitly – it is a smear, and I advised him to leave it for a bit and see how it goes. I will see what I can do to help him.

Before Economic Strategy Committee I said to Merlyn Rees, 'You told me the other day you wondered whether you were really in charge of the Home Office, a remark which made a great impression on me. Is that true of the two deportation orders you put on Hosenball and Agee?'

'No, no,' he said, 'I dealt with them both personally. They were in touch with foreign agents – Cubans and Russians.'

* Agee, a former CIA operations officer, who exposed CIA activities in a book, and Hosenball, a radical American journalist also writing about Intelligence matters, were deported in 1977 by Merlyn Rees as security risks. A large and vocal campaign for their defence was waged.

'Well, it looks as if the Americans have put pressure —'

'Oh, nothing to do with the Americans at all, they were damaging to our security.'

I took very careful notes at the Committee. Jim began by saying there was sympathy for us in America and Germany, that Harold Lever was on a mission to the USA to explain our position, but everybody believed that the PSBR was the key. We must be very secret about this, though we will have to find ways later of telling the Cabinet, later still of telling the Party and the TUC.

'We need a package,' said Jim, 'and I will describe this myself before Denis speaks. First, IMF backing for the industrial strategy, and I must tell you that the IMF does not think that sterling is undervalued. Second, we need a safety net by way of funding the sterling balances, and thirdly we want to have some policy on imports. Import deposits are one option but I am thinking of something else. Don't ask me more.'

Then Denis said, 'I want a mandate to talk to the IMF. They have seen the forecasts. Len Murray and Methven of the CBI have been to see them and supported the Social Contract and the industrial strategy. The IMF confirm our balance of payments forecast for 1977. They say there will be lower growth next year because of world trade and depreciation but the PSBR will be higher because of the lower growth.

'The PSBR is the key to the IMF loan. If we can get it down in 1977 and 1978, it would be better, so I want to discuss a tax and public expenditure balance with Treasury officials to this end. We must decide before Christmas because we have to have a contingent agreement on the PSBR from the Cabinet by next Tuesday, it will take two weeks to implement and we should aim to agree to something not less than a £9 billion PSBR target.'

Jim said, 'Nine billion is the minimum.'

Denis agreed. 'The unanimous belief of our friends and colleagues is that the PSBR is too high. I will have to have a package deal: regulator powers if used to the full would give us £750 million with some employment effects but public expenditure would have manpower effects.'

'The PSBR seems to be becoming a sort of God,' snorted Roy Hattersley.

I said I wanted to look at the problem entirely politically, and not technically. I welcomed the idea of a package but it had to hang together and if the PSBR was the key to external confidence, it was also the key to internal confidence, because if you cut the PSBR it would be deflationary in one sense but push up some prices, rents and rates for example; it would push up unemployment, a danger to the Social Contract; and it would endanger investment. The idea that the PSBR was the key factor was not surprising since some people in the

Treasury had wanted to cut it for ages anyway. We *were* treating it like a God. Denis believed the IMF was angry with us and we had to cut more hospitals and schools and that would be sufficient. The trouble was that it would be unpredictable.

Then, of course, if we agreed to a £9 billion limit or whatever on Tuesday, we were absolutely committed to deliver. This was a test of political will and I said, 'If I may make a point about psychology, I think sacrifices to earn the right to borrow money from abroad with which to buy goods from abroad and, in the process, destroy our own industry is mad, absolutely mad. Letting the Germans lend us money to buy their German cars, when imports are now 43 per cent is crazy, and if you add to that that you not only have to satisfy the IMF but the market, then of course it is the complete abandonment of our responsibilities. There is a sense of national revulsion at the proposal that we sell BP shares, or the National Gallery – it is a feeling of national pride. We must stand on our own feet. It's rather a Victorian sentiment to introduce, I know, but we can't buy from abroad more than we can pay for abroad, and that points to import controls.'

I don't think that pleased Jim very much, so he said we had to decide now and that was the end of it. He was a bit crabby with me, frankly. We finished with that item and we came on to Denis's specific papers. The first one was in effect to sell the Government's shares in BP.

With our policy on participation, and our own BNOC, a state-owned oil company like BP is very important to us. I said that we had pledged in the Social Contract to stick at 51 per cent ownership of the shares. Churchill had bought them and I never thought I would have to quote a Churchill speech to a Labour Cabinet committee, that even in the darkest days of the war he would never sell them. In fact, in Scotland, where the Forties field is regarded as Scottish oil, there would be a tremendous row, if an English government – as they saw it – sold off their assets.

Jim interrupted, 'Well, I let BP fall below 51 per cent when I was Chancellor and nobody made a row.'

'Well, it will be seen as a piece of de-nationalisation,' I said.

Thursday 18 November

At 10.15 went to Cabinet at which Jim said, 'We'll have an oral report on the IMF. There is not much I can say, Harold Lever has been in Washington,' and he repeated the points made at the meeting yesterday by him and Denis, stressing that the PSBR was the key. The PSBR quantum had to be agreed next Tuesday.

Stan asked about import controls and I said we *must* talk to the TUC. 'We haven't got time. Chequers next week might be possible, but that is after we have decided on the quantum,' Jim said.

Then we came to two Cabinet papers, one on Cabinet security and the other on the Official Secrets Act which discussed lifting the criminal sanctions from documents that didn't touch defence or foreign security, or commercial confidence or personal records. It wasn't exactly open government, but Peter Shore was passionately against this. 'You cannot discuss things openly.' He really is a Transport House bureaucrat. I said I didn't think it mattered very much. Not having criminal sanctions was hardly open government.

Anyway the two documents were agreed. One other issue came up – the health and safety committees to which we are absolutely pledged. The story is very simple: the private sector is prepared to run and fund them but the local authorities, Government, Defence Department and health authorities don't want them, because they involve a big expansion of industrial democracy.

So officials tried to fight it by putting enormous inflationary costs in, based on the need to train everybody in fire and safety drill, and recruit more workers. The cost was put at £88m and then reduced to £44m, then the Government agreed £25m and Albert said, 'Let's make it £10 million.' In the end we haven't done it at all because of public expenditure cuts. Albert has got to tell the TUC, who will be really upset that this can't be done. Another nail in the coffin of the Social Contract. Really awful. You wonder whether you're in a Labour Government at all.

Went over to the House and Elliott Richardson came at 4. Now that he is a lame duck Secretary for Commerce in the US Administration, the PM is being told not to see him, he's not important. But Jim said he would like to meet him.

Elliott told me about Carter's energy strategy and I asked him about nuclear power. 'Well, there are these obscurantist groups, the environmentalists, who are against change and they are the real conservatives, they ignore the needs of the people.'

We discussed economic growth and I said, 'For about a hundred years, people in this country have really rejected the idea of high growth anyway.'

'Well, that is wasteful,' he said, 'and not in their interest.'

'I'm all for eliminating waste, but what we've never done here is really accept the values of the market economy. Capitalism is a sort of heart transplant that has never quite taken.'

'Well, you sure said a mouthful!' he said.

'We don't like people being made factors of production, we just don't like it, morally we object to it.'

I took him down to Jim, then discovered he left behind on my desk his brief for his visit. I was dying to look at it, and so I took it to the lavatory, sat down and turned to the 'Personality' page. There was a picture of me, with a description of the various posts I held. 'Leading socialist, in favour of nationalisation and state control. Caused great anxiety to business interests. However, carrying on current policy of the Department of Energy. Moved from the Department of Industry.' Then it said I was an energetic and enthusiastic person married to an American from Cincinnati with four children. I didn't drink but was a generous host. It wasn't as bad as I expected, it might have been a hell of a lot worse. I would love to have photocopied it but I didn't have the guts. It was amusing.

Today Jim sent me a note that because I couldn't give him an assurance that Brian Sedgemore would support the Government he was not prepared to allow me to appoint Brian Sedgemore. I wrote back saying:

Dear Jim

I have never been asked to seek personal assurances from a PPS, nor has my choice ever been queried. The fault, if fault there be, is mine because I didn't feel it right to ask Brian Sedgemore. You didn't ask me when you appointed your Cabinet. Confidence has to be assumed between colleagues.

But I didn't ask him to reverse his decision.

Came home and the minutes which I had asked for of the fateful 1931 Cabinet meeting arrived. They were not all that different from today's minutes – very uninformative – but that five day period from 19–24 August 1931 was fascinating, and a complete repeat of what is happening now.

There was the appeal for absolute secrecy, the wide consultation with the Bank of England, the Federal Reserve and the New York bankers, and the Bank of France. Of course they were discussing the crisis with the Tories which we haven't done. The NEC then was leaving it all to the Government. The TUC was critical. There was talk about a revenue tariff, that's to say import controls. Snowden was warning against any depreciation in the standard of living of workers. MacDonald was urging cuts, mainly of unemployment benefit which the Tories and the Bank of England insisted upon, though the Tories resisted cuts in the fighting services. Important members of the Cabinet were refusing to agree cuts in unemployment benefit.

1931 had always been a horror to me but reading these papers I could see that it was a perfectly normal Cabinet crisis, the difference being that then we had a genuine minority Government so you did have to talk to the Opposition. In the end some senior Ministers couldn't go along with it but the majority could. So Ramsay went and formed a Coalition Goverment. He said it wouldn't last long and that normal Party activity would resume later; and then, having formed a Government, he dissolved Parliament a few weeks later, denounced the Labour Party and destroyed it.

I don't think Jim will do the same. It is hair-raising reading and it makes me shiver but seeing them in the same format as present-day Cabinet minutes and knowing that Father attended all those meetings, is also somehow thrilling.

Saturday 20 November

Rang Dick Clements and told him about the 1931 Cabinet minutes. He dashed over to see them and I said, 'Look you could reproduce the whole thing in *Tribune* if you wanted to in a single issue.' He said he'd publish them in two weeks but I said it had to be quicker than that.

Sunday 21 November

I went to the London Weekend Television studios to discuss the House of Lords with Chairman of the Conservative Party, Lord Thorneycroft, for Peter Jay's programme. Before we began, I gave Peter the minutes of the 1931 crisis and he was spellbound.

I got across the points I wanted to make about class structure and the conservative nature of the Lords. I was asked about the monarchy and I said, 'Australia and Canada have a monarchy but they have no House of Lords, and the constitutional monarchy doesn't use its powers against the Commons so it's quite secure.'

Got in the car and was driven to Park Lane where I joined the TUC/Labour Party anti-racialism march. The whole family was there. We saw Neil Kinnock, Michael Foot, Joan Lestor and David Pitt. It was frightfully cold as we listened to the speeches. Merlyn Rees was really booed and shouted at over the Hosenball and Agee deportations. It angers everybody with any decent liberal instincts.

Went to Anne Armstrong's reception for a delegation from the US. She was terribly friendly to Caroline. I got the feeling that it was really members of the security community that had come over on a visit. I think they're called the Western European Security and Cooperation Committee of the Senate. They had been round Western Europe probably assessing whether Western Europe was stable or not.

Norman Atkinson and his wife were there as was Hugh Jenkins [Labour MP for Putney] and his wife, and Neil and Glenys Kinnock. I think the American Embassy wanted the Senate Committee to get a look at the Left.

Monday 22 November

At 7.45 am Ron Vaughan drove me to Claridges where I had breakfast followed by oil talks with the President of Venezuela, Carlos Andres Perez. There was a great crowd outside, with TV cameras, tape-recorders and security officials and so on. Jack Rampton and Bryan Emmett came with me and I suppose there were twenty-five present there including our Ambassador, Perez Guerrero, who is a former head of UNCTAD, and the Foreign Minister, Escovar. Perez is older than me, about fifty-five, with sideburns, a tough, determined, dynamic man, leader of a radical, reforming nationalist party, the Action Democratic Party. He doesn't speak a word of English.

The cameras withdrew finally and I had next to me a tall fifty-five-year-old English interpreter, a Mrs Anderson, who was extremely good though I could hardly hear her voice, since Perez boomed out in Spanish. He got quickly on to the oil question, the relation between the oil price and the new international order and how necessary it was for Venezuela to fight on behalf of the developing countries and for the industrialised countries to be sympathetic. We shouldn't be parochial.

'Well, Mr President,' I said, 'if you intended to invite to breakfast somebody who believes in British capitalism, then I'm afraid you invited the wrong man.' He roared with laughter.

I repeated Julius Nyerere's remark when he was criticised by American journalists for having one party, TANU, in Tanzania, that in America they have a one-party state but with typical American extravagance they have two of them.

Perez is a charming man and it was a friendly meeting. We talked about the new economic order in the world and in Britain, and I told him that the Labour Party was committed to a fundamental and irreversible shift in the balance of wealth and power in favour of working people and their families. He said they'd take that as a slogan for the North-South dialogue, and I replied that was fine.

Before lunch I sat in on the Aircraft and Shipbuilding Nationalisation Bill in the House of Lords on which they were solemnly deciding, by 190 to 90 votes, that they would delete ship repairing. They knew they were engaged in a major constitutional crisis by rejecting such an important Bill and I heard Fred Peart saying that it was inadvisable to do this. My presence at the bar was noticed by some Tory peers; they must hate my guts.

I went back to the House and looked in to see Peter Shore. Nicky Kaldor was with him, trying to persuade him to resign tomorrow. Peter was very preoccupied. He has given up about £480 million on housing in the last couple of weeks and he was worried.

I took Nicky to my room and we talked. He said he had impeccable information – from a source he couldn't possibly disclose – that there was no agreement in the Treasury about what we should do tomorrow. 'It is absolutely essential for the life and safety of the Labour movement that you stand firm, collectively reject the imposition of the cuts, and call Jim's bluff.' He also said that Sir Douglas Wass, the Permanent Secretary of the Treasury, and Leo Pliatzky were both very sympathetic to us and it was Alan Lord and Derek Mitchell at the Treasury who were putting the knife in.

I went over with Caroline to Number 10 for a dinner for Perez. Talked a bit to David Steel. Jim made a good speech. I told him that he looked very boyish and he said he'd washed his hair for the occasion! I also had a long talk to John Biffen whom I really like. He said he spent a lot of time defending me and the idea that I was an authoritarian was a load of old codswallop.

Caroline and I enjoyed it very much. When we arrived home, the paper that is being discussed at Cabinet tomorrow was in my red box. It is absolutely terrifying. £1.5 billion cuts, including the sale of BP shares and delaying the upgrading of pensions. I just feel that it is unacceptable.

Tuesday 23 November

Frances and Francis arrived at 8 to discuss today's Cabinet paper. We went over the ground carefully and I reported what Nicky Kaldor had said yesterday. We concluded that the right line to take today was the national interest.

At Cabinet the first item was Rhodesia and Tony Crosland had a paper calling for a British presence in Rhodesia to help an interim Government. Jim reported that this had been put to a committee which had been evenly divided. Crosland said a British presence was absolutely essential but he hoped no one would think that we were being drawn into another Vietnam. Michael Foot and Elwyn Jones agreed.

I said, 'We are told it's a modest proposal. But is it really? If you look at para four, the FO say that if we don't go in we'll lose goodwill and influence in black Africa, we'll lose our European reputation, risk a racial guerrilla war and make it more likely that South African and Cuban intervention takes place, and Rhodesia will become a shambles. If these really are the things we're going to prevent, then the policy advocated would be a major exercise of power. If it were to be used, if we were to attempt to use it, it would be well beyond our capacity and if we abandoned it and guerrilla warfare resumed, then our reputation would be gone for ever and our impotence would be proved. It is territory extremely conducive to guerrilla warfare. What we'd be doing is internalising the Rhodesian situation and creating a crisis in the heart of British politics.

'Awful as it is for the whites to accept, the whites have got to come to terms with the blacks. If you look at our colonial history, we always claim that Attlee gave colonial freedom to India and Pakistan. The truth is that the majority always took their freedom and we didn't resist. The mythology is that we were generous and we have to do it again but, in reality, these people have got to be helped to come to terms with the situation. That does not mean a British presence.'

I also asked if it was not the case that the Rhodesian troops and Intelligence Services were closely integrated in a common military and intelligence community with South Africa, and that if we were there as Commander-in-Chief of the Rhodesian troops and Intelligence, we'd be caught up in the same net.

Jim said he couldn't discuss that. He summed up that we were going to go ahead with it. It wasn't the major item today but still I was glad I had made my point.

Then we came to the IMF. Jim gave another warning about secrecy and leaks and he regretted the story in the *Guardian* that the Cabinet was going to discuss the IMF terms today. The question was could we afford to pay the price that the IMF were asking of us. Either way we could go into the abyss. There was no certainty and we had to decide in twenty-four hours.

Denis said this timescale was a new dimension. We have been negotiating hard and we can't wreck the relations with either the CBI or the TUC. The IMF think a dramatic improvement is possible. They say that by 1978–9 we can get the PSBR down to £6.5 billion and accept that our starting point is £10.5 billion next year. The IMF would accept £9 billion next year and £6.5 billion the year after. He said 7 December was the best day to announce; it was painful but at least we'd have an endorsement from international sources for our policy, it would transform our international position and take us out of current account deficit next year, and domestic confidence would resume as interest rates came down.

Tony Crosland said he couldn't defend the package and senior economists had written to *The Times* to say this. As to the politics, whatever Jack Jones may say, NALGO, NUPE and the NUT would in effect pull out of the Social Contract, and the PLP would produce opposition that came from a far wider group than the Tribune Group. 'We know it's wrong and what would happen to confidence if we really saw the end of the Social Contract? We would be savagely split and it would have a serious effect in the House of Commons. So what are we to do?'

I said, 'I suggest we accept £1 billion off the PSBR, find half of it in Burmah oil shares, a quarter by cuts in public expenditure that would not be deflationary, and a quarter (£250 million) in real cuts.'

Crosland suggested we should ask the Americans and the Germans whether by their pressure they want to drive us to a policy of protection and defence cuts. Our weakness was our strength, it was a test of nerve, and the IMF must give us the loan.

Jim Callaghan reminded us that the question really before us was whether to authorise Denis to discuss £9 billion with the IMF and we ought to decide it by lunchtime.

Reg Prentice didn't see any alternative, and therefore thought we should cut the PSBR. He thought we needed a bigger cut than the IMF figure. If the Labour Party wouldn't face up to its responsibilities, we might have to have the support of other parties or make way for a Government that would do it.

Peter said, 'Well, we're being asked to bite the bullet but in fact we'll blow our political brains out. The confidence of the markets is no basis.' Denis had produced an alternative strategy himself and Peter suspected the figures produced by the Treasury.

Peter continued that he thought that unemployment would be about 2 million, and he didn't agree with Tony Crosland; he was in favour of the alternative strategy of import controls, beginning perhaps with deposits, and of exchange controls.

Roy Hattersley saw the loan as a first step in a radical change in our economic strategy and he was prepared to pay some price. He disliked the alternative strategy but we couldn't pay this price. Tony Crosland was right, trade union loyalty to the wage policy would end. We should make some concessions to confidence but there would be a wide rejection of this package and it would spell the destruction of the Government and the Labour Party. If that were the price, he wanted to examine the argument about import controls and exchange controls.

I said the gravity of the issue was beyond dispute and that our prime duty was to the British nation who had elected us to govern. It was a historic choice and we had to look back at past history and at the future. I'd been through the Cabinets for 1931 over the last five days and there were many lessons to be learned. It is said that history never repeats itself, but it certainly had done so in this case.

We had to look at the future of the country and the Party and we couldn't let the IMF supervise our economy right up until the next Election. We needed time to consult the TUC, as happened before; the NEC, as happened before; the PLP, as happened before; and we had to have a political strategy based on getting this through the House of Commons on Labour votes. The Chancellor was asking us to reverse his policy and adopt deflation and cuts when there were already 1.75 million unemployed, 16 per cent inflation, 8 per cent fall in living standards this year and low investment. All of these would be exacerbated and if the money were all taken in cuts, I didn't believe there would be light at the end of the tunnel.

'But,' I said, 'my real objection to it is that it betrays our national interest in terms of growth and jobs and introduces deflation and a slump. It will undermine the Social Contract because it would be making pensioners pay for the crisis, which is unjust. Being a supervised economy it will undermine national confidence and pleading for money is very demoralising.' Therefore, we couldn't get it through the Commons on Labour votes because it would be divisive, and blind and unthinking loyalty were not enough.

So what was the alternative? I was strongly in favour of the alternative strategy. But the other alternative was for the PM to take it up with the IMF. The PM should argue the case and keep the alternative policy in reserve.

I said I didn't like Governments that threatened people but at the same time if we couldn't get help in dealing with these problems then we would have to draw people's attention to the fact that we'd have to defend ourselves. We'd better tell them that no Government in Britain – Labour or Tory – could govern without the goodwill of the trade union movement because these were the people who create the nation's wealth; and we must have good relations with management. We had a prime duty to the nation and we should discharge it in the way suggested by the PM, arguing for the policy that the Cabinet had adopted.

Winding up, Denis said we didn't want publicity about this if we could avoid it and there would be a lot of pressure, but if we adopted the course the Cabinet seemed to want to adopt, then it would invariably lead to the alternative strategy.

Wednesday 24 November

Decided to dictate a Cabinet paper, with Francis by my side, to be classified as Top Secret, in which I spelled out the choices facing the Cabinet, the dangers of the IMF route and the alternative strategy, ending with a long passage on the problems of implementation.

To the Energy Committee chaired by Merlyn Rees, where the first item was Windscale. A year ago we agreed to the siting of an oxide reprocessing plant for Japanese nuclear waste. I had held it up for some months to allow public discussion, as a result of which it was alleged that the French had been offered the contract. I held inquiry hearings in Windscale itself, and in London, and finally recommended to the Cabinet that we go ahead with it.

It is of course a major planning issue and the Cumbrian Council, who are interested in the jobs, approved it, but Peter Shore as Minister of the Environment had the right to call it in for a decision by himself. He wrote a paper for today's meeting calling it in, although the whole of Whitehall had briefed their Ministers against doing this because it would involve delay.

I described how, on a visit to Tokyo a year ago, I was told that Windscale had had a fire in 1957 and that part of it was not operating yet, something I had never been told by my officials. I said it was not a problem of middle-class cranks versus solid workers. It was the scientific community trying to get its way with political Ministers.

We were discussing the statutory rights of people to have such matters properly looked at, and we should be very careful before we tell a Minister to blank out these statutory rights.

Peter got very hot under the collar and said he was calling it in anyway. Anyway it was agreed that it would go to Cabinet and meanwhile Peter would extend the decision time.

When the history of nuclear power comes to be written, I think this discussion will turn out to be a significant one.

The second item was what we should do about Burmah and the BP shares. In 1974, when Burmah got into difficulties the Government offered to buy their BP shares which were then at a low price. They've rocketed since and we have made about £450 million profit for the Government. Now Burmah are suing us for the shares. Meanwhile in order to get the PSBR down below the level which the IMF want, the Chancellor wants to sell off the shares – but because Burmah shareholders are in the process of suing the Government, Denis can't sell the shares so the Government are now planning to sell its original BP shares.

Edmund Dell thought we should sell the shares but not to foreign Governments. Harold Lever said we should sell to the highest bidder.

I went back to my room and Frances and Francis came over with the paper 'The Real Choices Facing the Cabinet'. I took it with me at 5.30 to see Michael Foot, Peter Shore, Albert Booth and Stan Orme. We agreed that we would have to stand firm, and they were all very optimistic about Tony Crosland's position, saying we should rally round him. Obviously Stan was a bit uneasy at my putting in a paper on the alternative strategy for fear that it would not win a majority. But he also admitted that the Crosland proposals would involve ending earnings-related benefit because of the cuts that were imposed on the DHSS.

Peter has been playing round with a paper for Economic Strategy Committee for a long time but he has not finished it yet, so my paper is the only one that is going in. I told them I was not asking them to support me but I wanted to set out the case quite clearly tomorrow.

Michael was worried and thought that Jim was going to come down against Denis, and Denis might resign. Of course if he does resign, the pound will go through the floor, even if we get the IMF loan. In order to keep Denis you have to have more deflation but the trick is to keep Denis and have less deflation.

It was quite a useful discussion and as for once I had marked everything absolutely secret, I hoped they would treat it as such. I later found out that the paper I'd written and was about to circulate to all Ministers, had been sent to Number 10 and Number 10 had decided to recommend to the PM that it should not be circulated. Jim had looked at it and agreed. So I am now in the position of having shown a paper to colleagues which the Prime Minister does not wish them to see, in which I refer to exchange controls and so on. It is very top secret but it is at least available and if Number 10 won't let it be seen, it just shows that Cabinet has ceased to operate at this moment of crisis, just as it did in 1929/31.

Thursday 25 November

Lazy start. First Cabinet at 10.30. *Tribune* came out with the 1931 minutes printed extensively over two pages, and the *Guardian* had a full story indicating that Jim had withdrawn his support from Denis. Things are very difficult at the moment and I'll keep my head down at Cabinet. I'll put in my paper and leave it at that. The *Guardian* story by Peter Jenkins about Callaghan taking over the helm from Denis probably came from Harold Lever who is a close friend of Jenkins. Peter Jay had an article in *The Times* based on the 1931 minutes.

Went over to Number 10 early and Ken Stowe, the PM's Private Secretary, said that my paper was not going to be circulated today but would be for a key Cabinet meeting next week.

Stan Orme showed me a minute he'd had from Brian Abel-Smith, adviser to the DHSS, concerning the alternative strategy, which stated that Nicky Kaldor had told Abel-Smith that the Treasury did have a complete plan for import controls and exchange controls – a full wartime plan locked away in a cupboard. It was known as 'the unmentionable'. Kaldor had told Abel-Smith that these were not bits of dream unreality from Benn, but were serious reserve proposals!

We discussed the Social Security Bill and whether we would be able to get the Party to support a bill which takes away the statutory rights of people who had paid for unemployment benefit all their lives to receive it where they are in receipt of occupational pensions. Stan Orme said this saved £87 million and it was forced on him in an earlier savings campaign.

But it is an absolute scandal to take money away by law from people who are entitled to receive it and I think we may not get it through. If we don't that will be a clear indication that the other savings planned by the Treasury won't get through either.

When we came to the IMF, Jim said that after the Cabinet on

Tuesday, he and Denis had carried out the necessary action. He had sent messages to President Ford and Schmidt, Denis had personally seen Alan Whittome, the head of the IMF's European Department then Whittome had been to see the Prime Minister and the Chancellor together. Jim said that the IMF knew about our fear of deflation and we faced a serious dilemma between retaining on the one hand the confidence of the TUC and, on the other, the confidence of the markets. He said that Ford and Schmidt did not want a decision today.

He went on to say that he had met Len Murray on another matter but since Len was a Privy Councillor, Jim felt able to tell him about the situation and the dilemma. Whittome had asked us to look at three scenarios for 1977/8: one was the PSBR at £8.5 billion, another at £9 billion and a third at £9.5 billion.

As to the time-table, Jim thought that we should perhaps have a decision by Wednesday's Cabinet because he was going to be at the European Council on Monday and Tuesday. He felt nothing further could be said today. Tony Benn had put out a minute and in view of its sensitive nature, he was not going to circulate it in conditions of top security until next week.

Denis said that when he met the IMF he had expressed the Cabinet view powerfully and his own motive was to ensure minimum damage to the British economy but he said we had to satisfy three groups: the staff of the IMF; the United States and Germany; and the markets.

Tony Crosland said Jim had been very successful with Ford and Schmidt and they were obviously responsive. The *Washington Post* and the *New York Herald Tribune* had written friendly leading articles, and he hoped that we'd get the papers in time to study them in detail before the Cabinet meeting at which we decided.

The Chancellor said that he would be putting in a joint paper with the Prime Minister. That will be the final stage at which we shall either be voting for or against the Prime Minister. On that there is no doubt whatever that the PM will carry the day.

Jim stated that none of these measures were going to be attractive. All the packages before us would be unpopular but he took the point about extra time for discussion and agreed that we should have two Cabinets next week, using Wednesday for discussion and Thursday for the decision.

I hoped the real options would be before us on Thursday and not just a Yes or No to the IMF proposals. We had to have broad discussions about the political implications of various courses of action. There were things that the IMF could do to us which we might accept but would involve taking away our seals of office, we would be a Government without power. Thatcher would then get in and the people we look after would suffer terribly.

Denis summed up and in reference to me he said he didn't want to intervene in the dispute between God and Mammon (me being God and Harold Lever being Mammon). We had to remember that the money-lenders did determine the value of our currency. We were spending more than we were earning and one of the things we had to go for was the real value of protected benefits because workers' earnings were not protected. This was the problem.

Stan intervened to say we had to create more jobs and Denis said it was the falling value of the pound that was losing jobs. So long as we lived in an open and a mixed economy, we shall depend on the market judgment to determine our future. If we couldn't persuade our followers that these were the facts we would fail in our leadership and then another Party would have to take over. This was the first serious threat which was, in effect, bringing the Government down. We would have proved that our brand of social democracy doesn't work.

Speaking for himself, Tony Crosland concluded that rationally he didn't believe that further cuts were sensible or necessary.

Jim didn't accept what I had said about the IMF taking away our seals of office because, he said, the IMF was there to support the Government of the day. But he did want to say that the sterling balances depended on the loan; and the reason he had included in the Queen's speech in the House yesterday a note of warning to the country, was that he thought it was only fair to give people some indication before the forecasts were published. To this extent he agreed with Tony Benn about providing more information. The situation was very grave but somebody once said you shouldn't ever lose sleep over public affairs, and Jim agreed with that.

Saturday 27 November

I read today that the CIA had a taped recording of Lee Harvey Oswald, the man arrested for shooting Kennedy, talking to the Russian Embassy before the assassination and this implied that the CIA knew more than they had ever admitted. They apparently say that they destroyed the tape when Oswald himself died – a most improbable explanation.

I must admit that the impact of the CIA story and Watergate on my thinking about the US has been profound. I am tremendously pro-American and believe passionately in the democratic ideas which they developed against the British monarchy in 1776. But the more I hear about the way in which the Intelligence Service operates in the US, the more deeply disillusioned and suspicious I get. Mind you, British Intelligence is no doubt much the same, though Merlyn Rees denies it. When I spoke to him about Agee, he said how different MI6 was from the CIA, which may be true but we don't know. At least the Americans have all these things out in the open and we don't.

In my box, there was a note of a question tabled by a Dutchman at the European Parliament asking the Commission to report on whether British oil policy is compatible with the Treaty of Rome. The Commissioner concerned is evidently going to respond that an inquiry is to be made. I added the point that if there are any official or unofficial comments by the Commission, I am to be told at once before any official or unofficial responses are given. If this is the case, the worst fears of the anti-Marketeers are going to turn out to be justified.

Sunday 28 November

An extract from Dick Crossman's *Diary* appeared in the *Sunday Times* today. It was all about who got what job. Most unattractive – personal, gossipy, unrooted in political principle and disconnected from the labour movement. It showed Crosman and politics in a bad light, and correctly so. The awful thing is that my diary for 1968, which is now being typed, is equally unattractive; but it does reveal the corruption of power and, in the long run, it is important that people should know these are the factors that influence Cabinets.

Monday 29 November

Tea with Brian Sedgemore and I told him about the refusal by Jim Callaghan to let him be my PPS and he agreed to let it rest till after Christmas. I'll get back to Jim then.

Went to dinner at 1 Carlton Gardens, the Foreign Secretary's official residence. My opposite number, D'Ornano was there. I've met him in Paris a couple of times and he is charming and amusing. He comes from a long aristocratic line of French landowners, has three Marshals of France in his antecedents, and tells me he is a Count. A businessman, he set up business in France selling perfumes.

I questioned him closely on the French system of Government, where the PM is just the dogsbody, and the President, elected by popular mandate, claims to have legitimacy at least as great as the Parliament. The PM presents the business and Ministers comment but in the end the President is not obliged to accept the majority of ministerial views because he appoints them. The Parliament can pass a Motion of Censure on the Government, but the no-votes have to be half the total Assembly plus one to pass the Motion. The President can dissolve the Assembly but only once in twelve months. It is in effect an institutionalised elected monarchy. It has none of the characteristics of deep democracy and it is quite different from the British system. Indeed the EEC Council of Ministers is being driven to follow French governmental practice. Nothing to do with the sort of democracy we have built up here. It is interesting to realise how we are being sucked in.

Tuesday 30 November
To Michael Foot's room. Jill was there, with Albert, Stan Orme, Peter Shore and John Silkin. We talked about tomorrow's Cabinet now all the papers have come round, fourteen of them including mine. We talked things through in depth, agreed on tactics and decided to meet again tomorrow night.

Wednesday 1 December
An item in the papers caught my attention this morning – a report about civil servants and military officers who throughout the 1930s leaked secret papers to Churchill so as to keep him informed about the weakness of our defences. These papers were found among Churchill's papers. An eighty-year-old retired airforce officer called Richardson is reported to have said that he sent these papers to Churchill because he was deeply disturbed at the lack of preparedness of the British forces. Frederick Lindemann, who later became Lord Cherwell, actually photographed these secret papers so that Churchill could see for himself what was in them and not rely on verbal reports. Here you have a serving airforce officer, a distinguished scientist who became a Privy Councillor and a peer, and Churchill himself actually associated with systematic leakages of secret papers in order to promote a policy contrary to that of the Government of the day. It is an astonishing story.

Francis and Frances came for breakfast and I spent from 8 till 9.30 going over the papers for the Cabinet.

We agreed that I must be careful to distinguish myself from Crosland and Healey, hoping that I wouldn't be called till later in the morning, by which time Crosland and Healey would have knocked each other out, then I'd come in with the alternative strategy, saying what we needed was reflation instead of high unemployment. So we sketched out a line of approach.

Frances came in the car with me to the Cabinet which was delayed from 10 till 10.30. This made us a bit suspicious. You don't normally delay a Cabinet of that importance unless there's some hiccup, and we wondered whether Jim and Denis were having a set-to; in fact when we went into the Cabinet Denis was just coming out, so I think they must have had a talk. Whether it indicated a row or a make-up I don't know.

The Cabinet meetings of 1 and 2 December which finally sealed the fate of the Labour Government's economic, and therefore industrial and social, policy are reproduced here virtually in their entirety to give as full a picture as possible of how the decisions were arrived at.

When the Cabinet met finally at about 10.40, there were no officials present, a thing that hasn't happened since Jim has been PM. He said, 'I want to draw special attention again to the need for secrecy. Some of the press reports have been very damaging and very accurate, for example, the blow by blow account in the *FT* last Friday called "An Honest Man in a Labour Cabinet". (That must have been a reference to Healey.) 'I know who gave it to the *FT* and I shall take the necessary action to deal with the matter when I next have a reshuffle.' He went on to say, 'We are in a position where we shall have to rally to the majority view, whatever it is, or it will not be possible for me to go on. We have to remember that we have some critical by-elections coming up.'

Denis said, 'I'm glad you've said what you've said because I've been the victim of many of these leaks and colleagues who have tried to make themselves out to be heroes at my expense have done themselves, as well as me, a lot of damage.'

At that point, officials were brought in, and Jim tried to call me, shrewdly concluding that it would be better to get me disposed of first. He said he wanted to conclude the general discussion today.

But Denis declared at once, 'I disagree with Tony Benn's paper,' and Jim replied that he would have his opportunity in a moment. Then Edmund Dell asked Jim when we were going to get a report about his discussions since last Thursday's Cabinet.

'Well, there's not much I can say. The formal position is that the IMF is considering the matter, but the IMF is not the only leg, it's a three-legged stool, and Schmidt is impressed with the gravity of the situation, though his fears are more global and are not really restricted to problems about us.'

I said, 'I too would like a report as to what happened. After all, Denis has seen Simon of the US Treasury over the weekend. Couldn't we have the report before we start discussion?'

'Well,' Denis said, 'I talked to Simon and a German official, and trying to bully the Fund won't help us. The US are being very difficult, there is no bilateral borrowing available to us, even if the Fund helps us, but if a safety net is required, the US would be prepared to look at it. Henry Reuss, Chairman of the House Banking Committee, is being very helpful. If the Fund does provide a loan, he'd try to clear it through Congress.'

David Ennals asked if there had been any discussion on import deposits, and Jim said again that he hadn't done any briefing. Denis said, 'All I can say is that they would look on import deposits with disfavour.'

Jim again then invited me to speak.

'Prime Minister, I think we're all aware that this is a political decision as grave as any in our history, that we cannot really rely on others to help us, particularly Ford, who is a lame duck, or Schmidt, whose view is pretty monetarist in character. I base myself on the telegram that came in after the Socialist Congress in Geneva in which our officials there said that Schmidt had warned about inflation and said that public expenditure not properly financed had been the cause of unemployment. I assume that represented his view. Carter wouldn't want to get too involved until he becomes President, therefore we have to rely on ourselves and trust our judgment. I entirely share the view that the survival of the Government is in the national interest, but in this context we must consult our partners – the TUC and the Labour Party.'

Jim interrupted me, 'I perhaps should tell the Cabinet that I have seen Len Murray about something else last Tuesday and I also keep in pretty close touch with Jack Jones.'

'Well, that's better than nothing,' I said, 'but I want to emphasise this very much indeed, because they've put their reputations at risk in supporting us and if we take decisions unacceptable to them, it would not be fair. If we are going to carry the movement and defend the national interest we've got to reflate the economy. We are in the middle of a slump with high and rising unemployment, we've got to reflate. We've got to reduce unemployment in Scotland, Wales and elsewhere, we've got to expand our manufacturing base, we've got to safeguard benefits of the welfare state and find the means to do so. Nobody is suggesting we continue with the existing policy. There are two alternative strategies, the Chancellor's and mine, and there is a very big choice to make. My paper warns against deflation of any kind, imposed or self-imposed. I have been driven to the conclusion, very reluctantly, and I hope the Cabinet will believe me, that expansion requires protection.

'In 1974 when we were elected, I was very keen on our industrial policy which I played some part in formulating but I did come to the conclusion that this would not work while our industry bled to death. I simply do not believe that it cannot be made to work. In 1931 the Chancellor warned the Cabinet that import duties or revenue tariffs were not acceptable, and that if we came off the Gold Standard, the standing of living of workmen would fall sharply. Yet two months later, both were done. Someone from that Labour Cabinet subsequently said that we were never told we could do it. Peter's paper draws attention to the fact that all import controls are legal under the General Agreement on Tariffs and Trade and under the EEC and I think we should seek international support on that basis for that alternative strategy. It would be inexplicable to our movement that we had never even tried on our alternative strategy with the IMF and yet more inexplicable that in order to get the loan we have promised not to undertake that alternative strategy. Our political stance would be untenable if we

deflate in a slump because it would undermine the industrial strategy,
involve accepting international control and, if cutting benefits were
thrown in, it would be impossible.

'We cannot fudge this issue. Everybody will know what we've done,
and cuts and deflation even on a lower level will not be acceptable.
Therefore I suggest that we follow the alternative strategy which is of
import controls fed in by a period of import deposits, and exchange
controls which would certainly be necessary in the short run. This
would permit us to have a differential interest rate for official holders
of sterling. We'd need a capital issues committee, control of bank
borrowing and to keep an eye on the direction of investment – and
planning agreements under reserve powers – more money for the
NEB. But the most important thing is that we should consult the
TUC.'

I was then subjected for about half an hour to the closest cross
examination. First, Jim asked, 'Do you think we need the loan?'

I said I would prefer to have the loan rather than not. I reminded
the Cabinet of the famous cartoon in 1940 of a soldier after Dunkirk
waving his fists and saying 'Very well, alone.' I said that I thought the
IMF would help us because it would be in their interests to do so.

Shirley asked if the import quotas would cover raw materials and
food as well as manufactured goods and I said no, they would only
cover manufactured goods; raw materials and food would come in as
before.

'Well,' said Shirley, 'we have a trading surplus in manufacture,
therefore we'd be exposed to retaliation.'

'Of course we have a trading surplus in manufacturing because we
are a manufacturing country, which means we don't feed ourselves,
but still millions of pounds worth of goods are sold to us, and I don't
see why anyone should want to cut off supplies and thus lose the trade
entirely. I am aware of the risk of rotting quietly behind a protective
tariff but of course, that's what the planning agreements are designed
to prevent and David Basnett pointed this out when we discussed it at
the TUC-Labour Party Liaison Committee. It is a political choice we
have to make.'

Jim Callaghan intervened half-mockingly and said, 'Tony Benn is a
putative Chancellor and should be listened to with respect,' so I laughed
and said, 'Don't leak that.'

Bill Rodgers asked what my policy would do to unemployment, and
I replied that although I hadn't got a Treasury computer to mislead
me the one thing that was absolutely clear was that unemployment
would rise under existing policy and would get worse under extra
cuts. Import controls would substantially improve the unemployment
situation. The big difference now was that with unused resources we

would not need cuts on the scale forecast by the Cambridge School, of which I am not a member, in order to go for the alternative strategy because these resources could be brought into play.

Fred Peart asked if we could get compulsory planning agreements through and would that be right? This was one reference in my paper that allowed me a backward look at my period in the Department of Industry and I said I was absolutely sure that we could have had planning agreements if we hadn't said that under no circumstances would we insist on them. I knew one or two firms that would have been ready to sign them rapidly. As it is, we had none and that was a great weakness. We could get them if we had the reserve powers. Industry was entitled to say to us that they would cooperate if we had legislative power, otherwise they weren't going to volunteer.

Harold Lever wanted to know why I thought we could survive politically. If we could get it through the Cabinet, could we get it through the House of Commons? What would our stance be electorally?

My opinion was that nothing would be more fatal to our electoral chances (and I had no crystal ball) than the Party going to the country having laid off employees in the manufacturing industries and in the public service sector on the grounds that the bankers wanted unemployment to restore confidence. I said it would be much better to present this in a vigorous way. I thought we would get support nationally, even in the House of Commons, and have a far better chance of winning.

I was also asked about exchange controls by Harold Lever. I said I knew very well that the Treasury had a secret emergency plan. I didn't know the details but it was there and we would need it, certainly in the short run.

Denis said, 'Yes, but where would you get the foreign currency to fund us immediately if we had exchange controls?'

Jim replied that it could be that new sources of money would become available in the short run for that purpose.

I mentioned the export of capital being on a large scale but they disputed that, saying these were profits made by British firms abroad.

Shirley Williams asked if my strategy was a threat or a real policy. I answered that I'd adopted it reluctantly, I would much rather we didn't have to do it but I thought it was inescapable. Mrs Thatcher would do it and in a way she would probably find it easier because no one would suspect her of wanting to make it an entry point into a full siege economy. We had to make it clear that we would be prepared to adopt this strategy in order to release the money. It would be absolutely inexplicable if we didn't try it out.

Peter was called next. He said we had two alternative strategies: the earlier policy had failed and we could either go for deflation or import controls. Denis was for deflation which would encase us in a two-year tomb. The IMF tranches would come bit by bit; we would be drip fed to police us and it was all very well to tease and hound Tony Benn, but the alternative policy needed to be looked at properly. Jim wouldn't accept that I was being teased and hounded – I didn't think so either – but I suppose that's how it looked.

Peter's position was slightly different from mine. He believed we were not paying our way and the easiest way to deal with that was to control imports. As to retaliation, we would have to look at our rights. The GATT and EEC provisions allowed any country to take these protective measures where there was a risk to its currency or to forestall a fall in its monetary reserves – they had almost been written specially for us!

Jim said the fear wasn't exactly of retaliation but of a possible trade war.

Peter Shore believed the Italians would retaliate, the Americans and the Germans would have no grounds, nor would the Japanese, and he wasn't sure about the French.

'What about the small countries? Would they follow suit?' asked Shirley.

Harold Lever asked which of the industrial countries had adopted this course.

Finland had import controls and so did Italy – they were the only OECD countries. Peter was convinced we could get away with them – we did it in 1966 with the surcharge. Our real problems were the short-term ones – how to get additional finance in the interim period. Only the Treasury technicians would know the answer to this. We knew emergency plans existed and the IMF would help because they could not humiliate and break a democratic Government. If they did, the whole IMF position would be untenable, and Roy Mason commented that perhaps they'd be pleased if we fell.

Peter ignored that comment and said the world was following a deflationary road. We could finance our imports by deposits and controls but there would be risks taken on both sides.

'What would we do about the PSBR?' asked Denis.

Peter said he was concerned about this and we had got to reduce it, but he preferred to use taxation mainly. Denis commented that that would mean more deflation earlier.

Shirley pointed out the risk of emulation by, for example, Australia, New Zealand and Canada if we took the GATT line and Peter didn't rule that out because there would have to be another world economic conference quite soon. The world system was seizing up.

Elwyn asked about the mid-term position. We had to return 1.6 billion dollars to the central bank on the 9th, we had to finance the external deficit and we had a £2.5 billion deficit expected next year.

How would we deal with the immediate borrowing or were we prepared to risk the bankruptcy of the UK?

Peter said the current account would be closed in 1977 under his proposals. Second we could push forward the impending dollars repayment for three months. Thirdly we would get the IMF's backing, but if we didn't we might have to mobilise our assets and then release them in an orderly way. We would have to guarantee the sterling balances as we had done before.

Jim said he was particularly worried about these survival problems, and Bruce Millan couldn't understand why import controls were on the basis of now or never. Was some pledge required?

Denis came in saying it would be a two-year programme with quarterly IMF missions and we would never need to draw beyond the first tranche because we might borrow elsewhere, the limits would be lifted and our obligations would be liquidated to the extent that we didn't borrow more. But we might get an agreement on import deposits of some kind. At that point Jim intervened to say this was all very secret and Denis shouldn't say any more.

The third gladiator in the ring, Tony Crosland, began with marvellous arrogance. 'I think the proposals I wish to put forward will command more support than Tony's or Peter's. I want us to stick to our existing strategy. We have had deflation, we have had devaluation, we've got a wages policy and it will work. There is no case for a change. New cuts would have a disastrous effect on investment because they'd damage wages policy and destroy confidence.

'But we live in the real world of expectation and there are two scenarios to consider. One is the £1 billion net cut which is unacceptable, and the IMF won't really press us for it. If they do, we should resist and theaten a siege economy, or talk about our role in Cyprus or our troops in Germany, or our position in Rhodesia, membership of the EEC, etc. Schmidt and Ford would soon give way.

'The other alternative is tolerable: to get £1 billion off the PSBR by selling the Burmah oil shares, having import deposits which are a bit deflationary and have political advantages, and to do a presentational job to the IMF by announcing now the cuts we had decided on in July but which have not yet become known, and possibly some extra cuts.'

'What if the IMF say no?' I asked.

'We won't accept it.'

Denis pushed him. 'But what if they stand firm?' Tony believed that they would, but that we would have to defend ourselves.

Stan Orme thought that the market might require even greater cuts than the IMF.

'They will be real cuts,' said Tony, 'but we are going to discuss all of that tomorrow.'

Fred Mulley said all we needed was a certificate of good management to release other borrowing. If the IMF were against us, would a grudging OK from them help us with the markets?

'We must have a safety net,' said Tony, 'because the market on its own couldn't give us stability.'

John Morris said that confidence was the key issue, and if we had to choose between a generous and a grudging approval by the IMF, he favoured a generous approval – which meant more cuts.

Edmund Dell asked Tony why he played down the negotiating power of the IMF. How would confidence be restored? These were all matters of political judgment, Tony said, and he believed in our present policy, and that confidence would be restored.

Denis said that to announce the July decisions on cuts didn't help because, although they hadn't been made public, the IMF had already counted them in the PSBR forecasts.

David Ennals agreed with Tony Crosland except that he was not in favour of confrontational challenges. He said we should discard Denis's proposals and alternative strategies because they would fail. It would be crazy to try them.

'All I am suggesting is that we put it to the IMF and try to sell them the idea that this is the best strategy,' he said.

Ennals understood that but said that the Party would not accept the cuts and deflation and therefore import deposits were best because that reduced the PSBR and would make the other cuts tolerable.

We then had a tremendous speech from Roy Mason. He thanked Denis for his courage and imperturbability, his intellectual resilience, his strength and moral fibre, at a time when the country is bankrupt and the Party is at its lowest ebb. He said we'd had the militants of NUPE, the disastrous Labour Conference, the NEC which was the laughing stock of the country, Transport House which some people seem to think has 2000 employees because it writes so many embarrassing reports. There was no buoyancy in the Party.

'We have to keep the Cabinet and the Party together and Tony Benn at least has a clear alternative. But we can't survive alone. How can we finance and support ourselves? Peter Shore and Tony Crosland are looking for a painless way out.'

On quotas he reminded us of the wrath of the European Free Trade Association when he was President of the Board of Trade. We were the biggest fish in EFTA at that time. Now we were very small fish in the Common Market. Threatening was no use to us now because it would put a break on world trade and there would be no lubrication to keep it going.

GATT was sympathetic, he thought, but the EEC would react to Tony Benn's measures by saying they are subsidising us. They would not allow the green pound to remain at its present level, we would lose £500 million a year, inward investment particularly in semi-manufactured goods would be threatened, the protection in inefficient industries would go on and managers don't want a siege economy. Import deposits were not on, and unemployment would rise anyway because of our strategy. 'After all, why did we nationalise the aircraft industry, the shipbuilding industry, the car industry, if it wasn't to rationalise them and cut jobs? As to the mining industry, we have put in tons of money to make it efficient and we have to go back to pit closures. Steel was the same. We've taken the misery out of unemployment but we're not taking the credit. What we need are selective investment measures and we try to eliminate the balance of payments deficit, we rally round the tax cuts, we rally round a cut in inflation for our wage policy. We should be emphasising these things.'

Fred Peart supported Roy Mason because he opposed import controls. He said the EFTA anger would erupt again. The green pound would be jeopardised and the risk of doing too little led him to support Denis. He rejected a siege economy as proposed by Tony Benn and Peter Shore.

John Morris said Crosland was too weak. We needed the loan and the IMF wanted to help us. The alternative strategy just involved waiting for something to turn up. The PLP was a political hurdle and so was confidence, but Crosland's plan wouldn't restore confidence. He was fed up with so many bites of the cherry and he supported Denis, with lower taxes later for our own people. Middle managers, some of whom were emigrating to Europe, were 'cabin'd, cribb'd, confin'd, bound in' by the present tax levels and the incomes policy squeeze. Denis may have overbid a bit but he supported him.

'Nothing is easy politically,' Fred Mulley said. 'A loan without strings would be attractive but our friends abroad doubt us. The Germans say the Italians had problems and admitted it, the British have problems but they don't admit it.' There was no queue of lenders coming along. There was a conflict between the short and long term and pay was a good example because, in the short term, pay policy was advantageous, but in the long run we wanted differentials; so a tax discount for manufacturing industry might be worth considering. We had to cut the PSBR. A VAT increase would be best and he accepted Crosland's paper. He would cut some benefits, particularly in the public sector, because of the interrelationship with pay. We had to get the IMF loan to safeguard the Government's position. Therefore we had to face the problems and put across the seriousness of the crisis.

Thursday 2 December

Slept late, because I didn't get to bed until 2.30 in the morning.

Cabinet at 10. Parliamentary business as usual, followed by Foreign Affairs. Tony Crosland reported the Geneva Conference on Rhodesia saying that a date for reconvening it in January had been agreed.

We came to the IMF negotiations. 'We now come to a decision on the quantum,' started Jim.

'Can I ask a procedural question?' I said, 'Are you going to decide things bit by bit ad referendum at the end; or are we going to have to reach a final decision today?'

Jim replied that he would be dealing with that in his summing up. Then Peter Shore said, 'Are we going to be discussing a paper from Shirley which has just come round?'

Jim said, 'Well, I should never have yielded but I did to a woman. She said she would do a one-page paper but in fact it is longer than that.'

Denis opened today's discussion which lasted throughout the whole morning. He said there had been a general feeling yesterday in the Cabinet that had led to a rejection of the alternative strategy and the siege economy, and therefore we would have to seek agreement with the Fund. We only had £2 billion left next week and if we failed to agree with the Fund, it would be a disaster. Then much more drastic measures would have to be taken, and there would be higher unemployment. The question was: what adjustments should we make and would they satisfy the Fund and meet criticism at home and abroad?

He said the PSBR must be cut below the forecast of £10.56 billion because otherwise we would either have to print money or we would have to have higher interest rates. If the PSBR forecast remained, we couldn't borrow abroad and none of our friends abroad believed that even if we cut the PSBR to £5 billion, it could be regarded as deflation. Schmidt may be to the right of Friedman but all the countries in the world agreed with him. Friends and creditors thought we were not creditworthy.

Options of cutting the PSBR to £9.5, or £9 or £8.5 billion had been discussed with the Fund. Denis said, 'I now recommend that we go for a £500 million sale of Burmah shares; for a net reduction of £1 billion in the PSBR in 1977–8, mainly by cuts, with another £1.5 billion reduction in 1978–9. Therefore the PSBR would be £8.7 million in 1977–8, it would reduce the GDP by 0.5 per cent, but the GDP would go up by 3.5 per cent in 1978; it would only add 0.5 per cent to the retail price index; unemployment would rise by 30,000 by the end of 1977 and by 110,000 by the end of 1978; but these would be offset by micro measures of a kind that Albert Booth has suggested.

'Shirley has said that a £1.5 billion cut would increase unemployment, but the GDP is not affected by the sale of the shares; interest rates which are a very big factor would only come down if we made big cuts, and lay-offs in the construction industry would involve a very high unemployment rate.

'The Fund and the Government at the moment have not reached an agreement: they disagree about the impact on the interest rates. The IMF claim that the return of confidence would offset any deflationary effect these measures have, because interest rates are the key – if they can be reduced, then the economy will recover. The balance of payments deficit would, in any case, reduce to £1 billion next year and we would have a £2.5 to £3 billion surplus in 1978. But I would like more help for industry and I think that the advance project schemes and the employment schemes could be advanced though not necessarily on the scale that Albert suggests.

'Anything less will not restore confidence even if the IMF accept it. The latest PSBR forecast now stands at £10.5 billion. The National Institute of Economic and Social Research and the Phillips forecast think the PSBR is already about £9 billion. But if I do an overkill, I'll feed it back in income tax reductions in the spring. We must do that anyway to get the support of the TUC for our pay policy and we must also get tax reductions at the upper end of the bracket. The overlap of low pay and benefits is a major problem and this would be partly offset by an increase in indirect taxation.

'Now, all this is in our interest, but can we persuade the IMF that it is right? We might succeed with a bit of political help. Crosland's package is quite unsaleable, and the markets would remain unconvinced. If we can do this, we will get the borrowing and the safety net and possibly import deposits. But the snag is that the reverse effect on the PSBR, when the import deposits were removed, would be very serious and the CBI would be hostile. The Crosland plan is unacceptable to the IMF, to other countries, and to the markets; it only offers a 20,000 gain in jobs; there is a risk of another demand for a package and it is better to overkill now.'

Jim Callaghan then said, 'I think the time has come for me to give my view. I read the Hansard on the Tuesday debate in the House and I noticed the speeches by Heffer, Maudling, Oonagh McDonald, Enoch Powell, and Eric Ogden [Labour MP for Liverpool, West Derby] which were very interesting and well informed. I must admit, I am not sure about what to do, but I think the time has come to make my position clear.

'I want to look at it from a political and economic angle. It is very hard to judge what will happen. These measures could have an adverse effect on the PLP and the unions but the public may take a different view. The Chief Whip sent me a minute to say that there is an absolute need that, whatever we do, we must avoid any legislation following from this package because it is not possible to rely upon the Parliamentary Party support to carry it through. But Denis's proposals do need legislation and the Cabinet had better face it. The PSBR approach alone is not enough and my view, therefore, is as follows.

'First, we should go for a quantum with £1 billion of cuts; and to this extent I support Denis. But this will help by allowing interest rates to fall which will assist industry and house owners. Secondly, we must reduce tax levels at the top and bottom, and for this we can expect wide public support. Thirdly, we must deal with social security benefits because if the choice is killing the construction industry or uprating social benefits, there is no doubt which would be more harmful in terms of jobs. We are committed to raising benefits by statute, either related to earnings or to prices, and pensioners have therefore got a 16 per cent increase this year which is more than those at work have got under the pay policy. But that can't go on on that basis. There is a good case in logic for saying that if we have to choose between the construction industry or deferring the increase in benefits, we should defer benefits; but that would require supporting legislation, and it would put the life of the Government at risk.

'Denis has fought very hard and I must tell the Cabinet that there is no agreement with the IMF yet. I must also tell you very confidentially that the Managing Director of the IMF, Johannes Witteveen, came to London yesterday and I had a long meeting with him. I read him Article 12 of GATT which provides for exemptions; it amused me yesterday, when I was told by Tony Benn that we had never put the possibility of import controls to the IMF. So I read it to him and he was very unyielding and he wants £2 billion of real cuts. Schmidt was going to phone me this morning but it was an abortive call. But I had a word with President Ford yesterday on the telephone and he said that if the Fund came through he would try to help with the safety net. He said he felt sure that it would be acceptable to the Congress.'

Then Jim read out – because Prime Ministers appear to like to show how well they get on with Presidents – the last few words of his exchange with Ford which ran something like this:

Jim: Sorry to bother you, Gerry.
Ford: Well, don't worry, Jim, I expect you're busy.
Jim: Well, it's just a question of which of us remains in office longer.
Ford: Well, I sincerely hope you succeed. When will the Cabinet decide?
Jim: By 1 pm.
Ford: You might be out of office first . . .

An almost exact reproduction, of course, of the telephone call on 23 August 1931 in which the Prime Minister announced that he had had a call on the phone from our Ambassador in Washington. That stuck in my mind as I listened to Jim.

Denis said, 'Congressman Henry Reuss will help.'

The Prime Minister continued, 'What I said to Ford is this. I would like to propose a three-legged stool: a cut of £1–1.5 billion in the PSBR; a safety net; import deposits on the same basis as Italy. I might be able to sell it.' Ford said their attitude was to be firm but fair.

Jim then added, 'I have also told Schmidt this, but if we can't sell it then we have a completely different perspective. I support this policy because: first, it will allow lower interest rates; second, the uprating of benefits will be reduced in a way that will be sensible; third, we will be reducing tax at the margins; fourth, we will perhaps be dealing with indirect taxation; fifth, our industrial strategy will be strengthened. But we do put our lives to the test and our life as a Government could come to an end. We must all understand that if we reject this, our overseas friends and critics will bring the life of this Government to an end and the tremors will shake us.'

Then Michael Foot spoke for the first time this week. He began very quietly by saying he was grateful to the Prime Minister, 'But I must tell you that your proposals are not satisfactory. £2 billion cuts and all the consequences that will flow from that, are inconceivable. The whole position has been changed by unemployment rising to 1.75 million in the forecasts and we would be accepting an increase in that. As to pay arrangements, the Party believes in egalitarian approaches to pay and you can't unscramble that. If you tried to deal with benefits by statute, it would destroy TUC support. The legislation would not be passed and we would be in a position where, if the Government was defeated, Labour candidates would be fighting an Election in favour of cuts in social benefits. The Party and public opinion can't be divided in that sense.

'The Labour Party and TUC links are the key, whether in Opposition or in Government. Schmidt takes a neolithic view of all these matters and thoroughly upset the Socialist International when he said it in Geneva. Therefore, you should go back to the IMF with a different package. Argue the employment case, propose a few cuts, maybe on roads, maybe on mortgage relief, plus import controls, plus the protection of the exchange rate as Tony Benn suggested. The Cabinet has got to try to hold together but if it can't hold together on an anti-deflationary policy in Government, then it will have to try to hold together in Opposition.'

He said he recoiled in horror from the unemployment effects and the cuts in benefits. 'If we followed this course we would forfeit our agreement and our association with the unions and would be ground to death. We must connect what we do to our own beliefs. We may not get the loan but we have better prospects than a course that would be a disaster for the movement. We need more time; we want to sustain the Government; or, if forced into Opposition, sustain ourselves in unity rather than be split into snarling groups.'

Crosland said that the Prime Minister's statement was a very grave one. He had thrown his judgment in with the Chancellor and this was a completely new factor. He thought it was wrong economically and socially, destructive of what he had believed in all his life. Also it was politically wrong. He doubted the judgment of the Cabinet and what was proposed was wrong. 'But the new factor is your view, Prime Minister. What would be the consequence of rejecting the Prime Minister? The unity of the Party depends upon sustaining the Prime Minister and the effect on sterling of rejecting the Prime Minister would be to destroy our capacity. Therefore I support the Prime Minister and the Chancellor.

'However, there is massive overkill: £0.5 billion from oil; £1 billion real cuts; and import deposits would be another £1.5 billion; and that would reduce the PSBR to £7.5 billion in the current year. Or, if you start from the lower base of the NIESR, we are being asked to accept a £5.2 billion PSBR at the current rate. But Denis said that there was overkill and therefore he hoped that there would be tax remissions and that these tax remissions would be announced virtually now at the same time as the package to help industry, to help jobs, and maybe even to reverse the cuts. That was the only presentational way of dealing with the proposal put forward.'

Denis answered, 'Look, I have agreed with the Fund that if the growth is lower than we thought, then we will reverse the cuts.'

David Ennals spoke. 'This is a grave statement by the Prime Minister and I don't know what significance to read into what he has said. I hope it doesn't mean that we are all expected to sign along the dotted line. I agree with Shirley and her balance is better. I have moved up progressively as I thought about it from Crosland's original cuts, up to £500 million, but we can't go above that. The Chief Whip was right. A modest adjustment in benefits is possible but I don't think we could save more than £40 million on that and we can't ask for discretion on benefits because it would look as if we were retaining the right not to raise them at all.'

'We will make it clear that we are going to uprate them in line with wages. And the TUC would certainly support it because they would not like to feel that wages were being held below benefits. Anyway, the union leaders are completely out of touch with the rank and file,' said Denis.

David Ennals replied, 'You might have to rely on Opposition support for these measures but if you are going to nail your colours to the mast, the question is what colours? Because in the end there would be no Party to sustain us.'

Next to speak was Albert Booth and he said that unemployment was now higher than in Sweden, France and Germany, was approaching the levels of America and Canada and indeed would overtake that in North America. In fact, if you looked around the whole Western world, the greatest increase in unemployment that had occurred in the last two and a half years had occurred under a Labour Government in Britain. The national income forecast had overtaken us. What he was proposing for relief was in the belief that it would be supported by the trade union movement and the CBI.

'My measures would involve no net cost to the PSBR because it costs so much to keep people out of work that it is really no cheaper to throw them out now than to keep them in work. But if we cut the flat-rate benefit in the depth of a recession, the Government would have broken the Social Contract and would be totally opposed.'

Jim pressed, 'It's getting late now. We must know by 1 o'clock where we stand.'

'There is only a £500 million difference, surely, between us,' said Elwyn Jones.

'The choice,' said Jim, 'is between hitting the construction industry with the high unemployment that would follow or reducing the upgrading of the benefits. It is a stark choice and even if we adopted Tony Benn's proposal for import controls, it would only defer the decision, because in fact you would still have to make serious cuts.'

Shirley Williams then said she accepted the £1.5 billion; the gap was not as wide as was thought; it can be bridged, she was not jibbing at reality. The problem wouldn't be solved easily and a shift to indirect taxation was necessary but we mustn't destroy the movement and there was still room for compromise. But if Denis asked for the whole pound of flesh, it would kill us.

Harold Lever said, 'We need the loan. We don't need deflation because it could kill the Government. We can face the difficulties. How do we get the loan? It would be a quick death for us to reject the Prime Minister and the Chancellor. My solution, therefore, is £1 billion cuts immediately, an absolute must; then tax cuts for the poorest workers.'

'I cannot accept the Prime Minister's and the Chancellor's view.' Stan Orme said. 'It would be deflationary, it is not acceptable. We talk about the people living on benefits – what are they actually getting? A single man on a flat rate benefit gets £12 a week. A married person gets £22. A married couple with two children gets £27 at present compared to the average wage of £70 per week.

'The TUC were very keen on increased pensions, fought very hard for them and they would never accept this. Of course, if you restricted uprating it would also be deflationary because people on benefits spend all their money and it is inconceivable that you could have a situation in which 2 million unemployed were to be sanctioned by the Cabinet. I can't credit a Labour Cabinet discussing these things and I must tell you that less than one in three of the PLP would vote for it. It is not on,' said Stan.

Fred Mulley hoped there would be no leaks. On the benefits he said it was difficult but it would be disastrous if we didn't get the IMF loan. We must pay the price. He was not against import deposits and he hoped we wouldn't take it all on public expenditure. Selective benefit changes were okay. But many of our local Party workers were pensioners, and we shouldn't forget that; we relied on the pensioners to fight the young Trotskyites who had come into the local Parties and if we deprived them of their uprated pensions, they would leave and the Trotskyites would get control.

This was the level of the discussion!

Eric Varley said, 'In July, I forecast that there would be one more package and I am now for making that package for £1.5 billion. We will just have to face benefit cuts.'

Reg Prentice said he accepted the three-legged stool; there was a risk of overkill but that was less than the risk of underkill. He was against helping benefits at the expense of the construction industry. As to the Party versus the people, we were elected to look after the people and we couldn't run away from that.

Peter Shore warned that unemployment in 1978–9 would be disastrous and the whole thing was a national humiliation. He said it was wrong, Tony Crosland had said it was wrong and it was wrong for a Cabinet Minister to support what he knew to be wrong.

'We have got no bargaining power left; we must accept it,' Bill Rodgers said.

Roy Hattersley then spoke. 'We must support the Prime Minister. I do so with apprehension and no conviction, because it will involve reducing the social programme. I am pro-public expenditure but we must face the fact that there are some members of the Parliamentary Party who would rather lose in a good cause. Edmund Dell says the Fund believes it has a case, and so do I. The IMF won't budge. If we have a choice of seeing the Government destroyed by the markets or by ourselves, I think it is better that we should not allow it to be destroyed by the markets.'

Elwyn Jones supported the Prime Minister and the Chancellor but he said that the Chancellor did say we had given a pledge that we would uprate benefits with our commitment to keep them in line with earnings and prices, and how were we going to deal with a complete breach of the Queen's Speech so quickly? He felt this was a point we had to turn our attention to.

John Morris supported Denis.

Merlyn said, 'We must have the loan. We can survive politically and, of course, if we overkill we can have a popular Budget.'

'The mind conditioning is now over,' Roy Mason declared. 'The Party and the country are ready and we must do it. Then we must be ready for tax cuts in the spring.'

Bruce Millan said he was in favour of the sale of Burmah and import deposits, but he was against trying to cut the benefit.

Then I spoke. 'Yesterday, Prime Minister, one crisis plan was put to the Cabinet and was rejected. Today another crisis plan – the true nature of which is now dawning on us – is before us; and it is based on the fact that we throw more people on the dole, and we then cut the dole but give tax remissions for people who are better off.

'This plan is based on two things: on Treasury forecasts that have been systematically wrong and on a monetarist theory that we don't, for one moment, accept ourselves and are only having foisted on us by others. Denis tells us now that if it is worse than we think it is going to be, we'll ease it up later. But it is already much worse than we thought it was going to be in July and the Treasury remedy is to increase the cuts. I therefore don't believe that we will ease up.

'Second, we are told that the trade union movement will welcome the cuts in benefit in order to help to reduce the pay differential for their workers. But they won't do anything of the kind. They will say, "If you bust your side of the Social Contract, we'll bust our side." And what they will say is let's go for big wage claims because that way we can keep the benefits up and we can reflate the economy to correct the deflation that the Government has imposed upon us.

'Then there will be only two weapons left in our armoury. One is monetary policy where you don't have to bother with what the trade unions say, Mrs Thatcher's view, because you turn off the taps of money and leave them without any power; or a statutory pay policy. Those are the only two things left. There is an eerie parallel with 1931.'

Jim interrupted and said, 'There is no such parallel. I don't accept it. I have been reading the minutes you have been circulating, every one of them, and I don't accept it.'

'I am very sorry but if I am in the Cabinet I must say what I think and I think there is a parallel with 1931 because then, too, the loan hinged upon cutting the benefits.'

Jim interrupted again and said, 'Well, I lived through it. You didn't.'

'Well, my dad was in that Cabinet. They voted for the cuts in benefits, and I won't accept them and I make that absolutely clear.

This policy will have one of two effects. Either it will defeat us in the House of Commons. Perhaps I may make this parallel: you have often told us, Jim, that your feeling about being Prime Minister is mixed, that you will do it while you feel you can do a good job. I think there are many Members of Parliament who feel the same about being MPs: they will do it while they think they can do a good job. But they will not accept this.

'Or, alternatively, if we are not defeated in the Commons, we shall be supported by Tory MPs who will prop us up like a boxer props up a sagging man for one final blow, keeping us there until they are ready. It will be the death warrant of the Labour Government if we accept this. The form in which it goes, how it goes, when it goes, is still a matter that can't be conjectured. But it is not acceptable to the TUC or to the PLP and should not be acceptable to the Cabinet.'

Fred Peart supported the Prime Minister; Silkin was against.

Jim said, 'I want now to sum up as best I can by saying that I put in the import deposits because I thought it would make it more acceptable. Of course, it also provides another £1.5 billion reduction on the PSBR. So I now think we should authorise Denis to offer to the IMF £1 billion in cuts, £0.5 billion in sale of shares, and test out the import deposit argument.'

To this Denis replied, 'Let's be clear, we have not yet persuaded the IMF that we can get away with as little as £1.5 billion with only £1 billion cuts, and any tax component, if put in, would be very much less acceptable because they want cuts, not tax increases. As to construction, it would have the heaviest unemployment effect of all and the least of all benefit on the PSBR, whereas as far as the benefits are concerned, these would have much less effect on levels of employment, indeed none.'

He didn't say so but of course the reason for that is that everyone who is on benefit is either retired or out of work, and if you raise indirect taxation on goods like tobacco, you hit the pensioners.

Crosland said, 'Can I just ask this. Would Denis agree to put in the statement something to the effect that he would be ready to give tax remissions and virtually announce part of his Budget at the same time?'

Harold Lever concurred, 'Yes, and perhaps reverse the deflationary effects.'

Denis said, 'No, no, come on. We can't push this. I have got to negotiate. You can't push things of that kind on me at this stage.'

Michael Foot made one final point. 'We have had a discussion. Only a majority is for this view, it is not unanimous, and the Cabinet minutes always say, "The Cabinet noted with approval the summing up of the Prime Minister." Well we don't all approve of the summing up of the Prime Minister.'

Jim said, 'My summing up will say that a majority of the Cabinet agrees and therefore surely you could "note with approval that a majority of the Cabinet agrees".'

Michael came back to the point I had made at the very beginning and said, 'Is it clear that the Cabinet can suspend its final judgment until the very end of this whole business when we know the quantum, we know the response, we know the allocation, we know whether we can get import deposits; we know the whole acceptability?'

'Yes,' said Jim, 'I agree with that.'

With that the Cabinet adjourned at 1.15.

The foregoing diary was actually dictated in my room at the Department of Energy directly afterwards. Frances came in and wanted to know what happened so she sat while I dictated it. It is the moment of defeat and we have to recognise it. She said the *Titanic* was going down.

Frankly the union leaders are very suspicious. They have sacrificed their own reputations to help the Government and the idea that a Minister might be encouraging the union members to revolt against a Labour Government which they want to keep in power is not attractive to them.

We left it that she would ring Larry Whitty and I would try to have a word with David Basnett.

At 4.15 I went over to the House and thought it would be nice to have a word with Joe Ashton. Now he is Whip I'm able to be a bit more candid with him. I told him, not in great detail, that the forecasts on unemployment and inflation were very high, that in fact the Government was going to go for cuts and deflation and was attacking benefits.

He said the truth was that the Party was absolutely punch-drunk now on anxiety and had been conditioned to what was likely to happen. In effect he was telling me to relax and not to get steamed up. It had all happened before. Eric Heffer had written an article today also saying that whatever happens, the Government had to be sustained.

At 5.30 I saw Michael Foot who was distressed about this morning's Cabinet, and hoped he would have an opportunity of a word with Jack Jones whom he hadn't actually seen for two or three weeks.

I'm thinking hard about how to handle the situation. It is most important not to get it wrong and go out on a limb but at the same time to try to bring the movement in.

Into the Tea Room and had a word with Norman Atkinson at the 'Welsh table' beyond the cash desk and the food counter, through the little arch on the right. By chance there was no one in that part of the Tea Room so I said to Norman, 'I want to speak to you as a senior member of the NEC, as Treasurer of the Party with special responsibility for links with the trade union movement. The forecasts are of rising unemployment and there are going to be cuts and deflation with an attack on benefits.'

In the course of the evening, I talked to Joel Barnett. He said that he had read the 1929/31 minutes with enormous interest, and had noted what I had said about my father. Mik had read the whole thing and has written in *Labour Weekly* a tremendous piece: 'Ye Gods, don't we ever learn?' based on those minutes. So the publication of the minutes at the moment has played in its own way quite a significant role in influencing opinion.

I pulled Judith aside during a vote this evening and said, 'Don't ask me too much, but in effect the main decision has been taken about deflation and the cuts. The social democratic Right has crumbled.' Then, after the vote, I asked Michael Meacher to come up to my room. I have a lot of confidence in him – he is a very able guy. In about half an hour I gave him a complete briefing on everything that was happening.

I came home deeply depressed at the events, to consider what should be done next.

Sunday 5 December
The *Observer* had a complete account of Cabinet based on briefing by the anti-deflationist Right – that group of Ministers led by Crosland and Hattersley who, when it came to the crunch, capitulated totally to what Denis Healey wanted. It confirmed my view about candid discussions and that we had to be more open.

Monday 6 December
TUC-Labour Party Liaison Committee at Transport House, with Joan Lestor in the chair. Denis opened with the economic situation. Since the last meeting, inflation had risen, the volume of exports had fallen as had output since the summer. Next year demand would be lower still and output in trade forecasts were down. Therefore there would be lower growth and higher unemployment, although there would be a balance of payments surplus in 1978. He hoped to make a statement next week.

Norman Atkinson asked how high unemployment was going to be and what were we going to do about it. The deflation was simply not on and alternatives had to be looked at because the Cabinet deflation plans would not be acceptable to the movement.

In Len Murray's view we had to see this in the international context. We could put the screw on the IMF but the IMF had lots of other countries to deal with and were facing a worldwide situation of decay and crisis. If the IMF price was too high to pay, what were we to do?

'What does your group think of the latest IMF conditions?'

Evening Standard, 7 December 1976.

If the industrial strategy went, then you could kiss goodbye to the Social Contract as well.

To this Jack Jones responded that he didn't think Len meant quite that, when he said you could kiss goodbye to the Social Contract. It would be dangerous if that got leaked. Surely Len meant that the pay policy would be difficult?

So Jim said that we had had very candid talks in the Cabinet about the IMF and now it was very painful to see all the leaks. He wished he could talk openly here but if he were to mention import surcharges, all the Japanese would begin stuffing their boats with cars to get them in before the surcharges were introduced. Sterling was the key. What we were looking for was the seal of good housekeeping from the IMF and we could expect the stabilisation of the pound.

I said that we faced this situation against the backdrop of a deepening world crisis. An oil price increase was coming at the end of the month. Helmut Schmidt was an extreme monetarist and we couldn't rely on Jimmy Carter to help us because he didn't come to power until 20

January. It was against this background that we were all determined to keep the Government going. I said I wanted to pay tribute to Jim because he had permitted a more candid talk in the Cabinet than I had ever known in twelve years: the fact that it had all appeared in the *FT* and the *Economist* and the *Observer* didn't necessarily mean that we shouldn't have had these discussions.

After that I talked to Frances again briefly and went over to the Cabinet at 3.30. Not much to report except to say that we began the agonising process of cutting.

We finished at 6.20 and at 7 I went to Michael's room where Michael, Peter, Stan and Albert and I discussed the situation carefully. Stan Orme had come to the point of thinking he would resign. He said the Cabinet didn't agree with what it was doing, and he was deeply shocked by what Crosland had said. Michael would not resign and neither would Peter. Albert didn't want to resign. Stan said he had been walking in the Dales thinking it out and although he might just be a little brick he was worried that if he pulled himself out the whole edifice would fall.

I don't want to resign actually and suggested we fight hard on the cuts in benefits and on prescription charges, all the political issues like that. We should say that we were entitled to be listened to on these matters. If Cabinet wouldn't do that, then we would no doubt go round the table to be asked whether we agreed, and I was not prepared to say that I did. I didn't accept the policy, it would fail and do terrible damage to the movement.

If it went round the table a second time I would say I couldn't support it. I wouldn't resign because I didn't want to bring down the Government but I couldn't support it. Jim would then have to say that there was a minority in the Cabinet who opposed the policy.

Michael said Jim had considered the possibility of saying that, and that he had considered going to the PLP and putting it to them, that he would get a 60–40 vote in favour of the Cabinet majority view, and that he would then go to the Queen and give up his office, suggesting that the Queen calls someone else but NOT Mrs Thatcher.

I said it was absurd if the PLP had voted 60–40 in support of Cabinet at a Party meeting, that we should contemplate another Prime Minister.

Stan thought Thatcher might be asked, and then when she was in office carry these things through, be defeated and then call an Election with her timing.

They all went to dinner. I went up to my room and there were the next set of 1931 minutes, Ramsay MacDonald and the Coalition Government. Here were Ramsay and Stanley Baldwin and Herbert Samuel and Sir Austen Chamberlain and the Coalition. It was revolting to read, somehow, for me it is the most forbidden territory of all, the minutes of a coalition government.

Tuesday 7 December
At 10.30 Cabinet to make the individual cuts.

On benefits, Denis Healey said this was a central problem which had been raised all over the place. We would be swept out of office by the anger of the low paid if we didn't deal with the level of benefits.

David Ennals was opposed, Stan Orme said we would lose all credibility if we did cut them and Michael Foot feared it would destroy our links with the TUC. John Morris asked when we'd need to legislate and Denis answered by Easter or Budget time.

Shirley Williams asked why we couldn't tax benefits and Fred Mulley replied that the House of Commons wouldn't change the rules in the middle of the game. Joel Barnett said taxing the benefits would be administratively expensive, and Stan reckoned we'd need about 13,000 civil servants to cope with it. Harold Lever said there was a strong *prima facie* case for doing it but it needed further study and talks with the TUC. Reg Prentice said Denis had not only a strong *prima facie* case but also a strong real case. We were already hitting the weakest – nursery schools and geriatric hospitals – and this wasn't much more.

Albert Booth believed that the redundancies up till now had been cushioned by the measures taken on the redundancy payments, the earnings-related principle and tax rebates which were all based on the insurance principle and you couldn't change that.

Joel was in favour of abolishing the earnings-related principle altogether, which would save £140 million in the first year and £150 million in the next; we could also save £40 million by doubling the waiting period for unemployment pay to two weeks.

Jim Callaghan proposed deferring the point. We had £700 million already.

Fred Mulley asked about public sector inflation proofing relating to pensions, and Fred Peart thought we should defer, as there were a million public service pensioners. John Morris felt that if we deferred the public sector pensions uprating, there would be chaos.

David Ennals pointed out that the non-resident child tax allowance needed no legislation but it would breach the Government/TUC/Labour Party working party agreement on child benefits. There was a lot of cheating on this, Denis said.

Jim mentioned 'in strictest confidence' that other countries were going to postpone uprating their old age pensions. We wouldn't get help from the IMF if we didn't appear to be doing the same. I asked if we were going to see the IMF Letter of Intent, and what would Denis say to the IMF? Jim Callaghan said he'd deal with the procedure later.

On nationalised industries' capital investment, Joel Barnett said the

Treasury view was that it didn't count as public expenditure but we would get some saving of the PSBR. The total capital expenditure of the nationalised industries was £3.25 billion and the Treasury could trim this by £100 million this year and £150 million next year, but anyway there was a suggestion of an overspend.

We came on to nationalised industry pricing. On gas, there was an economic case for increasing it and an 8 per cent increase would give £50 million plus a saving of £50 million. On electricity prices we could do something, and on telecommunications, there was already a profit of £400 million, and 99 per cent of it was self-financing. But the effect would be felt on the supply industries. Crosland was in favour of this; he thought it was less difficult.

I said it was just not serious. We were supposed to have an industrial strategy which gives preference to industry whether public or private. You had to consider what effect an 8 per cent rise in gas prices would have. If you cut down the nationalised industries' investment it would affect the miners and make things very difficult at this moment, particularly in the heavy electrical industry. It just wasn't feasible.

Peter Shore agreed that it wasn't serious, but stated, 'Wounds were better than atrocities.'

Healey said the trouble with cuts was that they weren't directed at waste.

Eric Varley was against the nationalised industries' price increase because it ran counter to the main thrust of our industrial strategy.

Joel Barnett said he thought we could get £100 million net out of national industries' price increases and £200 million gross and do it again in 1978–9.

On the Regional Employment Premium, Joel Barnett suggested that we save £150 million by cutting development and special development areas. Eric Varley supported the ending of the REP because he wants to use the money selectively. Roy Mason said he had 10 per cent unemployment in Northern Ireland, 30 per cent male unemployment in some areas, and 10,000 to 15,000 jobs would go at once if we withdrew the premium there.

I interrupted and said if we did this it would be in effect a tax on the development areas. It wouldn't affect the Midlands and the South-East, only the areas of highest unemployment. It would be a political bombshell, especially in Merseyside.

'Everything we are doing is a bombshell,' commented Jim.

Albert Booth pointed out that the development area relativities were widening again and that the Temporary Employment Subsidy was effective.

Peter Shore argued that the Regional Employment Premium wasn't significant now. The Temporary Employment Subsidy swamped the

REP and the 20 per cent depreciation allowance had changed it all anyway because industry could afford to pay now. Unemployment was spreading like a blight and there would be a backlash in non-development areas.

Crosland said we couldn't reach £1 billion without cutting REP, and John Morris said it did help labour-intensive industries and commented that selective help tends to go to the Midlands and the large firms.

Bill Rodgers suggested we cut REP in development areas in 1977–8 and in special development areas in 1978–9. Fred made the point that it would save on civil servants.

By then we'd come to the end of the list and after a discussion of the Burmah shares, Crosland said it was crazy but we should sell the shares.

I raised a point of order asking if it was right for Cabinet Ministers to say things were 'crazy' and then still support them, but Jim over-ruled me.

It was clear we were not agreed, said the Prime Minister. We should go away and Denis and he would prepare a total for Thursday's meeting. Then the Cabinet would have to decide collectively whether to accept their total and individuals or groups could resign. We would have a Party meeting and he hoped that there would be no resignations before that; the IMF talks would be conducted by Denis and then reported back. There would be a statement next Wednesday. He hoped people would hold off from resigning till then. He ended by saying he hadn't any energy left (he did have a very bad cough) and that finished the first part of today's discussions.

Off to Cabinet again at 8 in the Prime Minister's room at the House. While waiting outside, I talked to David Jones who used to be Deputy Secretary at the Department of Industry and is now in the Cabinet Office. I asked him about what happened to the note books actually describing who said what in Cabinet and he told me that the Cabinet Secretariat's note books were destroyed. That's interesting because those are the only real records, comparable to the ones I'm doing now, of what actually happened.

Denis had a new paper to present and he was now asking for £1199.25 million in 1977, which was nearly £200 million over the billion requested by the IMF. Crosland pointed this out but Denis said that confidence had been undermined by the leaks and therefore we'd have to make more cuts in public expenditure to prevent further loss of confidence.

Then there was a long argument about the number of jobs that could be lost by the package. Denis said 30,000 in 1977–8 and 110,000 the year after.

Peter Shore thought we had been near enough to reach an agreement. But now we were told we had to produce another £200 million and

£1200 million simply was impossible. After much argument, we eventually got just over £1 billion for 1977 and £1.6 billion for the following year.

There was a division at 10 and as we came back Harold Lever said to me, 'I agree with you, it is all crazy but we will give it all back in tax relief.'

'Maybe we will, but they're all Tory measures, they only help the rich.'

'No, no,' he said, 'it helps more.' But he doesn't really believe that.

So we came to the final summing up by Jim, who repeated the list of cuts from the day's discussions. He reiterated the need for absolute secrecy because if it was known what the Treasury had asked, and what it had got (which was much less), it would damage the package. We weren't even to tell our political advisers. He continued, 'We have therefore given authority to the Chancellor to offer the IMF £1 billion cuts in public expenditure in 1977–8, £2 billion in 1978–9 of which half a billion will be in tax.

'We have agreed to sell the BP shares, we will consult on the Letter of Intent to the IMF, we will use the regulator to get £200 million in tax for the year just coming. On the addback, there will be a sub-committee on nationalised industries. We will try and negotiate the safety net and there will be a Party meeting on Thursday next week, and I think there should be a motion of support on the measures.'

'Well,' said Michael, 'I don't agree with the measures and I think we had better be careful about having a vote; I am doubtful about that.'

Denis suggested having a debate in the House on the Monday or Tuesday following.

'I don't support this,' I said. 'I am only going along with it out of loyalty to the Government, and an awful lot of members of the Party don't support it either, so loyalty is the only thing you are going to be living off from now on.'

Well, that was it. The end of the discussions, unless the IMF turns us down.

I haven't tried to get the mood of the meeting but we are all very tired, going to bed at 1 or 2 in the morning. Exhausting. The Cabinet has done a job of work, and I think we have achieved something. We haven't done badly – we have fought off the emotive things like social security cuts and increased prescription charges but the package will be wildly unpopular with the Party, even if the Tories do say it isn't enough and it will fail. It was agreed that I would write a united paper on emergency measures with Frances and Francis and produce it if anything went wrong. Now the only grounds for resigning are because one disagrees with the economic strategy of the Government over all.

Wednesday 8 December
I got the report on the Windscale incident. On 10 October, nearly two months ago, there was a leak of high activity waste material at Windscale which I was not told about. I wrote on Peter Shore's report that it was inexcusable and I would make a parliamentary statement tomorrow.

Thursday 9 December
This afternoon, the statement of seepage of radioactive waste at Windscale was published. This is an absolute scandal. It is unforgivable that I haven't been told for two months.

Monday 13 December
At 2.30 the two Nuclear Inspectors came about the Windscale episode. It was horrifying that neither of them had actually been up to Windscale to have a look, even though 100 gallons a day is seeping out. I was totally shaken and they were acutely embarrassed.

Went into the House which was pretty full because of the Devolution debate and I played it very low key. Just as I was leaving, Nicholas Ridley, Conservative MP for Cirencester and Tewkesbury, raised a question about the surveillance of trade unionists by the Secret Services, which must have severely embarrassed the Front Bench.

Tuesday 14 December
Cabinet at Number 10, where our Letter of Intent to the IMF was in front of us and also the future economic forecasts which are being published tomorrow, which exclude unemployment forecasts. So there is no indication of unemployment rising to 1.75 million, and the Letter of Intent included a phrase 'that the present levels of direct taxation are a disincentive' – an absolutely Tory view.

Denis described the Letter of Intent and said that domestic credit expansion was the key and we would have to promise not to introduce import restraints or exchange controls. In effect, we have got no safety net and we have got no right to introduce import deposits. We have lost everything.

Jim said he was disappointed. Ford and Schmidt had let him down and it was the first time in his life that he felt anti-American.

Tony Crosland asked, 'Are import deposits ruled out by the Letter of Intent, and Jim said Yes.'

I tried to raise the question of unemployment and this was ruled out. Then I queried the paragraph in the letter that the present levels of direct taxation were too high. 'It's pure Thatcherism,' I said and a great groan went around the Cabinet.

Wednesday 15 December
Today I had a report to the effect that some tritium had been found on the beach at Windscale a year ago which had not been explained. There didn't appear to be any link with the recent silo seepage but now they have discovered that there could be a connection and so this raises the question of how long the leak has been going on. Was it reaching the beach?

I asked for all the details and tonight I had a note in my box that a man had inhaled some plutonium a year ago at the radio-chemical centre at Windscale and was now being watched. Now that I have demanded that all nuclear incidents be reported to me, I realise I shall be absolutely swamped by them. I have to find a way of revealing them without causing a scare but in view of the fact that tomorrow morning Peter is going to try to get a Cabinet view on Windscale, I'm hoping I can use some of the information to good effect.

Thursday 16 December
The press universally denounced the package yesterday as being totally inadequate and so on. Even the *Mirror* had a hideous front page (from Denis's point of view) called 'The Rubber Chancellor'.

At Cabinet, Foreign Affairs, the first time Crosland had admitted there were Foreign Affairs for a long time. The FO is going to have talks with the Argentine on the Falkland Islands.

Then we began a discussion on Devolution and Referendum and Michael Foot wanted a statement today saying the Government had decided to have a Referendum in Scotland and Wales.

Windscale, and Peter made a twenty-five-minute speech, saying he really must call in the planning consent for the processing of waste place. Cumbrian County Council couldn't deal with the matter.

Jim said, 'Why can't we just take the Japanese waste and store it before we reprocess it?'

I came in. 'I would like to develop my argument, if I may, because this isn't a pro- or anti-nuclear issue, it is the handling of an expanding nuclear programme which inevitably follows from building power stations. I approved the project but I still support Peter. We shall need nuclear energy and what we need is confidence.' There was anxiety worldwide, and I gave a few examples. 'We need a pause for candour; I was shaken frankly by the Windscale seepage being kept from me and the tritium incident. We can't proceed without restoration of public confidence.'

'Sorry, loves – it seems we've already been too madly lavish!'

Daily Telegraph, 3 December 1976.

Fred Mulley introduced the defence interest which I knew was at the back of this nuclear business. He said the Anglo-American agreements provide that we sell them plutonium and they give us tritium for our bombs and you couldn't review such a sensitive matter so openly because it might affect the Anglo-American nuclear relationship. He talked about nuclear proliferation and the case for doing it here.

Fred Peart said, 'There's too much emotion over this, with the Friends of the Earth and talk of Nagasaki and Hiroshima. It is absurd.'

Denis's comment was: 'If you have a public inquiry, every intellectual exhibitionist in Britain will go there.' That is Healey's attitude to public opinion.

In the end, Peter won; it was a struggle but he won.

Went to the PLP meeting and arrived just as Denis was finishing his presentation. He said, 'The package is introduced on behalf of a united Cabinet.' (That was a bloody lie.) Then he said, 'We need nerve and solidarity and remember, in 1968 we had nerve and solidarity and we came through.'

Jim Callaghan wound up. He said, 'I would like to thank people for their response in the House of Commons because it is an agony to be attacked by your own side. I must tell you that in the Cabinet all the views were expressed and the alternative strategy and the papers to back it up were presented to the Cabinet but the great majority of the Cabinet agreed to reject it.' He addressed individual points that had been made, and went on, 'We need a greater link between industry and the Civil Service and for that reason I don't like to see middle management attacked; this is no time for the class war and I'll say that to anyone who tries to start it. I shall need help from the PLP, from the NEC, from the Tribune Group and from the Manifesto Group. Let's have unity and get together.'

It was an extremely skilful speech by Jim, spoken with great relaxation and he has put on the record that there was a big argument in the Cabinet; that, in a sense, is all one wants people to know.

Friday 17 December

There was an article by Peter Jenkins in the *Guardian* saying Jim Callaghan should sack me and get Joan Maynard, Lena Jeger, and Judith Hart removed from the Executive at next year's Conference.

Saturday 18 December

John Cunningham came to see me. He is desperately worried about Windscale because the plant is in his constituency.

Tuesday 21 December

Economic Strategy Committee met at Number 10 and we had a long and extremely good discussion on industrial democracy based on the first copy of the Bullock Report which we have all received. Jim Callaghan said the TUC was interested in this but it was important that we shouldn't lose the goodwill of the CBI, particularly as it might affect investment.

I thought this was possibly the biggest decision the Government had to take during its lifetime and it was comparable in importance to the extension and development of the franchise. I said we must not be mesmerised by German experience and I agreed that we needed time but we had discussed it for sixty years and we had entered our commitment to do it in the Manifesto. We must also be careful not to be too much affected by the CBI view because working management was quite different, it was quite sympathetic, and managers were joining the trade unions in large numbers now.

Jim Callaghan said, 'This goes to the root of relationships in industry as Devolution goes to the root of relationships in our constitution. Can we get acquiescence? I remember in 1947 that I was on a committee looking at company law and at the time I was much struck with the fact that capitalism has its fingers on the throats of the industry.' I rather emphasise that because it is the first time I have ever heard Jim Callaghan speaking about capitalism as capitalism, using the actual word, and it indicated that perhaps everybody is on the move.

I was pleased I attended. Jim was friendly and I felt things were relaxing a bit.

Friday 24 December

This evening at about 11.30 Mark and Val Arnold-Forster arrived. I took Mark into the front room and he drank whisky and we talked until about 1.45 am on Christmas morning. I told him I was concerned about the extent to which the Security Services were beginning to survey the whole of our public and political life and I didn't know whether it was MI5 or MI6.

He said, 'MI5 is espionage and MI6 is counter-espionage.' I knew that but I pretended not to in order to get him to explain it to me. 'MI5 can't tap telephones unless they have personal authority from the Home Secretary.'

I said, 'I don't believe that. I had known at the Post Office that was the case when I made inquiries, though I had never asked to see whose phones were tapped, but I just didn't believe it.' I said I knew my phone was tapped because Melissa heard her own voice when she picked up the phone and on another occasion Joshua had picked up my calls while I was making them with some apparatus he had set up. I told Mark I had mentioned it to my Private Secretary at the Department of Energy, Roy Williams, who was very shocked but nothing had happened so presumably he had discovered that there was nothing that he could do about it.

Mark didn't really take this on board. So I said, 'Why are we getting all this subversion stuff now about trade union leaders and so on?'

He said the story about Brian Crozier in the *Guardian* was due to the zealous left-wing investigations of a guy called Martin Walker. I somewhat doubt that.

I said I did know that trade union leaders were tapped or bugged and recalled the dinner I had had with Harold Wilson, Harold Lever, Roy Jenkins and Peter Shore and the CBI in 1971 when Harold had boasted about it.

Mark said certainly the Cabinet papers that he had studied revealed that in the Twenties and early Thirties trade union leaders had been carefully watched lest they were under the influence of the Russians. Well I knew that was the case but I wanted to indicate that I knew it was going on now and that it was very damaging.

Then he told me what I suspected but didn't know, that he had worked for MI6. 'You must promise never to say this to anybody but

I have dropped spies into Russia on several occasions, my area is electronic surveillance. I tried to drop somebody in the Black Sea but failed and I finally dropped him off Vladivostok from a ship and then we discovered that he was a double agent who had been recruited by Philby; so I had to get round to everybody who had been on board the ship and to warn them against going to Eastern Europe, lest they disappeared.'

I said, 'I fully understand the need for spying against the Russians. They spy against us and so do the French and so does everybody, everyone knows that. The only anxiety I have is that the Americans might destabilise us.'

'I don't think that,' he said. 'There is a historic and very close link between Britain and the United States.'

'I think you are right but the CIA activities have certainly done a great deal of damage in shaking people's confidence.'

He said that after he had tried to drop the double agent in Russia, he had actually had to go and see Harold Wilson and Harold had been marvellous and had laid on the search for all the members of the crew, and had even found the cook who was running a fish and chip shop in Canada.

Sunday 26 December

Caroline gave each of us a copy of the *Communist Manifesto* in our stockings, published in English in Russia, and she gave Josh a book called *Marx for Beginners* and gave Hilary Isaac Deutscher's three volume biography of Trotsky. I read the *Communist Manifesto* yesterday, never having read it before and I found that, without having read any Communist text, I had come to Marx's view. It is some confession to make in a diary but the analysis of feudal society, the role of the Church and religion, the class struggle, the impact of technology in destroying the professions, and religion, the cash society, the identification of monopoly and the internationalisation of trade and commerce, all these things had been set out absolutely clearly by 1848 by Marx and Engels. It is a most astonishing thing and I feel so ignorant that at the age of fifty-one as a socialist politican in Britain I should never have read that basic text before and I am shy to admit it.

There is no doubt that in the years up to 1968 I was just a career politician and in 1968 I began thinking about technology and participation and all that; it wasn't particularly socialist and my Fabian tract of 1970 was almost anti-socialist, corporatist in character with a democratic theme – management and labour working together. Up to 1973, I shifted to the Left and analysed the Left. Then in 1974 at the Department of Industry I learned it all again by struggle and by seeing it and thinking about it, and I have been driven further and further towards a real socialist position, not a Marxist position particularly because in reading about the Levellers and our own heritage I realise that so much of British socialism goes back quite independently into our history. But, except for the fact that the *Communist Manifesto* wasn't written with an understanding of British history and British society, it is a most amazing summary of the impact of the industrial revolution – Marx was writing within seventy years of Adam Smith. So the Industrial Revolution gave rise to capitalism, socialism and trade unionism at about one and the same time.

I record this now while I am reading all the basic texts in order to try to understand what is going on.

Tuesday 28 December

It has been a very remarkable year really in the aftermath of the Referendum when the Party was in a terrible state of depression and the Government appeared to be going forward with its own right-wing policy unchallenged.

The first great event was the resignation of Harold Wilson in March. It took everybody by surprise and yet at the same time he had predicted he was going to do it.

I decided to stand for Leader and managed to get my policy all out in the first eight days of the first ballot, picking up thirty-seven votes and when Jim was elected I tried very hard to establish a good working relationship with him which has been on and off all year – it's off at the moment.

For all that, Jim is a much better Prime Minister than Wilson. He is more candid and open with people and he does not try to double talk them as Wilson did. Wilson has just simply disappeared from sight. Once his patronage has gone, there's nothing left. Nobody thinks about him any more.

There has been of course the growth of confidence of the Labour movement in confronting the Government, and the Cabinet is now more out of sympathy with the rank and file and middle rank of the Party, although the PLP remains much as before, an instrument of the Right.

For the first six months of 1977 I become the President of the Energy Council along with all the other British Ministers and their respective Councils – Crosland and the Foreign Affairs Council of Ministers, John Silkin and the Agriculture Council, and so on. Jim will be host of the summit.

I must think about Europe. My concerns at the moment are how the Party should react to the Common Market and I think we should call for major reforms in the Treaty of Rome committing us to a democratic socialist association of states which will bring about a fundamental and irreversible shift in the balance of wealth and power in favour of the working people of Europe and their families. And it should be open to all countries and aim at dismantling all the federal parts so that it becomes an open association with none of the present centralisation and bureaucracy.

Next year I also want to try to re-state the case for parliamentary democracy and democracy against capitalism in the very strongest way possible, to show why it is that the Labour Party is committed to democracy and free speech.

I say little of the family in this diary. Caroline is terribly busy. She has got two or three major projects on all the time and is highly respected and regarded by all the people in the educational world. Stephen has just had three months in America working with Senator Eagleton and has to finish his thesis which is a big strain for him, particularly coming back to England after the glamour of Washington. Hilary is well established with Rosalind and his job with ASTMS will last as long as he wants it. Melissa has three years at LSE and Josh is kicking around until he goes to his polytechnic next year.

I'm very richly blessed with an extremely happy family life and could not be more content. I've had as much happiness and comfort and sustenance in my fifty-one years as any man could expect to have in two or three lifetimes, so even if things go wrong and I lose my seat – as I might well do in the next General Election – I have plenty to remember and a role to perform even if it isn't necessarily in the House of Commons.

Principal Persons
(I) Political and Official

Each person is named according to his or her status as the Diaries open. The complete list of Labour Shadow Cabinet and Government Members as at January 1973, February 1974, October 1975 and April 1976, is given in the Appendices.

ADAMSON, Campbell. Industrialist. Director General of the Confederation of British Industry and member of the National Economic Development Council, 1969–76. Seconded to the Department of Economic Affairs as industrial adviser, 1967–9. Subsequently Chairman of Abbey National Building Society.

ALLAUN, Frank. Chairman of the Labour Party, 1978/9, and Labour MP for Salford East, 1955–83. Vice-President of CND and President of Labour Action for Peace.

ARMSTRONG, Robert. Principal Private Secretary to Edward Heath and Harold Wilson, 1970–75, Home Office Deputy Under-Secretary, 1975–7, and Permanent Under-Secretary 1977–9. Secretary of the Cabinet, 1979–87 and Head of the Home Civil Service, 1983–7. Treasury official 1950–70; Principal Private Secretary to Chancellor of the Exchequer, Roy Jenkins, 1968. Created a life peer, 1988.

ARMSTRONG, Sir William (1915–1980). Head of the Home Civil Service and Permanent Secretary of the Civil Service Department, 1968–74. Joint Permanent Secretary of the Treasury, 1962–8. Created a life peer in 1975.

ARNOLD-FORSTER, Mark (1920–1981). Senior journalist and political commentator on the *Guardian*, the *Observer* and ITN, 1946–81. Distinguished service with the Royal Navy while engaged on secret missions during the Second World War. Married to Val Arnold-Forster, journalist. Family friends.

ASHTON, Joe. Principal Private Secretary to Tony Benn, 1975–6. Labour MP for Bassetlaw since 1968.

BALOGH, Lord (Thomas Balogh) (1905–1985). Oxford economist of Hungarian birth. Minister of State at the Department of Energy, 1974–5, and Deputy Chairman, British National Oil Company, 1976–8. Close adviser to Harold Wilson in the 1950s and early 1960s, and Economic Adviser to the Cabinet, 1964–8. Created a life peer in 1968.

BANKS, Tony. Head of Research, Amalgamated Union of Engineering Workers, 1968–75, and Assistant General Secretary, Association of Broadcasting and Allied Staffs, 1976–83. Last Chairman of Greater London Council, 1985–6. Labour MP for Newham North West since 1983.

BARNETT, Joel. Chief Secretary to the Treasury, 1974–9. Labour MP for Heywood and Royton, 1964–83. Created a life peer in 1983.

BERRILL, Sir Kenneth. Economist. Director General of the Central Policy Review Staff ('Think Tank'), 1974–80. Special Adviser and subsequently Chief Economic Adviser to the Treasury between 1967 and 1974.

BESWICK, Lord (Frank Beswick) (1912–1987). Minister of State for Industry, 1974–5, subsequently Chairman of British Aerospace. Labour Co-operative MP for Uxbridge, 1945–59. Created a life peer in 1964. Government Chief Whip in House of Lords, 1967–70.

BISH, Geoff. Research Assistant at Labour Party Research Department, 1968–74. Head of Research, subsequently Policy Director, of the Labour Party since 1974.

BOOTH, Albert. Minister of State, Department of Employment, 1974–6, and Secretary of State, 1976–9. From 1966 to 1983 he was Labour MP for Barrow-in-Furness, a shipbuilding constituency which he lost after his principled stand against the construction of nuclear submarines there.

BROCKWAY, Fenner (1888–1988). Life-long campaigner for peace and founder of the Movement for Colonial Freedom in the 1950s. Labour MP for East Leyton, 1929–31, and for Eton and Slough 1950–64. Leading member of the Independent Labour Party between 1922 and 1946. Created a life peer in 1964.

BUTLER, David. Political scientist and broadcaster, whose special subject is the study of elections; the first person to coin the term 'psephology'. Has published study of every British General Election since 1951. Life-long friend. Married to Marilyn Butler, lecturer and subsequently professor of English Literature.

CALLAGHAN, James. Foreign Secretary, 1974–6, Prime Minister 1976–9 and Leader of the Labour Party until 1980. Held junior posts in the 1945–51 Labour Government, was Chancellor of the Exchequer, 1964–7 and Home Secretary, 1967–70. Chairman of the Labour Party 1973/4 and Labour MP for South, South-East and again South Cardiff, 1945–87. Father of the House, 1983–7. Made a Knight of the Garter and a life peer in 1987. Married to Audrey Callaghan.

CAREY, Peter. Second Permanent Secretary at the Department of Trade and Industry, subsequently at the Department of Industry, 1973–6, and Permanent Secretary at Industry, 1976–83. Deputy Secretary in the Cabinet Office, 1971–2. Chairman of Morgan Grenfell Group.

CARR, Robert. Home Secretary, 1972–4, Secretary of State for Employment, 1970–72, PPS to Anthony Eden, 1951–5. Conservative MP for Mitcham, 1950–74, and Carshalton, 1974–75. Created a life peer in 1975.

CARRINGTON, Lord (Peter Carrington). Secretary of State for Defence, 1970–74, and Energy, 1974. Foreign Secretary from 1979 until his resignation at the start of the Falklands War in 1982. First Lord of the Admiralty and subsequent Leader of the House of Lords, 1959–64. Succeeded to the peerage in 1938 and held all his posts in the Lords. Secretary General of NATO, 1984–8.

CASTLE, Barbara. Secretary of State for Social Services, 1974–6, dismissed by James Callaghan when he formed his Government in 1976. Minister of Overseas Development, 1964–5, Minister of Transport, 1965–8, First Secretary of State at the Department of Employment and Productivity, 1968–70. Chairman of the Labour Party, 1958/9. Labour MP for Blackburn, 1945–79. Leader of the British Labour Group in the European Parliament, 1979–85. Her late husband, Ted Castle, was created a life peer in 1974.

CHAPPLE, Frank. General Secretary of the Electrical, Electronic Telecommunications and Plumbing Trade Union, 1966–84. Member of the National Economic Development Council, 1979–83. Created a life peer in 1985.

CLAPHAM, Sir Michael. Industrialist. President of the Confederation of British Industry, 1972–4, member of the National Economic Development Council, 1971–6.

COATES, Ken. One of the founders of the Institute for Workers' Control and a director of the Bertrand Russell Foundation. Senior Tutor, subsequently Reader, in the Adult Education Department, Nottingham University. Author of numerous works on socialism and industrial democracy. Elected to the European Parliament, 1989.

CRAIGIE, Jill. Author and journalist, married to Michael Foot.

CRIPPS, Francis. Economic adviser to Tony Benn, 1974–9. Founder member of the Cambridge Economic Policy Group.

CROSLAND, Anthony (1918–1977). Secretary of State for the Environment until 1976, then Foreign Secretary up to his sudden death in February 1977. In the 1964–70 Government he was Minister of State for Economic Affairs, 1964–6, Secretary of State for Education and Science, 1965–7, President of the Board of Trade, 1967–9 and Secretary of State for Local Government, 1969–70. Labour MP for South Gloucester, 1950–55 and Grimsby, 1959–77. Married journalist Susan Barnes in 1964. A personal friend from the war years.

CROSSMAN, Richard (1907–1974). Minister of Housing and Local Government, 1964–6, Lord President of the Council and Leader of the House of Commons, 1966–8, Secretary of State for Health and Social Security, 1968–70. Chairman of the Labour Party, 1960/61. He published three volumes of Cabinet Diaries covering 1964–70. Labour MP for Coventry, 1945–74. An Oxford academic, he wrote *Government and the Governed*, 1939. Editor of the *New Statesman* after the 1970 Election. Married to Anne Crossman.

CUDLIPP, Hugh. Succeeded Cecil King as Chairman of Daily Mirror Newspapers, 1963–8. Deputy Chairman, then Chairman of International Publishing Corporation (IPC), 1964–73. Created a life peer in 1974.

CUSTIS, Ronnie. Private Secretary to Tony Benn at Department of Energy, 1975, later Under-Secretary and Director General of Offshore Supplies.

DALYELL, Tam. PPS to Richard Crossman 1964–70. Labour MP for West Lothian, 1962–83, and Linlithgow since 1983.

DAVIES, John (1916–1979). Chancellor of the Duchy of Lancaster with resposibility for Europe, 1972–4. Director-General of the Confederation of British Industry, 1965–9. Elected as an MP in June 1970 and went direct into Cabinet as Minister of Technology from July to October 1970, when Mintech was abolished. Secretary of

State for Industry, 1970–72. Member of the National Economic Development Council, 1962–72. Conservative MP for Knutsford, 1970–78.

DELL, Edmund. Joint Parliamentary Secretary at the Ministry of Technology, 1966–7, Joint Under-Secretary of State at the Department of Economic Affairs, 1967–8, Minister of State at the Board of Trade, 1968–9, and at Employment and Productivity, 1969–70. Secretary of State for Trade 1976–8, resigning to become Deputy Chairman of Guinness Mahon; later joined the SDP.

DONOUGHUE, Bernard. Senior member of staff at the London School of Economics, 1963–74. Senior policy adviser to the Prime Minister and head of the Policy Unit at Number 10, 1974–9. Created life peer in 1985.

EADIE, Alex. Parliamentary Under-Secretary of State at the Department of Energy, 1974–9. A former miner, Labour MP for Midlothian since 1966.

EMMETT, Bryan. Principal Private Secretary to Tony Benn at Department of Energy, 1975–6, subsequently Chief Executive of the Employment Division of the Manpower Services Commission, and Head of the Oil Division at Energy.

ENNALS, David. Minister of State at the Foreign and Commonwealth Office 1974–6, and Secretary of State for Social Services, 1976–9. Secretary of the Labour Party's International Department, 1958–64. Under-Secretary of State at Defence, 1966, and at the Home Office, 1967. Minister of State at the Department of Health and Social Security, 1968–70. Labour MP for Dover, 1964–70 and Norwich North, 1974–83. Created a life peer in 1983.

FEATHER, Vic (1908–1976). Assistant General Secretary of the TUC, 1960–69. General Secretary, 1969–73 and member of the National Economic Development Council. Created a life peer in 1974.

FOOT, Michael. Back Bencher during the 1964–70 Labour Government. Secretary of State for Employment, 1974–6, Lord President of the Council and Leader of the House of Commons, 1976–9. Deputy-Leader of the Labour Party, 1979–80, and Leader, 1980–83. Member of the National Executive, 1971–83. Labour MP for Devonport, 1945–55, Ebbw Vale, 1960–83, and Blaenau Gwent since 1983. Author and journalist; close friend and biographer of Aneurin Bevan. Married to Jill Craigie.

GEORGE-BROWN, Lord (1914–1985). Deputy-Leader of the Labour Party, 1960–70, and in that capacity member of the National Executive and Chairman of the Home Policy Committee. Held office in the 1945–51 Government, finally as Minister of Works. First Secretary of State at the Department of Economic Affairs, 1964–6, and Foreign Secretary 1966–8. Ardently pro-Common Market: tried to negotiate Britain's entry in 1967. Labour MP for Belper, 1945–70. Created a life peer in 1970. Resigned from the Labour Party in 1976 and later joined the SDP.

GOODMAN, Geoffrey. Industrial Editor of the *Daily Mirror*, 1969–86, and Head of the Counter-Inflation Publicity Unit, 1975–6. Former journalist on the *Daily Herald* and the *Sun* and member of the Labour Party Committee on Industrial Democracy, 1966–67.

GORMLEY, Joe. President of the North West Area of the National Union of Mineworkers, 1961–71, and subsequently of the NUM, 1971–82. Member of the National Executive, 1963–73. Created a life peer in 1982.

GRIFFIN, Ken. Appointed adviser to the Ministry of Technology, 1970, industrial relations adviser to Tony Benn at the Department of Industry, 1974. Subsequently a deputy chairman of British Shipbuilders.

HAILSHAM, Lord. As Quintin Hogg sat as Conservative MP for St Marylebone, 1963–70, after disclaiming his peerages in 1963 during the contest for the Conservative Party leadership. Previously sat as MP for Oxford City, 1938 to 1950, when he succeeded his father as 2nd Viscount Hailsham. Held ministerial posts in the House of Lords during the 1951–64 Conservative Governments, including Secretary of State for Education in 1964. Returned to the Lords with a life peerage in 1970. Lord Chancellor, 1970–74 and 1979–87.

HAINES, Joe. Chief Press Secretary to Harold Wilson, 1969–76, previously political correspondent of the *Sun*. Since 1977, a journalist on the *Daily Mirror*, subsequently Political Editor of the Mirror Group.

HART, Judith. Minister for Overseas Development 1974–5, sacked by Harold Wilson after the Referendum, and reinstated 1977–9. In the 1964–70 Government she was successively Joint Under-Secretary for Scotland, Minister of State for Commonwealth Affairs, Minister of Social Security, Paymaster General and Minister for Overseas Development. Chairman of the Labour Party, 1981/2. Labour MP for Lanark, 1959–83, Clydesdale, 1983–7. Married to Tony Hart, a scientist and leading anti-nuclear campaigner.

HATTERSLEY, Roy. Minister of State at the Foreign and Commonwealth Office, 1974–6, Secretary of State for Prices and Consumer Protection, 1976–9. Joint Parliamentary Secretary at the

Department of Employment and Productivity, 1967–9, and Minister of Defence for Administration, 1969–70. Deputy Leader of the Labour Party since 1983.

HAYWARD, Ron. General Secretary of the Labour Party, 1972–82; National Agent, 1969–72, previously a regional organiser of the Party.

HEALEY, Denis. Chancellor of the Exchequer, 1974–9, Secretary of State for Defence, 1964–70. Deputy Leader of the Labour Party, 1980–83. Labour MP for Leeds South East, 1952–5, and Leeds East since 1955.

HEATH, Edward. Succeeded Alec Douglas-Home as Leader of the Conservative Party in 1965. Defeated by Margaret Thatcher in 1975. Prime Minister, 1970–74. Back Bencher since 1975. Minister of Labour, 1959–60, Lord Privy Seal, 1960–63, and Secretary of State for Industry and Trade and President of the Board of Trade, 1963–4. Conservative MP for Bexley, subsequently Old Bexley and Sidcup, since 1950.

HEFFER, Eric. Minister of State at the Department of Industry, 1974–5, sacked by Harold Wilson over the Common Market. Chairman of the Labour Party, 1983/4. Carpenter/joiner by trade and Labour MP for Walton, Liverpool, since 1964. Married to Doris Heffer.

HESELTINE, Michael. Parliamentary Under-Secretary at Department of Environment, 1970–72, Minister for Aerospace and Shipping at Department of Trade and Industry, 1972–4 and Shadow Spokesman on Industry, 1974–6. Secretary of State for Environment, 1979–83, and for Defence until his resignation in 1986. Conservative MP for Tavistock, 1966–74, and Henley since 1974.

HILL, John. Chairman of the UK Atomic Energy Authority, 1967–81, and of British Nuclear Fuels, 1971–83. Member of the Advisory Council on Technology, 1968–70.

HOLLAND, Stuart. Special adviser to Judith Hart, Minister of Overseas Development, 1974–5. Chairman of the Labour Party Public Enterprise Group 1973–75, and contributed substantially to the National Enterprise Board proposals. Economic Assistant in the Cabinet Office, 1966–7 and Assistant to Harold Wilson, 1967–8. Labour MP for Vauxhall, 1979–89.

HOME, Lord (Sir Alec Douglas-Home). Foreign Secretary, 1960–63, in the House of Lords. Before inheriting his peerage, the Earldom of Home, in 1951 he was Conservative/Unionist MP for Lanark, 1931-51, using his courtesy title of Viscount Dunglass. He succeeded

Macmillan and renounced his title in 1963. Prime Minister from October 1963 until October 1964, and MP for Kinross and West Perthshire, 1963–74. In 1974 he was created a life peer and re-entered the Lords as Home of the Hirsel.

HOUGHTON, Douglas. Chairman of the PLP, 1967–74. Chancellor of the Duchy of Lancaster, 1964–6, Minister without Portfolio, 1966–7. Labour MP for Sowerby, 1949–74. Created a life peer in 1974.

HUGHES, Cledwyn. Chairman of the Parliamentary Labour Party, Oct 1974–9. Minister of State for Commonwealth Relations, 1964–6 and Minister of Agriculture, Fisheries and Food, 1968–70. Labour MP for Anglesey, 1951–79. Created a life peer, Lord Cledwyn of Penrhos, in 1979.

INGHAM, Bernard. Director of Information at the Department of Energy, 1974–8, Chief Information Officer at the Department of Employment and Productivity, 1968–73. Reporter on the *Yorkshire Post* and the *Guardian*, 1952–67. Chief Press Secretary to the Prime Minister since 1979.

JACKSON, Margaret. PPS to Judith Hart at the Ministry of Overseas Development, 1974–5. Secretary of the Labour Party Study Group into the National Enterprise Board. Labour MP for Lincoln, defeating Dick Taverne (see below), Oct 1974–9, and for Derby South since 1983.

JAY, Douglas. Leading anti-Common Marketeer. President of the Board of Trade, 1964–7. 'Resigned' in the reshuffle of August 1967 and returned to the Back Benches. Labour MP for North Battersea, 1946–83. Created a life peer in 1987.

JEGER, Lena. Labour MP for St Pancras and Holborn South, 1953–9 and 1964–74 and for Camden, Holborn and St Pancras South, 1974–9. Chairman of the Labour Party, 1979/80. Created a life peer in 1979.

JENKINS, Clive. General Secretary of the Association of Scientific Technical and Managerial Staffs, 1970–88. Member of the General Council of the TUC, 1974–8.

JENKINS, Roy. Home Secretary, 1974–6. In 1976 he became President of the European Commission. Minister of Aviation, 1964–5, Home Secretary, 1965–7, Chancellor of the Exchequer, 1967–70. Deputy Leader of the Labour Party, 1970–72, in which capacity he sat on the National Executive. Labour MP for Central Southwark, 1948–50, for Stechford, 1950–76. Leader of the SDP, 1981–3, and SDP MP for Glasgow Hillhead, 1982–7. Created a life peer in 1987.

JONES, Sir Elwyn. Lord Chancellor 1974–9. Attorney-General, 1964–70. Labour MP for Plaistow, 1945–50, for West Ham South, 1950–74 and for Newham South, February to May 1974, when he was created a life peer, Lord Elwyn-Jones.

JONES, Jack. Assistant General Secretary of the Transport and General Workers' Union, 1963–9, General Secretary 1969–78. Member of the Labour Party National Executive, 1964–7, and of the TUC General Council, 1968–78. Vice-President of Age Concern since 1978.

JOSEPH, Sir Keith. Secretary of State for Social Services, 1970–74, for Industry, 1979–81 and Education and Science 1981–6. From 1959–64 served as Parliamentary Secretary and as Minister of Housing and Local Government and of Welsh Affairs. Conservative MP for Leeds North-East, 1956–87. Created a life peer in 1987.

KAUFMAN, Gerald. Minister of State, Department of Industry, 1975–9. Labour Party press officer, 1965–70. Previously journalist on *Daily Mirror* and *New Statesman*. Labour MP for Manchester Ardwick, 1970–83, and Manchester Gorton since 1983.

KEARTON, Lord (Frank Kearton). A distinguished public servant. Chairman of Courtaulds, 1964–75, and served on the Atomic Energy Authority, and the Central Electricity Generating Board, 1955–81. First Chairman of the Industrial Reorganisation Corporation, 1966–8. Member of the Advisory Council on Technology. First Chairman and Chief Executive of the British National Oil Corporation, 1975–9. Created a life peer in 1970.

KEITH of Castleacre, Lord (Kenneth Keith). Industrialist and banker. Chairman and Chief Executive of Rolls Royce Ltd, 1972–80. Member of National Economic Development Council, 1964–71. Chairman of Hill Samuel, 1970–80 and of Standard Telephones and Cables since 1985. Created a life peer in 1980.

KING, Cecil (1901–1987). Chairman, International Publishing Corporation (IPC), 1963–8. A director of the Bank of England, 1965–8. Chairman of Daily Mirror Newspapers Limited, 1951–63.

LESTOR, Joan. Under-Secretary at the Foreign and Commonwealth Office, 1974–5 and at the Department of Education and Science, 1975–6 resigning her post over public expenditure cuts. Under-Secretary at the Department of Education and Science, 1969–70. Chairman of the Labour Party, 1977/8. Labour MP for Eton and Slough, 1966–83, and Eccles since 1987.

LEVER, Harold. Chancellor of the Duchy of Lancaster, 1974–79.

Financial Secretary to the Treasury, 1967–9, Paymaster General, 1969–70. Created a life peer in 1979.

LOVELL-DAVIS, Lord (Peter Lovell-Davis). Parliamentary Under-Secretary of State at the Department of Energy, 1975–6. Created a life peer in 1974.

MABON, Dickson (Dick). Minister of State at the Department of Energy, 1976–9. Chairman of the Labour Committee for Europe and the European Movement between 1974–6. Labour MP for Greenock from 1955. Joined the SDP in 1981 and sat as SDP Member, 1981–3.

McELHONE, Frank (1929–1982). PPS to Tony Benn, 1974–5. Under-Secretary of State for Scotland, 1975–9. Labour MP for Gorbals 1969–74, Glasgow Queen's Park, 1974–82.

McGARVEY, Danny (1919–1977). President of the Amalgamated Society of Boilermakers, Shipwrights, Blacksmiths and Structural Workers, 1965–77. Member of the National Economic Development Council, 1975–7. Knighted just before his death.

MacKENZIE, Gregor. Parliamentary Under-Secretary of State for Industry, 1974–5, Minister of State, 1975–6. Minister of State at the Scottish Office, 1976–9. PPS to James Callaghan, 1966–70. Labour MP for Rutherglen, 1964–87.

MACMILLAN, Harold (1894–1986). Prime Minister from 1957 until his retirement in October 1963, previously Minister of Defence, 1954–5, Foreign Secretary, 1955, and Chancellor of the Exchequer, 1955–7. Created Earl of Stockton, 1984. Conservative MP for Stockton-on-Tees, 1924–9, 1931–45, and for Bromley, 1945–64.

MADDOCK, Ieuan. Chief Scientist at the Department of Trade and Industry, 1971–77. Atomic scientist who worked at the Atomic Weapons Research Establishment, Aldermaston, and directed the research programme for the Nuclear Test-Ban Treaty, 1957–66. Controller at the Ministry of Technology, 1965–71.

MANLEY, Ivor. Principal Private Secretary to Tony Benn at the Ministry of Technology, 1968–70. Principal Establishment Officer, Department of Energy, 1974–8 and Deputy-Secretary since 1981. Member of UK Atomic Energy Authority, 1981–6.

MARSHALL, Walter. Director of the Atomic Energy Research Establishment at Harwell, 1968–75. Chief Scientist, Department of Energy, 1974–7, Deputy Chairman of the United Kingdom Atomic Energy Authority, 1975–81. Chairman of the UKAEA, 1981–2 and of the Central Electricity Generating Board since 1982. Created a life peer, Lord Marshall of Goring, in 1985.

MASON, Roy. Secretary of State for Defence, 1974–6, and Secretary of State for Northern Ireland, 1976–9. In the 1964–70 Government he was Minister of State at the Board of Trade, 1964–7, Minister of Defence, 1967–8 and of Power 1968–9, and President of the Board of Trade, 1969–70. Labour MP for Barnsley, 1953–87. Created a life peer in 1987.

MAYHEW, Christopher. Appointed Minister of Defence for the Royal Navy in 1964, resigned in 1966 in protest against naval cuts. Labour MP for South Norfolk, 1945–50, and for Woolwich East, 1951–July 1974, when he resigned from the Labour Party to join the Liberal Party. Sat as a Liberal MP for Woolwich East for three months. Created a life peer in 1981.

MAYNARD, Joan. Labour MP for Sheffield, Brightside, Oct 1974–87. Vice-Chairman of the Labour Party, 1980/1.

MEACHER, Michael. Parliamentary Under-Secretary of State for Industry, 1974–5, Health and Social Security, 1975–6, and Trade, 1976–9. Labour MP for Oldham West since 1970.

MELLISH, Robert. Opposition Chief Whip, 1970–74. Joint Parliamentary Secretary at the Ministry of Housing, 1964–7. Minister of Public Building and Works, 1967–9. Government Chief Whip, 1969–70 and 1974–6. Labour MP for Bermondsey from 1946 to 1982, when he resigned from the Labour Party and sat as an Independent until the by-election in March, 1983, which was won by the Liberals. Deputy chairman of the London Docklands Development Corporation since 1981. Created a life peer in 1985.

MIKARDO, Ian. Labour MP for Poplar, 1964–74 and for Bethnal Green and Bow, 1974–87. MP for Reading and South Reading, 1945–59. A distinguished leader of the Labour Left, he was Chairman of the Labour Party, 1970/71. A close associate of Aneurin Bevan and sometime chairman of the Tribune Group of Labour MPs.

MORRELL, Frances. Political adviser to Tony Benn, 1974–9. Press officer for the National Union of Students and the Fabian Society, 1970–72. Previously a schoolteacher, 1960–69. Leader of Inner London Education Authority, 1983–7.

MULLEY, Fred. Minister of Transport, 1969–70, and again in the Department of the Environment, 1974–5. Secretary of State for Education and Science, 1975–6 and for Defence, 1976–9. Deputy Defence Secretary, 1964–5 and Minister of Aviation, 1965–7. Minister of State, Foreign and Commonwealth Office and Disarmament, 1967–9. Chairman of the Labour Party, 1974/5. Labour MP for Sheffield, Park, 1950–83. Created a life peer in 1984.

MURRAY, Len. General Secretary of the TUC, 1973–84. Member of the TUC staff from 1947. Created a life peer, Lord Murray of Epping Forest, in 1985.

ORME, Stan. Minister of State, Northern Ireland Office, 1974–6, Minister of State for Social Security, 1976–7 and Minister for Social Security, 1977–9. Chairman of the PLP since 1987. Labour MP for Salford West 1964–83 and for Salford East since 1983.

OWEN, David. Parliamentary Under-Secretary of State, then Minister of State at the Department of Health and Social Security, 1974–6, Minister of State at the Foreign and Commonwealth Office, 1976. Foreign Secretary, following Tony Crosland's death, 1977–9. Parliamentary Under-Secretary of State for the Royal Navy, 1968–70. Labour MP for Plymouth Sutton, 1966–74 and Plymouth Devonport, 1974–81. Founder Member of the SDP, 1981 and sat as SDP MP, 1981–3; SDP MP for Devonport since 1983.

PANNELL, Charles (1902–1980). Minister of Public Building and Works, 1964–6. Labour MP for Leeds West, 1949–74. Created a life peer in 1974.

PART, Sir Antony. Permanent Secretary at the Department of Trade and Industry, 1970–4 and the Department of Industry, 1974–6. Previously Permanent Secretary at the Ministry of Public Building and Works, 1965–8 and the Board of Trade, 1968–70. Retired in 1976. Chairman of the Committee on North Sea Oil Taxation, 1981.

PEART, Fred. (1914–88). Minister of Agriculture, Fisheries and Food, 1974–6, Minister of Agriculture, 1964–8, and Lord President and Leader of the House of Commons, 1968–70. Labour MP for Workington, 1945–76. Created a life peer in 1976.

PITT, Terry (1937–1986). Head of the Labour Party's Research Department, 1965–74. Special Adviser to the Lord President of the Council, 1974. Later elected to the European Parliament.

PLIATZKY, Leo. Under-Secretary at the Treasury, 1967–71 and Second Permanent Secretary, 1971–6. Permanent Secretary at the Department of Trade, 1977–9.

POWELL, Enoch. Minister of Health, 1960–63. Resigned as Financial Secretary to the Treasury in protest at the Budget. Conservative MP for Wolverhampton South-West, 1950–74. Stood down as Conservative candidate in February 1974 in disagreement over the calling of a General Election. United Ulster Unionist MP for Down South, October 1974–87.

PRENTICE, Reg. Minister of Overseas Development, 1967–9, and again 1975–6. Secretary of State for Education and Science, 1974–5. Minister of State, Department of Education and Science, 1964–6. Minister of Public Building and Works, 1966–7. Labour MP for East Ham North, 1951–74, Newham North East, 1974–9. In October 1977 Reg Prentice crossed the floor and sat on the Conservative benches until 1979. In 1979 he was elected Conservative MP for Daventry and sat for Daventry until 1987; he was Minister for Social Security, 1979–81 in the Conservative Government.

RAMPTON, Sir Jack. Permanent Under-Secretary of State at the Department of Energy, 1974–80. Formerly a senior official at the Ministry of Technology and the Department of Trade and Industry, 1968–74.

REES, Merlyn. Secretary of State for Northern Ireland, 1974–6, Home Secretary, 1976–9. Parliamentary Under-Secretary of State at the Ministry of Defence, 1965–8, and Home Office, 1968–70. Labour MP for South Leeds, 1963–83, and for Morley and Leeds South since 1983.

ROBINSON, Geoffrey. Chief Executive of Jaguar Cars, Coventry, 1973–75, and consultant in a personal capacity to Meriden Motor Cycle Workers' Co-operative. Unpaid Chief Executive of Meriden, 1979–80. Senior Executive, Industrial Reorganisation Corporation, 1968–70. Labour MP for Coventry North-West since 1976.

RODGERS, William (Bill). Minister of State at the Ministry of Defence, 1974–6, Secretary of State for Transport, 1976–79. Parliamentary Under-Secretary of State at the Department of Economic Affairs then Foreign Commonwealth Office, 1964–8. Minister of State at the Board of Trade, 1968–9, and the Treasury, 1969–70. Labour MP for Stockton-on-Tees (Teesside, Stockton from 1974), 1962–81. Founder member of the SDP in 1981 and sat as SDP MP for same seat, 1981–3.

ROGERS, Herbert. Election Agent for Tony Benn, 1951–70. Secretary of the East Bristol Independent Labour Party from 1912. Agent for Sir Stafford Cripps, MP for Bristol East, and after wartime work in the Government became Secretary of the Bristol South East Labour Party.

ROSS, William, Secretary of State for Scotland, 1964–70, and 1974–6. Labour MP for Kilmarnock, 1946–79. Created a life peer in 1979.

ROTHSCHILD, Lord (Victor Rothschild). Director-General of the Central Policy Review Staff ('Think Tank'), 1970–74. Scientist and Chairman of Shell Research Ltd, 1963–70. Member of the Central Advisory Committee for Science and Technology, 1969.

RYDER, Sir Don. Chairman and Chief Executive of Reed International, 1968–75, Chairman of the National Enterprise Board (NEB), appointed by Tony Benn, 1975–7. Created a life peer in 1975.

SCANLON, Hugh. President of the Amalgamated Union of Engineering Workers, 1968–78. AEU organiser, 1947–63. Member of the National Economic Development Council, 1971–8. Created a life peer in 1979.

SEDGEMORE, Brian. PPS to Tony Benn 1977–8. Labour MP for Luton West, 1974–9 and for Hackney South and Shoreditch since 1983. Granada TV researcher, 1980–83.

SHORE, Liz. Civil Service doctor. Deputy Chief Medical Officer for the Department of Health and Social Security, 1977–85. Post-Graduate Medical Dean, North West Thames Region since 1985. Married to Peter Shore.

SHORE, Peter. Secretary of State for Trade, 1974–6, Secretary of State for the Environment, 1976–9. Head of Research Department of the Labour Party, 1959–64. PPS to Harold Wilson, 1965–6. Joint Parliamentary Secretary at the Ministry of Technology, 1966–7, Secretary of State for Economic Affairs, 1967–9. Minister without Portfolio, 1969–70. Labour MP for Stepney, subsequently Stepney and Poplar, and then Bethnal Green and Stepney since 1964. Married to Liz Shore.

SHORT, Edward. Deputy Leader of the Labour Party, 1972–6, and Lord President of the Council and Leader of the House of Commons, 1974–6. Government Chief Whip, 1964–6. Postmaster General, 1966–8. Secretary of State for Education and Science, 1968–70. Labour MP for Newcastle-on-Tyne Central, 1951–76. Created a life peer, Lord Glenamara, in 1976.

SILKIN, John (1923–1987). Minister for Planning and Local Government, 1974–6 and Minister for Agriculture, Fisheries and Food, 1976–9. Government Whip, 1964–6 and Chief Whip, 1966–9. Minister of Public Building and Works, 1969–70. Labour MP for Deptford, 1963–87.

SIMPSON, Bill. General Secretary, Amalgamated Union of Engineering Workers (Foundry Section), 1967–75. Chairman of the

Labour Party, 1972/3. Chairman of the Health and Safety Commission 1974–83.

SMITH, John. Parliamentary Under-Secretary of State, then Minister of State, at the Department of Energy, 1974–6. Minister of State in the Privy Council Office, with responsibility for Devolution, 1976–8. Secretary of State for Trade, 1978–9. Labour MP for Lanarkshire North, 1970–83 and Monklands East since 1983.

STANLEY, Bryan. General Secretary of the Post Office Engineering Union (later the National Communications Union), 1972–86; member of the National Executive 1973–8.

STEEL, David. Leader of the Liberal Party, 1976–1988, and co-Leader of the Social Democratic and Liberal Alliance during 1987. Liberal MP for Roxburgh, Selkirk and Peebles, 1965–83 and Tweeddale, Ettrick and Lauderdale since 1983.

STEWART, Michael. Secretary of State for Education and Science, 1964–5, Foreign Secretary, 1965–6, Secretary of State for Economic Affairs, 1966–7, Foreign and Commonwealth Secretary, 1968–70. Held junior office in the 1945–51 Labour Government. Labour MP for Fulham East, subsequently Fulham and then Hammersmith and Fulham, 1945–79. Created a life peer in 1979.

STONEHOUSE, John (1925–1988). Parliamentary Secretary, Ministry of Aviation, 1964–6. Under-Secretary of State for the Colonies, 1966–7. Ministry of Aviation, 1967. Minister of State at the Ministry of Technology, 1967–8. Postmaster General in 1968 and Minister of Posts and Telecommunications, 1969. Labour Co-operative MP for Wednesbury, 1957–74, and Walsall North, 1974, until his resignation in 1976. Imprisoned for fraud, 1976.

TAVERNE, Dick. Labour MP for Lincoln from 1962 until resigning in 1972. Regained the seat in a by-election in 1973, as Democratic Labour candidate, lost it in the October 1974 Election. Financial Secretary to the Treasury, 1969–70.

THATCHER, Margaret. Secretary of State for Education and Science, 1970–74, previously a junior Minister in the Ministry of Pensions and National Insurance, 1961–4. Leader of the Conservative Opposition 1975–9, Prime Minister since 1979. Conservative MP for Finchley since 1959.

THOMAS, George. Speaker of the House of Commons, 1976–83, (Deputy Speaker 1974–6). Minister of State at the Welsh Office, 1966–7, and Commonwealth Office, 1967–8. Secretary of State for Wales, 1968–70. Since 1983 Chairman of the National Children's

Home. A former Vice President of the Methodist Conference. Labour MP for Cardiff Central, 1945–50, Cardiff West, 1950–83 (sat as Speaker from 1976). Created a hereditary peer, Viscount Tonypandy, in 1983.

THOMSON, George. Chairman of the Labour Committee for Europe, 1972–3, appointed an EEC Commissioner, 1973–7. Minister of State at the Foreign Office, 1964–6 and Chancellor of the Duchy of Lancaster, 1966–7 and 1969–70. Secretary of State for Commonwealth Affairs, 1967–8. Minister without Portfolio, 1968–9. Chairman of the Independent Broadcasting Authority (IBA) since 1981. Labour MP for Dundee East, 1952–72. Created a life peer in 1977.

THORPE, Jeremy. Leader of the Liberal Party, 1967–76. Liberal MP for North Devon, 1959–79.

TUITE, Ray. Principal Press Officer to Tony Benn at the Department of Industry.

VARLEY, Eric. Secretary of State for Energy, 1974–5, exchanging Cabinet jobs with Tony Benn to become Secretary of State for Industry, 1975–9, while Tony Benn was responsible for Energy, 1975–9. PPS to Harold Wilson, 1968–9. Minister of State at the Ministry of Technology, 1969–70. Labour MP for Chesterfield, 1964–84. Retired in 1984 to become Chairman of Coalite Group.

VAUGHAN, Ron. Official driver to Tony Benn at the Ministry of Technology, 1968–70, and at the Departments of Industry and Energy, 1974–9.

WALKER, Peter. Secretary of State for the Environment, 1970–2 and for Trade and Industry, 1972–4. Minister for Agriculture, Fisheries and Food, 1979–83, Secretary of State for Wales since 1987. Deputy Chairman of Slater, Walker Securities, 1964–70. Conservative MP for Worcester since 1961.

WEINSTOCK, Arnold. Industrialist. Managing Director of GEC since 1963, of Radio and Allied Industries, 1954–63. Created a life peer in 1980.

WHITELAW, William (Willie). Secretary of State for Employment, 1973–4, previously Leader of the House of Commons, and Secretary of State for Northern Ireland, 1972–3. Chairman of the Conservative Party, 1974–5. Home Secretary, 1979–83. Created a viscount in 1983.

WHITTY, Larry. Assistant Private Secretary at the Ministry of Technology, 1965–70. Official of General and Municipal Workers Union, 1973–85. Since 1985, General Secretary of the Labour Party.

WILLIAMS, Marcia. Personal and Political Secretary to Harold Wilson since 1956. Created a life peer, Lady Falkender, in 1976.

WILLIAMS, Roy. Principal Private Secretary to Tony Benn, 1974. Under-Secretary, subsequently Deputy Secretary, of the Department of Industry (later the Department of Trade and Industry), since 1976.

WILLIAMS, Shirley. Secretary of State for Prices and Consumer Protection, 1974–6, Secretary of State for Education and Science and Paymaster General, 1976–9. Member of the National Executive 1970–81. In the 1964–70 Government she was Parliamentary Secretary at the Ministry of Labour, 1966–7, Minister of State, Education and Science, 1967–9, and the Home Office, 1969–70. Labour MP for Hitchin, 1964–74, for Hertford and Stevenage, 1974–9. Founder of SDP in 1981, President in 1982 and SDP MP for Crosby, 1981–3.

WILSON, Harold. Leader of the Labour Party, 1963–76. Prime Minister, 1964–70, and 1974–6. Resigned in 1976 and did not hold office again. President of the Board of Trade, 1947–51, when he resigned with Aneurin Bevan. Chairman of the Labour Party, 1961/2. Labour MP for Ormskirk, 1945–50, and Huyton, 1950–83. Created life peer, Lord Wilson of Rievaulx. Married to Mary Wilson, poet and writer.

WISE, Audrey. Labour MP for Coventry South West, 1974–9 and for Preston since 1987.

(II) Personal

BENN, Caroline. Born in Ohio and graduated from Vassar College, post-graduate degrees from the Universities of Cincinnati and London. Founder member of the main comprehensive education campaign group in Britain, and editor of *Comprehensive Education*. Author of many educational publications including *Half Way There* with Professor Brian Simon (1970) and *Challenging the MSC* with John Fairley (1986). President of the Socialist Educational Association. Adult education lecturer since 1965, currently teaching an Open University preparation course. Former member of the Inner London Education Authority, and governor of several schools and colleges. Married Tony Benn in 1949. Four children: Stephen, Hilary, Melissa and Joshua (see below).

BENN, David Wedgwood. Younger brother of Tony Benn; a barrister, worked for the Socialist International and later for the External Service of the BBC. Head of the BBC Yugoslav Section, 1974–84. A writer specialising in Soviet affairs.

BENN, Hilary. Born 1953. Educated at Holland Park School and Sussex University. Research Officer with the trade union MSF (formerly ASTMS). A past President of Acton Labour Party, elected to Ealing Council, 1979. Deputy Leader of the Council and Chair of the Education Committee since 1986. Also Chair of the Association of London Authorities' Education Committee. Contested Ealing North in 1983 and 1987 Elections. In 1973 married Rosalind Retey, who died of cancer in 1979. Married Sally Clark in 1982. Four children.

BENN, Joshua. Born 1958. Educated at Holland Park School. Founder of COMMUNITEC Computer Training Consultancy, 1984–8. Director of Westway Music Publishing, 1980–82. Former contributor to *Sound International, Beat Instrumental* and computer and electronics magazines. Co-author of *Rock Hardware* (1981). Executive member of Computing for Labour. Employed by the Housing Corporation since 1988. Married Elizabeth Feeney in 1984. One son.

BENN, June. Former lecturer; novelist writing under the name of June Barraclough. Married David Benn in 1959. Two children, Piers, born 1962, and Frances, born 1964.

BENN, Melissa. Born 1957. Educated at Holland Park School and the London School of Economics. Socialist feminist writer and journalist. Joint author with Ken Worpole of *Death in the City* (1986). Contributor to several essay collections on feminism, the media, the police and crime; her work has also appeared in *Feminist Review, Women's Studies International Forum* and several international publications (in translation). Contributes to the *Guardian, New Statesman, Marxism Today, Spare Rib*. On the staff of *City Limits* since 1988.

BENN, Stephen. Born 1951. Educated at Holland Park School and Keele University. PhD (1984) for 'The White House Staff'. Former assistant to Senator Thomas F. Eagleton. Secretary and Agent, Kensington Labour Party. Labour candidate GLC, 1981. Member GLC Special Committee, 1983–6. Chair, Brent South CLP. ILEA member since 1981 (representing Hackney North and Stoke Newington since 1986), and Chair of General Purposes Committee. School and College Governor. Court of Governors, Central London Polytechnic. Vice-Chair, ALA Education Committee since 1987. Parliamentary Affairs Officer for Royal Society of Chemistry since 1988. Composer. During the period covered by this volume, lived with

June Battye, a fellow student at Keele. Married Nita Clarke in 1988.

CARTER, Peter. Close family friend. Architect who worked in Chicago under Mies van der Rohe.

FLANDERS, Michael (1922–1975). Actor and writer. Contemporary of Tony Benn at school. Family friend who, with Donald Swann, formed the duo well known for its musical stage entertainments.

GIBSON, Ralph. University contemporary, a barrister who was later made a judge. He and his wife, Anne, are close friends of the family.

KHAMA, Sir Seretse (1921–1980). Founder and President of the Bechuanaland Democratic Party from 1962, becoming Prime Minister of Bechuanaland (Botswana) in 1965, and President of the Republic of Botswana in 1966. A barrister educated at Oxford, Seretse had become chief of the Bamangwato tribe in 1925, aged four. He was removed from the British protectorate by the Labour Government in 1950 over objections to his marriage to Ruth Williams, a white British woman, in 1948. Became close friends with the Benns who lent support in the 1950s. Seretse Khama was godfather to Melissa Benn, and Tony Benn godfather to Anthony Khama.

LAMBERT, Phyllis. A Canadian architect, a college contemporary of Caroline Benn, and long-time friend of the family.

RETEY, Rosalind (1953–1979). A contemporary of Hilary Benn at Holland Park School, graduated from Queen Mary College, London. They married in April 1973. Rosalind contracted cancer in 1978, and died at home in June 1979 after much suffering which she bore with immense courage. A fund in her memory has been established at Holland Park School under the control of the students.

STANSGATE, Lady. Margaret Holmes, born in Scotland in 1897, the daughter of Liberal MP, D. T. Holmes. Married William Wedgwood Benn in 1920. They had three children (the eldest son, Michael, was killed while serving as an RAF pilot during the war). A long-standing member of the Movement for the Ordination of Women, the first President of the Congregational Federation, served on the Council of Christians and Jews, and of the Friends of the Hebrew University. Fellow of the Hebrew University. Joint author of *Beckoning Horizon*, 1934.

STANSGATE, Lord (1877–1960). William Wedgwood Benn. Son of John Williams Benn, who was Liberal MP for Tower Hamlets and later for Devonport, and Chairman, 1904/5, of the London County Council of which he was a founder member. William Wedgwood Benn was himself elected Liberal MP for St George's, Tower Hamlets, in 1906. Became a Whip in the Liberal Government in 1910. Served in the First World War and was decorated with the DSO and DFC, returning in 1918 to be elected Liberal MP for Leith. Joined the Labour Party in 1926, resigned his seat the same day, and was subsequently elected Labour MP for North Aberdeen (1928–31) in a by-election. Secretary of State for India in the 1929–31 Labour Cabinet. Re-elected as Labour MP for Gorton in 1937. He rejoined the RAF in 1940 at the age of sixty-three, was made a peer, Viscount Stansgate, in 1941, and was Secretary of State for Air, 1945–6, in the postwar Labour Government. World President of the Inter-Parliamentary Union, 1947–57.

SWANN, Donald. School contemporary and family friend who wrote the music for and performed in many shows, including *At the Drop of a Hat*, which he and Michael Flanders staged in London and took on a world tour. Composer of church music.

WINCH, Olive (Buddy). Miss Winch was with the family as a children's nurse from 1928 until 1940, when she left to undertake war work. A life-long friend.

APPENDIX I

Parliamentary Committee (Shadow Cabinet), January 1973

Leader	Mr Harold Wilson
Deputy Leader	Mr Edward Short
Chairman, PLP	Mr Douglas Houghton
Chief Whip	Mr Robert Mellish
Department of Trade and Industry	Mr Tony Benn
	Mr Harold Lever
Foreign and Commonwealth Office	Mr James Callaghan
Environment	Mr Anthony Crosland
European Common Market	Mr Michael Foot
	Mr Peter Shore
Treasury	Mr Denis Healey
Defence	Mr Fred Peart
Employment	Mr Reg Prentice
Northern Ireland Affairs	Mr Merlyn Rees
Scotland	Mr William Ross
Home Office	Mrs Shirley Williams
Leader, House of Lords	Lord Shackleton
Chief Whip, House of Lords	Lord Beswick
Labour Peers' Representatives	Lord Champion
Secretary	Mr Frank Barlow

APPENDIX II

Her Majesty's Government
Complete List of Ministers and Offices

The Cabinet, February 1974

Prime Minister and First Lord of the Treasury	Mr Harold Wilson
Lord President of the Council and Leader of the House of Commons	Mr Edward Short
Secretary of State for Foreign and Commonwealth Affairs	Mr James Callaghan
Lord Chancellor	Lord Elwyn-Jones
Secretary of State for the Home Department	Mr Roy Jenkins
Chancellor of the Exchequer	Mr Denis Healey
Secretary of State for Employment	Mr Michael Foot
Secretary of State for Energy	Mr Eric Varley
Secretary of State for Social Services	Mrs Barbara Castle
Secretary of State for Industry	Mr Tony Benn
Secretary of State for Scotland	Mr William Ross
Chancellor of the Duchy of Lancaster	Mr Harold Lever
Secretary of State for Trade	Mr Peter Shore
Secretary of State for Prices and Consumer Protection	Mrs Shirley Williams
Minister of Agriculture, Fisheries and Food	Mr Frederick Peart
Secretary of State for Defence	Mr Roy Mason
Secretary of State for Northern Ireland	Mr Merlyn Rees
Secretary of State for Wales	Mr John Morris
Secretary of State for Education and Science	Mr Reg Prentice
Lord Privy Seal and Leader of the House of Lords	Lord Shepherd

Ministers not in the Cabinet, February 1974

Minister for Overseas Development	Mrs Judith Hart
Paymaster General	Mr Edmund Dell
Parliamentary Secretary to the Treasury	Mr Robert Mellish
Attorney-General	Mr Samuel Silkin
Solicitor-General	Mr Peter Archer
Minister of State for Energy	Lord Balogh
Minister for Transport	Mr Frederick Mulley
Minister for Planning and Local Government	Mr John Silkin
Minister for Housing and Construction	Mr Reginald Freeson
Minister of State for Urban Affairs, Department of the Environment	Mr Charles Morris
Minister of State for Sport, Department of the Environment	Mr Denis Howell
Ministers of State for Foreign and Commonwealth Affairs	Mr David Ennals
	Mr Roy Hattersley
Minister of State for Industry	Mr Eric Heffer
Minister of State for Northern Ireland	Mr Stanley Orme
Chief Secretary to the Treasury	Mr Joel Barnett
Financial Secretary to the Treasury	Dr John Gilbert
Minister of State for Agriculture, Fisheries and Food	Mr Norman Buchan
Minister of State for Defence	Mr William Rodgers
Minister of State for Education and Science	Mr Gerald Fowler
Minister of State for Employment	Mr Albert Booth
Minister of State for Health and Social Security	Mr Brian O'Malley
Ministers of State, Home Office	Mr Alexander Lyon
	Lord Harris of Greenwich
Minister of State for Prices and Consumer Protection	Mr Alan Williams
Ministers of State, Scottish Office	Mr Bruce Millan
	Lord Hughes
Lord Advocate	Mr Ronald King Murray
Minister of State for Civil Service	Mr Robert Sheldon
Minister of State for Industry and Deputy Leader of the House of Lords	Lord Beswick
Solicitor General for Scotland	Mr John McCluskey

The Cabinet, October 1975

Prime Minister and First Lord of the Treasury	Mr Harold Wilson
Lord President of the Council and Leader of the House of Commons	Mr Edward Short
Secretary of State for Foreign and Commonwealth Affairs	Mr James Callaghan
Lord Chancellor	Lord Elwyn-Jones
Secretary of State for the Home Department	Mr Roy Jenkins
Chancellor of the Exchequer	Mr Denis Healey
Secretary of State for Employment	Mr Michael Foot
Secretary of State for Energy	Mr Tony Benn
Secretary of State for Social Services	Mrs Barbara Castle
Secretary of State for Industry	Mr Eric Varley
Secretary of State for the Environment	Mr Anthony Crosland
Secretary of State for Scotland	Mr William Ross
Chancellor of the Duchy of Lancaster	Mr Harold Lever
Secretary of State for Trade	Mr Peter Shore
Secretary of State for Prices and Consumer Protection	Mrs Shirley Williams
Minister of Agriculture, Fisheries and Food	Mr Frederick Peart
Secretary of State for Defence	Mr Roy Mason
Secretary of State for Northern Ireland	Mr Merlyn Rees
Secretary of State for Wales	Mr John Morris
Secretary of State for Education and Science	Mr Frederick Mulley
Lord Privy Seal and Leader of the House of Lords	Lord Shepherd
Minister of Overseas Development	Mr Reg Prentice
Parliamentary Secretary to the Treasury	Mr Robert Mellish
Minister for Planning and Local Government	Mr John Silkin

Ministers not in the Cabinet, October 1975

Attorney-General	Mr Samuel Silkin
Solicitor-General	Mr Peter Archer
Minister of State for Energy	Lord Balogh
Minister for Transport	Dr John Gilbert
Minister for Housing and Construction	Mr Reginald Freeson
Secretary of State, Department of the Environment	Mr Denis Howell
Ministers of State for Foreign and Commonwealth Affairs	Mr David Ennals
	Mr Roy Hattersley
	Lord Beswick
Ministers of State for Industry	Mr Gregor MacKenzie

Ministers of State for Northern Ireland	Mr Stanley Orme
	Mr Roland Moyle
Chief Secretary to the Treasury	Mr Joel Barnett
Financial Secretary to the Treasury	Mr Robert Sheldon
Minister of State, Treasury	Mr Denzil Davies
Minister of State for Agriculture, Fisheries and Food	Mr Edward Bishop
Minister of State for Defence	Mr William Rodgers
Minister of State for Education and Science	Lord Crowther-Hunt
Minister of State, Privy Council Office	Mr Gerald Fowler
Minister of State for Employment	Mr Albert Booth
Ministers of State for Health and Social Security	Mr Brian O'Malley
	Dr David Owen
Ministers of State, Home Office	Mr Alexander Lyon
	Lord Harris of Greenwich
Minister of State for Prices and Consumer Protection	Mr Alan Williams
Minister of State for Civil Service	Mr Charles Morris
Ministers of State, Scottish Office	Mr Bruce Millan
	Lord Hughes
Lord Advocate	Mr Ronald King Murray
Solicitor-General for Scotland	Mr John McCluskey

The Cabinet, April 1976

Prime Minister and First Lord of the Treasury	Mr James Callaghan
Lord President of the Council and Leader of the House of Commons	Mr Michael Foot
Secretary of State for Foreign and Commonwealth Affairs	Mr Anthony Crosland
Lord Chancellor	Lord Elwyn-Jones
Secretary of State for the Home Department	Mr Roy Jenkins
Chancellor of the Exchequer	Mr Denis Healey
Secretary of State for Employment	Mr Albert Booth
Secretary of State for Energy	Mr Tony Benn
Secretary of State for Social Services	Mr David Ennals
Secretary of State for Industry	Mr Eric Varley
Secretary of State for the Environment	Mr Peter Shore
Secretary of State for Scotland	Mr Bruce Millan
Chancellor of the Duchy of Lancaster	Mr Harold Lever

Secretary of State for Trade	Mr Edmund Dell
Secretary of State for Prices and Consumer Protection	Mrs Shirley Williams
Minister of Agriculture, Fisheries and Food	Mr Frederick Peart
Secretary of State for Defence	Mr Roy Mason
Secretary of State for Northern Ireland	Mr Merlyn Rees
Secretary of State for Wales	Mr John Morris
Secretary of State for Education and Science	Mr Frederick Mulley
Lord Privy Seal and Leader of the House of Lords	Lord Shepherd
Minister for Overseas Development	Mr Reg Prentice
Parliamentary Secretary to the Treasury	Mr Michael Cocks
Minister for Planning and Local Government	Mr John Silkin

Ministers not in the Cabinet, April 1976

Attorney-General	Mr Samuel Silkin
Solicitor-General	Mr Peter Archer
Minister of State for Energy	Mr Dick Mabon
Minister for Transport	Mr John Gilbert
Minister for Housing and Construction	Mr Reginald Freeson
Ministers of State for Foreign and Commonwealth Affairs	Mr Roy Hattersley
	Lord Goronwy Roberts
	Mr Edward Rowlands
Ministers of State for Industry	Mr Gerald Kaufman
	Mr Alan Williams
Ministers of State for Northern Ireland	Mr Roland Moyle
	Mr Don Concannon
Chief Secretary to the Treasury	Mr Joel Barnett
Financial Secretary to the Treasury	Mr Robert Sheldon
Minister of State, Treasury	Mr Denzil Davies
Minister of State, Agriculture, Fisheries and Food	Mr Edward S. Bishop
Minister of State for Defence	Mr William Rodgers
Minister of State for Education and Science	Mr Gerald Fowler
Minister of State, Privy Council Office	Mr John Smith
Minister of State for Employment	Mr Harold Walker
Ministers of State for Health and Social Security	Dr David Owen
	Mr Stanley Orme
Minister of State, Home Office	Mr Brynmor John
Minister of State, Prices and Consumer Protection	Mr John Fraser
Minister of State for Civil Service	Mr Charles Morris
Ministers of State, Scottish Office	Lord Kirkhill
	Mr Gregor MacKenzie

Lord Advocate	Mr Ronald King Murray
Solicitor-General for Scotland	Mr John McCluskey

Changes made on 10 September 1976 by James Callaghan:

Lord Peart appointed Lord Privy Seal and Leader of the House of Lords.

Merlyn Rees replaced Roy Jenkins as Home Secretary.

John Silkin replaced Fred Peart as Minister of Agriculture, Fisheries and Food.

Fred Mulley replaced Roy Mason as Secretary of State for Defence.

Shirley Williams replaced Fred Mulley as Secretary of State for Education and Science.

Roy Mason replaced Merlyn Rees as Northern Ireland Secretary.

Roy Hattersley replaced Shirley Williams as Secretary of State for Prices and Consumer Protection.

Stan Orme appointed Minister for Social Security.

William Rodgers appointed Secretary of State for Transport.

APPENDIX III

Labour Party National Executive Committees 1973 and 1976

1972/3

Mr William Simpson	Chairman
Mr James Callaghan, MP	Vice-Chairman and Treasurer
Mr Harold Wilson, MP	Leader of the Parliamentary Party
Mr Edward Short, MP	Deputy-Leader of the Parliamentary Party
Mr Ron Hayward	General Secretary

Trade Unions' Section

Mr T. G. Bradley, MP (Transport Salaried Staffs' Association)
Mr J. Chalmers (Amalgamated Society of Boilermakers, Shipwrights, Blacksmiths and Structural Workers)
Mr A. Cunningham (National Union of General and Municipal Workers)
Mr J. Diamond (British Iron, Steel and Kindred Trades Association)
Mr L. Forden (Transport and General Workers' Union)
Mr J. Forrester (Amalgamated Union of Engineering Workers, Technical and Supervisory Section)
Mr J. Gormley (National Union of Mineworkers)
Mr A. Kitson (Scottish Commercial Motormen's Union)
Mr F. W. Mulley, MP (Clerical and Administrative Workers' Union)
Mr W. E. Padley, MP (Union of Shop, Distributive and Allied Workers)
Mr W. Simpson (Amalgamated Union of Engineering Workers, Foundry Section)
Mr S. Weighell (National Union of Railwaymen)

Socialist, Cooperative and Professional Organisations' Section
Mr J. Cartwright (Royal Arsenal Cooperative Society)

Constituency Organisations' Section
Mr F. Allaun, MP
Mr A. W. Benn, MP
Mrs B. Castle, MP
Mr M. Foot, MP
Mr D. Healey, MP
Miss J. Lestor, MP
Mr I. Mikardo, MP

Women Members
Mrs Judith Hart, MP
Mrs L. Jeger, MP
Miss J. Maynard
Mrs Renee Short, MP
Mrs Shirley Williams, MP

Labour Party Young Socialists' Representative
Mr P. Doyle

1976/7

Mr John Chalmers	Chairman
Miss Joan Lestor, MP	Vice-Chairman
Mr Norman Atkinson, MP	Treasurer
Mr James Callaghan, MP	Leader of the Parliamentary Party
Mr Michael Foot, MP	Deputy Leader of the Parliamentary Party
Mr Ron Hayward	General Secretary

Trade Unions' Section
Mr T. G. Bradley, MP (Transport Salaried Staffs' Association)
Mr J. Chalmers (Amalgamated Society of Boilermakers, Shipwrights, Blacksmiths and Structural Workers)
Mr J. Forrester (Amalgamated Union of Engineering Workers, Technical, Administrative and Supervisory Section)
Mr H. E. Hickling (Union of General and Municipal Workers)
Mr W. John (Amalgamated Union of Engineering Workers, Engineering Section)
Mr A. Kitson (Transport and General Workers' Union)
Mr S. McCluskie (National Union of Seamen)

Mr F. Mulley, MP (Association of Professional, Clerical and Computer Staffs)
Mr W. Padley, MP (Union of Shop, Distributive and Allied Workers)
Mr B. Stanley (Post Office Engineering Union)
Mr R. Tuck (National Union of Railwaymen)
Mr E. Williams (National Union of Mineworkers)

Socialist, Cooperative and other organisations' Section
Mr J. Cartwright, MP (Royal Arsenal Cooperative Society)

Constituency Labour Parties
Mr F. Allaun, MP
Mr J. Ashley, MP
Mr A. W. Benn, MP
Mrs B. Castle, MP
Mr E. Heffer, MP
Miss J. Lestor, MP
Mr I. Mikardo, MP

Women Members
Mrs Judith Hart, MP
Mrs L. Jeger, MP
Miss J. Maynard, MP
Mrs Renee Short, MP
Mrs Shirley Williams, MP

Labour Party Young Socialists' Representative
Mr N. Bradley

APPENDIX IV
The Alternative Economic Strategy in Outline

Early in 1975 I wrote this note setting out the economic choices which faced the Labour Government.

Our aims through 1974 were to sustain output and employment; to pave the way for a switch of resources into exports and investment; and to moderate the rate of inflation. The measures to implement this strategy included modest reflation; external borrowing in defence of sterling and subsidies to hold down the cost of living as part of a counter-inflationary programme based on price controls and voluntary wage restraint.

This strategy is coming under increasing pressure. It is more than possible that in the coming year we could face a severe recession in world trade; a continued deficit of £4 billion in the balance of payments; a budget deficit of about £9 billion; rising bankruptcies, closures, and retrenchment within industry; accelerating unemployment; and a continuation of price and wage inflation at a rate of 20% or more per annum, which is faster than our main international competitors. Action is clearly needed to avoid the possibility of the exhaustion of our external borrowing power, and flight of capital.

In considering measures, the various options centre on two broad alternative approaches, the first of which ('Strategy A' below) would be on conventional macro-economic lines, whilst the second ('Strategy B') would be more selective. Both would involve radical action justified by reference to the magnitude of the problems.

STRATEGY A

The objective of Strategy A would be to secure a relatively quick improvement in the balance of payments, and to reduce the rate of inflation without compromising our international obligations. It would involve imposing cuts in living standards with a view to improving employment prospects over the longer term. The main ingredients of this strategy would be as follows:

the reduction of the budget deficit by a combination of tax increases and public spending cuts totalling say £3 billion;

some form of enforceable pay restraint;

further transfers of cash into the company sector to encourage investment by general relief to liquidity and profitability.

The main effect of the strategy would be:

sudden and heavy deflation;

relatively quick improvement in the trade balance, through the shifting of resources into exports and reduced imports from falling consumption;

worse unemployment and associated further loss of industrial capacity;

a substantial cut in real wages;

enforced moderation in wage inflation through the loss of bargaining power and diminished capacity to pay;

the withdrawal of support from the Government by the TUC and the Labour movement.

STRATEGY B

The main emphasis of the alternative approach would be on saving jobs and preserving industrial capacity, while securing a slower improvement in the balance of payments. The policy would be more selective and it would be discussed in advance and in detail with the TUC. It is implicit that the strategy involves a higher rate of inflation than Strategy A.

The essential features of this strategy would be:

a full explanation by the Government to the nation of the reasons for the crisis, taking the people into its confidence;

immediate discussion with the Trade Union movement of a new overall economic strategy;

the maintenance of the Prices Code;

selective assistance to Industry on a larger scale through the Industry Act and the NEB. This assistance would be primarily to save jobs but would also help large firms more generally e.g., by financing stock-piling, and encouraging productive investment for the longer term. Separate measures would be needed for small firms;

selective import restrictions through quotas and high tarriffs on manufactured goods for which there is spare capacity in UK industry. In this connection, it should be noted that finished manufactures accounted for 24% (i.e., £5.5 billion) of the value of our total imports in 1974. During the year they rose by 20% (consumer goods by 8% and capital goods by 34%);

rationing and allocation of some imported materials and fuel; to keep them for essential purposes;

work sharing arrangements and a shorter working week coupled with transitional employment subsidies – to reduce the 'shake-out' of labour and redundancies;

tax increases on the basis of real equality of sacrifice, e.g., by surcharges on net income and on capital;

saving of foreign exchange on invisibles and capital account, e.g., by further and deeper cuts on overseas Defence commitments; control of capital outflows; and levies on investment dollars;

controls on banks and other financial institutions sufficient to support the National Enterprise Board and to help channel funds into the public sector and industry;

allowing a further downward float of sterling to bring internal and external price levels into line over a period of years;

the development of wider trading arrangements.

The main effects of the strategy would be:

greater preservation of jobs and industrial capacity;

a slower improvement in the balance of payments;

any reduction in overall living standards made more tolerable by the broader strategy and full consultation;

continuation of inflation at a higher level than under Strategy A;

straining of international relations, possibly including retaliatory measures;

further development of middle class opposition to the Government; and some strain on relations between the Labour Movement and the Government.

IMPLICATIONS OF CHOICE

There are variations on each of these strategies, and some of their respective features are not necessarily mutually exclusive. But the main purpose of this paper is to focus attention on the basic distinction between the two broad lines of approach on which a choice must be made. Strategy A and its variants entails, as a deliberate act of policy, a relatively sharp cut in living standards and employment, achieved by traditional, indirect, macro-economic measures of a broadly indiscriminate nature. Strategy B, by contrast, is intended to operate more slowly and more selectively by direct action at particular points of weakness and with greater emphasis on the preservation of employment and manufacturing capacity. Each approach has its risks and dangers, but on balance, Strategy B closes less options for further action than Strategy A in the event of failure, and is less likely to founder through a severe confrontation which would merely deepen the existing social divisions.

APPENDIX V
Abbreviations

ACAS	Advisory Conciliation and Arbitration Service
ACTT	Association of Cinematograph, Television and Allied Technicians
AEA	Atomic Energy Authority
AEOI	Atomic Energy of Iran
AES	Alternative Economic Strategy
AGR	Advanced Gas-cooled Reactor
APEX	Association of Professional, Executive, Clerical and Computer Staff
ASLEF	Amalgamated Society of Locomotive Engineers and Firemen
ASTMS	Association of Scientific, Technical and Managerial Staffs
AUEW	Amalgamated Union of Engineering Workers
BAC	British Aircraft Corporation
BBC	British Broadcasting Corporation
BNOC	British National Oil Corporation
BP	British Petroleum
BSC	British Steel Corporation
CAP	Common Agricultural Policy
CBI	Confederation of British Industry
CEGB	Central Electricity Generating Board
CIA	Central Intelligence Agency
CLP	Constituency Labour Party
CPAG	Child Poverty Action Group
CPRS	Central Policy Review Staff
CSEU	Confederation of Shipbuilding and Engineering Unions
DHSS	Department of Health and Social Security
DS	Devolution Committee (of Cabinet)
DTI	Department of Trade and Industry
EEC	European Economic Community
EETPU	Electrical, Electronic, Telecommunication and Plumbing Union

EFTA	European Free Trade Association
ENM	Energy Committee (of Cabinet)
ETU	Electrical Trades Union (subsequently part of EETPU)
EY	Economic Strategy Committee (of Cabinet)
FBI	Federal Bureau of Investigation
FBR	Fast Breeder Reactor
FFI	Finance for Industry
GATT	General Agreement on Tariffs and Trade
GEC	General Electric Company
GKN	Guest, Keen and Nettlefolds
GMC	General Management Committee
GMWU	General and Municipal Workers' Union
HSE	Health and Safety Executive
IBA	Independent Broadcasting Authority
ICI	Imperial Chemical Industries
IDAB	Industrial Development Advisory Board
IDV	Industrial Development Committee (of Cabinet)
ILEA	Inner London Education Authority
ILP	Independent Labour Party
IMF	International Monetary Fund
IPC	International Publishing Corporation
IPD	International Property Development (Industrial) Ltd
IRA	Irish Republican Army
IRC	Industrial Reorganisation Corporation
IS	International Socialists
ITN	Independent Television News
ITT	International Telephones and Telegraph
IWC	Institute for Workers' Control
KGB	Soviet Intelligence Agency
KME	Kirkby Manufacturing and Engineering Company (formerly IPD-Fisher Bendix)
LPYS	Labour Party Young Socialists
LSE	London School of Economics
MIRV	Multiple Re-entry Vehicle
MOD	Ministry of Defence
NALGO	National and Local Government Officers' Association
NATO	North Atlantic Treaty Organisation
NATSOPA	National Society of Operative Printers, Graphical and Media Personnel
NCB	National Coal Board
NEA	National Energy Agency
NEB	National Enterprise Board
NEC	National Executive Committee
NEDC	National Economic Development Council (Neddy)

NHS	National Health Service
NIESR	National Institute of Economic and Social Research
NIOC	National Iranian Oil Corporation
NIRC	National Industrial Relations Court
NRDC	National Research and Development Corporation
NUJ	National Union of Journalists
NUM	National Union of Mineworkers
NUPE	National Union of Public Employees
NUR	National Union of Railwaymen
NUS	National Union of Seamen
NUT	National Union of Teachers
NVT	Norton Villiers Triumph
OECD	Organisation for Economic Cooperation and Development
OPD	Overseas and Defence Policy Committee (of Cabinet – subsequently renamed DOP)
OPEC	Organisation of Petroleum Exporting Countries
PLO	Palestine Liberation Organisation
PLP	Parliamentary Labour Party
POEU	Post Office Engineering Union
PPS	Parliamentary Private Secretary
PRISE	Programme for Reform in Secondary Education
PSBR	Public Sector Borrowing Requirement
PWR	Pressurised Water Reactor
REP	Regional Employment Premium
RPI	Retail Price Index
RTZ	Rio Tinto-Zinc
SBAC	Society of British Aerospace Companies
SGHWR	Steam Generating Heavy Water Reactor
SPD	West German Social Democratic Party
STUC	Scottish Trades Union Congress
SWAPO	South West African Peoples' Organisation
TASS	Transport and Salaried Staffs Association
TES	Temporary Employment Subsidy
TGWU	Transport and General Workers' Union
TUC	Trades Union Congress
UCATT	Union of Construction, Allied Trades and Technicians
UCS	Upper Clyde Shipbuilders
UN	United Nations
UNCTAD	United Nations Commission for Trade and Development
UNESCO	United Nations Educational, Scientific and Cultural Organisation
UPW	Union of Post Office Workers
USDAW	Union of Shop, Distributive and Allied Workers
WEA	Workers' Educational Asssociation

Index

Trade Unions and other organisations that are commonly known by their abbreviated form or acronym are so indexed. In more ambiguous cases, they will generally be found under the full title with a cross-reference from the shortened form where appropriate. See page 728 for list of abbreviations. The sub-heading 'mentions', appearing under some persons and subjects, indicates minor references.

Abel-Smith, Brian 422n
Abortion Amendment Bill 422n
Achille-Fould, M 130–2
ACTT (Association of Cinematograph Television & Allied Technicians) 6
Adamson, Campbell 114, 118, 249, 316, 328; mentions 70, 240, 310, 327, 455
Adeane, Michael 94
AEA *see* Atomic Energy Authority
African National Congress (ANC) 255
Agee, Philip 645, 650
Agnew, Sir Godfrey 122–3
Aims of Industry 93, 205
aircraft industry 148, 186, 194, 549n; nationalisation 148, 186, 194, 236; 262, 263, 301, 572, 669; mentions 359, 574, 577, 642, 651; *see also* Hawker Siddeley; Lucas
Aitken, Ian 413
Aldermaston 76, 268
Aldington, Lord 586
Alfred Herbert Ltd 131, 169–70, 236, 243, 254–5
Algeria: oil 504
Allaun, Frank 23, 37, 42, 77, 204, 271, 293, 442, 468, 604; mentions 338, 443
Allen, Alf, 157, 373, 508
Allen, Sir Douglas 223, 279, 332–4, 416, 464, 584–5, 587; mentions 279, 464, 590
Allende, President 59, 138, 225, 319
Alternative Economic Strategy 302, 324–6, 551, 583, 588–9; debate 595–6, 602, 621, 631, 632, 638, 654, 656, 657, 661–71 *passim*, 690, *see also* import controls
Amery, Julian 511
Amis, Kingsley 109

Amouzegar, Jamshid 489
Angola: *see* South Africa, uranium
Annenberg, Walter 157, 431, 506
Appledore shipyard 185, 190, 230–1, 235n
Argentina 421, 540, 638, 688
Armstrong, Anne 531–2, 576, 626, 650
Armstrong, Sir Robert 154, 241, 560; mentions 175, 203, 327
Armstrong, Sir William 125–6, 149, 422, 520; mentions 118, 294, 510
Arnold-Forster, Mark & Val 49, 310, 691
Ashton, Joe: advice to author 367, 376, 397; PPS appointment 284, 467, 533n, 546; on Civil Service 328–9; industry & economy 392, 393, 529; leadership issue 535, 536–7, 538, 539, 544, 546, 615; miners 406; Party affairs 445, 494, 604, 638, 639, 679; Tribune Group 285; dismissal 530, 533; mentions 289, 318, 338, 360, 386, 398, 481, 482, 532, 616
Ashton, Maggie 536, 616
ASLEF (Associated Society of Locomotive Engineers & Firemen) 5, 8, 83, 90
ASTMS (Association of Scientific Technical & Managerial Staffs) 30, 32, 228, 383, 400
Astor, David 111
Atkins, Humphrey 429
Atkinson, Fred 418
Atkinson, Norman 451–2, 532, 538, 615, 644, 650, 679–80; mentions 28, 49, 318, 338, 467, 593, 604, 633
Atomic Energy Authority (AEA) 377, 406, 420, 454, 549n, 573, 581; mentions 466, 483, 524

Attlee, Clement 62, 272, 436, 625, 653; mentions 45, 240, 420, 436

AUEW: (Amalgamated Union of Engineering Workers): 13–14, 32, 60, 137, 167, 411; mentions 242, 276, 593

Austick, David 56n

Australia 459, 666

BAC (British Aircraft Corporation) 59, 61, 123, 158

Balcome Street Siege 477

Bale, Reg 110–11

Ball, George 151

Balogh, Lord (Thomas): Govt debate 65, 387–8, 467, 494, 518, 524–5; industry 60, 417–18, 450, 499, 527; mentions 15, 27, 242, 363, 403, 449, 498, 510, 526, 548, 574, 583

Banks, Tony 32, 60, 395, 521; mentions 15, 49, 73, 81, 276, 363, 397

Barber, Anthony 56, 79, 104, 593

Barclay Curle 161

Barnett, Joel: and author 176, 680; Civil Service 478; economic debate 591, 683, 684; industrial matters 158, 172, 175, 202–3, 326, 350, 559, 560; unemployment 513

Barratt Brown, Michael 77

Basnett, David 78, 105, 337, 442, 508, 522, 531, 616, 664; mentions 157, 276, 373, 615, 679

Bateman, Sir Ralph 174, 192, 240, 315, 317, 363; mentions 455

Battye, June 45, 82, 232, 368, 484, 536

BBC (British Broadcasting Corporation): and author 27, 82, 139, 201, 229, 233, 287, 384; programmes 22, 23, 39, 234, 308, 310, 377, 389, 407; reactionary stance 365, 377, 531, 614

Bearbrand Ltd 350

Beckingham, Bryan 514, 579, 601, 605

Beith, Alan 73n

Belgium: Common Market 142

Beloff, Nora 32, 64, 80, 248, 253, 279–80

Benn, Caroline: personal matters 57, 124, 146, 224, 237, 424, 531–2, 625–6; family affairs 43, 52, 57, 176, 227–8, 318, 320, 378, 484, 534, 638, 692; bomb incident 448; burglary 644; colliery visits 470–2, 634; ILEA and education 17, 309, 446, 548, 598, 616,

626, 629, 694; phone tapping & security 190, 335, 477; political stance 24, 87, 146, 227, 292, 331, 360, 390, 525; campaigning 107, 229, 386, 538, 539, 544; and Press 218, 276, 309, 370–1, 499; social occasions 141, 145, 242, 285, 287, 306, 339, 387, 403, 431, 462, 498, 510–11, 524, 526, 547, 652; mentions 66, 82, 110, 209, 214, 232, 296, 308, 368, 369, 371, 388, 397, 440, 510, 529, 536, 556, 562, 608, 650

Benn, Dave 318

Benn, Hilary 7, 17, 18, 205, 232, 467, 536–7, 692, 694; mentions 54–5, 109, 371, 386, 390, 398, 484, 539, 607

Benn, Joshua 118, 218, 220, 234, 335, 370–1, 398, 424–5, 440, 644, 691, 694; mentions 68, 209, 250, 291, 318, 320, 384, 397, 448, 537, 544, 692

Benn, Melissa 108, 217, 220, 384, 385–6, 390, 398, 422, 466, 499–500, 691, 694; mentions 68, 218, 250, 318, 320, 368, 413, 421, 424, 520, 521, 527, 536

Benn, Rosalind 7, 18, 54–5, 205, 484, 607, 694

Benn, Stephen: college 52, 68, 72; media 378; political interest 234, 524, 573; US visit & job 124, 232, 431–2, 608, 617, 633–4, 694; mentions 45, 52, 82, 108, 127, 237, 285, 368, 371, 386, 390, 397, 398, 484, 536, 539, 544

Berlinguer, Enrico 485

Berrill, Sir Kenneth: CPRS post 141n, 241, 497; policies 246, 265, 279, 380, 418, 501, 509, 640; mentions 141n, 417, 454

Bertrand Russell Peace Foundation & Press 66, 431

Beswick, Frank (Lord Beswick) 125, 126, 217; mentions 133, 135, 136, 158, 159, 205, 300

Bevan, Andy 20

Bevan, Aneurin 50, 293, 295, 526; mentions 369, 397, 447, 521, 613

Bevin, Ernest 62, 295

Bidwell, Sydney 97, 207, 318, 338, 544

Biffen, John 6, 76, 90, 499, 516, 534, 652; mentions 524

Binning, Ken 116

Birch, Reg 167

Bish, Geoff 11, 159, 454, 598; mentions 8, 120, 157, 293

Blackley, John 123
BL *see* British Leyland
Boardman, Tom 27
Booth, Albert 501, 555–6, 562, 586, 622, 648, 670, 675, 682, 683, 684–5; mentions 122, 158, 164, 413, 602, 639, 656, 661
Boots Ltd 350
Borschette, Commissioner 181
Bottomley, Arthur 540
Boyd, Johnny 136, 167, 443, 587–8
BP International 447, 448–9, 482, 505, 506–7, 559, 560, 571, 585; shares 647, 652, 656, 686; mentions 419, 450, 473
Bradlaugh, Charles 123
Bradley, Nick 275, 468, 566
Bradley, Tom 13, 88, 204, 544
Brahimi, Lakhdar 504
Brandt, Willy 140, 150, 224, 438–9
Bray, Jeremy 393, 637
Brezhnev, Leonid 45, 313, 423, 512, 539
Briginshaw, Dick (Lord Briginshaw), 84, 337, 362, 450
Brimelow, Sir Thomas 155
Bristol Channel Repairers 370
Bristol Evening Post 97, 103, 289
British Aircraft Corporation *see* BAC
British Gas Corporation 37, 481, 483–4, 504
British Leyland: debate 184, 191–2, 278, 279, 364–5, 367
British Leyland (BL): problems 115, 143, 276, 287, 293, 358; mentions 236, 264, 284, 320, 368, 379, 411, 466, 480
British National Oil Corporation (BNOC) 418, 420, 447, 448–9, 473, 482, 505, 507, 647; mentions 450, 483, 499
British Nuclear Fuel Corporation (BNFC) 484
British Nuclear Fuels Ltd (BNFL) 447
British Steel Corporation (BSC) 128, 174, 180, 281, 378, *see also* steel industry
Brookes, Sir Ray 131, 197
Brown, George 36, 207, 320, 331, 334, 383, 525–6; mentions 223, 293, 456, 553
Brown, Gill 434, 440
Brown, Hugh 131, 161, 165, 194
Brown, Wilfred (Lord Brown) 54, 76, 466, 548
Brunner, Guido 407, 440
BSC *see* British Steel Corporation

Buchan, Norman 165, 233, 363, 397
Buckton, Ray 5, 81, 83, 87, 276
Budgets: (1974) 127, 130, 142, 222; (1975) 383, 379–80
Bulletin, The 465
Bullock, Richard 184, 243, 320
Bullock Report 690
Bunster, Alvaro & Raquel 59, 66, 68
Burmah Oil Co. 469, 656; shares 653, 656, 667, 670, 677, 685
Burt, Sir Cyril 629
Butler, Adam 511
Butler, David 106, 534
Butler, Robin 82
Butt, Ronald 168, 230, 434

Callaghan, Jim: in Opposition 1973–4; relations with author 29, 37, 49, 60, 65; policy debates 11, 36, 77, 89; leadership prospects 60, 62, 67, 75, 99; IMF ambition 39, 46; Day of Protest debate 12–13; defence 18–19; energy crisis 78, 79, 84, 86, 99, 100; immigration debate 42; Israel vote 71; 'Twenty-five companies' 28, 42, 47; other nationalisation issues 4, 26, 32, 33, 43; union matters 8, 10, 14, 22, 61, 80, 96; election 92, 93, 107
in Government 1974–5; and author 191, 193; leadership prospects 196, 280, 281, 376; policy debates 115, 132, 140, 155, 196, 210, 239, 241–2, 325; coalition prospects 121, 226; arms for Chile 128, 135, 141, 146, 155; Clay Cross 133, 134, 204, 258; Common Market 142, 163, 177, 179–80, 184, 192, 206, 236, 305, 330, 341–6 *passim*, 352 *passim*, 369; Concorde 125, 160; Conference 275; Cyprus 201, 209, 223; defence 268, 269; fiscal matters 127, 286–7, 325, 357; industrial matters 114, 184, 187, 191, 194, 212, 326, 368; Israel 266, 268; NEC & resignation threat 252–3, 259, 272; Northern Ireland 138, 162, 273; press 314–15; South Africa & Rhodesia 246, 300; trade union affairs 278; US influence 266, 268, 332, 576; elections 225
in Government 1975–6; policy debate 530, 539; leadership contest 397, 404, 487–8, 535, 537, 542, 543, 544, 547, 549, 551; Conference 443; defence 476; economy 486; EEC 462,

516; foreign affairs 423, 516, 539, 540;
Northern Ireland 474; nuclear issues
454, 495–6, 509; oil 449, 453
   as PM 1976; premiership &
appointments 552–3, 555–7, 558, 566,
569, 690; relations with author 553,
554, 555–7, 558, 561–2, 566, 596–7,
599–601, 622–3, 691, 693; policy
debate 575, 576, 602–3, 613–14, 620–
3, 625, 634; collective responsibility
561–2, 564–5, 570–1, 638; Conference
611, 615, 617; economic crisis 577, 580,
582–3, 588, 592, 594–6, 598, 608, 621,
638, 640–3, 646–8, 653–9 passim, 662–
78 passim, 681–91 passim; education 577,
626, 627, 628, 629; EEC 631, 632–3,
658, 666, 693; energy matters 559,
565, 583, 593; foreign visits 612, 614;
Human Rights Charter 577; industry
577, 688, 690; leaks inquiry 581–2, 587,
590, 591, 653, 662; miners' case 622;
NATO 631; Rhodesia 614, 652, 653;
Sedgemore incident 639, 649, 660; US
Ambassador 648
   mentions 85, 94, 200, 227, 321, 329,
340, 365, 442, 475, 497, 525, 630
capital punishment vote 479
Callard, Sir Jack 167–8
Cambridge Group 504, 531, 580, 665
Campaign Committee 8, 89, 154–5,
224–5, 227
Campbell-Savours, Dale 635
car industry see Chrysler; Rolls Royce;
British Leyland and under
nationalisation
Carey, Peter 172, 292, 294, 296–7, 309,
313–14, 320, 337, 503; mentions 152,
181, 241, 282, 286, 434
Carr, Robert 89, 90, 319
Carrington, Lord 83, 86, 87, 89, 95, 104
Carter, (President) Jimmy 607, 626, 633,
635, 663, 682; mentions 551, 637, 648
Carter, Ray 23, 293
Carter-Jones, Lewis 306
Cartwright, John 88, 204
Castle, Barbara: and author 116, 172,
394, 397; on Crossman 402; Cabinet
reshuffle 396–7, 450; leadership issue &
resignation 536, 552, 557, 561; arms
for Chile 130, 136; Common Market
206, 305, 339, 340–1, 344, 348–9, 353,
363–4, 516; defence 268, 475–6; DHSS

451, 469, 476, 549, 630; economic
debate 416, 459, 479, 508, 594, 598;
energy crises 89, 516; Home Policy
Committee 293; nuclear issue 510;
Party matters 413, 502, 562–3; and
press 226, 450; Rhodesia & S. Africa
300, 353; Stonehouse affair 389; wages
& trade unions 172–3, 306, 459; welfare
schemes 41, 125, 141, 208; mentions
360, 375, 403, 434, 478, 602
Castro, Fidel & Raoul 401, 504
Catherwood, Sir Fred 66
CBI (Confederation of British Industry):
economic crisis 618, 636, 642, 671, 675;
investment 373; and Labour Party 103,
118, 248, 315–17, 653, 690; loss of
confidence 70–1, 295; NEB & Industry
Bill 113, 185, 249, 315–17, 327, 336;
pay policies 404, 411, 415; Social
contract 192; and TUC 86, 103, 114,
249; mentions 139, 328, 382, 456, 514,
547
CEGB (Central Electricity Generating
Board) 495, 551–2, 580
Central Policy Review Staff ('Think
Tank') 11, 141, 146–7, 163, 241, 265,
278–9, 454; mentions 477, 497
Chalfont, Lord 228, 229, 431, 501, 618
Chalmers, George 488, 489–90
Chalmers, John 42, 293
Channel Tunnel 73, 300
Chapple, Frank 185, 482, 501, 583
Charteris, Sir Martin 94–5, 576
Chile: Air Show 217; arms sales 127–30
passim, 135–6, 138, 139, 141, 146,
147–8, 155, 157; coup & CIA 59, 66,
224, 225, 227, 319, 377
China 198–9, 265–6, 338, 577, 633
Chirac, Jacques 185
Chou-en-Lai 198–9, 633
Chrysler 459–60, 466–7, 477–8, 479–80;
mentions 482
Churchill, Winston 196, 257, 502, 562,
607, 661
CIA (Central Intelligence Agency) 314,
425, 431, 441, 659; in Europe 53–4,
319, 332, 401, 423, 441, 446; Latin
America 224, 225, 227, 498; Middle
East 506; mentions 490, 492, 532, 607,
City (of London): in economic crisis 279,
551, 618; Labour plans 33, 38, 103,
145; Stock Market 276; Tory strength
32, 96, 401; mentions 518, 523

Civil Service: numbers & power 478, 479, 526; politicians compared 333, 560; vetting 296, 298–9, 308, 313–14; ways of working & author's views 267, 329, 416–17, 505, 508–9, 517, *see also* Part, Sir Antony; Trade & Industry, Dept of; Treasury

Clapham, Sir Michael 70, 86, 118, 130, 248–9

Clarke, Mary Lou 98, 132–3, 323, 537; mentions 115, 202, 227, 232, 248, 536, 544

Clarke, Otto 197, 416–17

Clay Cross question 6, 132, 133–4, 204, 258, 400, 426

Clements, Dick 445, 650; mentions 49, 73, 77, 338, 363, 386, 484

Clements, Julie 644

Co-op Development Agency 53

coal *see* mining industry

Coates, Ken 81–2, 118, 227, 230, 417, 431, 521, 561, 615, 645; mentions 27, 47, 77, 91, 164, 168, 237, 278, 547

Common Agriculatural Policy (CAP) *see under* Common Market

Common Market: Britain's entry 1–2, 48, 109, 236, 330, 382, 612; Labour policy in Opposition 2, 35, 60, 68, 116; policy & dissent in Office 236, 269–70, 320, 325, 342–9, 351–6, 360–4, 368, 384–5, 693–4; TUC policy 13, 167, 287, 346–7, 374; sovereignty issue 37, 135, 143, 153, 163, 178, 182, 236, 269–70, 288–92, 342–9 *passim*; debate 135, 142–3, 165, 175–9, 192–3, 206–7, 229; renegotiation 128, 151–4, 163, 177–81, 184, 186, 277, 282–3, 305, 339, 341–2; Referendum campaign 263–4, 267, 274, 277, 285, 288–92, 306, 322–3, 338–9, 351–5, 360–2, 367–8, 382–7; consequences 381, 382, 473, 474, 515–16, 541, 660, 663; CAP 142, 345, 347, 465, 578; Community budget 282, 283, 341; Economic & Monetary Union 341, 383, 407, 465, 578, 666; passport 473, 578, 579; Safeguards Committee 465–6; loan to Britain 631, 632–3, 668–9; author's tour 434–40; mentions 36, 204, 205, 492, *see also* Council of Ministers; European Commission; European Parliament

Communism 196, 312, 369–70, 501

Communist Party 23, 185, 517; foreign parties 251, 312, 315, 423, 436, 437, 440, 485, 511; and Labour Party 15, 425; Revolutionary Group 233; security 24, 299, 420, 441, 561, 579; mentions 66, 343, 569

Concannon, Don 28, 94, 168

Concorde aircraft 6, 29, 108, 125, 128; plans to scrap 116, 121, 123, 124, 159–60, 179; negotiations 130–2, 158, 162, 169, 185; success 201, 209, 214–15, 504

Confederation of British Industry *see* CBI

Confederation of Shipbuilding & Engineering Unions *see* CSEU

Congdon, Tim 98

Conservative party: policies (1972–3) 1, 2, 26, 53, 55, 121, 202, 295; coalition question 55–6, 75, 84, 234, 351, 365–6, 376, 464, 574, 630; 1974 elections 100, 107, 109, 110, 119; dealings with Liberals 113, 121; Opposition tactics 122, 225, 451, 487–8, 501, 514, 574; lack of resolve 168, 177–8, 319, 362, 420, 575; leadership contest 311; resurgence 625; Common Market 192–3, 204, 236, 322–3, 349, 362, 365–6; corporate power 32, 35, 96, 401; Devolution 432, 618; trade union relations 13, 103, 112n, 137, 262, 457–8, 520, 570, 574, *see also* Heath, Edward; Thatcher, Margaret

Cooley, Mike 505

Cooper, Jack 62

Cooper, Karen 230

Cork, Kenneth 195–6, 221

Council of Ministers, 407–8, 462, 578, 660, *see also* European Parliament

Court Line 184, 235n; negotiation 184, 190, 200–1, 216, 220, 425; Parliament & press 185, 218, 219, 426, 429; DTI 286, 408–9, 422, *see also* Appledore shipyard

Cousins, Frank 62, 256

Cox, Vera 230, 231

CPRS *see* Central Policy Review Staff

Craigie, Jill (Jill Foot) 49, 202, 287, 525, 527

Crane, Sir Harry 420

Crawshaw, Dick 9

Cripps, Francis 102–3; advisory post 115, 120, 211–12, 217, 256, 405–6, 487; Common Market 382, 384; economic ideas 580, 583, 588, 591, 598–9, 606, 608, 613, 617, 638, 652, 656; elections

Cripps, Francis—*contd.*
229, 230; energy proposals 508, 565; industrial proposals 148, 159, 172, 210, 245, 504, 528; leadership issue 535, 536, 538, 544, 555; media 227, 512; nationalisation 232, 302; security measures 590; Treasury matters 102–3, 149, 162–3, 222; mentions 82, 89, 115, 122, 237, 368, 383, 595, 687
Cripps, Sir Stafford 36, 233
Crosland, Susan 57, 193
Crosland, Tony: ambitions 18, 57, 97, 208, 576
    in Opposition 1973–4; policy debates 3, 34–5, 38, 47, 61; Common Market 73; Israel vote 71; NEC procedures 51; Poulson affair 5; industry 17, 32; union affairs 75, 80
    Wilson Government 1974–6; ministerial office 193, 238–9; policy debates 118, 240, 329; Channel Tunnel 300; Clay Cross 133, 258; Common Market 206, 330–1, 342, 347, 351, 354; economic affairs 132, 356, 379, 458, 461; housing 409; leadership contest 527, 537, 544–5, 567; nationalisation 194, 212; trade unions 329
    Callaghan Govt 1976; as Foreign Minister 556, 557–8, 561, 576, 688, 693; policy debate 578, 654; economic debate 589, 640, 653–4, 656, 658, 659, 667–71 *passim*, 674, 676, 678, 682–4 *passim*; education 598; EEC 612; Rhodesia & China 577, 609, 614, 626, 652 mentions 14, 172, 191, 207, 340, 396, 448, 478, 571, 593, 661
Crossman, Dick 41, 100, 134, 402, 488, 502; diaries 264–5, 309, 313, 409, 425, 434, 501, 549, 638–9, 660
Crowder, Petre 99
Crozier, Brian 501, 691
CSEU (Confederation of Shipbuilding & Engineering Unions) 143, 186, 226, 243, 255, 293, 297, 407
Cuba 504
Cudlipp, Sir Hugh 20, 46, 277, 280, 627
Cunningham, Andy 53, 111n
Cunningham, George 306
Cunningham, John 53, 690
Custis, Ronnie 450–1, 460, 467, 471; mentions 403, 419, 452, 465, 466
Cyprus: coup & invasion 197, 200, 201, 203n, 223

Czechoslovakia: Wilson's visit 19

Daily Express, The; and author 218, 220, 232–3, 523, 561, 610; elections 362; industrial issues 184, 210, 385, 426; leaks inquiry 582; Marxist article 154; mentions 312, 393, 440, 545
Daily Mail, The: and author 87, 199, 214, 370, 371, 413; elections 362; industrial matters 27–8, 210, 301, 426; mentions 107, 207, 403, 450, 479, 517, 526, 641
Daily Mirror, The: on author 190, 383–4, 446; Common Market 207, 382, 385; industrial affairs 30, 277, 301; Labour Party 617, 688; nuclear issues 447; worker participation 46; mentions 227, 234, 383, 616, 627
Daily Telegraph, The: on author 81, 175, 291, 372, 374, 560; industrial matters 28, 32, 165; trade unions 461
Daly, Lawrence 77, 81, 100, 278
Dalyell, Tam 165
Davies, Dai (Sir David) 136
Davies, John 185, 368
Day of Protest *see under* TUC
Day, Robin 66–7, 73, 212, 233, 382; mentions 49, 377, 628
de Camp, James Milton & Graydon 227–8, 288, 424
de Gaulle, General 401, 466, 612, 619
Deakin, Arthur 569
Deakins, Eric 194
Dearing, Ron 172
defence: Labour policies 18–19, 77, 267–9, 475–6, 507n; Procurement Executive 39, *see also* Chile; nuclear issues; South Africa
Dell, Edmund: economic debate 200, 637, 656, 662, 668, 676; foreign affairs 146; industry 17, 377, 382, 417–18, 449, 559; mentions 284, 327, 389, 449, 450, 499–500, 527, 602
Denmark: Common Market 142, 192, 345
Devlin, Tim 106
Devolution *see* Scottish National Assembly; Wales
Devolution Committee 286, 303, 304, 401
DHSS *see* health; Social Services
Diamond, Jim 13
Dimbleby, David 521
Dimbleby, Jonathan 200, 384
Diplock, Lord 16, 111n

Donoughue, Bernard 120, 425, 447, 454, 534, 640; mentions 394, 488

Doughty, George 9, 143, 148, 216

Douglas-Home, Alec (Lord Home) 55, 369, 543

Dounreay nuclear plant 406, 552, 565, 581, see also nuclear issues

Doyle, Peter 35, 41, 42

Drake, Sir Eric 95, 419, 453, 473

Driberg, Tom (Lord Bradwell) 608

Du Cann, Edward 384, 420

Duffy, Pat 539, 563–4

Duncan, Sir Val 484, 531

Eadie, Alex 400, 481, 494, 528, 535, 580

Eagleton, Tom 607, 608, 633

Eban, Abba 190, 528–9

Ecclestone, Jacob 98

Economic Strategy Committee 120, 208, 246, 253, 263, 277–9; (1975) 324, 329; (1976) 575, 579–80, 588–9, 636–8, 640–2, 646–7, 690

Economic Strategy Committee: mentions 191, 558, 580, 623

Economist, The: 237, 341, 628; mentions 205, 334, 454, 682

economy see Alternative Economic Strategy; import controls; prices & incomes; and under Callaghan, Healey, Wilson

Edelman, Maurice 169

Eden, Anthony (Lord Avon) 22, 543

Edinburgh, Duke of 285, 453, 506

education issues 476, 548, 577, 598, 606, 616, 626, 627, 628, 629

Edwards, George 169, 504

EEC see Common Market; Council of Ministers; European Commission; European Parliament

EFTA (European Free Trade Association) 668, 669

Elizabeth II, the Queen see Queen

Emmett, Bryan 533, 535, 555, 560, 571, 589–90; mentions 488, 490, 512, 518, 552, 585, 590, 604, 651

Employment Protection Act 60, 315

Energy Commission 600

Energy Committee 146–7, 406, 466, 499–500, 508, 559, 565, 655; mentions 497, 582

Energy Conference 577, 583–4, 585

Energy Council 693

energy crisis see three day week

Ennals, David 582, 662, 668, 674–5, 683

Etemad, Dr Akbar 489, 490

Etheridge, Dick 23

European Commission: lack of accountability 269–70, 304, 313, 330, 341, 343, 407, 439; strength 408, 462; and UK 321, 336, 364–5, 440, 609, 660; see also Council of Ministers

European Court of Human Rights 274

European Economic Community (EEC) see Common Market

European Free Trade Association see EFTA

European Parliament: elections 282, 283, 343, 462–3, 473, 516–17, 578; Labour boycott 13; sovereignty issue 264, 269–70, 283, 343, 346, 534

Evans, Alan 49

Evans, Harold 20, 75–6, 468

Evans, Moss 136, 202, 615

Evening Standard 173, 222, 254, 591; mentions 109, 214, 246, 253, 377, 385, 588, 681

Ewing, Harry 165, 233, 245

Exxon Co. 417, 420, 447, 450, 513, 617

Ezra, Sir Derek 25, 403, 464, 583, 621, 634

Falkland Islands 421, 516, 540, 688

Fanti, Giorgio 484–5

Farnsworth, Gordon 103, 123–4

Faulds, Andrew 9

Faulkner, Brian 162

FBI (Federal Bureau of Investigation) 424, 441, 492

Feather, Vic 10, 40, 383

Ferranti brothers 358, 374

Ferranti 225, 226, 236

Field, Frank 50, 82, 582, 587, 645

Field, Tony 25, 137

Finance for Industry (FFI) 264, 302

finance institutions see City; and under nationalisation

Financial Times, The: and author 416, 584; Common Market 207; Labour Party 159, 623, 636, 662; nationalisation 210; non-political claim 95; Rolls-Royce affair 32; mentions 96, 336, 606, 682

Finniston, Monty 136, 216, 370, 378; mentions 90, 216, 281, 464

Fisher-Bendix see IPD

Fitt, Gerry (Lord Fitt) 14, 133, 142, 495

Flannery, Martin 317–18
Fletcher, Alex 73n
Fletcher, Ted 603
Flowers, Sir Brian 565, 583, 625, 628
Flynn, Ross 515
Foot, Michael: in Opposition 1973–4;
    support for author 9, 27, 29, 68, 93;
    leadership prospects 54, 61–2, 67–8, 76;
    policy debate 4, 36, 92; Common
    Market 73; energy crisis 77, 84, 86, 91,
    100, 101; industry & nationalisation
    42, 47, 48–9, 58; NEC procedures 40,
    51, 63; on political apathy 16–17, 84
    in Government 1974–5; new office
    114, 115, 124, 166, 292; Press criticism
    154; Cabinet row 252, 254, 257, 259,
    260; Cabinet reshuffle 379, 387–8, 390,
    392, 393, 395–6, 399; leadership issue
    413, 443; arms for Chile 129, 130,
    135–6, 141; Clay Cross 133; Common
    Market 206, 207, 263, 264, 267, 274,
    283, 305, 341, 343, 347, 349, 351 passim,
    360, 369, 384–5; Concorde 125, 158;
    Conference 275; Cyprus 223; defence
    268; nationalisation 147, 302, 429;
    Northern Ireland 274; pay policy 120,
    122, 165–6, 278, 280, 286, 403, 404,
    442; Shrewsbury pickets 318;
    Stonehouse affair 389; union affairs
    136, 262, 315, 329, 335, 338–9, 415;
    elections 202, 226
    in Government 1975–6; illness 639;
    leadership contest 527, 536, 537–8,
    539, 541–7 passim, 549, 553; Leader of
    House 555–6, 633; policy debate 518,
    522, 525, 530, 532, 561, 564, 574, 640,
    682; Conference 615, 623; defence 476;
    economic debate 412, 415, 416, 448,
    458, 486, 498, 592, 595, 636, 656, 673,
    679, 683, 686; education 577; industry
    572, 574, 575; leaks inquiry 582;
    Northern Ireland 474, 495; nuclear
    issue 509–10; pay talks 562; Radcliffe
    report 497, 498, 501, 502, 569, 587,
    638; Rhodesia 614, 652; and Tribune
    464; unemployment 510, 589, 639
        mentions 21, 49, 100, 196, 207, 287,
        289, 360, 365, 372, 403, 413, 435, 602,
        604, 611, 650, 656, 661
    Ford Motors 288, 480, 580
Ford, President Gerald 218, 506, 551,
    576, 633, 658, 663, 672–3, 687;
    mentions 232, 551, 620

Foreign Office 175, 177, 309, 313, 321,
    631, 652
Forrester, John 20, 36
France: Common Market 142, 157, 283,
    348, 613, 666; Concorde 6, 108, 124,
    125, 130–2, 160, 162, 169; industry 346,
    435, 456, 675; NATO 267; politics 46,
    435, 612–13, 660
Francis, Dai 80, 385, 460, 472
Fraser, Lady Antonia 7, 22, 50, 54
Fraser, Hugh 7n, 53–4, 311, 448, 461
Fraser, Sir Ian 27
Frelimo 300
Freud, Clement 56n
Friedman, Milton 597, 644, 670
Friends of the Earth 447, 689
Frost, David 227, 548
Fuchs, Klaus 421

Gaitskell, Hugh 44–5, 62, 263, 331,
    420–1, 613; mentions 340, 553, 609
Garnett, John 285
Garrett, John 393, 538
Garvey, Ambassador Terence 159
Garvin, Cliff 474–5, 512, 513, 617
gas industry see British Gas Corporation
GATT (General Agreement on Tariffs &
    Trade) 666, 668, 672
Gaughan, Michael 164, 287–8
General Management Committee (GMC
    Bristol S–E) 57–8, 116, 311–12, 514,
    541, 605; mentions 600, 601, 602
Germany: Common Market 142, 283,
    345, 646, 666; industry & economy
    346, 379, 456, 612–13, 641, 675;
    NATO 267–8; politics 224, 438–9, 658
Gilbert, John 70, 158
Gilchrist, Bill 59
Gill, Ken 243, 244, 297, 501
Giro, 200
Giscard d'Estaing, Valérie 157, 423, 612;
    mentions 150, 186, 201, 277, 282, 437
GKN Ltd 197
Gladwyn, Lord (Gladwyn Jebb) 314
GMC see General Management
    Committee
GMWU (General & Municipal Workers
    Union) 421, 508, 616
Godfrey, Peter 57
Godley, Wynne 504
Golding, John 191
Gollan, John 243
Gooding, Wing Commander 234

Goodman, Lord 25, 26–7, 463
Goodman, Geoffrey 46, 144, 277, 280, 430, 534–5
Gormley, Joe 12–13, 102, 105, 460, 523, 548, 622, 634, 635; mentions 87, 101, 276
Graham, Andrew 210
Graham, Ken 85
Granada TV 89
Grant, Ted 20–1
Grantham, Roy 195, 243
Gratton, John 218, 261, 276
Gray, Bill 161
Gray, Lew 59, 123
Grayson, Victor 105
Green, Alan 514
Greendale, Walter 15–16, 47
Greene, Sir Hugh 277
Greene, Sidney 10, 78, 85, 373
Greenhill, Sir Denis 15, 532
Gregory, Arnold 54
Griffin, Ken 217
Griffiths, Eldon 182, 383
Grunfeld, Henry 131
Guardian, The: and author 83, 100, 385, 398, 375, 610; industrial topics 20–1, 28, 99, 190, 653; Labour Party 657, 690; mentions 49, 67, 413, 416, 498, 601, 636, 691

Haber, Donna 230
Hailsham, Lord 501, 590
Haines, Joe 25, 173, 191, 261, 463, 534–5, 542, 617; mentions 92, 120, 254, 308, 394, 447, 535
Hall, Sir Arnold 198, 202, 208, 244, 246, 260
Ham, Adrian 210, 487, 548–9
Hamling, Bill 307–8
Hammer, Armand 626
Hare, Alan 95–6
Harland & Wolff 197
Harmsworth, Vere 204–5, 403
Harris, Ennis 76, 227
Harris, John (Lord Harris) 362, 572
Harrison, Bob 405–6
Hart, Judith: and Wilson 48, 242–3, 258, 259, 260, 261, 395; press criticism 154; MI5 treatment 243, 244; Cabinet reshuffle 387–8, 392, 393, 395–6, 399, 400; leadership issue 538, 545–6; arms for Chile 140; Common Market 342; Conference 275, 443, 444; defence

issues 77; industry 34, 443; Party affairs 452, 469, 521–2, 680, 690; Simonstown issue 256; State Holding Company 12, 15, 17, 18, 37, 42; women's affairs 422; mentions 41, 49, 172, 363, 397, 423, 521, 570, 602
Hase, Ambassador Karl von 52–3
Haslam, Robert 167
Hattersley, Roy 571–2, 576; Cabinet member 609, 614; policy debate 37, 571; BP corruption 559; Common Market 186, 321, 324, 330; Day of Protest 23; economic debate 637, 646, 654, 676, 680; leadership issue 567; N. Ireland 572; South Africa 246–7, 377
Hawker Siddeley 197–8, 202, 208, 243–4, 246, 247, 260
Hawkins, Arthur 580, 583
Hawley, Glyn 202
Hayward, Arthur 471–2
Hayward, Ron: policy debate 47, 360, 566, 611; Cabinet row 260, 355; Common Market 248, 287, 306, 355; energy crisis 84, 99; industry debate 58; Israel vote 71; Party procedures 13, 40, 75, 270–1, 293; Rolls Royce issue 27, 29; union matters 30; on Wilson 548; mentions 15, 25, 49, 230, 240, 575, 604
Healey, Denis: and author 32, 46, 62, 97, 340, 442–3, 558, 580, 598, 610, 633
  in Opposition 1973–4: policy debates 36, 38; Common Market 35; Concorde 29, 124; Day of Protest 13; energy crisis 79, 86, 101; fiscal matters 3, 35; Israel vote 71; nationalisation issues 26, 42, 48, 70; NEC procedures 51, 75
  in Government 1974–5: leadership prospects 277, 280, 376, 397, 413; policy debates 242, 253, 265, 266, 325, 326, 373; arms for Chile 155; Common Market 142, 341, 347, 353, 382; Concorde 125, 159–60, 162; Conference 275; economic affairs 246, 279, 295, 325, 327, 328, 380–1; fiscal policies 127, 130, 207, 263, 341, 356–7, 379; pay policy 120, 373, 404, 405; foreign visits 612; Home Policy Committee 293; industrial matters 159, 184, 187, 188, 194, 206, 212, 222, 316–17, 367; Northern Ireland 274; Social Contract 324; welfare matters 125, 208; Winstanley affair 132

Healey, Denis—*contd.*
in Government 1975–6; leadership contest 425, 488, 527, 536, 539, 542, 544, 546, 549; policy debate 466–7, 508, 524, 530, 634, 640; Chrysler 479; Conference 443, 611, 616–17; defence 475; Devolution 401–2; fiscal policies 411–16 *passim*, 478, 480, 486, 531, 562, 575, 577, 580, 591, 594, 596, 621, 624, 632–3; economic crisis & IMF 521–2, 575, 582, 588, 591, 592, 599, 600, 613, 615–16, 620, 636–8, 646–7, 653, 655–9, 662, 665–78 *passim*, 680, 683–9 *passim*; EEC 578; energy issues 449, 454, 509; leaks inquiry 581, 582, 662; Northern Ireland 474; TUC matters 415; and Ham 548–9
mentions 41, 85, 102, 224, 227, 329, 359, 365, 437, 442, 498, 533, 542, 594, 602, 607, 661
Health & Safety Committees 648
Health Service 125, 413, 476, 497, 571, 582, 656; fluoridation 41; pay beds 450, 451, 469–70, 549
Heath, Edward: as PM 1, 109, 520, 534, 543, 560, 579; attacks on author 173–4, 365; three-day week 77, 78, 82–3, 90, 93, 102, 104, 115; Govt defeat 80, 83, 89, 91, 104, 105, 106, 114; coalition issue 113, 377, 379, 404; displaced as leader 236; 311, 319, 322, 420; in Opposition 424; 575; smear campaign 230; visit to China 198–9; Common Market 1, 323, 369–70, 372, 612; industry & nationalisation 182, 231, 301, 368, 422; union affairs 5, 46, 120, 351, 422, 523; US bicentenary 399; Wilson tribute 536; mentions 14, 265, 369, 416, 446, 511, 526, 630
Heenan, Cardinal 51, 52
Heffer, Doris 9, 49, 122, 250
Heffer, Eric: ministerial office 115, 120, 128, 139, 159, 173, 217, 322; Cabinet row 257–8, 260; leadership issue 536, 541; return to Back Benches 250, 324, 342, 362; arms for Chile 127, 129, 138, 139, 140, 147–8; Common Market 135, 179, 207, 362; Conference 275, 443, 444, 616; economic issues 132, 148, 322, 529, 540, 594, 602, 604, 671; elections 202, 679; industrial matters 84, 280, 337, 393; Italian Communist party 440; law & trade unions 3, 22–3,

68, 468; nationalisation 17, 28, 53, 171, 172, 188, 302; Shrewsbury pickets 284, 318; mentions 9, 49, 122, 133, 134, 164, 189, 196, 205, 215, 221, 222, 260, 298, 378, 451, 532, 533
Henley, Sir Douglas 211–12, 284, 332–4
Herzig, Chris 452, 533, 573, 611–12
Heseltine, Michael: behaviour in House 572; and Heath 89; author & nationalisation 231, 301, 336, 516; Industry Bill 310, 319, 366–7, 393; BL 379; Court Line 185, 286, 429; KME 287; Meriden 337; Rolls Royce 34, 38, 301; on DTI 323; terrorist threats 87, 89
Hetherington, Alastair 20
Hetherington, Arthur 481, 515, 583
Hill, Charlie (Lord Hill) 277, 280
Hill, Sir John 552, 573, 583, 586, 625
Hird, Roger 169, 175
Hiss, Alger 39
Hobsbawm, Eric 484
Holland, Stuart 8–9, 11, 17, 60, 501; mentions 15, 49
Hollom, Sir Jasper 131, 145
Home Policy Committee 11, 26, 170–1, 293, 556, 597–8; mentions 252, 513, 532, 564
honours system 117, 216, 363, 513, 562, 570
Hooberman, Ben 73
Hosenball, Mark 645, 650
Houghton, Douglas: policy debate 65; Common Market 35; Israel vote 71; miners' strike 99, 101; Rolls Royce 27; union matters 40, 61, 75, 80; mentions 2, 39, 85
House of Lords 32, 372, 632, 650, 651
Housing Finance Act 21, 47, 240, 258, 400
Hoveyda, Prime Minister 492–3
Howe, Sir Geoffrey 45, 55, 311, 349, 420, 588
Howell, Denis 250
Huddie, David 57
Huddleston, Trevor 107
Hughes, Bob 259
Hughes, Cledwyn 318, 319, 533, 535, 540, 544–5, 553
Hughes, Roy, 207, 385
Human Rights Charter 577–8
Hunt, Gilbert 149, 216
Hunt, Sir John 147, 434–5, 451, 556, 617; mentions 215, 327

Hurd, Douglas 564
Hussein of Jordan, King 221
Hyde, Montgomery 41

Iceland: cod war 469
ICI (Imperial Chemical Industries)
  167–8, 188
IMF (International Monetary Fund):
  Govt debate 575, 580, 588–92 passim,
  595, 636–7, 646–7, 653–9 passim, 662–
  3, 666–73 passim, 676, 681, 684–7
  passim; loan 551, 616, 631, 632, 638,
  653, 654, 666, 678; mentions 46, 325,
  620, 656
immigration issues 42, 92n, 588, 618
import controls: urged by author 302,
  380, 384, 458, 554, 595, 621, 642;
  debate 443, 459, 478–80, 498, 531, 613,
  620, 637, 646, 662–7 passim, 673, 676,
  678, 687; mentions 515, 518, 528, 594,
  598, see also Alternative Economic
  Strategy
incomes see prices & incomes
Industrial Democracy Act 60
Industrial Development Advisory Board
  243, 287, 288, 466
Industrial Development Committee
  (IDV) 187, 193, 202, 222, 301, 306,
  326, 327, 349–50, 422
Industrial Policy Committee 17, 60
Industrial Powers Bill 32–3
Industrial Relations Act (1971) 1, 13–14,
  105, 112n, 136; plans to repeal 10, 40,
  60, 78, 114, 262
Industrial Society 285, 392
Industry Bill 58, 116, 236, 249; debate
  121, 301, 315–17, 319, 336–7, 366–7,
  372, 392–4, 445; and EEC 309–10, 341;
  mentions 237, 300, 359, 374, 397
Industry Group of Labour
  businessmen/MPs 54, 392
inflation 55, 144, 335, 356–7, 411, 457–8,
  529, 632, 636, 654; countermeasures
  404, 414–16, 424, 430, 515, 599, 661,
  675, 680; mentions 381, 442, 448
Ingham, Bernard: and author 414, 452,
  460, 463–4, 555, 560; economic
  matters 412–13, 416; mentions 398,
  419, 434, 512, 518, 535, 552, 604
Institute for Workers' Control 15, 118,
  431, see also workers' control
International Committee 18, 155, 496
International Marxist Group 23

International Monetary Fund see IMF
International Socialists 23, 50, 343, 372,
  433
IPD (Fisher-Bendix) 167, 172, 195–6,
  203, 221, 222–3, 242; mentions 29, 159,
  183, 221, 259, see also KME
IPU Conference, 430
IRA: bombing campaign 9, 80, 137,
  164n, 270, 390, 430, 431, 519; Govt
  policy 273, 477, 519, 572
Iran: author's visit 488–94
Ireland (Eire): Common Market 142,
  192, 345, see also Northern Ireland
Israel 69, 74, 135, 189–90, 266, 268, 430,
  528–9
Italy: Common Market 142, 613, 666;
  industry 346, 436; politics 420, 436–7,
  440, 484–5
ITN (Independent Television News) 6,
  24, 231, 234, 431
Ivens, Michael 220–1

Jackson, Margaret 11, 258, 467, 533, 615;
  mentions 8, 49, 362, 397
Jackson, Tom 18, 433, 442
Japan: nuclear waste 447, 655, 688; trade
  326, 370, 379, 456, 666
Jay, Douglas 285, 368n, 374, 387
Jay, Mary 285, 340, 367
Jay, Peter 99, 368, 457, 464, 481, 635,
  650; mentions 106, 510, 597, 657
Jeger, Lena 41, 186, 276–7, 426, 608, 690
Jellicoe, Lord 41, 48, 112n
Jenkin, Patrick 91
Jenkins, Clive 425–6; support for author
  105, 229, 237, 400; Common Market
  369; Concorde & unions 6, 128;
  industrial matters 285, 397, 426, 443;
  nationalisation issues 30, 32, 109;
  telephone tapping 195; mentions 78,
  136, 276, 341, 383
Jenkins, Dick 167, 221, 242
Jenkins, Hugh 554, 650
Jenkins, Jennifer 92–3
Jenkins, Peter 636, 657, 690
Jenkins, Robert 505
Jenkins, Roy: in Opposition 1973–4;
  resigns deputy leadership 2, 609;
  political prospects 54, 55, 57, 69; policy
  debate 89; support for author 92–3, 97,
  107; Common Market 46; economic
  affairs 56; Stonehouse affair 302; union
  matters 80, 137

Jenkins, Roy—*contd.*
Wilson Govt 1974–6; political position 121, 125, 221, 376, 377, 393, 397, 404, 416; Policy debates 265, 303, 324, 394, 480, 530; leadership contest 527, 542, 544, 546, 553, 556, 567; arms for Chile 146; Clay Cross 133; Common Market 142, 206, 207–8, 229, 267, 325, 349, 352, 361, 369, 383, 384, 516; Concorde 160; Devolution 401, 432; economic & fiscal 335, 357, 404, 412, 458–9; industry 262, 309, 326; Northern Ireland 138, 163–4, 273, 274, 390, 473–4; nuclear issues 500, 509; Prentice affair 433; on Press 314; Radcliffe report 501, 502, 549n; Shrewsbury pickets 318; 390n; quits Govt/Presidency of EC 609–10
Wilson Govt 1976; Davis case 566; economic debate 589, 592; EEC 578–9, 609; Human Rights Charter 577; leaks inquiry 581–2; Radcliffe Report 569, 587
mentions 73, 165, 190, 205, 227, 240, 329, 332, 340, 435, 442, 446, 572, 593, 691
Johnson, Dennis 119, 171, 218, 219, 261, 278
Johnson, President Lyndon 3, 151, 422
Johnson, Walter 27, 288
Jones, Alec 604, 652
Jones, David 116, 125, 202, 685
Jones, Elwyn: Common Market 344, 355; Concorde 159; Crosman's diaries 309; economic debate 666, 675, 677; education authority case 577; Human Rights Charter 577; industrial relations 136, 137, 262, 639; Lords case 632; Northern Ireland 273–4, 474; nuclear issue 510; security case 303–4, 587, 590, 592; Stonehouse affair 389
Jones, Jack 422, 426, 482; support for author 237, 385, 388; role in Labour Party 3, 30, 46, 62, 124, 166, 360, 413, 452; and Foot 67, 679; Common Market 287, 360, 386; Concorde 127; Conference 276, 443, 444, 445, 583, 615, 616; industry 40, 182–4, 444, 508; Meriden 147, 158, 182; miners' dispute 77, 78, 90; nationalisation issues 49, 329, 336; pay & economy 403, 411, 445, 522, 530, 643, 663, 681; Prentice row 10, 13; security risk 296, 318, 481,

498, 559; mentions 23, 39, 119, 123, 157, 196, 202, 285, 292, 372, 455, 486, 607, 653
Jones, Ken 470
Jones, Philip 452
Joseph, Sir Keith 244–5, 420
Judd, Frank 30, 50, 548

Kagan, Sir Joseph 54
Kaldor, Nicky 27, 82, 88–9, 120, 481, 651–2, 657; mentions 102, 368, 527
Karamanlis, Konstantinos 203
Kato, Mr and Madame 463
Kaufman, Gerald 25, 68, 94, 419, 425, 447
Kearns, Freddie 165
Kearton, Lord 421, 447, 448–9, 450, 473, 507, 586, 617–18; mentions 505
Keating, Justin 408
Keith, Sir Kenneth 122, 125–7
Kennedy, President John 151, 559, 659
Kennedy, Ludovic 39, 66
Kent, Duke & Duchess of 221, 482, 634–5
Kerry, Michael 246, 408
KGB 155, 158, 159, 401
Khama, President Seretse & Ruth 368, 369
Kidd, Vicky 487
Kilbrandon Report 46–7
Killick, Sir John 155
King, Cecil 56, 62, 383, 627
King, Mackenzie 95, 467
King Murray, Ronny 274, 309
King, Tom 378
King, Tony 102, 383
Kinnock, Glenys 481, 650
Kinnock, Neil: and author 93, 259, 384, 426, 467, 615; leadership issue 539, 545–6; *Tribune* rally 445, 616; mentions 471, 532, 576, 650
Kirillin, Academician 149, 156, 157, 158–9, 568
Kissinger, Henry 318, 332, 423, 493, 528–9, 614, 626; mentions 266, 268, 424, 505, 576
Kitson, Alex 157, 615
KME (Kirby Manufacturing & Engineering Co) 287, 292, 294, 296, 309, 498–9, *see also* IPD
Knight, Jill 99, 661
Kosygin, Alexei 157

Labour Party: 'caring' party 48, 52, 103–4, 291–2, 402, 613, 651, 694; coalition debate 55–6, 75, 84, 234, 351, 365–6, 375–6, 574, 641, 654; 1974 elections 101, 106, 107, 109–10 *passim*, 234–6; policy reviews: (1973) 1, 11, 32, 34–8; (1974) 113–14, 154–5, 168–9, 186–8, 193–4, 205–6, 225, 265–7; (1975) 302, 324–6, 351–5, 404–5, 411–12, 414–15, 451, (1976) 507–8, 521, 530–1, 534–5, 566–7, 575 *see also* Alternative Economic Strategy reshaping 221, 280, 313, 383, 417, 433, 434, 529, 603, 619; self-betrayal 397, 416, 430, 455, 457, 501, 611, 654–5, 661; Conferences 270, 275–7, 369, 442–6, 611, 614–17, 623–4; Constitution amendments 13; industrial policies 16, 26, 85, 165, 182, 320; other policies *see under* Common Market; defence; media; nationalisation; prices & incomes; leadership contest 535–49 *passim*, 615; relations with business 119, 144, 320, 327, 456; relations with TUC 1, 10, 30, 61, 85, 87, 477, 523, 565, 617, 650, 673, *see also* trade unions; TUC-Labour Party Liaison Committee *see also* NEC; PLP; Social Democrats; Young Socialists

Labour Weekly 23, 64, 245, 680
Laird, Gavin 72, 232
Lambie, David 263
Lambton, Lord 41, 48, 112n
Lamond, Jimmy 538, 544
Langham, Cyril 57, 227, 233, 601, 603–4, 605
Lapworth, Bill 119, 171, 218, 261
Lawson, George 165
Lawson, Nigel 43n
Le Cheminant, Peter 488, 490, 492, 620
Lea, David 60, 85, 148, 338, 569
Legislation Committee 299, 309
Leighton, Ron 465
Lestor, Joan: policy debates 36, 451–2, 469; smear campaign 228; Cabinet row 257, 258, 259, 260, 261; energy crisis 81; nationalisation issues 42; press criticism 154; Rolls Royce 30; Simonstown issue 256; resignation 520, 521, 533, 538–9; mentions 50, 73, 413, 446, 459, 604, 650, 680
Lever, Harold: and author 176, 232, 627; Common Market 283, 330, 331, 344, 346, 354; Defence 71, 269; DHSS 450,
451, 470, economic debate 580, 589, 592, 637, 659, 665, 666, 675, 678, 686; taxes & salaries 70, 127, 286, 675, 683; industry debate 188, 212, 213, 262; Chrysler 478; IPD 203, 222; Meriden 171, 172, 175, 183, 326; Triang 350; oil 389, 417–18, 447, 449, 450, 559, 656; leaks 582, 657; miners' dispute 75; nationalisation 32, 33, 36, 301, 417, 418; Northern Ireland 474; nuclear issues 455, 509; union affairs 70, 80, 301; US mission 646, 647; mentions 68, 212, 378, 380, 565, 691

Levin, Bernard 25–6, 572, 618
Liberal Party: 1974 elections 109, 110, 111, 234, 574, 575, 618–19; negotiations with Tories 113, 121, 234, 376; and Labour 125, 574, 610; press attack 533, *see also* Thorpe, Jeremy
Lidbury, John 202, 208, 260
Liverman, John 417, 512, 518
Llewelyn-Davies, Patricia 372
Lloyd of Kilgerran, Lord 86
Lloyd, Richard, 145, 455
Longford, Elizabeth 22
Longworth, Alice Roosevelt 232, 617
Lord, Alan 172, 241, 306, 320, 652
Lovell-Davis, Peter (Lord Lovell-Davis) 409, 467, 514, 516, 528
Lovelock, Douglas 313–14
Lucas Aerospace 262, 505, 549–50n
Lunkov, Nicolai 147, 149, 157, 510–12, 539, 633
Luxembourg: Common Market 142

Mabon, Dick 603, 626
McBride, Sean 509, 510
McCluskie, Sam 275, 469
McCone, John 53–4
Macdermot, Niall 304, 390n
MacDonald, Margo 73n, 494n
MacDonald, Ramsay 100, 233, 405, 457, 649–50, 683
McElhone, Frank: and author 62, 120, 132–3, 237, 245, 250, 278, 280–1, 536; illness 604; industry affairs 28; Joseph speech 244–5; media 26–7, 584; PLP liaison 17, 102, 263, 278, 281; Scottish Office 434; Simonstown issue 255–6, 258; mentions 34, 45, 72, 115, 123, 131, 160, 161, 363
McGahey, Mick 97, 99–103 *passim*; mentions 335, 343, 460, 523

McGarvey, Danny 297, 371, 455, 456, 537

McIntosh, Ronnie 456

MacKenzie, Gregor 115, 217, 307, 499, mentions 135, 194, 205

Mackie, Allister 161, 335, 358, 363

Mackintosh, John 369

McLaren, John 605

Maclennan, Bob 97, 540

McLennan, Gordon 425, 482

Macmillan, Harold (Lord Stockton) 369, 456, 612, 628

McNally, Tom 88

Macpherson, Hugh 9, 81

Madden, Max 393

Maddock, Ieuan 320, 420

Maitland, Donald 534

Makarios, Archbishop 197

Malta 143–4

Manifesto Committee 47

Manley, Ivor 450–1

Mann, Tom 100, 105–6

Mao Tse-Tung 45, 198, 338, 524, 609

Marchais, Georges 485, 511

Margach, James 101, 176, 295

Marre, Sir Alan 408–9

Marsh, Richard (Lord Marsh) 65, 68, 90, 240, 373

Marshall, Walter 491, 570, 573–4, 586, 620, 625

Marten, Neil 56, 285, 387

Martin, Paul 467

Marxist Party & Marxism 15, 52, 98, 154, 233, 365; mentions 335, 611, 628

Mason, Roy: ability 68; arms for Chile 130; Common Market 305, 348, 354–5; Concorde 160; defence 268, 454–5, 476, 563; economic debate 287, 666, 668, 669, 677, 684; miners' strike 101; Northern Ireland 142; nuclear issue 509; Party affairs 480, 530; pay policy 287; South Africa 246, 253, 377, 509; mentions 65, 370

Mass Media Group 30–1, 98

Maudling, Reginald 2–3, 111n, 319, 322; mentions 361, 377, 671

Maxwell, Bob 335, 358, 363

Mayhew, Christopher 98–9, 194, 207, 229, 302

Maynard, Joan: Party policies 4, 271, 566; arms for Chile 129; Clay Cross 204; nationalisation 42; NEC 615, 690; pensions debate 41; mentions 15, 604

Meacher, Michael: Common Market 135; energy crisis 81, 82; Industry Bill 318, 319, 393; leadership issue 536, 541; leaks inquiry 582, 605, 645; motorway incident 362–3; nationalisation issues 172, 184, 302; as PUS 115, 159, 160, 217, 570, 680; saving jobs 294; mentions 9, 49, 89, 122, 136, 164, 205, 227, 237, 260, 376, 392, 413, 451

Meacher, Molly 9, 49, 582, 605

media: author's relations with 19–20, 115, 176, 375, 398, 527–8, 604; anti-Labour stance 24, 48, 64, 113, 165, 184, 265, 358, 430, 534; Labour policies on 30–1, 98, 228, 248, 253, 688; Common Market 370, 382, 386–7, 486; election coverage 7, 227; trade union coverage 4, 314–15, 366, see also BBC; ITN; individual papers; Mass Media Group

Meir, Golda 74

Mellish, Bob: and author 326–7, 372, 429; policy debates 34, 38, 100, 226, 468, 530; Cabinet row 254, 256–7, 259; leadership issue & resignation 535, 557; arms for Chile 130; Common Market 267, 346, 354, 361; Defence issues 269; Industry Bill 309, 372; Northern Ireland 162, 274, 474; Stonehouse affair 302; women's affairs 422; mentions 85, 99, 117, 208, 250, 272, 276, 305, 434

Mendelson, Jack 50, 318

Mendes France, Pierre 526

Meriden cooperative 118, 121, 146, 147, 235n, 261–2, 337, 425; fight to save 146, 147, 171, 172, 174–5, 331, 423; operations 218–19, 276, 308, 326, 356; mentions 119, 163, 183, 259, 308, 370

Merseyside 132, 213, 214, 223, 684

Meyer, Cord 225, 332, 532

MI5 see Security Services

MI6 15, 446, 532, 659, 691, see also Security Services

Mikardo, Ian: policy debates 35, 205, 251, 522, 604, 680; attacked by Skinner 6; Cabinet row 259, 260; Common Market 186, 204, 206, 207, 342; Conference 275, 445, 446, 611, 616; defence issues 18, 19; energy crisis 86; Home Policy Committee 293; leadership issue 536, 544; nationalisation 15, 37, 185, 616; press criticism 154; mentions 245, 314, 340, 352, 393, 514, 602

Miles, Dame Margaret 309

Millan, Bruce 161, 233, 500, 579, 667

Miller, Maurice 72

Mina, Parviz 488, 490

mining industry: author's pit visits 470–2, 634–5; coal imports 495; industrial action (1973–4) 1, 75, 77, 79, 82–9 *passim*, 93, 96, 97, 99–105 *passim*, 114–15, 472, 520; Common Market 374; pay demands 278, 406, 622; pit disasters 400; review 424, *see also* NUM

Mintoff, Dom 143–4

Mitterand, François 71, 91, 435, 485

Molloy, Mike 531

Monitoring Committee 251–2

Morning Star 23, 28, 83, 291, 312; Security Service case 296, 299, 303, 308, 314; mentions 323, 457

Morrell, Frances: political advisor post 60, 115, 120, 217, 256; personal advice to author 124, 132, 360, 376, 486; criticism of 278, 510, 531, 541; and Callaghan 590; Civil Service 152, 169, 267, 517; Common Market 250, 288, 289, 366, 384, 386; Concorde 319; Devolution 494; DHSS 451; economic matters 210, 211, 216, 218, 245, 405–6, 529, 588, 598–9, 613, 638, 652, 656; elections 106, 228, 229; energy policy 508, 565; foreign trips 434, 436, 438, 488, 490; leadership issue 535, 536–7, 538, 541, 544; media 227, 322, 335–6, 512, 597; nationalisation 66, 172, 232, 302, 306; repatriation 618; security 224, 446, 492; social events 9, 49, 73, 190, 528, 555; and Wilson 139, 173, 176–7, 192, 204, 250, 259, 395, 454, 487; mentions 81, 151, 221, 237, 285, 322, 363, 383, 388, 413, 433, 570, 595, 655, 679, 687

Morris, Colin 65–6

Morris, John: defence & nuclear 130, 269, 500; economy & industry 350, 668, 669, 683, 685; EEC 349; Wales 402, 432; mentions 474, 620, 677

Morrison, Herbert 272, 293, 295, 553

Mosley, Oswald 23–4, 220, 438, 512, 588

Mountbatten, Lord 506, 511, 627

Mueller, Anne 148, 150, 320

Mulley, Fred: policy debate 37, 41, 89, 458, 561, 564; defence 689; economic debate 480, 668, 669, 676, 683, 685; education 393, 476, 479, 564, 577, 598; energy matters 147; Northern Ireland 474; Tribune Group 170; mentions 13, 205, 399

Mullin, Chris 390n

multinationals 150, 172, 429, 482, 635

Murray, Len: and author 86, 238, 385; education debate 629; energy crisis 78, 79, 86, 114; NEB & industry 336, 338, 456, 482, 507–8; pay & economy 411, 414, 522, 565, 646, 658, 681; Scottish Action Committee 226; union relations 134, 166, 168, 327, 512, 569, 639; mentions 131, 292, 372, 452, 535, 602, 607, 663

NALGO (National & Local Government Officers' Association) 653

Namibia *see* South Africa

National Coal Board (NCB) 114–15, 403, *see also* mining industry

National Council for Social Services 497

National Economic Development Council *see* NEDC (Neddy)

National Enterprise Board (NEB): concept 113, 163, 209, 215, 458, 508, 664; debate 17, 37–8, 121, 171–2, 184, 187–8, 193–4, 213–14, 336–7, 370; media 220–1; and other bodies 180, 181, 249, 302, 316–17, 327; positive vetting 318; mentions 42, 169, 240, 264, 275, 277, 300, 310, 455, 466, 631; *see also* State Holding Company

National Executive Committee (NEC): procedures 21–2, 40, 51, 443, 615; Cabinet/TUC relationships 80, 115, 251–2, 270–1, 272, 564–5, 583, 596, 690; and PLP 47–8, 63–4, 240, 251–2, 407, 468–9, 563, 566–7; Common Market 177, 251, 340, 342, 351–8 *passim*, 633; Day of Protest (1973) 12–13, 14, 18; import controls 598; and media 528, 614, 668; miners' strike 96; Social Contract 595, 604; other meetings 8, 41, 141, 185, 422, 523, 544, *see also* Home Policy Committee; International Committee; Monitoring Committee

National Front 97, 109, 110–11, 433, 434, 605

National Iranian Oil Company 488–9

National Union of Sheet Metalworkers 164

nationalisation: Labour policy 63, 180, 209, 213, 350; debate 4, 29, 115, 183, 212–13, 240, 398, 641, 684; car industry 24–5, 26, 191–2, 478, 480, 660, *see also* Rolls Royce; finance institutions 4, 33, 38, 43, 302, 325, 604, 611, 616, 642; land 42, 103, 279, *see also* aircraft; National Enterprise Board; oil; shipbuilding; steel; 'Twenty-five Companies'

NATO (North Atlantic Treaty Organisation) 476, 612; mentions 77, 267, 423, 631, 632

NATSOPA (National Society of Operative Printers, Graphical & Media Personnel) 84

NCB *see* National Coal Board

NEB *see* National Enterprise Board

NEC *see* National Executive Committee

NEDC (National Economic Development Council; Neddy) 119, 192, 373, 455; mentions 456, 526, 592

Neild, Robert 510

Nenni, Pietro 436–7, 485

Nethercott, Ron 123

Netherlands: Common Market 142, 345; nuclear power 612

Newens, Stan 540–1

New Society 63, 581, 582, 587

New Statesman 156, 340, 381

Nield, Sir William 116–18, 125

Nigeria 411, 412

Nixon, President Richard 524, 532; arms to Israel 189; bugging 492, 493; Wallace affair 227; Watergate & departure 21, 22, 24, 39, 53, 69, 72, 111–12n, 151, 157, 215–16, 217–18; mentions 45, 332, 409, 432, 441, 506

North Sea Renegotiation Committee 417–18, 447

Northern Ireland: industry & unions 166, 197, 684; law issues 111n, 133, 273–4, 473–4; politics 162, 457, 526, 536, 574; withdrawal lobby 137–8, 142, 164, 457, 459, *see also* IRA

Norton Villiers Triumph (NVT) 119, 121, 158, 174, 235n, 261–2, 288, 326, 495, *see also* Meriden

Norway: Common Market 192, 305

nuclear issues: commercial development 423, 533, 551–2, 570, 573–4, 586, 612–13, 625, 628, 688; safety aspects 565, 568, 580–1, 583, 594, 620, 656, 687, 688, 690; waste problem 447, 500–1, 655–6, 688; security 406, 466, 500, 524; military 76, 267–9, 552, 612, 689; Iran 491; S. Africa 377, 484, 487, 495–6, 509–10, 549n

NUJ (National Union of Journalists) 98, 314–15

NUM (National Union of Mineworkers) 74, 87, 96, 99, 403, 406, 460, 472, 606, *see also* mining industry

NUPE (National Union of Public Employees) 593–4, 653, 668

NVT *see* Norton Villiers Triumph

Nyerere, Julius 438, 614, 651

Oakeshott, Matthew 210

Observer, The: on author 7, 32, 230, 237–8, 597; Energy Conference 585; industrial matters 90, 310, 413; politics 434, 680; mentions 107, 319, 596, 682

OECD (Organisation for Economic Cooperation & Development) 79, 325, 500, 666

Official Secrets Act 102

oil: energy crisis 1, 74, 79, 81, 87, 92; Middle East 474, 488, 490–1; North Sea (production) 403, 419, 453, 506–7; (EEC & US interest) 347–8, 426–9, 515–16, 610, 660; (economy) 72, 266, 491, 551, 640; nationalisation 37, 161, 417–18, 427, 447, 448–9, 450; prices 216, 239, 356, 444, 516, 527, 626, 628, 682; Falkland Islands 421; 540; mentions 108, 389, 460, 486, *see also* BNOC; OPEC; trade unions

Oman 490, 494

O'Neill, Terence 14

OPD *see* Overseas & Defence Policy Committee

OPEC (Organisation of Petroleum-Exporting Countries) 1, 92, 356, 483, 489; mentions 479, 516, 610, *see also* oil industry

Orme, Stan: Cabinet post 609; economic debate 2–3, 262–3, 643, 647, 656, 657, 659, 667, 675–6, 682, 683; leadership issue 536, 603; security 477, 590, 605; mentions 28, 413, 533, 614, 639, 643, 661

Ortoli, François 151–4, 181–2, 321

Overseas & Defence Policy Committee (OPD) 146, 247, 454, 495, 509

Owen, David 572, 601–2, 605, 630–2

Padley, Walter 42, 422, 468
Page, Bruce 228, 531
Page, Derek 54
Paisley, Revd Ian 14
Palestine 189–90, 266
Palestine Liberation Organisation (PLO) 273, 430–1
Palliser, Sir Michael 407, 439
Pannell, Charlie 30, 34
Pardoe, John 106, 231, 533
Park, George 169
Parker, Peter 61, 90
Parliamentary Labour Party see PLP
Parry, Terry 481
Part, Sir Antony: personal matters 205, 311, 359; relations with author 123, 138–9, 174, 186–7, 211, 245, 247–8, 270, 294, 409–10, 503; coalition government 190–1; DTI affairs 152, 198, 236–7, 282, 296–7, 298, 327, 334, 520; industrial matters 147, 154, 169, 171–2, 197–8, 210–11, 219; nationalisation & jobs 151, 186, 241, 294, 303, 359; on Treasury 201; TUC grant 232; vetting procedures 116–18, 127, 160, 174, 197, 363; mentions 114, 115n, 141, 148, 217, 238, 246, 254, 280, 284, 477
Partridge, Sir John 70, 240
pay policy see prices & incomes
Peacock, Professor Alan 148, 152, 191
Pearce, Tin 474, 512–13
Pearson, Sir Denning 57, 126
Peart, Fred: airport security 89; Common Market 165, 348; defence 476, 689; economic debate 665, 669, 678, 683; energy crisis 87; Israel vote 71; in Lords 609, 632; nationalisation issues 29, 212, 651; Northern Ireland 138, 162, 474
Peddie, Lord (Robert) 197, 580, 581
Pennell, Monty 505, 506, 507, 571
Pentonville Five 133–4
Perez, President Carlos 651, 652
Peston, Maurice 210
Peyton, John 311
Phillips, Alan 465, 517, 566, 573
Phillips, Fred 480
Piachaud, David 82
Pitt, Terry 13
Plant, Cyril 592–3
Pliatzky, Leo 284, 417–18, 593, 652
Plowden, Lord 240

PLP (Parliamentary Labour Party): author's relations with 17, 97, 403, 624, 693; Common Market 206, 284, 340, 354–5; industry & economy 53, 80, 592, 616, 653, 669, 671–2, 676, 678, 682, 689–90; and NEC 14, 47, 270–1, 468–9, 530, 563, 583; other meetings 245–6, 317, 342, 426, 524, 540–1, 544, 553, 594; see also Labour Party; NEC
Pompidou, President 131, 132, 150, 612
Ponamarev, Boris 633
Pontillon, Robert 435
Poore, Dennis 119, 121, 158, 171, 172, 261, 331
Pope-Hennessy, James 22
Portugal 314–15, 318, 423, 613
Post Office Engineering Union 5
Poulson, John 5, 6, 53, 111n, 322
Powell, Enoch: political role 14, 56, 76, 79, 109, 574; Common Market issue 44, 46, 96, 285; energy conference 583–4; fiscal matters 55, 104, 671; and Heath 91, 105; immigration & attack by author 8, 92, 356, 618; N. Ireland 526, 536, 574; three-day week 79; mentions 204, 314, 387, 486, 607
Pravda 464
Prentice, Reg: in Opposition 1973–4; policy debates 3, 34, 74; NEC procedures 63–4, 65; union affairs 8, 10, 13, 60, 80, 97, 99; three-day week 74, 85–6, 87, 101
    in Government 1974–6; attacks on 335, 501; Party matters 121, 271, 480, 502, 605; Clay Cross 133; Common Market 207, 330, 344, 347, 354, 372; Concorde 160; defence issues 268; economic debate 654, 676, 683; Northern Ireland 474; nuclear issues 455; Overseas Development office 393; rejection by constituency 423, 424, 433–4, 443, 468, 469; departure 221, 596
Prescott, John 467
Price, Dolours & Marion 163–4
prices & incomes policy: Tory 1, 2, 4, 10, 104, 145, 295; early warnings 96, 119, 120, 122, 280; debate 165–6, 292, 394, 403, 404, 411–12, 457–8, 528, 562, 588, 667, 671–8 passim
Primarolo, Mike & Dawn 601
Prior, James 84–5, 104, 311, 592
PRISE (Programme for Reform in Secondary Education) 446

Profumo, John 54

Proops, Marjorie 481–2

Prosser, Raymond 241

Public Accounts Committee 237, 294, 333–4

Public Enterprise Committee 134, 158, 172, 219

Queen, the: and author 399; constitutional position 94–5, 120, 122, 459, 563; oil ceremony 453; projected visit to Russia 313; US bicentenary 576; wealth 323

Rabin, Itzhak 189–90

Race, Reg 593

Radcliffe Report 497, 498, 501, 502–3, 549n, 569

Radice, Giles 393

Raine, Neale 170, 254–5

Ramelson, Bert 66, 501

Rampton, Sir Jack: and author 451, 463–4, 533, 556; coal 495; nuclear energy 508, 573–4, 580; oil 571; Scanlon security 481; mentions 417, 483, 512, 520, 563, 620, 651

Rayner, Derek (Lord Rayner) 39

Red Star 510, 511

Red Weekly 23, 547

Ress, Merlyn: arms for Chile 130; Clay Cross 133; Common Market 339, 348; economy debate 637, 642, 677; Home Secretary 609, 643–4, 645–6, 650, 659; Israel vote 71; Northern Ireland 137, 142, 162, 273, 457, 473–4, 526; mentions 567, 655

Rees-Mogg, Lord (William) 98–9, 100, 101, 618; mentions 73, 433

Regional Development Fund 134, 330

Regional Employment Premium 684–5

Reid, Jimmy 243, 517

Remuneration Charges & Grants Bill 423

Reserve Powers Bill 418

Reuss, Henry 662, 673

Rhodesia 300, 377, 614, 626, 652–3, 670

Richardson, Elliott 332, 339, 376–7, 426–7, 431–2, 450, 477, 506, 648–9; mentions 72, 403, 425

Richardson, Gordon 641–2

Richmond, Alf 25

Ridley, Nicholas 687

Rippon, Geoffrey 439, 529

Roach, Bert 57

Robens, Alf (Lord Robens) 66, 95, 437, 531

Robertson, James 92, 93, 109, 111, 148, 530

Robertson, John 165

Robinson, Ambrose 105

Robinson, Geoffrey 285, 320; mentions 146, 158, 172, 216, 219, 261

Rocard, Michel 435

Roderick, Caerwyn 385, 393

Rodgers, Bill: Party matters 54–5, 398, 572; Cabinet post 609, 614; economic debate 664, 676, 685; EEC 69; nuclear issue 500; S. Africa 246–7; mentions 572

Rogers, Herbert; as agent 102, 227, 233, 465, 537, 597, 603–4; EEC & other issues 57–8, 245, 291, 311–12, 340, 514, 605

Rolls Royce 125–6; Tory dealings 1, 5, 25, 57; Labour plans 25, 26, 27–9, 31–2, 34; trade unions 30, 32, 59, 61, 109, 228; and Concorde 122, 124, 158, 162; Chile contract 155, 157; US proposals 151

Rooke, Denis 481

Roosevelt, Eleanor 626

Rootes Motors, 149

Rosedale Industries Limited 470

Ross, Donald 82, 83, 84, 89

Ross, Willie: policy debate 38, 86, 269; Common Market 305, 307, 330, 345, 349, 353; Crossman's diaries 309; Devolution 242, 303, 401, 432; industry affairs 188, 212, 477–8; Israel vote 71; Northern Ireland 138, 162, 474; nuclear security 466; Rhodesia 300; US bicentenary 399; resignation 557

Rothschild, Lord 141–2, 163, 241; mentions 146, 147

RTZ (Rio Tinto-Zinc) Co 484: 549n

Rudderham, Bishop 51

Russell, Bertrand 66, 100, 431, 468, 526

Ryder, Sir Don 263, 267, 274, 277, 279–80, 282, 358, 481; mentions 284, 310, 320, 327, 374, 464, 584

Ryder Committee & Report 358, 364, 367

Ryland, Bill 140, 146, 267

Sadat, President Anwar 529

Sainsbury, Tim 73n

Sapper, Alan 73, 74, 98
Saragat, Guiseppe 436–7
SAS (Special Air Service) 406, 500
Saudi Arabia 411, 411, 412
Scales, Prunella 44
Scanlon, Hugh 644; role in Labour Party 3, 14, 62, 639; support for author 238, 424, 552–3; BGC appointment 481, 483–4, 498, 520; Common Market 167; Conference 615, 616; industrial relations 13–14, 40, 90, 166–7, 336, 426; pay & prices 10, 442, 522; and press 13–14, 154; mentions 126, 157, 179, 196, 276, 297, 372, 455
Scarbrow, Ernie 505
Scargill, Arthur 101, 222, 278, 374, 400, 520, 523, 606, 635; mentions 84, 266, 329, 335, 460
Schmidt, Helmut 150, 423, 670, 673, 682; and Britain 277, 473, 475, 476, 524, 551, 658, 662, 663, 687; mentions 282, 551, 620, 624, 631, 672
Scotland 72, 647, 663, see also Scottish entries
Scott, Nicholas 25
Scott, Norman 512, 533, 565
Scott-James, Anne 222
Scottish Daily News project 161, 226, 233, 335, 358, 359, 363, 459
Scottish Development Agency 278
Scottish National Assembly & Devolution 242, 278, 303, 304, 343, 346, 401–2, 432, 494, 688
Scottish Nationalist Party 73, 134, 263, 345, 432, 434, 508, 618; mentions 281, 463, 494, 575
Security Services 691; & Civil Service 296, 299, 308, 318; leak inquiry 590, 605; MPs 243, 244, 285, 304, 323, 390n, 420, 441, 466, 617; trade unions 441, 481, 498, 687, 691
Sedgemore, Brian 538, 639, 649, 660; mentions 393, 421, 467, 544
Selby, Harry 73
Service, Jack 148, 226, 243, 358
Shackleton, Eddie 484
Shah of Iran 488, 489, 490–2, 506
Shaw, Rev Geoff 161
Shawcross, William 228
Shell Co 417, 447, 450, 617
Shepherd, Malcolm (Lord Shepherd) 348, 350, 465, 466, 469, 474, 478, 500
Sheppard, Bishop David 44

shipbuilding industry 161, 201, 632; nationalisation 184, 194, 209, 210, 235n, 236, 286, 301, 370, 371, 572, 651, 669; mentions 359, 574, 577, 642, see also Appledore; Court Line
Shore, Peter: in Opposition 1973–4; Party politics 4, 56; support for author 9, 29; support for Foot 76; Common Market 60, 73; Rolls Royce 27, 29; three-day week 74, 86, 99
  Wilson Govt 1974–6; new office 114, 115, 122, 292, 375; Party policies 200, 377, 498, 518, 524–5; Cabinet reshuffle 387–8; leadership contest 527, 540, 597; arms for Chile 130, 136, 146; Common Market 150, 263, 264, 267, 283, 289, 344, 348, 349, 352, 355, 356, 363–4; Concorde 160; Court Line 220, 422, 429; defence 268, 377; economy 279, 356, 405, 412, 416, 486, 498; energy 392; industry affairs 188, 338, 350; nationalisation 302; Northern Ireland 138, 162, 474, 495; nuclear issues 455, 496, 509; Press 315
  Callaghan Govt 1976; Policy debate 563; economy 579–80, 586, 594, 620, 637, 654, 656, 663, 665–70 passim, 676, 682–7 passim; EEC 579; energy issues 655–6, 688, 689; housing 651; Human Rights Charter 577; leaks inquiry 581, 587, 648; on Tory policy 574, 579
  mentions 49, 157, 172, 194, 279, 287, 360, 365, 372, 413, 423, 465, 484, 604, 639, 661, 691
Short, Renée 36, 422
Short, Ted: smear campaign 201, 226; party policies 4, 246, 266, 373–4; leadership issue & resignation 535, 536, 542, 552, 557; arms for Chile 130; Civil Service 478; Clay Cross 400; Common Market 208, 344, 345, 355, 360; Cyprus 223; defence 77; Devolution 286, 304, 401, 432, 508; energy crisis 79, 80, 101; Industry Bill 394; nationalisation 28, 212, 301; nuclear issues 455, 509; Stonehouse affair 389; TV programme 524, 544; mentions 70, 71, 94, 268, 354, 372, 397, 399
Shrewsbury Pickets 277, 284, 317–18, 390n, 530
Shrimsley, Anthony 199, 204, 370
Sieff, Edward 81
Sieff, Marcus 165

Silkin, John 75, 84, 269, 348, 361, 495, 609, 678, 693; mentions 74, 172, 363, 396, 403, 405, 546, 639, 661
Silkin, Sam 273, 402, 409, 422, 577
Sillars, Jim 46, 73, 494, 530; mentions 263, 517
Silverman, Julius 23
Simonet, Henri 180, 407, 440, 632
Simonstown Agreement 251, 252, 255–6, 272, 275
Simpson, Bill 12–13, 40, 205, 275; mentions 3, 41, 293
Singer, Aubrey 308
Sissons, Peter 499
Skeet, Trevor 630, 633
Skinner, David 6
Skinner, Dennis: support for author 93, 367, 459; Clay Cross 6, 258; Common Market 284; economic issues 10, 421, 575; leadership issue 536, 538; nationalisation 28; Tribune Group 170
Smirnovsky, Ambassador 11
Smith, Cyril 533
Smith, George, 75, 85
Smith, Giles 499
Smith, Ian 300, 300n, 614
Smith, John 245, 467, 481, 527; mentions 417, 528
Smith, T. Dan 111n
Soames, Christopher 330, 420
Soares, Dr Mario 315, 318, 423, 445–6
Social Contract 113, 120, 192, 206, 324, 604, 641, 647; breached 411, 653, 655, 675, 677, 681; mentions 239, 291, 335, 357, 403, 508, 592, 595, 636
Social Democrats 15, 263, 443, 680
Social Security Bill 657
Social Services 116, 208, 476, 497; benefit cuts 581, 596, 657, 672–8 passim, 680, 683, see also unemployment
Socialist Environmental Resources Association 523–4
Socialist Education Association 616
Socialist International 436, 438
Socialist Labour League 23, 50
Socialist Worker 23, 372, 379, 547
Solzhenitsyn, Alexander 526
Soper, Donald (Lord Soper) 107
South Africa: Air Show 217; political plot 528, 565–6; RN visit 246–7, 251, 257–8, 271; Russian plan 539; trade 128, 129, 377; uranium 454, 484, 487, 495–9–10, 549n, see also Rhodesia

Soviet Union: civil rights 91; Common Market views 155, 157, 312, 345; defence 268; Angola plan 539; and Britain 11, 157, 312–13, 692; relations with China 199, 265–6, 633; Cuba 504; Germany 511; Portugal 423
Spearing, Nigel 338
Spiers, Ronny 403, 477, 626
Spinelli, Altiero 180, 181, 309–10, 388, 439–40
Spriggs, Jack 167, 195–6, 398, 498–9; mentions 167, 221, 222, 242
Stacey, Tom 431
Stalin, Joseph 199
Standring, Keith 27
Stanley, Bryan 73, 74, 191, 271, 277, 293, 441, 442, 443; mentions 237, 611
State Holding Company 12, 15, 17, 26, 163, see also National Enterprise Board (NEB)
Steel, Sir David 449, 453, 505, 506–7, 571, 585–6
Steel, David (Liberal) 533, 610, 652
steel industry 128, 136, 180, 189, 370, 378; mentions 161, 311, 336, see also British Steel Corporation
Sternberg, Sir Rudy 54
Stewart, Mr (Private Secretary) 289, 290
Stirling, Colonel David 220
Stock Exchange see City
Stockwood, Bishop Mervyn 456–7, 482
Stokes, Donald (Lord Stokes) 90, 191–2, 264, 278, 287, 367
Stonehouse, John 272–3, 277, 285, 301–2, 359, 389, 521, 607
Stott, Roger 639
Stowe, Ken 465, 507, 657
Strang, Gavin 500–1
Strauss, George 544, 553
Straw, Jack 50, 363, 451, 487
Summerskill, Edith 625
Sun, The: and author 106, 190, 503; other articles 30, 83, 382; mentions 207, 479
Sunday Express, The: on author 382, 424; other articles 219, 369, 590; mentions 10, 183
Sunday Mirror, The 375
Sunday Post, The 54
Sunday Telegraph, The: and author 32, 562; other articles 128, 237, 487, 574, 597
Sunday Times, The: and author 81, 87, 190, 227–8, 230, 237–8, 253, 562; BP

corruption 559; Common Market 207;
Crossman diaries 264, 313, 409, 660;
Labour Party 177, 190, 226, 253, 434,
542; Tory Party 168–9, 520, 523;
three-day week 91; mentions 53, 75,
101, 468, 629
Suslov, Mikhail 158, 159
SWAPO (South-West Africa People's
Organisation) 495, 496, 509
Sweden: economy 641, 675
Swingler, Stephen 304, 390n

Targett, Reverend Ken 105
TASS 477
Taussig, Robert 521
Taverne, Dick 7; Bristol election 91, 92,
93, 102; Common Market 207, 362;
Lincoln win 9; Prentice affair 433–4;
mentions 23, 228
taxation 325, 461, 478–9, 583, 594, 669–
78 *passim*, 683, 687–8, VAT 341, 465,
669; wealth 127
Taylor, A.J.P. 41
Tebbit, Norman 99–100, 554–5
Teller, Dr Edward 628–9
Terry, Walter 154
TGWU (Transport & General Workers'
Union) 30, 137, 287, 421, 444, 445,
569, 616; support for author 32, 147;
mentions 442, 593
thalidomide issue 259
Thames Television 83
Thameside Education Authority 577
Thatcher, Margaret: Party leadership
236, 311, 322, 420, 440, 487, 533, 579,
645; policies 379, 531, 579, 592–3, 619,
677; tactics 403, 502, 530, 570, 572,
625, 665, 682; 'Iron Lady' 507, 510–
11, 632; Common Market 319, 322–3,
341, 349, 360, 367; economic debate
416, 593, 642; industry 319, 572;
Wilson's resignation 536; Australia
visit 614; mentions 105, 366, 432, 443,
513, 522, 538, 607, 626, 630, 639
Theology 607
'Think Tank' *see* Central Policy Review
Staff
Thomas, Captain Dan 552
Thomas, George 513, 572
Thomas, Professor Hugh 22
Thomas, Ron 59, 544
Thompson, Peter 275–6
Thomson, George 134, 181, 192

Thomson, Lord 98
Thorne, Stan 538, 544
Thorneycroft, Lord 650
Thorpe, Jeremy: blackmail case 482, 512,
528, 533, 565; Appledore shipyard
185, 190; coalition prospects 55, 234,
377, 404; Selwyn-Lloyd tribute 513;
Wilson tribute 536; mentions 7, 14, 446
three-day week 77–9, 81, 82, 85, 90
Times, The: on author 6, 53, 108, 159,
173–4, 251, 370, 584, 610; bugging
605; Common Market 207, 291, 365;
foreign affairs 140; industrial topics 27,
30, 51, 190, 210, 292, 481; miners' strike
98, 99; politics 434, 457, 645; (1912)
coverage 100; mentions 3, 26, 96, 107,
606, 619, 628, 653, 657
Tindemans, Leo 578
Tinsley, Bishop John 514
Toffler, Alvin & Heidi 332
Tombs, Frank 580
Tomkins, Bishop Oliver 514
Tomkins, Sir Edward & Lady 130–1, 434
Tomlinson, Ricky *see* Shrewsbury Pickets
Trade & Industry, Dept of 139, 152, 198,
220, 296–7, 313, 323, 383, *see also* Part,
Sir Antony
trade unions: background & strengths
195, 285, 298, 477, 482, 597, 655;
control of power 96, 103, 119, 145, 239,
240, 278, 301, 329, 421, 461; Labour
Opposition backing 3–4, 8, 61, 80, *see
also* Labour Party 404; Labour Govt
policy 134, 136–7, 166, 216, 292, 306,
335, 403, 458, 570; resistance to Tory
law 2–3, 8, 13, 16, 112n; Industry Bill
& NEB 310, 321, 405, 460;
nationalisation issues 169–70, 226, 287,
482; oil rigs 419, 444, 467–8, 516; pay
deals & economic measures 445, 457–
8, 522, 610, 653, 654; security
surveillance 441, 481, 498, 687, 691;
European context 13; grants for
research 191, 211, 232, 238, 296, 333;
commemorative stamp issue 122, 140–
1, 146, 364, *see also* Conservative Party;
TUC
Treasury, the 594, 603; procedures 102,
127, 201–2, 223, 284, 422, 453; Budgets
& fiscal measures 222, 478, 575–6, 593,
595, 621, 643, 657, 665, 677; Counter-
Inflation Unit 430, 534; energy matters
147, 600; Giro 200; hold on economy

Treasury, the—*contd.*
279, 299, 328, 414, 448, 451, 551, 631;
industrial policy unit 383, 425;
industrial problems 162–3, 243, 244,
317, 469; leaks 588, 591

Trend, Burke 505

Triang Toys 349–50

Tribune, 26, 250, 445, 650, 657; mentions
464, 532, 616

Tribune Group 46, 67–8, 170, 285, 398,
529, 530, 538; mentions 397, 444, 579,
653, 690

Trotskyites 113, 196, 469, 605, 617,
623–4, 676

Trubshaw, Brian 214, 215

Trudeau, Pierre 150

TUC (Trades Union Congress): power
222, 276, 405, 518; three-day week 78,
79, 85–7, 90, 93, 102; Day of Protest
10, 12–13, 22–4; industrial relations
policies 40, 60–1, 85, 114, 262, 690;
Social Contract 120, 206, 324, 381,
595; Industry Bill & industry 136, 317,
327–8, 336–7, 378; pay policies 403,
405, 411–12, 414, 415, 562, 583, 588,
636, 671; Common Market policies 13,
167, 287, 346–7, 374; Energy
Conference 583; import controls 515,
531, 637; in NEDC 373; (1976)
economic crisis 589, 595, 599, 616–17,
632, 636, 637, 639, 640, 653, 663, 673–
9 *passim*; Scottish 73, 161; Welsh 191,
211, 232, 238, 296, 333, *see also* trade
unions; *and under* Labour Party

TUC-Labour Party Liaison Committee:
policy matters 8, 75, 80, 157, 452, 507–
8, 521–2, 602–3, 629, 680–3; leaks 13,
170; other meetings 39, 78, 85, 96, 366,
664

Tucker, Brian 406, 452, 483, 580, 620

Tuite, Ray 168, 191, 199–200, 321, 383,
398; mentions 160, 161, 200, 214

Turner, Sir Mark 403, 484

Tuttie, Ernie 230–1

'Twenty-five Companies' 1, 113, 163,
182; debate 17, 42, 47–51 *passim* 63, 64

UCATT 442

Ulbricht, Walter 199

Ulster Unionists 574

Workers' Council 166, 303

Unemployment: rise of 379, 404, 486, 502,
599, 619, 639, 673, 680; debate

(Wilson Govt) 381, 414, 510, 528, 531;
(Callaghan Govt) 574, 632, 642, 654,
661–5 *passim*; 670, 674–80 *passim*, 685–
7 *passim*; counter-measures 378, 457,
508, 598, 636; benefit 380, 513, 657, *see
also* Social Services; mentions 415, 448,
456, 683

United Nations 223, 345

Urwin, Harry 23–4, 119

USA (United States of America):
author's visit 518–20; destabilising
fears 225, 318–19, 332, 376–7, 423, 485,
692; bicentenary 364, 399, 477, 518,
576; elections 635–6; British political
scene 607, 610, 612, 631, 633, 646, 658,
662; Cuba 504; economic matters 150–
1, 379, 636, 666, 675; European
industry 149, 150, 151, 347, 460, 479;
oil & nuclear interests 265, 426–9, 551–
2, 570, 573–4, 628, 689; NATO &
defence 18–19, 267, 423, 552, *see also*
CIA; Watergate scandal

Vahidi, Iraj 488, 490

Varley, Eric: and author 390;
Government office 114, 115, 278, 452;
Chrysler 466, 477–8, 479; Clay Cross
133; Common Market 347–8, 349,
354, 361; economic debate 456, 458,
459–60, 480, 637, 676, 684; Lords case
632; Meriden 425; NEC Treasurer 615;
North Sea oil 266, 427, 449; nuclear
energy 552; pay policy 287, 329; S.
Africa 377, 509; trade unions 301;
mentions 68, 74, 81, 83, 94, 99, 399,
496, 630

Vaughan, Ron 398, 472, 477, 497, 534,
543, 603; mentions 162, 173, 232, 356,
399, 404, 539, 576, 600, 607, 624, 651

Veil, Simone 434

Vietnam War 151, 359, 518

Vile, Martin 200, 219, 275–6

Villiers, Charles 43

Vorster, Dr B.J. 300

wages *see* prices & incomes

Wagner, Mr (Shell) 617

Wainwright, Richard 533

Walden, Brian 44–5, 103, 115

Wales 278, 343, 401–2, 432, 663, 688

Walker, Martin 475, 691

Walker, Peter 27, 34, 90, 91, 319, 368,
372; mentions 84, 98, 575

Walker, Gen Sir Walter 220
Wallace, Governor George 227
Wardle, Mr (Lib candidate) 234
Warne, John 161
Warren, Des *see* Shrewsbury Pickets
Warrington, Anthony 246
Wass, Sir Douglas 383, 560, 652
Watergate scandal 21, 22, 39, 53, 72, 111–12n, 157, 215–16, 493
Watkinson, Harold (Lord Watkinson) 249, 456, 583
Watson, Jack 514, 605
Watson, Sam 62
Wedgwood, Josiah 100
Weekend World 90
Weighell, Sid 42, 293
Weinstock, Sir Arnold 5, 25, 38–9, 511, 580, 586
Welsh Development Agency 278
Western Daily Press 289, 467
White, James 422
White, John 165
Whitehead, Phillip 7
Whitehorn, Sir John 70
Whitelaw, Willie: coalition issue 75, 83, 84, 86, 430; Common Market 366; Court Line 429; leadership bid 311; miners' strike 104; mentions 361, 420, 432
Whitlam, Gough 71, 287, 459
Whittome, Alan 658
Whitty, Larry 105, 405, 679
Wigdor, Lucien 70, 103, 240
Wigg, George 285
Wilcox, Desmond 308
Williams, Alan 84
Williams, Sir Len 2
Williams, Marcia 25, 137, 160, 244, 409, 447–8, 526–7, 543, 627; mentions 409, 548
Williams, Roy: and author 176, 248, 275, 294, 334, 390, 392, 691; Common Market 163, 203; and Part 232, 296, 298; and PM 154, 168, 277, 289–90; mentions 123, 160, 161, 175, 214, 300, 358, 376
Williams, Shirley: author's opinions 21, 379
    in Opposition 1973–4; policy debates 36, 63–4, 65, 89; industry 25, 26, 32, 42; poll ratings 54
    Wilson government 1973–5; policy debate 121, 155, 373, 468, 480, 530, 539; resignation proposed 221, 222, 229; Chrysler 478; Clay Cross 204; Common Market 204, 207, 229, 230, 253, 267, 339, 346, 349, 351, 352, 541; Conference 275; defence 269; Home Policy Committee 293; industry 188, 198, 212, 309, 350; leadership issue 535; Northern Ireland 162; pay & prices 132, 394, 457; Prentice affair 433; S. Africa 377, 510; Stonehouse affair 389; trade unions 301; women's affairs 422
    Callaghan Govt 1976; Policy debate 561, 579; economic debate 637, 641, 664, 665, 666, 670–1, 674, 675, 683; education 609, 626, 627, 628, 629; women's affairs 577; mentions 41, 80, 102, 250, 353, 413, 531, 564
Williamson, Tom 62
Willis, Norman 85, 569
Willis, Ted 468
Wilson, David 319
Wilson, Des 44
Wilson, Harold: anecdotes & quirks 52–3, 305, 421–2, 432, 474, 505–6, 562–3, 691, 692; Dimbleby interview 521; and Marcia Williams 25, 160, 244, 526–7, 543, 627; honours given & received 480, 523, 560, 562, 570, 571, 615, 624–5
    in Opposition 1973–4; friction with author 8, 9, 26, 37, 39, 48, 58, 64, 92, 501; decline of popularity 55; policy statements 4–5, 34, 80; CBI dinner 70–1; concern with leaks 13, 40, 64, 65; Czechoslovakia visit 19; Day of Protest debate 12–13; election campaign 91–2, 106, 108–9; fiscal matters 36, 41; Iranian lunch 94; Israel vote 71–2; 'kitchen cabinet' 25, 41, 62, 68, 617; miners' dispute & energy crisis 75, 78, 82, 83, 90, 99, 100, 101, 102; nationalisation issues 26, 28, 29, 33, 38, 66, 103; 'Twenty-five Companies' 1, 47–8, 51, 63; NEC procedures 40, 51, 53, 63–5, 75; prices & incomes 2, 10; TUC affairs 85, 167
    as PM 1974; policies & tactics 113–14, 122, 124–5, 155, 173, 205–6, 212; ministerial appointments & 'Procedures' 114, 115, 116, 120, 137, 139, 142, 154, 177, 207, 235n; press on author 115, 118, 156, 168, 175–192, 200, 203, 214; arms for Chile 138, 146, 155; CBI relations 130

Wilson, Harold—*contd.*
   Cross 133; Common Market 140, 177–
   8, 184, 185–6, 192, 230, 439; Concorde
   121, 127, 160, 201; Court Line 219–20;
   elections 225, 226, 230, 237; energy
   conservation 147; industrial affairs 137,
   182, 187–8, 189, 193–4, 206, 212, 213,
   215, 222; Meriden coup 147; Northern
   Ireland 133, 162; Russian negotiations
   157
      as PM 1974–5; Ministerial
   responsibility 239, 246, 250, 251–3,
   255, 259, 261, 290, 357; showdown
   with author 237, 238, 253–4, 256–60;
   further relations 289–90, 294, 307–8,
   328, 334, 372, 375, 379, 390; other
   Cabinet problems 242–3, 262, 277, 290,
   351–5, 375, 387–8, 584; policies 245,
   246, 266–7, 323, 325–6, 355, 375;
   Common Market 236, 267, 277, 282–
   3, 305, 307, 330, 339–49 *passim*, 351–4
   passim, 358, 360–1, 367, 369, 388–9;
   Conference 275; defence 267, 269;
   Devolution 286, 303; economic
   situation 279, 329, 381–2; industrial
   affairs 240–1, 301, 368; Industry Bill
   & nationalisation 316, 317, 318, 327–
   8, 336–7; IRA bombings 270, 273;
   media 314, 315, 337; Moscow visit 312–
   13, 318; official cars ruling 368–9, 543,
   624; South Africa & Rhodesia 253, 300,
   377; trade union matters 278, 292, 362
      as PM 1975–6; Cabinet reshuffle
   393, 394–6, 399, 467, 478; ministerial
   dictates 454, 465, 468, 487, 496, 497,
   502, 513, 546, 509n; and author 409,
   425, 447, 507, 525, 527, 532, 534–5,
   541, 547, 554; policy debates 455, 456,
   475–6, 479, 530, 531; car industry 460,
   478, 479; Conference 443; defence 476;
   DHSS 451, 469–70, 476, 478; economic
   situation 400, 411, 412, 415–16, 457,
   461, 480, 486; EEC 462, 473, 579;
   foreign affairs 423, 430–1, 476;
   inflation 414, 430; N. Ireland 526;
   nuclear issue 509, 510; oil issue 449,
   505, 507; pay & prices 404, 405,
   8; Thorpe affair 528;
   ...nt speculation 403–4, 446,
   ...7, 532; resignation 535–

7, 539–40, 542–3, 544, 548, 553, 554,
   627–8, 693
      as backbencher (1976) 554, 557, 565,
   693
Wilson, Mary 276, 548, 560, 627
Wilson, Tony 442
Windscale nuclear plant 406, 500–1, 655–
   6, 687, 688, 690 *see also* nuclear issues
Winnifrith, Sir John 165
Winstanley, Dr Michael 132
Wischnewski, Herr 321
Wise, Audrey 16, 170, 421, 459, 538;
   mentions 338, 393, 544
Witteveen, Johannes 672
Wood, David 380
Wood, Mr (Electricity Council) 515
Wood, Sir Frank 149, 280
Woodcock, George 131
Woodcock, Leonard 202
Woosey, Brian 106
Worcester, Bob 102
Workers' Action Committee *see Scottish
   Daily News*
workers' control 61, 151, 154, 156, 187,
   189, 301, 338, 398, 635; cooperatives
   46, 236, 255, 266, 371, 406; EEC
   policies 182, *see also* Institute for
   Workers' Control Bulletin 118
Workers' Educational Association 156,
   564
Workers' Press 23, 198, 547
Worsthorne, Peregrine 190, 296, 461, 574

Wright, Bob 226, 254, 255, 358
Wright, George 232, 385
Wright, Sir Oliver 611
Wright, Peter 113
Wright, Roy 75
Wyatt, Woodrow 73, 375, 501

Yamani, Sheikh 474, 483, 489
Yates, Ivan 319
Yom Kippur war 69, 74, 135, 189
Young, Hugo 75–6
Young, Michael 394, 395, 455
Young Socialists 15, 20–1, 53, 66, 111,
   116, 311

Zander, Michael 49
Zuckerman, Sir Solly 627